THE CURRENCY OF EMPIRE

THE CURRENCY OF EMPIRE

MONEY AND POWER IN SEVENTEENTH-CENTURY ENGLISH AMERICA

JONATHAN BARTH

CORNELL UNIVERSITY PRESS
Ithaca and London

Thanks to generous funding from Arizona State University and George Mason University, the ebook editions of this book are available as open access volumes through the Cornell Open initiative.

First published 2021 by Cornell University Press

Library of Congress Cataloging-in-Publication Data

Names: Barth, Jonathan, 1984– author.
Title: The currency of empire : money and power in
    seventeenth-century English America / Jonathan Barth.
Description: Ithaca [New York] : Cornell University Press,
    2021. | Includes bibliographical references and index.
Identifiers: LCCN 2020037661 (print) | LCCN 2020037662
    (ebook) | ISBN 9781501755774 (paperback) |
    ISBN 9781501755781 (pdf) | ISBN 9781501755798 (epub)
Subjects: LCSH: Money—Political aspects—United
    States—History—17th century. | Mercantile system—
    United States—History—17th century. | Fiscal
    policy—United States—History—17th century. |
    United States—Foreign economic relations—Great
    Britain—History—17th century. | Great Britain—
    Foreign economic relations—United States—History—
    17th century.
Classification: LCC HG221 .B329 2021 (print) |
    LCC HG221 (ebook) | DDC 332.4/97309032—dc23
LC record available at https://lccn.loc.gov/2020037661
LC ebook record available at https://lccn.loc.gov
    /2020037662

Hee that brings mony in his hand,
Is sure to speed by sea or land.
But he that hath no coyn in's purse,
His fortune is a great deale worse.
    —Martin Parker, "There's Nothing to be had without Money"
    (London, 1633)

Contents

THE CURRENCY OF EMPIRE

Introduction

This book examines the pivotal role that silver and gold money played in the formation and working out of England's American colonial project in the seventeenth century. The book argues, first, that money was the primum mobile, or prime mover, of English imperial action and overseas activity, including the impulse for colonization, the regulation of colonial trade, and the introduction of certain fundamental changes in imperial colonial administration. Second, the book argues that money was also a chief catalyst for colonial resistance to that same mercantilist order, an order that many colonists believed prejudiced or wrongly subordinated their economies to imperial or London interests. This colonial resistance, propelled in large measure by money-related matters, grew stronger and more virulent as the century proceeded, until much of it dissipated with the onset of a new imperial age after the 1690s.

By analyzing the close relation between money, trade, and political power, this book seeks a more comprehensive explanation for the many tensions that prevailed in the seventeenth century between empire and colony. New perspectives on a number of seminal events and developments arise from viewing the early empire through a currency lens. John Pollexfen, a founding member of the Board of Trade, argued in 1697 that "Trade and Coyn have such a dependence one upon the other, that they could not well be consider'd distinctly."[1] I agree with that statement but extend it to also include empire and politics, both of which have such a dependence on money—and vice versa—that the study of one requires considering the other. Money, as an object of historical study, possesses unique explanatory power. This book will demonstrate how and why pecuniary matters—matters of or relating to money—were so critical to this period. In so doing, I hope to shed additional light on many of the most important economic and political hallmarks of the first one hundred years of England's empire in America.

The passing of Queen Elizabeth in 1603 closed an important first chapter in the history of the early English empire. The city of London, formerly a peripheral outport confined to simple exchange across the Channel, was now a major commercial hub, home to a host of cosmopolitan-minded merchants with direct trading relationships in Mediterranean, Baltic, and East Indian markets.[2] Silver, gold, and negotiable paper instruments representing silver and gold mediated exchange within these new Elizabethan trade networks. The profits therefrom resulted in a singular increase in the circulating money supply in England and most especially in London, equipping merchants with investment capital to finance further overseas ventures.[3]

Still, the achievements of the Elizabethan age paled in comparison with what was to come. In the seventeenth century, England's overseas dominions and commercial interests transformed in ways that few earlier could have imagined possible. By the final decades of the seventeenth century, London seemed poised to become "the General Emporie of the World," as one writer put it.[4] Over the century, England's exports and imports each rose more than sixfold; particularly lucrative was the reexport trade of North American, Caribbean, and East Indian commodities.[5] After 1660 especially, transoceanic commerce with the East Indies and Americas grew spectacularly, and none faster than transatlantic commerce. Traffic to and from colonial America accounted for nearly one-fifth of London's overseas trade by the end of the century.[6]

The interests of trade and state had never been so tightly wrapped together as they were in the seventeenth century. Overseas trade was indispensable to the English government, boosting its revenue and helping to finance the growth in state institutions. In turn, English government—the navy, bureaucracy, and laws protecting English commercial interests—proved indispensable to the ever-growing troop of cash-loaded merchants in London, of whom approximately one thousand had some sort of trading connection to colonial America by 1700.[7] By that date, England's commercial interests and dominion spanned the world: an empire of trade, an empire of money.

Silver and gold were the currency of empire. They drove imperial action; they made the empire move. "Money is the *primum mobile* which moves the

Spheres," a prominent English merchant wrote in 1679; ". . . it's the sovereign cordial, which gives life to all noble Actions and Designs."[8] The reasons for this were plain. To quote a few contemporaries of that age, silver and gold money was "every where coveted, and never out of fashion"—of "general Use almost every where," the "common receipt, and standard of all the world," a "vitall spirit of trade" that "answereth all things, and commandeth all things under the Sun."[9] This was true whether one was in Europe, the Middle East, India, or China; silver, in particular, had become "as merchandise the basis of the greatest commerce in the world."[10] "Money is as necessary for the carrying on of Trade, as Nerves and Sinews are for the motion of the Natural Body," said Sir Josiah Child in 1694.[11]

As prime mover, silver and gold figured prominently, even centrally, in England's dealings abroad. This was particularly true in colonial America, and that is the central concern of this book. Whether the enterprise was private or public, commercial or political, much of England's overseas activity in this period had as its general goal or justification the promise of a quantifiable increase of silver and gold in public and private coffers in England, especially London. This pecuniary motive and rationale—the *raison d'argent*—found its intellectual basis in the predominant mercantilist ideas of the day. Experience and conventional wisdom taught that a greater supply of silver and gold—procured through a favorable balance of trade, or trade surplus—was the most important prerequisite in securing national power, prestige, security, and plenty. Mercantilist ideas about money and foreign trade informed everything from overseas commercial regulations to war and diplomacy, the conquest and colonization of faraway lands, and the administration from London of colonial dependencies. Greatness, wealth, and glory were the end, money was the indispensable means, and colonies were among the most important means to acquiring that money.

One reason for the mercantilist fixation on silver and gold was their preeminent role in state formation. The two metals financed the building of vast armies and navies, sustained expansive bureaucracies, and nourished a relatively prosperous people and mercantile community primed for taxes and lending to government. Merchants financed state activity through loans and taxation. A stronger, more robust state, in turn, secured expanded markets for merchants, which fattened their pockets and made them all the more ready to finance state activity: "Money being," as one writer described it in 1693, "the very Life of War, and Sinews of all Publick Action."[12] "In the Language of Trade, Money is the Alphabet that forms the Sound," declared Daniel Defoe in 1706.[13] In the language of empire also, money ruled the day. Money and imperial power enjoyed a symbiotic relationship: each benefited the other. "Profit and Power ought joyntly to be considered," reasoned Child.[14] The country's merchants, landowners, and even masses enjoyed greater prosperity by consequence, and the resulting tranquility made for more stable government: "the People will be Contented," said another writer, "and the Exchequer maintained in a Full Spring Tide."[15] Child, a prominent East Indian merchant, summed up the benefits nicely: "Foreign Trade produceth Riches, Riches Power, Power preserves our Trade and Religion, the security of the Liberty, Property, and Protestant Religion of this Kingdom."[16]

Yet there also existed a certain scarcity to silver and gold, even as they emanated so profusely from Mexican, Peruvian, and Japanese mines. The supply was necessarily limited; a state could not simply will more into existence like paper money from a printing press. Thus, in the wake of new mining discoveries in the Americas and Japan in the sixteenth century, rival empires positioned themselves to become masters of the world's metallic output. The major economic question of the day regarding foreign trade was how to acquire more of the two metals and then how to retain them. This, in turn, led to the corollary question of how the state might optimally intervene to support such economic action, usually through restrictions or prohibitions of some sort or another.

The international scramble for money in the mercantilist age rested not on mining per se but on the so-called balance of trade. The balance-of-trade doctrine was the chief cornerstone of mercantilist thought. Mercantilist prescriptions for the economy were numerous, highly varied, and often incongruous. Yet all derived from this fundamental axiom. All mercantilists agreed that a country ought to export more goods on balance than it imported. Trade deficits drained money from the country, trade surpluses provided a country new money; the former was "unfavorable," the latter was "favorable," and the state should always stand ready to intervene on behalf of that balance. Subscribing to this principle was what made a mercantilist a mercantilist. Despite frequent and vehement disagreements on particular points of policy, consensus reigned among mercantilists on the issue of the trade balance. The doctrine provided a coherent, cohesive element to mercantilism, which otherwise was quite heterogeneous.

A favorable trade balance fulfilled the pecuniary imperative. It rendered mines entirely unnecessary. The English learned this lesson early in North America. Some at first were severely disappointed in the lack of mines on the eastern part of the continent. And yet through proper control and economic regulation, England's American empire soon proved a mercantilist bonanza, vastly improving the kingdom's overall trade balance and hence England's supply of money. All depended on this balance and on proper use of state power to improve it. "The Theory of Trade is a Princely Science, and the true Regulation of it the Key of Empire," wrote William Wood, one of the most prominent mercantilist thinkers of the early eighteenth century.[17]

This scramble for silver and gold, however, did not ensue only between rival kingdoms and empires. The competition ensued also within the *same* empire, between different men of different regions and of different interest groups, espousing different visions of political economy. This competition arose between metropole and periphery, between neighboring colonies, and often within the same colony.

In this book the intraimperial struggle for money is as important as the international struggle. Imperial policymakers designed the colonial system to center money in England. This made sense at the time, given the international contest for money. But in designing it in this fashion, imperial policymakers inadvertently created the groundwork for immense economic tension between London and the colonial periphery. In the second half of the seventeenth century especially, many leading colonists acutely resented their subordinate economic position. They believed that absent mercantilist controls, their colony might be wealthier and in command of more coin. And thus far, their subordinate station seemed to offer them comparatively little in return.

Colonies were among the greatest assets in any mercantilist empire. Colonies supplied the empire with goods, necessities, or luxuries not native to the home country but formerly imported from other countries. This supply improved the kingdom's trade balance. Additionally, colonists imported merchandise from the home country, sometimes comprising the kingdom's most dependable overseas market—again, improving the trade balance. The ideal colony primarily served the economic needs of the mother country (as contemporaries so often labeled England). Economic regulations were meant to secure this service. Colonies were in every way subordinate to wider imperial goals, operating as total dependencies, at least in theory. Whether or not that colony had a robust, secure, and uniform money supply was of little to no concern to most mercantilists, for it had no bearing at all on England's trade balance. If anything, a plentiful supply of silver coin in a colony evinced that something had in fact gone wrong with England's management of the empire, as most coin ought to center in England. "It is not expedient for England to give the Plantations opportunities of laying up great Banks of Treasure among themselves," wrote an anonymous author in 1701.[18]

But the bulk of England's colonists wanted wealth and money too: or at least a competent sum of it. It is necessary here to define our terms. By *wealth*— or affluence—I mean a suitable or plentiful possession of things of value. By *money* (at least here) I mean the predominant money of the seventeenth century: silver and gold coin. Money is a form of wealth, but not all wealth is money. Wealth, for example, might include fine nonmetallic imports from abroad or any other commodity of relative value and worth. Colonists, in general, wanted both: they wanted nice things, and they wanted a suitable medium of exchange. They wanted money for the many reasons that people and communities for thousands of years have wanted money—for private purposes, yes, but also for the public purpose of stimulating trade and the local economy. The circulation of money was as necessary for commerce as the circulation of blood in one's body. So earnest were colonists for money that in the absence of coin they often resorted to alternative, nonmetallic commodity monies to mediate commercial exchanges, including tobacco, sugar, and all sorts of grain. Of course coin was preferable to these, if available—desired for its portability and near-universal demand. If coin was not to be had, then many colonists still desired, at least, a higher standard of living: the capacity to acquire more imported goods, for example.

England's American colonists resorted to a variety of means to increase their stock of coin or standard of living. Some were licit, others illicit. They included import substitution, export expansion, smuggling, piracy, colonial mints, and coin devaluation. Many colonists wished to trade freely with the buyers and sellers who offered them the most competitive prices, whether or not that buyer or seller fell within the English mercantile orbit. Sometimes the best price could be found through legal avenues of trade, but often foreign tradesmen offered a better price for the goods they sold or for the goods they bought. Here, colonists found themselves directly at odds with England's mercantilist program, which barred such trade. The question at this point was whether to obey or to disobey.

When imperial regulations interfered with the colonists' innate desire for greater affluence and more money, illegal trade proved a powerful temptation. Imperial officials could tolerate illegal trade if sporadic and not terribly widespread. But when it increased or became better organized—with colonial governments even colluding in the act—the integrity and functioning of the whole mercantilist order was at risk. A forceful hand seemed to many imperial officials the only sensible option. At this point, the economic and monetary squabble transformed into a political fight. One of the founding principles of England's early American empire was that colonies were economically subordinate to the fiscal and monetary needs of the mother country. When colonists subverted this agenda and pursued their own pecuniary interests, they undermined one of the chief reasons for England having an empire in the first place. This subversion warranted, from the empire's perspective, an authoritative response, including major political and institutional reforms and reorganization. Political coercion, it was hoped, would solve the economic problem, bringing even the most obstreperous colonist or colony into line.

In both England and colonial America there prevailed an intense desire to secure a workable, vibrant, and relatively uniform currency. A perusal of the century's many documents, treatises, statute books, and private and public correspondence reveal these monetary desires unequivocally. These desires, however, were not always reconcilable: they often clashed. In the second half of the century in particular, competing economic and monetary demands placed England and its colonies on a collision course that resulted in a series of tumultuous political battles and other like episodes. Many of the major political contests from this period bore a direct relation to the pecuniary conflict that arose from mercantilism and colonial resistance to the colonies' subordinate economic status. This struggle became especially stark after 1675 and even threatened to break up the empire a full one hundred years before the American Revolution. Not until the grand settlement of the 1690s did the crisis finally begin to subside, with most colonists tentatively accepting, on a conditional basis, their subordinate place within a mercantilist empire that promised greater benefits and a more persuasive bargain than anything the earlier Stuart kings had offered them before 1688. The consequence was the thriving of a reconstructed mercantilist empire for almost three-quarters of a century.

In this book I pursue three chief investigative questions. First, was there an organizing principle behind England's pursuit and sponsorship of overseas colonies, and, if so, what was it precisely, and was it coherent? Second, how did that principle, over space and time, direct or influence the regulation and administrative management of colonial America? Third, what were the repercussions for the colonial sphere, and how, over space and time, did the organizing principle influence colonial attitudes toward imperial authority?

This book does not pretend to contain exhaustive answers to any of these questions, of course. Instead, it insists that the answers cannot be arrived at in any remotely comprehensive manner without taking the question of money seriously. Currency alone cannot provide all-encompassing answers to these questions. But money possesses exceptional explanatory power: first, of the imperial project as a whole and, second, of the ever-changing relationship between empire and colony. The lens of currency offers a new perspective on this critical early period of American, English, and imperial history. By identifying money as a common denominator in many of the most significant episodes of the seventeenth century, I aim in this book to supply new insights into colonial development, the broader Atlantic economy, and the ever-evolving politics and constitution of the early English empire.

First, was there an organizing principle at all behind England's early empire? Did it have a functional purpose? Historians have long debated this question. Those who argue against the existence of a coherent organizing principle emphasize the role of disparate private interests in promoting and maintaining much of the early empire. The fiscally strapped state played only a reactive role and, even then, only intermittently, ad hoc, and often reluctantly, yielding way rather to dissimilar initiatives of competing private interests: all resulting, these historians argue, in "a patchwork mosaic of measures adopted through expediency or accident"—an empire, in short, that was "rather unsystematic."[19]

This book, by contrast, maintains that there was indeed a coherent, organizing principle behind the early English empire. The book does not deny, of course, the unusually decentralized character of the early empire, nor the prevalence of ad hoc experimentation, the centrality of private initiative, or the existence of ulterior motives. The book does not deny that fiscal constraints limited what the early English state could accomplish overseas, nor that those constraints contributed to the aforementioned patchwork mosaic of colonial governments. But fiscal weakness—the state's lack of money—is precisely what underscored the need for an empire. This, I argue, justified the organizing principle. Decentralization, from the empire's vantage point, was certainly less than desirable, yet necessary given the fiscal constraints at the beginning. Imperial officials soon deeply regretted this framework; after 1660 especially, it was ever obvious that decentralization precluded the successful operation of a well-managed mercantilist empire. But the organizing principle was always there.

The organizing principle was that colonies existed primarily to support the economic, fiscal, and monetary needs of the mother country. The latter included English merchants but, above all, the state. Colonial economic subordination was the intention from the start, even when private initiative undertook such projects. John Cary, a merchant from Bristol and political economist, described it this way in his massively influential *Essay on the State of England* in 1695: "This was the first Design of settling Plantations abroad, that the People of England might better maintain a Commerce and Trade among themselves, the chief Profit whereof was to redound to the Center." "These are our Golden Mines," he said of the colonies, "and have helpt to support the Ballance of Trade."[20] Cary's view, as we will see, was not an isolated opinion, nor was it a novel one in the 1690s. Rather, his view was about a century old. It existed from the beginning, even as far back as the age of Elizabeth, before a permanent colony had yet been established. As the century proceeded, the impulse only strengthened, corresponding to the growth and rising significance of the American colonial economies.

Colonial economic subordination—the answer to the second part of our first inquiry—derived from a body of economic thought known retrospectively as *mercantilism*. It would be challenging to think of a more contentious term in the historiography of early modern economies than *mercantilism*. Some historians embrace its use wholeheartedly, others use it only very reluctantly, still others reject it outright. Probably the worst thing to happen to the term was carelessness by economic historians who expanded its definition to include beliefs characterizing the views of only *some* of the proponents of the balance-of-trade doctrine, and yet these historians treated those positions as additional, essential tenets of mercantilism. An inaccurate, crude caricature of mercantilism prevailed for many decades among economic historians, opening the way for a torrent of criticism by scholars (mostly British) who soon pointed out that many of the early-modern thinkers traditionally classified as mercantilists did not hold many of those views at all. For example, some historians held (and some even now hold) that all mercantilists believed that international trade was a zero-sum game, that gold and silver alone were wealth, that internal trade was sterile, and so on. We know now that those positions—while held by some men—were not even close to representative of the economic thought of the wide range of thinkers traditionally identified as mercantilists. Thus, the critics rightly dismantled the amorphous parody that the term *mercantilism* had become. Economic thought in the seventeenth and early eighteenth century, they argued, was not stale or suffocating, but innovative, rich, and dynamic, and it encompassed many opinions and views. In this, they were mostly correct, but they went a critical step too far by denying that there was any coherence *at all* to mercantilism, calling for the term to be either discarded altogether or, if retained, stripped of any real meaning. This book dissents strongly from that view.[21]

Mercantilism, on the whole, was a coherent, diverse, forward-thinking, and rational way of approaching and conceptualizing the economy in the early-modern period. Whether or not mercantilism was successful or sound we can leave to economists to debate. That lies far beyond the purview of this book. Nonetheless, the term *mercantilism* is as indispensable to descriptions of empire and foreign trade in this period, as the term *capitalism* is when describing the history of Western economies since the nineteenth century. Like capitalism, mercantilism permitted widely divergent views and policy prescriptions underneath the wider umbrella that comprised its distinctive, essential tenets. If nonuniformity means that we must rid ourselves of the term *mercantilism*—as some have argued—then we must also rid ourselves of the terms *capitalism*, *feudalism*, and *socialism*. Have socialists ever uniformly agreed on policy? Obviously not: there are varying schools of thought within the broader yet meaningful, coherent framework that people call *socialism*. In the same manner, we may speak of different mercantilist schools of thought, and of different mercantilist visions, all of which consciously or unconsciously adhered to a broader mercantilist consensus. The balance-of-trade doctrine, and its corollary argument for a regulatory state (on behalf of supporting that balance), was important enough in economic history to justify historians distinguishing this period of economic thought from preceding and subsequent bodies of opinion. One of the goals of this book, then, is to encourage historians to use the term *mercantilism* carefully, precisely, but also confidently and without apology.

In early-modern England a motley of commercial and political interests concurred in a broad yet far-reaching agenda endorsing the use of state power to secure greater trade surpluses. The precise methods for doing so were immensely complex and controversial; debate, disagreement, and animosity characterized many of the economic discussions of the day, as disparate groups within England clashed over strategy and method. There was no single, exact blueprint for how to proceed; there was no single mercantilist pressure group. Some of them undoubtedly had naked private interest primarily in mind, but they always couched their arguments in rhetoric concerning the public good, framing their policy prescriptions in the common language of mercantilism. Many, perhaps the majority, knew they might privately benefit from the adoption of a particular policy or regulation yet sincerely regarded their interests as aligned with the public, national goal of achieving or retaining a favorable trade balance. The bulk of them were true believers. By the latter decades of the seventeenth century, colonial America figured prominently on most of their minds.

The second inquiry—the ways in which this organizing principle (mercantilism and colonial economic subordination) directed or influenced imperial policy toward the colonies—permeates every chapter of the book. The hallmark, of course, was the famous series of Navigation Acts authorized by Parliament in 1651, 1660, 1663, 1673, and 1696. Nevertheless, expression of this influence began even before the mid-seventeenth century. Moreover, it was not limited to the Navigation Acts but included royal decrees, the creation of executive or advisory councils, the appointment of new emissaries, and continual attempts at political reorganization and reform. It was not a coincidence that major imperial reforms followed the eruption of significant monetary or fiscal crises in England, whether in the early 1620s, at the middle of the century, in the 1670s, or in the 1690s.

The answer to the third inquiry—the impact of this organizing principle on imperial-colonial relations—lies at the heart of the book. Mercantilism required compliance. First, mercantilism required compliance from groups within England itself, whose private interests often ran contrary to the purported interest of the whole. More important, for our purposes, mercantilism required compliance from a colonial sphere whose economic interests often ran contrary to England's purported economic interests.

It was not easy to persuade colonists in a far-flung decentralized empire to surrender economic self-interest, particularly when it was not entirely clear what they might gain in return. Many colonists possessed a radically different vision for empire than the one endorsed from London. This alternative vision insisted on the application of equal economic rules throughout the empire. It rejected the London-imposed mercantilist vision that used economic constraints to center money in England.

This incongruity of visions, rooted in competing economic and monetary ambitions, resulted in intense political conflict between England and much of colonial America in this period. It began most conspicuously in the 1650s, intensified after the Crown's Restoration in 1660, and then erupted into full-blown political warfare in the 1670s and 1680s, when imperial administrators responded to colonial resistance by suppressing many of the colonists' most cherished political liberties. But this tumult was rather short-lived. After 1688 many, though notably not all, of those political liberties returned, and a new war with France rendered imperial protection that much more valuable to many of England's colonists. A powerful new sensibility toward empire appeared widely throughout the colonies in this latter period. Colonial attitudes changed—not overnight, but perceptibly and fairly quickly. During and after the 1690s, colonials, by and large, came to tacitly accept their subordinate station within the mercantilist empire. This acceptance helped to ensure the survival and singular success of Britain's mercantilist empire through much of the coming eighteenth century. The new, more effective administrative model of empire that arose from the reforms of the 1690s—and especially those from the all-important year of 1696—functioned, not perfectly or seamlessly, but very impressively for nearly seventy years. In light of the many stresses of the seventeenth century, this was a remarkable achievement.

Why was the impulse for colonization so strong in England in the early modern period? Why settle colonies overseas? What stimulated imperial action, administration, and regulation? Why did certain stages of imperial development occur when they did? What was the catalyst for administrative change? What motivated the many varied colonial responses to these changes? All of these questions I hope to answer, in part, by investigating more closely the relation between money and power in early English America.

CHAPTER 1

Silver, Mercantilism, and the Impulse for Colonization

Silver and gold coin and bullion permeated world markets as never before in the sixteenth and seventeenth centuries. The inexorable current of metals, especially of silver, from the Americas and Japan permanently transfigured some of the most important political, economic, and social institutions in Europe and across much of the globe. Affluent merchants and companies in select cities in western Europe controlled much of the global silver trade; in silver, they finally possessed a good as highly in demand in China and India as Eastern goods were in Europe. The economic advantages accruing to these merchants and companies, and the political advantages accruing to the countries to which they belonged, were extraordinary. Silver and gold not only provided merchants and consumers with the means to buy an unprecedented abundance of merchandise abroad, but also financed the steady accretion of state power and military might in the several Atlantic-bordering countries in Europe—all resulting in the formation of a highly competitive, multinational, European managed, global empire of silver.

The underlying significance of silver and gold to the state and economy— to power and to plenty—provoked a calculated scramble between rival European empires for the two coveted metals. By the early decades of the seventeenth century, in England especially, a new way of thinking about the state and economy—an order retrospectively labeled *mercantilism*—came to dominate most ideas and conversations about the general benefits but also potential pitfalls of foreign trade. This development carried vast political implications. Mercantilism emphasized the role of the state in managing trade so that silver and gold accumulated and remained within national borders. For this accumulation of metals, a favorable *balance of trade* was most necessary. Exports, on balance, must exceed imports. Only through an overall trade surplus would silver and gold enter into and, on balance, remain within a country. Mercantilists no doubt were a heterogeneous bunch, particularly in England, deviating broadly on specific strategy and policy prescriptions. All agreed, however, on the balance-of-trade doctrine, and all agreed that while the incoming current of silver and gold was not the end in itself, it was in fact the optimum way to enhance national power, prestige, security, and plenty. Money was the means to secure the empire's chief ends.

Mercantilism, as such, became as good as sacrosanct in most economic and political thought in seventeenth-century England. An often tense alliance of merchants and government—of capital and coercion—propagated, debated, and furthered the predominant principles and divergent methods of mercantilism, resulting in the growth of an English empire that functionally benefited both groups, broadly considered. Colonial plantations, in particular, ranked among the most emphasized and prized of all mercantilist assets.

On the eve of the sixteenth century, the world's most lucrative trade routes passed through the Middle East into Asia. Porcelain, silk, cotton, and spices traversed hundreds and thousands of miles, with gold and silver mediating, as money, a great bulk of this exchange. Most gold derived from West Africa, with smaller sums produced in Nubia, Ethiopia, Zimbabwe, the Balkans, the Caucasus, and Southeast Asia; the bulk of silver derived from central Europe, with smaller quantities arriving from Persia and China.[1] China and the Indian subcontinent each boasted populations exceeding one hundred million; China comprised the world's largest economy even after the recent turn of the Ming dynasty inward from maritime trade and overseas exploration. The Ottoman Empire governed a smaller, more diffuse population of twenty million; Ottoman rule, nonetheless, brought much-needed stability and order to overland trade routes, its merchants profiting signally as middlemen between Asia and Europe, even before the empire's conquest of Constantinople in 1453.[2]

Europe was on the periphery of this semiglobal trade network. Approximately seventy million inhabited the continent, but with a much lower population density than either China or India and with greater political fragmentation than any other core region. During the High Middle Ages, however, and accelerating through the fifteenth century, Europe's political and economic condition had rapidly altered. Its princes fielded larger armies and mobile artillery, rendering castles and fortifications less secure while encouraging more consolidated political units capable of extracting the money required to finance these new, more expensive methods of warfare. European rulers still extracted the bulk of their revenue from tribute, fees, and land rents, but an increasing number of states now also turned to merchants for loans, and some foresaw tremendous revenue potential in taxing commercial enterprise.[3] European market activity had widened considerably in recent centuries; more and more capital accumulated in mercantile hands, centered in towns and cities where a budding class of urban and semiurban artisans and tradesmen signaled the onset of a more commercial future for Europe. Though the peasantry remained rural and mostly bound to the land, the older feudal world in which static, immobile landholdings constituted the highest form of wealth was already giving way gradually to a commercial world demanding fluid capital and a vibrant merchant class for the distribution of international goods, setting the stage for silver and gold to supplant land as the most desired commodity in Europe.

Italian merchants, centered largely in Venice, handled vast sums of gold and silver coin in this period. Like the Ottomans, they functioned as commercial middlemen, but between the rest of Europe and the Near East. The continent's overall trade deficit compelled Venetian merchants to exchange European silver to the eastern Mediterranean for imported goods; from there the silver either remained in Ottoman hands or flew further eastward to Persia and onward to India. Europe's silver supply derived primarily from the mines of present-day Germany, Austria, and the Czech Republic; Hungary and Transylvania supplied moderate quantities of gold, but most gold in Europe arrived from the western Sudan and Gold Coast (Ghana), traveling by caravan across the Sahara, passing through Ottoman hands before settling in Italian trading centers, whence the gold then dispersed across continent.[4] The stock of gold in Europe had grown appreciably since the late twelfth century, and though European silver mining languished in the fourteenth and early fifteenth centuries, the continent's silver mines rebounded after the 1460s in spectacular fashion, providing merchants and consumers with still more currency to purchase imported goods.[5]

The sequence from here is very familiar. Anxious to break Venetian and Muslim hegemony over currency and trade, Portuguese explorers ventured southward to and around Africa: first to access gold from the western part of the continent, and then to establish direct commerce with the Indies. Bartolomeu Dias rounded the Cape of Good Hope in 1488, and only ten years later Vasco da Gama reached the Indian subcontinent. The length of the voyage still made it too impractical to carry on the bulk of Europe's trade with the East; that trade carried on via overland routes long afterward. The inexpediency of the route around Africa had already prompted Christopher Columbus to undertake a daring voyage west for Asia. But in doing so, Columbus inadvertently unveiled an entirely new world, presaging a shift in the balance of power from Mediterranean to Atlantic. Less than three decades later, Ferdinand Magellan's crew had circumnavigated the globe for Spain.

Few could have anticipated the coming monetary windfall for Spain in the Americas, yet Columbus and his men received strong hints of it on their inaugural voyage. Many of the people they encountered, Columbus said, wore "very large rings of gold on their arms and legs," claiming knowledge of lands possessing "more gold than earth." Within only a three month period, Columbus's diary mentioned the quest for gold no fewer than sixty-five times. "Without doubt," he concluded one month after his arrival, "there is in these lands a vast quantity of gold": enough, indeed, to return to Spain in 1493 with 64 pounds of the metal; his second voyage the following year yielded 141 pounds of gold.[6]

The invasion of Mexico in 1519 revealed the main fount of this gold. In the thriving metropolis of Tenochtitlan, Hernán Cortés and his men saw in the marketplaces, temples, and palaces such indescribable marvels of gold and silver ornaments, buckles, headdresses, necklaces, and other jewelry, that they could hardly believe their eyes: "things so remarkable," Cortés wrote, "that they cannot be described in writing nor would they be understood unless they were seen"—"so marvelous," indeed, "that considering their novelty and strangeness they are priceless."[7] An indigenous witness later recounted that upon seeing these items, "the Spaniards grinned like little beasts and patted each other with delight . . . they hungered like pigs for that gold."[8] Cortés quickly seized Montezuma and "begged him to show me the mines," demanding a ransom of gold for the emperor's release. After a months-long struggle, Tenochtitlan fell in 1521, the city razed and the gold confiscated, with a fraction of the treasure, the "Royal Fifth," consigned to the Habsburg king of Spain, while "the remainder of the gold was divided up between myself [Cortés] and the other Spaniards."[9] The conquerors then spent the next several years scouring the land for gold, notoriously wreaking havoc over much of the population to satiate their lust for more metal. Francisco Pizarro's conquest of Peru in 1532 inflicted similar cruelties.

Before the 1530s, treasure confiscation accounted for most of the incoming silver and gold to Spain from the Americas, and of that treasure, gold dominated (about 70 percent of the total value of metals).[10] But the land now subdued, the Spaniards soon opened up mines across the country, forcibly recruiting many of the natives to labor under extraordinarily strenuous and often deadly conditions. Mining, at first, was mostly limited to the areas surrounding Mexico City, where the first colonial mint opened in 1536. But in

April 1545 the Spaniards uncovered massive silver deposits deep in the mountain of Cerro Rico, at Potosí in Upper Peru (present-day Bolivia). The following year, the Spaniards discovered additional silver deposits at Zacatecas, about 350 miles northwest of Mexico City, and a decade later, smaller silver deposits at Guadalajara, in western Mexico. A major technological advancement, the separation of silver from other minerals via mercury amalgamation, further aided the boom after 1557, together with the amazingly convenient discovery of mercury deposits in Peru in 1563. A second mint opened at Lima two years later.[11] Mines in Ecuador, Chile, and New Granada (northern South America) also produced copious quantities of gold, but already by the 1570s, silver made up almost 90 percent of the value of all metals shipped from the Americas to Spain.[12] The silver mountain at Potosí alone supplied an estimated 40 percent of all the silver mined *in the world* between 1580 and 1610.[13]

The numbers indeed are staggering. Between 1550 and 1700, the total output of silver from American mines exceeded 40,000 tons.[14] This is all the more incredible when one considers that at the beginning of the sixteenth century, the estimated global stock of silver was only 35,000 tons.[15] The data from the eighteenth century is even more impressive, approaching 50,000 tons of newly extracted silver. Peru, for many decades, was the source of most silver production, but after 1670 Mexico jumped ahead and accounted for almost 70 percent of all American silver production in the eighteenth century.[16] It was the most phenomenal expansion in the silver money supply in all of human history: "so prodigious a quantity of gold and silver," observed Montesquieu, "that all we had before could not be compared with it."[17]

The principal coin to emerge from this profusion of American silver was the "piece of eight," so-called because it had the silver content of eight *reals* (royals), a smaller denomination of Spanish money (see figure 1). The coin contained roughly one ounce of silver and measured nearly four centimeters in diameter. Between 1520 and 1700, the silver extracted from American mines supplied nearly 1.5 billion pieces of eight: Mexico produced 634 million and Peru 855 million.[18] Through the entire colonial epoch, from 1520 to 1810, the sum totaled 3.5 billion pieces of eight.[19] The coin utterly dominated commercial exchanges in America and the Atlantic, and even in the Pacific, China, and other parts of East Asia. Though most European nations, including England, required the reminting of foreign coin before entering domestic circulation, English law never prohibited the use of foreign money within England's colonial possessions. Consequently, the piece of eight became the most commonly used coin in English America (once established), remaining in circulation there well into the nineteenth century, until the Coinage Act of 1857 finally revoked its legal tender status in the United States.[20]

FIGURE 1. Silver piece of eight, Potosí, 1637. (ANS 1969.111.42. Courtesy of American Numismatic Society.)

The rich silver deposits in New Spain and Peru rendered the two viceroyalties enormously profitable for the Spanish Crown. Output reached its highest levels in the 1590s, when silver accounted for 95 percent of total American exports (including nonmetallic goods).[21] Spain was now the most powerful state in Europe. Having recently humbled France after decades of warfare, the only close rival was the Ottoman Empire, presiding over the eastern Mediterranean, Red Sea, Persian Gulf, and other principal zones in the older but still vital Eurasian trade routes. Spain, nevertheless, had the greater momentum, armed with a seemingly boundless stream of American treasure and exercising sovereign control over Portugal, the Netherlands, the Philippines, Mexico, Peru, and large segments of Italy.[22]

Such a rapid turn in geopolitical affairs astounded, impressed, and also panicked the rest of Europe. Lacking the financial means to conventionally confront Spanish military might, some European states resorted to privateering. Privateers sailed under government-granted letters of marque and commissions of war, with permission to keep a portion of the spoils of any captured enemy vessel. These privateers constituted a private, leased navy of sorts.[23] Of the 197 English vessels used to stop the Spanish Armada in 1588, for instance, only 34 belonged to the Royal Navy: privateers made up the remainder.[24] In England, France and the Low Countries, affluent merchants and landowners sponsored scores of privateers to plunder Spanish silver fleets crossing the Caribbean Sea and Atlantic Ocean on their way to Cádiz and Seville. The French were the first to sponsor such attacks, deploying the so-called corsairs to the Caribbean Sea beginning in the 1520s. The English and Dutch joined after the 1560s, culminating in a massive spike in English privateering with the opening of the Anglo-Spanish War in 1585.[25] Sir Francis Drake was the most famous of these Elizabethan sea dogs, raiding coastal towns across Spanish America in the early 1570s and then plundering an estimated £600,000 worth of bullion, coin, spices, and other valuables while circumnavigating the globe from 1577 to 1580. Upon his return to England, Drake received a knighthood from Elizabeth, whose half share of the plunder exceeded the rest of her entire royal revenue from that year.[26]

Even when the two metals passed safely across the Atlantic, however, Spain still suffered a hemorrhaging of silver and gold, as Spanish merchants relentlessly exported silver to other merchants in Europe for imported woolens and linens. In a vain attempt to contain silver within Spain, the government made it a capital crime to export coin without a license. Tradesmen continued to do so anyway, only more furtively.[27] Ironically, to keep the silver within Spain would have been proven worse. The influx of silver precipitated a dramatic rise in domestic prices in Spain, forcing consumers to spend greater sums of coin to purchase the same quantity of goods. One visitor to the country remarked that it was a popular saying there that "everything is dear in Spain, except silver."[28] Wages rose, but at a slower rate than inflation, causing a sharp decline in real wages. Spanish industry suffered immeasurably, as Spanish-made cloth and other manufactures were now far more expensive (in terms of silver) than foreign competition. This price differential discouraged other Europeans from buying expensive Spanish-made goods, and encouraged Spaniards to buy cheaper Dutch-, French-, and English-made goods. The result was a flight of money from Spain, a lagging manufacturing sector, a depressed economy, and the beginning of the long decline of Spanish hegemony.[29]

Like water overfilling its container, silver and gold spilled across much of the European continent, resulting in a monumental uptick in continental prices. Inflation rates varied from region to region, but prices generally began their ascent after 1515, rising with particular speed between 1540 and 1600, then advancing at a slower rate until the end of the 1640s.[30] In England between 1515 and 1650, prices rose nearly 700 percent.[31] A concurrent boost in population levels and urbanization played a complementary role in the so-called Price Revolution, but the extreme profusion of American silver, and its subsequent fall in value, contributed most of all to this price phenomenon. Observers in England noted this in the early-seventeenth century. Spain had become the "Fountain of Mony": "the Cistern and Receptacle of almost all the Gold and Silver, which is thence dispersed into the rest of Europe." "This treasure passeth from them as if it were conveyed by a channel," a merchant in England marveled in 1601.[32]

Both metals fell considerably in value, but silver fell at a greater rate than gold. Between 1500 and 1700, American mines yielded 289 tons of gold—an impressive sum, no doubt (roughly 20 percent of world output in the same period)—but more than 42,000 tons of silver.[33] The gold-silver ratio responded accordingly: in 1519, in Europe, 11 ounces of silver purchased one ounce of gold; by 1640, one ounce of gold required at least 15 ounces of silver.[34] The sharp reduction in silver's value shortly bankrupted many of the old central European mines, ending the once great European silver mining boom of the fifteenth century.[35] If household consumption of wrought silver had not risen concurrently as another use for silver than coin—in plates, bowls, utensils, tankards, and other goods made formerly of iron, tin, and brass—the price of silver would surely have plunged even further.[36]

The silver influx initiated more than the Price Revolution; it revolutionized, also, global commerce between West and East. Key to this development was the so-called "silverization of China" in the fifteenth century. Through much of the medieval period, succeeding dynasties in China had successfully emitted the world's first paper currency. This paper system, with bronze coins, worked reasonably well through the end of the twelfth century. But the value of the paper money severely depreciated in the thirteenth and fourteenth centuries, inducing Chinese merchants and tradesmen to thereafter use silver bars as their favored medium of exchange. By the sixteenth century, the Chinese economy—serving nearly one-quarter of the world's population—had landed upon silver as its predominant medium of exchange. Historian Richard von Glahn labels the period between 1550 and 1650 China's "Silver Century."[37] But silver was unusually expensive in China. Because domestic silver mining was far too insufficient to quench domestic demand, the price of the metal in China skyrocketed, especially relative to gold. By the mid-sixteenth century, the gold-silver ratio in China was 1:6, compared with 1:8 in India, 1:10 in Persia, and 1:11–12 in Europe.[38] European merchants, now inundated with silver, and eager as ever for Chinese imports, proved happy to export their silver to a land where it fetched such a high price. Nor was China the only burgeoning market for silver: in Mughal India (where the population exceeded that of Europe and the Middle East combined), the silver *rupee* became ever more predominant in trade, and like the Chinese, Indian merchants possessed valuable merchandise—pepper and cotton textiles—to trade for silver.[39] Silver became the first global currency. "In any Country that hath Commerce with the rest of the World," Locke correctly noted in 1692, "it is almost impossible now to be without the use of Silver Coin."[40]

The Chinese, at first, received most of their incoming bullion from Japan, known as the "Silver Islands" since the 1530s discovery of extensive silver deposits at Iwami in western Honshu (the largest and most populous Japanese island). Between 1550 and 1650, the Japanese produced eight thousand tons of silver, making Japan the second largest producer of silver in the world.[41] Because the Ming Dynasty prohibited all direct trade between China and Japan, however, the Portuguese stepped in as the predominant middlemen between the two countries, purchasing Chinese silk with Japanese silver and then selling the Chinese silk in Japan for additional silver to export to China for additional silk, and so on.[42] When Dutch intermediaries replaced the Portuguese in the early seventeenth century, the export of Japanese silver by the Dutch East India Company to both China and India averaged some 150–200 tons per annum. The trade abruptly declined in the middle decades of the seventeenth century, but only because the Japanese shogunate sequestered its seaports from outsiders.[43]

The Americas furnished the remaining silver for China's currency conversion. Most of the American silver exported from Europe to China in the late sixteenth and early seventeenth centuries traveled along the traditional routes: the Baltic route (Russia to central Asia) and the Levant route (the Red Sea and Persian Gulf to the Indian Ocean). But as the seventeenth century progressed, the Pacific route (from Mexico to the Philippines) and the Cape route (around the coast of south Africa and then across the Indian Ocean) witnessed remarkable growth in traffic. The Cape route especially flourished as the Dutch and the English entered the business.[44] By the early eighteenth century, nearly seventy vessels a year made the trip around Africa, surpassing all other routes to Asia and removing up to one-third of Europe's incoming supply of American silver, now dispersed across a multitude of trading stations on the coasts of India and the South China Sea.[45]

The silver shipments from Europe to Asia were astronomical. In the seventeenth century they approximated 150 tons per annum—generally in the form of silver bars or Spanish pieces of eight.[46] Of the 42,000 tons of American silver produced between 1520 and 1700, an estimated 31,000 tons—three-fourths—headed straight to Europe (the rest stayed in the Americas or ventured across the Pacific). Of this total, 12,000 tons—that is, 40 percent of Europe's total importation of American silver—left promptly for Asia.[47] This number does not include the unknown yet undoubtedly high quantities of silver exported by smugglers, whether via the Pacific route, the Cape route, or Eurasian land and sea routes. As one Portuguese merchant wrote in 1621, "Silver wanders throughout all the world in its peregrinations before flocking to China, where it remains, as if at its natural center."[48]

The silver trade to Asia, not surprisingly, provoked a considerable backlash from many critics in Europe. When silver traded between different European kingdoms, at least it "continued within the bounds of Christendome," English merchant Edward Misselden wrote in 1622, but with the traffic to Asia, "the money that is traded out of Christendome . . . never returneth againe"; "the treasure of Christendome is wasted." Not that Europeans should abstain altogether from purchasing Asian commodities: far better, he argued, if "in stead of Money for Wares, we may give Wares for Wares."[49] The problem, of course, was that Chinese and Indian merchants did not demand many European wares, leaving European tradesmen little choice but to pay in silver. One English merchant, Gerard Malynes, noted in 1601 the hypocrisy of Europeans ridiculing Native Americans for trading gold for glass beads, iron, and needles, when "nay, we ourselves are guilty of the like simplicity," exchanging American treasure for "dainties and delicacies of superfluous things."[50]

Global trade was never the same again, and despite the large volume of silver leaving Europe for Asia, western European merchants, especially the English and Dutch, gained prodigiously from these new commercial networks. For the first time, European merchants possessed en masse a commodity that Chinese and Indian merchants desperately wanted. This granted European merchants unparalleled access to Eastern desirables, far beyond anything their most recent forebears could have possibly imagined. They acted, in large measure, as middlemen. With American silver, European merchants and companies purchased silk, cotton, porcelain, spices, and other items (including undervalued Chinese gold) in the East, sold them in Europe for additional silver, and then repeated the cycle, profiting handsomely along the way. Both parties purportedly benefited: on one end, the Chinese and Indians received the silver they so greatly demanded; on the other, Europeans won access to the goods they had coveted for centuries. And yet these English, Dutch, and later French merchants and companies enjoyed a distinct and lucrative advantage. They controlled, competitively among themselves, the international distribution of silver. Though fierce rivals, often searching to gain against the other, they together comprised the focal power centers and trading hubs of a new international empire of money.

Not all Atlantic-bordering states were so fortunate. As global trade flourished, the Spanish Empire prolapsed into a period of protracted decline. Besides the aforementioned fallout that inflation wreaked on Spanish exports, wages, and manufacturing, a series of continental wars, occupations, and a prolonged Dutch rebellion against Spanish rule severely sapped the Habsburg treasury, now deep in debt to Genoese bankers. When American silver production unexpectedly dropped by almost 25 percent in the 1640s, the Spanish treasury received only a third of the money that it had taken in during the 1590s.[51] Financial crisis ensued, the public debt exploded, and the Spanish Crown habitually defaulted on its debt obligations: the most "celebrated bankruptcy known to all the world," Montesquieu later called it.[52] The monarchy still administered a sprawling global empire; gold and silver mining, especially in Mexico, achieved new heights in the eighteenth century. But, by this time, the kingdom had long descended from the top tier of the European power structure, having fallen into the trap that Aristotle once warned of two millennia earlier. "He who is rich in coin may often be in want of necessary food," he said, ". . . like Midas in the fable, whose insatiable prayer turned everything that was set before him into gold."[53]

Gold and silver remained extremely desirable—indeed, as indispensable as ever. Long after the peak of Spain's power, the wealthiest, most powerful, most prestigious nations on Earth owned much of it. But for silver and gold to have real utility and worth, the nation or kingdom in possession of these metals must also *produce*. It must domestically produce many nonmetallic goods: first, to refrain from spending too much money on goods from abroad and, second, to sell a surplus of those goods to merchants abroad for gold and silver money. The mere possession of gold and silver was not enough, as Spain had so vividly illustrated. Enter mercantilism.

Out of the monetary revolution of the sixteenth century arose a potent, dynamic new creed: a body of economic opinion known by later generations as *mercantilism*. Mercantilism was the cardinal economic philosophy of empire in early modern Europe. According to mercantilist doctrine, the national quantity of money bore a direct relationship to the nation's economic and political health. The role of the mercantilist state, therefore, was to order and regulate commerce so as to optimize the stock of silver and gold within the state's borders. The most efficient means to achieve this optimization was through a favorable balance of trade, in which exports, on balance, exceeded imports. The balance of trade became the principal gauge to determine the relative benefit or harm of particular commercial activities abroad; the state restricted or prohibited any branch of overseas trade deemed pernicious by that measure. The needs of the national economy always came first, superseding private interests if the latter adversely affected the trade balance. In this way, mercantilism in its ideal state constituted a joint and sometimes sacrificial enterprise, undertaken by every merchant, consumer, and producer in the nation—under force of state management—to better the national welfare by helping to increase the money stock.

Money was the key to national power, prestige, security, and plenty. An incoming current of silver and gold, first, empowered government to finance extravagant state-building programs, vast armies and navies, and extensive colonization projects. Second, as the "Spring and Life to all our Trades," silver and gold also broadened the general prosperity and comfort of ordinary citizens, from merchant to manufacturer, sailor, planter, laborer, and shopkeeper.[54] This effect in turn made the public more able and willing to bear higher taxation and to lend money to the state, enabling the first goal. The whole nation benefited, ensuring for the body politic greater "Strength, Power, Riches and Reputation."[55]

The perceived link between money on one hand and power and plenty on the other was certainly not new to mercantilism. Prior to the seventeenth century, a general body of thought called *bullionism* found favor in much of Europe. Bullionism championed the acquisition of money, in bullion form, through either mining or the conquest of metal-rich lands, while also endorsing state prohibitions on merchants exporting any bullion or coin from the country.[56] Spain, of course, was the prime example of bullionism in action, and its later disgrace did much to discredit the bullionist emphasis on mining. "Whatever we do, let us not imitate the Spaniards," urged one Englishman in 1690, for though "Millions in Specie come in yearly to them," in matters of external trade, they are but "the Fools of the World."[57] Bullionism did not fully disappear in the seventeenth century: some English and Dutch investors still excitedly anticipated the acquisition of new mines in the Americas, and the English government still flatly prohibited the unlicensed export of bullion and foreign coin from the country until the 1660s. Nevertheless, by the early seventeenth century, the new, more sophisticated mercantilist alternative proved vastly more alluring. Gold and silver remained the "great and ultimate effect of Trade," English political economist Sir William Petty wrote in 1676. But now, under mercantilist theory, the optimal means to this end was neither mining, nor blanket prohibitions on exporting bullion from the country (bullion that might, after all, be spent on goods to reexport, such as those from the East Indies). Rather, the most optimal means to increasing the national money stock was the balance of trade: "a more infallible method to secure their Treasure," economist John Pollexfen declared in 1699.[58]

The balance of trade was the mercantilists' central fixation, its study imperative to the country's economic health and vitality. A country's foreign trade was not unlike a "paire of Scales," explained Edward Misselden in 1623. When exports "waigh down and exceed" the value of imports, he said, "the overplus thereof must needs come in in treasure." But when deficits predominate, another writer warned, "impoverishment seems unavoidable, for then our ready Money must go out to even the Ballance." The basic household accounting principle of earning more than one spends was thus applied to the nation. "Wee must ever observe this rule," Thomas Mun wrote in *England's Treasure by Forraign Trade,* "to sell more to strangers yearly than wee consume of theirs in value." The subtitle of Mun's influential 1628 tract in England encapsulated concisely the mercantilist position: *The Ballance of our Forraign Trade is the Rule of our Treasure.*[59]

By the early part of the seventeenth century, the balance-of-trade doctrine enjoyed near-universal acceptance among economic theorists, retaining its prized position as the central pillar of economic thought for the next 150 years. The number of English and European authors who articulated and promoted this doctrine was almost incalculable; indeed, one is hard-pressed to find a single commercial tract ignoring the principle. "It is agreed by all that pretend to understand Trade that a Country doth grow rich, and then only, when the Commodities exported out of it are more in value, then those that are imported into it," one Englishman stated in 1689; indeed, he continued, "there is no way in the World for a Country to grow rich by Trade but by setting this Balance right." "Almost ever since the Revival of Commerce in Europe, there has been a great deal written upon the general annual Balance of a whole Nation's Commerce," Adam Anderson of Scotland wrote in 1764. Anderson agreed with this fixation on drawing an "Over-balance of Money from other Nations," arguing that "it is undoubtedly our great and most important Interest incessantly to pursue it." "The Wealth of a Country now is the Ballance," argued Charles Davenant in 1695, ". . . a Nation which looses in the Generall Ballance had better be without Trade then with it." The doctrine, indeed, remained so pervasive, for so long, that in 1734 the author of *Money Answers All Things* declared it "almost self-evident."[60] "If a King would desire to behold from his throne, the various revolutions of Commerce," Misselden wrote in 1623, ". . . he may behold them all at once in this Globe of glasse, *The Ballance of Trade.*"[61]

Mercantilist preoccupations with the "Grand Ballance of Trade"—as one writer called it in 1652—excited, necessarily, economic jealousy between rival states. Commercial warfare occasionally resulted, each power "striving to undermyne and beate each other out of their trades."[62] Mercantilists generally wished to avoid actual warfare—wars, after all, drained a country of money—but economic warfare (e.g., tariffs, prohibitions, and regulations) was nearly always an appropriate strategy if the outcome was an upgraded trade balance.[63] The stakes were high: the victor of the contest would purportedly emerge the most powerful state in Europe and possibly the world.

European monarchs and state policymakers embraced mercantilism for its promised benefits of military might and political stability. Customs revenue and other commercial taxes increased in proportion with trade; a wealthy merchant community could also lend money to the king at low interest. "When

Trade flourisheth, the Kings revenue is augmented," Misselden noted in 1622. "Rich Subjects can make their King Rich when they please," argued another in 1693, "If He gain their Hearts, He will quickly be Master of their Purses." "Gold and Silver is a Kingly Merchandize," wrote a London merchant in 1660, ". . . the chief Strength of the Kingdom . . . the Sinews of Warre . . . the great Wheell of the State": "the undoubted Interest of his Majesty," said another merchant in 1671.[64] A broad understanding prevailed now among European rulers that political power depended, in part, on a highly monetized economy, a thriving commercial sector, and the possession of capital by private men expected to collaborate with the state.[65]

The changing nature of warfare in Europe—the burgeoning armies, navies, and bureaucracies to oversee them—required that the state have unprecedented access to money and credit. "The Wars now adays seem rather to be waged with Gold than with Iron," one Englishman stated in 1695; "War is become rather an Expence of Money than Men," said another two years earlier, "and Success attends those that can most and longest spend Money."[66] "'Tis the longest Purse that conquers now, not the Sword," Defoe noted in 1728, ". . . if they have but more Money than their Neighbours, they shall soon be superior to them in Strength, for Money is Power."[67] The relation between power and money was reciprocal: money extended power, and power generated more money. "Riches always follow Power," said Charles Davenant in 1695, "and the Iron does draw to it the Gold and Silver."[68] "Since the Wealth of the Indies came to be discovered and dispersed more and more, Wars are managed by much Treasure and little Fighting," said another Englishman in 1680, ". . . the Prince and Nation which hath the greatest Treasure, will finally have the Victory."[69] "Money, and not merely Multitudes of Men, as in old Times," wrote Anderson in 1764, was "now the great Measure of Power."[70]

Governments played a vital role in molding national trade objectives to secure the specie (gold and silver) so requisite for military might. "All the Happyness and Glory of England depends upon the Encouragement and good Management of Trade," said one writer in 1693. Trade was now "the Darling of State," another stated in 1682: "a principal Piece of State-policy." "Is there any thing in the World that should be more thought a Matter of State than Trade?" Davenant asked in 1696: "the bent of all the laws should tend to the Incouragement of Commerce." Of course the balance of trade was the predominant measure, and because of that, Mun argued in 1628, "this balance of the Kingdoms account ought to be drawn up yearly," informing various modes of state action and regulation.[71]

State intervention became the rule of the day. "All Nations under well constituted Governments, are vigilant and careful to preserve what they esteem their Treasure," John Pollexfen asserted in 1699, "and in their Councils advise and concert, how to restrain and discourage such Trades as they suspect will exhaust their Wealth."[72] State intervention entailed a host of miscellaneous schemes, including prohibitive duties on foreign imports, subsidies for domestic industry, restrictions on foreign shipping, and other "numberless bars, obstructions, and imposts," David Hume later derided, "which all the nations of Europe, and none more than England, have put upon trade, from an exorbitant desire of amassing money."[73]

Mercantilists deemed economic intervention necessary because "private advantages" in trade too often breached "publick profit."[74] For the mercantilist, the "benefit of the whole" was always in view, at least rhetorically.[75] "It should not be left in the Liberty of Trading men to Traffick by such ways and in such a Manner as may bring Mischief to the Publick," Davenant argued in his *Memorial Concerning the Coyn of England*.[76] Merchants may indeed be "very wise and good men," Josiah Child presumed in 1689, but "they are not always the best Judges of Trade, as it relates to the profit or power of a Kingdom"; "oftentimes," another said, "the Merchant may get when the Publick looses."[77] Consider, for instance, a London merchant employing a Dutch shipmaster who charges less money for freight than competing shipmasters in England. Though the London merchant undoubtedly gained from his use of Dutch shipping, the silver he expended on freight went straight to Holland, thus damaging (allegedly) the public interest of England. Consequently, according to many (though not all) mercantilists, government policy ought to bar this temptation altogether. "A Country cannot Increase in Wealth and Power but by Private Men doing their Duty to the Publick," Davenant insisted in 1699. "Private Interest is that many headed Monster," wrote another in 1680: "a private Trade may be very beneficial to the private Trader, but of hurtful, nay of very ruinous Consequence to the whole Nation."[78]

In spite of it all, regulatory policy was the point at which the mercantilist consensus entirely broke down. Mercantilists unanimously believed that governments ought to stand ready and willing to intervene on behalf of the trade balance, but where, how, and to what extent remained wildly controversial. "Tho' we are agreed that Trade is the main Spring from whence Riches flow," English clothier William Carter explained in 1700, "yet we do as much differ in the Method of acquiring thereof."[79] Some mercantilists supported protection for shipping; others argued that such restrictions rendered freight more expensive, damaging the overall balance by stifling trade. Some championed manufacturing protection (via new import duties); still others wished to prohibit altogether the importation of luxury items such as wine, tobacco, silk, and other "superfluous Commodities that drain our Treasure."[80] Some supported monopoly companies; others believed trade should be open to all the kingdom's merchants. Most supported overseas colonization, but some argued that colonial settlements unnecessarily depopulated the home country and "decoy'd away to New-England and Virginia" the country's main source of labor.[81] Most controversial of all was the trade to China and India: some defended the export of silver to the East as ultimately gainful—pointing to the lucrative reexport trade—while others blasted the trade for draining the country of money.

Nearly all mercantilists abandoned the earlier bullionist emphasis on discovering mines replete with silver and gold; most also objected to blanket prohibitions on exporting bullion. But these objections signified only a shift in strategy, and not any real decline in the desire to acquire precious metals. Indeed, mercantilist policymakers demanded coin even more than their bullionist predecessors. The mercantilists simply better understood now how best to acquire it and then how to retain it. William Wood, a merchant in England in the early eighteenth century, explained succinctly the difference between mercantilism and bullionism. England's "trading Mines," he argued, consisted of industry, commerce, agriculture, and labor. These were in fact superior to actual mines because they make a "perpetual Addition" to the money supply, whereas countries that acquired specie simply through digging faced the ultimate problem of depleted mines and thereafter "become Beggars, notwithstanding their first Property of all the Gold and Silver in the World." Disdain for mining was quite common among the mercantilists; one English politician, in 1711, surmised that the English discovery of gold and silver mines "would only destroy our industry, and make us a lazy Generation." Far better, he argued, was the alternative of "exchanging our Goods for Bullion."[82] "Trade is a richer and more dureable Mine than any in Mexico or Peru," declared another writer in 1696.[83]

Economic ideas, concepts, and issues ventured from the periphery of intellectual and political discussion to the forefront. Niccolò Machiavelli had once argued in 1513 that princes "should have no care or thought but for war . . . for war is the sole art looked for in one who rules." But such was no longer the case. Now, as William Wood remarked, it was the "chief Wish, to have a Prince on the Throne, who, Ruling over a Trading People, may know the Grand Concern of Trade." It was "the Indispensable Concernment of the Government," said another, "to make it their utmost Care and Labour to Understand, Preserve, and improve this one thing necessary." As Roger Coke announced in 1670, "Trade is now become the Lady, which in this present Age is more Courted and Celebrated than in any former by all the Princes"; "surely matters of State and of Trade are involved and wrapt up together," said Misselden.[84]

Seventeenth-century English and European writers heaped innumerable praises on commerce, trumpeting statements unthinkable, even heretical, in the century preceding it. A small sample of these accolades—all in the seventeenth century—illuminate the truly radical nature of this transformation. "Trade and Commerce are the Pillars of Prosperity, and safety to England"; the "true and intrinsick Interest of England, without which it cannot subsist"; the "glory, strength and security of the English Nation"; "as useful in the body Politick as blood in the veins of the body," that which "moves, maintains, and enlivens the whole Body of the People from the meanest Cottage, to the Royal Throne."[85] One English author, in 1608, even spoke of the "sanctified Altars of publique Commerce," a phrase that would have utterly dumbfounded readers only a few decades prior. "Love doth much, but Money doth all," another writer acclaimed positively in 1615.[86]

With attitudes toward commerce shifting so profoundly and suddenly, the social and political status and influence of the profit-minded merchant also enjoyed significant advances. Historically, the rank and prestige of even the wealthiest merchant stood far below that of the landed gentry. According to the prevailing view, a landed man who "engaged any of his younger children in a Trade . . . debased his family for ever"; indeed, better to raise a child "up for the Gallows" than to "be dishonoured by a Trade."[87] A strong remnant of this antimercantile sentiment prevailed well into the eighteenth and even nineteenth centuries, but the dawn of the commercial revolution steadily eroded these prejudices, beginning in the sixteenth and seventeenth centuries.[88] As one English merchant wrote in 1601, European states were finally coming to realize that "a Prince may use this kinde of men, I meane Merchantes, to the great benefite, and good of his state . . . without losse of one jote of honor."[89] Many merchants, by the early seventeenth century, unabashedly championed purely commercial matters in their published writings and outward conversations. "Every man almost is taken with the attention to profite," one merchant exclaimed in 1615—that "sweete fountaine of profite" that brought with it a "continual spring of great gaine."[90] Thomas Mun, in like manner, in the 1620s, labeled trade a "Noble vocation," a "laudable practise . . . the very Touchstone of a kingdoms prosperity"; Slingsby Bethel, in 1671, even called it "the most honourable of all professions."[91]

All the while, in the midst of this commercial and monetary revolution, European governments converged rapidly on the nation-state model. The process assumed a variety of forms but generally sought to work coercion and capital together. Coercion, on the one hand, found expression in the great consolidating states, boasting centralized armies, navies, and administrative structures. Capital located itself in the great commercial cities and urban centers, forming an often uneasy alliance with the state—one that required much bargaining, often extraordinarily tense, between both parties. State concessions to merchants including affording them some sort of representation in government—whether in parliaments, committees, or advisory roles—together with relative freedom of trade within the state's borders. Mercantile concessions to the state included a general acceptance of new taxes on commerce, precarious loans in wartime, and state oversight and restrictions on certain market activity, especially in their trade with foreign countries. The impromptu result was the early dawn of the modern European state.[92]

American silver and gold accelerated the transition to modern statehood, and mercantilism was the favorite mode of state-economic organization. As Charles Tilly, historian and sociologist, once wrote: "war made the state, and the state made war." But the state also made money—and money, for certain, made the state. "Money in the State quickens its Actions," Sir William Petty remarked in 1664.[93] By the start of the eighteenth century, Britain appeared on the winning end of this mercantilist contest. The seeds of this ascendancy were first sown in England's remarkable commercial rise in the latter half of the sixteenth century, sprouting further in the seventeenth century as English officials struggled to forge and then to master a new mercantilist empire of power and money.

England was a highly unlikely candidate in the early sixteenth century to win the upcoming contest for silver and gold. London, in the 1520s, counted only 60,000 residents, far fewer than Antwerp, Naples, Paris, Venice, or Lisbon. The two next largest towns in England, Norwich and Bristol, each counted only 10,000 residents. The country's 2.5 million inhabitants labored primarily in agriculture and sheep herding, scattered across the many villages that peppered the English countryside, extracting wool and producing coarse textiles. Woolens accounted for nearly four-fifths of all English exports; tin and lead made up the remainder. The Company of Merchant Adventurers, a London-based mercantile guild founded in the early fifteenth century, sent the bulk of these across the Channel directly to Antwerp, a city situated near the province of Flanders, in the southern half of the Spanish Netherlands. Flemish merchants reexported English woolens across most of the European continent at considerable profit and then gainfully reexported continental European goods—wines, linens, and metalwares—to the English.[94]

The early Tudor kings lacked both the resources and the will to finance overseas exploration and expansion. The country was still recovering from the dynastic Wars of the Roses (1455–1485) when Columbus entreated King Henry VII in 1487 to finance the former's voyage across the Atlantic. "In those dayes we had no great need to follow strange reports, or to seeke wilde adventures," recalled one writer in 1609.[95] In 1496 Henry awarded a patent to John Cabot, a Venetian, to explore North America, but failed to capitalize on Cabot's discoveries. King Henry VIII (r. 1509–1547) displayed even less concern for transatlantic ventures, notwithstanding promises from a few of his English contemporaries that American colonization assured the kingdom "perpetuall glory," "great profite," and the "richest lands and Ilands of the worlde of Golde"—a statement reflecting the still-dominant bullionist view. Henry VIII did not stir on the question, immersed rather in domestic affairs, religious controversies, and continental wars.[96]

Still, woolen exports—"our Golden Fleece," as it was commonly known—enjoyed a spectacular boom in the early Tudor period, resulting in a major influx of coin into England, boosting state revenue as well as popular perceptions of the general benefits of commerce.[97] The second half of the century looked even brighter for English wool. Despite a devastating bust in woolen exports at midcentury, the market rebounded by the 1560s, and for the first time, English exporters looked beyond the Flemish middlemen at Antwerp and traded heavy woolens directly from England to the Baltics, Hamburg, and other northern European states. Moreover, in the 1560s, English clothworkers began steadily producing "new draperies": lighter woolens more suitable for southern Europeans. By the late 1570s, English merchants had secured a direct trade to Mediterranean markets, exporting new draperies to Spain and Italy and tin and lead to the Ottoman Empire, and purchasing silk, sugar, raisins, cotton, and drugs to bring back to England, altogether bypassing Antwerp (a city now besieged by the still-dominant Spanish).[98]

Under Queen Elizabeth (r. 1558–1603), England embarked on a prolonged period of political stability and commercial expansion, the peak of which extended from the 1560s through early 1580s. The period featured the creation of private, joint-stock companies armed with monopoly charters from the Crown, including the Muscovy Company (to Russia), the Turkey Company, and Venice Company (the latter two merged into the Levant Company in 1592). Other companies functioned not with a common stock of capital but with a regular set of entry requirements, including the Eastland Company (to the Baltics and Scandinavia), the Spanish Company, and the older Company of Merchant Adventurers. The new overseas ventures allotted English merchants invaluable experience in capital accumulation, long-distance trade, and large-scale company organization.[99] The establishment in 1568 of the Royal Exchange of London signaled the onset of this commercial transformation. Here, cosmopolitan merchants eagerly assembled to distribute commodities and money from all over the globe, conversing excitedly over new opportunities for trade and profit.[100] Moreover, in 1570 Parliament legalized the lending of money at interest, enabling further development of credit markets in London. The city now boasted more than 200,000 residents, including "a great number of wealthie, and well experimented Merchants," many of whom proudly entered the House of Commons.[101]

Foreign coin and bullion proceeded steadily into the Elizabethan mint. Between 1559 and 1601, the royal mint in London coined money to the value of £5.2 million, of which nearly £4.5 million was silver; gold comprised under £800,000.[102] The silver coins struck under Queen Elizabeth included the crown (5s), half-crown (2s6d), shilling (1s), sixpence (6d), groat (4d), twopence, penny, and halfpenny—each containing the sterling standard of 92.5 percent silver.[103] The coins attained common circulation in the towns and cities; £4.5 million of silver money makes 18 million crowns, or 90 million shillings, circulating—unequally of course—among a population of four million people. This was no small sum, and certainly far greater than the currency in previous decades.

The winnings of English privateers, plundered from Spanish galleons on the high seas, comprised a sizable portion of this incoming silver. Though England and Spain were not formally at war until 1585, the strain between the two kingdoms had grown intensely since the late 1560s. Elizabeth was deeply conservative in most matters of foreign policy, but she was also wary of Spanish attempts to dominate France and the Protestant Netherlands, the former decapitated by religious civil war and the latter in active revolt against Spanish rule. The Queen implicitly endorsed Drake's plundering of Spanish ships in the 1570s and explicitly commissioned privateering with the formal onset of war in 1585. The Crown possessed no more than a couple dozen ships exceeding one hundred tons, and commissioning privateers was much less costly to the Crown than expanding the royal navy.[104] Some 100–200 privateers annually set out from England in the years after 1585, many venturing to the Caribbean (the West Indies). During this high period of Elizabethan privateering, the sum of prizes averaged £200,000 in value per annum; a good portion of this windfall, in turn, funneled into mercantile enterprises and other commercial investments.[105]

A spirit of pride, destiny, and solidarity consumed England as never before in the 1570s and 1580s. The public image and reputation of the English monarchy soared to near-celestial heights. American exploration, hitherto unconsidered, played well into this Elizabethan zeitgeist. The Anglo-Spanish conflict had focused English attention, for the first time, on the enticing possibilities of the still-mysterious Atlantic. Though most English merchants attended exclusively to opportunities in Mediterranean and intra-European trade, a growing and vocal contingent of interests urgently promoted North American colonization as the surest way to usher into England more silver and gold, whether through mining or, increasingly, through colonial economic production designed to improve the national trade balance.[106]

English claims to North America dated back almost a century to Cabot's expedition, but the ensuing dearth of activity exasperated proponents of colonization. By this time, there were nearly two hundred Spanish towns and cities in the New World; French explorers, moreover, had made substantial discoveries in the 1530s and 1540s, including, most significantly, the Saint Lawrence River, linking the Atlantic Ocean to the Great Lakes of North America.[107] Time was running desperately short; the kingdom might later regret inaction, as Henry VII's notorious rejection of Columbus's offer had already evidenced. The hour indeed had come, Sir George Peckham insisted in 1583, for England to awaken "out of that drowsie dreame wherein we have so long slumbered."[108]

The English adventurers who crossed the Atlantic in the 1570s and 1580s anticipated discovering mines and a Northwest Passage to the so-called South Sea, or Pacific Ocean. Wild rumors of indigenous cities of gold enraptured the public imagination, including of many of the adventurers, hoping to emulate the still seemingly successful Spanish model.[109] The Northwest Passage, for its part, promised roundabout access to silver and gold. As of yet, the Portuguese still monopolized the East Indian trade, forcing the English to buy spices at marked-up prices from merchant-middlemen in Lisbon. A westward passage to Asia would not only grant the English direct access to Oriental goods but also open a remunerative carrying trade with Europe, seizing continental markets for English merchants and ushering in, as Sir Humphrey Gilbert forecast in 1576, "great aboundance of gold and silver." Sir Francis Drake, for this reason, celebrated the illusory passage as "the path to Fame, the proofe of Zeale, and way to purchase golde."[110]

In June 1578 Queen Elizabeth granted a private patent to Sir Humphrey Gilbert to plant and govern a colony in North America. Though the Crown did not finance the project, the patent provided that the queen receive the customary royal fifth of all gold and silver discovered, extracted, or seized in said lands. Significantly, the patent also specified that colonists "enjoy all privileges of free denizens and persons native of England."[111] Gilbert selected the island of Newfoundland for colonization. Itinerant fishermen already embarked on seasonal, migratory trips to Newfoundland, but Gilbert desired a permanent, year-round settlement, with ambitions to later move southward along the coast. Meager resources, poor planning, and unrealistic expectations impeded the project, however, ending in September 1583 when Gilbert was lost at sea in a storm. Sir Walter Raleigh, his half-brother, inherited the patent and focused his attention further south. He too fantasized of golden cities and a passage to Asia, as well as a New World base to supply privateers against Spanish treasure fleets. In April 1585, seven ships, together with more than one hundred passengers, departed England to colonize Roanoke Island, in present-day North Carolina. Ralph Lane, the deputy governor, encapsulated the prevailing view well when he declared that "the discovery of a good Mine . . . or a passage to the South-sea, or some way to it, and nothing else can bring this Countrey in request to be inhabited by our nation." The settlement vanished, abruptly terminating the Elizabethan colonial epoch in 1590.[112]

Most of the original English adventurers to America were martial, not commercial, in orientation. Despite this fact, however, and notwithstanding all the talk of mythical golden cities, a number of Elizabethan proponents of colonization eschewed the bullionist impulse in favor of a new, more sophisticated mercantilist model. The most outspoken advocate for colonization, Richard Hakluyt, wrote very little about discovering precious metals but argued that colonies instead ought to produce goods that the English imported from foreign countries. Colonial proponents of the mercantilist type cast doubt on the endless speculation that North America abounded with gold, believing such rumors to be merely hype to make investors "more willyng to furnishe their money," as George Peckham chided in 1583.[113] Bullionist tunnel vision, they believed, obscured the true value of colonies. The trade balance, not mining, would optimally strengthen the national money supply.

Naval stores were among the goods most urgently needed to improve England's trade balance. The recent surge in shipbuilding in the Elizabethan period had worsened England's trade deficit with Baltic and Scandinavian countries for pitch, tar, flax, hemp, masts, and timber. The deficit precipitated from London a flight of coin and bullion to Sweden, Norway, Russia, Poland, and northern Germany. Most of the woodlands in England were long depleted, leaving the kingdom utterly dependent on other countries for naval stores and timber, "so absolutely necessary, that we must have them, though purchased for Bullion," one writer later said.[114] The Baltic trade "exhause this Realme of treasure," one Englishman noted in 1549.[115] The problem intensified in the latter half of the century, as England's growing commerce with the Mediterranean called for vessels of far greater tonnage—between 200 and 400 tons—than the smaller watercraft used in North Atlantic trade. Shipbuilding in general had soared in recent years. Between 1560 and 1582 the number of English vessels between 100 and 200 tons more than doubled, from 71 to 155; the number of ships over 200 tons tripled in the same period, from six to eighteen.[116] The trend continued so that between 1582 and 1609, total shipping tonnage in England amounted to more than one hundred thousand tons per annum—an increase of almost 50 percent—forcing the Muscovy and East-land Companies to import naval stores far in excess of the woolens they exported to those countries.[117]

Colonization, then, might be the answer to the problem of naval stores. In 1576, Richard Hakluyt predicted that if the English settled North America, they would no longer stand dependent on Baltic countries "for flaxe, pitch, tarre, and mastes, so we should not so exhaust our treasure, and so exceeding inrich our doubtfull friends." Indeed, the coming Gilbert and Raleigh expeditions to America unveiled a land replete with pine forests, "enough to serve the whole Realme," argued George Peckham in 1583.[118] North American pine trees extended as high as 100 to 250 feet—large enough for a single tree to serve as a mast—whereas Baltic fir required the piecing together of several trees to form a single mast.[119] Such "plentie of excellent trees," Hakluyt predicted in 1584, would soon contribute to the "great inrichinge of the realme." Another like proponent in 1583 looked forward to a day when the English could build ships "without being in any sort beholding to a King of Denmarke."[120]

American fishing was also immensely promising; one contemporary estimate claimed that the English exported £100,000 in coin and bullion every year to purchase herring from Holland and Zeeland.[121] The Dutch, by consequence, reportedly reckoned the northern European fisheries "their Chiefest Trade and gold-Mine."[122] "This is their Myne, and the Sea the source of those silvered streames," wrote Captain John Smith of the Hollanders' "trade of fish."[123] Happily, according to reports, the northernmost parts of America boasted "great store of excellent Cod fish"; the "most famous fishing in the world."[124] Itinerant English fisherman had frequented Newfoundland since the early sixteenth century, but a permanent settlement would further secure the trade; as one Englishman argued in 1615, the kingdom, through fishing, "may get treasure in aboundance . . . we shall stay the unnaturall tyde of the departure and transportation of our gold . . . which, to our shame and losse, the Hollanders carry away."[125]

The land of Virginia, for its part, promised an entirely different set of goods for England, including wine, silkworms, and olives. Production of these goods would further boost the kingdom's already favorable trade balance with southern Europe. Ever the optimist, Hakluyt excitedly listed sugar, oranges, lemons, and figs among Virginia's prospective commodities, goods currently purchased from the Mediterranean, Iberian Peninsula, and Barbary Coast.[126] Reports slowly surfaced that Virginia contained soil that was "most plentifull, sweete, fruitfull and wholsome": a "paradise of the world" that will assuredly "supplie of those defects which this Realm of Englande most requireth."[127] For precisely this reason, one frustrated Englishman, in 1588, lashed out against the Roanoke expedition for losing their enthusiasm "after golde and silver was not so soone found."[128]

Fantastic tales of gold and silver mines in North America persisted nonetheless. In 1588, reports surfaced that the natives at Roanoke had boasted of "mountaines and rivers that yeelde white graines of Mettal."[129] Following the failed colonial expeditions, and after the crushing defeat of the Spanish Armada in 1588, little else was done on that score, however—notwithstanding Raleigh's determined quest to find the legendary "great and Golden Citie" of El Dorado, in Guiana, South America.[130] Adam Smith likely had Raleigh in mind when he later disparaged "the search after new silver and gold mines" as "the most disadvantageous lottery in the world": a project of "absurd confidence" and "strange delusions."[131]

The 1590s turned out to be a grueling decade for England, discouraging any further colonial projects. A rise of vagrancy and urban poor, together with the outbreak of food riots in the midst of a series of terrible harvests in 1594–1597, alarmed the middling and upper orders in England, already dealing with the eruption of plague in 1592–1593 and the inauguration of a nine-year Irish rebellion in 1594. The Anglo-Spanish War (1585–1604) dealt a serious blow to Spanish power, but the short-term, domestic consequences for England were considerably onerous. Though privateers brought considerable sums of Spanish coin into England, the war abruptly halted English exports of new draperies (lighter woolens) to the money-rich Iberian Peninsula, causing widespread unemployment in England. The financial demands of war also far outstripped the government's revenue, forcing Elizabeth to sell royal lands, borrow money, and summon an ever independent-minded Parliament to levy new taxes.[132] Further sullying matters, England's trade deficit with the Baltic for naval stores reached new heights. Indeed, England's trade with all of Europe approached a deficit of £200,000 per annum in the 1590s, causing Queen Elizabeth in 1600 to issue a proclamation ordering stricter enforcement of laws prohibiting the unlicensed export of coin and bullion.[133]

The rapid accretion of Dutch commercial power caused further uneasiness in England in the 1590s. The decline of the Flemish entrepôt of Antwerp had indeed benefited London (as well as Hamburg), but the chief successor to Antwerp was Amsterdam, the most prominent city in Holland, itself the mightiest province in the United Provinces of the Netherlands. The Dutch had lived under the Habsburg yoke since the late fifteenth century, but beginning in 1566 the northern, Protestant half of the Spanish Netherlands initiated a decades-long rebellion against Habsburg rule. Though the Spanish Crown did not formally relinquish sovereignty until 1647, the Dutch rebels had virtually won their independence by 1590. De facto independence was almost immediately accompanied by an aggressive push by Dutch merchants into European commercial traffic. Amsterdam, whose population doubled between 1570 and 1600, became the center of a thriving reexport trade between northern and southern Europe. Enterprising Dutch merchants bought, stored, and then reexported a wide variety of goods between the Baltic and Mediterranean: bulky grain and timber from the former, and valuable silk, sugar, cotton, and drugs from the latter—pocketing, in the transfer, great sums of silver and gold, in a form of traffic called the *carrying trade*.[134] The 1595 launch of the Dutch *fluit*, a new lightweight vessel, further enhanced Dutch economic competitiveness. The fluit boasted a longer, shallower hull; fewer masts; and a flat bottom, allowing maximum carrying capacity. Built at only half the cost of conventional vessels of the same size, the fluit also required only half the number of working crew, sharply reducing Dutch operating costs in shipping goods from one place to another.[135] Consequently, even in London in the year 1601, Dutch ships outnumbered English ships by 74 percent, 360 to 207.[136]

East Indian commerce was the shining centerpiece of the Dutch carrying trade. The inaugural Dutch fleet reached the Spice Islands (Indonesia) in 1595. After seven years of fierce competition between rival Dutch merchants—including eight different Dutch companies—the States-General of the United Provinces granted exclusive rights to the United Dutch East India Company (Vereenigde Oostindische Compagnie, or VOC). Three years later, in 1605, the VOC ousted the Portuguese from the Spice Islands. The VOC now presided over a maritime empire stretching from the Cape of Good Hope to Japan and East Asia, with a string of military garrisons erected across much of Southeast Asia, and with a virtual monopoly over the trade in nutmeg, mace, and cloves. Much of these spices the VOC reexported to England and France. Furthermore, the VOC marketed a great bulk of these spices throughout East Asia, especially Japan. In Japan, the VOC bought silver with spices, sold the same silver to China for porcelain and silk, and then returned to Europe with Chinese commodities—all accomplished with virtually no silver exports from Holland.[137]

The English answered with their own East India Company (EIC), founded in 1600 with monopoly trading rights between the Cape of Good Hope and the Strait of Magellan. Funded largely from profits generated in Mediterranean commerce, the EIC constructed so-called factories (warehouses and trading settlements) on the Persian and Indian coasts, purchasing valuable pepper to ship back to England in ships weighing up to five hundred tons. As of yet, the company had purchased only limited sums of Indian cotton: pepper predominated the company's trade in the first half of the seventeenth century.[138]

To purchase the pepper (and later cotton), the EIC, with royal license, exported from England immense quantities of silver (and sometimes gold). The company's specie exports, up through the 1660s, varied between £30,000 and £80,000 per annum, but in the final quarter of the seventeenth century, the company exported, every year, £300,000–£600,000 of coin and bullion to the East Indies.[139] The amount constituted a near-unimaginable transfer of specie to the East, but as EIC defenders so eagerly pointed out, the company's reexport of pepper and cotton to European markets was so lucrative that it offset the initial export of silver from England. That said, the Dutch VOC remained substantially more profitable than its English competitor, outstripping the number of English ships in the Indian Ocean, and boasting far more contacts in intra-Asian trade networks.

The new Dutch commercial ventures enriched the Netherlands as rapidly as the discovery of Potosí enriched Spain. Sir Josiah Child later called the Dutch East Indies "more profitable to them than are the Mines of Gold and Silver in America."[140] The Netherlands commanded few natural resources, and as late as the 1580s Dutch involvement in high-value commerce was negligible at best. Yet by the beginning of the seventeenth century, the Netherlands had clearly burst ahead of all other European states in the race for silver and gold. By this point in time, Spanish economic decline was already evident, and religious civil war had practically paralyzed France, leaving a vacuum of economic power for the Dutch to contentedly fill, to the jealous envy of English merchants and administrators.

Despite the many problems vexing England at the close of the sixteenth century, Queen Elizabeth left the country far more secure and commercially advanced than she had found it. Between 1561 and 1603, the circulating stock of silver and gold in England rose by more than 140 percent, from £1.45 million to £3.5 million.[141] Still, the 1590s were a troubling decade, and no permanent settlement had yet been made in America. Elizabeth's Stuart successor, King James I (r. 1603–1625), soon found himself in a better position. Peace with Spain in 1605 allowed the renewal of England's silver-begetting trade of light woolens to the Iberian Peninsula, alleviating some internal economic anxieties. The government's fiscal difficulties continued, but the early part of James's reign witnessed a run of good harvests, considerable growth in East Indian traffic, and a further extension in the export of new draperies to southern Europe. All of this permitted English eyes to once again peer across the Atlantic.[142]

On April 10, 1606, James chartered the Virginia Company of London and the Virginia Company of Plymouth. The London company was to settle lands in the southern half of the North American coast; the smaller, less affluent

Plymouth company was to settle more northerly regions. The charters commanded the companies to "dig, mine, and search for all Manner of Mines of gold, Silver, and Copper," yielding "the fifth Part" to the Crown. Significantly again—as with the Gilbert patent—the king declared that "all and every" person inhabiting the colony, including succeeding generations, "have and enjoy all Liberties . . . as if they had been abiding and born within this our Realm of England."[143] An Englishman inhabiting America was thus no different from an Englishman inhabiting England—at least for now.

As the two companies solicited shareholders, many investors excitedly awaited the discovery of mines, the Northwest Passage, or both. Others scoffed at the supposed credulity of these claims. In the preceding year, 1605, a play entitled *Eastward Hoe* premiered in London, mocking the company's more fanciful outlook. "I tell thee, golde is more plentifull there then copper is with us," alleged one of the fools in the play. "All their dripping-pans and their chamber-potts are pure gould," he said, provoking laughter from the audience. The satire was amusing, though some in the theater, no doubt, must have wondered whether the stories were not at least partly true.[144]

No serious shareholder in the Virginia Company of London went quite so far as the fool in *Eastward Hoe*, but many came awfully close. "We are fall'n upon a land that promises more than the Land of Promise!" an investor exclaimed in 1607, adding, in allusion to Israel, "instead of milk, we find pearl, and gold instead of honey!"[145] Virginia was the "most stately, rich kingdom in the world," another investor rejoiced in 1607, boasting "rocks and mountains that promiseth infinite treasure."[146] In 1606 the poet Michael Drayton dedicated one of his works "to the Virginian Voyage." "Britans you stay too long," he quipped, "quickly aboord bestow you . . . to get the Pearle and Gold, and ours to hold, Virginia, Earth's onely Paradise."[147] Even the aging Richard Hakluyt, in 1609, believed "rich mines of gold" may indeed "lie beyond the mountaines" of Virginia. "There are hilles and mountaines making a sensible proffer of hidden treasure, never yet searched," another writer promised the same year.[148]

Only with the realization that no such mines existed would the English finally abandon the bullionist model for the new mercantilist model of colonization. The shift in strategy, completed in full by the mid-seventeenth century, proved eminently successful. Money remained the empire's primary objective. But in place of mining, England's American plantations procured tobacco, sugar, timber, and other lucrative goods, earning, for the mother country, great "Riches and Money, since it makes the Exportation greater, or the Importation less," to quote an English merchant in 1659. Decades later, in 1725, one writer boasted that trade and commerce had proven "better than the Mines of Peru and Mexico"; the colonies, in particular, yielded "more Treasure than the Mines of Potosí," another said in 1696.[149]

Such prodigious sums of treasure, of course, were not intended for circulation within the colonies themselves. Silver and gold were for England, for the mother country: for the parent, not the child. Colonies are a "vast Advantage to us in the General Balance of Trade," stated merchant William Wood in 1718, ". . . a Spring of Wealth to this Nation, since *they* work for us, and *their* Treasure centers all *here*." Indeed the colonies were nothing short of an "inexhaustible Mine of Treasure to England," said Charles Davenant in 1698. "These are our Golden Mines, and have helpt to support the Ballance of Trade," John Cary, Bristol merchant, wrote of the colonies in 1696.[150]

Henry VII's rejection of Columbus's proposition had proved a blessing after all—that is, only so long as colonial trade served England's interests, and only so long as the bulk of the silver and gold that resulted from colonial trade accumulated in England. Colonial economic interests, from the start, were secondary and subordinate, but such subordination would later prove a hard sell for those who risked everything in crossing the Atlantic. They too wanted a portion, and thought that they had earned it—and were they not also English? It was not long before the development of competing political economies, and of divergent conceptions of empire, caused a growing rift between the metropole in London and the money-famished colonial periphery. The rift had its root in mercantilism—in the empire's central principle of subordinating the colonial world to England's fiscal and monetary needs. Few could have predicted this outcome, however, when the first colonists disembarked at Jamestown.

The Spanish Crown, in the sixteenth century, had chanced upon a spectacular fountain of silver and gold. The discovery initiated a price revolution, a geopolitical revolution, and finally a commercial revolution spanning most parts of the globe. By the turn of the seventeenth century, however, it became abundantly clear that something had gone seriously wrong. Spain lost control of the greater part of her money-holdings, and the empire's prestige declined almost as rapidly as it formerly arose. Mercantilism, thereafter, became the champion theory in most economic thought—the balance of trade became the surest measure in the quest to acquire metallic currency.

Despite looming problems for England at the beginning of the seventeenth century, the English economy enjoyed a record quantity of coin in circulation, some £3.5 million. The trend continued into the seventeenth century. By 1640, the circulating money stock in England exceeded £10 million; by 1700, it reached £14.5 million (in coin, not including paper notes).[151] The American colonies played a crucial role in this gathering of treasure, but the following chapter commences with more humble beginnings: the founding of a perilous settlement in Jamestown, Virginia. The year 1607 marked the beginning of a new epoch in English colonization, one that ultimately propelled the British Isles to the status of world's premier superpower.

CHAPTER 2

The First Decades of English American Settlement, 1607–1639

After about a quarter century of delay and false starts, the English American project finally achieved some permanence at Jamestown, Virginia, in 1607. Extreme hardship, frustration, and reluctant shifts in economic strategy marked the first decade of settlement in Virginia. And yet, some few years later, by the end of the 1630s, English companies and colonists had successfully planted settlements across much of the Eastern Seaboard of North America and in a few of the West Indian islands. The settlers uncovered no gold or silver mines, but the new mercantilist mentality found much to commend in the goods that colonists landed upon instead—goods that promised to indirectly boost England's gold and silver supply by advancing the kingdom's balance of trade.

There was no set precedent yet for running the nascent empire. The king's Privy Council—a deliberative body of a dozen or so men—managed most imperial administrative issues, handling all letters, petitions, and reports to, from, and regarding the colonial settlements and governments. The council did so with neither marked expertise nor clear courses of action. Consensus prevailed that colonial commerce ought to primarily benefit the mother country; nevertheless, the precise means to that end, especially with regard to imperial management, remained vague, uncertain, and inconsistent. The ambiguity resulted, in part, from the inconvenient fact that much of the economic activity that colonists engaged upon, while certainly not antithetical to mercantilism, confounded and disoriented many of the original planners, as well as the Privy Council. Furthermore, these were yet small settlements, not nearly as significant to England's overall trade balance as they later would prove; moreover, centralized direction required money the Crown did not have.

Decentralization, coupled with ad hoc experimentation and a variety of colonial governmental forms, thus characterized the empire during this early Stuart period. At no point, however, did this belie the presence of a central principle behind the formation of this empire. Colonies, from the beginning, were meant to be subordinate to the economic and monetary interests of the mother country. What eluded so many of the planners and administrators was the question of how to optimally manage those colonies for mercantilist ends. The principle was coherent, just not the precise strategy. Notwithstanding, as early as 1621, the principle translated into direct action when the Privy Council prohibited Virginia planters and the Virginia Company from shipping their most valuable staple crop, tobacco, to or through any place but England. The regulation foreshadowed, even at this early date, imminent tension within the empire over whether English colonials could freely trade as they saw fit.

Silver coin rarely penetrated the colonial economy in this early period. When it did, trade deficits resulted in the coin leaving almost as quickly as it arrived. A currency of some sort or another in the colonies remained necessary for internal trade. Alternative monies thus arose in place of silver. In Virginia and the early West Indies, English settlers adopted tobacco money; farther north, in New England, farm produce or "country pay" circulated as money, alongside wampum beads and beaver skins. Most colonists, for now, quietly tolerated the several shortcomings that attended these alternative monies. Colonists always preferred coin, of course, and before too long insisted upon it.

On December 20, 1606, the Virginia Company of London dispatched to North America three vessels of 144 passengers under command of Captain Christopher Newport, a former privateer and still-celebrated navigator. Five months later, the reduced, fatigued party of 105 passengers landed on the banks of the James River, erecting a fort of palisades, some tents, and a church. Almost immediately, the new inhabitants cast about anxiously for any sign of gold or silver. The sooner the better, claimed the resident Jamestown Council in June 1607, "lest that all devouring Spaniard lay his ravenous hands upon these gold showing mountains."[1] Newport was especially zealous in this bullionist mission. Two months after arrival, the captain departed again for England with a cargo full of sparkling dirt, found to be entirely void of silver and gold upon its receipt in London. After returning to Virginia in January 1608 (this time with two goldsmiths, two refiners, and a jeweler), Newport artlessly packed the vessel again with valueless rocks and earth, embarking for London in April. Nearly half of the original settlers, meanwhile, had already died of disease and malnutrition.[2]

Failure bred desperation, and then heedless delusion, as the Jamestown settlers probed tirelessly for metals at the expense of cultivating the soil and maintaining a basic subsistence. "Golden promises," recalled Captain John Smith in 1624, forged an atmosphere in Jamestown where "there was no talke, no hope, nor worke, but dig gold."[3] Starvation and disease placed annual death rates at 50 percent, reaching 80 percent during the cannibalistic winter of 1609–1610.[4] Astoundingly, the following October, in 1610, company officers commanded a large band of men "to march towardes the mountaines, for the discovery of gold or silver mines." They returned to Jamestown empty-handed.[5] Reality finally began to sink in, though as late as 1613 some investors still believed there were "probable likeliehoods of rich Mines" a mere "three dayes journey" from Jamestown.[6] Yet by this date, most immediate hopes for a belated discovery had all but vanished.

With the mythical mines nowhere to be found, the company grudgingly turned to the next best alternative: staple commodities that England currently purchased from foreign powers. The new mission delighted Captain John Smith, long frustrated with the wanton futility of singularly focusing on precious metals. Smith epitomized the new mercantilist mindset, rejecting altogether the cruder bullionism of Raleigh and Newport. "To thinke," he argued, "that gold and silver Mines are in a country otherwise most rich and fruitfull, or the greatest wealth in a Plantation, is but a popular error." Spain's ongoing decline substantiated this view. "The first conquest of the Spaniards," Smith recalled, "got great and mighty store of treasure," but now that money was "exceedingly wasted . . . so that all things considered, the cleere gaines of those metals . . . is but small, and nothing neere so much as vulgarly as imagined." Sir Francis Bacon, the famed philosopher, shared this view. "The Hope of Mines is very Uncertaine," Bacon wrote of colonial settlements in 1625, rendering "the Planters Lazie in other Things."[7] The balance of trade, not mining, was the most efficient way to boost England's money supply.

The kingdom's most pressing need was to correct its dependence on timber and naval stores from Baltic and Scandinavian countries. When Newport sent a silver-hunting mission far west of the settlement in autumn 1608, Smith instructed the group of men who stayed behind in Jamestown to cut timber and to make glass, pitch, and tar. The next year, 1609, when a councilor proposed sending to London more cargoes of dirt, Smith wisely intervened and forwarded cedar instead.[8] Smith's focus on cedar, indeed, was quite timely: only four years later, King James I decried the fact that English merchants exported an "exceeding great quantitie" of "Spanish Moneyes" to northern European states for naval stores and timber.[9] Moreover, another predicted, Virginia might also prove "capable of wine, of oyle, of silkes," improving the already favorable trade balance with Mediterranean countries.[10] "Many hundreth of thousands of pounds are yearly spent in Christendome in these commodities," the company stated in a 1610 promotional pamphlet, indicating, already, the beginnings of this shift in approach.[11]

The situation in Virginia remained depressingly bleak in the early 1610s. Many deemed the colony a colossal failure. Mortality rates remained extraordinarily high, and the settlement had yet to produce any exports of note. The colony, for some time, was even overshadowed by the vastly more successful and populous settlement of Englishmen on the lush Bermuda Islands, accidentally discovered after a hurricane diverted and then shipwrecked a vessel on way to Virginia.[12] The sudden appearance of tobacco, however, soon forever changed the colony's economic destiny.

English consumers had first familiarized themselves with tobacco during the late Elizabethan period, though the leaf was still prohibitively expensive for many Englishmen. Most tobacco initially came from the Spanish Caribbean; in 1615 alone, English merchants imported nearly £13,000 worth of tobacco from the Spanish.[13] The trade jeopardized England's favorable balance of trade with Spain, a frightening prospect given the fact that England's trade surplus with Spain had long supplied the kingdom with much silver. Virginia tobacco might mitigate English dependency on the Spanish product. Yet the Virginia Company proved extremely reluctant to latch onto this "deceavable weede," as they called it, urging instead "more staple and honorable comoditytes," to no avail.[14]

Within a few years of the first tobacco shipments from Virginia in 1614, tobacco production eclipsed all other economic activity. Between 1617 and 1624, Virginia's tobacco exports jumped more than tenfold: from just under 10,000 pounds weight to nearly 120,000 pounds.[15] English settlers on Bermuda also entered the trade; indeed Bermudan tobacco production even exceeded that of Virginia until the latter surged permanently ahead in the 1630s.[16] Tobacco mania swept both colonies, despite the company's foremost efforts against it, and despite the king's famous censure of smoking as "poysonous and dangerous for the bodies and healths of Our Subjects."[17] Cultivating the leaf was simply too great a temptation for most planters to resist, especially where no other option presented itself. Tobacco production required neither skilled labor, nor significant sums of capital. Besides, tobacco was money in Virginia, in the most literal way.

Tobacco became money very early in the Virginia tobacco boom. Because the crop was in constant demand for export to England, the possessor could discharge it at practically any moment to practically any person, making it a natural choice for currency in a land where coin was all but nonexistent. Tradesmen in Virginia accepted tobacco in payment for goods—with no intention at all of consuming the crop themselves, but rather to use it solely as a medium of exchange to acquire something else. Tobacco became practically the only money in existence in Virginia. "All this Summer little was done but securing themselves and planting Tobacco, which passes there as current Silver," Smith wrote in 1622.[18] "That Comoditie is become their monny," the Virginia Company regretted at a meeting of shareholders in London in 1621. The company, at the same meeting, urged that "some course be taken that some other Commoditie may be made their Coyne," lest tobacco become a permanent staple.[19]

One of the first acts of the Virginia House of Burgesses, in 1619, was the legal recognition of tobacco currency. The Burgesses fixed the value of higher grades at three shillings (3s) a pound and lower grades at one shilling six pence (1s6d), thus allowing familiar English denominational units to still govern trade.[20] Nevertheless, most Virginians and Bermudans maintained their accounts, contracts, and bookkeeping entries in pounds of tobacco, not in shillings. The Virginia governor, House of Burgesses, and government clerks, for example, all received their salaries entirely in pounds of tobacco, generally recorded in book as a credit to the receiver's account.[21] The Burgesses declared tobacco legal tender in all public payments: the penalty for missing church, for instance, was a pound of tobacco, and a fifty-pound fine awaited anyone absconding services for a month. "Pounds of Tobacco" even settled the "yearly Salary of the Ministers."[22] It was the "usuall custome" in Virginia, the Burgesses acknowledged in 1633, "to make all bargaines, contracts, and to keepe all accounts in tobacco, and not in money [silver]."[23]

It is unclear how often payments between individuals took place in physical units of tobacco, versus those recorded simply on account without any physical transfer. Were tobacco payments mostly recorded in book, with physical units delivered or transferred only later to clear or to settle accumulated debts? Or was it routine to see men walking into the tavern with pockets of tobacco, plunking the leaves down on the bar to buy a drink? Book accounts and transfers were almost certainly the predominant way to use tobacco currency; nonetheless, Smith's aforementioned comment that tobacco "passes there as current Silver" may indicate that it sometimes, if not frequently, functioned like coin. One Bermudan account, in 1624, called "tobacco (our only money)."[24] "Tobacco answers all the uses of Silver and Gold in Trade," said one observer later in 1708: "the Money of that Country which Answers all Things," affirmed another account at the end of the seventeenth century—"the money as well as the staple of Virginia."[25]

Whether transferred in book or in physical units, tobacco was far from an ideal currency. As a perishable good, it lacked the durability of other historical monies, including not only silver and gold, but also the cowrie shell, the cacao bean, brass, and copper. Tobacco was also a bulky commodity, requiring large bundles or casks for transport, rendering payments unusually cumbersome. Extreme deviations in quality caused further inconveniences, as acknowledged by the Burgesses' decision in 1619 to assign higher grades of tobacco a value nearly three times the "second sorte."[26] The curing process made a key difference in quality, with the worst sort thrown into large heaps upon the ground, causing rankness and discoloration, and with the better sort carefully hung on racks to dry for several weeks. "If it had not been perfectly Dryed," one writer observed, "it will certainly Rot, Perish, and become good for nothing."[27] Many traders concealed casks stuffed with lower-grade tobacco, lining higher-quality leaf near the top, notoriously settling exchanges and clearing debts with "trash" tobacco.[28]

Inflation, for a period, was among the most destructive symptoms of tobacco money. The value of tobacco plunged in the 1620s and 1630s, amounting, effectively, to an atypical form of currency devaluation. In the early 1620s, Virginia tobacco production generally fell below 100,000 pounds weight every year. By 1628 production in Virginia exceeded 369,000 pounds, and by the late 1630s exceeded 1 million pounds every year, even surpassing 2.3 million pounds in 1638. The value of the crop fell accordingly. The farm price of tobacco (the sum the planter received for his crop) sank from a high of 3s (36d) per pound in the late 1610s, to less than 8d a pound in the late 1620s, to less than 3d a pound in the late 1630s: a depreciation of 90 percent over twenty years.[29] The inflation was steep enough to force the Virginia government by 1629 to raise the amount of tax per poll from one pound to five pounds of tobacco and to now provide casks to each taxpayer to deliver it.[30] The founding of a new tobacco colony at Maryland in 1632 further aggravated the situation, as did the onset of tobacco cultivation in the English West Indies (Caribbean), including Barbados and the Leeward Islands (St. Christopher, Nevis, Antigua, and Montserrat), where tobacco also functioned as legal tender.[31] In all of these colonies, the use of tobacco as currency, ironically, only reinforced the glut, worsening the inflation. Settlers could literally grow money from out of the ground—a virtual printing press on each acre of farmland.

The use of tobacco currency also discouraged the development of a wage economy. Toward the end of the calendar year, after the crop had shipped overseas, little tobacco remained for internal circulation. During this seasonal lack of tobacco, the "People want Money for traveling Expences, and for paying the small Jobbs of Labourers, and Artificers," noted one later observer.[32] "Workemen and laborers are discouraged," the Virginia governor wrote in 1636, ". . . there is no means to paye them untill the crop of Tobacco be ready." The previous governor of Virginia agreed, declaring in 1626 that "nothing has hindred the proceedings of Arttes, mannuall Trade, and Staple comodities more than the want of money amongst us. . . . There is not Tobacco (which is our mony) all the yeare for us to pay workemen."[33]

Some possible alternatives to tobacco currency existed, but none sufficient to solve the colony's monetary woes. Bills of exchange alleviated the problem for a small minority of men in Virginia, but in this early period, even bills of exchange arrived from abroad only intermittently, and when they did, they only infrequently, if ever, changed hands before departing the colony to buy imported goods. Bills of exchange operated much like a modern-day check: they were written orders directing a transfer of money held elsewhere on account. The chief difference from a check was that a bill of exchange was transferable and assignable to multiple parties and could thus circulate widely before the final settlement of that bill in specie (gold or silver coin). Nevertheless, bills of exchange—despite their essential role in overseas commerce—did not function well as a common currency in early America; they were mostly used by merchants and tradesmen to settle debts owed to someone outside of the colony or to purchase goods from abroad.[34] Book credit, as formerly mentioned, mitigated some of the cumbersomeness of tobacco money, but only in an immediate sense. Shopkeepers or merchants who recorded the debt in their account books still required an eventual, physical delivery of the leaf to settle the tab, compelling them, often, to precariously "go about among the Planters that owe them Tobacco" and, after tracking them down, incurring "the Charge of carting this Tobacco" back to the town, warehouse, or shop.[35]

Tobacco warehouses proved a partial though still insufficient expedient to currency impediments. In 1633 the Virginia House of Burgesses ordered planters—on pain of confiscation—to store their tobacco in the nearest of five warehouses erected throughout the colony. All tobacco remained in the warehouse "until such tyme as the same be laden away aboard some shipp" to England. At the warehouse, government officials inspected the leaf, with any "badd and ill conditioned" tobacco "instantlie" burned and the farmer now barred from planting leaf in the future—"for the better upholdinge the price of this commoditie." In addition, large payments and debt settlements in tobacco could now be made at the warehouse, accomplished by the mere transfer of tobacco notated in record books from one name to another.

Notwithstanding this innovation, most people apparently still retained some leaf on their person for monetary exchange: the same law in 1633 included a clause stipulating that planters keep on their person any tobacco "reserved for his or theire owne spendinge to use in his familie."[36]

The idea for a colonial coinage briefly came to mind. Nor was it the first time. Between 1616 and 1619, settlers in the Bermuda colony utilized a metallic currency minted in England and designed exclusively for the Bermuda islands. The composition of the Bermuda coinage was a low-grade brassy copper, brimmed with a thin wash of silver to enhance its appearance. A wild boar appeared on the front of the coin, commemorating the multitude of feral hogs discovered on the island by the English castaways in 1609; on the reverse of the coin was the famous galleon that had shipwrecked off the island's coast (see figure 2). The "hogge mony," as people called it, fell out of favor sometime around 1619, after tobacco became the island's predominant currency; the minting of copper tokens terminated shortly thereafter.[37] As for Virginia, the original charter in 1606 explicitly conferred on the company a right to mint coins, "for the more Ease of Traffique and Bargaining." But the revised charters for Virginia in 1609 and 1612 conferred no such right, nor did the colonial government possess minting privileges after Virginia became a royal colony in 1624.[38]

Now, with the inconveniences of tobacco money so apparent, Virginia's leaders revisited the possibility of a colonial coinage. In 1636 Governor Sir John Harvey lobbied the Crown for a metallic coinage designed exclusively for use in Virginia. His petition was modest: the governor simply asked that "some farthing

FIGURE 2.   Sixpence coin of Bermuda, ca. 1616. The images are not of the same piece. (Obverse, ANS 1934.25.6; Reverse, ANS 1956.104.29. Courtesy of American Numismatic Society.)

tokens may be sent," for "the means of exchange is a very principall part of trade, which Virginia wants."[39] Harvey likely had something akin to the old Bermuda hog-money in mind. King Charles I assented to this request, and granted the governor permission "to stamp farthing tokens of Copper or Brasse," under condition that the coins be minted in England by a particular nobleman in special favor with the Crown. But Charles did not stop there. Remarkably, he ordered that special copper tokens be minted for *every* colonial plantation, including New England, the West Indian islands, and Bermuda, so that all English colonials may "not totally be driven to trucke with Comodities for another."[40]

If enacted, the king's grandiose plan would have altered the course of colonial economic and monetary history. The plan would have established, for the first time, the beginnings of a uniform policy from the Crown concerning money in the colonies—one consistent with the mercantilist goal of retaining silver and gold for England. The king's plan fell apart, however, almost as soon as the king agreed to it, and in the most anticlimactic manner. After word reached Virginia of the royal assent, the Burgesses pleaded for £5,000 in *silver* coin instead, deeming it "more portable" than copper. Colonists, they said, would "bee altogether dishartened" to use a debased copper currency, whereas a silver coinage would help shift their economy toward "more honorable employments," including artisanal crafts, fishing, and shipbuilding, "which may not well bee accomplished without a Coyne."[41] Charles balked at their rejoinder, and nothing else came of the prospective coinage. Whether or not the king still would have gone through with the plan for a colonial copper token coinage is uncertain; the eruption of civil war in England soon after quite obviously precluded any further action on the subject.[42]

Tobacco thus persisted as the currency of Virginia, symbolizing the colony's utter dependence on the staple from the 1620s onward. Tobacco was a crude medium at best, yet satisfactory enough, evidently, to cause Virginians to use it well into the eighteenth century; as late as 1743 a lawyer from Philadelphia who traveled to Virginia and Maryland noted that tobacco remained "the currency of these Provinces."[43] Virginia, indeed, was the final British mainland colony to adopt paper currency, doing so in 1755. English officials had little reason to discourage this anomaly. Despite its flaws, tobacco money reduced the need for silver in the Chesapeake region and encouraged cultivation of a crop that progressively drew metallic currency to London. The bullionist dream suffered a significant blow with the realization that no mines existed in Virginia. But it was progressively evident, by this time, that England would be a mercantilist empire, not a bullionist one on the model of Spain. Why fret over mines when gold and silver could just as easily be acquired through regulated trade? The key qualifier, of course, was that such trade be regulated.

In the early 1620s, as tobacco mania first swept Virginia, a harsh economic depression battered the English economy. An unprecedented monetary crisis and great "Decay of Trade" despoiled England during this period, "exhausting the treasure of the Realm," King James proclaimed in 1622.[44] The depression resulted in the first installment of mercantilist regulations over colonial commerce.

The causes of the depression were several. First, the opening of the Thirty Years' War in 1618 severely hampered the export of English woolens to continental Europe. Second, international currency exchange rates were greatly disrupted after German and Polish princes in various stages devalued their respective coinages to finance the war. Continental currency devaluation greatly prejudiced English exports, making them artificially expensive in Europe, while European goods became artificially cheap for the English to import. All told, the "disturbance of the Cloth-trade" wreaked havoc on England's overall trade balance.[45] "A great quantity of our money hath beene carried out of the Kingdome," Thomas Mun, merchant and economist, deplored in 1621; "the want of money hath caused divers Merchants and Tradesmen to Break," Gerard Malynes, another merchant, noted in 1622.[46] After a spirited debate over the underlying causes of the crisis, Mun's position, which emphasized the role of the kingdom's trade deficit in causing money shortages, won the day against Malynes's endorsement of statutorily regulating rattled currency markets and others who backed a corresponding devaluation of the English pound. Mun chided devaluation as "not only fruitless but also harmful"; instead, he argued, "Treasure only will be brought in or carried out of a Commonwealth, as the Forraign Trade doth over or under balance in value."[47] The king's Privy Council agreed, identifying the "over-ballansing of late Trade" as the predominant source of the crisis.[48]

England's monetary trouble in the early 1620s, and the debate surrounding its causes, highlighted a number of things. First, it signaled the onset of a new epoch in English mercantilist thought. From this point forward, the balance-of-trade doctrine assumed almost unquestioned preeminence in English economic opinion. The trend in this direction was already unmistakable before the crisis—mercantilism was most certainly on the rise during the latter decades of Queen Elizabeth's reign—but the events and debate of the early 1620s affirmed and cemented its dominance. Second, the depression underscored the need for the Crown and the Privy Council to consult merchants and private experts on trade and monetary policy. Thus, in the throes of the crisis, King James directed that a special commission of experts (not privy councillors) inquire into its causes and potential remedies. Shortly after, in 1625, his son, the newly crowned King Charles I, directed the formation of a temporary "Commission about Trade." He pointedly charged the expert commission to advise the Privy Council on how to improve England's balance of trade; of particular concern was the kingdom's continued reliance on foreign naval stores, and especially on any imported product that was not of any practical or necessary use.[49]

Not surprisingly, England's growing addiction to imported tobacco, especially from the Spanish Caribbean, suffered an onslaught of criticism, especially in the context of the early 1620s depression. The recent introduction of Virginia and Bermuda tobacco did little, initially, to lessen English consumption of the Spanish American variety, which many consumers deemed superior. King James, who already staunchly opposed tobacco before the crisis—citing its "corruption both of mens bodies and maners"—possessed more reasons now to oppose that "weede of no necessary use." In June 1620, he enacted new licensing restrictions on importing Spanish tobacco. Merchants trading in the leaf, he said in the proclamation, "doe transport much Gold bullion and Coyne out of Our Kingdomes"—a "great waste and consumption of the wealth of Our Kingdomes."[50] The king was hardly alone in this conviction: many observers deemed Spanish tobacco a "wastfull expense" that "doth hinder the importation of Bullion."[51] "Corruptible smoking things," Malynes wrote in 1620, ". . . draweth away our treasure and ready Moneys to the incredible loss and impoverishing of the Realm"—"debarring us from Spanish *realls*," he said again two years later. Another prominent merchant, Edward Misselden, agreed, listing the "Tobacco of the West Indies" as a "cause of our want of money": one of several "discommodities . . . bought with ready mony, which otherwise would be brought over in treasure."[52]

England's importation of Spanish tobacco represented a dead loss to the nation, especially now that Virginia and Bermuda produced the same. Sir Edward Sandys, a member of Parliament and (quite importantly) treasurer of the Virginia Company, estimated in 1621 that imports of Spanish tobacco cost the kingdom an annual average of £120,000 in silver coin. Sandys reminded Parliament that England once enjoyed an overwhelming trade surplus with Spain, but now "the rayne of their silver to us hath beene in a manner dryed up." Restricting consumption to the Virginia and Bermuda variety, he argued, "will be a double profit to us," aiding Virginia while simultaneously ensuring that "England shall be better stored with money."[53]

Most members of Parliament (MPs) agreed with Sandys, but, under the banner of saving additional money, some MPs sought to prohibit the importation of *all* tobacco, including the English colonial product. When one MP objected that this would "overthroweth the [Virginia] plantation," a supporter of the ban retorted that Parliament ought to "loveth England better than Virginia." "Thousands have died of this vile weed," urged another MP, "tobacco hindereth all the kingdom, in health, and otherwise . . . pull it up by the roots." The total prohibition of "smoake," another Englishman argued, would save England enough "mony" to "make this Kingdom happie in her selfe, and dreadfull to her neighbours." "The company restraineth it by all means it can," an opponent of the ban replied, ". . . give it some time."[54] After long debate, the House of Commons, in 1624, requested that James prohibit the importation of foreign tobacco only, which the king promptly did. His successor Charles—ever mindful of the customs revenue—later legalized the importation of Spanish tobacco, but with much higher duties than the Virginia product. The duty on Spanish tobacco was 1s10d (22d) a pound, and the duty on English colonial tobacco, after 1632, was 4d a pound—a virtual prohibition on foreign leaf for anyone but wealthy consumers.[55]

There was no fear that English merchants might export silver or gold to Virginia for tobacco; the colony's total dependence on imports from London was such that English merchants would invariably pay for Chesapeake tobacco with goods, not coin. While this pattern barred the possibility of Virginia ever gaining a viable circulating supply of silver coin, the higher duties on Spanish tobacco awarded English colonial planters with a de facto monopoly of the tobacco market in England. Trade restrictions thus occasionally worked to a colony's advantage, encouraging the flourishing of a colonial product at the expense of the foreign variety.

Colonists soon discovered, of course, that trade restrictions could also impede, rather than benefit, the colonial economy. Direct trade with foreigners was one such restriction. Few parties in England were happy that Virginians fixated on tobacco instead of other goods—naval stores, silk, or wine—that might alleviate trade imbalances elsewhere. Nevertheless, so long as tobacco was Virginia's main staple, it ought to at least benefit England primarily, and not a foreign power like the Dutch.

Virginia-Dutch trade was the first casualty of English mercantilist regulation on colonial commerce. In 1621 the Privy Council received word that the Virginia Company was shipping tobacco directly to Dutch merchants in the Netherlands at Middelburg, in the province of Zeeland. The trade completely bypassed England and hence avoided the customs duty. At this time, the duty was 12d (1s) a pound, with no drawback (or rebate) on its reexportation to foreign countries. The Crown was always extra sensitive when it came to customs revenue; a sufficient sum of it permitted the king to rule without Parliament, as James in fact accomplished between 1614 and 1621. Fiscal necessity compelled James to summon Parliament in January 1621. Just a few months later, information emerged of a direct trade between Virginia and the Netherlands. When the Privy Council demanded an answer from the Virginia Company, its officials replied that they did indeed trade directly with the Dutch but reminded the Privy Council that it was the "libertie and freedome" of English subjects "to be free to carry their Comodities to the best Marketts."[56] Days later, on October 21, the Privy Council ordered the immediate cessation of any Virginia-Dutch trade. Such commerce, they wrote in a strongly worded rebuke, violated "the honor of the state" and represented a severe "losse unto his Majestie in his Customes." Hereafter, according to royal instructions, colonial tobacco could only be transported to England and "shall not be carried into any forraine parts until the same have been first Landed here and his Majesties Customes paid."[57]

The Privy Council order of October 1621—continued under King Charles I—was the first regulation to explicitly prohibit the trade of a colonial product directly to a foreign power without first going through England. The prohibition did not simply apply to Virginia Company merchants venturing directly to the Netherlands; it also, importantly, prohibited colonists from selling tobacco to Dutch tradesmen who ventured to the coasts of Virginia. As of yet, only a small number of Dutch vessels appeared off Chesapeake shores; nevertheless, the temptation for planters to sell tobacco directly to the Dutch—who, after all, delivered the first slaves to Virginia in 1619—was a very real and incipient peril.[58] In June 1621—shortly before the Privy Council order—the States General in the Netherlands chartered a West India Company (WIC), with ambitions to expand Dutch trade and military might in the Atlantic. Shortly after, the Dutch company dispatched a vessel to Virginia. Though the WIC soon proved only a lackluster trading company, initial word of the charter alarmed English authorities, who feared it might match the success of the all-powerful Dutch East India Company.[59] English authorities were determined to not allow the Dutch to capture Virginia markets. It would rob the king of far too much revenue and would deny English merchants several profitable branches of trade—the export of merchandise to Virginia and the reexport of tobacco to continental Europe—all damaging, in turn, the trade balance and money supply at a time of great economic depression.

Dutch trade, nonetheless, was a marvelous temptation for many colonial planters. The Dutch paid higher prices than the English for tobacco and charged lower prices for essential merchandise like textiles, shoes, hardware, and other goods. The reasons were several. For one, Dutch shipmasters charged the lowest freight rates in all of Europe: one-third to one-half cheaper than English rates. For low-value, bulk trades like tobacco, freight expenses made a critical difference.[60] Superior seafaring technology permitted this price reduction: the Dutch *fluit* was famously ideal for shipping tobacco; moreover, the Dutch acquired timber and naval stores from the Baltic more cheaply than the English.[61] Dutch price competitiveness in colonial America also resulted from the elimination of a merchant-middleman in London, who made handsome profits from reexporting tobacco to the European continent at a higher price than what he had initially paid for it. Virginia tobacco was therefore more expensive in Amsterdam than it was in London. In the mid-1630s, Virginia tobacco sold for less than 1s a pound in London but for 2s a pound in Amsterdam.[62] Thus, when Dutch tradesmen managed to circumvent the English middleman by venturing directly to Virginia, they proved willing to pay a slightly higher price for tobacco than the English, made possible also by the lower freight rates. For the same reason, but in the reverse, a Dutch tradesman in Virginia could sell continental European goods at far cheaper prices than could the English. The Virginian governor and council recognized this disparity in 1628, denouncing the "excessive rates" that "unconscionable and cruell [English] Merchants" charged for imported merchandise.[63]

Dutch trade, in short, saved the colonists money. In this particular case, in early Virginia, Dutch trade resulted not in a flow of silver coin into the colony, but rather in the colonists' ability to import more merchandise than would otherwise have been possible. Money is wealth, but not all wealth is money: wealth includes merchandise as well. Colonists wanted both money and merchandise, but, if they were forced to choose, imported necessities always assumed greater priority. Tobacco currency, in the meantime, could always serve in place of silver.

Virginia-Dutch trade was still comparatively light and infrequent in the 1620s through the mid-1630s. Planters had become "greatlie indebted" to English merchants, having bought so many of their goods in previous years. As Governor Sir John Harvey reported in 1632, the colonists' indebtedness to English merchant-creditors rendered the latter "most fitt to contract for all the tobacco of this place." But the appetite for change was strong. Hence, in the same letter, the governor complained to royal commissioners about the "most excessive rates" charged by the English for imported goods and for freight. The Dutch, he said, paid Virginia farmers a much higher price for their tobacco than the English: 1s6d a pound from the Dutch, he claimed, versus only a fraction from the English. Audaciously, the governor then asked "why we may not have the same freedome of his Majestie's other subjects to seek our best marquett?"[64]

The answer should have been obvious. English merchants and the Crown lost money from colonial-Dutch trade, practically ensuring its prohibition. To allow colonists to sell valuable produce directly to foreign nations—or, as the

Burgesses lobbied for in 1638, "the free benefitt and use of our comodity"—undercut the general principle that England's pecuniary interests assumed ultimate precedence over those of the colony.[65]

To discourage direct trade between Virginia planters and the Dutch, and to encourage English merchant-middlemen in the international tobacco trade, the Crown in 1631 introduced a drawback system, whereby the customs office rebated to the English merchant a fraction of the duty on imported Virginia tobacco (2d of the 4d tax) if he reexported the leaf to continental Europe.[66] The remaining duty, however, with the higher freight rates, the extra shipping involved in indirect trade routes, and the profits extracted from the English merchant-middleman, continued to incentivize direct trade between the colonies and foreign powers.

Thus the colonists' pecuniary motive to trade directly with the Dutch was strong, especially if a planter was not captive to an English creditor-merchant. What else was such a planter to do when a Dutch vessel cruised down the coastline offering prices that outcompeted the English?

Indeed, by the end of the 1630s, Virginia-Dutch commercial ties had slowly but conspicuously widened. In 1635 a visiting Dutch tradesman noted that of the thirty-six ships he encountered in Virginia, all were English; seven years later, however, he found "four Holland ships, which make a great trade here every year," and had, he said, since the late 1630s.[67] During this time, two well-renowned Dutch agents, the Stam brothers—representing a number of Amsterdam merchants and firms—bought almost nine hundred acres of land on Virginia's Eastern Shore, developing wide contacts among the colony's planters. In one year alone, 1640, the Stam brothers shipped at least 60,000 pounds of tobacco directly to Holland, and in 1641 their shipment reached 100,000 pounds.[68] Nor was it simply in Virginia that colonists encountered the temptation to trade directly with foreigners. Dutch vessels also frequented the English Caribbean, purchasing tobacco and extending credit to the islanders. The colonization by the Dutch West India Company of the nearby island of St. Eustatius in 1636, rendered this cruising trade with the English Leeward Islands particularly attractive.[69]

Nevertheless, English merchants still commanded the bulk of tobacco traffic in the colonies in the late 1630s. Tobacco proved a surprisingly remunerative crop for both the English state and London merchants. By 1639 the Privy Council reported that tobacco duties alone "payed his Majestie great Summes of money."[70] English imports of Chesapeake tobacco exceeded one million pounds weight every year in the late 1630s.[71] That amounted to a lot of customs revenue and a lot of money in merchant pockets, in what was certainly a welcome turnabout from the devastating first decade of settlement.

Significant questions remained. First, the new tobacco colonies completely failed to address England's trade deficit with the Baltic and Scandinavian countries for naval stores and timber. Second, the Dutch commercial presence in the colonies had grown patently in recent years, rendering those colonies less advantageous than they could yet be. Less immediately, but just as important, the Crown's initial efforts to stifle Virginia-Dutch trade sowed the early seeds of colonial discontent. Colonial protests against that restriction, for now, were for the most part reticent. Yet the tension and conflict of interests encouraged by mercantilism—the policy that subordinated the interests of the colonial economy to those of the mother country—signaled the likelihood for greater, more vocal protests later in the century.

Further north of Virginia, the colonial settlements in New England offered a unique set of problems for the mercantilist model. Unlike the tobacco colonies, New England never fully developed a staple export; the rocky soil and brief growing season encouraged settlers to focus on subsistence farming, livestock, and basic foodstuffs instead. After the mid-seventeenth century, New England acted more as a competitor to England than a subordinate partner, with vast trade networks sprawling all over the Atlantic, attended by colonial shipbuilding and the distant potential for colonial manufacturing—all detrimental (most mercantilists alleged) to England's economy and money supply.

Some mercantilists, in the decades preceding settlement, had great expectations for New England. The tall white pines of the region would make ideal masts for English ships, and London merchants might also reexport the "Riche Furres" of the country to continental Europe.[72] More important, the regional fisheries might finally stay the kingdom's purchase of herring from Dutch fishermen. "This is a most beneficial trade for money," an MP exclaimed of the New England fisheries in 1621. Indeed, in April of that year—in the midst of the economic and monetary depression—the House of Commons reported that American fishing might prove "a greate meanese of bringinge in of Bollion and Coyne from forreigne ptes into this Realme."[73] An English mariner, for instance, Tobias Gentleman—in a 1614 tract entitled *Englands Way to Win Wealth*—promoted fishing "for the bringing in of gold, and money," for the Dutch "carry away our money and best gold for fish and Herrings." Edward Misselden agreed. "A Mine of Gold it is," he wrote of fishing in 1623, "the Mine is deepe, the veines are great . . . another means, not inferiour unto any, for the recovery of our Exportations, in the Ballance of Trade."[74]

Captain John Smith, who coined the name *New England*, foresaw tremendous mercantilist value upon visiting the region in 1614. "Our plot," he recorded, "was there to take Whales and make tryalls of a Myne of Gold and

Copper," adding, with frustration, "For our Golde, it was rather the Masters device to get a voyage that projected it, then any knowledge hee had at all of any such matter." Smith was far more interested in "Fish & Furres" and "of woods, seeing there is such plenty of all sorts . . . that build ships and boates." To critics pestering him with constant inquiries about precious metals, Smith replied, "Now I know the common question is, For all those miseries, where is the wealth they have got, or the Gold or Silver Mines? To such greedy unworthy minds I say once againe: The sea is better then the richest Mine knowne." "Though I can promise no Mines of gold," he continued, look to the Hollanders, "whose wealth and strength are good testimonies of their treasure gotten by fishing." "Let not the meannesse of the word Fish distaste you," he urged, "for it will afford as good gold as the mines of Guiana or Tumbatu, with lesse hazard and charge, and more certaintie and facilitie."[75] Raleigh's bullionist strategy for drawing money to England was a relic of the sixteenth century; Smith's emphasis on the trade balance reflected the emerging mercantilist consensus of a new era.

Though itinerant fisherman had frequented the large island of Newfoundland since the early sixteenth century, attempts to colonize New England had thus far met bitter disappointment.[76] In 1608 an English colony at Sagadahoc, in present-day Maine—sponsored by the Virginia Company of Plymouth—floundered after only a single year of settlement. Permanent settlement did not begin again until the 1620 founding of Plymouth Colony, where nearly half the settlers perished in the bitter cold of the first winter. Indeed, by this time, the word in London was that New England was "good for nothing but to starve so many people as comes in it."[77] The population at Plymouth numbered no more than four hundred by the end of the 1620s; attention, for now, centered almost entirely on the tobacco-booming Chesapeake, Bermuda, and English West Indies.

The floodgates finally opened after 1628, when the Massachusetts Bay Company—an incorporated group in England of middling tradesmen and Puritan dissenters—founded a new colony. Over the next twelve years, more than fifteen thousand migrants landed on the shores of Massachusetts Bay; the population of New England, by the end of the 1630s, was nearly double that of Virginia, with numerous towns sprouting up across the eastern half of Massachusetts. The migration included middling Puritan families with modest sums of property in England, as well as not-always-so-pious tradesmen and artisans from the lower strata of London's commercial community, men who composed the first generation of New England merchants. English political affairs, at the time, were particularly agitated; King Charles I dissolved Parliament in 1629, not to call it again for eleven years. The strict persecution of Puritan dissenters had recently ramped up, and rising numbers of poor and unemployed—following a slump in the export of woolens in 1629–1631—cast a shadow over England's economy. Migration to a country with abundance of land promised to preserve the middling status of a family or individual; the right to practice one's own religious convictions was obviously another strong motivating factor. The prospect of being a part of something greater than themselves—the creation of a spiritual haven presumably divorced from Old World corruption—coupled with economic opportunity to encourage thousands of English men and women to flee to a distant, unknown land more than three thousand miles from home.[78]

Puritan ideals governed life in the early years of settlement, with a special emphasis on moral, communalistic, covenantal living. Organized into compact townships, each man, woman, and child, ideally, labored for the glory of God and for the good of the whole. Order, submission, tranquility, harmony, law, authority, property, patriarchy, and a fiery though carefully circumscribed liberty facilitated the inception and perseverance of this tight social fabric. Adult, male church members elected the governor and both houses of the assembly, the latter called the General Court. The compactness of settlement allowed for mutual defense, common schooling, public worship, economic cooperation, and communal supervision over the moral well-being of the covenantal people—a society in which men like John Baker, for instance, could be publicly "whipped for shooteing att fowle on the Sabboth day," with other like modes of social and spiritual discipline.[79] On the perimeters of town, families raised livestock and cultivated a wide assortment of crops, including wheat, peas, barley, corn, and rye. Along the New England coast a modest collection of tradesmen-turned-merchants distributed imported merchandise across the surrounding hinterland. Clearly, a medium of exchange of some sort or another would prove essential for such a settlement, but much like Virginia, the nascent colony could not yet rely on trade surpluses to acquire much silver. Unlike Virginia, however, New England had no single, obvious commodity to adopt as money in place of silver.

Exchange was indispensable for the first generation of New England settlers. The myth of the wholly self-sufficient farming family was rarely a reality at any place or time in colonial America. The early Massachusetts Bay Colony was no exception. Families here engaged in what historian Richard Bushman calls "composite farming." They produced, first, food and sundry items for the basic welfare and sustenance of the family. But the settlers also eagerly traded any surplus of goods—produced intentionally for that purpose—to others within the community and beyond. Such items of trade included corn, flour, textiles, butter, meat, cheese, grains, peas, salt, shoes, muskets, farming equipment, and other goods that, in the aggregate, no single family could produce entirely for themselves. A local division of labor thus characterized even the most outlying areas of settlement; very few, if any, families were truly self-sufficient. Neither was the community as a whole self-sufficient, for transatlantic trade procured essentials that could not be produced locally. Most middling families in this early period desired little more than a comfortable living, with perhaps a few luxury items if circumstances permitted: an economic state of being that historian Daniel Vickers calls "competency," or as Bushman calls it, "a modest prosperity." All the same, modest prosperity required at least a modest degree of market exchange; this, in turn, required some sort of medium to govern it.[80]

Direct exchange, or barter, made up a sizable portion of trade in early New England. Under direct exchange, each party consumed the item of trade for themselves: butter for flour, for instance, or pork for cheese. Indirect exchange, however, was necessary in cases where the wants of each party did not align. Silver was the preferred medium in such cases, but in early Massachusetts, coin was not always readily available. New England immigrants had imported small sums of coin with them, but the trade deficit with England often returned the same money back to England, leaving the land mostly devoid of an ample supply of circulating coin.

The colony's Puritan leadership first resorted to statutory measures to keep coin within the colony. Almost immediately, the Massachusetts General Court prohibited the export of money from the colony without a license, but enforcing the ban proved exceptionally difficult. In 1631 the assembly further banned the trading of silver and gold to Native Americans, and three years later prohibited the wearing of clothing with silver and gold lace. There was a moral element also to this latter prohibition—a Puritan condemnation of conspicuous wealth—but for a society in want of money, it was especially absurd, at least seemingly, for settlers to boast "newe & immodest fashions" that could otherwise circulate as money.[81]

A common silver and gold currency, for now, was out of the question, but other, nonmetallic commodities emerged instead to become the predominant media of exchange in New England. These media included Indian corn, furs, pork, peas, grain, and other produce. "Corne"—a generic term for grain, typically synonymous with Indian corn or maize—was among the first commodities deployed for this purpose. As early as 1624, according to Plymouth Governor William Bradford, colonists "begane now highly to prise corne as more pretious then silver, and those that had some to spare begane to trade one with another . . . for money they had none, and if any had, corne was prefered before it."[82] Corn was the first commodity other than coin to be acknowledged by the General Court of Massachusetts as a medium of exchange; in 1631 the assembly ruled that "corne shall passe for payement of all debts" at 6s a bushel, excepting any debt where payment in coin was "expressely named."[83] This statute did not initiate the colonists' use of corn as a medium of exchange— this use had already happened organically, outside of law. Four years later, in 1635, the assembly acknowledged the use of musket balls as small change— ruling that they would pass at one farthing a piece—and further resolved that beaver skins would pass at 10s a pound. The same statute also ruled that "merchantable corne" should be legal tender in all public payments, including all taxes, fines, and fees.[84]

Were these goods currency, as tobacco was in Virginia? Reverend John Wise seemed to think so. Decades later, in 1721, in a pamphlet on paper currency, Wise recounted the earlier use of "Corn Specie" in Massachusetts, reminding his readers that governors formerly received their salary in a grain medium. "When the Salary was changed from the Corn Specie to Money [silver]," he recalled, "there was such a muttering and grumbling in the Country, as tho' they were going into a mutiny. What! to Pay such a Salary, and pay it in Money!"[85] The reverend's choice of language was extremely significant. "Money" in the early-modern period was synonymous with silver or gold. By labeling bushels of corn "Specie," however, Wise implicitly attributed monetary properties to the bushel of corn. John Winthrop the Younger, governor of Connecticut, made a very similar observation in 1667. "Corne is not only the provision for subsistence," he wrote, "but that which is in use amongst us for payments instead of mony."[86] In 1655 the Commissioners of the United Colonies of New England remarked of the frequent "paiment of Indian Corn and other Cash" in the local economy. *Cash* could sometimes mean money box, but here it clearly meant currency.[87] Later in 1691, Captain John Blackwell of Massachusetts—an ardent supporter of paper currency—equated corn with actual money. "Why may not *Paper-mony* be as good as *Tobacco-mony*, *Potato-mony* and *Sugar-mony*?" he asked, "Yea, do not our Brethren at Connecticut find, *Corn-mony* will do their business for them?"[88] "Corn Specie," "Indian Corn and other Cash," and "Corn-mony": all indicate that something far more sophisticated than mere barter characterized exchange in early New England.

The common caricature of early colonial trade as dominated mostly by barter—if only because coin was not the medium of exchange—is fraught with problems. First, this caricature privileges coin as the only legitimate commodity money; second, this representation fails to differentiate between direct exchange and indirect exchange.[89] The difficulty, in part, lies in the often ambiguous, all-too-broad definition of *barter*: the exchange of commodities for commodities without the intervention of money. Such a definition, however, is extraordinarily confusing for an era in which most monies (including gold and silver) were also commodities. The question, rather, should center on whether these were direct or indirect exchanges. Some of them were the former, some of them were the latter, and the distinction made a big difference. A key contrast between direct and indirect exchange is that the latter involves more than one trade. Such was often the case with "Corn Specie," as forthcoming examples will demonstrate. Another distinction is that in a direct exchange—in a traditional barter transaction—both parties chiefly regard the subjective *use-value* of the good in question. That is, each party considers and subjectively determines whether the good in question contains value for his or her *own* personal use or consumption. Under indirect exchange, however, the person trading for silver—or tobacco, in the case of colonial Virginia—regards primarily the *exchange-value* of the tobacco or silver coin. He or she has no intention to consume it but rather intends to later exchange the coin (or leaf) for something else. Here, the party regards a value for the good that is strictly *extrinsic* to his or her person: a value assigned to the good not by the person himself or herself, but by society, the market, or by government. Exchange-value, not use-value, characterizes indirect exchange. When New Englanders utilized "Corn Specie" as a medium in trade, they regarded its exchange-value—as they also did with silver.

If the use of "Corn Specie" as a medium of exchange was altogether different from barter, the question still remains as to whether "Corn Specie" was money. Conventional opinion privileges gold and silver as the only legitimate commodity monies, but this is a faulty and ahistorical presumption. Money can take any form or shape, so long as the good is commonly or ubiquitously accepted enough within the community as a medium of exchange. As a lawyer in colonial Philadelphia later rightly stated, "That commodity for which the rest in the country are generally bought and sold, is the currency or money of the country."[90] The fact that the same good has uses other than money is completely beside the point: the very idea behind commodity currency is that the good also possesses nonmonetary functions—whether in jewelry (as with gold and silver), in a smoking pipe, or on the dinner table.

That being said, some goods might occasionally function as media of exchange but not commonly or ubiquitously enough to warrant the title *money*. The challenge for historians comes in exploring the precise extent to which men and women consistently accepted those items as media of exchange. This is an extraordinarily difficult task. Undoubtedly, tobacco was money in the Chesapeake and early Caribbean, but the case in New England is far less apparent. Nevertheless, we can still arrive at some proximity of knowledge. References to "corne" in this period typically signified maize: a popular mainstay in the colonial diet, making it a natural medium for trade. A colonial official who received his salary in one hundred bushels of corn (recorded, likely, in a book account) did not consume all or even most of that corn himself but rather used it as a medium to acquire other goods, transferring his ownership of the corn to somebody else for the things that he actually wanted. Corn mediated some of the trade with Native Americans, as Connecticut record books affirm. The Massachusetts General Court even collected bushels of corn to fund the initial construction and maintenance of Harvard College.[91] The 1635 order that musket balls circulate as a "farthing peece," or that a pound of beaver "shall passe att 10s," also imply currency status, at least in this early period; significantly, Connecticut mirrored the same ruling only three years later.[92]

But New England men and women also used a much wider variety of goods in payment than even these, thus complicating the picture. Harvard attendees paid their tuition with a broad range of produce and goods: in 1649, for instance, one student (later president of the college) tendered "an old cow" to cover part of his tuition payment.[93] Court records in Essex County, Massachusetts, affirm that as late as 1682, "fish as silver" settled a number of debts.[94] In 1657 a carpenter in Massachusetts contracted to build a three-chimney house for £45, to be paid "one-half in corn and cattle at or before the house was raised, and the remainder at the next wheat harvest."[95] Presumably the carpenter used a large portion of this corn to buy other goods or to settle debts with a local shopkeeper: in either case, corn was the medium of trade. In 1645, John Dunham of Plymouth bought a house and a garden for thirteen bushels of Indian corn and five bushels of wheat, with "three pounds more in Countrey pay" to be settled within the next twelve months.[96] Dunham likely acquired these bushels not from his own farm but from other sources or transactions—from someone like the aforementioned carpenter, for instance, or from a shopkeeper—passing the corn off again as money (whether delivered physically or transferred in a book account) to buy the house and garden.

New Englanders used the words "country pay" as a general synonym for agricultural money-produce. According to the Essex County Court, country pay was "valued heare as money in N. England." The Commissioners of the United Colonies of New England, in 1655, described "countrey pay" as "paiment of Indian Corn and other Cash."[97] The earliest recorded use of the phrase "country pay" was in Plymouth Colony in 1638; Massachusetts, at the time, still simply called it "corne." By the second half of the seventeenth century, however, the words "country pay" inundated nearly all New England record books, including those of Massachusetts.[98]

Colonists often denominated country pay in familiar English monetary units: "thirteen shillings in country pay," for instance.[99] One Plymouth resident bought a house and land for the sum of £9 2s6d, to be paid within the space of one year "in currant Countrey pay." The guard at the governor's mansion in Plymouth colony received his £30 salary in "currant countrey pay."[100] The printer of *New Englands Memoriall* received "twenty pound in countrey pay . . . towards the procuring of paper for the printing of the said booke."[101] Sometimes the sum was so high that payments had to be broken up. In 1668, a Plymouth real-estate purchase of £150 was set to be paid in three installments within the space of nine years, each installment to be settled in "current countrey pay."[102]

Country pay and tobacco money shared similar inconveniences of bulkiness, perishability, variations in quality, and higher transaction costs than silver or gold. In 1684 the Massachusetts General Court recalled that prior to their founding of a mint in 1652 (discussed in the next chapter), there was no other way "to pay debts or buy necessaries, but Fish and Corn, which was so cumbersom and troublesom as could not be born."[103] One story from 1693 highlighted the problem especially well. That year, the constable of Springfield, Massachusetts ventured into the country to collect taxes for the colony government, including a single payment of 130 bushels of peas. The bulkiness of the peas combined with the inadequacy of country roads to compel the constable to choose water carriage for his journey back to Boston. The constable loaded the bushels onto the watercraft, but when he encountered the Falls of Connecticut River, the water soaked the vessel and the peas became entirely unsaleable.[104] Furthermore, the quality of country pay, like tobacco, often varied wildly; in 1669, for instance, a man in Essex County purchased a horse for £8, "to be paid in wheat and malt." Following the deal, the buyer and seller disputed over the date of payment. After the seller sued for payment, the buyer called him "a knave" and replied that he would now "pay him in the worst pay in the country."[105]

Country pay, however, also enjoyed clear benefits over tobacco money. Relative price stability was one. But, more important, merchants did not export country pay out of the country, making the currency available year-round. In a multitude of New England documents, "workmens wages" were said to be "paid in corne," and, almost as frequently, Chesapeake documents decried the inability of Virginia colonists to do the same with tobacco.[106] Indeed, the rapid development of artisanal work in New England, unlike the Chesapeake, may have been partly the result of the year-round availability of country pay to settle wages.

The adoption of the shilling unit by users of country pay was simply a matter of convenience and uniformity, and should not distract historians from viewing the goods any less as currency. Indeed, the same was true in England, where people kept accounts in shillings, not ounces of silver. New Englanders, in like manner, maintained accounts sometimes in shillings instead of bushels of corn. Neither should the occasional use of book accounts and book credit deter historians from viewing country pay as anything less than money. It is impossible to know how often this happened, but if the payment of a salary in "Corn-mony," for example, was notated in book rather than physically delivered to the salary-earner, the bushels of corn still had to be accounted for, wherever they were stored—just as wages and salaries today are paid not in cash but transferred to the earner's account (only now at the bank, not at a shop). Whatever the extent to which tradesmen and ordinary folk used book accounts, the aforementioned statement from the General Court in 1684 that there was no other way "to pay debts or buy necessaries, but Fish and Corn, which was so cumbersom and troublesom as could not be born," indicates that in fact many transactions involved the physical delivery of country pay at the point of exchange. As for book credit, it was less frequent in the seventeenth century than in the eighteenth century, but in this context too, country pay still often functioned as money. Book credit was a convenient means of postponing payment by weeks, months, or even longer, depending on the soundness of one's reputation. If the debtor later cleared his account in coin, then silver or gold was the ultimate medium; if settled in produce, then country pay.[107]

If no single good was money in early New England, then country pay in the aggregate was money. Country pay was not a mere substitute for money, but rather money itself. As one Massachusetts writer recalled later in 1731, colonists in earlier decades settled "payments in *Pay* (as the Countrys produce was then called) . . . the Countrys produce was indeed as good as *Money*." Even in the eighteenth century, country pay was still money in peripheral areas of New England. In 1704, for instance, Sarah Kemble Knight passed through Connecticut on a journey from Boston to New York, remarking in her journal that "Pay is Grain, Pork Beef, etc . . . It seems a very Intricate way of trade." Clearly, Knight was referring to something other than mere barter, which can hardly be called "a very Intricate way of trade."[108]

Elementary barter no doubt existed in early New England, but the common assumption that it characterized most trade in this period obscures the pervasiveness of a multifaceted, elaborate system of indirect exchange: a web of alternative, locally produced monies that fostered the development of intracommunity commercial and social relationships. Country pay highlights that the early New England economy was not just commercialized but thoroughly monetized. Tobacco money and country pay were certainly less convenient than coin and later paper currency, but, all things considered, these alternative monies served the purposes of seventeenth-century America rather well, facili-tating commerce, albeit imperfectly, when coin was not readily available: an innovative colonial response to the vexing problem of silver shortages.

Wampum was another response to the dearth of coin, serving the role of a subsidiary, small-change currency in early New England. Produced by Native Americans, wampum beads (known also as wampumpeage, peage, or sewant) were smoothly polished, cylindrical pieces of shell, drilled through the center with a sharp stone and then strung together into belts or sashes. One fathom or belt of wampum comprised 360 beads, and a skilled indigenous craftsman in the pre-colonial era could produce up to 40 beads a day. Wampum beads differed in value, with the white beads (derived from periwinkle shells) worth half the value of the rarer purple beads (derived from quahog clams). Both shells prolif-erated off the coast of the Long Island Sound, and natives across eastern North America esteemed wampum belts for centuries preceding contact. Strung to-gether, the white and purple beads produced elaborate pieces of artwork; Na-tive Americans commonly used wampum belts in treaty protocol and for tribute, the redemption of captives, compensation for a crime, gift exchanges during marriage, and other ceremonies or rituals.[109] Some contemporary observers and later historians mistakenly believed wampum to be "the common Indian cur-rency" and the "moneyed medium among the natives," but as historian William Cronon notes, wampum functioned more as a "medium of gift giving" among Indians than as a medium of commerce.[110]

Native Americans used wampum as a money when trading with Europe-ans, however, and especially when trading with the Dutch at New Netherland. In 1625 the Dutch West India Company founded New Amsterdam at the mouth of the Hudson River, and the settlement's harbor conveniently bor-dered Long Island Sound. Here, Dutch traders exchanged European wares to local Indians for wampum; afterward, the traders sent ships 150 miles up the Hudson River to Fort Orange (present-day Albany), where they used the wam-pum to purchase furs from distant Iroquois nations. The trade was so suc-cessful that the Great Seal of New Netherland soon displayed a beaver encircled by wampum currency. "Wampum is the source and the mother of the beaver trade," wrote Peter Stuyvesant, director-general of New Netherland from 1647 to 1664; ". . . without wampum, we cannot obtain beavers."[111] Beaver pelts were extraordinarily valuable: the profits accruing from the sale of a single skin provided enough money to a tradesman to feed him for approximately three months.[112] Demand for the key to that trade, wampum, subsequently soared. Dutch colonists, quite naturally, soon utilized wampum as a money among themselves, alongside beaver skins, which the colonists called "beaver currency."

One writer in 1634 even called wampum "the currency of the country." "There has been no currency but Wampum among the common people in New Netherland," company officials remarked in 1650.[113]

Wampum was the lifeblood of the Dutch colonial economy, with the Long Island coast christened "the mine of New Netherland."[114] Also near Long Island Sound, however, was the colony of New Plymouth. Fearing English competition in the Connecticut fur trade if the people of Plymouth discovered the value of wampum independently, the Dutch West India Company deliberately introduced Plymouth colonists to the "trade of Wampampeake," so long as they traded in more easterly areas beyond New Netherland's reach.[115] Wampum saved and temporarily enriched New Plymouth in the late 1620s and 1630s, who used the shells to dominate the fur trade of southeastern New England. By the late 1630s, however, the New England beaver population was nearing extinction, and Plymouth settlers lacked the requisite capital to construct posts deep within the interior.[116]

Boston merchants hoped to fill the void left by Plymouth in the fur trade. The Massachusetts colony desperately needed an export to stymie the outflow of silver coin from Boston to England—an inevitable consequence of the colony's considerable trade deficit. To enter the fur trade, however, Massachusetts needed access to wampum currency, and Boston was distant from Long Island. Technology provided one answer, making the beads more plentiful. Dutch traders had recently introduced metal drills to the Indians, causing wampum production to soar to tens of thousands of beads per year by the mid-1630s. The introduction of English colonists to the trade further spurred indigenous production of wampum; Plymouth Governor William Bradford noted that the Indians "became rich and potent by it," as they now possessed powerful leverage in their dealings with the English and the Dutch.[117]

Wampum's meteoric rise bore wide implications for Indian culture; new leaders emerged among those who had greater access to shells, and the trade introduced European goods to the Indians on an unprecedented scale. The trade further encouraged Indians to inhabit the Long Island coast year-round instead of seasonally; moreover, the trade sparked a shift in native alliances and rivalries.[118] "Strange it was to see the great alteration it made in a few years among the Indians," Bradford wrote, ". . . it may prove a drugg in time." Another noted that the local Indians "delight much in having and using knives, combs, scissors, hatchets, hoes, guns, needles, awls, looking glasses, and such like necessaries, which they purchase of the English and Dutch with their peague."[119] The Pequots in particular thrived under these new economic conditions, exacting tribute in wampum from subordinate Indian groups in return for Pequot military protection from the Narragansetts, a rival Indian group that also produced and distributed wampum. More alarming, from the English perspective, was the use of wampum currency by some Indians to purchase firearms and other weaponry.[120]

Diplomacy between the Pequot and the Massachusetts Bay Colony completely broke down in the mid-1630s, escalating to war in the summer of 1636. The rival Narragansett and Mohegan Indians sided with the English against the Pequots. The notorious, bloody conflict ended in 1637 with a decisive English victory. The allied colonial governments exacted massive payments of tribute in wampum from the defeated Pequot, but the governments also exacted tribute from natives who had allied with the English during the war. Over the next three decades New England governments collected more than 21,000 fathoms of wampum in tribute: that is, seven million beads (equal roughly to £5,000—an enormous sum of money for any colonial government).[121] Standard use of wampum money in Massachusetts Bay followed shortly thereafter. In November 1637 the Massachusetts General Court officially recognized wampum as currency in the colony, equating six white beads (or three purple beads) with a penny. Connecticut followed a few months later.[122] The beads became a popular subsidiary currency within New England; by the early 1640s wampum achieved legal-tender status in all public and private payments.[123]

The Pequot War shifted the regional balance of power from New Netherland to New England, though not without much uncertainty still for the New England economy. After 1637, the Dutch West India Company had to purchase much of its wampum from New England sources to continue its fur trade; as one Dutch colonist warned, "the English will retain all the Wampum manufacturers to themselves and we shall be obliged to eat oats out of English hands."[124] Access to beaver remained a serious difficulty for Massachusetts tradesmen, however; even as the English strove "to monopolize all the profits of the Wampum trade to themselves," the Hudson River still afforded Dutch tradesmen premier access to distant fur supplies.[125]

The Massachusetts colony still sorely required a dependable export. Farm produce would not yet suffice as an exportable good. The export of codfish to Spain allowed for modest returns, but not in money; Boston merchants traded cod to Bilbao for fine Spanish wool, and then reexported the wool to England for manufactured goods to bring to and sell in New England. Boston merchants acquired most of this codfish from Newfoundland and Maine; Bay colonists, for the most part, did not yet apply themselves to fishing.[126] The colonial shipbuilding industry was still in its infancy, and though ample supplies of timber made for a possible export, transportation costs to England proved prohibitive: the voyage across the Atlantic was five times longer than the distance between England and Sweden. A reliable, colony-produced export was still urgently needed.[127]

Through it all, a robust contingent of middling merchants arose to some prominence in Boston and Salem, equipping the surrounding region with imported merchandise from England. This merchandise they purchased either by reexporting Spanish wool to England (through the aforementioned codfish trade) or by exporting coin and bills of exchange from the Massachusetts colony. The New England merchant occupied a dubious position in early Massachusetts society. On the one hand, he supplied the region with vital essentials, such as clothing and ironware; on the other, his open pursuit of private profit incurred automatic scrutiny in a community that emphasized covenantal unity, higher spiritual errands, and the public good. Merchants risked the charge of serving mammon over God.[128]

Reverend Cotton Mather later commented on this dilemma. "Tho the Love of Money be the Root of all Evil," he said, it is also true that "where the Use of Money has not been introduced, Men are brutish and savage, and nothing that is good has been cultivated."[129] Man indeed possessed God's mandate to till the earth, to labor, and to profit therein. Industry was not simply a virtue but a divine injunction, and private property received holy sanction from the eighth commandment. To delight in the harvest—the honest bounty of one's hard work—was in itself not sin. But avarice was among the worst of all sins, and the line between profit and avarice was quite ambiguous indeed. Mammon, not money per se, was the thing to be avoided: the elevation of riches and material pleasures over sacred concerns and one's spiritual welfare. "If Gold could speak," Mather said, "it would rebuke the Idolatry wherewith Mankind adores it."[130]

Gold was not sinful; idolatry was. Thus, the Puritan-dominated General Court in the 1630s authorized price controls, sumptuary legislation, and other curbs on commercial activity, while nonetheless legitimizing basic mercantile functions.[131] Few in the colony could question the need for commercial distributors, yet also few could deny that unbridled commerce menaced social and spiritual cohesion. As time proceeded, the merchant continued his steady advance; with each passing year, it seemed, his status elevated within New England society, scandalizing those who championed metaphysical profit over pecuniary gain. Money lay at the root of his power, but not even the strictest Puritan dared to deny the utility of money, and the colony's leaders proved exceptionally eager to increase the colony's silver supply. God over money was their creed. But money was still wanted, and still to be had.[132]

The first generation of English colonists in America faced immense difficulties in accumulating even a modest supply of silver coin. Their predicament was entirely predictable. In Virginia, few immigrants had carried any money at all with them from England. The coin that accompanied immigrants to New England was minimal; upon arrival, the family bought provisions from local colonists to get through the first year, and then the silver generally passed out of New England to buy imports from England. Most manufactured necessities had to be imported: clothing, shoes, nails, and ironware. Large trade deficits and only a diminutive supply of silver coin resulted, placing colonists in profound economic dependency on England.

Colonists responded, first, by adopting alternative commodity monies in local exchange, including tobacco, beaver, wampum, and country pay. As Sir Dudley North later stated in 1691, "Nations which are very poor have scarce any Money, and in the beginnings of Trade have often made use of something else; as Sweden hath used Copper, and the Plantations, Sugar and Tobacco, but not without great Inconveniences."[133] Yet despite these obvious deficiencies, alternative commodity currencies performed fairly well in facilitating local exchange—at least in this early stage. The middling farmer in early America had little need for coin, so long as tradesmen and tax collectors accepted country pay, wampum, or tobacco for money payments. Even so, the health of the colony's silver supply interested all residents by determining—when trade deficits prevailed—the colony's capacity to import merchandise from abroad.

English officials and merchants had money on their mind as well. The pecuniary interests of the English state and economy—the customs revenue, mercantile profits, and the balance of trade—assumed top priority, especially in the aftermath of the stark monetary depression of the early 1620s. The first mercantilist restriction on colonial trade appeared in the context of that depression in 1621—a practical prohibition on Virginia-Dutch commerce.

The English economy in the 1630s enjoyed an impressive comeback; the Tower Mint in that decade coined more than £3,000,000 of silver and £700,000 of gold.[134] The most booming sector was England's Mediterranean trade. The Thirty Years' War had temporarily paralyzed Dutch mercantile activity in the southern parts of Europe; England's abstention from the war, as well as England's conclusion of war with Spain and with France in the late 1620s, allowed English merchants to fill the void left by the Dutch.[135] The Dutch still outcompeted the English in the Baltic and northern European trades, but England's thriving commerce to the Mediterranean, southern Europe, and East Indies appeared to compensate. Average customs revenue surged from £600,000 per annum at the beginning of the 1630s to £900,000 by the end of the decade.[136] The kingdom's money supply, moreover, approximated £10 million by the end of 1630s, an increase of 150 percent from the £4 million figure at the end of Elizabeth's reign.[137]

It is vital not to overstate the importance and standing that most English administrators and merchants assigned to the American colonies in the early Stuart period. Imports from the American colonies accounted for only 3 percent of England's total imports in 1640. The reexport of American tobacco, meanwhile, represented only a slight percentage of total English exports to continental Europe.[138] The colonial population was still relatively small: 14,000 in New England, perhaps an equal number in Barbados, and just under 9,000 in the Chesapeake—large compared to the 400 colonists in New Netherland, but incomparable to the 5 million inhabitants of England.[139] Imperial-colonial administration was still fraught with ambiguity, haphazardness, and sometimes even a lack of interest, leaving colonists broadly free to pursue their own course. Virginia was the only settlement controlled directly by the Crown; the other colonies were run privately, either by proprietors (Maryland and the Caribbean) or by charter companies (Massachusetts and Bermuda). Connecticut and Rhode Island began without any authorization at all, but the Crown did not seem to mind one way or the other. King Charles I in 1625 expressed "full resolution" that "Our Royall Empire" consist of "one uniforme course of Government," but nothing of the sort had even remotely been accomplished, nor was it a top priority.[140]

The 1621 ban on Virginia-Dutch trade was one of the most important exceptions during this period; another exception occurred in 1634, when King Charles I established a new committee of the Privy Council to deal exclusively with matters concerning the colonial plantations. William Laud, the much-reviled archbishop of Canterbury, headed the new colonial committee; the commissioners, however, evinced little desire to wield any real administrative power.[141] On one occasion in April 1638, the committee considered whether Charles ought to revoke the Massachusetts charter and assume direct control over New England. When the Massachusetts General Court got wind of this query, the assemblymen replied that September that "if our patent be taken from us . . . the common people here will conceive that his Majesty hath cast them off, and that hereby they are freed from their allegiance and subjection, and thereupon will be ready to confederate themselves under a new government." And that was all that came of the matter.[142]

Fiscal exigencies continually handicapped the early Stuart crown, notwithstanding the general increase in customs revenue, especially in the 1630s. Both James I and Charles I indulged a far more expensive, extravagant court than Elizabeth had. Constitutional tension germinated with James's reluctant summoning of Parliament in the early 1620s, and the Parliament summoned by Charles in the late 1620s proved severely tense. Charles elected to rule without Parliament through the entire 1630s, relying instead on the advice of an isolated court of competing ministers, alienating the king from much of his country.[143] Finally, in April 1640, Charles summoned Parliament to grant him funds to combat a Scottish Presbyterian rebellion. The new Parliament refused to grant Charles the money unless the king made certain concessions regarding his more arbitrary abuses of power; three weeks later, he angrily dissolved the body. That summer, Charles desperately seized £130,000 of gold and silver bullion that English merchants had deposited at the Tower Mint to convert into coin. Charles called it a "loan," but the ensuing clamor forced him to return the bullion to its proper owners within only a few days. The utter failure of the "Forced Loan" embarrassed the king and irreparably bruised his already marred reputation among merchants. News soon leaked that the king was contemplating a 25 percent debasement of the silver coinage to finance his Scottish expedition; this news also sparked an outcry from merchants that compelled the king to abandon the proposal.[144] With no other choice, and on the heels of a humiliating defeat of the English army by the Scots (who now occupied northern England), Charles summoned a new Parliament in November 1640. Over the next year, the king agreed to a series of constitutional reforms. By the end of 1641 many moderates believed that the more liberal and radical elements in Parliament were pushing too hard and too fast, winning for Charles a modicum of renewed sympathy among some of the broader public. In December 1641, liberal Parliamentarians seized political control of the City of London, and a few months later Charles fled the city. The English political nation was now starkly divided between Royalists ("Cavaliers") and Parliamentarians ("Roundheads").[145]

Thus in 1642 England plunged headfirst into a prolonged, intense period of domestic strife—involving civil war, regicide, a Commonwealth government, and then a military state—only to see the Stuarts return again in 1660. It was during this period—the Civil War and Interregnum—that American colonials wrested themselves from the early trappings of English dependency. In the middle of the seventeenth century, England's colonists achieved a remarkable degree of economic and political autonomy—exercising, with near-total freedom, their newfound ability to acquire, and sometimes to create, silver money.

CHAPTER 3

Monetary Upheaval, Recovery, and the Dutch Infiltration, 1640–1659

Grave uncertainty clouded the English Atlantic in 1640. As an irate Parliament gathered for the first time in eleven years to demand constitutional reform, the English world found itself in the throes of a fierce monetary contraction. Credit disintegrated, capital fled the cities of London and Bristol, and silver coin retreated from circulation in England. The crisis reverberated across the whole Atlantic, causing a deflationary collapse in commodity prices in New England, Virginia, and the West Indian islands.

As the Civil War engulfed the mother country, colonial governments and leading colonial planters and tradesmen embarked on a concerted effort to recover from the depths of economic and monetary depression. Remedies included currency devaluation, new export trades, commercial contact with Dutch traders, and even the founding of a mint house in Boston. With the government at home so exceedingly distracted, colonists found themselves largely undeterred in pursuing this economic program, the centerpiece of which was free trade with the Dutch. The Netherlands were at their peak of commercial power at midcentury; much of the world's silver and gold centered in and around Amsterdam. England's American colonists fell gratefully into the Dutch web, coaxed by its many pecuniary benefits.

In England, by contrast, envy and hostility toward Dutch commercial power reached new heights at midcentury—here too, money was front and center. The Netherlands were England's foremost economic competitor and, as such, became the chief target of the first of a series of Navigation Acts in 1651. Though this first Navigation Act focused primarily on England's trade with continental Europe, it also targeted colonial-Dutch trade. Enforcement was initially lax, but the first Navigation Act heralded the onset of a new mercantilist era in English colonial history. The act codified mercantilism into law and set the important precedent of parliamentary interference in colonial economic matters. The Navigation Act of 1651 betrayed a growing disparity between English and colonial economic interests, presaging later political conflict. Distractions in England, for now, forestalled enforcement, permitting colonists a largely free hand in overseas trade in the 1650s—economic freedom that made it all the harder for colonists to adjust to new imperial realities in the season after.

An extreme monetary crisis shook England's economy to its core in the opening years of the 1640s. The political uncertainties of the Civil War encouraged large capital withdrawals from the country, the hoarding of money within, higher interest rates, and high trade deficits with continental Europe.[1] Woolen exports collapsed; the customs revenue foundered to less than £200,000 in 1643.[2] London merchants petitioned against the "great decay of trade in this kingdom and great scarcity of money"; "great discontent betwixt the King and Parliament . . . makes trade here very dead," another merchant remarked.[3] A 1641 anonymous pamphlet entitled *A Caution to Keepe Money: Shewing the Miserie of the Want Thereof*, declared the "want of Money to be an Epidemicall Disease . . . all from the highest to the lowest feeling the misse of it." "There is a general muttering that money is hard to come by," wrote a visiting Scotsman in 1643, "and that is because all kinde of trades and trading begin to decay, and they who have money keep it close."[4]

The financial support of the London business community was imperative to Parliament's wartime objectives. The population of London stood at 400,000, up from 200,000 at the beginning of the century; businessmen had allied with parliamentarianism since the late 1620s, disrupting the traditional alliance between the Crown and trading companies formed earlier under Elizabeth.[5] Royalists received some funding from the melted silver plate of landed nobility and gentry, but London's wealthy merchant-financiers awarded Parliament a clear fiscal edge.[6] Furthermore, Parliament's command of England's major seaports won for their cause the bulk of the customs revenue, however diminished.[7]

The lopsided fiscal conditions of the two warring sides manifested especially in the disparities in minting activity. In August 1642, Parliament seized the Tower Mint in London, forcing Charles to establish royalist mints in the

English countryside. Parliament, ironically, continued to strike coins bearing Charles's portrait, name, and royal arms; royalist mints stamped their coinage with a message asserting that royalist forces were fighting for the Protestant religion, laws of England, and a free Parliament.[8] The difference in output was staggering: between 1642 and 1646 Parliament's output of coins (mostly silver) made up more than 90 percent of all money coined in England.[9] So desperate was Charles that in March 1644, he took the unprecedented step of legalizing the use of foreign coin in domestic commerce.[10] The proclamation signified a total surrender of the most visible hallmark of royal sovereignty: the exclusive circulation of coin bearing the mark of the Stuart king. English men and women could now pass money bearing the stamp of a foreign prince: an outward testament to the waning authority of a monarch who commanded far fewer resources than Parliament in prosecuting the war.

Cries of a great "scarcity of Coine" still reverberated across England through most of the conflict-ridden decade. One member of Parliament, Thomas Roe, proposed reinstating the death penalty for any merchants caught exporting coin or bullion without a license. "If a man may justly suffer death for robbing of a private man," he argued in 1641, "I see no injustice or cruelty to inflict the same punishment upon him that robs a Kingdome." The proposition did not carry through; nevertheless, smugglers of coin—men who threatened "to damnifie the Common-wealth"—now suffered fines of up to £4,000. "By these deceits," wrote a London prosecutor, "commerce is spoil'd, Traffick decayeth . . . and the commonaltie, to speak all in a word, is brought to Povertie."[11]

New England confronted a similarly stark depression at the beginning of the decade. The convening of the Puritan-friendly Parliaments in 1640–1641 reduced the incentive for dissenters to leave England, abruptly terminating nearly all immigration to Massachusetts. Immigration was formerly the colony's chief supply of incoming coin; migrants used the money they brought with them to buy surplus provisions and produce from local farms.[12] Now, according to Governor John Winthrop in June 1640, inbound vessels transported "but few passengers (and those brought very little money)."[13] The closing of this monetary spigot coalesced with the empire-wide contraction of money and credit to create a perfect economic storm in the summer of 1640. Prices collapsed into a deflationary spiral, causing, according to the General Court, "a great stop in trade & commerce."[14] Between May and October 1640, agricultural prices in Massachusetts fell by almost half, tumbling further in the following months.[15] "He who last year, or but three months before, was worth 1000 pounds," Winthrop wrote, "could not now, if he should sell his whole estate, raise 200 pounds."[16] Colonial merchants who once accepted produce in payment of wares now demanded coin, as the potential for

further deflation had made country pay too risky to accept. Panic spread, causing farmers to desperately sell off their produce before an additional fall in
prices, contributing to a glut in supply that worsened the deflation. Most silver and bills of exchange in the colony were either hoarded or exported. The
deflationary plunge continued through 1641, so that "corn would buy nothing; a cow which cost last year 20 pounds might now be bought for 4 or 5
pounds."[17] Debtor-farmers defaulted on debts, thus losing the land they had
posted as collateral; local merchant-creditors, for their part, defaulted on the
silver debts they owed merchants across the Atlantic, as most coin and bills of
exchange were either hoarded or exported from the colony. "Many men in the
plantation are in debt," recorded the assembly in October 1640, "and heare is
not money sufficient to discharge the same."[18] The entire chain of credit had
utterly collapsed. "All our money was drained from us," wrote Winthrop,
"cattle and all commodities grew very cheap . . . the scarcity of money made
a great change in all commerce."[19]

Armed with sincere convictions of an obligation to rescue their flock from
temporal distress, the Puritan leadership in Massachusetts Bay embarked
swiftly on a multifaceted program for economic recovery. The program included short-term remedies as well as a long-term blueprint to boost the colony's productive capacity, with the goal of improving the colony's balance of
trade.

Among the most important of the colony's short-term remedies was currency devaluation. The General Court hoped to relieve debtors and to combat the general fall in prices. For this purpose, currency devaluation was
immensely attractive. It lowered the value of currency; it was, by definition,
inflationary. Colonial inflation in the eighteenth century involved the printing of paper money, but colonial inflation in the seventeenth century involved
raising the legal (or extrinsic) value of foreign silver coin. The procedure went
by a number of names—raising the coin, advancing the coin, devaluing the
currency, or depreciating the currency—all indicating the same procedure. One
later writer described it as the government's "attempting to increase Money,
by augmenting the denomination of it."[20]

The method was simple. Because colonists preferred familiar English denominations when using Spanish money, foreign coins required a legal valuation specifying the number of shillings and pence that the money passed for
within the colony. The silver content of the Spanish piece of eight was equal
to the silver content of 4s6d of English coin, and so Spanish dollars hitherto
passed in Massachusetts at 4s6d. In June 1642, however, the General Court declared that dollars would henceforth pass at 4s8d. Three months later, in September, they raised the dollar again to 5s.[21] Between these two acts—based

on the authority of the legislature alone—the number of shillings in Massachusetts Bay increased by 11 percent, though the quantity of silver in the colony was no greater. A shilling, in short, no longer represented as much silver as it once did—hence the term *devaluation*. The act allowed debtors to settle what they owed a bit more easily: they could clear money debts with only 89 percent of the coin required at the former rate. For those with obligations in country pay, the General Court similarly raised the legal-tender value of agriculture produce in the settlement of debts, to like effect.[22]

But the new rate for silver coin did not apply simply to the payment of debts. The new rate applied to all market transactions. In time, all goods within the colony increased in price, adjusting to correspond to the new rate for coin. "The inhauncing of our Moneys will increase the prices of all things," said Gerard Malynes, English economist, in 1623; "the Price of things bought with Money doth rise in Proportion," wrote another.[23] Yet the corresponding inflation did not occur evenly. Prices for imported goods rose first. Colonial merchants still required the same sum of coins to purchase goods from abroad, regardless of what the Massachusetts government had decreed about their shilling value. The foreign merchant who sold goods to a colonial tradesman did not care what denomination the Massachusetts government had placed on Spanish coin, whether five shillings or eight shillings: he still expected the same number of coins. Thus, following devaluation, the colonial merchant spent a higher shilling price (though the same sum of silver) for imported goods. This in turn compelled him to charge a higher shilling price when selling imported merchandise again to colonial consumers. In this way, the shilling price of imported goods typically rose before the price of any other good in the colony.

Prices for domestic goods rose later. If a bushel of corn was 4s on the eve of devaluation, it usually remained around 4s in the immediate aftermath. Only later, perhaps in a few weeks or even months, would the shilling price of domestic goods rise proportionally to match the rising shilling price of imported goods. The same was true of wages—the price of labor. Wages also increased following devaluation but lagged for a season behind the price increase for imported goods. This disparity in prices between the domestic and the imported was temporary, but it had tremendous and unmistakable repercussions for the local economy: an interim phase called the *lag period*.

Because of the lag period, devaluation, for a season, profited some groups more than others. Of course any debtor owing silver money benefited from a real decline in debts. But more than that, money-holders in general profited considerably. During this interim phase, colonists in possession of coin could suddenly purchase more locally produced goods with their coin than previously, as local prices had yet to fully correspond to the devaluation. Such circumstances could potentially grant a shrewd money-holder "extravagant Profit."[24] For this reason, many wealthy colonial merchants—including creditors—supported raising the rates for Spanish coin, even if it meant losing a modest sum of money from debts.[25] Thus one colonial critic of devaluation, Captain John Blackwell (an early supporter of paper currency), called coin devaluation a method by which "the poorer sort of people are oppressed by the wealthyer traders," who force them to buy "imported commodityes" at "a very Excessive rate."[26]

But devaluation did not simply benefit money-holders inside the colony. Money-holders outside the colony also took advantage of the situation—the interim lag period. Because Spanish money temporarily enjoyed greater real purchasing power inside the colony, outside money-holders had an incentive to bring coin into the colony to purchase cheap domestic goods. One eighteenth-century critic, for this reason, said that devaluation gave "strangers a vast advantage, by buying up goods for less than their value."[27] But such "strangers" bought these goods with coin, thus adding to the colony's money supply—one of the motives of devaluation. The chief difference between the local money-holder and the outside trader was that the former spent money already within the colony's borders; the latter brought silver *into* the colony.

In this way devaluation, for a time, stimulated a colony's exports and discouraged imports, resulting in a trade surplus that brought more coin into the colony than previously, not just in terms of nominal shillings, but in terms of actual silver. This surplus again resulted from the lag period. Imported goods had become more expensive, and domestic goods were temporarily cheap: a predicament that encouraged outside money-holders to bring coin into the colony and discouraged the colony's tradesmen from exporting coin from the colony. Money, temporarily, had greater purchasing power there than anywhere else, and imports, for now, were comparatively expensive. Once domestic prices adjusted to the devaluation, the incentive for outside tradesmen to bring money into the colony utterly ceased, as did the advantage for local money-holders.

Devaluation, therefore, did not constitute any real lasting solution to systemic issues within the colony's economy. Things eventually balanced out, but in the meantime there were certain winners and losers, and it was not always clear what the colony had even gained in the ultimate sense of things. Opponents of the practice thus frequently charged that the scheme was a "fundamentall Error" and "juggling trick," accomplishing little or nothing in the long run: the "Gayne would proove to be imaginary."[28] And no doubt, rent-seeking was a frequent motive behind currency legislation. Still, it was hard to deny the appearance of some positive changes for a struggling economy in the short term. Aside from the relief it offered debtors, the indisputable impact of devaluation on the balance of trade and on incoming coin—however ephemeral—made it much too alluring for most colonial governments to forgo.

Besides, many colonial governments perceived that they had no other choice but to devalue, in order to counteract the negative consequences of devaluation from a neighboring colony. The temporary stream of coin that accrued to the devaluing colony often came directly from neighboring governments, transferring silver from one colony to another. A critic in England, Rice Vaughan, for this reason called devaluation "an Art which States have used to rob one another of their Money, by setting on higher prices upon it." Not surprisingly, devaluation often provoked great economic tension and jealousy between various colonies, rousing neighboring governments to either match or exceed the new rates for Spanish coin. ("Other Nations out of the same Misconceipt," said Vaughan, "will raise the Money likewise, and so deprive you of your end.")[29] Competitive devaluations resulted, on occasion, in a not-so-subtle form of intercolonial monetary warfare. The animosity was not yet especially tense in the mid-seventeenth century but grew more and more so as the century proceeded, so that several colonies were soon at loggerheads over currency rates.

The coming rivalry was nevertheless already evident in the middle of the seventeenth century. When raising the Spanish dollar to 5s in 1642, the Massachusetts government cited the "oft occasions wee have of trading with the Hollanders" at New Amsterdam. By raising the coin, the government reasoned, more money would arrive at Boston from New Netherland.[30] Four months later, the Dutch West India Company petitioned the director-general and council of New Netherland that "the value of money be raised in order that it be retained here and not exported hence by foreign nations." The government agreed and raised the coin by 20 percent, surpassing the rate in Massachusetts.[31] In April 1643 the Connecticut government responded in kind by matching the Massachusetts rate, setting the dollar at 5s. The Virginia House of Burgesses, in 1645, eclipsed all three colonies by raising the piece of eight to 6s—an increase of 33 percent—though the burgesses inexplicably reduced the rate to 5s a decade later. Elsewhere in the English Atlantic, the government at Barbados established a 5s rate in 1646 and then raised it to 6s in 1651 (though the collapse of the island's royalist government shortly after caused it to fall again, later settling at 5s a piece). Bermuda too joined the inflationary trend, raising the coin to 5s in 1658.[32]

Currency devaluation was certainly not new to the Western or even global experience. The Ottoman and Mughal empires periodically devalued their currencies, as did the Romans at the twilight of their ancient empire. European states since the High Middle Ages intermittently reduced the silver content of their currency units, aiming to profit the king's treasury and to draw "abundance of money" from rival neighbors.[33] As one English writer said, one of the "common Reasons" against devaluation was that "others will raise as well as we, whereby the Design will be frustrated." Such actions, moreover, might "occasion Quarrellings and War from neighbouring Kingdoms and States, for draining their Money from them."[34]

Currency competition through devaluation thus dated back many centuries between rival states, yet the practice was altogether unheard of between colonies of the same empire. Devaluation also departed sharply from the practice of England herself at the time. Prior to the Great Recoinage debate of the 1690s, most economic thinkers in England possessed a staunchly negative view of devaluation, no doubt influenced by the memory of King Henry VIII's notorious devaluations in the previous century, which had culminated in the Great Debasement of 1545–1551. Queen Elizabeth restored confidence and stability to the pound through a recoinage in 1560–1561, and after a very minor devaluation in 1601, the pound remained constant at just under four ounces of sterling silver through the rest of the early modern period. England's colonies were therefore quite distinct from the mother country on this matter. The 1640s and 1650s marked the beginning of this new episode in American monetary history, and in the decades following, the currency contest excited no shortage of animosity, disunity, and resentment between neighboring colonial governments. For now, as governments generally stuck to a 5s rate, intercolonial tension on the issue was by and large muted, and not a top concern at the moment. That situation would later change.

To turn back to the depression in Massachusetts: The long-term agenda for economic recovery centered around improving the balance of trade. Fishing, shipbuilding, lumbering, and cloth and iron manufacture were all a significant part of this effort. As individuals or members of their immediate family, colonists pursued this work for personal gain, hoping to purchase additional goods at the store or perhaps to pocket some silver change. More broadly, however, the colony's government and leaders, in pursuing this economic agenda, had the trade balance and money supply primarily in view. "So long as our ingate exceeds our outgate," the General Court affirmed in 1646, "the ballance . . . cann leave us but litle money."[35]

Import substitution was a key part of this agenda. Cloth and iron made up the bulk of imported goods: coats, blankets, stockings, farming and building equipment, pots, pans, nails, and weapons. Producing these goods internally would decrease the colony's trade deficit with England, keeping some money

in Massachusetts. Thus the General Court, in October 1640, offered direct subsidies to colonists who produced homespun cloth, dispatching representatives to the various towns for "teaching the boyes & girles in all townes the
spining of the yarne." "God is leading us by the hand into a way of cloathing," the author of *New Englands First Fruits* reported happily in 1643.[36] Import substitution, however, confronted strict limits. A company founded for
ironwork in 1645, for example, lasted only seven years before folding. Textile
production encountered similar difficulties: the cost of labor, too high; the
slack season on the farm, too short; the quality of clothing, too coarse and
mediocre to allay demand for imported textiles.[37]

Export expansion proved far more successful, particularly in the fishing
trade; indeed fishing became one of the colony's most vital sources of silver
coin. Before the Civil War, New Englanders imported most of their fish from
itinerant English fishermen in Newfoundland and Maine, but the wartime im-
pressment of English sailors left an instant vacuum and temporarily doubled
the price of fish.[38] New England fishermen immediately took to the coasts of
Newfoundland, New Hampshire, and Maine. Within thirty years, they took
in an annual catch of 6,000,000 pounds of fish, up from a mere 300,000 in
1641.[39] Boston merchants expanded the now-thriving export trade of cod
across the Atlantic Ocean—not only to Bilbao in Spain, but to Portugal and
the Wine Islands. About one-third to one-half of the earnings from cod exports now returned to Massachusetts in coin or bills of exchange.[40] "The Fishery was then the N.E. Silver Mine," one eighteenth-century writer recalled,
". . . the principal Means to draw in Silver." "Some silver mine, if any here doe
wish, they it may finde in the bellyes of our fish," a colonist quipped in 1648.[41]

Shipbuilding developed into another cornerstone of New England's emergent economy, contributing further to monetary recovery. Timber was notably abundant in the region; Boston merchants had already made the habit of
exporting clapboards, planks, barrel staves, and other lumber products to the
deforested Wine Islands and Caribbean.[42] This made the building of ships a
natural enterprise. Money was a prime motivator behind the rise of New
England shipbuilding, as Governor Winthrop affirmed. "The general fear of
want of foreign commodities, now our money was gone, set us on work to
provide shipping of our own," he remarked; ". . . the work was hard to accomplish for want of money, but our shipwrights were content to take such pay as
the country could make." "Such pay as the country could make" was likely a
reference to shipwrights' accepting their wages in country pay; the General
Court in October 1641 declared that "for servants and workmens wages it is
ordered, that they may bee paid in corne."[43] By 1645 Boston shipwrights had
constructed six vessels of at least 300 tons—used primarily for transoceanic

trade—as well as many additional smaller craft of 45–90 tons for coastal trade with the Chesapeake and Caribbean.[44]

Shipbuilding retained money within the colony by relieving New England merchants from paying freight expenses to an English or foreign shipmaster. Freight expenses included hiring the vessel; victualing the ship; shipping insurance; and settling wages for the master, mates, cooks, and seamen—money that returned to the country of origin. Thomas Mun, in 1628, estimated that "fraight of Ships, ensurance of the Adventure" typically amounted to 25 percent of the total value of goods on board.[45] Economists today call these charges "invisible earnings" because they did not show up in the customhouse ledgers, which counted only "visible" imports and exports. A seemingly unfavorable trade balance, then, could be offset through high invisible earnings. Indeed, freight—according to some—was the "most certain Profit a Country can possibly make by Trade."[46]

The West Indian islands, especially Barbados, became a favorite trading partner of Boston's merchants. Barbados underwent an even greater transformation than Massachusetts Bay in the 1640s. Barbadians responded to the depression by switching their staple crop from tobacco to sugar. Sugar, in recent decades, had become wildly popular among the wealthier classes in England, but imported as it was from Brazil, the sweet additive was still very expensive. The Dutch had ruled Brazil—which they called New Holland—since the 1630s. But in 1645 the Portuguese planters in Brazil launched a near decade-long revolt against Dutch rule, shutting down the major sugar plantations and causing the price of sugar to shoot up nearly 50 percent in a single year, now trading at 6d a pound.[47] The English planters on Barbados responded accordingly, ditching the depressed tobacco crop in favor of sugar. The change was rapid and extraordinary, aided, in large measure, by the use of African slave labor. Over the next two decades, Barbadian planters imported more than forty thousand slaves; by 1660, Barbados became the first English colony with a black majority.[48] Sugar plantations required immense numbers of workers to plant, cultivate, cut, grind, and boil the cane. The productivity of each individual slave was substantial: up to six thousand pounds of sugar per annum. At 6d a pound this equated to £150 worth of sugar, and even after the price of sugar fell to 3d a pound by the late 1650s, this output amounted to an impressive £75 per worker (about three hundred pieces of eight).[49] The high capital requirements for starting and running a sugar plantation—not simply the labor but also the heavy equipment—transformed the demographics further by forcing small tobacco farmers off the island, consolidating ownership in the land in fewer hands.[50]

The Barbadian elite became fabulously wealthy, and yet silver remained in short supply on the island. Money and wealth were not synonymous. Money is only a *particular* type of wealth. Planters manifested their newfound wealth not in gold and silver coin, but in slaves, capital equipment, and imported luxuries, including furniture, wine, silk, books, clocks, and other goods intended for pleasure or conspicuous consumption.[51] The balance of trade thus remained heavily against Barbados, requiring the use of another medium of exchange than silver. Not surprisingly, the Barbadian planters replaced the tobacco money they formerly used with sugar money. The about-face occurred as suddenly as the transition on the plantation. The island's governor, Francis Willoughby, later called sugar "theire Coyne" and "our ready money."[52] Taxes, fees, fines, and salaries were all payable in sugar; for instance, any islander caught concealing a dagger or "pocket Pistol" paid a fine of 500 pounds of sugar, and a fine of 5,000 pounds awaited anyone who formally challenged another man to a fight. The government used sugar money to regulate social behavior: any freeman who traded with a slave without the master's consent was fined 500 pounds of sugar, as was anyone who knowingly entertained a slave not his own.[53] As one observer wrote at the end of the seventeenth century, "'Tis but of late years that any other way of buying and selling was us'd in those islands but for sugar, all their accounts being computed by pounds of sugar, and the Law of the Countrey allowing all debts to be paid in that Specie."[54]

Like tobacco money, sugar money was liable to various deceits in quality, prompting the Barbadian legislature, in 1652, to appoint a special officer to oversee disputes over "unmerchantable" sugar being "given and received in payment."[55] Also like tobacco money, not every transaction involved the physical hauling of sugar at the moment of sale. Transactions, initially, were often recorded in book, with payment completed once the crop was ready: "the Marchants keeping all their books & accts in Shuggr." In such instances, sugar still acted as money, for "those who need provisions & cloathing buy them with Shugr," explained the governor of the Leeward Islands later in the century.[56] Nevertheless, there were also many cases when a physical transfer of sugar immediately followed a transaction: decades later, in 1701, a petition for a silver mint on Barbados lamented the planters' "necessity of Carrying Sugar and Tobacco upon their Backs to barter for little Common Necessarys."[57]

The Barbadian sugar revolution came at the perfect time for Massachusetts. Sugar was so profitable that the islanders devoted as much land as possible for "that Noble Juice of the Cane": "so intent upon planting sugar," a planter told Winthrop in 1647, "that they had rather buy foode at very deare rates . . . soe infinite is the profitt of sugar workes."[58] Massachusetts merchants gladly responded to the call, and in coming years exported fish, barrel staves, horses, pork, beef, flour, cheese, corn, peas, and other provisions to the Caribbean,

returning sugar, rum, and molasses to New England. The merchants conducted this traffic most often with Massachusetts-owned vessels, advancing
the shipbuilding industry. Moreover, because New Englanders exported more
goods to the West Indies than they imported from the West Indies, the trade
also returned coin and bills of exchange to New England—another reason silver remained scarce on Barbados.[59] New England merchants profited also
from the Barbadian attachment to slavery, exporting fish and timber products
to the Canary Islands for slaves and then carrying slaves across the Atlantic to
Barbados to exchange for sugar, rum, molasses, silver, and bills of exchange.[60]

By midcentury, Massachusetts Bay had recovered quite spectacularly from
its earlier depression, out of which emerged a diversified commercial economy
in which no single staple dominated but rather a multiplicity of trades. The
most visible sign of this transformation was the growing presence of foreign
coin in Massachusetts, particularly in Boston and Salem; in 1647, for example,
the inventory of one modest, middling tradesman included nearly £5 in foreign
money, that is, twenty pieces of eight (the same tradesman also had £3 worth
of wampum).[61] New England merchants did not simply import Spanish money;
they also imported money minted in Portugal, the Holy Roman Empire, France,
and Holland, as well as small sums of Barbary and Turkish gold from the export of fish to the Mediterranean.[62] Even so, the general failure at import substitution kept the colony highly dependent on English and European imports,
exporting a great deal of this coin straight out of the colony. Those who possessed coin in Massachusetts generally inhabited the port towns, not the countryside. "Itt is true, some men have here Spanish mony sometimes," the General
Court affirmed in 1646, but trade deficits "leave us but litle mony."[63] Middling
farmers still relied almost exclusively on country pay, wampum, or direct barter
for trade; the government still levied taxes in wheat, barley, rye, peas, and Indian corn.[64]

Further south, in the Chesapeake, tobacco growers witnessed a mild recovery at midcentury: the Barbadian transition to sugar eliminated one of their
largest competitors in the English tobacco market. Virginia and Maryland became ever more dependent on tobacco, with a tenfold increase in tobacco
exports from 1638 to 1668, amounting to fifteen million pounds by the latter
date.[65] Signs of future economic diversification, however, slowly appeared. Virginians exported small numbers of livestock to Barbados (via ships owned by
Massachusetts merchants) and even engaged in limited shipbuilding projects
for coastal trade.[66] One traveler to Barbados, in 1648, noted that "New England
sendeth Horses, and Virginia Oxen" to the "rich men" of Barbados, who paid
them "excessive rates."[67] Life, on the whole, became more settled and favorable in Virginia at midcentury, with modest but genuine prospects available

for economic and social advancement—even for former servants—prompting the arrival of more migrants from England.[68] Tobacco currency still predominated exchange: in 1656 the Virginia House of Burgesses allocated salaries of 25,000 pounds of tobacco to the governor and 6,000 pounds to the speaker of the house; even clergymen received pay in tobacco.[69]

Tobacco money, by now, had governed Virginia's internal trade for the better part of three decades. Some leaders in the colony still wished to change that. In November 1645 the House of Burgesses passed a currency bill that accomplished two things. First, it raised the value of Spanish dollars from 4s6d to 6s: a devaluation of 33 percent, with the aim of drawing more silver into the colony. Second, the bill authorized the establishment of a Virginia mint. The mint was to issue copper coins, ranging from 2d to 9d, with an extrinsic value far exceeding the intrinsic value of the copper metal the coins contained (by almost fourteen times). The mint was to stamp the Virginia motto on one side of the coin, with the other side of the coin "stampted yearly with some new figure." According to the statute, each Virginia county would take turns in annually determining the particular figure on the coin's reverse.[70] In justifying the currency law, the burgesses declared "how advantageous a quoine current would be to this collony, and the great wants and miseries which do daily happen unto it by the sole dependency upon tob'o." The coinage would have mostly served the purposes of small change—tobacco money would not have been wholly supplanted—but even a limited metallic coinage held out least some relief to the colony. Mysteriously, however, the prospective Virginia coinage never came into effect, and no existing records explain the reason. Virginia remained strictly dependent on the tobacco medium.[71]

The English colonial economies rebounded quite impressively from the gloom of the early 1640s. The United Provinces of the Netherlands played a big role in the recovery of these economies. By the end of the 1640s, direct trade between English colonists and Dutch tradesmen had expanded far beyond the loosely organized, ad hoc arrangements of the 1630s and had proved a great benefit to the colonial economies. For England, however, this trade represented the gravest threat yet to the mercantilist order for the colonies. The Civil War, for now, left colonial-Dutch trade unimpeded. But England's colonists were set for a rude awakening whenever the mother country again focused her attention across the Atlantic.

English colonials, at first, traded with the Dutch out of sheer necessity. Colonial producers required markets to vend their exports, and colonial consumers required a dependable, affordable source for imported necessities. The Civil War disrupted no small part of this trade with England; capital was now largely unavailable and commercial vessels faced inordinate risk in English waters. Another European power would have to fill the void. Dutch merchants gladly stepped in, eager for additional markets to absorb the recent boom in Dutch manufacturing, especially of fine cloth and linens.[72]

After war erupted inside England in 1642, Dutch shipmasters from New Amsterdam, in the hire of firms in the Netherlands, scoured the North American coastline, buying produce and selling merchandise. The New England governments took immediate steps to secure and encourage this trade, sending coasting vessels down to New Netherland to invite Dutch merchants "to supply us with necessaries and to take of our commodities."[73] For the first time, in 1642–1643, the governments of Massachusetts and Connecticut recognized non-Spanish and non-English money as current—including silver ducatons and rijksdaalders—"considering the oft occasions wee have of trading with the Hollanders."[74] The Virginia House of Burgesses, in March 1643, declared that "it shall be free and lawfull for any merchant, factors or others of the Dutch nation to import wares and merchandizes and to trade or traffique for the commoditys of the collony."[75] Such a declaration openly violated the Privy Council order of 1621, but the Civil War left the burgesses no other choice—and, besides, what could the distraught empire do in response? The following year, 1644, the burgesses dispatched agents to New Amsterdam with the message that merchants in England were now completely "unable to Mannadg the affaires."[76]

Above all, however, pecuniary factors—not bare necessity—drove English colonists to trade with the Dutch, as evidenced by their participation in the trade even when trade with England was still viable. The Dutch were more competitive; they almost always paid higher prices for colonial produce, while selling imported goods at prices 30–40 percent cheaper than those offered by the English. The price disparity, on both ends—buying and selling—resulted primarily from the stark contrast in freight expenses.[77] "The Cheapness of their Freight enable them to under-sell us," an English administrator wrote in 1651, ". . . in our Plantations they have three, if not four Sail of Ships, for our one."[78] The reduced operating costs of the Dutch *fluit*—with fewer masts, fewer sails, and fewer crew members—allowed Dutch shipmasters to charge only £4 per ton of cargo. The English, for their part, charged £8–14 per ton.[79] Freight expenses were especially pertinent for bulky commodities like tobacco or sugar, for which the marginal profit per ton was far lower than for more valuable goods like spices or silk. As one Englishman recorded in 1652, the Dutch "carry all manner of bulkie Commodities (the fraight whereof rises high) so much cheaper."[80]

Hence, when London merchants petitioned Parliament in 1644 to "transport ammunition" to Virginia "to interrupt the Hollanders," the burgesses announced their determination for "the whole Collony to defend them [the

Dutch] with our uttermost power & abilitye."[81] The most prominent leaders in Virginia, including Governor Sir William Berkeley, were ardent royalists; Dutch trade, for them, served the additional purpose of undermining Parliament-dominated London, where most prewar trade had centered and where Parliament collected customs duties to support its part of the war effort. Political motivations aside, however, the practical and economic motivation was also undeniable. New Amsterdam was only a short journey away from Virginia; the trade made sense, and it subsequently soared. Between 1643 and 1649, at least thirty-three Dutch vessels sailed to Virginia, purchasing tobacco and selling "Linnen Cloth of all sorts . . . Stockins, Shooes, and the like things."[82] English-Chesapeake trade was not entirely eviscerated in the 1640s, yet imports of Chesapeake tobacco into England fell by nearly half.[83] "At last Christmas," one Virginian recounted in 1649, "we had trading here ten ships from London, two from Bristoll, twelve Hollanders, and seven from New-England."[84]

Dutch traders made even greater inroads in the English West Indies. By the late 1640s, more than a dozen Dutch vessels docked annually off the coast of Barbados, purchasing sugar and selling an assortment of provisions and merchandise to the islanders, particularly textiles.[85] The Barbadian council and assembly, in 1651, praised the Dutch for "how much cheaper they sell their Commodities to us then our owne Nation"; the following year, the governor confirmed that the island's trade "was most of all carried on by the Dutch."[86] The number of Amsterdam sugar refineries had nearly doubled in the second quarter of the seventeenth century—reaching fifty by the year 1662—and the loss of Brazil made the Dutch eager for new sugar sources.[87] But they were not only interested in sugar: elsewhere in the Caribbean, the tobacco of the Leeward Islands gained the Hollanders' interest. The Dutch even hired agents to inhabit the islands for part of the year, networking with local inhabitants and offering credit liberally to the most reliable planters. Some of the Dutch went so far as to build warehouses three to four stories tall on St. Christopher and Montserrat, storing produce, tobacco, and goods over extended periods.[88]

Price competitiveness was the predominant factor in colonial dealings with the Dutch. Freight expenses played a major role, but even absent the disparity in freight, the sheer presence of additional buyers and sellers off the colony's coast necessarily implied a great economic benefit for colonial planters and settlers. Additional buyers meant the competitive bidding up of prices for colonial exports; additional sellers meant the competitive bidding down of prices for imported goods. On the island of St. Christopher, Dutch captains reportedly sold shirts, shoes, and drawers each at the price of only 12 pounds weight of tobacco, whereas the English sold the same for 40–50 pounds.[89] No doubt, the Dutch manifestly benefited colonial economic interests. England's colonists, in turn, offered their warm embrace.

There was much to admire, besides, about the Netherlands. The country's Protestantism surely commended it, but one could not help but marvel, more particularly, at its recent commercial ascendancy. The Dutch, at present, were reveling in one of the greatest economic booms in human history. The population of Amsterdam had more than doubled since 1600—from 60,000 to 140,000—and its merchants had thoroughly mastered the global carrying trade. Massive warehouses lined the city's canals, storing goods imported from all over the globe, awaiting profitable reexport to foreign markets. The Bank of Amsterdam, or *Wisselbank*, had become the world's most powerful financial institution, supplanting Venice and other financial centers in Italy; London, for its part, had no incorporated bank at all. Once a possession of the foreign Habsburg monarchy, the Netherlands was now a "potent and flourishing Republick"; the "Store-keepers of the Goods of Foreign Nations." "They carry all before them like a mighty torrent," acclaimed one English contemporary.[90]

Commercial men in England especially envied the latest Dutch economic boom. In the 1630s English merchants had temporarily supplanted the Dutch in the carrying trade of rich Mediterranean goods to northern Europe. Holland's involvement in the Thirty Years' War, and English abstention, permitted this. But the Civil War abruptly ended England's commercial euphoria in the early 1640s, and the Peace of Westphalia in 1648 again unleashed Dutch economic might, with Dutch freight rates almost immediately being cut in half—well below the rates of English ships.[91] This rate cut, in turn, encouraged London merchants to buy Baltic and Mediterranean goods from the Amsterdam entrepôt; between 1647 and 1651, for example the number of English ships arriving in London from the Baltic Sea collapsed from 130 to a mere 22.[92] Dutch merchants now handled 70 percent of all Baltic exports and 80 percent of all Spanish exports. England's trade with Italy and the Levant also disintegrated, and Dutch cloth decidedly outcompeted English woolens in continental sales.[93] The combined tonnage of Dutch seapower—commercial and naval—now more than doubled that of England, and the Dutch had practically cornered Atlantic and East Indian markets.[94] "I believe forty times more gold & silver is here at this day in the Low Countreys than so in England," a resident of Amsterdam wrote a London correspondent in 1652, with some exaggeration. "Wee have in Amsterdam more English gold than you have," he said, ". . . great quantitys of heavy English silver hath weekly come over"; "as your business now stands, you have hardly money left to maintaine the Trade of the Nation."[95]

The most profitable branch of the Dutch carrying trade was its United East India Company (VOC), an unbridled tour de force that far exceeded all like English and Portuguese traffic. The VOC thoroughly dominated trade with China and other ports in east and southeast Asia, purchasing silk, cotton, and spices to reexport to European markets at a price three times the initial cost, a margin of profit far exceeding that of the English East India Company.[96] Worse still, the English company exported silver out of England's own stock to purchase items from Asia, while the Dutch "carry no Silver from Holland, but drive the Trade with the Silver they get from Japan in exchange for other Commodities."[97] The VOC further cemented its hegemony by founding Cape Colony on the southern tip of Africa in 1652; by this date, the Dutch company employed approximately 160 ships in Asian waters.[98]

Dutch activity in the Americas and West Indies appeared modest by comparison; nevertheless, by 1650, Dutch investment in Atlantic trade surpassed investments made even in East Indian trade. The key difference was that the trade was neither monopolized by a single company nor centered on Dutch-controlled territories. The Dutch West India Company (WIC) surrendered its monopoly over New Netherland's trade in 1640, and the coming Brazilian debacle forced the WIC to relinquish its claim to Brazil in 1654. Far from suffering, however, Dutch trade in the Atlantic actually expanded in the 1650s. What set the Dutch apart from other Atlantic empires was their reliance on trade with other colonials. Dutch tradesmen cruised continually down the coastlines of English and Spanish America, peddling a vast assortment of coveted merchandise at prices that merchants of other empires could not match. The WIC, at root, was not a trading company, but a military enterprise; as far as trade was concerned, the Dutch government had granted noncompany tradesmen complete freedom to trade anywhere they wanted to in the Atlantic. So they did, and quite spectacularly.[99]

The Dutch Republic, at midcentury, was vastly outpacing all of its competition in the international contest for silver and gold. "They alwayes have great store of moneys," Henry Robinson, English merchant and administrator, remarked enviously in 1652.[100] The Netherlands' remarkable metamorphosis from client state of Spain to world superpower reinforced the appeal of the balance-of-trade doctrine and solidified support even further for mercantilist ideas. At the beginning of the century the Protestant Dutch were natural allies to the English, but in this new mercantilist age, religious considerations increasingly yielded way to commercial consciousness.[101] As one Englishman recalled in 1651, not long earlier the "Design of Spain" had been the "Universal Monarchie of Christendom"; the Dutch, however, were more perilous, for they sought "the Universal Trade, not onely of Christendom, but indeed, of the greater part of the known world." "Where force fails, yet money prevails; thus hopes the Hollanders," Thomas Mun wrote a couple decades earlier.[102] Many English onlookers blended envy with admiration, extolling the commercial eminence of their new rival. Dutch merchants were "Masters of the Field in Trade": an "industrious People" who "court Trade as their Mistress," whose sudden rise "is the envy of the present, and may be the wonder of all future Generations."[103]

As the Civil War finally came to a close, England seemed poised to counterstrike. A republican form of government now ruled over the British Isles. The Rump Parliament had tried and convicted the king of treason, executing Charles on January 30, 1649. Seven days later, the Rump abolished the House of Lords and the following day resolved that "the office of a king in this nation . . . is unnecessary, burdensome, and dangerous to the liberty, safety and public interest of the people." In May 1649 the Rump declared England "a Commonwealth and Free State."[104] The Council of State was the sole executive institution, consisting of forty-one members (annually appointed by Parliament). The council's duties included examining ways and means to improve England's trade and navigation. Imperial-colonial administration also fell under its jurisdiction: the Council of State carried on most official correspondence with the colonies.[105] To aid them in this task, in August 1650, Parliament established a separate Council of Trade, reporting directly to the Council of State on commercial and colonial matters. Its secretary, Benjamin Worsley, was a London merchant with expert knowledge of colonial America. Parliament instructed the Council of Trade to take into "consideration the English Plantations in America," while keeping an exact account of "all commodities imported and exported through the Land, to the end that a perfect Balance of Trade may be taken."[106]

Fiscal and monetary uncertainty drove the new Commonwealth's fixation on mercantilist matters. "The Moneyes of this Commonwealth are in very great Sums transported," the Council of State reported in a July 1651 document expounding on the "many great Inconveniencies & mischiefs upon this Commonwealth by the freedome of Trade driven by the Dutch."[107] The government's need for money was extraordinary. The state's new administrative apparatus was vast and expensive. Oliver Cromwell's New Model Army of 70,000 soldiers cost the government more than £2,000,000 in 1651; between 1645 and 1651, Parliament paid out nearly £5,230,000 to Cromwell's army, which still numbered more than 40,000 soldiers in the late 1650s.[108] The Commonwealth navy was also very expensive; the fleet in 1652 required just over 10,000 men, and more than a hundred new ships were built in the coming decade to add to the fleet.[109] Where could the new government get that kind of money? Most agreed that mercantilism provided the answer: a managed, regulated trade designed explicitly to draw gold and silver into England, in public and private coffers alike. The Navigation Act epitomized this vision, and colonial-Dutch trade was among its many targets.

When the New Model Army won the Battle of Worcester in September 1651—finally ending the Civil War and compelling the flight of Charles's twenty-one-year-old son to France—the new English republic inherited an Atlantic empire vastly different from the one England had governed on the eve of the war. Massachusetts and Barbados had each undergone economic revolutions; Barbados, in particular, now produced a staple good, sugar, that Englishmen previously imported from abroad, and the crop was also exportable to continental Europe. The main roadblock, at present, was the Dutch. Dutch merchants and shipmasters were robbing the English Commonwealth of rightful gains from Atlantic commerce, and indeed also from Baltic and Mediterranean commerce. As Henry Robinson, leading merchant and Commonwealth advisor, urged in 1649, it was "now high time" to act on the matter, else the Dutch "must necessarily beat us out of all Markets."[110]

Empire-wide recognition of Commonwealth authority came first on Parliament's agenda. The task was particularly difficult in the fiercely royalist colonies of Barbados and Virginia. In October 1650, Parliament prohibited all outside commerce (English or foreign) with the two colonies until each recognized Commonwealth authority.[111] The reaction from both colonies was swift and defiant. The Barbadian government called it a "Slavish imposition" to "be bound by the regulations of the Parliament in which we have no representatives"; Virginia, led by Governor Sir William Berkeley, denounced the "Tyrannicall" proceedings and insisted they would "Protect all forraigne Merchants with our utmost force." "The Dutch found and relieved us," Berkeley said.[112] When the two governments surrendered to the new English government in early 1652, they purported to do so only conditionally, insisting on their right to trade with whomever they wished. The House of Burgesses stipulated that "the people of Virginia have free trade as the people of England do enjoy to all places and with all nations"; the Barbadian government, in like manner, provided "that all Trade be free with all Nations that do Trade" and claimed to retain "as great a freedom of Trade as ever."[113]

The Navigation Act of 1651 rendered useless these free-trade proclamations. Authorized by Parliament in October 1651, the Navigation Act inaugurated a new era of mercantilist controls over English and colonial commerce. First, the act stipulated that no goods were to be imported into England from the Americas or from the East Indies except in vessels owned either by the English or by English colonists; moreover, the vessel had to be manned by a crew at least three-fourths English or English colonial. Second, neither England nor the colonies could import continental European goods except in vessels owned by the English, English colonists, or the country of origin (the initial producer). This latter regulation effectively outlawed the Dutch carrying trade of Baltic and Mediterranean goods to England, as well as the Dutch carrying trade of European goods—German linens, French wines—to colonial consumers.[114]

Unlike later acts of navigation, the primary emphasis of the act of 1651 was not on the Atlantic, but on England's trade with continental Europe. American trade at midcentury counted for no more than one-tenth of England's total overseas commerce.[115] Consequently, the act of 1651 appears a bit lighter on colonial commerce than later versions, at least on paper. But this appearance is also somewhat deceptive. For example, the statute restricted the flow of imported goods to the colonies, but it technically left colonial exports alone. Tobacco and sugar planters could legally sell their crop directly to foreign traders. On the other hand, those same foreign traders who bought tobacco and sugar—primarily Dutch—also sold merchandise. The provision, therefore, that prohibited colonists from purchasing European imports from Dutch carriers, prohibited de facto the Dutch purchase of tobacco and sugar. What the Navigation Act of 1651 implied, the act of 1660 later categorically spelled out.

The Navigation Act of 1651 was not the first of its kind in English history, but it was altogether distinct from any preceding regulation. Almost three centuries earlier, for instance, in 1381, the parliament under King Richard II mandated that no English merchant "shall carry forth nor bring any Merchandises, but only in Ships of the King's Allegiance." Parliament repealed the statute in 1559, responding to new commercial realities in the early part of Elizabeth's reign.[116] In this sense, but in this sense only, the Navigation Act was a return to the old. What set the act of 1651 strictly apart from the medieval restriction was, first, its comprehensiveness and, second, its decidedly mercantilist character. The public aims of the law explicitly emphasized the balance-of-trade doctrine and specie objective. Benjamin Worsley, secretary to the Council of Trade and primary author of the law, described the act's primary objective as "Weakening [Dutch] Shipping, and dreyning them by degrees of their Treasure and Coin." Another one of the law's chief architects, merchant Henry Robinson, explained that Parliament designed it to bring "the Grand Ballance of Trade in favour of this Nation," "whereby the Money stock of the Nation may be encreased."[117] Other enthusiasts predicted that the Navigation Act would make "money as plentifull as dust," whereas without it, the Dutch will "become almost Masters, both of our Mony and Trade."[118] Samuel Lambe, London merchant, explained it this way: "He that commands the Sea, may command trade, and he that hath the greatest trade will have the most money, which is of such value, that it command all worldly things, both in War and Peace." "Gold and Silver is the Universall measure of all things, and the Staple of Commerce," a supporter of the Navigation Act wrote in 1653: it "drives the Wheel of Trade and Success."[119]

The new regulations appeared to pay off, moderately, in the Baltic and Mediterranean trades. Over the rest of the 1650s, the English navy intercepted approximately three hundred ships—mostly Dutch, and mostly in the Channel and North Sea—for violating the Navigation Act.[120] Dutch share of Baltic traffic fell from 70 to 50 percent, and English merchants recovered some of the carrying trade to and from the Mediterranean.[121] In this regard, the Navigation Act of 1651 was a modest success. Atlantic trade was a much different story, as we will see. Enforcement proved far easier in England than in America; nevertheless, even there, in the months after Parliament passed the Navigation Act, a single English naval expedition captured twenty-four Dutch vessels off the coast of Barbados (the island was still in rebellion), collectively worth about £100,000.[122] This operation, together with frequent interceptions of Dutch ships in English waters, fueled the outbreak of war with the Netherlands in May 1652, the first of three Anglo-Dutch wars in the third quarter of the seventeenth century.[123]

War between the two Protestant commercial powers was not inevitable. The Rump Parliament earlier pursued a close political union with the Netherlands in 1649–1650, urging a united, Protestant, republican political front. The Dutch, however, wisely perceived that union would disadvantage them politically and economically, and rebuffed the proposal. After William II, Stadtholder and Prince of Orange, unexpectedly died in November 1650, the Rump Parliament again appealed in 1651 for a close political union, but the States General balked. One month later, in October, Parliament retorted with the Navigation Act and a fresh round of confiscations of Dutch vessels on the high seas.[124]

The First Anglo-Dutch War (1652–1654) was waged almost solely on commercial grounds. Both sides combated largely in the North Sea and English Channel, though Dutch property on the Leeward Islands also suffered persistent attacks. The war concluded with only a nominal victory for England, with a highly lenient treaty for the Dutch. The States General feigned concessions to the Navigation Act, and the latter half of the 1650s proved one of the most prosperous periods in Dutch economic history.[125] Colonial-Dutch trade persisted after the treaty in 1654, exposing the absolute feebleness of enforcing the Navigation Acts across the Atlantic. After 1654 the various colonial assemblies repealed all wartime prohibitions on Dutch commerce. The wartime prohibitions were only symbolic anyway; even during the war itself, English colonists traded brazenly with the Dutch. "All freedom of trade shall be maintained, and all merchants and traders shall be cherished," the Virginia House of Burgesses declared in 1655.[126]

For the remainder of the 1650s, English colonials simply ignored the Navigation Act, exercising, in Berkeley's words, "our right of giving and selling our goods to whom we please."[127] Berkeley was no longer governor of Virginia—his outspoken royalism removed him from office—but free-trade sentiment remained strong in the colony, and for good reason. As the directors of the WIC told the director-general of New Netherland in 1656, English merchants paid Virginia planters a "lower price" for their tobacco, "and this, we think, should induce the Virginians to continue their commercial relations with you [the Dutch] under all circumstances."[128] Colonial-Dutch trade was even more buoyant after the war in the English West Indies: as many as thirty Dutch vessels a year embarked to Barbados alone, and some more to the Leeward Islands. On one occasion, in 1655, an English squadron captured two dozen such vessels on Barbados, yet the jury on the island acquitted the Dutch masters despite incontrovertible evidence.[129] The Barbadian government's sentiments in 1651 still rang true: "We will never be so ungratefull to the Dutch for former helps as to deny them or any other Nation the freedome of our Ports," they had said. To do so would be to "prostitute those Liberties and Freedomes to which we were borne."[130] New Englanders echoed similar sentiments. When an English captain seized a Dutch vessel off the coast of Massachusetts in 1655, the General Court condemned the action as tending "highly to the infringing of our liberties, discouraging of trade, and destructive to our comfortable being." The Rhode Island assembly went furthest of all. In 1657 the Rhode Islanders announced that "the Dutch may have lawfull commerce with the English in this colony"; the following year they made it a felony for any English captain to seize foreign vessels, rebuking the several "ill-disposed persons" who had dared to try.[131]

The English state had to find some way to secure common obedience to the Navigation Act—not only in the colonies, but also in England, where some English merchants found it in their private interest to evade the law. Obedience could be secured through one of two means: coercion or persuasion; strong-arm tactics or voluntary compliance. Coercion required the rigorous use of various enforcement mechanisms, designed to compel submission (even if reluctant) to the letter of the law. Persuasion, on the other hand, entailed getting tradesmen to *agree* with the public aims of the law and thereby comply with its terms willingly, without the immediate threat of force. In both cases—coercion and persuasion—the English merchant was more likely to obey the Navigation

Act than most colonial tradesmen. For one, compulsion was far more effective in England, where vigilant officials stood watch close by. But second, the English merchant was also more likely to agree with the public aims of the law, that is, of mercantilism—the aim to center money in England—even if it contravened his private interests. The English merchant, after all, enjoyed representation in the Parliament that authorized the Navigation Act.

Such was not the case on the peripheries of empire. Coercion was extraordinarily difficult in the colonies, especially in this early period when not a single imperial officer yet resided in the colonies to enforce economic regulations. Persuasion, too, was far less plausible. Parliament, in essence, demanded that colonists sacrifice economic self-interest so that silver and gold could accumulate in a land thousands of miles across the ocean. This was a hard sell, especially in the 1650s, when many colonists still harbored royalist sentiments. Even New Englanders, who overwhelmingly cheered on Parliament during the war, balked at the idea of surrendering economic sovereignty for the doubtful advantage of benefiting the Commonwealth government. The pecuniary incentive behind Dutch trade was simply too strong for many colonists to ignore, while the reasons to abide by the law were hollow and weak.

Smuggling thus proliferated in the colonies in the 1650s, and there was no effective maneuver taken in England to stop it. The executive Council of State had to grapple with other pressing concerns: subduing Ireland and Scotland, and fighting the First Anglo-Dutch War, to say nothing of settling the government at home. The Council of Trade, for its part, folded entirely in May 1653. Parliament was utterly swamped with fickle administrative duties, hardly able at all to conduct day-to-day business. The army was growing ever more impatient, and by December 1653 its commander, Oliver Cromwell, had assumed the executive office of Lord Protector of the Commonwealth, dissolving the Council of State. Cromwell welcomed mercantile opinion in his councils, committees, and government, but he never formulated any comprehensive plan for managing the colonial sphere. The one exception was Cromwell's grandiose design to conquer the Spanish West Indies, but it was done in the midst of a war with Spain that only further distracted his government from other affairs in the Atlantic. The disorderliness of it all rendered imperial control of most colonial activity practically null.[132]

In such circumstances, the Navigation Act could never hope to achieve adequate enforcement in America—although there were indeed voices in England, at the time, demanding major administrative changes in imperial-colonial relations. In 1654 a group of London merchants with wide-ranging investments in Virginia, New England, and the Caribbean petitioned for the formation of a single council with powers "to reduce all Colonies and Plantations to a more

certaine, civill, and uniforme way of government." The merchants cited the
desperate need of "shutting out all Strangers from that Trade," arguing that
doing so would permit English merchants to export colonial goods to Europe
"instead of Bullion."[133] Two years later, in 1656, Thomas Povey, a London gentleman with investments and family connections in the West Indian islands,
petitioned Cromwell's government on "whether it be not a prudentiall thing to
draw all the Islands, Colonies, and Dominions of America under one and the
same management here."[134]

The English government adopted none of these propositions, but not
because it disagreed on principle; rather, the impracticalities of implementing these ideas were yet far too great in the 1650s. It was ill-advised and dangerous for colonists to trade freely with other countries—of this, English
administrators were well aware. Colonial refusal to comply with the Navigation Acts was not only a matter of economic disobedience; it was a matter of
political disobedience. Colonial compliance would have signaled political allegiance and submission to imperial authority. Illicit trade, on the other hand,
signaled political infidelity, and even rebellion and de facto independence. In
1652 this colonial attitude assumed a very tangible form—in the proud figure
of a New England silver coin, bearing the image of a pine tree.

The Massachusetts pine-tree shilling was one of the most remarkable produc-
tions of the seventeenth-century Atlantic world. It was the boldest expression
of colonial autonomy and colonial sovereignty in any era preceding the American Revolution. In the most palpable manner, it drew broad attention to the
fact that a prominent, proud, and outspoken faction within the Massachusetts
Bay Colony considered themselves independent of practically all authority in
England.

In May 1652 the Massachusetts General Court authorized the coinage of a
new silver currency. Denominations came in one-shilling, sixpence, and three-
pence pieces. The original stamp, as issued between June and October 1652,
was remarkably simple: a mere *NE* on one side for New England, and the
denomination in Roman numerals on the other. The same law instructed,
further, that all residents bring their foreign silver into the newly constructed mint house, whereupon they received a paper receipt to later claim
their newly coined money.[135] Five months later, in October 1652, the General
Court arranged for a new, more comprehensive stamp, including, for the first
time, a double ring on both sides to discourage clippers from shaving silver
off the edge. On the obverse of the coin was a tree, encircled by the inscription *Massachusetts*; on the reverse was *AD 1652* and the denomination in Roman
numerals, with *New England* inscribed along the coin's outer edge. The species

of tree varied throughout the mint's history: a willow tree (1652–1660), an oak tree (1660–1667), and most famously a pine tree (1667–1682) (figure 3). It was during this latter period, if not earlier, that the coins became known as "pine-tree shillings," though people also commonly called them "Boston shillings" or "Bay shillings."[136]

The most immediate reason for establishing the Massachusetts mint was the growing irregularity of coins. Since the mid-1640s, foreign coin had arrived in the colony at levels unequaled in previous years. The Spanish piece of eight was the most common, but other silver coins from France, Holland, and the Holy Roman Empire also entered circulation, all with varying weights and even fineness. The Spanish dollar was the most widely used coin, but this too was irregular, as the Peruvian piece of eight was notoriously lighter than the heavier Mexican piece of eight, despite possessing the same face value. (For years, the mint masters at Potosí had deceptively and fraudulently issued debased coins with less silver than authorized, a scandal that went undiscovered until 1641, causing substantial confusion in global exchanges thereafter.)[137]

Clipping had further aggravated the colony's currency irregularities, as it did in most Atlantic commercial centers. Clipping was the act of cropping, with shears, small amounts of silver from a coin before passing it off at face value. Most coins did not yet have a milled edge, an invention of the mid-seventeenth century that placed grooves on the coin's rim; the old hammered money did not possess this safeguard. "Coinage by the Hammer exposes you much more to the danger of false Coin," John Locke later remarked, ". . . the pieces not being so round, even, and fairly Stamp'd, nor marked on the Edges." Clipped money was extraordinarily common in colonial America. As the new Boston mint master,

FIGURE 3. Twelve-pence pine-tree coin of Massachusetts, issued sometime between 1667 and 1682. (ANS 1944.94.2. Courtesy of American Numismatic Society.)

John Hull, testified in his diary, the General Court "ordered a mint to be set up . . . upon occasion of much counterfeit coin brought in the country."[138]

Nor was wampum any longer a reliable currency in Massachusetts, creating a need for small change, which the mint fulfilled. The use of metal drills in the production of wampum had resulted in a sharp increase in the number of beads in circulation, severely depreciating its value. Wampum manufacture had become far too easy; not only that, but "counterfeit shell" and "false peag" pro- liferated, with colonists and Indians sometimes dying the white beads purple to artificially double their value.[139] Colonists increasingly grumbled of "uncomely and disorderly" beads, with "breaches" and "deforming spots"; ministers regu- larly complained of congregants tithing with "refuse wampome."[140] In 1649 the Massachusetts General Court prohibited the use of wampum for all public payments, including taxes. Though the beads could still circulate "from man to man"—that was not revoked until 1661—wampum was no longer "currant with the marchants," and thus, very quickly, it became quite "unreasonable that it should be forced upon any man."[141] A uniform coinage in Massachusetts would avert the inconveniences of a depreciated wampum currency and the disordered jumble of clipped foreign monies. The economic argument for the mint was extremely compelling.

Devaluation also attended the mint act of 1652. Each new Massachusetts coin contained about 22.5 percent less silver than its denominational equiva- lent in England. For ten years, since 1642, the rate for Spanish dollars in Mas- sachusetts was 5s, only 11 percent above the rate in England. Under the new mint act, however, the silver content of six new Massachusetts shillings equaled, approximately, the silver content of a single Spanish dollar. The legislation, therefore, was not unlike raising the piece of eight from 5s to 6s. As for the value of the piece of eight itself, the same act ordered it down to 4s6d, thus incentivizing holders of Spanish money to bring their coin to the mint for con- version. Moreover, when circumstances compelled a merchant to export sil- ver from the colony, the merchant would invariably choose to export the undervalued piece of eight, not the highly valued Boston coinage, thus (in theory) retaining the pine-tree shilling strictly within Massachusetts borders.[142]

Keeping the new coin within Massachusetts proved an arduous task. De- spite a 1654 law banning its export from the colony—attendant with warrant- less searches and harsh penalties—merchants in Boston and Salem still occasionally exported the coin covertly, preferring their "owne gaine before the publick good."[143] The West Indian island governments of Montserrat and Nevis soon recognized the circulation of "New England Monies," followed later by the governments of New York, New Jersey, Maryland, Virginia, Pennsylvania, and Carolina. Massachusetts coins even appeared as far east as the Canary

Islands and the borders of the Mediterranean. Though completely unintended, this dispersion of Bay shillings served as a visible testament to Boston's integration into a much wider commercial network—the city's tentacles extending thousands of miles from its borders—communicating to the rest of the Atlantic world that Massachusetts merited greater respect and recognition.[144]

The iconography and symbolism behind the new money was extraordinarily powerful. It was a point of great pride for the colony. For one, prior to the mid-1640s, the establishment of a Massachusetts mint would have been unfathomable; the subsequent progress of the Massachusetts economy made it possible. The very design of the money, centered as it was on a simple tree, celebrated the successes of the growing shipbuilding industry. Such an image contrasted sharply with the English silver money of the Interregnum period, which bore a Caesar-like visage of Cromwell. Moreover, the New England inscription on the back of the coin testified to the colony's growing dominance throughout the New England region. Economically speaking, by midcentury, virtually all of New England relied on Boston merchants for European goods, and it was they who handled more Bay shillings than any other class in New England. Politically speaking, Massachusetts was the foremost leader of the recently formed United Colonies of New England, a military alliance of confederated colonies with Boston as its central meeting place. Boston first came to dominate southern New England in the 1640s, and in the 1650s the city's merchants and governing leadership strengthened their influence and control over much of northern New England. Historian Mark Peterson aptly labels it "the city-state of Boston."[145] "They call the money coyned in this colony, New England coyne," Edward Randolph, customs officer, reported some years later, ". . . thereby bespeaking the influence this small government would have over all the neighbouring colonys."[146]

The political component of the Massachusetts shilling was the most compelling trait of all. Historically speaking, coinage bespoke political sovereignty, a prerogative reserved only for monarchs, princes, and independent states. As one English author wrote in 1630, coinage is a "principal point of Soveraignty"; thus, it was nothing short of "dishonour" to utilize coin bearing the symbols or image of a foreign state.[147] Iconography is among the most public and visible manifestations of state authority. Because money is often the most circulated and coveted good within the community, it is also uniquely conducive for displaying state symbols and messages. As one writer later commented, "Though it be true that such a piece of silver is but a piece of silver, yet as it bears Caesar's image and superscription upon it, it is more significant."[148] Indeed, just one year preceding the founding of the Boston mint, Thomas Hobbes in *Leviathan* listed "the power to coyn Money" among the "Rights, which make the Essence of Soveraignty." The right to mint coins, he argued, "belongeth to the Common-wealth, that is to say, to the Soveraign."[149]

By unilaterally minting its own currency, the Massachusetts government asserted de facto political sovereignty. This was a conscious decision. For one, the coin bore no reference at all to English authority. Unlike the former "hogge mony" of Bermuda or the earlier petitions for a Virginia coinage, the Massachusetts General Court never bothered seeking permission for the mint. This by now had become a pattern for Massachusetts. The same year, 1652, the General Court decreed that all freemen take an oath of allegiance to Massachusetts, with no mention whatsoever of any political fealty or ties to England.[150] Political autonomy and monetary autonomy were inextricably linked. The Rump Parliament had executed Charles I only three years earlier; Cromwell would not become Lord Protector of the Commonwealth until the following year. Massachusetts' leaders, in the meantime, took advantage of the political ambiguities and assumed one of the most definitive characteristics of independent statehood.

The Boston coinage, on the one hand, manifested a growing pride and confidence in the colony's present and future; paradoxically, however, the coinage also came about in an era of immense religious uncertainty. This, too, factored deeply into the Massachusetts coinage. The colony's founding generation, in the 1630s, had not only sought to create a refuge of godly government in North America for persecuted Christians, but also hoped to serve as a beacon and model for the rest of the Protestant world, especially for Puritans who stayed behind in England. The outbreak of the Civil War in 1642, and the subsequent dissolution of the Church of England, gave the Bay colonists much optimism; indeed, in the early 1640s, many reformers in England considered emulating the particular brand of church and state as featured in Massachusetts. That dream quickly faded, however, as it became clear that parliamentary victory required a broad Protestant coalition. By the late 1640s, few if any English reformers—much less the New Model Army—seriously endorsed the Bostonian model of "universall Compulsion" on theological matters.[151] This chasm deepened in the early 1650s, as the victorious Commonwealth state tolerated virtually any Protestant loyal to the cause. Oliver Cromwell, though pious and Calvinist in doctrine, endorsed the freedom for English men and women to pursue a wide range of Protestant creeds, including Quakerism, Anabaptism, and use of the Book of Common Prayer. Even Catholics enjoyed a measure of freedom. Appallingly, in 1652, a former resident and founding member of the Massachusetts Bay Company, Sir Richard Saltonstall, urged Boston ministers to embrace greater inclusivity within their own province. New England had lost its primary audience, sparking a crisis of identity that, strangely enough, coincided with the colony's fantastic commercial boom.[152]

Economics was the mint's raison d'être, yet the date of its founding, 1652, came at too critical a time to not signify something deeper. The colony's divine errand—religious revolution across the English world—had seemingly fallen apart, betrayed by fellow reformers in England. The Massachusetts mint, and the novel shilling it produced, provided the disheartened colonists varying degrees of comfort and support: a refreshingly positive PR development in an age of bad news for the colony's theological agenda. The Bay shilling demonstrated—in the most tangible, material fashion—that Massachusetts Bay remained a formidable presence on the Atlantic stage. The coin saved, at least in part, the dignity of a spiritually demoralized and disillusioned colony.

But herein lay an apparent contradiction. The colony's commercial influence had never been higher, its religious influence had never been lower, and the Bay shilling overtly celebrated this commercial ascendancy. One might think the ministers would dissent or at least withhold their active support for this money. Yet some of the colony's most radical Puritan ministers became the mint's most zealous supporters. All the while, the same ministers issued scathing criticisms of commercial greed, condemning the growing primacy of money in the colony over spiritual concerns.[153]

On the surface, the Bay shilling and pious Puritan were strange bedfellows indeed. But the paradox unravels once one considers the coin's aggressive political and cultural symbolism. The Boston coinage meant different things to different people. For the moderate, less religiously minded merchant, commercial expediency was foremost on his mind when considering the utility of the mint. For the clergyman or independent assemblyman, the political and cultural symbolism held far greater significance. The colony's political sovereignty—expressed so plainly on the face of the coin—was more necessary than ever: it served as a buffer protecting spiritual purity from a corrupted England. Appropriately enough, the master of the mint, John Hull, inhabited both camps: an affluent merchant and leading silversmith, he was nonetheless a deeply pious, devout man who kept detailed notes of the sermons he heard at the Boston church he helped to establish.[154]

Cromwell made no mention of the Boston mint in any of his writings. No evidence exists that he was even aware of it, and if he was, he suffered no offense. The Caribbean was Cromwell's chief colonial concern; New England was barely an afterthought. The Massachusetts General Court had already declared formal allegiance to his government; that was enough for Cromwell. The colony's relationship with England was courteous while tenuous and distant. As John Hull recorded in his diary the day news arrived of Cromwell's death in 1658, the Lord Protector was "one that sought the good of New England; though he seemed to be much wanting in a thorough testimony against the blasphemers of our days."[155] Not until 1660 would the Boston coinage face any real challenges from England, and when it did, the problem lay not in its economic rationale, but in the subversive, political elements inherent within the stamp of the coin itself.

Massachusetts trade continued its rapid expansion into the late 1650s; overseas traffic was the key to the colony's wealth. More than thirty wharves now lined the Boston waterfront, serving the export trade not only of fish and provisions but also of pine-tree masts to England, supplying England's need for shipbuilding materials in the wake of the Navigation Act. The New England population had risen to approximately sixty thousand colonial inhabitants, more than double that of the Chesapeake. From the Boston city center, extensive road networks branched out into the hinterland, with townships and general stores peppering the countryside. Shopkeepers preferred coin in payment, but also accepted country pay and extended book credit. Goods from all over New England flocked to the bustling port towns of Boston and Salem: lumber from New Hampshire, livestock and horses from Rhode Island, and agricultural produce from Connecticut and rural Massachusetts.[156]

Most agrarian New Englanders still largely depended on country pay, direct exchange (barter), and book credit for trade, handling coin only occasionally. Country pay remained legal tender for tax payments in Massachusetts, though the treasurer, after 1658, offered a 25 percent discount to anyone tendering coin (moreover, "leane cattle" would no longer be acceptable for public payments).[157] It was not unusual for ordinary farmers to own at least a few pieces of coin; the inventory of one such middling farmer in 1654 included 10s in "N.E. silver," as well as nine pieces of eight.[158] Nevertheless, most coin centered in and around Boston and Salem, where merchants and tradesmen circulated Bay shillings among themselves and exported Spanish money to purchase goods from abroad. The further one got from the major port towns of Massachusetts, the more precious coin became. "Wee have not English coyne," reported the Rhode Island assembly in 1658, "but only that which passeth amonge these barbarians [wampum], and such comodities as are raised by the labour of our hands [country pay], as corne, cattell, tobbacco, and the like, to make payment in."[159]

Further south, Chesapeake planters still relied almost exclusively on tobacco money in the 1650s, though now at the price of just under two pence a pound.[160] For this low price some blamed the Navigation Act. "The thing complained of by the Planters is the prohibiting of Foreigners to trade thither," said Lionel Gatford, an English merchant with ties to Virginia, to Oliver Cromwell in 1657: "by which prohibition (say they) the English Traders thither will have the Tobaco at their own rates, and sell their own goods and commodities transported thither at their own prices." Gatford suggested that Virginia be allowed a "certain coyn." Metallic currency, he argued, is far superior to the "bulkness of Tobacco, the onely thing yet used instead of coyn in that Colonie." A Virginia mint would allow business to be transacted "with much less trouble and difficultie." Gatford, in suggesting this, was almost certainly familiar with the Massachusetts mint; the proposal, not surprisingly, fell on deaf ears in London.[161]

The West Indies were the chief exception to Cromwell's general neglect of colonial America. Cromwell was keenly aware of the Caribbean's vast money-making potential, and his government stood in dire need of it: military expenditures, especially naval, had soared in recent years, and the government's debt now totaled near £2,000,000, though taxes had also never been higher.[162] Cromwell figured that the islands might help rescue his government from fiscal disaster; little wonder then that nearly all of the Dutch vessels seized by the English navy in the 1650s for smuggling in the colonies were in the Caribbean.

Thus far the English had only settled the outer periphery of the Caribbean, known as the Lesser Antilles. Anxious to expand into the center, Cromwell in 1655 launched the Western Design, a military campaign against Spanish possessions in the Greater Antilles, with hopes, perhaps, of even launching an assault on the Spanish Main. After a disastrously failed attempt to seize Hispaniola, a fleet of about thirty English ships proceeded successfully against the comparatively defenseless island of Jamaica. The Jamaican conquest marked the first time the English government had forcibly seized an overseas colony from a European power; it was also the first instance in which the English government assumed direct control of a colony immediately, without the initiative of a company or private proprietor. Ironically then—given the overall neglect of the rest of America in this period—the conquest of Jamaica marked a real turning point in the history of the empire: arguably the most aggressive imperial move yet made by England.[163]

Geographically speaking, Jamaica's position proved a strategic blessing. Unlike Barbados and the Leeward Islands, Jamaica lay almost directly in the path of Spanish silver fleets. Jamaica was also the third largest island in the Caribbean, far larger than any other English island possession (4,411 square miles on Jamaica to a mere 166 on Barbados). Mountains as high as seven thousand feet divided the land between north and south, rendering vast portions of the island off-limits for agricultural production but permitting cool breezes to frequent the coastline.[164] In coming years, the large, sheltered harbor at Port Royal, on the southern coast of the island, enticed and drew in merchants, buccaneers, and Spanish silver alike; Jamaica's prime location, only a few hundred miles from the Spanish Main, awarded the English ready access to the most spectacular fount of silver in the world. Sugar eventually took off as the island's major staple crop, but not yet. Plantations required several years of clearing fields, and many of Jamaica's new settlers—numbering no more than 3,500 by the end of the 1650s—were either too poor or simply too rough around the edges, susceptible rather to buccaneering than to planting at the moment.

Barbados, for the time being, remained England's most highly prized colonial possession. The island's population had almost quadrupled since 1640, now exceeding fifty thousand people, mostly comprising enslaved African workers. By the mid-1650s, Barbadian planters exported nearly eight thousand tons of sugar every year to England, more than double the number in 1651.[165] The island's elites had even recently established a satellite sugar colony, Surinam, off the northeastern coast of South America.[166] And though the price of sugar roughly halved since the mid-1640s, dropping from 6d to 3d a pound, the crop remained enormously profitable for planter and empire alike.[167] "This little Spot of Ground," one English author later said of Barbados, ". . . has been as good as a Mine of Silver or Gold."[168]

The slave trade alone was a mercantilist bonanza. First, it stimulated England's trade to Africa, where English merchants, on English ships, sold English manufactures to African slave dealers: about £3 worth of manufactured goods (textiles and metalwares) for each adult male slave.[169] The English dealer then transported the slaves across the Atlantic Ocean to the West Indian islands to exchange for sugar, and then either exported the sugar to England or lucratively reexported the sugar to Europe for coin, bills of exchange, or merchandise that otherwise would have required money to purchase. "Barbadoes . . . to what a height it is grown in a very few years," one merchant in London marveled in 1659; "heretofore we had [sugar] from other Countries, and now we can and do furnish those same people with our sugars."[170]

If only colonial commerce could be rid of the Dutch, the potential profits for England would surely be greater. The restoration of the Stuart crown in 1660 promised new opportunities for embarking on such a project. The empire required closer, more centralized management; trade laws needed to be updated and more effectively enforced. What English administrators failed to appreciate was how deeply accustomed colonists had already become to autonomous action. In the 1640s and 1650s the colonies had functioned as virtual sovereigns in matters of government and trade, developing and pursuing their own distinctive political economies. Varied as they were, these colonial political economies could not be reconciled easily with the new imperial agenda after 1660.

CHAPTER 4

Mercantilism, Mints, Clipping, Smuggling, and Piracy, 1660–1674

King Charles II inherited an empire vastly different from the one his father had governed. The midcentury rebellion, though it ultimately failed at establishing republican government in England, succeeded in radically undermining the ancient grandeur and mystique of the Crown. Though restored, the Crown had to reconcile itself to a Parliament demanding greater accountability and input in decision making. Furthermore, England exited the Interregnum period a stronger, more aggressive geopolitical power than it had been under the early Stuarts, having seized Jamaica from Spain and won a naval war against the Dutch. Government expenditures, the military, the navy, and the administrative bureaucracy all witnessed extensive growth under Commonwealth rule. The colonies, for their part, were almost unrecognizable from the pre-1640 era; the colonial population had quadrupled its previous number, while entire new trades and lines of economic production flourished. Finally, the Commonwealth Parliament in 1651 had codified mercantilism into law with the first Navigation Act.

Despite all rhetoric to the contrary, Charles II accepted a great many of these structural and functional changes, pressing forward, in large measure, on the same imperial trajectory. Government policymakers still scrutinized the country's economic well-being through the mercantilist lens, prioritizing the balance of trade. Both the Parliament and Crown were eager to confirm and to update the earlier Navigation Act. As one English merchant, Samuel

Lambe, wrote earlier in 1657, the Navigation Act of 1651 had "breathed some refreshing to the decaying Trade of the English Nation, yet it hath not altogether cured her of her disease."[1]

Economic reform and regulation ranked high on the agenda for the new English government. With regard to the colonies especially, greater enforcement of mercantilist trade restrictions became a top priority. American commerce was substantially greater than what it had been before the middle part of the century. In 1664 alone, 43 English ships cleared London for the North American mainland, and 45 English ships cleared London for the West Indian islands.[2] Yet trade regulations were still largely evaded in the colonies; American trade was not nearly as profitable for England as it yet could be. The Navigation Acts of 1660 and 1663 attended to some of the deficiencies found in the earlier act of 1651. But many colonists continued to trade freely all the same. "If a Breach of the Navigation-Act be conniv'd at," Charles Davenant warned later in the century, "even our own Plantations may become more profitable to our Neighbours than to us."[3]

Colonial experience with de facto autonomy in the 1640s and 1650s primed colonial tradesmen, planters, and political leaders, after 1660, to advocate for and insist upon the right to continue steering their own economic and monetary course. This included free trade, colonial mints, currency devaluation, import substitution, and the countenancing of pirates. Many colonists paid far greater mind to the commercial and pecuniary interests of their own colony than to those of England, rejecting altogether England's insistence on colonial economic and monetary subordination. In so doing, these colonists undermined the central organizing principle of empire. They rejected the empire's application of mercantilism to the colonial sphere, unconvinced that the supposed benefits of imperial membership justified the degree of economic sacrifice demanded of them from London. This rejection of the empire's mercantilist vision was a stance that, for now, colonists could brandish. The Navigation Acts, in this early part of the Restoration period, still largely depended on persuasion and willing compliance. The coercive apparatus had not yet matured enough in the 1660s and early 1670s to adequately compel colonial obedience.

During these early years of the Restoration government, King Charles II pursued a mostly moderate approach toward colonial matters. He and his officials tacitly acknowledged or tolerated certain rights and privileges claimed by the colonial sphere—including the persistence of assembly government—in exchange for the colonists' outward allegiance to the restored monarchy. Tension between imperial and colonial interests was certainly evident, but for now it did not lead to any severe political conflict. Not until the 1670s did a greater political crisis erupt, when the Crown determined that coercion and political reorganization were the only adequate responses to colonial economic defiance.

Upon Charles's return to England on May 25, 1660, the kingdom's merchants and mercantilists wasted no time in pushing for a renewal and strengthening of the Navigation Act. "There was a Set of People in Trade," one merchant recalled later in the century, who "thought themselves never safe until they got the Act of Navigation confirm'd."[4] Commercial interest groups in England exercised far greater influence in the formulation of economic policy than they had before the Interregnum period. During the 1650s, English merchants—especially those who did not belong to the great monopoly companies—organized, for the first time, into voluntary associations for the chief purpose of influencing public policy. These associations met most frequently in London coffeehouses, including the Virginia-Maryland Coffee House, located only a block away from the London Exchange. After 1660, merchant interest groups and trade associations expanded further in membership, wealth, resources, influence, and organization, and played no small part in contriving new economic statutes like the Navigation Acts.[5]

The Navigation Act of 1651 had partly succeeded in eroding the Dutch monopoly of the carrying trade in the Baltic and Mediterranean. By the late 1650s, however, several mercantilists in England had grown extremely frustrated with the English government for apparently "sleighting the execution of that Act for Trade." One author, in 1659, called it one of Cromwell's most "visible miscarriages." "If it had been continued and duly Executed," he wrote, England would have "over-ballanced all the Exchange of the World; it would have made Trading abound, and money as plentifull as dust."[6] "Our Neighbours the Hollanders will soone over-ballance us, if not timely prevented," warned merchant Samuel Lambe in 1657. Throughout England, "even the greatest of her Gentry complain for want of Mony," said one writer; the whole country purportedly dreaded "the decrease, and exportation of English Coyn." According to John Milton—a staunch republican—trade had become "so miserably bad" by 1659 that a general belief prevailed "that nothing but kingship can restore trade."[7]

There were still some men in England who feared that commercial interests could not peaceably coexist with monarchial government; nevertheless, most merchants presumed that a restored Stuart monarch would appreciate anew the sweet benefits of commerce. Who could dispute now that "trade must be the principal Interest of England"? "Without trade, no Nation can be formidable," argued Slingsby Bethel, a prominent merchant, in 1671. "This is the undoubted Interest of his Majesty," he stated, "to advance and promote Trade . . . and giving it all manner of incouragement."[8] Customs revenue, after all, was easier to collect and to raise than land taxes, hearth taxes, or excise taxes; moreover, the customs revenue was the Crown's most critical source of money collected independently of Parliament—a great attraction for any king who wished to rule autonomously. Charles determined, not unwisely, that merchants and overseas trade could be a force for much good in his govern-ment. "Upon the king's first arrival in England," recalled his chief adviser, the earl of Clarendon, "he manifested a very great desire to improve the general traffick and trade of the kingdom, and upon all occasions conferred with the most active merchants upon it, and offered all he could contribute to the ad-vancement thereof."[9]

King Charles II was a mercantilist monarch, though his attraction to mer-cantilism was nakedly pragmatic. A royal proclamation in 1661 underscored his intention to use mercantilist means to solve the "present scarcity of Mon-eys." First, Charles outlined why gold and silver were so necessary: "for making and maintaining of just and honorable Wars . . . for adorning and furnishing Our Dominions in time of Peace, and strengthening the same with Reputa-tion, which followeth such Princes as are esteemed rich in Treasure." Second, Charles identified the balance of trade as the means to gold and silver. He praised the "rich Dowry of native and home-bred Commodities . . . the Ex-portation and Product whereof may bring great Treasure, both of Gold and Silver." Such money, he said, once "brought in, should there remain a perpet-ual Stock not to go forth again." This outcome, however, could only be achieved if "Foreign Commodities . . . could not possibly be Imported in greater quanti-ties, then the native Commodities of Our Dominions."[10] Charles's advisers no doubt authored the bulk of this proclamation; nevertheless, a more succinct delineation of the mercantilist program had never hitherto been uttered by an English monarch.

In the same spirit, near the end of 1660, Charles commissioned a Council of Trade. The Council of Trade was an advisory body to the Privy Council; it consisted of sixty-two men, predominantly merchants. The commission com-manded them to enquire "whether the Importation of forreigne Commodi-tyes doe not over-ballance the Exportations of such as are Native," in order "that the Coyne & present Stock of these our Kingdomes, may be preserved & increased." "Such a Scale & Rule of proportion," the commission said of the balance of trade, "is one of the highest and most prudentiall points of Trade, by which the riches & strength of these our Kingdomes, are best to be understood & maintained."[11] Around the same time, Charles also commis-sioned a Council for Foreign Plantations, which operated separately from the

Council of Trade and focused chiefly on colonies. It consisted of forty-eight members, charged with "rendering those dominions usefull to England" by ensuring "strict execution" of all commercial regulations and by examining how a stronger "ballance may be made for the better ordering and disposing of trade."[12]

In September 1660, a mere four months after arriving in England, Charles approved a new Navigation Act. The statute, enacted by Parliament, incorporated most of the principles of its 1651 predecessor but with stronger enforcement mechanisms, including, for the first time, an elaborate system of bonds and certificates. Most important, the statute contained greater constraints on colonial trade. Unlike the act of 1651, the act of 1660 prohibited the export of certain enumerated colonial commodities (tobacco, sugar, indigo, and others) directly to foreign ports. The colonial good had to first be exported to England, Wales, or Ireland and, upon arrival, the merchant there had to pay the appropriate customs (receiving a partial rebate or drawback if he chose to reexport the good to Europe). All other colonial exports, unenumerated by the act, could be sent directly to foreign lands without stopping in England, but the goods could only be transported on English (or English colonial) ships with English (or English colonial) crew members. Regarding imports, the act of 1660 specified that certain enumerated European goods—timber, naval stores, and wines—could be shipped only to English dominions in English-owned vessels, with a crew at least three-fourths English. For all other imports, unenumerated by the act, only the country of origin could deliver the goods, in its own vessels—outlawing, again, the Dutch carrying trade. Three years later, in 1663, a new Navigation Act added the more stringent requirement that most European goods stop first in an English port—the cargo unloaded, the duties paid, and the cargo reloaded—before crossing the ocean for colonial markets. The opening clause of the Navigation Act of 1663 (also called the Staple Act), explained that the goal was "keeping them [the colonies] in a firmer Dependance," "rendring them yet more beneficial and advantagious."[13]

Over time, the Navigation Acts assumed a near-sacrosanct character as founding documents of English commercial policy. Among other things, they unequivocally subordinated the American colonies to England's monetary interests. One later commentator, in 1696, called the acts of navigation the "Sea Magna Carta"; Sir Josiah Child, in 1692, called it "one of the choicest and most prudent Acts that ever was made in England"; Edmund Burke, on the eve of the American Revolution, described the Navigation Acts as "the corner-stone of the policy of this country with regard to its colonies." The Navigation Acts rendered America a most fundamental link in England's "Golden Chain of Commerce," one supporter told Parliament in 1666. The very "Bent and Design of that Law," Charles Davenant recalled later in the century, "was to make those Colonies as much dependant, as possible, upon their Mother-Country."[14]

As expected, the initial implementation of the Navigation Acts provoked much colonial resistance. Sugar planters especially loathed the new restrictions; prior to 1660, up to three-fourths of all vessels trading to Barbados had been Dutch, and the price of sugar—as it was—had already fallen in recent years. Hence in 1661 the Barbadian government petitioned King Charles for the freedom to sell sugar directly to foreigners, reasoning that if sugar be "forced to bee brought into one Markett," it would surely "result in a Glutt of the same, and by a necessary consequence, a great abatement of the price." "Free trade render the best Comodity and meanes of Liveing to any Collony," they petitioned seven years later, ". . . an open Market renders the most plenty and best penny worth to any Citty or Countrey." "The great Inconvenience lyes upon us by the Act of Parliament for Navigation & Trade," the government petitioned again in 1675, ". . . being constrayned to bring all our produce to one Markett, it soe beats downe the price of Sugars, and Advances the price of freight, that in a short tyme it must of necessity bring to Ruine your Majestys Plantations."[15]

In Virginia, Governor Sir William Berkeley (reinstated in 1660) launched a vigorous protest against the "Mighty and destructive" Navigation Acts—a "severe act of parliament," he called them in 1671.[16] Hoping to secure a repeal of the export restriction, Berkeley ventured to London in 1662 as agent for the colony; during his stay there, he penned A Discourse and View of Virginia, in which he said that "we cannot but resent, that [Virginians] should be impoverish'd to enrich little more then forty Merchants, who being the only buyers of our Tobacco give us what they please for it, and after it is here, sell it how they please."[17] As a committed royalist, Berkeley did not argue for more political autonomy, nor did he necessarily argue against mercantilism. As Berkeley saw it, a prosperous colonial sphere benefited imperial economic interests. "If this were for his Majesty's service," he said, "or the good of his subjects, we should not repine, whatever our sufferings are for it, but on my soul, it is contrary for both."[18] One of his most important allies in London, John Bland—a merchant with landed estates in Virginia—agreed that a small group of merchants had secured the restriction for "their own private interests." The "high freight" charged by English shipmasters, he said—relative to the "Hollanders cheap sailing"—imperiled the future of one of England's most valuable colonies. Bar foreign traders from Virginia, he predicted, and the Dutch will soon "plant Tobacco in their own Territories, whereby they will not need ours." "Forein trade makes rich and populous any Country," Bland argued, ". . . is it not then a madness to hinder the Hollanders or any else from trading thither?" Unshackle the trade, he wrote, and "riches will abound," both for England and for Virginia.[19]

Berkeley himself, however, betrayed the answer to the question of why the export restriction should not be repealed. "Let it be considered," he recounted in *Discourse*, "what summes of Money was in the last Age exhausted from [England] for Sugar, Cotton, Drugges, Dyings, and Tobacco, and how easily now we supply our selves with these, and also bring home enough to balance many other forraign necessities."[20] For Berkeley, this meant that Virginia and Barbados deserved special protection in the form of commercial leniency, but his point in fact corroborated the imperial position that tobacco and sugar should be funneled through England.

Berkeley was right to identify vast "summes of Money" with the tobacco and sugar trades. Presently, English merchants reexported about one-half of all sugar and one-third of all tobacco to continental Europe, winning, in turn, abundant middleman profits.[21] The royal revenue from customs was also sizable. The Crown collected 2d for every imported pound of English colonial tobacco, with a partial rebate (1.5d) on reexportation. This activity procured for the Crown an annual revenue of more than £75,000 in the 1660s and £100,000 by the 1670s.[22] (On foreign tobacco, the Crown collected duties of 6d a pound, providing a certain encouragement to the Chesapeake product—an instance in which Virginians benefited from mercantilism by affording them a practical monopoly of the English consumer market). From sugar, the Crown collected 1s6d on every imported hundredweight (cwt), again with a partial drawback on reexportation. The customs revenue from sugar was substantially less than the revenue from tobacco: roughly a quarter of the amount, ranging between £15,000 and £25,000 a year. Still, recorded imports of sugar to London approached 150,000 cwt in 1663, and exceeded 400,000 cwt by the 1680s, earning a modest but reliable sum of revenue for the treasury.[23] Moreover, when Charles converted Barbados and the Leeward Islands to royal colonies in 1663—dispensing with their private proprietorships—he placed a tax of 4.5 percent on all of their exports, procuring a total of more than £80,000 in royal revenue over the next two decades.[24]

Gold and silver coin circulated in and out of London, but even the wealthiest planters in Virginia and Barbados used tobacco and sugar for money—underscoring their unequal relation to England. Even Berkeley received part of his salary in tobacco (50,000 pounds of tobacco, plus £700 sterling money). Virginia courts still collected fines in tobacco; militia officers received salaries of 10–15,000 pounds of the leaf. Tobacco money financed the building of a new state-house at Jamestown—each worker receiving 2,000 pounds—and the burgesses in 1666 allotted nearly 100,000 pounds to construct a new fort at

Point Comfort, on the tip of the Virginia Peninsula, using the currency to pur-chase supplies and labor.[25] "There is not coyne in that countrey," a report stated frankly in 1672.[26] As for Barbados, sugar remained the "general Medium of Commerce"—"all their accounts being computed by pounds of sugar," ac-cording to one report, "and the Law of the Countrey allowing all debts to be paid in that Specie."[27] It was "for want of money," an imperial officer reported in 1660, that "the Inhabitants are driven to make theire payments in Sugar."[28]

Though free trade alone would not have been enough to earn a substan-tial sum of coin for Virginia, the Navigation Acts certainly rendered a silver currency less likely. Tobacco prices had become severely depressed in recent years. The wholesale price in England for Virginia tobacco was about 6–8d a pound, but the farm price of tobacco (the sum received by the farmer) had fallen from 2.5d a pound in the mid-1650s, to a mere penny in the latter half of the 1660s.[29] Some of this decline was owing to increases in farm productiv-ity, but one economic historian, Peter McClelland, estimates that the farm price of tobacco was nearly one-third less than it would have been without the ex-port restriction in the Navigation Act.[30] Indeed for many years, the duty ex-tracted in London on imported Virginia tobacco (a tax of 2d a pound) was about double what the planter received for his crop at the farm.[31]

Still worse, at the very time that export restrictions reduced the income of tobacco planters, import restrictions increased the cost of living. According to the Navigation Act of 1663, colonists had to purchase European imports at marked-up prices through a merchant-middleman in England. The indirect route, the duties collected in London, and the middleman's profits all amounted to higher prices for colonists. Among their most desired imports were linens from Holland and Germany. England did not yet have a satisfactory linen in-dustry; nevertheless, colonial access to continental linen cloth could come only through England. The same was true of other imports. One contemporary alleged that English merchants charged fifty pounds of tobacco for a pair of shoes; the Dutch, only twelve.[32] John Bland anticipated this problem in 1661 when he predicted that an import restriction would compel Virginians to "pay to them [English merchants] what prices and rates they pleased to require."[33] The same issue beleaguered Caribbean planters. Some time later, in 1682, the governor of Jamaica asserted that the Dutch "sell European Goods 30 percent cheaper than we [the English], & will paye deerer [a higher price] for Ameri-can Goods"; another source—a customs officer in the Caribbean—claimed that the Dutch "Sell 20 per cent. Cheaper than the English."[34]

The coin deficiency on Barbados was not solely the product of the Naviga-tion Acts, though planters often asserted so. Few planters, if any, blamed their own extravagant spending for the scarcity of silver money. Despite the boom in sugar exports, the island's trade deficit remained extraordinarily high, as the purchase and consumption of imported luxuries soared, precluding the accumulation of a domestic stock of coin. Formerly, in the early 1640s, houses were "generally meane with only things for necessity." But now, according to one report in 1667, their houses are "very faire and beautiful . . . like Castles," filled amply with "plate, Jewells and extraordinary houshould stuffs."[35] The island's elite imported furniture, books, clocks, gloves, swords, glass, olives, tapestries, "Cloth of all kinds," and "Wine of all sorts."[36] The planters, indeed, obsessed over wealth accumulation—not wealth as coin but rather wealth as *stuff*. To illustrate the difference: silver, ironically, was quite abundant on Barbados during this period, but nearly all of it was demonetized, taking the form of so-called "plate," that is, silver pots, silver dishes, silver tankards, silver buttons, and silver utensils. As one English writer complained (in this case, speaking on elite practices in England), the "super-abounding" of plate "tends to the decrease of Moneys."[37] The same was true on Barbados. The irony of owning silver plate while bemoaning the lack of silver coin is particularly striking. Having chosen to store their wealth in things other than money, the island's planters implicitly elected to cope with sugar currency.

African slaves were the most important store of wealth on Barbados. The importation of slaves worsened the island's trade deficit and rendered the accumulation of coin that much more difficult, even as slave importation boosted the island's sugar exports. The Barbadian slave population nearly quadrupled between 1650 and 1670, numbering forty thousand by the latter date, costing the islanders no paltry sum of cash.[38] Even here the planters tried to pass the buck, blaming the Royal African Company (RAC) for charging high prices for slaves. Founded in 1660 under a different name (the Company of Royal Adventurers Trading to Africa), the Crown awarded the company a legal monopoly over the West African slave trade. The monopoly prohibited noncompany men in England from trading slaves to the Americas and also prohibited the Dutch from selling slaves to English colonial planters.[39] The Dutch, at the time, were the leading transatlantic slave dealers, conducting three hundred such voyages between 1641 and 1670. When Brazil finally fell to the Portuguese in 1654, the Dutch were all the more eager to sell slaves to English sugar planters.[40] Thus, as Barbadian planters perceived it, the RAC monopoly made the price of slaves artificially high on the island—again, to benefit a select group of private investors in London. Before the RAC monopoly, they said, planters had slaves "at much cheaper rates," not the "excessive prices" since endured.[41] All this made a silver currency all the more difficult to achieve on Barbados. Eliminate the RAC monopoly, and eliminate the import and export restrictions in the Navigation Acts, and the planters—they believed—might enjoy luxury items, slaves, *and* money.

The settlements in New England, in stark contrast to the Chesapeake and Caribbean, initially benefited from the export restrictions in the Navigation Act of 1660. It was likely even responsible for a modest increase in the silver money supply in the greater Boston area in the 1660s. Colonial vessels and seamen all counted as English under the Navigation Acts, stimulating colonial shipbuilding, which centered, at this time, in New England. This allowance also granted New England merchants the freedom to purchase tobacco and sugar to carry over to England, shielding them from (legal) Dutch competition in buying the same. Pine-tree masts were the only New England commodity enumerated for export exclusively to England. It remained perfectly legal for New England merchants to export barrel staves and fish directly to Spain, Portugal, and the Wine Islands, so long as the goods were transported in colonial-built ships. The Act of 1663 required New England merchants to purchase European goods through an English middleman, yet, even here, exemptions written into the law mitigated its impact, as New England merchants were free to import salt directly from southern Europe for use in the colonial fishery.[42]

In spite of these advantages, however, New England merchants habitually evaded the unfavorable provisions. Many New England merchants illicitly carried tobacco and sugar to foreign traders in Newfoundland, New Netherland, and the Dutch and French West Indian islands. There, the same New England merchants defied the act of 1663 by purchasing European goods directly from foreign traders, including "linnen, Shooes, Stockins, [and] Cloathes," often reexporting the same to Virginia and Barbados at cheaper rates than English merchants.[43] In 1663 customs officials estimated that the New England sale of tobacco to New Amsterdam alone cost the Crown up to £10,000 per annum in lost customs revenue.[44] New England merchants countered by arguing that reexporting tobacco and sugar from an English colonial port was equivalent to reexporting the same from England itself. If something was not soon done about this activity, warned the president of the king's Council for Foreign Plantations, New England would become "mighty and powerfull and not at all carefull of theire dependance upon Old England."[45]

The Navigation Act of 1673, also known as the Plantation Duty Act, targeted the New England carrying trade of tobacco and sugar to European buyers. Besides clarifying the illegality of this traffic, the law arranged for the Crown to appoint customs officials to serve in the Chesapeake and Caribbean, with orders to collect duties on the intercolonial sale of tobacco and sugar (from one English colony to another). Parliament reasoned that the duty would dissuade New England merchants from carrying these goods to foreign markets, because the duty could be avoided only if the shipmaster posted bond to carry the same goods to England. Not surprisingly, New England merchants interpreted this provision to mean that once the duty was paid in Virginia or Barbados, the colonial shipmaster was free to carry the tobacco or sugar directly to foreign markets. The discovered loophole was clearly not the law's intent, but the wording of the law was ambiguous enough to make it a plausible interpretation, compelling the king's attorney general to further clarify the illegality of this activity.[46]

Direct trade between the Dutch and English colonists on colonial shores also persisted through this period, an even grosser violation of the law. Until 1673, colonial governors were solely responsible for implementing the Navigation Acts—men, like Sir William Berkeley in Virginia, who openly opposed it. Frequent complaints thus arose of a "secret trade driven by and with the Dutch, for Tobacco," owing to the "neglect of those Governors . . . not taking a View of all forrain-built Ships which come into their Plantations."[47] The Crown's appointment of a resident customs collector in the Chesapeake and West Indies—as provided in the new Navigation Act of 1673—made smuggling a little more difficult, but Dutch shipmasters found a way around even this safeguard by feigning English names upon landing on shore. The lack of an empire-wide ship registry made this deception quite easy. Planters welcomed the Dutch, knowing that the tradesmen—whether buying or selling—usually offered more competitive prices. Legal fish and flour often concealed these illegal goods; interloping vessels found regular refuge in a number of clandestine areas. Large vessels generally parked further outside of the port, while smaller ships ventured into less-frequented harbors, bays, rivers, or creeks.[48] To top it all, the lowly paid, little-respected customs officials were highly susceptible—as one Englishman relayed in 1677—"to take Bribes, and comply with those Smugglers."[49]

Smuggling, nonetheless, was a hazardous endeavor—even in this period—for both buyer and seller. Illicit vessels and goods were liable for seizure and forfeiture; one often had to seek remote places of landing. Presumed friends or allies along the way could duplicitously turn into informants. Crews on interloping ships expected higher wages. Trust was often low, and cheating abounded; written documentation could later prove incriminating, so verbal assurances ruled the day—but a man's word was not always his bond.[50] Why would merchants and tradesmen undergo such peril and inconvenience? The simple answer was that doing so was profitable. The pecuniary motive was strong on both sides of the transaction—for the buyer and for the seller—making the hazard often worth it, especially in that period of imperfect enforcement. Meanwhile, for the colony as a whole, tolerance for smuggling prevailed, because many people personally knew smugglers in town and benefited from the sale of their goods. Furthermore, many colonists also understood that freer trade made a sizable difference in the colony's overall wealth—as measured in merchandise, coin, or a combination of both. It was no secret among the broader public that illicit trade meant more goods and possibly more money.

The proximity of the Dutch colony of New Netherland aggravated the situation, making enforcement of the Navigation Acts of 1660 and 1663 especially difficult. Situated between New England and the Chesapeake, the colony was a constant source of temptation for English colonial tradesmen and planters. Dutch firms in Amsterdam and Rotterdam routinely coordinated with New Amsterdam merchants to fit out small watercraft to trade in Virginia. English officials found this extremely obnoxious. According to a committee of the Privy Council in 1663, the New Netherland settlement allowed "greate quantities of tobacco to the Dutch."[51] If only the Acts of Trade could be more adequately enforced, George Downing of the Exchequer declared in 1664, then "good night Amsterdam."[52]

The Second Anglo-Dutch War (1665–1667) broke out soon after. English seizures of Dutch interloping vessels had steadily risen of late; the slave-trading companies of both powers recurrently clashed off the West African coast, the rival East Indian companies increasingly came to blows in Asia, and a new Danish-Dutch alliance imperiled England's access to the all-important Baltic Sea.[53] In the spirit of the mercantilist age they now lived in, King Charles II announced to Parliament that the war's objective was the "advancement of the trade of this kingdom." While praising the Dutch for "their very commendable industry," Charles insisted that war was necessary because "these States have found out to make themselves monarchs of the sole trade of the whole East and West Indies." The House of Lords agreed, alleging that in the previous four years, illegal Dutch trade across the board had cost England—between the customs revenue and private profits of English merchants—as much as £800,000 sterling in money.[54]

The English, astoundingly, conquered New Netherland before the war had even officially begun. In August 1664, an expedition of four frigates and three hundred English soldiers seized New Amsterdam, bringing the city's 1,500 residents—and the colony's total 8,000 residents—under English control. The English rechristened it New York, after the king's younger brother, James, duke of York, now proprietor of the colony. But those who hoped for a swift end to Dutch smuggling were deeply disappointed in the war's aftermath. Not much changed in New York; the Dutch smuggling trade still operated out of the city in forthcoming years. The Treaty of Breda in 1667 permitted Dutch inhabitants to remain in New York, and the new English governor, Francis Lovelace, openly tolerated illegal trade and even invested money in it throughout his 1668–1673 tenure, going so far as to appoint the former secretary of the Dutch West India Company as head officer for collecting duties and administering commercial regulations.[55]

The Second Anglo-Dutch War, like the first, accomplished very little in stamping out Dutch-colonial trade. England began the war with great military triumphs, but the nation's fortunes sagged toward the end of the war, inducing Charles to conclude it without any real commercial concessions from the Dutch. In compensation for the loss of New Netherland, the Treaty of Breda recognized the recent Dutch conquest of Surinam from the English, a promising settlement off the northeastern coast of South America that soon became one of the most flourishing sugar colonies in the New World.[56] The conquest of New Netherland established an uninterrupted string of English colonies along the North American seaboard, but the persistence of colonial-Dutch trade glaringly underlined the need for a more concentrated, forceful effort from London to stamp it out.

Money was at the heart of the interloping trade between English colonists and foreign tradesmen. The competitive prices that the Dutch in particular offered on imported and exported goods increased the colony's access to imported merchandise, coin, or to both. If the money supply did not increase with smuggling, it was only because colonists elected to buy more imported goods than otherwise possible; either way, the colony materially gained.

But there were other more immediate, direct approaches to improving the currency supply. Colonial mints were among these. Proponents anticipated that a local mint would, first, occasion uniformity in the currency; second, provide small change to the colony; third, encourage the importation of foreign silver—coined into money with a higher shilling value than what the same silver earned outside of the colony.

What the supporters of colonial mints underestimated, however, was the certain and adamant opposition these proposals would elicit from the Crown. Reasons for this opposition were several. For one, administrators feared that colonial governments might trifle with the weight and fineness of the silver in their currencies, distorting and confusing the colony's internal and external trade. The real peril, however, was not economic, but political. Colonial mints were politically dangerous because of the historic link between coinage and political sovereignty. Massachusetts Bay, the sole colony with a mint, exemplified this tendency. The Massachusetts pine-tree shilling smacked of independency, insubordination, and even rebellion. Better to not allow other colonies to create their own coinages.

Barbadian planters and government officials were especially eager to establish a colonial mint, "as in New England and else where is Practised," the assembly requested. The island was England's wealthiest colony and yet almost entirely devoid of coin. The government first sought royal permission in a petition in May 1661. It met swift rejection. In 1667 the assembly petitioned the king again for a mint, arguing that "Money is the life of trade . . . in Forreigne Plantations especially, it is needfull." This petition also failed. Undeterred, the assembly petitioned the Crown again in 1668, "to Sett up a mint within this Island for Coyning money." Notably, for the first time, the assembly specified that the said coin be stamped with an "Impression as your Majestie shall appoint or approve to be proper." Though clever, the attempt to placate the regal prerogative proved ineffective.[57] "This noble Island wants a Money trade," a planter privately urged Charles in 1669, requesting, to no avail, that he "lett us have a Mint as they have in New England, which I beleeve the Assembly have craved." The following year, in 1670, the assembly solicited the governor that they might petition a fourth time—"incase his Majestie will be pleased to graunt a mint for Coyning of monney"—but the governor refused to provoke the king any further, and so nothing came of it. In one final, vain attempt, in 1673, a grand jury on the island requested "licence to coyne sylver to supply the wants of this place, without which there can bee noe certaine assured florishing trade."[58]

Jamaica likewise entreated the Crown repeatedly, and unsuccessfully, for a mint. In 1664 Governor Sir Thomas Modyford petitioned for the right to make coins of the "weight of that of New-England." His rationale was that the island suffered a scarcity of small change, namely of pence. Privateers brought many pieces of eight to Jamaica, but they weighed about a full ounce of silver and were equal in value to fifty-four pence. The smallest available coin on Jamaica was the Spanish *real* or "bitt"—worth about 7d—but these smaller coins were not nearly as common, and still too high, besides, for transactions calling for two or three pence. Some Jamaicans resorted to halving or quartering coins—an illegal practice known as "cutting"—but this obviously created substantial irregularities in the currency, which a mint could remedy. To the governor's surprise, the Privy Council rejected his request. Modyford, in reply, wondered aloud why "Coyning is not thought reasonable." Again in 1670 he petitioned for "a Coyne allowed us, either by a Mint sett upp here" or in England, so that the islanders might enjoy money "with similar marke on it." The Crown again refused.[59]

Like efforts in Maryland to establish a mint also failed, though under much different circumstances. Maryland was a private colony, and the coinage began on the eve of the Stuart Restoration. In 1659 the Maryland proprietor—Cecil Calvert, second Lord Baltimore (a royalist)—secretly coined silver money at the Tower Mint in London, intending it for the people of Maryland. Calvert's face was on one side of the coin, his family arms on the other (figure 4); he coined the money, he said, at "Great paines and Charge" but believed it "would be a very great advantage to the Colony." Calvert promptly sent a "Sample of the Maryland money" on a ship bound for the colony, but a clerk at the Tower Mint informed on him, and the Council of State issued a warrant for his arrest in October 1659. The arrest warrant cited the treasonous act of coining a "great quantity of Silver," and the crime of having "transported great sums of money" to Maryland. To Calvert's good fortune, however, Charles II ascended the throne only a few months later and restored his proprietorship. Charles allowed Calvert, a royalist, to transport the remainder of his coins to Maryland but sternly forbade him from creating additional coins or establishing a colonial mint.[60]

The Maryland assembly dispersed Calvert's coins by requiring that each taxable citizen exchange sixty pounds of tobacco to the treasurer for 10s of the new money, thereby placing roughly £2,500 of silver money into circulation.[61] Because this was an insufficient sum to constitute a common currency, however, the assembly in May 1661 authorized "the Setting up of a Mint for the Coyneing of money." In doing so, the assembly argued that the want of silver coin was the "mayne hindrance to the Advancement of this Collony in Trades

FIGURE 4.   Twelve-pence coin of Cecil Calvert, second Lord Baltimore, ca. 1658–1659.
(ANS 1950.185.1. Courtesy of American Numismatic Society.)

Manafactors Townes and all other thinges."[62] The extent to which the assembly knew of the king's instructions to Calvert is not known, but Calvert dutifully obeyed the king's orders and repealed the new mint act. Eight years later, an English visitor to the colony affirmed that tobacco remained the "general way of Traffick and Commerce," though some utilized "his Lordships own Coyn . . . which his Lordship at his own Charge caus'd to be Coyn'd and dispers'd throughout that Province." Even this use of the coins could not last: trade deficits soon resulted in the money's total disappearance, and the short-lived coinage never returned.[63]

England, for certain, was not alone in rejecting the concept of colonial mints. In the early 1670s, King Louis XIV denied similar requests from the government of New France to establish a mint in Montreal, and the Dutch West India Company denied the same to New Amsterdam officials in 1661.[64] Spain was the only power to allow colonial mints, and the decision derived entirely from the convenience of coining money adjacent to the mines of Mexico and Peru. Otherwise, these empires understood two things about coining money: first, the age-old practice of European mints tinkering with the weights and fineness of metal in coins (why permit a rogue colony to do the same?); second, the association—engrained deeply in the European mind—between coinage and political sovereignty. It was no accident that Massachusetts was the only colony to have a mint; it was a private colony that boasted near-complete political autonomy. This status made the Massachusetts coinage all the more offensive to English officials.

Upon the king's restoration, the quasi-independence of the Massachusetts government fell under instant scrutiny. Samuel Maverick launched the opening salvo in late 1660, publishing a pamphlet entitled *A Briefe Discription of New England*. Maverick was a disgruntled former resident of the colony and alleged that he had suffered persecution there for his royalism and Anglicanism. No oaths of allegiance and supremacy to England or to Charles II had yet been taken in Boston, he wrote: officials "swearing theire subjects to submite to lawes made only by themselfes." "Indeed," he continued, "to Alleage a Statute Law of England in one of their Courts would be a ridiculous thing."[65] It was true indeed that colonists had not taken the required oaths of allegiance or supremacy. The colony's reaction to the Stuart Restoration was certainly less than enthusiastic. After word reached the colony in November 1660 that the Church of England was back in operation, Boston mint master John Hull held a private "day of humiliation at our house, for the state of our native country . . . the church countenancing the old liturgy, and formalities again to be practised," he wrote down in his diary.[66] Boston officials still implicitly and dutifully accepted the return of the monarchy, but many did so only grudgingly.

At minimum, Bay colonists hoped to continue undisturbed their peculiar form of government.

The Massachusetts mint, of course, also suffered immediate scrutiny. "They likewise long since fell to coyning of monies," Maverick continued, "melting downe all the English Coyne they can gett." The Privy Council too, received news in 1661 that the mint master, Hull, had treasonously allowed "the King's Coyne to be bought and melted downe in Boston to be new coynd there."[67] The reason for this, purportedly, was the higher valuation accorded to silver at the Boston mint than at the English mint: every 12d of English money made 15d of Massachusetts money.

Yet the greatest offense of the Boston mint was not in its occasional melting down of English money—most of the melted coin was Spanish—but rather the mint's political symbolism. Two enemies of the colony—the proprietor of New Hampshire and the former governor of Maine—raised this matter in a joint petition to the king in 1662. "For these many yeares together past," they said, the people of Massachusetts "endeavoured to model and contrive themselves into a free state." As evidence, they cited the "coyning of money with their own stamp and signature." The same proposition was affirmed by a much more neutral observer, Director-General Peter Stuyvesant of New Netherland, when he reported in October 1660 that though other colonists were "good Royalists," Boston "remains faithful to its old principle of a free state."[68] The Massachusetts coinage manifestly and materially celebrated the colony's de facto independence.

A story of Charles's encounter with the Bay shilling suggests that the mint, to a small degree, offended the king personally. In 1662 Sir Thomas Temple, proprietor of Nova Scotia, conversed with King Charles and his Privy Council on the "state of affairs in the Massachusets." "In the course of the conversation Sir Thomas took some of the money out of his pocket, and presented it to the King." The money was none other than the Boston shilling. Upon seeing the coin, Charles exhibited "great warmth against that colony; among other things he said, they had invaded his prerogative by coining money." Temple, who resided in Boston in the 1650s—"a real friend to the colony"— promptly defended the mint, claiming that economic reasons alone lay behind the coinage. "The colonists had but little acquaintance with law," he insisted, "they had no ill design, and thought it no crime to make money for their own use." Charles took a second look at the money and then "inquired what tree that was?" Temple disingenuously replied that it was the "royal oak," the same material used to build the ship that carried younger Charles across the Channel into exile in 1650. "The Massachuset's people," he told the king, "not daring to put his Majesty's name on their coin during the late troubles, had impressed upon it the emblem of the oak which preserved his Majesty's life." Temple now conceded a political rationale behind the coin but entirely flipped its meaning, cleverly suggesting that the Bay shilling was in fact a masked cry for royalism. Charles, indeed, had hidden away in an oak tree upon Cromwell's victory at the Battle of Worcester in 1651; images commemorating this event were not uncommon in the early 1660s. Of course, this was patently *not* the reason behind the placing of a tree on the Boston coinage, and the king's advisers knew it. (The oak tree had only been placed on the coin in 1660 [see figure 5]; the coins minted in the 1650s featured a willow tree, and coins minted after 1667 a pine tree.) The story, nonetheless, "put the king into good humour, and disposed him to hear what Sir Thomas had to say in their favour." As Temple defended the province, Charles grazed the shilling between his fingers, chuckling as he "called them a parcel of honest dogs." Clearly, after all was said and done, this was not an issue of high importance to the king.[69]

Yet the offense of the Massachusetts mint went far deeper than insulting the person of the king. The mint challenged the power of the imperial state. This challenge, more than anything, explained the Crown's growing antagonism toward the mint. Henceforth, the Boston mint became a central target of the Crown for elimination.

In 1664 Charles instructed four commissioners, including Samuel Maverick, to survey New England, with a particular eye for colonial observance of the Navigation Acts. The commissioners also bore secret instructions to try to convince political leaders in Massachusetts to consent to a new requirement that the Crown approve all future governors. Accompanied by nearly four hundred troops, the commissioners first trekked through Connecticut, Rhode Island,

FIGURE 5. Six-pence oak-tree coin of Massachusetts, issued sometime between 1662 and 1667. (ANS 1957.23.1. Courtesy of American Numismatic Society.)

and the Plymouth colony, where each government "made great promises of their Loyalty and obedience." However, upon their arrival in Boston in spring 1665, the General Court declared the commission illegal, refused their cooperation, and, according to the commissioners, "proclaymed by sound of Trumpet that the Generall Court was the Supreamest Judicatory in that Province." "Seditious Speech" was apparently replete among the assemblymen, and though, according to the commissioners, a moderate group of "loyall Subjects" still existed, "it is now with them as was with the Kings Party in Cromwells time." Indeed, in Massachusetts "their way of Government is Common-wealth like."[70]

One of the many demands of the royal commission, besides enforcing the Navigation Acts, was that the "mint house . . . be repealed, for coyning is a royall prerogative." Maverick reportedly lashed out at one of the locals, telling him they were "rebels and traitors for minting money and printing, which was treason for the country to do."[71] The colonial government did not seem to mind: the colonists responded by defiantly petitioning Charles that they would never abolish their mint—to do otherwise, they said, was contrary to "the liberties of Englishmen, so wee can see no reason to submit thereto."[72] Bay colonists undoubtedly retained a strong commitment to Englishness—to English culture and to English notions of economic and political rights. Their problem, rather, was with a centralized empire, administered principally out of London, that treated English colonists as subordinate. The Massachusetts charter derived its authority from the Crown, but many Bay colonists interpreted it as having granted them autonomous powers to manage the colony as they saw fit, believing—as the royal commissioners alleged—that they were "free to use their priviledges," and "not obliged to the King but by civility."[73]

Jolted by these reports, Charles instructed the General Court to send agents to London at once for an explanation. The assembly briefly considered an overtly defiant reply, but a growing moderate faction begged the rest of the assembly to refrain. Indeed, the younger generation of New England merchants, many of whom were not Puritans, were more and more coming to resent the political dominance of the commercially skeptical, theocratic faction on the General Court (only church members could vote) and began yearning for royal intervention. The assembly bowed to moderate pressure and instead sent the Royal Navy a gift of "two very large masts," hoping to mollify the Crown despite the colony's refusal to send agents. Charles and his Privy Council elected not to pursue the matter any further, and from 1666 to 1674 all official communication between Old and New England ceased.[74]

The Boston mint persisted onward: to abolish it overnight threatened an unwanted political war with the colony, and the English state had far greater concerns at the moment than picking a fight with a province that, relative to the tobacco and sugar plantations, contributed little to the mercantilist system. On the heels of the commission came the Great Plague of London (1665–1666), the Great Fire of London (1666), two additional years of warfare with Holland, and the Third Anglo-Dutch War in 1672–1674. The Boston mint, of course, paled in comparison. In this early half of the Restoration period, imperial dictates still required a significant degree of voluntary compliance from the colonists, and if they refused, there was little else the Crown could do; it could expend valuable time, money, and resources on a peripheral nuisance or begrudgingly tolerate the headstrong New Englanders. The Crown, after 1665, chose the latter option, ushering in a decade-long malaise in English-Massachusetts relations. The pine-tree shilling, all the while, remained a troublesome and aggravating reminder of de facto sovereignty within Massachusetts. When commercial men in London, the Caribbean, and elsewhere in the Atlantic encountered the Bay shilling in trade, the coin no doubt impressed upon many of them that the Massachusetts colony had effectively achieved and maintained a degree of economic and political autonomy unmatched in the empire. As one colonial administrator noted in 1666, the task yet remained "to find out a way to bring downe the pride of the Massachusetts."[75]

The Massachusetts people had solid reason to be proud. In the 1660s alone the colony's population nearly doubled in size, primarily from natural increase. New England shipbuilding boomed in the wake of the Navigation Acts, which required use of ships built either in England or in English colonies. New England's provisioning trade of lumber, food, and fish to the Caribbean, Wine Islands, and Iberian Peninsula expanded even further from its midcentury levels, returning greater sums of coin and bills of exchange to Massachusetts and allowing the importation of additional goods from abroad. The colony's merchants unabashedly pursued Atlantic trade with a free hand; court records even reveal that New England sailors occasionally received wages in "sterling money of France."[76]

And yet the colony's currency complications remained precarious. The trade deficit with England was still considerably large; the pine-tree mast was the colony's only significant export to the mother country, excepting the carrying trade of tobacco and sugar from other colonies. Import substitution proved insufficient. The silver money that Boston merchants earned from the provisioning trade—even after going to the mint for conversion—rarely circulated more than a few months before the money left the colony to purchase imported merchandise. The export of pine-tree shillings had been illegal since 1654, when the General Court authorized the searching of boxes, trunks, and chests of outgoing vessels. In 1669 the assembly increased the number of searchers and instructed them to also check the "pocket, cloake, [and] bag" of any person leaving the province overland on "horse back," demonstrating the severity of the issue.[77] "Coyninge hath not fully answered the Court's expectations," the assembly noted with regret a few weeks later; ". . . there still remaynes great want for a further supply."[78] The amount of coin had certainly increased in recent years, yet few rural inhabitants enjoyed regular or even semiregular access to silver money. Coin still generally centered in the towns; country pay remained the dominant tender for tax payments, though the treasury abated rates one-fourth if taxes were paid in silver.[79]

So acute was the currency problem in Massachusetts that a reverend named John Woodbridge proposed, during this time, a paper currency backed by land mortgages. The idea garnered enough support locally to impel the Massachusetts council to formally consider his proposal in 1667. The council did not adopt the scheme, and so a few years later, in 1671, Woodbridge announced that he would establish a private land bank instead, issuing "Bank-Bills," backed by land mortgages, without any support from the government. Nevertheless, for reasons unspecified, the private bank suspended operations shortly after the announcement "when bills were just to be issued forth." The project evaporated, but not the need for a real currency solution. The mint alone was not enough.[80]

Perhaps for this reason, in October 1672 the General Court once again allowed the domestic circulation of Spanish pieces of eight. Spanish dollars had not circulated in the colony since the founding of the Boston mint in 1652; the original mint act had lowered the price of Spanish dollars to 4s6d, thus making them vastly undervalued vis-à-vis the pine-tree shilling. In October 1672, however, the assembly raised the value of a Spanish dollar to 6s, thus placing it on par (roughly) with the Bay shilling. The move came only months after the termination of Woodbridge's paper project and one day after the government in New York raised the Spanish dollar from five to six shillings.[81] Ironically the plan backfired, causing, inadvertently, the export of pine-tree shillings. At 6s a piece, the Spanish dollar was not exactly on par with the pine-tree coinage. Six Massachusetts shillings contained 400 grains of silver, but one Spanish dollar—which also passed at 6s—contained only 387 grains of silver. Thus, the new valuation slightly *overvalued* Spanish coin and slightly undervalued Massachusetts coin. The difference in silver content was only 3 percent—imperceptible to the average colonist—but enough to incentivize merchants to spend the lighter Spanish coin internally instead of the heavier Massachusetts coin and to (surreptitiously) export the latter instead of the former when settling overseas payments. Not until ten years later, in 1682, did the General Court finally correct the mistake by ruling that Spanish coin would pass at 5s10d.[82]

The 1672 remonetization of foreign coin in Massachusetts also had the inescapable effect of causing new confusion in the currency. The domestic stock of money was less uniform than earlier, much as it had been before 1652. Coins of varying weight, fineness, and origin again entered circulation: Mexican dollars, lighter Peruvian dollars, French money, Dutch money, Barbary and Turkish monies, clipped monies.

Clipping—the cropping of silver from the coin's edge with shears before passing it off at face value—was a severe problem in the seventeenth century, on both sides of the Atlantic (see figure 6). Clipping had been around since the Middle Ages; it was a capital crime in England, bringing "Pains of Death" to any convicted offender. Defacing the "King's coin" had long been considered a treasonous act—indeed, "High Treason in the Highest degree," wrote one commentator.[83] In colonial English America, clipping money was not a capital crime (it is not treason to deface the coin of the king of Spain), but a serious crime nonetheless. Some years later, for example, in 1692, the Massachusetts General Court ordered that all convicted clippers shall "stand in the pillory . . . and then have one of his ears cut off."[84] The remarkable ease of clipping, however, along with the great difficulty in catching clippers in the act, encouraged people to continue the practice whatever the possible punishment. As Locke later said, "Clipping is so gainful, and so secret a Robbery, that penalties cannot restrain it."[85] Merchants dealt with the proliferation of

FIGURE 6.   *Left to right, top to bottom*: Eight real, Mexico City, ca. 1665–1700 (ANS 1935.36.834); eight real, Mexico City, ca. 1665–1700 (ANS 1935.36.809); eight real, Mexico City, ca. 1665–1700 (ANS 1942.107.1); eight real, Mexico City, 1650 (ANS 1964.158.1); eight real, Mexico City, ca. 1700–1746 (ANS 1964.198.2); eight real, Lima, 1687 (ANS 1972.244.3); eight real, Mexico City, 1639 (ANS 1986.25.48); eight real, Mexico City, ca. 1621–1665 (ANS 1990.49.5). (Courtesy of American Numismatic Society.)

clipped money by weighing the coin on scales, adjusting their prices accordingly. Most common people, however, accepted the money at face value despite the diminished silver content; from this acceptance arose the "excessive Profit" from clipping.[86]

Only a fraction of circulating coin in America was full weight—especially if the money passed first through the Caribbean, where clippers habitually reduced the amount of silver by as much as one-third. Years later, in 1691, the governor of the Leeward Islands estimated that no more than "one in a 100" pieces of eight on the islands were full weight; on Barbados, according to its council in 1678, "bad & light money" was practically the only coin left in circulation.[87] From there, the clipped money spread across much of the North American seaboard; "few or no peeces of eight" went unscathed, the General Court in Massachusetts reported in 1672.[88] One can therefore understand the immense attraction of a colonial mint: if nothing else, it would provide some semblance of uniformity to the deformed currency—a great bulk of which originated from Caribbean buccaneers.

Most silver money in the West Indian islands had come into contact with privateers or pirates at some point or another. The distinction between privateers and pirates (collectively called buccaneers) was often blurred and not well understood. Privateers bore official letters of marque granting them permission to capture enemy ships and to raid enemy ports during times of intense rivalry and war. The intensity and frequency of privateering activity ebbed and flowed. First, the golden age of the Elizabethan sea dogs in the 1580s and 1590s yielded way to an almost complete disappearance of English privateers in the Caribbean Sea in the first half of the seventeenth century. By the late 1650s and early 1660s, however, England's use of privateers gradually returned, induced by Spain's refusal to recognize English control of Jamaica. Finally, in 1665, the onset of the Second Anglo-Dutch War inaugurated a new era of marauding at sea. Commissioned privateers exploded in number, targeting Dutch and Spanish ships alike in the West Indies.[89] The strategy was certainly effective when privateers targeted enemy ships. As official state policy, however, it proved highly precarious, for once hostilities ended, few marauders wished to cease their looting entirely, even without a letter of marque. At this point in time privateering became piracy, but the exact boundaries between privateering and piracy were notoriously vague, especially when rogue, corrupt, or negligent colonial governors granted privateering commissions in times of peace. This practice, in turn, caused quite a few diplomatic headaches; sometimes the targets of supposed privateers included friendly vessels or even vessels belonging to English merchants.[90]

As governor of Jamaica from 1664 to 1671, Sir Thomas Modyford invited buccaneers in droves to Port Royal, liberally handing out privateering commissions. Jamaica lay perfectly positioned in the path of Spanish silver fleets, in contrast to other English islands that were too far out on the periphery of the Caribbean Sea. "Barbadoes could never boast of equal Advantages with Jamaica," an author later remarked in 1708, ". . . and had never such Resort of Pyrates, who are the Men that make Silver plenty."[91] Jamaica had already attracted buccaneers prior to Modyford's tenure as governor: a band of marauders in 1659, for instance, had visited the island with more than £50,000 of plundered Spanish coin; another group the same year brought in "twenty-two chests of the King of Spain's silver," containing over "12000 peeces of Eight."[92] But privateering under Modyford compounded to a more spectacular degree. The most famous instance was the governor's sponsoring of a 1668 land raid by Captain Henry Morgan against Porto Bello, Panama; the raid netted more than £75,000 worth of plunder, with each of Morgan's men taking in roughly £60 in silver coin (more than 260 pieces of eight).[93] By 1670 at least twenty privateering vessels operated out of Port Royal, counting some two thousand men, with Modyford celebrating "the Greate Occasions his Majestie might have for them."[94]

Silver money was the chief motive for turning Jamaica into a privateering haven in the 1660s. Modyford's council, in 1666, defending the move by stating (correctly) that it "replinisheth the Island with Coin"; it also afforded the island commodities "at cheap and easy rates."[95] "So great is the scarcity of money," wrote a Jamaica resident at the beginning of Modyford's governorship in 1665, "that unless there be free trade or war with the Spaniards, the colony will never flourish or hardly be kept."[96] Upon a successful expedition, most sea rovers returned to Port Royal to spend their silver and gold, whether in taverns, brothels, or shops. The freebooters were "very welcome guests in Jamaica," recalled an eighteenth-century text; they "fought with the most desperate bravery and spent their plunder with the most stupid extravagance." "They often brought two, three, and four hundred thousand pieces of eight at a time, which were immediately squandered in all the ways of excessive gaming, wine and women. Vast fortunes were made, and the returns of treasure to England were prodigiously great."[97]

Port Royal became the most boisterous, garish town in the whole English empire, and the buccaneers were no less welcome because of it, at least initially. In their relations with the people in town, the buccaneers often proved uniquely charismatic and easygoing. One of the most detailed accounts that we have of their behavior at Port Royal comes from Alexander Esquemeling, a former Dutch privateer and surgeon under Captain Morgan, who authored a multivolume book in 1684 entitled *Bucaniers of America*. "All these prizes they carried into Jamaica," he said, ". . . wasted in a few days, in Taverns and Stews, all they had gotten." Some of them would "spend two or three thousand pieces of eight in one night"; "I saw one of them given unto a common Strumpet, five hundred pieces of eight, only that he might see her naked." "My own Master," he continued, "would buy, in like occasions, a whole pipe of wine, and placing it in the street, would force every one that passed by to drink with him, threatning also to Pistol them, in case they would not do it. At other times he would do the same with Barrels of Ale or Beer." All in good spirits, however—as the former privateer explained, "among themselves, and to each other, these Pirates are extreamly liberal, and free. If any one of them hath lost all his goods, which often happeneth in their manner of life, they freely give him and make him partaker of what they have." And of course, "in Taverns, and Ale houses, they always have great credit."[98]

From Port Royal, the plundered silver and gold often made way to the North American seaboard. From Jamaica, the coin ventured northward in payment of provisions and goods to supply and to build the island's budding sugar plantations. In 1671 for instance, a vessel sailed from Port Royal to New York with nearly £4,000 worth of pieces of eight onboard, a large portion of which, no doubt, had been earlier plundered by privateers.[99] Much of the coinage output from the Boston mint was likely from pirated silver; one writer in 1675 remarked that when Boston merchants "trade with Jamaica, as they do sometimes with Provisions, they bring home pieces of 8." "Their Money is of pretty good Silver," the writer continued, "in the middle of it is a Pine-tree . . . with this Silver they are wholly supplyed from Jamaica."[100] Quite the unlikely alliance—puritanical Massachusetts and freebooting Jamaica.

Increasingly, however, by 1670, it was no longer evident that privateering was a profitable use of Jamaica, whether for imperial interests or for private, commercial interests. For one, Jamaica was ideally suited as a depot to supply African slaves to Spanish America. Spain had no trading bases on the West African coast, forcing the Spanish to buy slaves from foreign merchants. The Spanish wanted slave labor for the gold, silver, and copper mines. Rather than permit an unrestricted slave trade with foreign powers, however, the Spanish Crown awarded a highly coveted contract called the *asiento* to select foreigners for the exclusive right to supply slaves to Spanish America. Portuguese merchants held the *asiento* from 1580 to 1639, during which time the country was under the dynastic rule of the Spanish Habsburg family, but a revolution in Portugal in 1640 abruptly ended this arrangement. A while later, in 1662, two Genoese merchants received the *asiento*; they, in turn, subcontracted with the Dutch and English African companies to supply the Spanish. The Royal African Company used Port Royal as its primary base to transmit slaves to Spanish America, up to 2,400 slaves a year (according to the RAC's contract with the Genoese). The Dutch West India Company used Curaçao as its primary base, an island just thirty-five miles from the coast of present-day Venezuela. The rivalry this generated between the RAC and WIC contributed in part to the Second Anglo-Dutch War.[101] The reexport trade of slaves to Spanish America promised prodigious sums of wealth and money—for England in general, but more specifically for RAC investors (many of whom belonged to the Stuart court) and for interested merchants residing in Port Royal. Spanish traders paid £18–22 a slave: the value of twenty gold guineas, or eighty silver pieces of eight.[102] As Charles's privy councillors predicted in 1663, the *asiento* would "be an occasion of importing Bullion to Our Mint"; the RAC likewise promised the king that the *asiento* would earn "Silver and Gould in great Quantities, both which Your Majestie hath not from any other Commerce."[103]

A second possible rival source of money was the contraband trade of cloth, ironware, and other manufactures to Spanish America. Here too, Jamaica was excellently suited as a base for operations. Since 1504, Spanish law prohibited Spain's American colonists from trading directly with foreign powers. Yet merchants in Spain were not able to adequately supply colonial demand for imported goods, especially in remote, underpopulated areas off the Spanish Main (the Spanish American coastline). Not surprisingly, interloping tradesmen and ships from rival nations found numerous ways around the ban. At midcentury, Dutch merchants monopolized most of the contraband trade, having acquired Curaçao not long before in 1634. But, after 1655, with Jamaica in a more ideal geographic position for this silver-begetting traffic, the contraband trade between Port Royal merchants and Spanish colonial tradesmen flourished, the latter paying in silver and gold. Part of the reason, indeed, that the English and Dutch so highly coveted the *asiento* was that it invariably opened more doors for the illicit but immensely valuable traffic in manufactured goods.[104]

The RAC and the Port Royal merchants who trafficked in slaves and contraband goods to Spanish America came more and more to despise the buccaneering interest. The constant raids obviously outraged Spanish officials, encouraging Spanish American traders to shun Jamaica for Curaçao. Jamaica was more accessible than Curaçao to most of the Spanish Main—freight costs were approximately 20 percent lower to and from Jamaica—yet the buccaneering threat practically nullified the lower transportation expense.[105] The Dutch, for this reason, never used Curaçao as a privateering base. King Charles II initially wavered on the privateering question—none could deny that it procured much silver and gold—but by the early 1670s it became evident that *trade* with Spanish America was far more remunerative for English interests than buccaneering.[106]

A new imperial era was slowly dawning in Jamaica, albeit in fits and starts—an era that favored commerce, sugar, and slavery over high-seas robbery. In July 1670, England and Spain signed the Treaty of Madrid, with Spain acknowledging English control of Jamaica in return for England's suppressing the buccaneers. Modyford's days were now limited as governor; ironically, however, the most fantastic privateering attack still lay ahead. Having been commissioned by Modyford at an earlier date, Henry Morgan and a fleet of thirty-six vessels ventured toward the Spanish Main, sacking Panama City in January 1671. Morgan and his crew of 1,400 men returned to Port Royal with £70,000 in silver and gold.[107] "We doe the Spainards more mischeife in one hour then they can do us in seven yeares," an English diplomat boasted, "it is incredible what loss the Spainards received by us in the last expedition at Panama. . . . Spanish Gold and Silver is the only cause of the Quarrel."[108] Having instructed the governor to abstain from sponsoring further attacks, King Charles immediately removed Modyford and imprisoned him in the Tower of London. Charles replaced him with Sir Thomas Lynch, a local rival of Modyford, who promptly repudiated the privateering commissions.[109] Governor Lynch's instructions from the king included pardoning "all belonging to any of the Privateer Shippes" who peaceably return to Port Royal and "apply themselves unto Planting and Merchandizeing." Lynch was to also divert the island's attention toward "Plantations of Sugars," indigo, dyewoods, ginger, cocoa, and vanilla.[110]

Lynch moved decisively against the buccaneering interest, but a third and final Anglo-Dutch War (1672–1674) afforded the freebooters new opportunities for plunder. Privateering commissions again proceeded—this time reluctantly—from the governor's desk. Not surprisingly, the privateers did not limit their attacks to the Dutch; one Jamaican privateer, at the beginning of the war, looted fourteen thousand pieces of eight from a neutral Spanish vessel.[111] Meanwhile, in England, Henry Morgan charismatically pleaded ignorance of the 1670 treaty with Spain during his Panama expedition; was knighted by the Crown in 1674; and, after promising to refrain from further piratical adventures, returned to Jamaica the following year as lieutenant governor, second in command to Lord Vaughan, the newly appointed (and antibuccaneer) governor. The move appalled Lynch—now out of office—who was unnerved by the Crown's still ambiguous position on privateering.[112]

Two factions, the buccaneering interest and the merchant-planter interest, now contended for power on the island. The planter interest had previously not been at odds with the buccaneers: privateering money had supplied much of the initial capital to finance sugar and indigo plantations; Modyford himself was among the greatest planters on the island. A great shift occurred, however, in the 1670s. Already by 1671, the number of sugar plantations on Jamaica had risen to 57, from only 7 in 1659.[113] But over the next decade, sugar exports grew nearly tenfold, from 500 tons in 1669 to roughly 5,000 tons by 1683 (Barbadian sugar exports remained constant during this period at around 10,000 tons).[114] By 1685 the island had 246 sugar plantations.[115] Attitudes toward privateering altered just as rapidly. Buccaneering imperiled commercial stability, discouraged slave traders from visiting the island, and attracted runaway servants and slaves from sugar plantations. Jamaican wealth was no longer contingent on buccaneering but was endangered by it. The buccaneers, soon banished from Jamaica, found welcome refuge on the money-hungry shores of eastern North America.

During the 1660s and early 1670s, the supply of silver coin in colonial commercial centers undoubtedly increased, namely in Port Royal and Boston, though more moderately in the latter. Most of the rest of the English Atlantic world remained almost entirely dependent on nonmetallic commodity currencies—particularly among rural folk, including in Massachusetts Bay, where debts were still "paid in merchantable fish," as well as in "wheat, barley and pork."[116] A few examples will suffice to illustrate. An inventory in Essex County, Massachusetts, in 1668, calculated the value of a particular man's estate at £656, yet the "Silver in his purse" was only 19s8d, just barely under £1.[117] In 1675 the building of a new meeting house in Salem, Massachusetts was financed "one third part in silver, one third in goods & one third part in provisions."[118] In nearby Plymouth Colony, a private real estate purchase in 1668 involved the sum of £150 of "current countrey pay." "Good currant Countrey pay" even financed a 1673 military expedition from Plymouth during the Third Anglo-Dutch War.[119] Even in outlying parts of Jamaica, country pay circulated alongside coin, the governor having established, in 1662, official money values for sugar, cocoa, and tobacco, rendering them legal tender "in all Contracts, bargains, buying & selling."[120]

Sugar money remained the predominant medium of exchange in the Lesser Antilles. "Wee have noe other payments to make, there being noe Money," the governor of Barbados wrote a committee of the Privy Council in 1664.[121] On the Leeward Islands, emergent sugar planters replaced the former tobacco money they had formerly used with sugar currency; "they have little Money, but Buy and Pay with Sugars," one visitor to Nevis remarked in 1688.[122] Coin devaluation was one solution in the Leeward Islands. Between 1670 and 1672, the governments on Montserrat, Antigua, and Nevis—after having "seriously considered the great Necessity of Money"—each passed laws raising pieces of eight from 5s to 6s. (A clause in the Montserrat law stipulated that any person refusing the new valuation would suffer a fine of 1,000 pounds of "good Muscovado Sugar.")[123]

The transition from tobacco to sugar planting on Antigua ended a brief experiment on the Leeward island of a tobacco-backed paper currency, which had lasted from 1669 to 1675. The Antigua assembly had authorized the issuance of paper receipts, representing tobacco deposited in official warehouses. At any time the holder of these "storehouse notes" could present them to the warehouse for the specified sum of tobacco. The storehouse notes could be transferred at any time, to any person. The experiment lasted six years, abolished in 1675 when sugar supplanted tobacco as the staple crop and currency. Nevertheless, two years later, a writer in England, Mark Lewis, specifically cited the Antigua currency experiment to support establishing a similar scheme in London, with paper notes backed not by tobacco but by pawned merchandise.[124]

To turn back to the mainland: in Carolina, a private proprietary colony founded in 1663, the new colonists were also almost solely dependent on alternative commodity currencies. Many of the first settlers came not from England, but from Barbados, now an overcrowded island. They settled along the Ashley River, in the southern part of the province, spreading thinly across the humid landscape. Possessing little to no coin, the settlers adopted deerskins as their chief medium of exchange. Deerskins were the colony's most valuable export, valued in England for making gloves and leggings, and in Carolina "there is such infinite Herds, that the whole Country seems but one continued Park."[125] Besides deerskins, Carolinians exported livestock and lumber to the Caribbean, returning negligible sums of coin to the province, most of which went directly to Boston to purchase reexported merchandise originating from England and from Europe. For now, the colony had to forgo any realistic prospects for obtaining a silver currency. As the colony's surveyor told the proprietors, "Ports and Markets" would flourish in Carolina only "provided there be a course taken for procuring a coine, without which no Towne nor Markett can well subsist." Procuring coin, in turn, he said, "can no way be effected but by the ballance of Trade."[126]

In the northern part of Carolina, recently freed indentured servants had migrated from Virginia in considerable numbers, bringing with them experience using tobacco money. By the end of the 1670s about five thousand of them had settled the northeastern corner of Carolina, in a backwater region called the Albemarle.[127] Tobacco was the predominant medium of exchange in both public and private payments; in 1673, for instance, a gallon of rum sold in the Albemarle for twenty-five pounds of the leaf.[128] Only small watercraft could maneuver through the shifting shoals and sandbars of the North Carolina coast, and so notwithstanding the occasional visit from a New England coasting vessel, the Albemarle, for now, was practically cut off from the wider Atlantic world.

In Virginia, the planters' absolute reliance on tobacco money was detrimental enough when the crop earned scarcely more than 2d a pound in the 1650s. Now, tobacco fetched barely a penny a pound.[129] Tobacco taxes in 1677 took in nearly 1.2 million pounds of the leaf, but the sterling value of this levy did not even reach £5,000.[130] To combat overproduction—essentially, the depreciation of tobacco money—the burgesses tried repeatedly to convince the neighboring government in Maryland to restrict the planting of tobacco, but to no avail: the proprietor, Lord Baltimore, vetoed the action despite approval from the Maryland assembly.[131]

In Maryland, tobacco planters sought desperately for a solution to the great "Scarcity of money in this Province," to quote the assembly in 1669.[132] In 1671 the Maryland assembly raised the value of the piece of eight from 4s6d to 6s, well surpassing the 5s rate in Virginia. The statute explained that because the crop is "att so Low a Rate," "payment cannot Soe well be made in Tobacco"; instead the assembly wished, via coin devaluation, to offer "Encouragement to those that shall bring monys into this Province." The same act, moreover, banned the export of silver money from the province.[133] Lord Baltimore repealed the statute, but not until five years later in 1676, after which the piece of eight returned to 4s6d, 10 percent lower than the standard in Virginia and 25 percent lower than the standard in Massachusetts and New York; prices in the colony tumbled down with the coin.[134] The coins minted earlier by Lord Calvert had almost all disappeared.

In New York, silver and gold circulated primarily among the city's merchant classes, most of whom were Dutch. Farmers in the hinterland relied on country pay, peltry, and even wampum for currency; indeed, the first currency legislation under English rule stipulated that "payments for goods imported shall be paid as formerly in Bever Pay . . . at 13s4d a Bever."[135] King Charles II placed the colony under the private, proprietary rule of his younger brother, the Duke of York (future James II). It was the only English proprietary colony without a representative assembly; any currency legislation would have to come from the governor, in this case, Edmund Andros, and his council. A military man fluent in Dutch, Andros became governor of New York after England reclaimed the colony from the Netherlands in 1674, after having temporarily lost it during the Third Anglo-Dutch War. Andros was a major shareholder in the Royal African Company, thus placing him on good terms with the Duke of York, who was also the RAC's governor. In part because smuggling was so rampant in New York under the previous English governor, Francis

Lovelace, the Crown installed a customs collector named William Dyre to oversee enforcement of the Navigation Acts. Not long into his administration, Governor Andros cozied up to the city's Dutch merchant elites, relying on them for local administration and instructing Dyre to look the other way when favored merchants smuggled Dutch goods into the colony.[136] Andros even lobbied the Duke of York, unsuccessfully, to exempt the city's importers from the Navigation Acts, requesting that "ships trade directly from Holland."[137] When the city's merchants approached Andros about raising the value of Spanish coin, the new governor was all ears.

Andros resolved first to lobby for a New York mint. Only a few months into his administration, in April 1675, he wrote the Duke of York of the "want of money for ordinary commerce," requesting permission to create a coinage with a "stamp or marke" of the duke's choosing. Andros and his merchant allies wanted New York to compete with Boston as an entrepôt for Atlantic trade; a New York coinage would mark the symbolic arrival of the port as a dominant presence in the region. The duke was less than enthusiastic. "There appeares not any present remedy for the inconvenience," the duke wrote of the apparent scarcity of money, adding, "'tis not Convenient for me" at present to push for a New York mint. "Indeed if money were coyned," the duke reasoned, the Crown might require that it share the same weight of silver as the shilling in England, and thus "it would soone be carryed away againe from you." The duke's secretary agreed, arguing that to coin money at weights different from the English standard required "the Kings express authority," which he thought was highly unlikely to be granted. "It is not worthy your further thoughts," the duke's secretary assured Andros, suggesting "brass farthings" instead.[138]

Unable to secure a mint, Andros floated the idea of devaluing the Spanish piece of eight. The New York government, in 1672, had already raised the coin from five to six shillings, a move calculated specifically to compete with Massachusetts.[139] Andros now proposed a rate of 6s6d for the dollar, nearly 45 percent above the rate in England and nearly 10 percent above the official rate in Boston (as well as the current New York rate). The move, if carried through, would have favored Andros's commercial friends and acquaintances, especially the city's elite Dutch merchants, who were the largest holders of silver money in the province.[140] The amount of nominal pounds and shillings in their possession would have increased overnight by almost 10 percent; this increase, in turn, would permit the merchants, temporarily, to purchase more domestic goods than previously, whether for export or for personal consumption, until domestic prices adjusted to the new rate. Precisely for this reason, one English critic of devaluation argued that it "giveth only Profit to a few Monied Men, whose Hands are full, at the time of the Raising."[141]

Indeed just a few years earlier, monied men in Port Royal, Jamaica, had taken similar advantage of the government's decision to devalue the currency. In October 1671, the Jamaican council announced that the value of a piece of eight would rise from 4s6d to 5s but that the change would not take place until five months later, in March 1672. Predictably, in the weeks following the announcement, those in possession of money began to eagerly "hoard up their Spanish mony, whereby Trade is very much lessened and abated." The council hastily intervened and switched the date of the change to December.[142]

Whatever Andros's motives, his plan, like the mint, never came to fruition. James, Duke of York, rejected the proposal; his secretary called it a "certaine way of debaseing the Comodityes of that Country, and therefore a kind of impoverishing it." The dollar in New York remained at 6s a piece, still tied with Massachusetts.[143]

By the mid-1670s the towns in English America where silver coin circulated commonly were Boston, Port Royal, and to a lesser extent New York. Everywhere else, country pay either circulated concurrently with silver money or constituted the only medium of exchange. Coin generally centered in the towns; colonies without large commercial centers—Virginia, Maryland, Carolina, the Leeward Islands, Connecticut, and New Hampshire—had virtually no silver or gold at all for internal circulation.

Colonial remedies to the currency problem were several. Smuggling was certainly a favorite remedy; so too was devaluation, as well as the erection of colonial mints, all of which the Crown steadfastly opposed. The Massachusetts mint remained in operation but encountered growing hostility from royal officials. In Jamaica, buccaneering, initially, was the most popular method to augment the currency, but growing internal and external opposition in the 1670s spelled its ultimate end, as the *asiento*, contraband trade, and planting of sugar was more consistently profitable.

English imperial policy unequivocally prioritized the improvement of its own trade balance and money supply over all colonial interests. But though king and Parliament issued mercantilist decrees and regulations, England's colonists wielded considerable power in determining whether or not to obey those dictates. For mercantilism to properly work, colonists must be persuaded to willingly comply or else face the coercive power of the imperial state. As of yet, England's colonists, on balance, were not inclined to freely concede economic and monetary subordination to England, at least fully, and in some cases even partially. Compelling obedience, however, required time, money, men, and resources that the Crown was simply not yet able or prepared in the 1660s to commit.

The Crown's patience would soon evaporate. In the early to mid-1670s, a new fiscal and monetary crisis beset the kingdom of England. A semiautonomous colonial sphere was no longer something the Crown could passively tolerate. A new, more coercive imperial approach was now in order, requiring a massive political and economic reorganization of of the whole of colonial America.

CHAPTER 5

Empire in Crisis and Flux, 1670–1677

A new fiscal, economic, and monetary crisis jolted England in the early to mid-1670s. Cries of a scarcity of money resounded through much of the country; the Crown defaulted on its debts in 1672; and a new imperial rival, France, was suddenly eclipsing England in the contest for New World metals. Mercantilists responded to this crisis by discussing and debating the most fitting means to improve the kingdom's trade balance and money supply. The challenges were extraordinary, but many mercantilists remained hopeful. "The Metropolis of London, so great and glorious, seems designed for all manner of riches and the seat of Empire," remarked one English author in 1674, ". . . if we but industrious no Nation can exceed us."[1]

A comprehensive reorganization of the colonial world appeared most requisite to secure fiscal and monetary strength and stability in England. This reorganization involved weakening the political autonomy of the several colonial governments. Had these governments adhered to mercantilist economic regulations, their political autonomy might have proved tolerable. Yet smuggling abounded, making a mockery of the rule that most transatlantic trade "should goe only from England."[2] The colonies' insubordination on economic matters demanded administrative and political reform. In light of this need, in 1675, the Crown commissioned the Lords of Trade and Plantations, a standing committee of the Privy Council, devoted to the task of better harnessing

America's moneymaking power. The commissioning of the Lords of Trade heralded a new imperial era.

On the heels of this reform, over the following months and next couple of years, English colonial America exploded in a fit of rebellion and conflict. In New England, a debilitating war with the Indians devastated several colonies and nearly emptied the Massachusetts treasury. In Virginia, the gross misuse of tobacco money by the Jamestown government incited a revolt that threatened to overturn the entire colony. In Jamaica, a newly combative planter-assembly defied the mercantilist designs of the king's appointed governor and Royal African Company. These crises added further support to the already formulated plans for imperial centralization.

Historians, in explaining why the Crown embarked on this centralization project in the mid-1670s, have too often neglected the role that contemporaneous fiscal, economic, and monetary anxieties in England played in provoking this action. At first glance, fiscal and currency predicaments in England might seem to have no obvious link to developments in colonial America. A closer examination of the matter, however, reveals the opposite. Fiscal, economic, and monetary uncertainty in England provoked this newly aggressive imperial stance. The colonial chaos in 1675–1677, though significant in shaping and informing the Crown's particular strategy in the late 1670s, did not provoke the initial move. Imperial consolidation would have occurred even absent these rebellions. The colonial crises, rather, vindicated to the Crown and its officers the wisdom in continuing forward with this agenda.

The new administrative regime after 1675 demanded unqualified submission to the mercantilist aims of the empire and mother country. Imperial officials aimed to utterly subordinate the colonial sphere to England's economic, fiscal, and monetary benefit. This subordination required coercion and, if necessary, even the toppling of existing colonial institutions. Quasi-independent colonists were robbing the empire of coin and of revenue. The power, stability, reputation, and treasure of England were all on shaky ground in the 1670s; far too much was at stake not to act. Critically, however, in the forthcoming period, imperial officials underestimated the colonists' resolve in countering that move.

England's economic condition was greatly discomfiting to many men and women, in city and country alike, in the early to mid-1670s. Woolen exports had fallen to only a third of their former value in the 1630s; the trade deficit, especially with respect to France, had widened substantially of late.[3] Scientific advancements in agriculture, though positive on the whole, resulted also in a tumbling of grain prices, land values, and rents, panicking landlords and driving much the peasantry from the countryside to urban centers, where under-employment, idleness, and poverty smothered the growing city of London.[4]

Economic pessimism, even despair, pervaded much of the public discourse in 1670s England. The depression and fears were not unjustified. "All people are experimentally sensible of the loss and decay of Trade," recorded the author of *An Essay to the Restoring of our Decayed Trade*, published in 1677, ". . . the general complaint now, being what shall we do, there is no Money stirring." The same year a London shopkeeper remarked that according to common opinion, "there is not a penny stirring," and "if these times hold we shall be all undone." Many people in England feared that "the whole Kingdom grows every day poorer and poorer," Sir William Petty reported in 1676, the sentiment prevailing "that there is a great scarcity both of Gold and Silver . . . that Trade in general doth lamentably decay." According to Robert Murray in London in 1676, the scarcity of money was the singular "cause of the many lamentable Calamities and ruinous Effects that are found amongst us."[5]

Silver money in England appeared scarcer and of lesser quality by the day: the scarcity caused by mounting trade deficits, the decline in quality by clipping. Clipping had become a full-blown crisis in England, corroding the currency to an almost intolerable degree by the 1670s. The decade before, in 1663, the royal mint installed rolling machines, which placed grooves on the edge of each coin to produce what became known as milled money.[6] Milled coins discouraged clipping, but much of the old hammered money remained in circulation. The restored Crown, after 1660, had ordered merely the recoinage of Commonwealth money from the 1650s. The Commonwealth coinage had only totaled £800,000, no more than one-seventh of the English money supply in 1660. Meanwhile, the mass of hammered money from earlier periods—from before the Civil War—remained legal tender, though these coins, on average, had lost about one-tenth of their silver through wear and through clipping.[7] Even the century-old coinage of Queen Elizabeth still actively circulated and likely exceeded £2 million in worth—that is, about one-third of all the silver coins in Restoration England.[8]

A striking disparity emerged in Restoration England between the hammered, clipped silver of the Tudor and early Stuart periods, and the "weighty, fine and beautiful Money" of the time after 1660 (see figure 7).[9] Gresham's Law, the principle that bad money chases out good money, promptly went into effect. Merchants and goldsmiths either hoarded the milled money or illegally melted it down into bullion to export abroad, spending only the clipped, hammered variety internally in England, where ordinary people often accepted the currency at face value.[10] The "Crime of Melting," though strictly illegal,

FIGURE 7. *Top row*, silver crown (five-shilling piece) of Charles II, 1672 (ANS 1957.117.4); *bottom left*, silver crown of Elizabeth I, 1601 (ANS 1893.14.850); *bottom right*, silver shilling of Charles I, issued sometime between 1625 and 1640 (ANS 1940.70.30). (Courtesy of American Numismatic Society.)

was nearly impossible to catch, with only a "small risk of discovery, and at a small expense."[11] The "fine new-milled coin" all but disappeared from common circulation, leaving "light and false money in abundance."[12] "There is very little remaining, but what is much Clipped, or worn" reported one Englishman in 1680; "this Nation, for many Years past, hath groaned, and still groans under the abuse of clipt Money," a merchant remarked later in 1691; "the Melting-Pot devours all."[13]

Gold was fast becoming the choice currency of English elites. In 1663 King Charles had authorized the creation of a new gold coin called the *guinea*, named after the Guinea Company, which imported West African gold into England.[14] The English market, for now, valued guineas at approximately

£1 (20s) a piece. The guinea was thus too far out of reach for the ordinary man or woman in England; even a skilled artisan made on average £14 a year, and so a single guinea represented an entire month's wages.[15] Older, clipped silver coins remained the money of small tradesmen, shopkeepers, craftsmen, and wage earners; denominations included the 5s piece (silver crown), 2s6d (half-crown), 1s, and 6d piece. The poor and destitute primarily used copper far-things (introduced in 1672) and tokens made of lead.[16] Small tradesmen in England typically earned between £20 and £50 a year—not enough to regularly use guineas—and many transactions, besides, called for small change. The typical merchant in London (there were roughly eight thousand of them at the time) possessed an average cash holding of £250: it was merchants, therefore, and other wealthy commercial men, who made regular use of guineas.[17]

The coinage of England degraded, it seemed, with each passing year in the Restoration era. Some proposed devaluation. Decreasing the silver content in each shilling might remedy the "scarcity of Money," they argued, and would thereby "enrich the whole Nation." Memory of the notorious Tudor debasements, however, made most English administrators understandably reluctant to repeat such an episode.[18] Others, like economist Samuel Fortrey, in 1663, called for a general recoinage of *all* the old money, "by the way of milling, whereby not onely the coin will be more beautifull, but also more equal in weight, and much more difficult to be clipped."[19] Yet the monumental task of a general and total recoinage seemed so insurmountable that few, for now, wished to think of it.

The government's fiscal situation was no better. In January 1672 the Crown defaulted on its debts, suspending, for a twelve-month period, most payments to the government's creditors. The Stop of the Exchequer was one of the most humiliating events in English financial history; it was, in effect, a declaration of state bankruptcy. English goldsmiths (unincorporated bankers) had lent nearly £2.25 million to the Exchequer, at 8 to 10 percent interest, mostly during the Second Anglo-Dutch War (1665–1667). Two goldsmiths alone, Sir Robert Vyner and Edward Backwell, together lent the Crown more than £645,000. The impact of the Stop was enormous: it bankrupted four goldsmiths and severely crippled many others, ruining, by extension, several hundred depositors, including men and women who had deposited their life savings and inheritances.[20] "The Bankers were broke," recalled Bishop Burnet, "and great multitudes, who had trusted their money in their hands, were ruined by this dishonourable and perfidious action." "The Famous stop upon the Exchequer almost blasted their very root," another author wrote of the goldsmiths in 1676.[21] The Stop was supposed to last for only one year, but the Crown was not ready to lift the suspension of payments in December 1672; instead, it delayed until March 1675, and even then payment occurred only in installments and at a lower rate of interest than originally stipulated.[22] For Charles, the default "not only lost the hearts of the subjects, and ruined many widows and orphans, whose stocks were lent him, but the reputation of his Exchequer," said diarist John Evelyn, which "did exceedingly discontent the people." Indeed, the king's councillors observed in December 1675 that "there was now by this late disorder among the Bankers so generall a distrust that it was in vayn to expect any money on credit."[23]

Nevertheless, alarming as all of these events truly were—the trade slump, the degradation of the coinage, the Stop of the Exchequer—the economic picture on the whole, according to some, was not all so gloomy. These events were little more than temporary setbacks on an otherwise upward trajectory, the optimists believed. "The Buildings of London grow great and glorious," Sir William Petty, economist, recorded cheerfully in 1676: "the American Plantations employ four Hundred Sail of Ships; Actions in the East-India Company are near double . . . the King has a greater Navy . . . and the Price of Food so reasonable." "That some are poorer than others, ever was and ever will be," he conceded; nonetheless, "the Interest and Affairs of England are in no deplorable Condition." Indeed far from it: "the Power and Wealth of England hath increased this last forty years," Petty said. John Houghton, London shopkeeper, agreed, insisting that "we have more Wealth now, than ever we had at any time before the Restauration."[24] The total tonnage of English shipping had more than doubled since the 1630s; the reexport trades of sugar, tobacco, and East Indian goods to continental Europe were all thriving. That woolens no longer monopolized English exports was in fact a sign of greater dynamism. The coal, iron, lead, glass, ceramic, and tin industries had all advanced markedly of late, and England had nearly caught up to the Dutch in urbanization. Brick buildings, glass windows, paved streets, and growing public consumption of fruit, cocoa, tobacco and sugar all signaled the rise of an emergent middle class in England, as well as a general rise in the standard of living.[25] Problems were certainly manifest, this no writer could deny—just look at the coinage— yet considering the progress already made, according to Petty, "the Impediments of Englands greatness are but contingent and removable."[26]

No matter how one felt about the true state of England's economy, the overwhelming consensus in the 1670s was that England's trade balance required much improvement. Richard Haines, a gentleman farmer, reiterated this mercantilist maxim in the 1677 edition of his popular book, *Prevention of Poverty*. "When in any Nation Commodities are Imported to a greater value than what are Exported," he said, "Impoverishment seems unavoidable, for then our ready Money must go out to even the Ballance." "Trade is the true and intrinsick interest of England," Slingsby Bethel, merchant and economist, wrote in 1679: the kingdom is "more or less enriched by the ballance of its foreign Trade." To better this balance, private interests must yield to public interests. "Merchants are like fire and water, Good Servants, but bad Masters," Thomas Violet, a goldsmith, stated earlier in 1660.[27] One of the many roles of government was to ensure that merchants made for "Good Servants." Precisely *how* the government was to regulate and intervene was the point on which the mercantilist consensus broke down.

Most mercantilists agreed that England's addiction to imported luxuries, particularly those from France, was especially harmful to the national trade balance. Among the urban middle classes and gentry in England, French commodities had become extremely fashionable as an outward sign of refinement and gentility. Eighteenth-century moralists later referred to this period as the "luxurious Age of King Charles II."[28] English consumption of French velvet, linen, silk, lace, looking glasses, furniture, jewelry, perfume, wine, and brandy all greatly increased during this period, fueling a general panic that "all the money of this Nation will be drawn into France," to quote Slingsby Bethel.[29] Contemporary estimates placed the annual trade deficit with France at the astonishing figure of £1.6 million.[30] Many men in England, including the anonymous author of *The Uses and Abuses of Money* in 1671, deplored "that we should pay ready Coin for French Nut-crackers, and give excessive Rates for the Wine which doth in truth intoxicate us, and makes us the more ready to give them Money for it."[31] Agitation arose for "extraordinary customs" against French imports, else "no doubt our treasure will be soon exhausted."[32] Parliament responded accordingly: having already raised the duty on French wine and brandy in 1666, it banned the importation of French goods outright in March 1678. "The Wealth and Treasure of this Nation hath been much exhausted by the Importation and Consumption of the French Commodities," the statute read.[33]

The East India Company (EIC) also bore much criticism for England's monetary problems, though on this matter mercantilists were deeply divided. To begin, silver and gold made up more than two-thirds of the value of all of the company's exports from England, because of the lack of demand in India for English manufactures. The EIC exported more than £2.2 million of silver and gold from England to the East Indies in the 1670s, almost 200 percent more than the £740,000 exported in the 1660s, itself an astronomical amount surpassing previous decades.[34] The stark increase reflected a shift in the company's trade in India, from importing pepper to importing cotton—a softer, lighter, more durable fabric than woolens and linens. The EIC in 1670 purchased 544,692 pieces of Indian cotton fabrics, up from only 28,000 pieces in 1664–1665.[35] In the early

1670s, the company sent artisans to India to train indigenous weavers to produce printed textiles geared specifically for English and European markets, including tapestries, bedspreads, draperies, shirts, and dresses. From the mid-1670s onward, these inexpensive, lightweight Indian fabrics—known as calicoes and muslins—became enormously fashionable in English and European circles, abating demand for traditional fabrics such as woolens.[36]

Alarmed by the threat of Indian imports to the woolen industry, English manufacturers launched a full-scale attack against Indian cotton. In so doing, they utilized mercantilist language. Calicoes were "fully Manufactured abroad," they said, imperiling the trade balance by undercutting woolen exports—"Englands Golden Fleece"—for a commerce "chiefly carried on with Gold and Silver sent from England."[37] English woolens, they argued, were the only way to "inrich this land with store of Coyn and Bullion." Thus one clothier, in 1672, called woolens "the richest Treasure in his Majesties Dominions."[38]

Other mercantilists vehemently defended the EIC, highlighting the profitable reexport trade of calicoes and pepper to continental Europe. The money earned from reexporting Indian goods to continental Europe overbalanced the money expended in purchasing those goods initially in India. In other words, English merchants could purchase European imports with Indian goods rather than with specie. Furthermore, English consumption of Indian calicoes abated English demand for European linens, further improving the trade balance with Continental rivals. "Though the Company send great quantities of Treasure to the East-Indies," Roger Coke conceded in 1675, "yet the returns of them, in the Trade to Spain, and other places, produce greater quantities of Treasure." Samuel Lambe compared the trade to a farmer sowing seed to reap a greater harvest, so that "the East-India Company have not wasted, but rather increased the English coins." "We [are] Gainers by the whole, and in the General Ballance," Charles Davenant later asserted; critics of the trade, he said, "Object against the Motion of one Wheel, without knowing and seeing how the whole Engine moves."[39]

Nonetheless, the functioning of that "whole Engine" seemed to come at too high a cost—the entire textile industry in England, which employed so many people and which still supplied the kingdom's most valuable native export. Support burgeoned for a protective tariff or even outright prohibition on foreign textiles; as of yet, there were no tariffs explicitly designed to protect English industry. One proponent predicted in 1677 that in saving the woolen industry, protective tariffs would "bring in more profit to the Kingdom of England . . . than all the Spaniards Gold and Silver Mines in America." Absent protection, he said, and "much of the Treasure of the Kingdom is exhausted and drawn to other lands."[40] Another supporter of tariffs, Carew

Reynell, argued in 1674 that a tariff will not only "set at work millions of people . . . it saves likewise mony in our purses by lessening importation, and brings mony in by exportation."[41]

This was just the beginning of the now classic debate between protectionists and free-traders; it is telling, however, that both sides in this period framed the debate with mercantilist language. Historians, understandably, emphasize the quarrel. But the shared assumptions are of equal, if not greater importance. The consensus was that a plenteous supply of silver and gold, achieved through a positive balance of trade, merited the utmost attention in economic policymaking. On the means to that end, there was certainly no shortage of disagreement.

On matters of war and diplomacy, also, English mercantilists diverged radically. Who posed the greatest threat to England's national interests: Holland or France? Which of these two powers more greatly imperiled England's commercial prowess, political power, military might, and money supply? The answer at midcentury was Holland—no question. By the late 1660s, however, a growing number of people in England doubted whether the Netherlands posed any significant danger at all. For one, Dutch merchants had lost considerable ground in the carrying trade of Baltic naval stores and timber. Sweden had recently enacted mercantilist legislation targeting Dutch carriers— legislation modeled closely after the English Navigation Acts—and similar anti-Dutch legislation followed shortly after in Norway, Russia, and Prussia.[42] The ratio of English to Dutch vessels in the Baltic Sea was 1:4—much improved from the 1:10 ratio at midcentury.[43] Dutch control of the slave trade from Africa was also losing ground, as the Royal African Company of London expanded its business and established a series of impregnable forts along the West African coast.[44] The Dutch East India Company (VOC) remained the most powerful company in East Indian trade; nevertheless, Dutch access to Japanese silver had declined severely in recent years, necessitating greater shipments of silver from Holland to continue the company's trade.[45]

France, all the while, grew stronger, more confident, and more aggressive than at any time since the mid-sixteenth century. Under King Francis I (r. 1515–47), France had proved a capable challenger to the Spanish-Habsburg juggernaut. But France lost that war to Spain in 1557, and three decades of feeble monarchs and religious civil war followed. A modicum of stability returned to France under the first Bourbon monarch, King Henry IV (r. 1589–1610), and, under King Louis XIII (r. 1610–1643), chief minister Cardinal Richelieu successfully reorganized the administrative apparatus, expanded the army and navy, and resurrected Atlantic colonization, settling tobacco colonies in the

Leeward Islands. Nonetheless the Thirty Years' War crippled the kingdom financially, and at midcentury France could still not match the power of Holland or England. Louis XIV was yet a child when he ascended the throne in 1643, but after the death of Cardinal Jules Mazarin in 1661, Louis—now twenty-three years old—elected to rule without a chief minister.[46]

Louis, at first, signed a treaty of alliance with the Dutch in 1662, aiming to finally dislodge the Spanish from the neighboring Low Countries. As many Dutch correctly suspected, however, Louis harbored secret ambitions to territorially expand into the southern Netherlands.[47] He loathed the fact that French merchants had grown dependent on Dutch commercial power. The Dutch even dominated the carrying trade of French wine, brandy, and salt to other European countries. Louis thus commanded his minister of finance, Jean-Baptiste Colbert, to formulate a new mercantilist agenda for France. Colbert's aim was to utterly destroy Dutch commercial hegemony, ushering in a new order of French economic supremacy—one that would saturate French public and private coffers with silver and gold, permitting Louis to consummate his dream of erecting a French superstate.[48] "Trade is the basis of finance, and finance is the sinews of war," Colbert said.[49]

In 1664 Louis and Colbert launched their *guerre de commerce* against the Netherlands, first, by establishing the French West and East India Companies and, second, by increasing the duties on goods imported traditionally from the Dutch, namely East Indian products and refined sugar. Three years later, in 1667, Colbert doubled rates on imported Dutch linen and raised the duty sevenfold on Dutch-processed tobacco. The same month, Louis ordered French troops to occupy part of the Spanish Netherlands. When the Dutch retaliated in 1671 with an uncharacteristically high tariff on French goods, Colbert raised the tariff again.[50]

In April 1672, Louis declared war on the Dutch Republic. King Charles of England likewise declared war the next day—on the side of France, against the Dutch. Charles had recently signed a secret treaty with Louis, wherein he promised to support French action in the Netherlands in exchange for an annual pension of £150,000.[51] A French army of 130,000 infantry and cavalry marched across the Spanish Netherlands to the north; they outnumbered the Dutch army four to one. Soon after, a joint Anglo-French fleet of 146 warships surrounded the Republic, sparking an immediate, two-year cessation of Dutch maritime commerce. The Amsterdam stock market crashed, including shares in the Dutch East India Company, and immense sums of capital fled the country. The Dutch Republic seemed on the verge of total collapse. Pandemonium swept the Dutch provinces the summer of 1672, and a hysterical mob seized, tortured, and executed the De Witt brothers, the government's lead-ing republicans.[52]

The Third Anglo-Dutch War was highly unpopular in England. Many be-lieved that it was "the utmost excess of madness" to ally with Louis, that "mas-ter of absolute dominion," against a now seemingly benign Dutch power.[53] "The King of France will gain all the traffic, and increase his power at sea," warned Algernon Sidney.[54] The year 1672 coincided with the Stop of the Ex-chequer and the consequent credit crisis in England; the same year, a London tradesmen complained "that trading was dead, money scarce, and this the worst war that was ever made."[55] England's most pressing trade deficit, ironi-cally, was with France, not Holland; every year, silver bullion flowed across the Channel to that powerful, popish, militaristic, absolutist state. By the end of 1673 especially, there was in England a "universal hatred against this French alliance"; reports of French military defeats were even received "by the gen-erality of the people as good news."[56]

Much of the European continent had also grown extremely apprehensive over Louis's territorial and geopolitical ambition. The entry of Spain and Aus-tria in the war, on the side of Holland, diverted the French army away from the Low Countries. Under extraordinary pressure from Parliament, Charles signed a peace with the Netherlands in February 1674. Dutch trade in the Baltic re-vived shortly thereafter, and in 1676 a joint Dutch-Danish fleet successfully de-feated the chief naval arm of France's ally Sweden. Under the treaty that ended the war in 1678, France agreed to repeal the 1667 punitive tariffs against Dutch goods, and Sweden agreed to allow Dutch vessels back into its ports.[57]

The United Provinces had barely escaped what otherwise would have spelled a disastrous end to their very existence as an economic power, if not as an independent state. The VOC still dominated East Indian commerce, and Dutch trade with Spain and with Spanish America revived shortly after. But Dutch commercial power no longer matched the phenomenal levels achieved in earlier periods. Despite periodic booms in forthcoming decades, including the late 1680s, the Netherlands embarked on a gradual, prolonged period of economic decline, extending long into the eighteenth century.[58]

Meanwhile, Colbertian mercantilism had transformed France into an eco-nomic powerhouse. Silver and gold inundated French state and mercantile purses, financing a naval and commercial marine unmatched at any other time in France's history. Louis's unbounded thirst for power and for metal—his will, drive, and unyielding energy, exemplified most spectacularly at Versailles—impressed and terrified many. His army now numbered 450,000 troops; his navy counted some four hundred ships and one hundred thousand men; military expenditures made up two-thirds of the state budget. Louis's revenue almost doubled between 1661 and 1688, and France boasted the largest taxpaying base of any country in Europe.[59]

In pursuit of these mercantilist objectives, Louis and Colbert also eyed North America and the West Indian islands. The French were largely dependent on the English and Dutch for sugar imports; the French consumer market was a major reason why English merchants reexported close to half of the sugar imported from the English Caribbean.[60] But that era was approaching an end. The French Caribbean colonies of Guadeloupe and Martinique had newly converted from tobacco to sugar, and the French had also recently acquired the sugar colony of Saint Domingue, on the island of Hispaniola. The French posted regular patrols throughout the Caribbean to protect against smuggling; the English had no such patrols. French colonial administration was far more centralized than that of the English; the French crown appointed all governors and colonial officials, with no obstinate assemblies and other autonomous colonial institutions. Furthermore, on the North American mainland, the French founded a string of new trading posts along the Saint Lawrence River and Great Lakes region; in 1678 Robert de La Salle voyaged down the Mississippi River and claimed the whole valley for France.[61]

Nevertheless, even after 1672, many English writers still adamantly insisted that Holland remained the greater commercial and geopolitical threat. These anti-Dutch men in England found a political home in the emerging Tory faction in parliament and court. The Tories, as they soon became known, championed an exceptionally high view of the regal prerogative and consequently enjoyed the king's unfettered favor. Charles was certainly not inclined to make an enemy of France; far from it. He was a cousin and friend of Louis and received a secret subsidy from Louis even after the end of the Third Anglo-Dutch War. Louis designed the subsidy to preclude Charles from having to summon a contentious, anti-French and anti-Catholic parliament. French fashion was all the rage at Charles's court; in the early 1670s, Charles unabashedly consorted with a French mistress. He yielded slightly in 1677 by arranging a marriage between his niece Mary (daughter of James, Duke of York) and his nephew William, Prince of Orange and Stadtholder of the Netherlands. But it was plain that Charles and his Tory allies viewed the Dutch as far more inimical to English interests, both politically and economically.[62]

Nor was this an implausible view. As Sir William Petty remarked in 1676, it was still common opinion that "the Hollanders are at our heels, in the race of Naval Power."[63] The Dutch mercantile fleet still exceeded the *combined* fleets of France and England.[64] In Asia, the Dutch East India Company still easily surpassed its English competitor, the latter enjoying close connections to

Charles's court. Dutch merchants, moreover, were the most competitive suppliers of African slaves and manufactured goods to Spanish America, both in volume and in price. Their chief English rival, the Royal African Company, also enjoyed close connections to Charles's court. France was not even a mild competitor in this field. The Dutch recently founded sugar plantations at St. Eustatius, Tobago, and Surinam—the latter won from England in 1667. Of course, Dutch tradesmen and smugglers in English America remained a constant thorn in the side of those who desperately wished to more strictly enforce the Navigation Acts.[65] Finally, the Dutch Republic's eccentric political and social character—its religious pluralism, laissez-faire attitudes, and toleration of radical dissenting viewpoints—purportedly undercut the stability of England's monarchical settlement after 1660. As one writer clamored in 1672, the Dutch have "not only undermin'd the Trade of the English in all parts, to the diminution of his Majesties Revenue . . . but have labored to soil his Glory, and lessen his Dignity."[66]

Popular opinion in England, however, was rapidly turning against Louis XIV. The so-called Whigs—the emergent, rival political faction to the Tories—railed zealously against England's near-perpetual state of war with the Dutch, entreating rather for an alliance with Holland against France. Increasingly, many political moderates and even moderate Tories joined them, alarmed at the prospect of militant French expansionism.[67] Slingsby Bethel, merchant and Whig, was among the loudest voices in this movement and in 1679 authored *An Account of the French Usurpation upon the Trade of England*. Louis, he warned, was a king "so rich in Treasure . . . that Europe begins to bow to his Power." Silver and gold—acquired through Colbertian mercantilism—was key to Louis's potency. "Trade is the fountain from whence its Riches spring, and Money is the basis of its greatness and strength," Bethel said. Colbert was the master of mercantilism: "studious to accumulate money, and careful to bring in more daily. . . . France will in a short time draw into them all the moneys of Europe." "Other Princes," he wrote, "are enforced to beg for peace, and disband their Armies, because their Treasures are exhausted," but with France, "their stock of money doth not fall much short of the money of the rest of all Europe." Indeed, Bethel asserted hyperbolically, "the prodigious sum of money which he doth yearly drain out of the rest of Europe, is beyond my Arithmetick to tell you."[68]

War with France appeared a real possibility in the late 1670s. Yet further action in that direction stalled. Mounting internal divisions at home between Whigs and Tories, namely the Exclusion Crisis of 1679–1681—a vicious debate over the regal legitimacy of the Catholic Duke of York, future James II—allowed Charles to persuade most moderates of the impropriety of declaring war on France while the country remained so split.[69]

Ironically, for many Englishmen the solution to the growing problem of France was in imitating Colbertian mercantilism. Prohibitive tariffs; manufacturing protection; and a stronger bureaucratic, administrative, regulatory state appealed strongly to this group. As already mentioned, Parliament in 1678 banned the importation of all French wine, brandy, linen, and silk.[70] On the administrative end, Charles's lead minister, Lord Danby, enlarged the scope and size of the Crown's several departments, broadening executive and bureaucratic authority.[71] State revenue remained a big question mark: tax receipts in England amounted to only one-fifth of state revenue in France, the latter supported by a larger population and a per capita tax burden that was three to four times higher than in England. Yearly public expenditures in England averaged only £2 million—far less than those of the nation's modern, absolutist rival across the Channel.[72] "New Maxims must be framed, and Measures taken, for the retrenchment of the Power of France," Bethel urged.[73]

Colonial America figured prominently in these discussions. What was the proper relationship between empire and colony? What could be done to make the colonies more gainful for England? More than ever, England required in America a fruitful, subordinate, money-making arm of the imperial system. The prospect was certainly there but thus far had not been fulfilled—not for lack of tobacco or sugar plantations, not because of a dearth of settlers, but by reason of insubordination. Colonial tradesmen repeatedly and pointedly flouted the Navigation Acts, all with a wink and a nod from their respective colonial governments, which, despite outward expressions of loyalty to England, acted more like quasi-independent bodies than complaisant dependencies.

Stricter enforcement of the Navigation Acts, to start, was absolutely imperative. Customs revenue accounted for nearly 40 percent of royal income.[74] Royal revenue was a particularly sensitive issue after the Stop of the Exchequer, and Lord Danby, the king's chief minister from 1673 to 1679, was determined not to repeat that dreadful episode. Customs, moreover, was revenue collected independently of Parliament. But most members of Parliament, too, wanted colonial trade to funnel primarily through England. The Navigation Acts, after all, originated in Parliament; merchants were among the most powerful lobbies in the House of Commons, whose members had long endorsed a mercantilist vision for managing the empire. Even the most Whiggish politicians in the 1670s wished to see England's trade balance improve—to increase the money stock but also to counter France. "London will be the Emporium, and great Mart of Europe," Bethel predicted; with wise policy, "the Power of France will be retrenched" and "we shall be fit for any foreign Action, or new Conquests."[75]

Consensus thus prevailed in English politics that illegal trade in the colonies must be suppressed. The obstacle was the lack of colonial compliance. Competitive pricing was still too great a temptation. From a strictly economic standpoint, it was in the colonists' best interest to sell to the highest bidder and to buy from the lowest seller, regardless of nationality. Even Bethel acknowledged the common sense in this point of view. "The fewer buyers of Native Commodities, the cheaper they must be," he explained, and "the fewer sellers of Forein" imports, he said—linens, shoes, wares, and the like—"the dearer they must be," that is, the more expensive.[76] On either end of the spectrum, buying or selling, colonists had a clear and distinct interest in welcoming as many outside traders into colonial ports as possible. And indeed many colonists did so, with few to no repercussions.

But smuggling made a mockery of England's colonial empire. Smuggling undercut the chief principle for having colonies in the first place. Open trade privileged colonial interests over English interests; the persistence of smuggling, in spite of the law, encouraged and represented an unabashed defiance, if not rebellion, against imperial authority. Such defiance could no longer be tolerated—not in this time of economic, monetary, financial, and political uncertainty. Colonial submission to the economic order—from the perspective of a great many mercantilists in England—was emphatically requisite for the empire to strengthen and to thrive.

Preferably, colonists and their governments would submit voluntarily. At present, however, voluntary submission was unlikely, for it first required that colonists accept the *political* doctrine that England's economic interests superseded or even abrogated the narrower economic interests of colonial Americans. This was a vision of the imperial constitution that many leading colonists refused to accept. To be sure, some of the more cosmopolitan merchants in the colonies perceived that it was in their interest to fully cooperate with imperial authority, aware that cooperation might beget valuable commercial and political relationships and networks in London. A case could also be made that economic subordination was a perfectly reasonable price for colonists to pay in exchange for the benefits of imperial membership. Colonial merchants who held such views were more likely to favor a tighter, more consolidated colonial sphere and more likely to comply voluntarily with the Navigation Acts. As of yet, however, such merchants were in the minority. The bulk of colonial tradesmen and colonial planters either partly or wholly rejected the political doctrine that colonies ought to be economically subordinate to England. Most of the time, colonists' rejection of this doctrine was implicit—found in their eagerness to break the Navigation Acts—though some on occasion articulated their rejection more explicitly.

Two competing visions prevailed on the nature of the imperial constitution. The empire's vision—that of the Crown, most members of Parliament, and most merchants and mercantilists in London—placed the pecuniary interests of the mother country, England, ahead of all others. Political power and gold and silver money ought to center in England, this vision held. The empire's vision did not view colonial liberties and economic interests as intrinsically unimportant per se; rather, those interests and liberties ought to always yield to the ultimate interests and will of the empire—as defined by those in charge of the empire. Colonial plantations were dominions of the Crown—wholly distinct from lands in England—subject, therefore, to a far greater exercise of the regal prerogative. Colonial liberties existed solely by virtue of the king's good pleasure; these liberties could legally and justly be removed if shown to interfere with larger imperial goals.[77] "The Right of Colonies," Thomas Hobbes wrote in *Leviathan*, ". . . dependeth wholly on their Licence, or Letters, by which their Soveraign authorized them to Plant." The preamble to Charles's commission in 1670 to the Council for Foreign Plantations—discussed later—declared that colonies are unequivocally "the proper Right and Soveraigne Possessions of us."[78]

Many colonists, with some marked exceptions, embraced a rival vision of the imperial constitution. They championed a decentralized empire, with power located in a multiplicity of mostly autonomous colonies, sharing with the mother country a common culture and monarch and common political, civil, legal, and economic traditions and liberties. Colonists, under this vision, owed allegiance to England but retained substantial autonomy in political and economic affairs, including the general freedom to prioritize—within reason—the colonists' own economic interests. Many leading colonists believed that *all* English subjects, whether at home or abroad, enjoyed the same immemorial rights guaranteed in the much lauded and unwritten ancient English constitution. Such rights included participation in lawmaking, representation in the legislature, and consent to taxation. Colonial laws could still be subject to royal oversight, perhaps—though many disputed even this idea—yet colonial laws were not subject to oversight from parliament, as colonists enjoyed no representation there. The early proliferation of locally elected colonial assemblies—a sort of provincial house of commons—corroborated this vision. The Navigation Acts, on the other hand, undermined it; many of its restrictions applied only to Englishmen in America, not to Englishmen in England, and colonists had no say in its passage. To quote the Boston mint master John Hull, if the English succeeded in better enforcing the Navigation Acts, it would be "as the cutting off our hands & feet . . . this orphant Plantation will be Crushed."[79] Hyperbole no doubt, but a sentiment widely shared. Notice the choice of words: "this orphant Plantation"—a colony that once had a mother but no longer, not by choice but by compulsion.

The colonial case for a decentralized empire was strong. In migrating across the vast ocean, colonists had risked their fortunes and lives; moreover, the hazard continued even after arrival, as they dangerously subdued the uncharted wilderness. In taking on this monumental task, they certainly never agreed to surrender their rights. They were in fact happy and zealous to affirm their utmost loyalty to England, the king, and even to empire—an empire that acknowledged their lawful birthright as Englishmen. This birthright included their right to self-governance, yes, but also to trade as freely as anyone residing in England. The colonists, in short, did not oppose empire, nor did they oppose imperial order; they simply believed a more liberal, decentralized form of it to be the best for all sections.[80]

One of the greatest disadvantages that colonists labored under was that they were poorly organized in America and poorly represented in London. They comprised over a dozen separate governments, often in intense rivalry with one another; moreover, it was an expensive ordeal to send special agents to London or even to pass a petition through Parliament. Not so for London mercantile interests. Increasingly, English merchants with commercial interests in America organized into voluntary associations, appearing regularly before the Lords of Trade (discussed later) to lobby on behalf of their interest group. But the interests of English merchants trading with America were often directly at odds with the interests of the colonists themselves. Colonial governments and leadership enjoyed little to no contact or cooperation with merchant interest groups in London and little direct contact with key policymakers. There was no colonial interest group in London. Colonists had practically no voice at all, for instance, in the drafting of the Navigation Acts, nor in the empire's administrative reformulation in the 1670s and 1680s. Officials at Whitehall and Westminster worked with scant information obtained directly from the colonists themselves; this lack, in turn, left imperial officials largely ignorant as to how colonists might respond to particular policy changes, resulting, in coming years, to some highly imprudent decisions from London.[81]

By the 1670s, those in charge of administering the empire—the Crown, bureaucracy, lobbies, members of Parliament—had concluded that coercion, not persuasion, was necessary to achieve the objectives of their centralized, hierarchal, mercantilist vision for empire. Persuasion had already been tried and had thus far failed. In a 1667 circular to colonial governors, for instance, the treasury had emphasized the importance "to his Majesty's revenue in particular that those laws [the Navigation Acts] should be duly and strictly observed"; but it was all to no effect.[82] Colonial refusal to faithfully abide by acts of Parliament and royal instructions left imperial administrators no other choice, from their perspective, but to compel submission, like a parent with an unruly child.

It was not yet clear what coercion might entail. Political reformation of some sort or another was manifestly in order, including, at the bare minimum, greater scrutiny over colonial lawmaking. In private colonies like Massachusetts this would prove a difficult task, but even there the Crown, for example, might appoint resident officials to survey the New England coast for smugglers, convey information to the colonial government from London, and report back to England of any illicit or disagreeable activity. If this procedure proved inadequate, the next recourse might involve something more serious—if need be, the toppling of any subversive political elements within the colony, including even representative government. This latter recourse would be extreme but entirely within the king's prerogative. As the Crown saw it, the abrogation of colonial liberties—which existed not by right, but by grace—was not only lawful but prudent if it meant furthering the interests of empire.

Administrative restructuring was the first step on this road to reform. Earlier, in 1660, Charles had commissioned a Council for Foreign Plantations to deal with the colonies, but the body of forty-eight members proved unwieldy and languished after only four years of irregular meetings (its sister body, the Council of Trade, also terminated around the same time).[83] In July 1670 Charles reconstituted the Council for Foreign Plantations. This time it comprised only ten regular members, and unlike the previous body, it convened about twice a week, proving a more eager, diligent, and inquisitive body than its predecessor. Their commission instructed them to discover "all prudentiall wayes and Meanes so to Order, Governe, and Regulate the Trade of our whole Plantations." They were to keep "a continuall correspondence" with each colony, requesting from each governor "a Coppy of all such Lawes, as have been at any time made." They were also to examine any supposed defects in the colonial charters, and if "the same cannot be friendly and amicably ended," they were to advise the Crown on how best to proceed. Finally, the council was to investigate the methods by which foreign governments (read France) administered their colonies and to inquire whether the same methods might be applied to England's plantations.[84]

In September 1672 Charles commissioned a broader Council of Trade and Foreign Plantations. Its membership remained nearly the same as the previous Council for Foreign Plantations, but the new council had the additional task now of considering all of England's domestic and foreign trade. The new commission borrowed much of its language from the 1670 instructions; on colonial matters, it commanded the council to deliberate on "the best wayes and Meanes for the encourageing, settling, and Improoving the Trade and Commerce of Our sayd Collonyes."[85] A few months later, parliament enacted the Navigation Act of 1673, also called the Plantation Duty Act, on advice of the Council of Trade and Foreign Plantations. The Navigation Act of 1673 aimed primarily at quelling the New England carrying trade of tobacco and sugar to foreign markets, to the "great Hurt and Diminution of your Majesty's Customs," the statute read, "and of the Trade and Navigation of this your Kingdom."[86]

In December 1674 Charles revoked the commission of the Council of Trade and Foreign Plantations. The revocation resulted neither from a change of imperial purpose, nor from a loss of enthusiasm within the council, but rather from a major shake-up at court. Lord Ashley, Earl of Shaftesbury, was president of the Council of Trade and Foreign Plantations, but he had fallen out of favor at Whitehall over his zeal against Roman Catholicism. Charles expelled Shaftesbury from the Privy Council in May 1674 and elevated Thomas Osborne—whom the Crown made the Earl of Danby—in June. Danby sought to strength executive, church, and royal authority at nearly all turns. He consolidated court control over politics; dispensed patronage to secure working majorities in Parliament; reduced the power of rival ministers to that of functionaries; and sought virtually any way possible to flex executive muscle in most domestic, foreign, and colonial matters. Financial solvency was near the top of his agenda; Danby objected to the earlier Stop of Exchequer, and now, as Lord High Treasurer, he aimed to boost the Crown's independent revenue—of which customs was most important—to the point that Charles would no longer be beholden to Parliament.[87]

Danby solicited for an entirely new body on trade and colonial affairs. He desired this body to carry executive power. The former standing councils, including the most recent, were advisory only, issuing mere recommendations to the Privy Council, which bore executive authority to either act or abstain from acting on those recommendations. Danby reasoned that the new body should consist of men who sat concurrently on the Privy Council, thus giving the body far greater weight. Charles agreed, and in March 1675 established a new standing committee of the Privy Council, the Lords of Trade and Plantations. Known commonly as simply the Lords of Trade, the committee's commission instructed the councillors to monitor and manage all colonial affairs, with particular regard "for Matters relating to trade."[88] The quorum for business was only three councillors, and so in practice, work generally fell under the oversight of a small number of councillors who consistently attended the weekly meetings and possessed special knowledge of colonial matters. In its first decade of existence, the committee averaged fifty sessions a year. It prioritized the systematic reformation of nearly all elements of imperial-colonial relations, pursuing virtually any measure that promoted colonial uniformity, centralization, dependency, and submission.[89]

A young, ambitious man named William Blathwayt quickly distinguished himself as one of the most influential figures within the Lords of Trade. Blathwayt, with Edward Randolph, typified the new ascendant professional class within the English civil service. Blathwayt was not a privy councillor; he joined the Lords of Trade as a clerk in September 1675 at the age of 25. Through great ambition, enthusiasm, industry, and dedication, he rose to the rank of secretary in 1679, wielding extraordinary influence over the committee's proceedings. The following year, 1680, he became surveyor and auditor-general of the Crown's revenue in America, serving in this capacity until his death in 1717. A strong admirer of the French model of imperial governance, Blathwayt rejected decentralization as the way of the past. The present, modern mode of administration was governance through strength, bureaucracy, energy, and centralization. The American colonies, he insisted, must be inextricably bound to the imperial will.[90]

Work proceeded quickly. The Lords of Trade, first, arranged for a host of new officers to venture to the colonies to guard against smuggling and to strengthen the customs service. The Navigation Act of 1673 already provided for customs officials in the tobacco and sugar colonies, but the Lords of Trade wanted them in all colonies, including New England. Second, the committee demanded written reports from governors of royal colonies—Virginia and the West Indian islands—with greater frequency and detail, threatening to remove any governor impudently evading instructions. The committee also preferred to appoint governors who possessed no estates in America and were thereby less likely to empathize with colonial elite concerns, unlike the earlier appointees Berkeley, Willoughby, and Modyford. The committee's preference was for military men accustomed to rule, take orders, and command—a mode of administration that one historian, Stephen Saunders Webb, describes as "garrison government."[91]

The Lords of Trade resolutely discouraged the founding of any further private colonies, whether by charter or proprietorship. Such settlements, by definition, were notoriously hard for the Crown to control. They were more likely to boast liberal or popular forms of government, often instituted by profit-minded proprietors eager to allure settlers; by consequence, they also commonly ran roughshod over the Navigation Acts. For those private colonies already in existence, the committee recommended their conversion into royal colonies, as Charles had already done with Barbados and the Leeward Islands and as Louis had done with private French colonies in 1664. Here, the committee faced tremendous obstacles. Charters were inviolable in court of law. Moreover, earlier in his reign, King Charles—ever desperate for short-term financial remedies—granted to Court favorites private proprietorships and land grants in Carolina, New Jersey, and in portions of Virginia. The Lords of Trade also failed to block an upcoming proprietary grant to William Penn in 1681, an action Charles took only to settle a major debt to Penn's deceased father; nevertheless, the committee managed to ensure that the Pennsylvania charter included tighter restrictions than earlier endowments.[92]

One way or another, reform was imminent; indeed it was already underway. And then, almost as if to underline the desperate need for reform, an unprecedented series of colonial crises broke out in 1675–1677, threatening to overturn the entire colonial project. When the dust finally settled, the move toward consolidation accelerated.

If English America had not erupted in chaos in 1675–1677, the Crown would still have proceeded with this consolidation program. But chaos erupted all the same, in New England, Virginia, Jamaica, and northeastern Carolina. The timing was such that historians have sometimes been tempted to identify these crises as the chief impetus behind the Crown's decision to tighten its grip over the colonies.[93] Yet these crises were not the spark; they rather vindicated the wisdom in continuing forward with already developed plans for imperial reform. Nevertheless, a strong vindication these crises certainly were, and currency played a major role in each of them.

King Philip's War broke out in New England in the spring of 1675. The namesake of the conflict was Metacom, a Wampanoag sachem known by the English as King Philip. The Plymouth Colony had recently executed three Wampanoag Indians accused of murdering a paid Indian informant in the service of Massachusetts Bay. The executions sparked a string of retaliatory Wampanoag attacks on English homesteads along the western frontier, unleashing among the Indians a fury of anti-English resentment. Other native groups swiftly joined the rebellion, and in the summer and fall of 1675, Indian insurgents attacked at least fifty-two New England villages, utterly destroying twelve. The course of the war altered only in early 1676, after the New England governments formed a military alliance with the Pequot and Mohegan Indians. Following a series of brutal counterattacks from the English and their allies, the insurgency in southern New England disintegrated in the spring and summer of 1676. More than one thousand New England settlers and approximately three thousand Indians died in the war, the former mostly in 1675 and the latter representing nearly a quarter of the native population in southern New England.[94]

The fiscal toll of the conflict was extraordinary. The governments of New England spent at least £50,000 sterling prosecuting the war, and property damage far exceeded that sum.[95] King Philip's War, in fact, was the last major Indian conflict fought in colonial North America without the aid of paper currency. War finance, absent paper currency, was a far slower, more tedious endeavor; it required cooperation from local merchant-creditors, who lent silver coin to the Massachusetts treasury in exchange for a paper receipt certifying the colony's indebtedness to the merchant. Indian land was the government's collateral in case of default. The treasurer (who so happened to be John Hull, the mint master) then used the borrowed coin to settle soldiers' wages and to purchase supplies.[96] The complications were exhausting and uncertain; if that were not enough, Hull failed to acquire an adequate sum of coin from merchant-lenders. "Moneys are much wanting," the Massachusetts assembly reported in October 1676. Country pay thus financed most of the war effort, with extraordinary taxes levied in "all sorts of corne."[97] After collecting the cumbersome produce—called "Stock in the Treasury" while it remained in storage—Hull exchanged it for coin.[98] Decades later, in 1721, one Massachusetts writer, John Wise, suggested that a paper currency might have helped the colony achieve a swifter victory in King Philip's War. "If this had been Projected and wisely used Twenty or Fourty Years before it was," he reflected, "it seems to me as tho' Thousands of Lives . . . would have been saved. . . . that a parcel of poor Naked Indians, had never attempted our Ruin, or prevailed as they have."[99]

Some six hundred miles south, a separate calamity struck the colony of Virginia. Bacon's Rebellion was a far more alarming event, for the Crown, than King Philip's War. Virginia was one of England's most profitable mercantilist assets. Annual imports of Chesapeake tobacco into England approached twenty million pounds in the mid-1670s. English merchants reexported approximately one-third of this leaf to the European continent. Furthermore, Virginia tobacco yielded more than £100,000 in customs revenue to the Crown per annum, more than the revenue from any other colony.[100] "Virginia is of as great importance to his Majesty as the Spanish Indias are to Spaine," an English merchant urged the Council of Trade and Foreign Plantations in 1673.[101] The collapse of Virginia would spell disaster for England: for its revenue, the finances, the merchant's pocketbook, the balance of trade, the money supply. The Crown thus approached the Virginia question with grave seriousness. A legion of problems plagued Virginia on the eve of Bacon's Rebellion. Tobacco prices at farm rarely exceeded a penny a pound, sometimes less.[102] During the two most recent wars between England and the Netherlands, the Dutch had incessantly attacked and captured tobacco ships sailing down the James River. Moreover, a string of natural disasters in the late 1660s and early 1670s—

hailstorms, flooding, and hurricanes—inflicted mass destruction on property, cattle, and crops.[103] Corruption was rife in the colony; Berkeley's reputation as governor had severely declined; with age he became impatient, irritable, arbitrary, and domineering, deploying patronage to bribe members of the House of Burgesses, a body that had not faced a general election since 1662, making it grossly unrepresentative of the will of most people.[104] A considerable bulk of the population comprised former indentured servants, recently freed—ever-restless families enduring a precarious state of existence in scattered frontier settlements to the north and west of the James River, far beyond the capital at Jamestown. Taxes fell most heavily and regressively on the most vulnerable farming families in Virginia, averaging between one-quarter and one-half of their tobacco crop. Farmers rightly accused the government of waste, fraud, and corruption in the spending of that tobacco money.[105] Obnoxiously, the cost of keeping a single delegate in the House of Burgesses— and each county required two—was an astounding 250 pounds of tobacco *per day* (the average farmer produced between 1,200 and 1,500 pounds a year).[106] The expense was so costly that some counties refused to send more than a single delegate to the burgesses, compelling the assembly in 1670 to threaten fines of 10,000 pounds of tobacco for any county that did not send two delegates to Jamestown.[107]

The breaking point came when a series of Indian raids and English counterattacks erupted on the Virginia frontier, reaching emergency levels in early 1676. Many folks sensed a conspiracy between Metacom's rebels in New England and the Chesapeake Indians; Berkeley, meanwhile—a prolific trader with the Indians in beaver skins—appeared altogether passive in the face of this threat, wasting tobacco money on the construction of expensive fortifications in areas entirely useless for countering potential Indian assaults.[108] At just the right moment, a young, brash, charismatic, conniving planter named Nathaniel Bacon—having arrived from England only two years before— emerged to channel the farmers' many grievances. In April, Bacon—without any commission from the governor—led a band of frustrated men to wage offensive war against the Indians. Berkeley, to appease the population, called for new elections in May 1676—the first general election in fourteen years— but also declared Bacon a rebel and traitor. Voters, nonetheless, elected Bacon unanimously to the House of Burgesses, whose members were now largely supportive of Bacon.[109]

After a series of plots, escapes, and back-and-forth negotiations with the governor, Bacon—on June 23—led a march on Jamestown of several armed men and women, prompting their allies in the burgesses to pass reform legislation and declare Bacon commander in chief. Bacon departed west again with an army of more than one thousand men to combat the Indians, but when Bacon received word that Berkeley was raising an army against him, Bacon and his men marched again toward Jamestown, prompting Berkeley to flee the capital.[110] With Berkeley gone, Bacon, at the end of July, drew up a declaration "in the Name of the People." The declaration, first and foremost, listed "great unjust taxes" as the cause of rebellion. "No visible effects" arose from these taxes, the declaration said, but rather, the government had traitorously "emboldened the Indians."[111] Bacon renewed his military campaign against the Indians, but returned to Jamestown weeks later after hearing that Berkeley and his soldiers had regained control of the capital. Bacon's men prepared a siege, but the governor fled a second time, and to prevent Berkeley from ever again making Jamestown a base of operations, Bacon's men burned the capital to the ground on September 19. They proceeded north to engage Berkeley's troops, but weeks later, Bacon fell ill with dysentery. He died on October 26. Lacking a leader, the rebellion dissipated shortly after, and by January 1677, after several courts-martial and hangings, Berkeley regained full control of the colony.[112]

The depreciation and extreme misuse of tobacco money was one of the chief drivers behind Bacon's Rebellion. The king's investigative commissioners soon found this to be so. In 1677 they solicited the people's grievances in order to better understand the cause of the revolt. The several counties, by and large, listed "great taxes" and their misapplication as the "cause of our riseing." "Whereas formerly it was accounted a great leavie that was 40 or 50 pounds of tobacco per each," read one petition, ". . . yet wee paying neer two hundred a head yearly, but for what we know not."[113] The value of tobacco currency had fallen to unprecedented lows, taxes had soared to unprecedented highs, and the corrupt government in Jamestown expended it on fruitless and fraudulent endeavors. Years later, in 1705, Robert Beverley, Jr.—the son of Berkeley's right-hand man during the rebellion—identified the first cause of the rebellion to be the "extream low price of Tobacco, and the ill Usage of the Planters in the Exchange of Goods for it": that is, the depreciation of tobacco currency. The second cause, he said, was "extravagant Taxes" that "fell heaviest on the poor People." "There was nothing to be got by Tobacco," Beverley recalled, a consequence, he argued, of the "heavy Restraints and Burdens laid upon their Trade by Act of Parliament in England."[114]

Compounding matters, another revolt, Culpeper's Rebellion, broke out in northeastern Carolina (called the Albemarle) in November 1677, overthrowing the imperial customs collector, who resided there according to the Navigation Act of 1673. Months after Bacon's Rebellion, Albemarle settlers imprisoned the customs collector and installed a local man, John Culpeper, in his place. Culpeper not only refused to collect any duties, but he and his supporters also convened a new legislature, made Culpeper governor, and for nearly two years governed the northern half of Carolina with full autonomy. The revolt purportedly came at the behest of several New England merchants who trafficked in the region. Two years later, in 1679, reports surfaced in London that "some New England men then there tradeing" had at least tacitly supported the revolt, having warned the Albemarle settlers that "it would be a great inconvenience for them to submit to this paymt"—that is, the customs duty—and that they "did intend to raise their commodities double if such paymt . . . were exacted from them." "Through their interest with the people," another reported, a few New England merchants "have factiously made one Mr Culpeper" governor.[115]

To top it all off, England's most valuable colony—Jamaica—endured the flaring up of a nonviolent but no less dangerous political crisis in the mid-1670s. A military regime governed Jamaica in the years after the English conquest in 1655; the island had no representative assembly at all until 1664, and even then only one that had a very brief existence. After 1664, Governor Modyford went seven years without an assembly.[116] Economic prosperity quelled most political agitation during this period, the lack of an assembly blunted by the continual stream of silver and gold from privateers. With the arrival of Governor Sir Thomas Lynch in 1671, however, the island's emergent class of elite sugar planters initiated a push for representative government. The following year, at the start of the Third Anglo-Dutch War, Lynch summoned the island's first assembly in eight years, calling on the assembly to raise additional money to strengthen fortifications. The assembly dutifully raised the necessary funds but not before also raising the value of the Spanish piece of eight from 4s6d to 5s. Lynch obliged, but the devaluation diminished all planter debts to the Royal African Company by 11 percent.[117] Moreover, "two or three obstinate and factious persons stirred up the Assembly," Lynch reported, ". . . to rayse questions about the Governour and Counsell's power." Another unruly assembly convened and dissolved in 1673. "Assemblyes are apt to bee refractory, when they are not restrayned by an absolute Power," Lynch wrote administrators in England.[118] Governor Lynch, nonetheless, had no choice but to call another assembly in 1674. Previous royal instructions directed that all Jamaican laws, including acts of revenue, be in force no longer than two years unless confirmed by the Crown.[119] The Crown had yet to confirm the 1672 laws, and they were now set to expire. Boasting the power of the purse, the new 1674 assembly upped its demands. Besides renewing the 5s valuation for pieces of eight, the assembly tacked the "free importation of negroes" onto the revenue bill—yet another attack on the Royal African Company.[120] Lynch, again, had little choice but to approve the new revenue bill; the government desperately required funding, and the assembly refused to cooperate under any other condition. The law had its desired effect: two years later, in 1676, when the RAC took an interloping shipmaster to court for carrying more than three hundred slaves illegally to the island, the judge threw out the case on the ground that the assembly had recently passed a "Statute against Monopolyes." Furious, the newly constituted Lords of Trade declared in response that the 1674 statute had stripped "the King of his Prerogative."[121]

King Philip's War, Bacon's Rebellion, Culpeper's Rebellion, and Jamaica's political turmoil rocked the English American world at precisely the time that England at home faced mounting concerns over its currency, finances, trade, and foreign relations. Control, coercion, and centralization seemed the logical and optimal path forward, and indeed was the path that English administrators had already decided on. Yet not all in England saw things this way; in fact, some Englishmen began questioning the propriety of having any colonies at all. Skeptics of colonization in this period based their concerns largely on England's purported demographic problems. England's population, after a century of growth, stopped increasing around the mid-seventeenth century, resulting in declining rents and rising labor costs. "The Condition of England is worse by our Plantations," argued Roger Coke: "Scarcity of People Diminish Trade," and "those multitudes of hands which are imployed abroad . . . are not imployed here." "Nations are observed to be rich and populous," said Carew Reynell, "who waste not their People in Foreign parts . . . decoy'd away to New-England and Virginia."[122] Two decades later, one prominent member of the Board of Trade, John Cary, affirmed that it had once "been a great question among many thoughtful Men whither our Foreign Plantations have been an advantage to this Nation"—whether overseas plantations "drained us of Multitudes of our People who might have been serviceable at home."[123] The colonial crises of 1675–1677 corroborated this view.

Most onlookers in London nevertheless welcomed the "clear Profit to the Kingdom" accruing from the colonies, and particularly from the tobacco and sugar plantations. Sir William Petty estimated that England's trade with America and Africa employed more than forty thousand tons of shipping per annum—an obvious boon to "the Power and Wealth of England," he said. William Penn, in 1681, decried the "vulgar opinion" of anticolonial skeptics, maintaining that colonists on profitable plantations are "worth more than if they stay'd at home." Tobacco and sugar colonies in particular, he argued, were to England of "extraordinary Profit," because "we Export it to other Countries in Europe, which brings in Money."[124]

Substantial reform, however, was clearly necessary. A more centralized empire, politically, would make for a more profitable empire, economically and monetarily. As Petty argued, "small divided remote Governments" represent a clear "Burthen" to the empire, so that "instead of being Additions, they are really Dimunitions." Petty proposed consolidating each colony into "the whole Empire," uniting England, Ireland, and the Americas into a single political body. "May not the three Kingdoms be United into one," he asked, "and equally represented in Parliament?"[125] The Crown's position on consolidation diverged quite radically from Petty's, however. Representative government in the colonies ought to be curbed and even vanquished if necessary. Some of the king's advisers hoped to reorganize the colonies into three general governments, each ruled directly by the Crown without any assemblies but modeled closely after France's colonies and the viceroyalties of New Spain and Peru.[126]

Colonial legislatures bore the brunt of the Crown's reform effort after 1675. First, in Virginia, Bacon's Rebellion demonstrated to the Crown the pitfalls of a strong House of Burgesses: it oppressed the people, incited rebellion, and then served as a vehicle to be captured by Bacon's men on behalf of rebellion. In Jamaica an upstart class of sugar planters had captured the local assembly and aggressively wielded the power of the purse to undermine the Royal African Company. Massachusetts Bay represented a very different type of problem: its people had already long established an autonomous government, and an entire generation had grown up under it. If Boston inhabitants had only kept to themselves, the Crown might not have minded. But Massachusetts, on the contrary, extended its commercial tentacles into virtually every corner of the Atlantic world, defying the Navigation Acts not only in New England but in the Chesapeake and Caribbean. The Lords of Trade launched their opening salvo against Massachusetts Bay in 1676. They did so by sending a previous unknown, Edward Randolph, to survey the region.

CHAPTER 6

Showdown in English America, 1675–1684

Economic, fiscal, and monetary uncertainties in England in the 1670s combined with the rise of new geopolitical anxieties to make comprehensive political and economic reform in the colonies appear categorically necessary. The several colonies had not approached anywhere near their full moneymaking potential; they were profitable, indeed, but too often for the wrong people; the wealth was not channeling as intended to England. Beginning in the 1670s, the Crown embarked on a more zealous and assertive reform program than in any previous era of English imperial history. The program began with the reconstitution of the Council for Foreign Plantations in 1670 and then accelerated in 1675 with the establishment of the Lords of Trade and Plantations.

Consolidated coercion was the order of the day, but many colonists embraced a rival vision for empire: one of free trade and political decentralization—a close familial relationship with England, attended perhaps by some modest and sensible controls or regulations, but certainly not in line with the imperial vision that thoroughly subordinated all colonial economic interests and political liberties to the will of the mother country, where money, trade, and power all centered. Leading figures at Whitehall, of course—the seat of English executive government—believed control and consolidation to be the modern and necessary order of things; if hostile colonial legislatures must be sacrificed in the process, so be it—a small price to pay for the greater imperial project.

Now was not the time to humor backwater, sentimentalist assertions of colonial free trade and liberty.

The chief obstacle to this coercive approach was that colonial political institutions had already been firmly established by 1675 and in some cases enjoyed a multidecade existence. It would not be easy to topple such institutions. The people of Massachusetts Bay, in particular, had long developed a highly distinctive brand of political economy, one jealously guarded by the General Court, the most opprobrious of all colonial legislatures. The independent members on the Massachusetts General Court insisted on total autonomy in economic, monetary, and political matters, perceiving virtually all royal interference as menacing and even alien, unlawfully imperiling their political birthright as Englishmen. But the Massachusetts government was not alone in earning the Crown's high disfavor; the colonial assemblies in Virginia and Jamaica also acted quite independently of imperial control. "The New England disease is very catching," a prominent Virginian warned the Crown in 1674. In Jamaica also—according to a member of the Lords of Trade in 1677—assemblymen "flew high & were in a fair way of treading, in time, in the steps of New England."[1]

New England was truly the most troubling, indeed puzzling, section of the empire. Its peculiar political and religious institutions, manifest smuggling, presumptuous coinage, and utter absence of any overt contribution to the mercantilist system discomfited even the most enthusiastic supporters of colonial empire. "Their Trade is no way managed to the Advantage of His Majesties Crown," the Privy Council reported in 1661; "the Government of New-England (both Civil and Ecclesiastical) doth so differ from that of His Majesties other Dominions, that 'tis hard to say what may be the consequence of it," wrote Sir William Petty in 1676.[2] In 1671 John Evelyn, a member of the Council of Trade and Foreign Plantations, recorded notes on a frank discussion within that council on the state of New England. The councillors believed that Massachusetts had grown "very independent as to their regard to Old England, or his Majesty, rich and strong as they now were." "There was fear of their breaking from all dependence on this nation," he recorded, ". . . Some of our Council were for sending them a menacing letter, which those who better understood the peevish and touchy humour of that Colony, were utterly against. . . . We understood they were a people almost upon the very brink of renouncing any dependence on the Crown." The council even inquired into whether the people of Massachusetts "were of such power, as to be able to resist his Majesty and declare for themselves as independent of the Crown, which we were told, and which of late years made them refractory."[3]

The Puritan character was famously conservative in its reverence for authority, submission, and hierarchy; on the other hand, the Puritan character was also intensely jealous of constitutional rights, privileges, and liberties, resolute on self-defense against perceived arbitrary or unlawful rule.[4] But from the empire's viewpoint, Massachusetts colonists surrendered their privileges (subject to the king's prerogative anyhow) by routinely sabotaging the Navigation Acts while acting unapologetically as a quasi-independent state. Their subversion was all the more irritating in light of the colony's growing prosperity, which many English officials attributed (not unfairly) to the colonists' free pursuit of illicit, overseas commerce. Boston was "a Magazine both of all American and European Commodityes," the Lords of Trade reported in 1675, leaving the navigation in England "unspeakeably prejudiced" and robbing the king of "an immense sum of Money yearly in his Customes."[5]

Political drama at home in England substantiated the Crown's general suspicion of representative assemblies. In Parliament, a new Country faction of independent MPs had lately introduced a slew of anti-Catholic bills aimed clearly at James, Duke of York, the king's younger brother and heir to the throne who had recently revealed himself a Roman Catholic. Charles prorogued Parliament for fifteen months between November 1675 and February 1677, but his need for money—despite secret subsidies from Louis XIV—compelled Charles to summon parliament again. (All the while, reports streamed into Whitehall of extensive colonial smuggling, which diminished the customs revenue.) The late 1670s were an extremely tumultuous time in English politics, including accusations of a popish conspiracy, impeachment proceedings against leading court figures (including Lord Danby), and a new general election in January 1679, followed by a Habeas Corpus Act and a bill to exclude all Catholics from the throne. Charles dissolved Parliament again in July 1679, but the new election brought in even more Country members, followed by another Exclusion Bill that passed the Commons at the end of 1680, stopped only by the House of Lords. Charles dissolved Parliament again in January 1681, followed by new elections; the new Parliament in March introduced another Exclusion Bill before the king dissolved the body a week later. From that point forward—April 1681 to his death in February 1685—Charles managed to rule without any Parliament, relying instead on the French king for renewed subsidies.[6]

Colonial assemblies would not fare well in such a hostile environment. James, Duke of York, thus warned the governor of New York, Edmund Andros, in 1676, not to allow any representative assembly to convene in New York, a colony that had never had a representative assembly. A New York assembly, James said, "would be of dangerous consequence," for it was common knowledge that parliaments "assume to themselves many priviledges which prove destructive."[7] Experience elsewhere in the colonies corroborated this view; all one had to do was look at the recent history of the Virginia House of Burgesses, the Jamaica planter-assembly, and the Massachusetts General Court. It was in this latter colony that the Lords of Trade conducted their boldest campaign. An eager upstart named Edward Randolph led the charge.

Edward Randolph was born in 1632 to an affluent family in the English county of Kent, the son of a physician and the cousin of Robert Mason (proprietor of New Hampshire and decided enemy of Massachusetts). In early 1676, as the final months of King Philip's War ravaged New England, the Lords of Trade commissioned Randolph to deliver a letter from the king to the Massachusetts General Court demanding that agents be sent to London at once for questioning. Randolph, during his stay, was also to investigate and report on the colony's social life, politics, unlawful expansion into northern New England (Maine and New Hampshire), and overseas trading habits.[8]

Randolph arrived in Boston in June 1676, inaugurating one of the most controversial careers of any imperial official in American history. From the beginning, Randolph conducted himself in a way that many of the colony's leaders considered altogether repugnant. His persona was one of pretension and hubris; his opponents in Boston viewed him as little more than a sycophantic busybody, stirring up trouble and meddling noxiously into affairs not his own. The Massachusetts council dismissed Randolph with firmness and haste upon receiving the king's letter; this time, however—in contrast to the answer given to the royal commission eleven years prior—the council sent the two requested agents to London.[9]

For the next several weeks, Randolph journeyed throughout the colony to gain a general sense of the social and economic landscape. To his delight, he found a moderate merchant minority within the colony longing to wrest political control from the parochial Puritan government and quite eager to establish closer ties to cosmopolitan London. Such men tended to occupy the upper echelon of Boston's trading community and chiefly belonged to the younger generation. If they participated in smuggling—and many of them did—they might be willing to forgo it in the future if it meant better access to political power in Boston and greater imperial connections abroad. The colony's dogged independence imperiled profitable relations with England, as well as the social distinction that accompanied it. For these moderates, freedom of trade might be a reasonable (though reluctant) sacrifice if it meant gaining the benefits of imperial membership.[10] Several merchants of high standing belonged to this minority; nevertheless, they were a decided minority. Most of the Massachusetts electorate, including the majority of government officials, cherished the colony's independence to the absolute utmost. This majority included John Leverett, the popularly elected governor (and former captain under Oliver Cromwell). When Randolph confronted Governor Leverett about the recent arrival of five vessels from France and the Canary Islands, with wine and brandy onboard, Leverett (according to Randolph) replied "that the Laws made by Our King and Parliament obligeth them in nothing but what consists with the Interest of New England."[11]

On returning to London in October 1676, Randolph submitted a lengthy, confidential report to the Lords of Trade. On nearly every page, Randolph portrayed Massachusetts in a negative light, continually attacking the colony's "pretended charter." Hyperbolic claims littered the text; historians, consequently, must handle his account with care. One of Randolph's greatest distortions was his depiction of a populace anxiously awaiting royal government, falsely insinuating that this minority opinion prevailed throughout most of New England. Nevertheless, great kernels of truth pervaded much of Randolph's report, and in any event, the Lords of Trade certainly accepted the account as trustworthy enough to inform their next steps in New England.[12]

The Massachusetts mint was one of the first subjects discussed in Randolph's report, and for good reason. The coin's stamp, he argued, was the most prominent symbol for all that was wrong with the colony. "As a marke of soveraignty they coin money," he told them, "stamped with inscription Massachusets and a tree in the center, on the one side, and New England, with the year 1652 and the value of the piece on the reverse." The stamp 1652 was a bit of a mystery. Since the opening of the mint—even a quarter-century later—the date on the back of newly minted coins was 1652. Ever keen to accuse the colony, Randolph happily explained its meaning. "All the money is stamped with these figures, 1652," he said, "the year being the aera of the commonwealth, wherin they erected themselves into a free state . . . which year is still commemorated on their coin."[13]

Quite the charge, but was it true? No doubt many Massachusetts colonists looked back on the 1650s as a time of greater political autonomy than the present. Neither the Massachusetts governor nor the mint's officers bothered explaining the 1652 date, and so Randolph's explanation is compelling. Five years earlier, in 1671, the Council for Foreign Plantations offered a slightly different explanation: "they still continue to coine money there," the council said, "but putt the date of 1652 on the stamp of it, that they might not seeme to trespass on his Majesties Prerogative."[14] In other words, the Boston mint master, John Hull, may simply have used the inscription to render the coinage less treasonous than otherwise. The year 1652 was still eight years distant from the crowning of Charles II, with no regal prerogative to violate; a 1676 stamp would have constituted a more flagrant assault on this ancient monarchical right.

The meaning behind the 1652 inscription—and the colony's reasons for retaining it two decades later—might have also comprised heavy spiritual components, though Randolph did not consider this possibility. Throughout the 1660s and 1670s, a narrative of provincial decline pervaded Massachusetts sermons and literature, known as the jeremiads. Reverend Increase Mather and other ministers inveighed powerfully against the perceived moral decay of New England's second and third generations. The original Winthropian vision in the 1630s had centered on the modeling and spread of Reformed theocratic government from Massachusetts to England and beyond. This vision collapsed in the 1640s and 1650s, as Cromwell and his followers chose a different path. Nevertheless, at least public morality remained strong in Massachusetts in the 1650s. The first generation of Massachusetts settlers still dominated provincial affairs in 1652, and Winthrop himself had been governor as recently as three years before. Jump forward a quarter-century, however, and one found a shockingly different story. By 1676, New England, as the ministers saw it, was virtually unrecognizable. Greed, covetousness, Sabbath-breaking, fornication, apostasy, vanity, conceit, and a devastating Indian war all plagued the colony: "New-Englands Calamity," Mather called it—"the strange degeneracy that is in the spirit of the present Generation."[15] Like Israel, New England had forsaken her original mission and turned headlong to worldly pursuits. Babylonian captivity was near; the hour was late, though the money bore the date 1652.

It was odd, perhaps, to use money a means to hearken back to a more spiritual era; money, no doubt, had been a corrupting force. Yet it surely did not escape the ministers' purview that money stamped with such a year might indeed serve a useful social purpose. Randolph had not stayed in the colony long enough to realize it, but the Bay shilling stamp, wittingly or not, reminded money-holders that a greater spiritual errand had once prevailed in Massachusetts Bay, a colony now under mounting imperial pressure. Merchants were the ones who most frequently handled money, and they, more than any other class in New England, required this reminder. Indeed the mint master, John Hull belonged to both groups: a wealthy merchant and treasurer of the colony, he was also a pious man and devoted church member. In targeting the mint, Randolph was tackling a very sensitive subject—an institution for which many Bay colonists had a remarkably deep affinity. Randolph was not the first imperial officer to denounce the Boston mint; the royal commissioners in 1665 had also demanded that the "mint house . . . be repealed, for coyning is a royall prerogative."[16] The same month that Randolph departed England for Boston, his cousin Robert Mason—proprietor of New Hampshire with a personal vendetta against Massachusetts for encroaching on the northern parts of New England—petitioned the king on the Bay colony's practice of "coining money with their own impress, raising the coin of England, and acting in all matters in a most absolute and arbitrary way." Sir Joseph Williamson, secretary of state, remarked in 1675 that the Boston mint masters "melt down all English mony brought in there, into their owne coyne." In like manner, the Lords of Trade, in December 1675, recorded that "so soon as any English money is brought thither . . . it is immediately melted down."[17] This charge of melting down English money was owing to the lighter silver content in the Bay shilling. 12d of English money made 15d of Boston money, thus incentivizing—supposedly—English merchants to export silver money to Boston for conversion. (Note that this charge came at precisely the time that England suffered a shortage of good silver money.) Now, with Randolph's report, the mint with its pine-tree shilling was further confirmed, in the eyes of the Crown, as a rebellious, treasonous institution—the most visible, tangible symbol of Massachusetts sovereignty.

Free trade, in spite of the Navigation Acts, was sovereignty in action. It implied a total rejection of England's authority to regulate the colony's economic affairs. "No law is in force or esteeme there but such as are made by the generall court," remarked Randolph in his 1676 report; "it is accounted a breach of their privileges and a betraying of the liberties of their commonwealth to urge the observation of the lawes of England." Boston merchants, he wrote, distributed illegally obtained European goods to other colonies at prices "much cheaper than such who pay the customes and are laden in England, leaving little left for the merchants residing in England to import into any of the plantations." "This kingdome hath lost the best part of the western trade," he warned, ". . . Boston may be esteemed the mart town of the West-Indies."[18]

The Bay colonists had therefore become spectacularly wealthy, he said, producing "rich men of all callings and professions"; the merchants in particular enjoyed "considerable estates and very great trades." "There is a reasonable quantitie of silver money in the colony, but no gold," he observed (again, at a time in which England suffered a languishing silver currency). A great deal of this Boston silver belonged properly to England and *would* belong to England if only the imperial government would take the requisite steps to secure it. "That government would make the world believe they are a free state," he continued, ". . . all nations having free liberty to come into their ports and vend their commodities, without any restrain." Randolph, in concluding the report, urged the king to annul the Massachusetts charter and establish a "general government" over all of New England, under "his Majesties authority."[19]

Randolph excitedly awaited a response from the Lords of Trade. But as the months rolled on, he sullenly found the committee preoccupied with crises afflicting the two predominant staple plantations: Virginia, where Bacon's Rebellion had recently erupted, and Jamaica, where political dissension between the governor and assembly had reached a boiling point. Even the most egregious trade offenses in New England seemed paltry by comparison. Restless, Randolph submitted a second report to the committee seven months later, charging the colony with having "formed themselves into a Common Wealth." Even more abrasively, he contended that the colony's governor and assembly "have noe right either to Land or Government in any part of New England and have allwayes been Usurpers." "They Coine money with their owne impress . . . They violate all the Acts of Trade and navigation, by which they have ingrossed the greatest part of the West India Trade." Boston smuggling, he now estimated with wanton embellishment, damaged the customs revenue "above £100,000 yearely and this Kingdome much more."[20]

With this second report, the Lords of Trade, in July 1677, finally launched a formal investigation. Out of twenty-four alleged "crimes and assumed powers not granted in their Charter," the *first* crime listed by the committee was the Boston mint. "They have erected a publick Mint in Boston and Coined money with their own Impress," the committee charged: the symbolic capstone to the ensuing twenty-three grievances, including the refusal to take oaths of allegiance and supremacy to King Charles II, and having "declared themselves a Common Wealth."[21]

The Massachusetts agents, having only recently arrived in London, faced an onslaught of merciless questioning. Regarding the Boston mint, the Lords of Trade asked "whether Treason be not herein Committed," and if so, whether this alone was enough to have the "Corporation dissolved and Charter forfeited?"[22] The two agents, William Stoughton and Peter Bulkeley, replied by insisting that the singular purpose of the mint was economic, not political; the mint was a benign project designed simply to support commercial activity. Their response was not entirely disingenuous: Stoughton was one of Boston's wealthiest merchants, and Bulkeley—though speaker of the House of Deputies (the lower house of the General Court)—was also a merchant of more moderate political leanings. Regarding the mint, they told the Lords of Trade that the colony was "necessitated to it, about the yeare 1652, for the support of their Trade, and have not, hitherto, discontinued it, as being never excepted against, or disallowed by His Majesty." This latter point was entirely false— perhaps unknowingly—because the 1665 commission had explicitly demanded the mint's repeal. Nevertheless, the two agents "beg pardon if they have offended." On the question of illegal trade, they conceded some smuggling in the colony but attributed this to a mere misunderstanding among its participants. "There are perhaps some private persons who trade indirectly," they said, "by reason they have not understood those Acts"; notwithstanding, the damage to the customs "is very inconsiderable in comparison of what is reported." In the future, they promised, the government would "readily apply themselves" to enforcing the Navigation Acts, and would promptly administer the required oaths of supremacy and allegiance to England.[23]

After several days of review, the Lord of Trade delivered their verdict, insisting on the absolute "necessity of bringing those People under a more palpable declaration of their obedience." Of the more egregious offenses, the colony "had transgress'd in presuming to Coyne Money, which is an Act of Sovereignty, and to which they were by noe Grant sufficiently authorized." Nonetheless, the committee recommended that the king compromise on the matter of the mint. The General Court must simply "sollicit His Majesties Pardon for the offence that is past," and "upon due application," the king might graciously allow the colony to continue the mint under *his* authority, thus maintaining the regal prerogative and completely eviscerating the coin's political attributes. The Navigation Acts, moreover, must be "religiously observed." If the colonists obeyed these and sundry other instructions, "His Majestie will not destroy their Charter, but rather by a Supplemental one to bee given them, set all things right that are now amiss."[24]

The judgment of the Lords of Trade was surprisingly moderate, and their position on the mint embodied this restraint. Imperial sanction of the Boston coinage, coupled with an apology and revised stamp—likely bearing Charles's visage—would enhance royal authority, not diminish it, while also avoiding much of the resentment (especially from commercial men) that would no doubt arise from outright abolishing the mint. The economic expediency of a distinctive Boston currency would no longer contradict the empire's larger political agenda but rather complement it. The coin would mutate from a symbol of colonial independence to one of imperial strength, power, and centralization. Relieved, the agents gladly agreed to "humbly Implore his Majesty's gratious Pardon" for the "extreamely usefull" mint, so the coinage "may be continued to them under what Impress He pleases."[25]

Had the plan gone through, it would not have been the first instance of an empire using a colonial coinage to buttress imperial authority. Seven years earlier, in 1670, King Louis XIV instructed the Paris mint to issue a series of coins for the colony of New France. Louis had recently rejected a request to allow a Montreal mint, but a colonial coinage minted in Paris suited the king just fine. The stamp was all the difference, displaying, as it did, the splendor, majesty, and sovereignty of the emerging French empire: on the obverse of the coin, the laureated bust of Louis XIV, the sun beaming above his glorified image; on the reverse, the French coat of arms, topped with a crown, encircled by the Latin phrase *GLORIAM REGNI TUI DICENT*—"They shall speak of the glory of thy kingdom" (figure 8). Perhaps the Lords of Trade had some-

FIGURE 8.   Silver fifteen-sols coin of New France, 1670. (Courtesy of Gord Carter, National Currency Collection, Bank of Canada Museum.)

thing similar in mind for the Boston mint. Whatever they intended, it was certainly not a pine tree.[26]

Had the Massachusetts General Court followed the agents' advice and apologized for the mint, the entire character of the coinage would have irrecoverably changed. The General Court thus rejected the offer, audaciously assuring the two agents upon their return that the Lords of Trade had simply misunderstood the issue of the coinage and mint. Once the king was truly "informed of the symplicity of our actings, the publicke joy thereof to his subjects here, and the great damage that the stoppage [of the mint] will inevitably be to our necessary commerce . . . his majestye will not account those to be friends to his crowne that shall seeke to interrupt us therein." The stamp was paramount, the General Court explained to the two agents. "And for the impress put upon it, wee shall take it as his majesties signall ouning us, if he will please to order such an impresse as shall be to him most acceptable."[27]

The mint controversy was a battle over symbols of two competing visions of empire. The battle was waged not only between England and Massachusetts but also within Massachusetts itself. The Lords of Trade recognized, correctly, that for royal authority to properly assert itself in Massachusetts Bay, the symbolic power of the Boston mint had to be turned on its head. The independent faction on the General Court opposed compromise for this very reason, exposing the mint for the political institution it truly was. From the perspective of the moderate faction, however, such intractability represented the height of absurdity, risking the existence of an economically useful mint on the basis of a mere stamp and simple apology.

Word of the Lords of Trade's judgment arrived in Boston late in 1677. Most Bay colonists greeted the news that "His Majestie will not destroy their Charter" with extreme delight and relief; the government even proclaimed an official day of thanksgiving.[28] Rumors had circulated that the Lords of Trade might abrogate the charter altogether; instead, it appeared that the committee had implicitly acknowledged the charter's legitimacy. With fear of a royal takeover now passed, the General Court went on its way and ignored virtually all of the demands made by the committee, expecting English officials to acquiesce as they had in 1665. Trade was the only issue on which the General Court partly relented, yet even here, the assembly (cleverly) managed to assert its own sovereignty by passing a colonial statute almost identical to the Navigation Acts, thus implying that laws of Parliament were valid only by the sovereign will of the colonial legislature.[29] Of course, trade continued on its ordinary course as though nothing had happened, even with the new Massachusetts law. Merchants traded freely, the mint continued onward without any apology, and government officials refrained from taking the required oaths of allegiance and supremacy to England and the king.[30]

Things appeared to return to normal, until months later, early in 1678, the General Court made a massive blunder. Upon receiving, for the first time, a leaked copy of Randolph's once-confidential report of 1676, the incensed assembly ordered that Stoughton and Bulkeley prepare a belated rebuttal, disproving the "several falshoods." To the shock of the General Court, however, when Stoughton and Bulkeley told the Lords of Trade that they possessed a copy of the report, the committee was indignant, demanding an explanation for the leak.[31] Randolph, still in London, happily pounced on this new opportunity, pointing out that the Massachusetts government had heretofore ignored virtually all of the committee's very moderate demands from the previous summer, having neither taken the necessary oaths nor "suspended the worke of their minte." Moreover, he continued, by passing a law nearly identical to the Navigation Acts, the assembly "doe encourage" the people "to beleive that noe Acts of Parliament . . . are in force with them until such a tyme as their Governors in General Court doe enact and order them soe to bee."[32]

Facing this renewed tide of criticism, the two agents desperately defended the colony, claiming Randolph's 1676 report to be full of "great mistakes & invidious misrepresentations." "Mr. Randolphs stay in New England was so short," they argued, that he could not have possibly portrayed the country accurately. Randolph, for instance, had claimed that at least thirty merchants held estates of £10–20,000; the agents rejoined that there were no more than a dozen whose estates exceeded even £5,000. "He speakes of only at randome," they urged, and "made it his businesse wherever he came, to disaffect the people as much as he could."[33]

The rebuttal proved entirely ineffective. Infuriated with the colony's determined incompliance, the Lords of Trade appointed Randolph collector, surveyor, and searcher of the customs for all of New England—the first imperial officer to serve full-time in the region. Stoughton and Bulkeley begged the committee to grant them "liberty to recommend a person," calling Randolph "a person extreamly obnoxious" who had "notoriously trespassed upon truth," "not likely to continue unbiassed." But the committee would hear none of it, and in September 1679, after some delay, Randolph sailed again for Massachusetts.[34]

After stopping first in New York and New Hampshire, Randolph arrived in Boston in January 1680, to a predictably hostile reception. A popular poem at once circulated across town, sardonically welcoming the "wicked" Randolph back to the Bay Colony. "Welcome now back againe," the poet proclaimed; "as is the whip, to a fooles back; as water in a ship. . . . If you doe understand your occupation, 'Tis to keepe acts of trade from violation." "I am received at Boston more like a spy, than one of his majesty's servants," Randolph wrote shortly after arrival, ". . . [they] have prepared a welcome for me, by a paper of scandalous verses, all persons taking liberty to abuse me in their discourses."[35]

Never one to back down, Randolph hurriedly went to work prosecuting purported smugglers, courageously boarding suspicious vessels in the face of violent threats and harassment. All the while, the ever-visible pine-tree shilling persistently badgered him. "The Government of Boston continue still to Coine money," he noted days after arrival, the city's "Merchants trading as freely as formerly."[36] Local jurists acquitted each of the thirty-four captains and merchants whom Randolph prosecuted for smuggling; worse, the colonial magistrates charged Randolph court fees as high as £10 a case, amounting to £257 in just two years, all without a single conviction.[37] Apologists for the colony later insisted that "upon the Tryall," Randolph's "proofs were so very defective, that the Juries would not find for His Majestie."[38] This explanation might have been true for a handful of cases, but the majority of the accused were most likely guilty. Several magistrates in the colony denied altogether that English law applied in the Massachusetts courtroom, a position shared by Deputy Governor Thomas Danforth, leader of the independent faction.[39]

Members of this independent faction, at best, believed that they owed only a minimal, circumscribed allegiance to king and parliament, and the sincerity of even this conviction was questionable. Though members of the General Court hastily, and for the first time, took the oath of allegiance in October 1678, that *very day* they also affirmed—on public record—that "the lawes of England are bounded within the fower seas, and doe not reach Amerrica." "Being not represented in Parliament," the assembly reasoned, "wee have not looked at ourselves to be impeded in our trade by them."[40] The statement mirrored a like declaration during the 1665 visit of the royal commission, when the assembly "proclaymed by sound of Trumpet that the Generall Court was the Supreamest Judicatory in that Province." One colonial magistrate in 1681 even openly declared that "His Majestye [has] nothing to doe here, for wee are a free people of our selves."[41] With this context, Randolph's near-fanatical hostility toward the Massachusetts mint makes a lot more sense. The colonists' abhorrence for the idea of placing the royal stamp on the Boston coinage had demonstrated unequivocally their commitment to a radically decentralized vision of their place within the empire.

Drastic reform was obviously looming. "There is an absolute necessity of Erecting a Great Councill" and "Generall Governor," Randolph ominously wrote the governor of New York, Sir Edmund Andros, in January 1680; "it is in every man's mouth that they are not Subject to the Laws of England." The Lords of Trade were also rapidly losing all patience. "They yet continue to carry on their Mint," the committee reported in September 1680, ". . . continuing their irregular Trade to the great prejudice of your Majesties Revenue" and taking "not the least notice" of royal instructions.[42] Delighted at this turn of events, Randolph (still in Boston) petitioned King Charles in April 1681 that the colony's "unparralell'd misdemeanors & contempts" amounted to "no lesse than High Treason." "United under one generall Government," he urged the committee again, New England "will be more serviceable to the Crown." Such a move, he argued, would instill proper "dependance and Submission," finally eviscerating the colonists' "Liberty in Trade." The mint alone, he reasoned, constituted a "great crime & misdemeanor," one of several offenses "sufficient to void their Charter ."[43]

One can only imagine the look of extreme aggravation on Randolph's face when he inevitably encountered "New England coyne" in day-to-day trade. Randolph was not the only imperial appointee in America disgusted with the matter. The new governor of Virginia, Thomas Lord Culpeper, wrote the Lords of Trade in 1681 that "as to the Mint erected at Boston . . . it is extreamly prejudicial to all his Majesty's Subjects, in all other places whatsoever that deale with them." The higher valuation that silver received at the Boston mint, he said—compared with the rate of foreign silver in Virginia—drew coin away from the Chesapeake, discouraging the colony's economic advancement.[44] Following this complaint from Virginia, the Lords of Trade, in October 1681, again berated the Massachusetts General Court for the "great crime you are answerable for in coyning money" and for the "fresh complaints" of smuggling. "You presume to continue your Mint without regard to the penalties thereby incurred," they warned, threatening, finally, to revoke the charter if instructions remained unheeded.[45]

The Crown's incessant demands of Massachusetts beg the question why the General Court had so many opportunities to compromise. Why was the mint still in operation as late as 1682? For one, the king at this time faced a torrent of internal political crises in England—perils of almost infinitely greater importance, namely the Popish Plot and Exclusion Crisis of 1679–1681. The New England question was a subject on which the Crown could afford at least some patience. Even within the colonial sphere, Jamaica and Virginia appeared more worthy of the Crown's immediate attention. Randolph profoundly disagreed, but most mercantilists deemed Jamaica and Virginia more critical than Massachusetts to England's finances and money supply. Once these other crises finally simmered down—and they mostly had by 1682—the Crown could spare more attention for New England.

Sensing a change in momentum, the moderate faction in Massachusetts, led by Governor Simon Bradstreet, desperately urged the independent members of the General Court to cooperate with the Crown, else the charter be forfeited. Moderates included merchants like Richard Wharton who already possessed considerable wealth, with much more to gain from closer ties with England than they had to lose by stricter enforcement of the Navigation Acts. Even Fitz and Wait Winthrop, grandsons of John Winthrop, Sr., were counted among the moderate group.[46] But the independent faction still controlled the judicial system and lower house of the General Court; in 1681 the General Court even reverted Governor Bradstreet's salary back to country pay to rebuke his relative moderation. The previous governor, John Leverett, had taken a much firmer stand against Randolph, but Leverett died in 1679, shifting the center of resistance from the governor to the General Court. "The factious party are against the Governor," Randolph reported, "and have ordered his salary to be payd in Indian Corn at 3s6d per Bushell, which is above the market" price per bushel (a not-so-subtle way of reducing his actual salary).[47]

Finally, in February 1682 the moderate faction on the General Court persuaded the independents to authorize the two agents, Stoughton and Bulkeley, to "begg pardon for the fault of coining" and to humbly vouch that the "Acts of Trade shall be duly observed." The apology for the mint went as follows: "We took up stamping of silver meerely upon necessitie, to prevent cheats by false peeces of eight. . . . If that be a Trespasse upon His Majesties Royal Prerogative, of which wee are Ignorant, wee Humbly beg His Majesties pardon and Gratious Allowance therein, It being so exceeding necessary for our Civil Commerce, and no way, as wee humbly Conceive, detrimentall to His Royal Majestie."[48]

Four months later, in June 1682, John Hull's contract as Boston mint master expired, after which there was no talk of renewal. Hull died the following year. Whether or not the mint shut down immediately after June 1682 is not known. Just one week after the contract expired, Randolph reported that the Boston government was currently "engageing the whole plantation in the matter of their mint." What precisely he meant by this statement is difficult to say. There might have been popular calls to defiantly renew the mint. Nevertheless, in June 1686, Joseph Dudley—council president of the Dominion of New England—remarked that the mint "hath long time discontinued," and so the coinage likely died with Hull.[49] A contract renewal after 1682 would have constituted too gross a violation of royal instructions, at too dangerous a time for the colony's charter. The sheer fact that the Boston mint lasted thirty years—an entire generation—was remarkable in itself.

Following a protracted series of tense exchanges between the Lords of Trade, the General Court, and Massachusetts agents, the Lords of Trade finally recommended a writ against the charter in June 1683. Randolph had recently submitted seventeen "articles of high misdemeanour" against the colony, and in the draft version, the now defunct mint made up the first article of complaint, followed by familiar charges of smuggling and political subversion. "We in Boston are threatened with a Condemnation of our Charter and consequently the Loss of all our Priviledges," deplored the independent reverend Increase Mather, including the "necessity of Coyning money with a peculiar stampe of our owne."[50]

Remarkably, despite the recommended writ, the General Court had still *another* chance to compromise after June 1683. The following month, King Charles II stipulated that the charter might indeed survive if the Crown revised its specific articles. If not, the king's attorney general would take the colony to trial, upon which the charter would almost certainly be found null and void.

Violent debate erupted in the General Court on whether the body should agree to a charter revision, with the moderate faction angrily urging that it was sheer madness to continue resisting the imperial impulse for centralization. The independent party won out, and in December 1683 the lower house voted against Charles's offer, vowing to fight the king in his own court. The effort was unsuccessful—the Massachusetts attorney even failed to arrive on time for trial—and on October 23, 1684, the Crown dissolved the Massachusetts charter.[51]

Even before Bacon's Rebellion in 1676, conditions in Virginia deeply perturbed numerous authorities in England. Hostility toward the Navigation Acts was so great in Virginia that during the Third Anglo-Dutch War (1672–1674), some

English officials feared that Virginia colonists might defect to the Hollanders. One English merchant who traded with the colony begged the Council of Trade and Foreign Plantations in October 1673 to oversee the construction of a string of fortifications along the Virginia coast, so that "the planters may thereby be secured from revolting to the Dutch, as it is much to be feared they will." "It is said that the planters there doe generally desire a trade with the Dutch and all other nations," he reported, so as to "not be singly bound to the trade of England." The planters in particular resented the new Navigation Act of 1673, which placed duties on the intercolonial sale of tobacco and installed a resident customs officer to enforce collection. The planters "speake openly there that they are in the nature of slaves," the merchant continued, "soe that the hearts of the greatest part of them are taken away from his Majesty." "Consequently his Majesties best, greatest and richest plantation is in danger with the planters consent to fall into the Enemies hands," he warned.[52]

Of particular controversy among the planters was the colony's gradual conversion from a Crown possession into a private proprietorship. The move alarmed virtually all colonists in Virginia, and for good reason. In 1669 Charles granted the northernmost peninsula of the colony—the so-called Northern Neck, bounded by the Potomac and Rappahannock Rivers—to a group of royal favorites, allowing them rights to divide the land, levy fines, and collect quitrents. The quitrent was a fee of 1s for every fifty acres of settled land, paid by the farmer or settler. Four years later, in February 1673, Charles—seeking to settle a long-standing debt—granted a patent to two other favorites for all land south of the Rappahannock River. The patent awarded Henry Bennet, Earl of Arlington, and Thomas Lord Culpeper the right to nominate all ministers, sheriffs, and other regional officers in the land for a period of thirty-one years. Worse still, Arlington and Culpeper had rights to collect quitrents on the land, again for a period of thirty-one years. Previously reserved for the king—who claimed ultimate ownership of all the soil—quitrent revenues were now being allocated to private noblemen in England.[53]

At first glance, the Arlington-Culpeper patent in 1673 appeared to violate the Crown's centralizing agenda. A closer look, however, shows the opposite. The two recipients were of unquestioned loyalty to Charles. Arlington was a privy councillor and one of the most active, regular members of the Council for Foreign Plantations (1670–1672). More important, from 1662 to 1674, Arlington was secretary of state for the Southern Department, which possessed supreme jurisdiction over colonial America. Culpeper, for his part, served as vice president of the Council of Trade and Foreign Plantations from 1672 to 1674. Viewed from this angle, the patent, though technically private, was nothing short of an imperial power grab.

The Arlington-Culpeper patent sent shock waves through Virginia. Pan-icked, the House of Burgesses instructed its agents in London to petition the Crown for a new charter that would more explicitly guarantee certain long-held rights. In November 1675 the colony's agents requested the Crown for such a charter. First, they entreated that "no tax or imposition" should be levied except but "by the grand assembly"; indeed, the Crown must explicitly recognize in the proposed charter "the authority of the grand assembly." Representative government, they said, had given the colony a "government more easy to the people, and more advantageous to the crown"; indeed, among the people, they claimed (again, in November 1675), there had "not been one law complained of as burthensome." In short, the continuation of representative government was "absolutely necessary for the peace and quiet of that country."[54]

More audaciously, the Virginia agents endorsed the concept of political equality within the empire and insisted that the principle be included in a new charter. Colonists, they reasoned in the petition, "ought to enjoy by law, in such plantation, the same liberties and privileges as Englishmen in England." The colonists still desired "perpetual immediate dependence"; this desire, the agents said, set the Virginians apart from the "example of New-England," where the people "endeavored as much as they could to sever themselves from the crown." But as "natural born subjects of England"—which, as colonists, "they ought by law to be"—the Virginia agents appealed for more explicit as-surances of the colonists' most basic political liberties. Such assurances, the agents promised, would make the colonists more cooperative to imperial in-terests and even toward the Navigation Acts.[55]

To some surprise, the agents persuaded the Lords of Trade to draft a new charter for Virginia in the winter of 1675–1676. The draft was impressive. It explained that Virginians would remain dependent on the king only, not on distant proprietors. More important, the draft stated that "no Impositions or Taxes shall be laid or imposed . . . but by the Comon Consent of the Gover-nour, Council and Burgesses."[56] Pragmatism thus won the day; despite their known enmity toward representative government, the Lords of Trade knew that an overbearing imperial program in Virginia might backfire, even to the point of driving the colonists to a foreign power like the Dutch. The Naviga-tion Acts had already antagonized the planters, suffering as they were from low tobacco prices; the Arlington-Culpeper patent only intensified this anxi-ety and anger. It was in the Crown's best interest for such a valuable colony to remain content and affectionate. A liberal charter, in other words, might se-cure obedience more effectively than a coercive route.

Despite this seeming victory, however, negotiations on the new charter mys-teriously stalled early in 1676. The interruption confounded the agents. "We can by no means find the cause," they petitioned; "we know not the reasons."[57] In April Charles finally directed that he would approve the new charter. But before doing so, Charles received a sudden petition in England from the mother of Giles Bland. Bland was the resident customs collector in Virginia, installed under the Navigation Act of 1673 (his father was also a prominent merchant in London, with estates and trading connections in Virginia). Giles's mother complained of the "unexampled severity" that her son had received from the governor, council, and burgesses, who proceeded "arbitrarily, violently & injuriously" against him on several occasions. Charles referred the petition to the Lords of Trade to investigate.[58] New suspicion arose that the draft charter's clause on taxation and representation might give Virginians cause to ignore the Plantation Duty Act of 1673 (in spite of the fact that the charter explicitly confirmed parliament's authority to levy taxes on "Comodities or Merchandizes which come from Virginia").[59] Stunned, the colony's agents replied that "the objection is too weak to stand," but to no effect: on 31 May, Charles killed the anticipated charter.[60]

In the weeks after, incoming reports of Bacon's Rebellion affirmed the wisdom of the Crown's recent decision. In response to incoming word of this rebellion, the colony's agents desperately insisted that Virginians were "eminently Loyall to the crowne" and that Bacon's actions had nothing at all to do with "any disaffection to your Majestie or your Government either here or there." Rather, the poorest in the colony were simply "misledd." This problem could be fixed very easily, the agents said, by resurrecting the liberal charter: "the most effectuall [way] to reduce that collony to a lasting obedience." The "better sort of people" in the colony, the agents argued, simply desired a firmer guarantee of their "just priveledges," and it was those people, most of all, "in whom lies the only security of the country."[61]

The agents' spurious narrative on the causes of Bacon's Rebellion collapsed upon further investigation. Farmers rebelled because of the oppressive government in Jamestown, not out of concern about overweening power from London. As Giles Bland correctly informed the Lords of Trade, the "greatest number" of people in Virginia had "soe little Reverence" for the House of Burgesses. (The Crown did not yet know it, but Bland soon joined the rebels and even led an armed expedition against Governor Berkeley.) "They complaine that great Taxes are Imposed upon them every yeare," Bland reported, a result of "the often meeting of the Assembly" and the extravagant salaries of its members. Moreover, as customs collector, "I have suffered many hardshipps and Discouragements" from the governor and burgesses, and unless the power of the assembly be reduced, the royal customs arising from tobacco "must of Necessarie Consequence cease or abate." The surest way to "Advance" the

Crown's revenue, Bland said, was to compel an immediate "Redresse of the great and heavy Burdens and taxes" levied by the Jamestown government; otherwise, the customs revenue will "bee much lessened," contributing to "the Ruine of the most beneficiall Plantation that belongs to his Majesties Crowne."[62]

By the end of summer 1676, the Lords of Trade concluded that an insolent colonial assembly had brought the empire's most profitable mainland colony to the brink of destruction. So much for the proposed liberal charter. As William Blathwayt, secretary of the Lords of Trade, wrote in 1679, "the Rebellion of Virginia was occasioned by the Excessive power of the Assembly." Berkeley himself admitted that the rebellion was "not against any particular Person but the whole Assembly."[63] A new charter was still necessary—the Crown increasingly wished to transition away from a quasi-proprietary model in any event—but the charter that resulted fell depressingly short of what the agents and burgesses had hoped.

In October 1676, King Charles affixed the Great Seal to a new Virginia charter. It ensured that colonials would "have their immediate dependance upon the crown of England," not on private proprietors. Crucially, however, the charter omitted any explicit confirmation of the authority of the House of Burgesses, including their claimed right to consent to taxation.[64] Furthermore, the king granted "grace and mercy" to all the rebels except for Bacon—a move designed to pacify the people—and then, for like reason, instructed that Berkeley "reduce the salary of the assembly" to a "moderate proportion," so that taxes (levied in tobacco money) will prove "noe grievance to the countrey." The House of Burgesses should be summoned "only once in two yeares," the king continued—not annually as before—sitting no more than fourteen days at a time.[65]

All told, Bacon's Rebellion incurred great expenses for the Crown. Besides the cost of sending one thousand English soldiers to Virginia, the customs revenue severely declined during the course of the conflict, contributing to Charles's reluctant summoning of Parliament in February 1677 (after fifteen months of prorogation) for new revenue.[66] "The ill news from Virginia and New England doth not only alarm us but extreamly abate the customs," a member of Parliament stated in December 1676, "so that notwithstanding all the shifts the Treasurer can make, this Parliament or another must sitt."[67]

News from Virginia did not get any better in the rebellion's aftermath. In spring 1677, the Crown's commissioners to Virginia reported that Berkeley and his "rapacious" supporters in the House of Burgesses ignored the king's pardon of Bacon's rebels and tried some of its leaders by court-martial (even hanging Giles Bland in March 1677), while resisting any effort to limit their salaries and the frequency of their meeting.[68] Berkeley finally and belatedly left his post as governor in May 1677, dying just two months later in England, but he left behind a loyal band in the House of Burgesses, led by a man named Robert Beverley. Beverley and the pro-Berkeley faction now pitched themselves as defenders of colonial liberty against royal encroachment. The new Crown-appointed governor, Thomas Lord Culpeper (no relation to the Carolina rebel, but the same man who held the much-hated land patent in Virginia), took his oath of office in London in July 1677 but failed to depart for the colony until more than two years later. In the interim, Culpeper left his job to a succession of four inept lieutenant governors.[69] The burgesses, in the meantime, persisted in levying heavy poll taxes on the population, leading one of the royal commissioners to tell Blathwayt that "the arrogancy of Virginia Assemblies" was the main factor precluding a lasting and profitable peace in the colony. "The great presumption" of the burgesses must be fully combated, the king's privy council reported in October 1678, "bringing said Assembly to a due sense and acknowledgment of their Duty and submission toward his Majesty."[70]

Governor Culpeper finally arrived in Virginia in May 1680, carrying instructions to impose Poyning's Law on the colony. Poyning's Law was an old act of Parliament, from 1494, for governing Ireland. That law had instructed that the Irish assembly could be summoned only with the king's permission, and even then could vote only on laws drafted by the king; lastly, it provided for a permanent revenue, thus eliminating the assembly's power of the purse. King Charles had tried to impose Poyning's Law on Jamaica the year before; now, he wished the same for Virginia—expecting, of course, the burgesses' "cheerfull and ready complyance," as he put it.[71] Impressively, Culpeper muscled the assembly into passing the permanent revenue bill: a two-shilling tax on every hogshead (five hundred pounds) of bulk tobacco exported from Virginia. But he failed to sway the burgesses to surrender their ability to initiate laws, and because the permanent revenue alone was insufficient to fund all public expenses, the House of Burgesses retained the power of the purse.[72]

A dispute over the value of silver coins inflamed the conflict even further. In July 1680 the House of Burgesses passed a bill prohibiting the export of all coin from the colony and then raised the price of Spanish dollars from 5s to 6s, an increase of 20 percent. Culpeper rejected the bill, insisting that the "best way of doing it is by address to his Majesty."[73] The Burgesses and Council thus petitioned the king to secure his approval; Culpeper, meanwhile, departed for England on personal business, leaving executive authority with a lieutenant governor. The Crown did not receive the burgesses' petition until July 1681. Five months afterward, Culpeper, in London, asked the Lords of Trade if he might "raise the price of Monyes" in the colony. The committee, in January

1682, agreed to his request, but on condition that it happen only by proclamation of the governor, so as to not give the House of Burgesses authority to
legislate on currency matters.[74]

Planters in Virginia were more desperate than ever to acquire a common
silver currency. Tobacco money—that "meene drugge," to quote Culpeper—
had depreciated so wretchedly in value that its farm price was now even lower
than it was on the eve of Bacon's Rebellion.[75] The colony's tobacco exports
had risen almost 50 percent between 1669 and 1681, from 15 million to more
than 22 million pounds. By this latter date, the leaf could not earn even a single penny a pound; this condition lasted until the mid-1680s, when the price
finally returned to a penny.[76] For this reason, when the burgesses petitioned
Charles in July 1680 to approve their raising the piece of eight, they also requested that the king order "a Totall Sessation from planting tobaccoes this
Next yeare" in Virginia, Maryland, and northern Carolina.[77] Many months
passed without word from the Crown, on either the piece of eight or the cessation of tobacco planting. Meanwhile, the economy was more deplorable
than ever. Rebellion, again, reared its head. In April and May 1682, bands of
armed plant-cutters stormed one plantation after another, cutting and pulling
up tobacco plants and destroying, in the end, some three million pounds of
tobacco, valued at more than £10,000.[78] Hearing of the new tobacco insur-
rection, Culpeper returned hastily to Virginia in December 1682, bearing the
Crown's new instructions on the piece of eight.

In January 1683 Culpeper issued a "Proclamation for the Raiseing the Price
of Forraign Coyne," to take effect in March. The proclamation advanced the
piece of eight from 5s to 6s; moreover, "the Coyne comonly called New England
money shall pass att one shilling." "The management of Trade and Comerce
is much impeded, for want of Coyne," the governor said; the proclamation
will "Encourage money to be brought into this Collony and afterwards kept
here."[79] The colony had finally secured a higher price for Spanish coin, or so
it seemed, but in September 1683, the Lords of Trade abruptly and inexplicably repealed the proclamation, instructing the governor to return the coin to
5s.[80] The committee's action seemed arbitrary, inexplicable, even bizarre;
as recently as January 1682, the Lords of Trade categorically permitted Culpeper to raise the dollar, but apparently no longer. Charles recalled Culpeper
to England in fall 1683; purchased back the remaining rights of the 1673 patent; and commissioned a new governor, Francis Lord Howard of Effingham,
in his stead.[81]

A devout Catholic with no personal stake in Virginia, Effingham was thoroughly hostile to representative institutions; his four-year administration
proved more overbearing to the House of Burgesses than even that of his pre-

decessor.[82] Prior to leaving England, Effingham persuaded the Lords of Trade to send a frigate of forty men and twelve guns to patrol the Chesapeake for smugglers, and upon his arrival in early 1684, the new governor made instant enemies among the planter elite.[83] Over his tenure, Effingham centralized most authority in the office of the governor, making no secret of his aristocratic disdain for even the slightest form of democratic governance. He insisted that any references "to the Publique" in forthcoming legislation be eliminated, replaced with language that specified that the statute was intended rather "for the benefit of his Majesties Dominion." "The Publique," he reasoned, was "a name certainely most odious under a Regal Government," and does "but little differ from that detestable one (Republick)."[84] Here was a man fully cut out for the imperial vision of the 1680s; he, with Sir Edmund Andros, epitomized the cavalier governor of the high Stuart period.

The House of Burgesses was ready for combat. In May 1684, three months after Effingham's arrival, the assembly drafted a petition to the king protesting the Crown's frequent use of the veto against Virginia laws, such as the one against a 6s piece of eight. The burgesses urged that the Crown refrain from repealing future statutes until the burgesses were given a chance to offer their "Grounds & Reasons for making those Lawes." Effingham, of course, was not amused; their petition was utterly "unfitt to be presented to his majestie," he said, and the proposal itself represented "soe great an entrenchment upon the royall authority that I canot but wonder you would offer at it." Effingham advised the burgesses to "better temper your selves"—to start acting like "dutifull Subjects." The burgesses sent the petition anyway—it was, they said, their "undoubted Right & priviledge"—but Charles never received it; the Lords of Trade determined not to present it to the king and commended Effingham for scolding the assembly.[85]

One reason for the Crown's upper hand against the burgesses was the late improvement of conditions (however modest) for less prosperous planters in Virginia. Tobacco prices, for one, moderately increased after the plant-cutting fiasco. After 1684 the wholesale price of Virginia leaf in London and Amsterdam markets recovered slightly from the lows of the early 1680s.[86] Second, the Crown wisely reformed the colony's tax code. For all his faults, Culpeper persuaded the Lords of Trade to compel the burgesses to enact "a juster manner of Taxe," overturning levies that had proven "high, unequal, and Burthensome to the people."[87] The Crown instructed Culpeper to secure "a more equal and easy way for levying money" and to "reduce the Salary of the Members of the Assembly to such a moderate proportion as may bee no grievance to the Countrey."[88] When Culpeper returned to Virginia late in 1682, he demanded that local officials give full account of all public expenditures, that taxes be

"Rightly Applyed and duely Administred," and that "nothing be Raised upon the Inhabitants but what is absolutely necessary."[89] Effingham continued this trend, ensuring the passage of a new law for "abateing and takeing off the greatness of the levies and taxes laid by the poll."[90] Imperious royal government apparently came with some benefits—in Virginia, for the frontier farmer; in puritanical Massachusetts, for the cosmopolitan merchant.

The Crown could not entirely suppress or eradicate the House of Burgesses; nevertheless, the Crown tempered the burgesses, safeguarded the customs revenue, and mollified most popular unrest. In doing so the Crown ensured the continuance of one of England's most profitable plantations. Further south, in Jamaica, the Crown won a similar victory, humbling an assembly that once seemed almost impossibly intractable.

It would be difficult to overstate the magnitude of Jamaica's economic role in England's mercantilist empire. Sugar, of all the staple crops, was by far the most lucrative commodity. Besides stimulating the profitable slave trade, it canceled the kingdom's dependence on foreign sugar and constituted one of the kingdom's most valuable exports to continental Europe. Between 1669 and 1683, Jamaica's sugar production increased tenfold, to roughly five thousand tons a year (now half the amount produced on Barbados, instead of only one-twentieth).[91] What placed Jamaica above Barbados in imperial importance was Port Royal's status as the preeminent emporium for England's trade with Spanish America. More than half of the ships that docked at Port Royal left afterward for the colonial Spanish Main, where Spanish traders offered silver and gold to the English for slaves and manufactures.[92]

The results were spectacular. From Jamaica alone, merchants in England imported £100,000–200,000 of silver and gold *per annum*.[93] To put this amount into perspective, the Tower Mint in London coined an average of £370,000 per annum in the 1670s and £543,658 in the 1680s.[94] As one promotional tract put it in 1683, Jamaica was "the Store-house or Treasury of the West-Indies," an island "most commodiously seated in the midst of the Spaniards, so that we drain the benefits of their Gold and Silver Mines without their Labour and expences."[95]

And yet, of course, many difficulties lingered on the island, obstructing Jamaica's full moneymaking potential. For one, the transition from privateering was haphazard and still ongoing; privateering still imperiled the contraband trade with Spanish America and distracted the island from further sugar planting. But even more urgently, the planters themselves were a hazard. The island's leading planters, in control of the assembly, persistently and zealously countered the authority and privileges of the royal governor and Royal African Company. Here, the Lords of Trade approached the standoff with exceptional caution, wary of unnecessarily breaking an otherwise profitable island; nevertheless, they coupled this caution with singular resolve, determined to fully subordinate Jamaica to England's imperial program.

The Royal African Company, as indicated by its name, enjoyed the unequivocal backing of the Crown. By the mid-1670s, the company paid its shareholders a handsome dividend of ten percent; many of these shareholders belonged to the Stuart court, including the king's younger brother James, Duke of York, who was the RAC's governor and largest shareholder.[96] More than one-third of the company's slave cargo went to Spanish America, where traders paid £18–22 a slave (the value, again, of twenty gold guineas, or eighty silver pieces of eight).[97]

Jamaica's planters detested the company's monopoly. First, they alleged, the RAC undersupplied the island by favoring other markets; second, the company, through its artificial monopoly, inordinately drove up the price of African labor. Some years later, in 1690, the English House of Commons resolved that the RAC charged whatever "price they please; and have actually sold their negroes at above double the price they may be imported for."[98] The allegation was not inaccurate; it made economic sense for the company to charge higher prices, if possible, and to favor the Spanish Main as a market. The Spanish, on average, paid the RAC about 25 percent more for slaves than what Jamaicans typically paid. Furthermore, the Spanish paid in coin and bullion and demanded no extensive credit from the company, unlike the credit-starved Jamaicans who often paid the company in sugar.[99] But even within the English West Indies, the RAC conspicuously favored Barbados over Jamaica (the Leeward Islands, for their part, were almost wholly neglected).[100] The number of slaves sold by the RAC to Jamaica had nearly doubled in the late 1670s, but sugar exports during the same period had risen nearly fivefold, with further expansion in the early 1680s.[101] Jamaica's leading planters were ever anxious, ever ravenous, for a significant increase in their bound labor supply. In their eyes, the Royal African Company was an oppressive imperial institution.

Illicit traders, on the other hand, sold Africans rather more cheaply to the islanders. These traders were not burdened by the RAC's extensive operating costs in erecting and maintaining forts along the West African coast.[102] Some of the smugglers included New England captains who sailed around the Cape of Good Hope to acquire slaves off the coast of Madagascar.[103] Thus in 1674— as mentioned in the previous chapter—the Jamaica legislature legalized the "free importation of negroes" from non-RAC dealers, attaching the brazen statute to a much-needed revenue bill that the governor, Sir Thomas Lynch, had no choice but to sign.[104]

A new governor, Lord Vaughan, arrived in March 1675 to replace Lynch. Immediately, Vaughan called a new assembly to repeal the repugnant legislation.

The planters dutifully reinstated the RAC monopoly, understanding rightly that a statute in such gross violation of imperial law would never stand. But the smuggling continued, and when illicit tradesmen came to court, they most often won acquittal; one judge in 1676 even proudly cited the overturned "Statute against Monopolyes" to declare that planters had a right to buy slaves from whomever they wished.[105]

In 1677 the Jamaica assembly had a new opportunity to write the "free trade" in slaves into law. Because all laws on the island automatically expired after two years, Vaughan had to summon another assembly in 1677 to confirm the laws of 1675. This time, the planter faction tacked a "Bill of Privileges" onto the revenue bill that funded the government. This "Bill of Privileges" declared all the laws of England to be in force on the island, a shrewd way to legalize non-RAC dealers who stayed within the bounds of the Navigation Acts by still using English ships and English sailors. After battling with the assembly for months on the bill, Vaughan—desperate to fund the government and tired of fighting with the planter faction—conceded to the Bill of Privileges.[106]

Incensed with Vaughan's acquiescence, the Lords of Trade prepared one of their own to quell the assembly, fellow committee member Charles Howard, Earl of Carlisle. The committee instructed Carlisle to summon an assembly immediately on arrival and to get them to authorize—by demand from the king—a perpetual revenue act and forty permanent laws authored directly by the Crown, negating the need for future assemblies. The Lords of Trade modeled this plan after Poyning's Law for governing Ireland—the same strategy deployed, unsuccessfully, the following year in Virginia.[107] In endorsing this radical step, the king's attorney general assured the Lords of Trade that Charles was the "absolute Soveraigne" in Jamaica and therefore "may impose what forme of constitution both of Government and Lawes he pleaseth." Colonial liberties, he said, existed "but by the meer Grace & Graunt of the King."[108]

Presuming success, the Lords of Trade promised Carlisle that he could afterward erect a mint on the island. Months before departing England for Jamaica, Carlisle had requested that "a Mint may bee allowed . . . coyned here with particular marke." Sir Thomas Modyford had ineffectually petitioned for a mint in 1664 and 1670, but this time, the Crown approved the request, even permitting the mint to operate on the island, not in England, so long as the "Coines have Our Image and Inscription engraved on them."[109] After some delay, Carlisle arrived in Port Royal in July 1678, and a few weeks later motioned the Crown for permission to begin setting up the mint. Silver abounded in Jamaica, but small change was scarce. "The least coin here is sevenpence halfe-penny," he said, "soe that the Inhabitants suffer much in their way of Trade."[110]

The contrast between the proposed Jamaican mint and the mint in Massachusetts could not have been starker. The economic rationale was essentially the same: the need for currency uniformity and small change. But the Jamaican coinage would bear the king's image with the current date, not a colonial staple with a Commonwealth year. The Jamaican mint also aligned with the regal prerogative. If the assembly had independently authorized the mint and had stamped a sugar cane on the coin instead of Charles II, the money would have been utterly unacceptable, even treasonous. Such was not the case here, and so the mint won the Crown's license. Implicit in that approval, of course, was that Carlisle ensure the passage of royally authored, permanent laws for Jamaica, especially the perpetual revenue act.

On arrival at Port Royal in July 1678, Carlisle summoned the seventh assembly to meet on the island since the year 1672. Not surprisingly, the planters voted down each and every one of the proposed statutes, with special emphasis against the perpetual revenue act. The planters understood that the power of the purse—no longer extant on Barbados and the Leeward Islands—tied the governor most strongly to planter interests.[111] "Popular discourses prevail here as in England," Carlisle wrote the Lords of Trade shortly after; "they will not consent to loos theyr deliberative power."[112]

Nevertheless, the assembly's grievances struck a chord with Carlisle. A mere four months after arrival, Carlisle shockingly wrote the Lords of Trade that the Crown's strategy was "very impracticable besides very distastfull to the sense of the people here."[113] Permanent laws were inadvisable in any colony, he argued, especially a growing one. The distance was too great, he insisted, between Jamaica and England, to respond to sudden changes that might occur on the island; a few of the statutes, besides, had flaws requiring amendment.[114] The committee, appalled, interpreted the governor's about-face as nothing short of betrayal. His timing could not have been worse. Contemporaneous events in London—the Popish Plot, Exclusion Crisis, and recent dissolution of Parliament—made the committee, in early 1679, more wary than ever of headstrong assemblies. "The assembly have endeavoured to grasp all power," the Lords of Trade warned Charles II. Exasperated, they responded to Carlisle by charging him with "defective" behavior, demanding that he try again to secure approval for the perpetual laws.[115]

With the governor now defecting, the Lords of Trade revisited the question of the mint. The committee had previously granted Carlisle permission to set whatever value on the money he "thought most agreeable"—meaning that he could arrange for the Jamaica shilling to contain less silver than the English shilling. But the Lords of Trade now reconsidered this option, asking the Commissioners of the Royal Mint to weigh in on the matter.[116] In February 1679, the mint commissioners replied that a Jamaican mint would be of "Dangerous Consequence" if not required to adhere to the "Standards of His Majesties Gold and Silver Moneys."[117] The Lords of Trade agreed, reporting to Charles thereafter that "the preserving of one certain Standard in weight . . . is very much for the security and advantage of Your Majesty"; to do otherwise would cause "eminent prejudice" to the other colonies. Charles, likewise, agreed; moreover, the king instructed that any expenses in setting up the mint—"all necessary tooles and engines for coyning, with salaries for the usefull Officers"—must now come from Carlisle's own pocketbook, and not from the Royal Exchequer as previously.[118]

Carlisle received the new instruction in May 1679. The governor had no problem stamping money with the "Royall Superscription," but he found the new conditions completely intolerable. Since 1672, Spanish dollars had passed on the island at 5s a piece, 11 percent above the 4s6d rate in England. The 1672 devaluation had temporarily boosted the island's money supply, both in nominal terms and in real terms. For a period, it stimulated the island's export economy, incentivizing outsiders to bring their coin into Jamaica to buy goods that had not yet inflated fully in price to match the new 5s rate. Compliance with the Crown's new order to use the standard for money in England, however, would mean a 10 percent currency *appreciation*, with the opposite effect from the 1672 action. Money would temporarily flow *out* of the colony until prices finally deflated to match the new standard. Only after a period of deflation would the hemorrhaging of money finally stop. Exports, in the meantime, would suffer, and newly minted Jamaican coins would depart from the island almost as soon as they left the mint. "Should our Coine bee of the same standard in weight and fineness to the King's Coine in England," the governor protested, "wee should never keep any money in the Island"; it would assuredly "carry off this Island all our ready money to other plantations."[119]

The Crown's irritation with Governor Carlisle's performance undoubtedly prompted this new requirement; the official reasons given were altogether specious, if not disingenuous. Every colony except for Maryland had devalued the shilling; there was anything *but* one "certain Standard in weight" across the whole empire. The Lords of Trade had told Carlisle that "the altering and debasing of the said standard . . . cannot bee practised or allowed in any part of His Majestie's Dominions," so that no "prejudice arise to the rest of his Dominions."[120] But New York, Massachusetts, and the Leeward Islands had each raised the Spanish piece of eight to 6s, one-third above the English standard. Virginia, Carolina, Jamaica, and Barbados each valued the piece of eight at 5s, 11 percent above the English standard. New Jersey devalued the shilling beyond any other, assigning the dollar, in 1676, a value of 7s8d—roughly 70 percent above the English standard. Even the sole exception, Maryland, assigned a 6s rate to the dollar between 1671 and 1676, until the proprietor forced a return to the English standard.[121]

Discouraged, Carlisle called off all plans for the mint, fearing the impending deflation would render the entire project worthless. Not having a mint at all— and retaining the freedom to set a higher shilling value on foreign coin—was preferable, he believed, to having a mint under the English standard. Indeed, such a mint might have spelled disaster for the island, at least temporarily. "I shall forbeare giving your Lordships any further trouble in this till I have a fairer opportunity of offering it more advantageously," the governor replied in June 1679.[122] The opportunity never came. Betrayed by his former compatriots at the Lords of Trade, Carlisle isolated himself further from the Crown by espousing the planters' grievances more overtly than before. In the same letter in which he regretted the news about the mint, the governor insisted that the island's most respected planters and gentlemen are "generally dissatisfied with haveing the deliberative part of makeing Lawes taken from the Assembly." Three months later he told the committee that the islanders would "never consent to make chaines (as they terme this Frame of Government) for their Posterityes."[123] Carlisle was soon out of office; nothing more came of the mint.

In London, however, reality soon sank in: Jamaica's planters would indeed never approve a permanent revenue and permanent laws. By the end of 1680, the Lords of Trade concluded that some other way must be found to check the assembly. Sir Thomas Lynch, the former governor, played a major role in this tactical shift, as he carefully advocated compromise in front of the committee in London. Lynch argued that the growth of the French West Indies meant that Jamaica required all due encouragement, including assurances to the planters of representative government. Reluctantly the committee gave in, promising such a government on condition of a seven-year revenue bill.[124]

The Crown had overreached; its more aggressive efforts backfired, compelling the Lords of Trade to finally accept the deliberative power of the assembly. In July 1681 the Crown commissioned Lynch to serve again as governor, with instructions to lobby the assembly for a seven-year revenue bill. Upon arrival in June 1682, Lynch wielded his diplomatic talents to persuade the assembly to compromise and agree to a seven-year revenue bill or lose all legislative privileges whatsoever. The assembly approved the revenue bill, and after the Crown approved of most of the assembly's new laws—including the 5s valuation for Spanish coin—political dissension on the island mostly evaporated. Despite loud opposition from the RAC, the Crown even approved a new law that set a price ceiling of £18 on all slaves sold within the colony. To show its gratitude, in October 1683, the assembly—in spite of "some few malicious persons"—extended the revenue to twenty-one years, which the Lords of Trade had privately induced Lynch to push for all along. The following year, after Lynch passed away in August, the Crown appointed an RAC agent, Sir Hender Molesworth, governor of Jamaica.[125]

Between 1675 and 1684 the Lords of Trade and Plantations inaugurated a newly aggressive imperial policy in the colonies, with particular focus on Virginia, Jamaica, and Massachusetts Bay. The mercantilist drive to center treasure in England was the common denominator in all three cases, motivating, in turn, the political solution of centralization and the consequent repression of autonomous colonial institutions and assemblies. Most colonists vowed sincere political allegiance to England, radical independents in Massachusetts notwithstanding. But the colonists had so far resisted the empire's demand that allegiance required them to relinquish the prioritizing of their own economic self-interest.

Coercion, wisely deployed, was the apparent solution, including the drastic reform or elimination of any unmanageable colonial forces: hostile assemblies, autonomous governors, venal officeholders, magistrates and jurists acquitting pirates and smugglers, and any other headstrong officeholders or institutions. By the end of 1684, the Crown could truly conclude that the program was thus far quite successful. On Jamaica, the royal governor had secured a twenty-one-year revenue bill, and the RAC monopoly remained intact; in Virginia, the Crown had humbled the House of Burgesses and compelled the assemblymen to accept a permanent revenue bill, tax reform, and the veto of legislation devaluing Spanish coin. In Massachusetts Bay the charter was voided, and the much-hated mint had finally folded.

An accelerated push for further centralization accompanied the latter half of the 1680s. Big questions remained. First, a new form of government must be settled in Massachusetts. As for the other, smaller, private colonies, those too must be dealt with. Indeed, only weeks after revoking the Massachusetts charter in October 1684, the Crown inquired into whether the private colonies of Connecticut, Rhode Island, Maryland, and Pennsylvania could also be lawfully absorbed into a new royal government.[126] As William Blathwayt told Governor Effingham of Virginia in December, the coming action "will bring about that Necessary union of all the English colonies in America, which will make the King great & Extend his real Empire in those parts."[127] A new king, James II, would spearhead that endeavor.

CHAPTER 7

Economic Rebellion, Competition, and Growth in English America, 1680–1685

Edward Randolph manifestly exaggerated when he claimed in 1676 that Massachusetts was brimming with silver. Even the most bustling mainland colonial towns in the 1670s possessed only a trifling sum of coin compared with most port towns and cities in England, itself concerned with its money stock. Nevertheless, this exaggeration, like most of Randolph's wild assertions, contained an element of truth. By the early 1680s in particular—as colonial economies matured and trade accelerated—mainland colonists enjoyed a greater circulation of coin than at any previous time in their history. Colonials did not retain all of this incoming coin—they exported much of it to buy imported goods on a scale eclipsing any previous era—but they did indeed keep a significant portion for internal circulation. Neither was this just a smattering of coin, nor did the coin center merely in Boston or Port Royal. Across much of the Eastern Seaboard of North America, and even in the surrounding countryside, coin became more readily available in the early 1680s than ever before, with ordinary men and women pairing silver coin with country pay to mediate day-to-day exchanges. The chief exception to this trend was the Chesapeake region, yet even Virginians might have enjoyed the beginnings of a metallic currency had they imported silver, not slaves, from their provisioning trade with the West Indies.

The West Indian islands were the source of most of the silver money that arrived in eastern North America in the 1680s. The mainland colonies sold a

vast array of supplies and provisions to Jamaica, Barbados, and Dutch Curaçao, including wheat, flour, barrel staves, timber, beef, pork, beer, biscuits, and
horses. Silver coin and bills of exchange made up most of the balance, flying
uninterrupted to bustling seaports on the eastern mainland seaboard. "All ships
from Ireland, Bermudas, New England and New York, loaden with provisions,
carry off for the same ready money," Governor Carlisle remarked in Jamaica
in 1679.[1] Even when sugar made up the balance instead, its subsequent carriage to London by Boston merchants had the roundabout effect of increasing the colony's money supply by diminishing the colony's trade deficit with
England for imported goods.

The provisioning trade, in most cases, was perfectly legal, and absolutely
necessary for the sugar islands. If that were the only major source of coin for
the mainland colonies, imperial officials might have left them alone. But there
were other, illicit sources of coin. Buccaneering was one. Though the buccaneers were largely banished from Jamaica by the early 1680s, they were driven
not out of existence but to North American seaports. The buccaneers arrived
there not to pillage but to spend pirated silver. Most colonists earnestly welcomed them in; the pirates indeed had a hugely positive impact on the colonial
money supply. Colonists used some of this coin for internal circulation; in
other cases to buy more imported goods—either way, it was an economic
benefit. To attract outside money, some colonial governments also competitively devalued their currencies, hoping to outdo their neighbors by offering
pirates—as well as legal traders—the highest shilling value for their pieces of
silver. Furthermore, several settlements developed nascent plans for colonial
manufacturing, designed specifically to quell the export of coin. However distant the prospect, colonial-made textiles threatened to undercut England's most
dependable overseas market (the colonies themselves) for the same goods.
Finally and most maddening of all, smuggling still proliferated across virtually
all of English America.

Put together, these colonial efforts to better themselves economically and
monetarily posed an extremely grave danger to the mercantilist program.
These actions persuaded English administrators of the need to bring the colonies under much stricter discipline. There was no doubt that English America
had grown more prosperous in recent years; the colonial money supply reflected this growth. Colonists attributed this growth to greater economic
productivity and to legal, just means of commerce. Absent mercantilist restrictions, many colonists believed, they would be even wealthier. The Lords of
Trade attributed colonial affluence to illicit activity: to piracy, currency manipulation, the ominous birth of colonial manufacturing, and most critically
smuggling. From the Crown's point of view, economic subversion was made

possible by the rebellious, independent political spirit of the colonial world. For the former to end, the latter had first to be extinguished. The Crown's conviction on this point hardened in the final years of Charles II's reign.

By the early 1680s, the worst of the political storm on Jamaica had passed; the Crown and the planter-assembly had broadly reconciled their severest differences. Part of the reason was their united front on another key point of the Crown's agenda: antipiracy. The planter-assembly, royal governor, local merchant community, and Royal African Company all had a stake in eradicating what remained of the buccaneering interest in Port Royal. No longer privateers with legal commissions, the freebooters had crossed unequivocally over into the criminal realm of piracy. Their continued forays disrupted the island's trade of contraband and slaves to Spanish America, raised the cost of shipping insurance and freight, discouraged vessels from stopping at Port Royal, and attracted hosts of runaway slaves from the sugar plantations.[2] Here the planters found common ground with the otherwise-hated RAC; even the two rebel leaders of the assembly, Samuel Long and William Beeston, agreed with the company that buccaneers had caused "irreparable damage" to those "imploying themselves in planting and Merchandize."[3]

Privateering commissions were already on the outs under the first governorship of Sir Thomas Lynch in the early 1670s. In recent years, however, Jamaica's buccaneers turned to the warring French and Dutch powers in the Caribbean to secure privateering commissions; nevertheless, they still returned to Port Royal with looted silver.[4] Their resilience undermined the entire plantation system. "The onely Enemy to Planting is Privateering," Governor Lord Vaughan declared in 1676. Vaughan made it a capital offense to sign a privateering commission with a foreign power, but for those who had already done so, he offered amnesty to any who surrendered within a year. About three hundred privateers turned themselves in. But Vaughan knew this action to be insufficient. "These Indyes are soe Vast and Rich, and this kind of Rapine soe sweet," he told the Lords of Trade, "that it is one of the hardest things in the World to Draw those from it which have used it so long."[5]

So long as the problem of buccaneering persisted, the Spaniards' eagerness to buy slaves and contraband goods from the English correspondingly diminished. One pirate raid in 1677, for instance, robbed the Spanish of nearly 50,000 "peeces of Eight"; another confiscated at least 20,000 pieces.[6] The Lords of Trade scolded Vaughan for his apparent inability to get a handle on the situation, telling him, "the King intendeth to make a Plantation of Jamaica and not a Christian Algiers." Buccaneering, said Sir Thomas Lynch in 1677, "hinders correspondence and a secret Trade with your neighbouring Spanyards, which brings infinitely more profit."[7] In 1680 the Jamaican Council demanded immediate action to "reduce the Privateers," so that Spanish traders might "bring us store of Mony and Goods, wherewith to purchase our English Commodityes."[8] A string of new silver strikes in Mexico in the 1680s made Jamaica's trade with the Spanish Main all the more alluring and the persistence of buccaneering all the more reprehensible.[9] "The Spaniards hate us for the multitude of English that here preys on them," Governor Lynch told the Council in 1684, "and in Spain they had rather the Dutch should have theyr Money then wee."[10]

Even Sir Henry Morgan, the former face of privateering, changed his mind on the matter. Morgan had recently become a substantial plantation owner, possessing more than one hundred slaves.[11] In 1680–1681, he again served as the deputy governor of Jamaica, having replaced the Earl of Carlisle. Morgan now disavowed the buccaneers as "vagabonds" and "Ravenous Vermin": men who "discourage Spaniards from private trade with us," and "presume even to plunder and take vessels belonging to this Island."[12] Indeed, under Morgan's leadership in 1681, the planter-assembly passed the most stringent antibuccaneering laws in the island's history.[13] "Our losses and troubles through pirates are intolerable," Lynch remarked two years later. Pirates had lately raided English vessels in Cuba, Hispaniola, the Bay of Honduras, and the Spanish Main—losses calculated at £50,000—including an assault in which "they tooke 65 pounds of Gold."[14] Yet the Spanish were still the primary target; in one such attack near Panama, English pirates allegedly "put the Spaniards to torture to discover if there were more silver." The most famous assault of the period was a land raid against Vera Cruz in 1683, conducted by an assortment of English and Dutch pirates aboard thirteen vessels. The incursion yielded 960,000 pieces of eight (£216,000 sterling), allotting each participant 800 pieces of eight (£180 sterling).[15]

By the mid-1680s, Lynch's aggressive antipiracy campaign had mostly succeeded in throwing the buccaneers out of Port Royal. But the pirates found refuge elsewhere, first in other parts of the Caribbean—the Leeward Islands, Bahamas, and Central American lagoons—and then in places far beyond.[16] "We have many villanous wretches amongst us who would be glad of any occasion to gett mony," remarked the governor of Bermuda in 1684, ". . . to make this country a Refuge of Pyrats is the Intention of the people." Carlisle had warned the Lords of Trade back in 1679 that the buccaneers had told him they "would leave their Interest in the Island, and sail for Road Island, or to the Dutch, where they could bee entertained."[17] This they did, and before long they sprawled across much of the North American seaboard, as well as the Indian Ocean, even forging a sanctuary settlement on Madagascar. Located 250 miles off the southeastern coast of Africa, Madagascar was prime estate for raiding East India Company vessels carrying boatloads of silver to India or expensive spices and fabrics on the return trip. There seemed few places the marauders would not trek; even a Pacific raid in 1686 allotted three hundred pieces of eight to each participant.[18]

But North America was the buccaneers' favorite destination to spend looted coin. Pirates were already frequenting North American seaports as early as 1680, but within a few years they were such regular guests that they ranked among the mainland's most important sources of money. Buccaneers who had once returned to Port Royal after a successful venture now opted for Newport, Charles Town, Boston, New York, Philadelphia, and the Albemarle region of northeastern Carolina. "The Law wee have made against privateers," Governor Lynch reported in 1684, "neither discourages them nor lessens their Number, while they have such retreats as Carolina, N. England and other Colonyes." Gold and silver, he said, was the colonists' chief incentive, for "they are now full of Pyrats money, and from Boston they have told me, the Privateers have brought in £80000."[19] This figure was almost surely exaggerated, but the point stands that tolerating the arrival of pirates into one's seaport made monetary sense. Pirates sold confiscated goods at bargain prices; they spent silver and gold money lavishly in taverns, brothels, and shops. Moreover, colonial merchants and labourers earned a handsome sum of coin repairing and victualing ships belonging to pirates; lucrative profits awaited any savvy colonial merchant willing to bear the risk.[20]

One of the more dramatic illustrations of the support that pirates received comes from Boston, in the year 1684. William Dyre, the newly appointed surveyor general of the customs in America, seized a vessel that plainly belonged to pirates. In doing so, however, he was "much discouraged and severely Threaten'd by many, but more especially by one Mr. Samuel Shrimpton, a merchant of this place, to have my Brains beat out or a stab for seizing said ship." Shrimpton was the wealthiest merchant in Boston and the purported recipient, Dyre said, of "Great Quantitys of piratically plundered Gold, silver and plate."[21]

Private colonies like Rhode Island were most notorious for harboring pirates, and here the Crown had little to no means to check the practice. The royal governor of New Hampshire, Edward Cranfield, recorded one such incident in Rhode Island in 1683. Upon his visit there, "two Pyrates came in" with a supposed commission from Lynch. The governor of New York, Thomas Dongan, was also present, and both Cranfield and Dongan recognized Lynch's signature as an obvious forgery; neither were his titles even correctly given. "Dongan and my self desired the Government to secure them, but they refused"; the governor of Rhode Island "was of another Opinion and Declared the Ship a free bottom."[22]

Massachusetts Bay, expectedly, bore a reputation as a "Receptacle of all piratical and uncustomed goods," to quote William Dyre in 1684.[23] Several of the men involved in the aforementioned attack on Vera Cruz in 1683—yielding 960,000 pieces of eight—apparently spent some of their money in Boston.[24] The governor of New Hampshire, in 1684, described an incident in Boston when a French privateering ship arrived with £700 of silver and gold per man. "The Bostoners no sooner had intelligence of her being upon the coast but they dispatched a messenger and pilot to invite and convey her in," he said; "the pirates are likely to leave the greatest part of their [silver] Plate behind them, having bought up most of the choice goods in Boston."[25] Randolph, of course, routinely called Massachusetts a "common receptacle of pyratts," claiming they "brought great bootyes to Boston . . . money, plate, and rich commodityes." Worse still, he said, the Boston mint "encouraged pyratts to bring their plate hither, because it could be coined and conveyed in great parcells undiscovered."[26]

Piracy became such a vital source of coin for New England that, years later, supporters of a colonial paper currency reasoned that the recent decline of piracy made silver an impractical currency in New England. One Boston pamphleteer in 1716 cited the buccaneers and fishery as having formerly been the two most "principal Means to draw in Silver . . . the Privateers did bring in considerable Quantities." Another writer, in 1720, remarked that of the money then in circulation, "it came great part of it from Pyrates."[27]

Buccaneering was practically the only source of coin for Carolina; several merchants in Charles Town earned generous sums of silver and gold servicing and victualling pirate vessels. The Carolina proprietors required their quitrents in coin, strengthening the incentive for tolerating piracy. After a succession of two openly pro-pirate governors in the early to mid-1680s—appointed by the merchant-dominated council—the proprietors sent a new antipirate governor, James Colleton, to govern the colony in 1686. Resistance to his governorship was so strong that he dismissed the entire council and declared martial law, though he still failed to fully stamp out the practice.[28] "It may be said, that formerly Silver was very plenty here," a defender of paper currency remarked to hard-money critics in South Carolina in 1732; "I answer thereto . . . the Privateers brought in great Quantities of Spanish Silver."[29]

Virginia and Maryland comprised the two main exceptions. The tobacco economy made the Chesapeake a target rather than a beneficiary of piracy; buccaneers sometimes raided the slow-moving tobacco vessels traveling to and from the lightly guarded Chesapeake, sometimes absconding to the northern colonies after a successful looting. "The last yeare and this present yeare this Government hath been ill Infested with Privateers, or rather Pyrates, of whom wee have very ill Apprehensions," the Virginia secretary wrote the Lords of Trade in 1683.[30] The Chesapeake also had no significant seaports for pirates to spend their money; moreover, the 5s valuation for Spanish coin (4s6d in Maryland) was lower than anywhere else on the Atlantic seaboard.

The response from England to this new outburst of piracy, at first, was astoundingly weak. The legal apparatus for dealing with pirates was not yet developed; the onus for enforcing antipiracy laws was still on each colonial government. Not until 1684 did a shift begin to occur. That year, King Charles commanded all governors to prosecute any persons who "knowingly entertain, harbor, conceal, trade, or hold any correspondence" with pirates.[31] Dutifully, each colonial government passed the antipiracy legislation. Enforcement was another matter. Colonial juries habitually delivered acquittals, convicted pirates curiously "escaped" from colonial jailhouses, and governors and magistrates recurrently accepted bribes from merchant allies.[32] The problem was so pervasive that in 1687 King James II commanded governors to no longer permit colonial magistrates to hurry pirates "immediately to their Tryals before any Evidence could be produced."[33]

Buccaneers considered a host of factors when determining which North American seaport to visit. Was it a private colony or a royal colony? What was the reputation of the governor? What of the merchants? And how many shillings could a piece of eight earn there?

Colonial governments raised the value of Spanish money to new heights in the early to mid-1680s. Coin devaluation, indeed, became the most popular means in colonial America to attract foreign silver, whether from pirates or ordinary tradesmen. The timing conveniently, though not accidentally, aligned with the pirate ascendancy in eastern North America; pirates were more likely to bring their coin into a port for 6s apiece—or better yet, 6s9d apiece—than, say, 5s apiece. Colonial leaders knew this fact well, and their governments, by consequence, actively competed over which province could offer pirates, merchants, tradesmen, and anyone else with coin the most bang for their buck.

In 1682, on the eve of this new devaluation wave, the rates for a Spanish dollar (piece of eight) were as follows: 4s6d in Maryland (the same standard as in England); 5s in Virginia, Carolina, Jamaica, and Barbados; 6s in New York, Massachusetts, and the Leeward Islands; 7s8d in New Jersey.[34] Rates changed rapidly thereafter. In 1683 alone, four colonies—Pennsylvania, Connecticut, New Hampshire, and Carolina—raised the piece of eight from 5s to 6s.[35] The following year, 1684, the New York assembly—meeting for the first time in the colony's history—advanced the dollar from 6s to 6s9d. The new rate was

12.5 percent higher than in Massachusetts. James, Duke of York, elected not to repeal the new statute, but less than two years later, as king, he warned Governor Dongan that "you shall not, upon any pretence whatsoever, permit any [further] alteration to bee made in the value of the current coyn."[36]

To somewhat complicate matters, however, devaluation could also be secured more discreetly. By ordering clipped coin to pass at face value, some governments permitted colonists to accept Spanish money at rates higher than the law, at first glance, suggested. An unclipped piece of eight, if minted in Mexico or Spain (though not in Peru), contained 17.5 pennyweight (dwt) of silver. Clipped coin was often as light as 12 dwt—one-third lighter than a full-weight dollar. Yet during this period, a number of colonial governments declared clipped money legal tender at the same rate as full-weight coin, allowing clipped money to pass at face value. This method of valuation was called *currency by tale*, as opposed to *currency by weight*. Virtually all pirate money was clipped to some degree—often by the same pirates—and so governments that allowed clipped money to pass at the ordinary rate—currency by tale—significantly enticed buccaneers with clipped money. The opposite approach—currency by weight—deployed a sliding scale of valuation, deducting a certain number of pence for each missing pennyweight from the coin. Pennsylvania, West Jersey, Barbados, and the Leeward Islands enacted currency by tale; New England, New York, East Jersey, and Carolina, currency by weight. The decision on which way to go—tale or weight—made a colossal difference in each colony's currency, sometimes for better and sometimes for worse.

Pennsylvania, for example, enacted currency by tale. After 1683, clipped dollars were legal tender in Pennsylvania at 6s a piece, the same rate for unclipped money. The assembly voted down a motion that dollars "goe by weight," and so, in reality, the Pennsylvania valuation for Spanish coin was far higher than the 6s rating suggested, for the law assigned a 6s rating for *clipped* money. The New England and Carolina governments also priced full-weight dollars at 6s but deducted a certain number of pence for each missing pennyweight. Consequently, though Pennsylvania and Massachusetts each rated the dollar at 6s, the de facto rating in Pennsylvania was substantially higher. A 12 dwt coin in Massachusetts passed at only 4s2d; the same coin in Pennsylvania passed at 6s. Barbados, like Pennsylvania, instituted currency by tale (though at 5s, not 6s); New York, like Massachusetts, instituted currency by weight, but at 6s9d for unclipped money and 4s8d for coins weighing 12 dwt (higher than Massachusetts, but lower than Pennsylvania).[37]

The greatest downside to currency by tale was that it banished full-weight coin from circulation, flooding colonies like Pennsylvania and Barbados with clipped money. Clipped money also circulated in New York and Massachusetts, of course, but at a discount, appearing alongside full-weight coin that did not receive a discount. In Pennsylvania and Barbados, however, no trader in his right mind would spend full-weight money when he could spend lighter coin at the same rate. In such colonies, "not one piece in a hundred weighs so much" as a full-weight dollar; "none but extreme light pieces will be brought in."[38] When a typical tradesman encountered full-weight money in a colony with currency by tale, he either exported the coin, hoarded the coin, or clipped the coin before spending it. Hence the governor of Pennsylvania complained to William Penn in 1689 that the law "incourages vile persons to clip all those species of moneys."[39] Some years later, when New York joined Pennsylvania in rating currency by tale, a merchant there reported that after the change, "none remain'd with us but such as was lessened by others."[40] Those who wished not to clip money—the vast majority of tradesmen—simply exported full-weight coin from the colony when purchasing imported goods and saved the clipped money for internal circulation. For this reason, the East Jersey assembly in 1686 repealed currency by tale, arguing that it had detrimentally caused "the continual draining of silver money that is most valuable. . . . The best of the coin is carried away."[41]

Currency by tale could lead to amusing predicaments, such as occurred in Boston at the beginning of the eighteenth century. Beginning in 1696, Boston merchants agreed in concert to adopt currency by tale because the Crown had refused to allow their government to increase the rating for full-weight dollars. A few years later, a certain English shipmaster ventured into town to "pay a sum of money," seeking provisions and other victuals. A local wharfman, upon seeing the shipmaster with "heavy pieces of Eight, asked him what he was to doe with that money." The shipmaster replied that he intended to spend it. To this, the man laughed and "told him if he would let him have it for a few hours, he would bring it to him with advantage." True to his word, the wharfman returned with all the coins clipped and with the remaining sum of silver that he had shaved off: a significant quantity. With a wink and a grin, the wharfman assured the shipmaster that the money would be accepted at the same rate as if it were unclipped, and the wharfman was right.[42]

Currency by weight suffered a critical disadvantage, however. The inconvenience of having to repeatedly weigh coins on scales, and then calculating their precise shilling value, was particularly taxing, even unbearable for some. Currency by weight, too often, caused inordinate "Trouble in receiving and paying": "'tis hardly possible to weigh or compute every groat and sixpence we pay."[43] In rural areas especially, where few to no scales existed, most men and women still relied on face value only, irrespective of silver content or the law. Locke summarized the dilemma well: "nothing can make Clipping unprofitable," he said, "but making all light Money go only for its weight"; nevertheless, "the weighing of Silver to every one we had occasion to pay it to, would be very troublesome, for every one must carry about Scales in his Pocket."[44]

Given the many discrepancies, then, between currency by tale and currency by weight—as well as the many variations in how many pence each currency-by-weight colony deducted for each missing pennyweight—it is an extraordinary task for the historian to draw up a comparative chart of the precise rates at which silver passed in the several English Atlantic colonies in any given year. It suffices, then, to note that money passed at the highest rates in the Middle Colonies; at slightly lower rates in New England, Carolina, and Barbados; and at the lowest rates in Jamaica and the Chesapeake.

How aware were pirates of the various rates and methods for valuing coin in each colony? It is not possible to say with any real certainty, but pirates were likely more aware of this information than some today might credit them. News traveled slowly in the early modern Atlantic world, but travel it did, and for pirates possessing hundreds or thousands of pieces of eight, this was knowledge well worth possessing.

Of course there were many other reasons for wanting to devalue the dollar. The antipirate colonies of Virginia and Jamaica were also zealous to devalue the dollar in the 1680s. As before mentioned, the House of Burgesses petitioned the king on the matter in 1680, applauded Governor Culpeper for advancing the dollar to 6s in January 1683, and then watched the Crown repeal his proclamation in September (despite having previously granted him permission to devalue). In Jamaica, beginning in 1683, the planter-assembly also struggled relentlessly to advance the dollar to 6s. The goal was not to encourage piracy but to ease debt payments to the Royal African Company. Jamaican planters collectively owed more than £130,000 to the RAC, and the proposed devaluation would abate their debts by 20 percent.[45] But Governor Lynch, now armed with a twenty-one-year revenue, refused his consent, detailing sixteen reasons against the bill. The next governor, Sir Hender Molesworth (1684–1687), simultaneously worked as the RAC agent for Jamaica. Needless to say, this doomed the assembly's effort.[46]

Cleverly, Jamaicans responded by undertaking de facto devaluation. They did so by mimicking, extralegally, the Barbadian example of currency by tale. Late in 1682, planters and tradesmen reached a voluntary agreement to institute currency by tale, as in Barbados. They did so outside of law, as such a bill would never have passed the governor's desk. Full-weight coin soon vanished from the island, and RAC agents howled at being pressured to accept clipped money at 5s for debt payments.[47] Governor Lynch warned the islanders that the RAC had already complained to the Lords of Trade about "the Light Money at Barbados."[48] Sure enough, the company petitioned the king that "light Spanish monys pass there without any determinated weight" and is "every day introduced lighter & lighter." The assembly, in reply, characteristically denounced the RAC as a monopolist company that had notoriously mismanaged its business; besides, they said, most debt was settled in sugar, not coin, and so the "lightnes of mony can be no prejudice to the Royall Company" and "may be refused" if offered (by this they meant that clipped money might be refused in favor of sugar money, not the full-weight silver desired by the company).[49]

Meanwhile, as the Crown battled efforts in Jamaica and Virginia to raise the dollar to 6s, the same imperial administrators expressly permitted a 6s valuation in New Hampshire, now a royal colony. In 1683 the governor, Edward Cranfield, followed the recent lead of Connecticut by raising the dollar to 6s. He did so, however, by mere proclamation, without a corresponding act from the assembly, which subsequently opposed the action. The next year, several New Hampshire residents petitioned against the proclamation, to which the governor insisted that six shillings was a "just value" for the coin, and that his decree had been an "advantage to the Province by bringing that money [in] more than formerly, and herein these people have no reason to complain."[50] The Lords of Trade, in early 1685, rebuked the governor for advancing the coin without royal permission, but let the proclamation stand.[51] Their decision came less than two years after they repealed a like proclamation in Virginia for which the governor *had* received permission.[52]

On the surface then, imperial currency policy seemed almost entirely arbitrary in the 1680s. The Crown, though it had demonstrated an undeniable disposition against devaluation, had little option but to tolerate it in private colonies, and in royal colonies the Crown fluctuated between allowing devaluation and prohibiting it. And yet there was also a degree of logic to the apparent inconsistency; it was not as capricious as may seem at first sight. The Crown most actively resisted devaluation in the tobacco and sugar plantations, citing a possible reduction in the customs revenue. The RAC also played a major role in blocking devaluation by law in Jamaica, and in Virginia the Crown's quitrent revenue was a principal factor. Either way, royal income was at stake, an especially pressing issue as the king sought to continue ruling at home without Parliament (which he had successfully done since dissolving parliament in 1681). Still, from the standpoint of colonial planters, the Crown's policy on devaluation seemed utterly haphazard and discriminatory; it proved immensely frustrating to watch neighboring colonies advance the rates of coin without the ability to follow.

The Crown also had much intellectual support in its anti-devaluation posture. Devaluation carried little favor among most prominent economic thinkers in England. Recently in 1675, a London printer published, for the first time, a decades-old economic treatise by Rice Vaughn, entitled *A Discourse of Coin and Coinage*. The members of the Lords of Trade had almost certainly read the book, and in it, Vaughn blasted the altering of currency rates, calling it an act of "Injustice and Oppression" against "all which are forced to receive less in Intrinsical value than is due unto them." A few years later, in 1684, when a customs officer on Nevis complained of the 6s rating in the Leeward Islands, the Commissioners of the Mint in London forwarded their opinion that trade was "in no wayes to be ballanced by notions and names of money or things, but by the real and intrinsic value of money and commodities truly answering each other." Prices will rise in proportion to the raising of coin, they argued, and so the law will not attain its purported end. This was the consensus among most economic thinkers in England in the 1670s and 1680s.[53]

More important, from the Crown's standpoint, competitive currency devaluation undermined any notion of a united English empire. Devaluation prompted intercolonial quarreling, suspicion, and jealousy. If the Lords of Trade could have banned the practice everywhere in the 1680s, they would have. For now, however, there was little the Crown could do to prevent private governments from autonomously determining their own rates for coin. As for New Hampshire, it was a royal colony surrounded by private New England governments, and as it had little consequence to the mercantilist system, the Crown saw no use in challenging its 6s rate.

The fact that devaluation was an issue *at all* in the colonies—together with the proliferation of piracy—served as further evidence to the Crown that consolidation was absolutely necessary. In both cases, piracy and coin devaluation, imperial administrators encountered the quagmire of a decentralized colonial sphere outside of its immediate control, whose actions, at any moment, could seriously jeopardize the empire's whole mercantilist foundation.

The relatively flourishing economic state of colonial America in the early 1680s made the Crown's push toward imperial consolidation all the more tempting. With sound reason, the Lords of Trade believed that England's colonists were thriving as never before. Smuggling and piracy played no small part in this relative prosperity; so too did the lawful provisioning trade to the West Indies for silver. But one way or the other—through legal or illegal means—colonists were better off economically. Imperial officials saw this prosperity as reason to bring colonists under stricter discipline and to channel more of that wealth into England. On the other end, many colonists resolutely believed that the empire had already overburdened them economically and that anything additional would add all the more to the injustice.

In Massachusetts Bay, silver and even gold coin become more common in the late 1670s and early 1680s. Historians have underestimated the extent to which Bay colonists in this period used coin to settle routine exchanges. The court records of Essex County—home of Salem, Massachusetts—reveal a surprising number of instances of colonists' even possessing gold money. One Martha Haffield, for instance, owned at least £21 in gold; others owned smaller sums of gold.[54] The same court records prove the consistent use of "money silver" in daily exchanges: a saddle, for instance, earned for one seller "12s in silver"; a doctor's visit cost a patient "in silver, 2s6d."[55] A merchant in Salem rented his twenty-ton vessel for "£12 10s per month in current silver of New England": an expression that could include pine-tree shillings, foreign coin at New England rates, or a combination of the two. In this case, monthly rent for the vessel was 250 pine-tree shillings, or almost 42 pieces of eight. Also in Salem, in 1681, a yeoman farmer sold four oxen and twenty lambs for "£18 10s in silver money of New England": 370 pine-tree shillings, or 62 pieces of eight.[56] The more well-to-do certainly possessed and spent on a regular basis. The inventory of a wealthy tradesman, Edward Wharton, in 1678, included £99 4s in "new England money": nearly 2,000 pine-tree shillings, or 330 pieces of eight.[57] Another estate, in 1685, included £580 in foreign coin and plate, £60 in English coin, and £23 in Bay shillings (460 pine-tree coins).[58] Even a more modest estate, such as that of Anne Burt, calculated at £47, included £2 10s of silver money (50 pine-tree shillings) and another £3 of debts owed to her expressly in silver.[59]

Even in the most rural areas of New England, coin gradually entered circulation. The governor of Connecticut, in 1680, attested that the provisioning trade of food and timber to the Caribbean islands had procured "some money" for the colony.[60] When the governments of Connecticut and New Hampshire revalued the dollar in 1683, both colonies, for the first time, assigned different values to the heavier Mexican piece (6s) and the lighter Peruvian piece (5s), indicating that enough of these coins now circulated to warrant such distinction.[61] In New Plymouth, for the first time, the government was now able to collect fines in silver; for example, the penalty for fornication, previously settled in country produce, could now only "be payed forthwith in Mony." Silver now settled a wide range of lawsuits in Plymouth: one defamation case in 1686 involved the astounding sum of "two hundred pounds of silver money," or more than 650 pieces of eight.[62]

Often times, payment was split between silver money and country pay. In 1679 the £10 stipend of a widow in Essex County was met "half in New England silver money and half in corn."[63] A Boston bricklayer in 1675 agreed to build two brick arches for an ironworks company for £20: "half in silver money of New England as soon as the work was finished, and half in English goods at money price delivered at Boston within a month after the work was finished."[64] In 1680 a millwright contracted to build a windmill for £160, "half in silver and half in fish or other goods at money price."[65] In 1676 a debtor owed a £12 payment to one Susanna Satchwell, payable "in silver or fat cattle fit for slaughter."[66] In Ipswich in 1678, two carpenters agreed to build a barn for £10: 10s was tendered "in silver," and the remainder "in corn and pork."[67]

To be certain, country pay still utterly dominated the rural economy. One should not venture to the opposite extreme and claim that silver coin was more prolific than it truly was. Indian corn, wheat, peas, malt, barrel staves, and even fish were all still regularly tendered in public and private payments. Many private payments, wages, court settlements, and salaries included no coin at all, only produce. Until 1680, neither the clerk nor secretary of the Massachusetts General Court received coin for their pay, and even after 1680, they still received three-quarters of their salary in country produce.[68] Grammar school teachers in New Plymouth received "att least twelve pounds in currant marchantable pay"; in the same colony, in 1682, the two surviving daughters of a man recently deceased were to receive "eight pounds in current country pay when they come of age." Also in Plymouth, a man and woman who had cared for a six-year-old orphan in "destitute condition" received "five pound in good currant country pay" for their "considerable charge and trouble in the keeping of her."[69] The Rhode Island assembly in 1687 declared "sheep's wool" legal tender at 7.5d a pound, alongside other country "species," including butter, corn, and pork.[70] Such remained the norm in the most rural areas of New England; nevertheless, especially as one drew nearer to the port towns, there is no doubt that by the early 1680s, ordinary New Englanders enjoyed far greater access to coin than in any previous era.

The known output of the Boston mint is also incredibly revealing. In 1679 alone, the mint produced approximately 20,000 pine-tree shillings, or about £1,000 worth of the coin. The only precise records available on the mint's output are from 1671 to 1680, during which time John Hull produced 74,777 shillings worth of Boston coin of varying (and unknown) denomination, amounting to some £3,738.[71] Historian Mark Peterson says that for the years between 1652 and 1682, "we can conservatively estimate that Hull produced 225,000 shillings' worth of sterling-grade Massachusetts money and as many as 300,000 individual coins," amounting to approximately six shillings of silver coin for every man, woman, and child in Massachusetts. "The Boston mint clearly produced a workable supply of small change for New England," Peterson writes, "even if we allow for the likelihood that substantial quantities of Massachusetts shillings were exported out of the region."[72]

By contrast, most southern colonies had practically no coin at all in circulation, even in the 1680s. The one exception was in Charles Town, where pirate money supplied the bulk of the silver, with the rest supplied from a small provisioning trade with the Caribbean; other than that, coin in Carolina was negligible. "Money here is but little, and that Spanish," reported one Charles Town resident in 1682, on the eve of the pirate ascendancy; ". . . our pay is what the Countrey affords."[73] No wonder residents soon proved so eager to welcome pirates in with chests full of silver.

In Virginia a common silver currency was a real possibility in the 1680s but never came to pass. The House of Burgesses, in 1683, even recognized the circulation of "Coyne comonly called New England money."[74] Many middling farmers on the Eastern Shore and lower James River had finally diversified from tobacco monoculture, shifting production either partly or entirely toward the Caribbean provisioning trade. Approximately seventy vessels—mostly hailing from New England—sailed annually from the Chesapeake to Barbados, carrying livestock, pipe staves, tobacco, and pork and other foodstuffs to the sugar planters. A nascent shipbuilding industry had even emerged in Virginia, producing thirty-ton sloops, ketches, and other small watercraft.[75]

Several economic factors precluded Virginians from acquiring anything close to a common silver currency. For one, tobacco monoculture remained the standard economic pursuit, even as the price of tobacco still hovered around a penny a pound. Two, the manipulation of silver rates by neighboring colonies, with no freedom to compete in like manner, impaired the effort; Virginia, more than any other colony (excepting Maryland), was the greatest loser in the intercolonial devaluation wars of the late Stuart period. Buccaneering, as before mentioned, did not increase Chesapeake access to money as it did for the rest. But more important, African slaves, not silver, constituted a majority of the returns from the Chesapeake's trade with the Caribbean. Ships belonging to the Royal African Company rarely visited the Chesapeake; planters had to acquire slaves from intercolonial trade.[76] Slaves still counted for less than 10 percent of the Chesapeake population at the end of the 1680s; nevertheless, their numbers had increased threefold since 1670, primarily as a result of Virginia's trade of livestock and provisions to the Caribbean.[77] If elite planters had desisted from purchasing African labor in this period, it is not unreasonable to suggest that Virginians might have enjoyed the beginnings of metallic currency in the 1680s, with returns from the Caribbean coming over in coin and bills of exchange, just as the trade functioned for other colonies. Virginia planters, instead, opted for slaves over silver.

On Barbados, silver coin finally displaced the islanders' total dependence on sugar money and book credit. Now, even among skilled workers, "no Man will doe business here but for ready Money," the governor remarked in 1682; three years later, he called silver the "Currant money of this Island," regretting, however, that most of the coins were clipped by about one-third, circulating at 5s a piece as if they were full-weight.[78] The council had prohibited the "Importation of bad & light money" in 1678, but currency by tale doomed the effort.[79] Clipped or unclipped, however, the appearance of any coin at all on Barbados was a welcome change. It certainly benefited North American colonists who did business on the island; in 1674, for instance, a Barbadian resident bought a thirty-ton ketch from a Massachusetts shipbuilder for £250 "in silver"—that is, about one thousand (clipped) pieces of eight.[80] Silver, to be sure, was still far from plenteous; though Barbadian planters were by far the wealthiest colonists in the empire, they still held most of their assets in valuables other than gold and silver. By way of comparison, per capita imports of English goods in the 1680s were as follows: £3.47 on Barbados, £2.06 on Jamaica, £0.63 in the Chesapeake, and £0.59 in New England.[81] Slaves and land made up the rest of their assets. By this time, three-quarters of the island's inhabitants were African slaves; as for the land, the top 7 percent of property holders owned more than half of the island and presumably the majority of silver.[82]

Sugar, by contrast, remained the predominant currency on the Leeward Islands until the end of the century. The planters there had gradually adopted the same consolidation model as Barbados for plantation agriculture, attendant with a black majority by 1680. But of coin the planters were lacking. "They have little Money, but Buy and Pay with Sugars," one visitor to Nevis wrote in 1688. As late as 1699, the council on Montserrat paid the island's Anglican minister an annual salary of twenty thousand pounds of sugar, recorded for him in book. "In the Leward Islands there is very little money," the governor wrote in 1691; ". . . those who need provisions & cloathing buy them with Shugr." By contrast, "in Barbadoes," he said, "tis true they have a money Trade."[83]

Jamaica still boasted more silver and gold than any other colony, notwithstanding the island's export of coin to North America for provisions. Almost all of the island's coin holdings were the result of the Spanish contraband trade. "We have much Money imported by our Trading Sloopes" from "all along the coast of the [Spanish] Mayn," remarked Governor Lynch in 1682, adding the following year, "Wee have had more Money coming this year than ever."[84] Incoming coin included pieces of eight, but also gold Spanish doubloons and French pistoles, both of which passed on the island at 20s (£1), the value of an English guinea. As one planter bragged in 1683, the islanders imported from the Spanish "bars and cakes of Gold, wedges and piggs of Silver, Pistols, Pieces of Eight and several other Coyns. . . . Almost every House hath a rich Cupboard of Plate." "Whereas most other Plantations ever did and now do keep their accounts in Sugar," he continued, ". . . it is otherwise in Jamaica, for in Port Royal there is more plenty of running Cash."[85]

The Middle Colonies—New York and Pennsylvania being chief—enjoyed a marked increase in coin in the early 1680s. Regional exports had advanced notably in the past two decades. As late as the 1670s, furs were still the dominant staple of New York, but with the market price for peltry now severely depressed, New Yorkers turned steadily to food provisioning. Middling merchants abandoned the transatlantic fur trade and focused instead on the coastwise trade with New England, the Carolinas, and the West Indies. All along the Hudson River, interior settlers sold small agricultural surpluses of grain and flour to sloops headed first to New York City and then to ultimate destinations far elsewhere.[86] Some wealthier merchants exported the produce all the way to Lisbon and Madeira, the ships returning from across the Atlantic with Portuguese silver and gold.[87] Most of the New York grain, flour, and staves, however, went to Dutch Curaçao, one of the most vibrant commercial entrepôts in all of the Caribbean—heavily engaged in the Spanish contraband trade but in desperate need of food and provisions. Because New York had retained much of its original Dutch character, the two were natural trading partners.[88] "Flour from New-York is counted the best," one visitor to Curaçao remarked; by the end of the 1680s, New Yorkers exported approximately sixty thousand barrels each of flour and grain to the Caribbean, especially Curaçao, every year, importing, in turn, pieces of eight, bills of exchange, and also Dutch-minted "lion dollars," more commonly known as "dog dollars" (the stamp was known to resemble the figure of a dog more than that of a lion; see figure 9).[89] By the end of the century,

FIGURE 9.   Silver leeuwendaalder coin of Holland, 1662. (ANS 1959.207.112. Courtesy of American Numismatic Society.)

Curaçaoans imported about £50,000 worth of goods each year from New York, Rhode Island, and Pennsylvania.[90]

Though New York now commanded a prominent space on the commercial map, its position remained humble and still largely dependent on the Boston entrepôt. Few English vessels, as of yet, traded directly with the Middle Colonies; merchants in New York, the Jerseys, and Philadelphia purchased most of their imported goods from merchant-middlemen in Boston, who siphoned away some of the coin that New Yorkers had received from Curaçao. Additionally, many of the small watercraft deployed by New York merchants for West Indian trade were built in Boston, though a growing number of Curaçao-bound vessels were now New York owned and New York built.[91]

A New York mint, if established, would effectively signal to the rest of the Atlantic world that the province indeed merited attention. But would the Duke of York, future King James II, approve? The duke, in 1675, had already turned down Governor Andros's proposal for a mint, but in 1684, Governor Dongan and the new representative assembly sought again to woo the duke, this time armed with new reasons. First, irregularity in the local currency had undoubtedly grown in recent years—from the influx of pirate money, no doubt, but also from the concurrent circulation of dog dollars, Mexican pieces of eight, and Peruvian pieces of eight, all arriving from West Indian trade. But second, and perhaps most important, the founding of a mint would bring to the colony great prestige. A New York coinage, with a New York stamp, would unquestionably boost the repute and confidence of the colony. New York had changed a lot since 1675; the duke appeared to recognize this fact, replying to Dongan that he was "inclinable enough to assent to your motion for a Mint" but would "resolve further to consider of the matter."[92] Months later, in February 1685, the duke became king. All talk of a mint fell through. Three years later, New York merged with the Dominion of New England, and a coin bearing the distinct symbols and markings of New York was now out of the question.

The population of the Middle Colonies had advanced rapidly since the 1670s. Word spread through much of the Atlantic and to England of the "great and rich Tracts of land" available in the region: an opportunity for ordinary men and women to "get Land of their own, and live exceeding well."[93] By the end of the 1680s, the combined populations of New York, Pennsylvania, and the Jerseys—though counting only one-third of the populations of either New England or the Chesapeake—almost equaled the free population of the entire English Caribbean. New York still had the most residents, 14,000; but the Jerseys had 8,000 settlers, and even more impressively Pennsylvania's population had soared from a mere 700 settlers in 1680 to more than 11,000 in 1689.[94] Proprietor William Penn brilliantly marketed more than 750,000 acres to six hundred subscribers, including entire companies that freighted scores of immigrants: Germans, English Quakers, and Dutch and Scotch-Irish Presbyterians. The immigrants were overwhelmingly of middling status, establishing farms across the several rural townships west and north of Philadelphia along the Delaware River. Philadelphia, the City of Brotherly Love, showcased a host of artisans, craftsmen, and a tight-knit community of middling Quaker merchants. The soil was more fertile than that of New England; the climate more temperate than that of the South; the easy, rolling hills well adapted for tillage; the many pleasant streams ideal for milling grain.[95]

Silver coin was difficult to come by in the first few years of the Pennsylvania settlement. The trade deficit with neighboring colonies and England was predictably great; exports from the colony were still largely underdeveloped, causing a "notorious scarcity of money in the province"; indeed, "almost all the money goes out," said a recent arrival.[96] As expected, the Pennsylvania assembly, in 1683, declared "Country-growth or produce" to be legal tender in public and private payments. "There is a Necessity for the Sake of Commerce in this infancy of things that the growth & produce of this Province & territories thereof, Shall pass in Lieu of Mony," they said. Such produce included "all marchantable Wheat, Rye, Indian-Corn, Barley, Oats, Pork, Beef [and] Tobacco," thereafter "accounted current pay."[97]

Penn craved the circulation of a common silver and gold currency for his infant colony, even telling friends that he planned to erect a Pennsylvania mint.[98] In one promotional pamphlet in 1685, Penn instructed forthcoming immigrants that it was "most advisable" to bring along estates at least "one-third in Money, and two thirds in Goods." On the same page, he appealed to the colony's high valuation for coin—6s per dollar, irrespective of weight— "so that a man worth £400 here [England], is worth £600 there, without sweating."[99] To Penn's delight, the sum of silver coin in Philadelphia increased considerably in the middle and latter years of the 1680s. Quaker merchants exported growing quantities of wheat, flour, beer, biscuits, horses, and barrel staves to Barbados and Curaçao—returning silver to the colony, not slaves— and some of the more ambitious merchants established an export trade with the Wine Islands and southern Europe. Pennsylvania wheat, flour, and bread made way to New England and Newfoundland; beef, pork, and barrel staves to the Chesapeake and Carolinas. A small shipbuilding industry even surfaced in Philadelphia, confined mostly to small watercraft.[100] Some newcomers, most notably the Quaker merchant Thomas Budd, hoped also to introduce the colonial manufacture of linen, which might abate the trade deficit with England and even provide enough "quantities to sell to the Inhabitants of our own neighbouring colonies."[101]

Colonial manufacturing, on a scale even closely resembling that of large-scale production, was, in truth, a distant prospect. The cost of labor was far higher in America than in England or Europe; the enormous acreage of land available made colonists less likely to enter wage work, despite the higher pay. "Poor People both Men and Women, will get near three times more Wages for their Labour in this Country, than they can earn either in England or Wales," said one writer from Pennsylvania.[102] Small-scale production of homespun cloth had grown in recent years, but this could only partially satisfy local demand, and the production certainly fell short of the quantity needed to dispense the cloth widely to other parts of America.[103] But as one resident of New York predicted, if they only had "more Tradesmen amongst them, they would in a little time live without the help of any other Countrey for their Clothing."[104] And colonists surely had strong pecuniary incentives to manufacture cloth; otherwise—as Thomas Budd said in 1685—they must be "supplied from England, where it must be dear [expensive], after Freight, Custom, and other charges."[105]

Nevertheless, however unlikely the prospect for now, colonial manufacturing was a definite menace to England's mercantilist empire. Manufactured goods accounted for 90 percent of all exports from England to the Americas. Of these, English manufactures were of the utmost importance; between 1660 and 1686, the export of English-made goods to the American colonies had nearly doubled—amounting now to a value of £211,933.[106] No mercantilist in England wished to hear of Americans making "Shooes and Hats" (as one report said of West Jersey in 1681); the English mercantilist or manufacturer trembled at news that colonial shoemakers were now supplying most of the internal market in New England and that a growing number of craftsmen inhabited rural townships.[107] The word from New York was of "every one making their own Linnen, and a great part of their woollen-cloth for their ordinary wearing."[108] If Americans demanded less imported merchandise, England's trade surplus with the colonies would suffer, and colonists would keep a far greater proportion of the coin that they earned from the Caribbean provisioning trade. Worse, they might expand this Caribbean trade by exporting to the islanders colonial-made textiles, not simply flour, bread, and barrel staves—a legal trade under the Navigation Acts. Considering that London merchants then exported more than £100,000 in English-made manufactures every year to the Caribbean, the thought of a cheaper colonial competitor in this area was a particularly dreadful one.[109]

Smuggling, nevertheless, remained a far more immediate concern to the mercantilist empire. The problem was decades old; it had yet to be resolved in any meaningful way, despite multiple efforts, including most conspicuously the appointment of resident customs officers in the Americas. Most colonial tradesmen had little to no scruples at all with smuggling. For the individual tradesman, illicit commerce boosted opportunities for gain; for the colony, more collectively, it increased either the provincial money supply or the volume of imported merchandise. It was in the colonists' immediate economic self-interest to pursue free trade, so long as they could get away with it.

In recent decades, some colonial historians have argued that smuggling had waned considerably by the early 1680s. By this time, they contend, smuggling was mostly confined to luxury goods. As evidence, these historians cite the recorded increase in England's transatlantic trade after 1660, maintaining that this increase indicates greater colonial compliance with the Navigation Acts. Furthermore, because enforcement mechanisms were still extraordinarily weak during this period, these historians argue that the supposed increase in colonial compliance implies that the economic incentive to smuggle had diminished: the price of English goods and of English freight was no longer higher than the Dutch competition, or smuggling would have continued unabated. Consequently, these historians argue, the Navigation Acts were not nearly as burdensome to colonists in the 1670s and 1680s as historians had initially thought.[110]

First, the statistical increase in English transatlantic trade and shipping after 1660 does nothing to prove any real, or at least substantial, decline in smuggling. The simultaneous rise in colonial population, and the consequent rise of colonial consumption and production, necessarily increased the volume of transatlantic trade across the board. The New England population nearly tripled between 1660 and 1689, from 32,000 to 86,000; the Chesapeake population grew from 26,000 to 82,000; the slave population in the English Caribbean went from 34,000 to 98,000. Consumption, in turn, multiplied.[111] Furthermore, improvements in agricultural efficiency, especially in the growing and curing of tobacco—the average crop size per worker rose from 1,514 to 1,829 pounds between 1660 and 1680—boosted colonial production beyond the natural increase received from the rise in population alone.[112] Even if smuggling *increased* after 1660, the volume of England's trade with the colonies still would have grown extensively.

Regarding the supposed decline in English freight rates, the records on freight rates are thin and highly disparate, rendering any surefire estimation impossible.[113] Still, even if rates for English shipping declined in the latter half of the seventeenth century, a probable estimation, that decline does not mean that smuggling was no longer a materially attractive option—even if English freight rates fell below the competition. Direct trade between colonists and foreigners obviated four payments: first, the customs duty; second, the profits accruing to the merchant-middleman in London; third, the many costs involved in clearing the goods out from England before reexportation (unloading, weighing, trucking, warehousing, and then reloading the goods for reexport); fourth, the additional expenses attendant on shipping the goods via an indirect route. As one colonist explained, the Navigation Acts required "making a double voyage . . . instead of going their voyages direct."[114] While this law benefited English merchants and supposedly the empire more generally, the requirement undoubtedly cost the colonial world a considerable sum of money.

One might object that Boston merchants were often middlemen between the Dutch or French on one end, and the Chesapeake or Caribbean on the other, and these merchants too took middlemen's profits, whether in the reexport of colonial produce to foreigners or of foreign merchandise to colonial buyers. Unlike the English, however, Boston merchants avoided paying customs on those goods; moreover, they carried the goods directly from buyer to seller without clearing out from England. As Randolph explained, Boston merchants bought produce and merchandise "Customs free," and therefore ". . . they were enabled to bring those Goods 50 per Cent. Cheaper to their Market there, than our Merchants could."[115] In this way, Massachusetts became "a Magazine both of all American and European Commodityes," the Lords of Trade reported in 1675—all "without carrying to England."[116]

Lastly, if smuggling indeed diminished as much as some historians claim, this diminishment begs the question why the Stuart Crown exhausted so many resources to stamp out a phantom problem. It was not inexpensive for the Commissioner of Customs to deploy full-time English agents to ports across Europe in 1683 to watch closely for inbound vessels from the colonies that had not stopped first in England.[117] The action was apparently not very effective: three years later, James II alleged that "several ships and vessels have carried great Quantityes" of colonial produce "to Holland, Hamburgh, and other places without first landing the same in England." Months earlier, the Privy Council urged another costly undertaking: that the royal navy be sent to the colonies to "seize all vessells belonging to strangers."[118] Clearly the Crown did not believe that smuggling had abated, at least in any significant way. The Crown treated smuggling as epidemic.

Furthermore, English mercantilists themselves conceded— unapologetically—that the Navigation Acts contravened the colonists' narrower economic self-interest. Sir Josiah Child even estimated, in 1693—with clear hyperbole—that were it not for the Navigation Acts, "you should see forty Dutch Ships at our own Plantations for one English." More extremely, one English opponent of Massachusetts, in 1689, proudly boasted that the "Parliament of England have never by any Act of theirs favoured the Plantations" but have always ensured that colonists be "restrained and burthened beyond any in England, as appears by the several Acts made for the increasing of Navigation."[119] Finally, there is no reason to doubt the accounts of men such as Governor Sir Thomas Lynch in Jamaica, who said in 1682 that smuggling prevailed on the island because the Dutch "sell European Goods 30 percent cheaper than we [the English], & will paye deerer for American Goods."[120]

The evidence is clear that illegal trade remained a significant fact of life in much if not most of the English colonial world in the 1680s. The colonists' provisioning trade to the French and Dutch Caribbean islands, in particular, offered numerous opportunities to illegally obtain European-made goods. Historian Cathy Matson has found that New York merchants regularly landed French and Dutch goods in the coves and inlets of East Jersey, Connecticut, and Long Island, avoiding detection by use of small watercraft. Wealthier merchants in New York even continued a direct trade with Amsterdam.[121] In East Jersey the customs collector, William Dyre, encountered fierce opposition from local merchants. In 1685 Dyre seized a vessel there for refusing to make entry at the customs office. Upon inspection, he found that one of the two shipmasters was French, and there was "but one English man on board." The cargo included all sorts of "European Goods," including gloves, linens, and Persian silks. The owner of the sloop, a Jersey man, publicly "railed at me and strangely contemned the Custome house." Dyre brought the case to court, but "the Jury (who bought much of the goods) found for the Defendant." The judge ordered Dyre to pay court fees, and after he refused to pay, the judge took Dyre "into his Custody." "I still remain prisoner," he wrote the Commissioner of Customs weeks later; ". . . to complain to the Governor is to no purpose." Such incidents were not unique to New Jersey. In October 1684, the acting governor of Maryland, George Talbot, astoundingly stabbed to death the king's customs collector.[122]

Direct trade between Virginia planters and Dutch tradesmen had declined somewhat since the 1650s; nevertheless, another illegal trade—a more indirect form—prevailed between the two, now mediated by carrier vessels from New England and New York, whose masters purchased the tobacco en route to French Newfoundland or to the Dutch Caribbean islands of Curaçao and St. Eustatius. The Navigation Act of 1673 required that colonial buyers of tobacco or sugar post bond to deliver the same to England. To avoid this requirement, shipmasters often covered the tobacco with legal fish or flour, and also did so when carrying European goods to colonial markets. "Under Colour of a Trade to Newfoundland for fish, great quantities of Wine Brandy and other European goods are imported," the Lords of Trade reported in 1687.[123] Five years earlier one member of the Virginia Council informed William

Blathwayt that "not one in ten payeth" the duty required by the Navigation Act of 1673.[124]

Scottish tradesmen steadily infiltrated the Chesapeake economy during this period. Until the Act of Union in 1707, this too was an illegal form of commerce. By the 1680s, Glasgow merchants collectively imported as much as 250,000 pounds of tobacco a year, entirely sidestepping the English customs and paying the planter a higher price than the legal English trader.[125] Because the Scots enjoyed close commercial ties with the Dutch, the Scots often carried this tobacco directly for Holland. Scottish freight rates were demonstrably lower than rates for English ships, and in bulk trades like tobacco, freight was often the greatest expense. Scottish shipmasters passed easily for Englishmen and "seldome faile [as] counterfeit masters," Randolph later recorded; even Dutch shipmasters quite frequently feigned English names, to the wink and nod of a knowing official.[126] Scottish tradesmen also penetrated southeastern Carolina, selling goods to buyers at comparatively low prices. A Charles Town jury acquitted one such trader in 1687, doubting (supposedly) that the crew was not English. Nevertheless, according to the customs collector, the jury "declared, that if it had been never soe evident" that the crew was indeed Scottish, the Carolina charter "gives them full Power to Trade with Scotland and Ireland." Money was the chief impetus to this refractory behavior, the customs collector explained in the aftermath of that trial: Scottish merchants "are evidently able to undersell the English, their Goods being either much Courser or Slighter . . . and will be sure to goe off there, being cheap."[127]

Well into the 1680s, English sugar planters in the West Indian islands still recurrently welcomed "forreign Vessels" into their ports. Some of these vessels belonged to the nearby French islanders, selling wine and luxury goods; others included Dutch traders selling linen and buying "great Quantitys of Sugar." The many shrouded inlets, coves, and bays in the area made it extraordinarily difficult, if not impossible, for imperial officers to monitor the full spectrum of commercial activity.[128] This difficulty was especially pronounced in the English Leeward Islands, positioned practically at a stone's throw distance from St. Eustatius (Dutch), St. Thomas (Danish but Dutch-dominated), Martinique (French), and Guadeloupe (French). One customs official in 1687 estimated that the Hollanders come "to St Christophers twice or thrice a week"; the French sell "brandys and french wines . . . our Merchants who pay his Majesties Customs being not able to supply them at near the Price they so illegally get them."[129]

Sugar planters courted illicit slave dealers, most of all, with the utmost zeal. This activity increased dramatically in the 1670s, so that by the early 1680s, English planters bought as many as one-third to one-half of their slaves from interlopers instead of the Royal African Company. Slave prices, consequently, fell to their lowest levels ever.[130] Dealers generally smuggled Africans into port at night, or on the back part of the island; with courts made up of planter juries, moreover, the RAC faced profound difficulties in successfully prosecuting these smugglers.[131] In one instance in 1682 a Jamaican judge awarded more than £1,600 in damages to an interloper seized by the company.[132] One RAC agent in 1681 reported of a smuggler in Barbados "bringing about 100 Negroes which were then put on shore without Interruption"; the smugglers' confidence and reputation has "growne very high," he said.[133] Leeward planters, largely neglected by the company, were especially eager for smuggled slave labor, and the planters' successful embrace of this illegal traffic played a significant role in granting the Leeward Islands a black majority by 1680.[134]

Those who maintain that there was a severe decline in smuggling in the 1670s and 1680s do not deny the interloping trade in slaves and luxury goods. But smuggling of *all* sorts remained common through this period. To be clear, the extent of this activity did not match the extraordinary levels of the 1650s, but that indeed was a truly exceptional decade. After 1660, enforcement was marginally stronger than before, increasing the risk of seizure. The trade after 1660 was more dependent on subterfuge and oftentimes chance; the networks between buyer and seller were less stable and less permanent than they had been at midcentury.[135] Mild efficiency improvements in English shipping may have also made smuggling slightly less worth the risk. In some cases, it was just as profitable to simply follow the law; in other cases, perhaps more numerous, there was much profit and money to be made in breaking it. One way or the other, however, English administrators and mercantilists took the problem of colonial smuggling very seriously, and for good reason. More and more they concluded that political coercion of the more extreme type was the only realistic solution.

When James II ascended the throne in February 1685, England was in the midst of a trade boom unparalleled in the nation's history. The extreme economic pessimism of the early to mid-1670s had long vanished.[136] The economic tide began to turn after 1674, when Charles signed a peace treaty with the Netherlands. The French and Dutch fought on for another four years, priming neutral England to vend textiles abroad. The kingdom's trade balances with Germany, the Low Countries, Portugal, Spain, and of course colonial America were all very favorable, offsetting England's trade deficit with France, the Baltic countries, and India. The English East India Company enjoyed record-setting profits; the company reexported more than half a million calicoes a year to continental Europe.[137] By the mid-1680s, the "grand Emporium" of

London had become the world's foremost commercial entrepôt, supplanting even Amsterdam, equipping the city's several thousand merchants with a "greater quantity of new Money."[138] The output of coin at the Tower Mint averaged £370,820 per year in the 1670s; in the 1680s it averaged £543,658 per year, an increase of nearly 50 percent.[139] Furthermore, the enlarged revenue from customs was adequate enough for Charles to rule independently; he last convened a Parliament in March 1681, dissolving it a week later. Charles governed without any Parliament in the final four years of his reign.

Despite persistent smuggling, England's trade with the Americas was exceptionally dynamic in the 1680s. From London, several hundred merchants traded extensively every year with the American colonies; at least nine of these London merchants in American trade possessed estates exceeding £30,000 in worth, and at least eight others possessed estates between £10–30,000.[140] By comparison, no more than a dozen merchants in Massachusetts had estates reaching even £5,000, and of those, fewer than half reached even £10,000.[141] Between 1663 and 1686, the number of ships clearing London for North America and the Caribbean nearly tripled, from 88 to 257. This trade now accounted for 37 percent of all of England's overseas tonnage (up from 29 percent in 1663).[142] One-third of all goods imported by English merchants for English consumption now came from the American colonies; only one-half came from continental Europe—a drastic reversal from previous decades. On the export side, the colonies represented 40 percent of the overseas market for English-made goods; at midcentury, by contrast, fewer than 10 percent of English-made exports went to England's American colonies.[143] Exports to the colonies included woolens, hats, glassware, paper, wrought leather, saddles, clocks, anchors, cordage, ironware, guns, gunpowder, nails, brassware, wrought copper, gloves, shoes, silks, calicoes, Dutch and German linens, spectacles, looking glasses, playing cards, books, curtains, and carriages.[144]

The reexport trade of colonial goods from London to continental Europe was a mercantilist treasure trove. As Dalby Thomas, English sugar merchant, wrote of the colonies in 1690, "they never draw from England Gold or Silver, but on the contrary"—through the re-export trade—". . . either occasion the Enriching of England by monies brought from Foreign parts for the sales of their product, or by Bartering for other Goods which must have been purchased by monies."[145] Another writer, the same year, boasted that because of colonial trade, "we buy less yearly of Forrainers to the value of half a Million [pounds sterling] at the least, and we export and sell, out of the same Produce, a good deale more than another half Million, which is the same thing in effect, as Mines of Silver yielding above a Million yearely." The colonies, and sugar plantations especially, made "a great alteration in our Trade and Money for the better," the writer said.[146]

The West Indian islands were still the most profitable sector of the mercantilist Atlantic. In 1686 sugar accounted for approximately 66.5 percent of the value of all colonial exports to London.[147] That year alone, nearly 1,300 London merchants imported, collectively, almost £675,000 worth of Caribbean goods—sugar dominating (87 percent)—in some 275 oceangoing vessels. (By way of contrast, just over 600 London merchants imported goods from North America to the value of £207,131, of which tobacco made up 68 percent.)[148] Sugar exports to London had nearly tripled between 1663 and 1686, amounting, by the latter date, to more than 22,000 tons.[149] Barbados produced about 55 percent of this sugar; exports from Barbados alone exceeded the value of all exports from mainland North America.[150] English merchants reexported approximately one-third of the incoming sugar to continental Europe.[151] "Heretofore we had all our Sugars from Portugal," Dalby Thomas recalled in 1690; this trade had formerly cost the kingdom "yearly about £400,000." "Now that great Leak is stopp'd," he said, and the reexport of sugar "brings us in yearly near the same Summe."[152]

The Royal African Company reaped handsome profits from the contraband trade of English manufactures and African slaves to Spanish America. Shares in the RAC yielded for its investors an annual divided of 10 percent in the years between 1676 and 1688.[153] James, Duke of York, was president and chief stockholder of the RAC, sweetening the company's success all the more. In the 1680s the company exported double the value of manufactured goods to West Africa than it had in the previous decade: exports to Africa included English woolens, metalwares, and cotton fabrics from India.[154] Between 1673 and 1688, the RAC exported approximately twenty thousand slaves to Spanish America; at £20 a slave this trade amounted to nearly half a million pounds sterling over a fifteen-year period.[155] The additional, clandestine export of textiles and metalwares to Spanish America tilted the balance even further in England's favor; the contraband trade alone was likely worth more than £100,000 every year.[156] Supporters of the company celebrated the "great quantity of the Gold and Silver we have of the Spaniards for Negroes and English Manufactory."[157] Jamaica, as the chief base of RAC operations, was thereby "the Key of the Indies, and naturally the seat of Riches and Empire . . . lying in the very Belly of all Commerce . . . facing to the South and West, the richest Continent in the World."[158]

The tobacco colonies of the Chesapeake benefited the mercantilist empire in different ways. Tobacco imports into London were a little less than one-quarter of the value of sugar imports (£141,606 to £586,528).[159] Nevertheless, between 1670 and 1686, tobacco imports had almost doubled, amounting now to an astounding twenty-eight million pounds.[160] Of this sum, English merchants reexported more than half to Europe; formerly, English merchants reexported only one-third of Chesapeake tobacco.[161] One contemporary estimated that this reexport trade in tobacco earned for England some £200,000 each year (in coin, bills of exchange, or merchandise).[162] The customs revenue on tobacco, meanwhile, far exceeded the revenue from sugar. Before the duty increase of 1685—discussed in the next chapter—the duty on tobacco earned about £150,000 per annum; after 1685, the revenue from tobacco exceeded £320,000.[163] Virginia's planters did not fail to take notice. "Our staple Commoditie tobacco accrues to your Majesties Revenue more then twice soe much as we our selves have," the burgesses petitioned the king in 1684.[164]

New England remained a serious question mark, of course. Whigs and Tories, for the most part, agreed. "Among these Plantations," said John Cary, a Whig, "I look on that of New-England to bring least Advantage to this Kingdom"; another Whig, John Pollexfen, called the region "of little use to us." Josiah Child, the court Tory, called it the "most prejudicial Plantation to the Kingdom of England"; their "Liberty of Trading," he argued in 1693, came at the "total exclusion of the old English Merchant."[165] Though the region supplied valuable pine-tree masts to English shipbuilders, New England shipbuilders competed against their English counterparts by constructing as many as thirty vessels a year for English merchants. The cost of constructing a ship in Massachusetts was 40 percent less than in England; adjacent timber supplies offset the higher wages.[166] "There is nothing more prejudicial, and in prospect more dangerous to any Mother Kingdom," Child declared, "than the encrease of Shipping in the Colonies." Carew Reynell, a Whig, agreed, arguing in 1674 that the New England settlements "breed no good Commerce," and "are rather a disadvantage, than advantage to us."[167]

Yet even in these northern settlements—New England, New York, and Pennsylvania—consumer demand for imported goods clearly benefited English mercantile interests. From London alone, in 1686, just over £100,000 worth of English-made goods went to mainland North America; of this quantity, £40,700 went to New England and £17,152 to the Middle Colonies.[168] Nor do these numbers include reexported goods from continental Europe. Northern colonists imported an "infinite Quantity of Iron Wares," "all sorts of Tin-ware," plowshares, axes, "Saddles and Bridles," and "many Barrels of Nails" (large spikes to hold wooden houses together).[169] Besides improving the kingdom's balance of trade, this commerce helped to diversify English industry beyond the mere export of woolens. Thus even the northern colonies offered much mercantilist value. The export of English-made goods to the

Caribbean islands were not that much greater than that to mainland North America: in the year 1686, the value of English-made exports to the Caribbean was £111,392, compared with £100,541 to North America. Furthermore, of this total, textiles comprised a far greater percentage of the exports to North America than to the Caribbean (53 percent versus 36 percent).[170]

By most metrics, England's trade with the American colonies was extremely favorable in the early to mid-1680s. Nevertheless, the persistence of smuggling and other adverse economic and monetary practices in the colonial world represented a pressing thorn in the side of England's mercantilist Atlantic empire. The kingdom's newfound prosperity in the 1680s did not abate imperial criticism of these practices; on the contrary, the drive to rein in colonial autonomy intensified. There was yet more money to be made, if only the colonists could be brought to obedience. "Though we are a Nation already pretty substantial," wrote Carew Reynell in 1674, "yet it's easie for us to be ten times richer."[171] To increase the "National Home-Treasure," to secure "Plenty, Glory, and Prosperity to a whole Nation"—said another English writer in 1680—that was the goal of the imperial project, and unlawful colonists ought not to obstruct it.[172]

Things had come a long way since 1607 and even since the early 1670s. No longer was there any real question of whether colonial plantations increased or decreased the national wealth. Most now agreed that colonies were "highly beneficial, and of vast advantage." "By a kind of Magnetick Force," said one author in 1689, "England draws to it all that is good in the Plantations: it is the Center to which all things tend."[173] Charles II died in February 1685. His younger brother, now King James II, was thoroughly convinced that colonial economic obedience could finally and only be attained through a drastic, sweeping, coercive reshaping of American colonial governance.

CHAPTER 8

Revolutions of 1685–1689

When James II ascended the throne in February 1685, the economic pessimism of the early to mid-1670s was little more than a distant memory. England's trade overseas was booming; money was more plentiful than previously; gold, in particular, streamed into the Tower Mint at unprecedented levels, resulting in the coinage of tens of thousands of guineas, liberally filling royal and mercantile coffers.[1] Two great monopoly companies, both fiercely loyal to the Stuart court, lorded over two of the most profitable branches of overseas trade, earning spectacular returns. Yet the nation's political life was extraordinarily tense, to put it mildly. James had long been one of the most controversial figures in all of England. A convert to Roman Catholicism in the late 1660s, he unabashedly envied the French absolutist state, and as late as 1681 he was almost excluded from the royal succession by Whigs in Parliament. Nevertheless, the English public, in early 1685, appeared altogether willing to afford the new king a fair opportunity. Most of the public, at this early stage, trusted that his reign would not represent too great of a departure from that of his older brother.[2]

James proceeded rapidly with a daring agenda for both domestic and colonial reforms. Like his predecessor, James's ultimate aim was to boost the Crown's independent revenue—namely the customs—thus liberating him from reliance on Parliament. With respect to the colonies, James determined to boost the customs revenue by first increasing the duties on tobacco and sugar and by finally enforcing the Navigation Acts. To achieve this end, James and his courtiers endorsed, first, the consolidation of smaller, private colonies into larger, royal ones and, second, the immediate subjugation of any restive, rebellious, or upstart elements within the colonial population. The plan was ambitious but poorly executed. The Crown's efforts in the Chesapeake and Caribbean excited a furious backlash from the money-starved tobacco and sugar planters; in Massachusetts, the king's brash decision, first, to end representative government and, second, to rebuff the colony's land speculators and small freeholders alienated nearly all men of standing in the colony, even those merchants who previously desired royal government.

The money supply of the American colonies diminished conspicuously during King James II's reign. This diminishment resulted primarily from the appreciable decline in smuggling and piracy and contrasted sharply with the relative prosperity of the colonies in the first half of the 1680s. Economic and monetary stagnation thus accompanied the colonists' many political grievances against James during his reign. This stagnation prepped them for revolution in 1689, a factor often neglected by colonial historians of this period. Economics, of course, was not the only reason why colonists greeted James's ouster with near-universal joy, but money's role in the drama was indeed monumental.

James's life story was a highly unusual one, even for English nobility or royalty. He was not even nine years old when the English Civil War broke out and only fifteen years old when his father was beheaded for treason. James had spent the early part of his adulthood as an exile in France, even serving in the French and Spanish armies before returning to England in 1660. Eight years later, at age thirty-five, the duke converted to Roman Catholicism, a decision not made public until 1673 when Parliament passed the Test Act, which required officeholders to reject central aspects of Roman Catholic doctrine; James subsequently resigned from his post as Lord Admiral. The duke's personality deviated sharply from that of his older brother, Charles, whose lighthearted charm, indulgence, worldliness, and political pragmatism (and sometimes artifice) set the prevailing mood of his court; the duke, by contrast, was austere; devout; stubborn; sober; and more ideological and rigid in worldview. He was remarkably more candid and sincere than his brother; James abhorred duplicity, opportunism, and personal machinations. He had a penchant for credulity, leaving him vulnerable to disappointment upon learning that those within his inner circle were not as authentic or principled. Cavalier to a fault, he was nonetheless forthright and courtly in demeanor and resented the permissive, undignified turn that the court had purportedly taken under Charles.[3]

Above all, the new king was a visionary. A mere reactionary he was not; his vision for England was decidedly modern, dynamic, innovative, and intensely fixated on future progression. France was his obvious exemplar; the siren song of Catholic absolutism had long enchanted the duke. His cousin, Louis XIV, possessed astonishing wealth, dazzling Europe with his palaces, military, political initiative, and power. The English and Dutch political models, by comparison, seemed quaint and outmoded. State centralization, James believed, was the way of the future: empire superintended by an aggressive, prestigious monarch—one jealous of prerogative and relentless in enforcing the will of the state, of which he was unequivocally head. From James's perspective, Louis and his finance minister Jean-Baptiste Colbert exemplified, most magnificently, the natural, reciprocal partnership between economic mercantilism and political hegemony. Money begat power, and power begat money; James pursued both with unqualified vigor (see figure 10).[4]

Having promised to uphold the prevailing constitution of church and state, the newly crowned James II—the first Roman Catholic monarch of England since Queen Mary, more than 125 years earlier—enjoyed considerable support at the outset of his reign. The general election in May 1685 turned out an overwhelmingly Tory parliament, styled the Loyal Parliament. Ready as they were to support the new king, most Tory MPs, nonetheless, were men of moderate views; they agreed with the basic Tory tenets of irresistible Crown authority and an authoritative Church of England but opposed the French model of absolutist, Catholic government. Such men trusted that James's governing style would not represent too great of a departure from that of his brother.

FIGURE 10. Gold five-guinea coin of King James II, 1687. (ANS 1957.172.19. Courtesy of American Numismatic Society.)

Indeed propertied men all over England—wary of another civil war—sided with conservatism and welcomed with open minds the new king.[5]

James commenced his reign with a swiftness and resolve that astounded most observers and panicked many others. Between February and December 1685, he expanded the size of the army from 9,000 to 20,000 men; within three years, the army numbered 40,000 soldiers (approaching Cromwellian levels), and military expenditures had more than tripled.[6] James ordered the quartering of troops in public houses—taverns, inns, and coffeehouses—and exempted soldiers from being tried according to English common law. He violated the Test Act of 1673 by commissioning a large number of Catholics into army and civilian posts, though Roman Catholics made up less than 2 percent of the population. When Parliament objected that his actions violated the law, he prorogued the body in November 1685, never to summon it again. Within weeks of his coronation, he established a Catholic Cabinet Council, whose members publicly and proudly espoused French absolutist theory, and he relied on this council for advice instead of the traditional Privy Council. In nearly every facet of political life, he placed absolute royalty at the center; this pattern was particularly true in the counties, previously the sphere of local elites, as James wantonly purged any magistrates, jurists, and justices of the peace not in his favor, achieving what historian Steve Pincus calls a "total reshaping of English government."[7]

Such ambition required new sources of money. Here, customs revenue was paramount, for once the rates had been established by Parliament, the Crown collected this revenue independently, freeing the royal purse from unwanted interference. Independent revenue had permitted Charles to dissolve the unruly Exclusion Parliaments in 1679–1681; James might not have summoned a parliament at all in 1685 if he could have legally assumed the customs revenue that Parliament had granted his older brother. No matter, however: the new Parliament was of loyal disposition, and James soon found himself in a very pleasant fiscal situation. Besides Parliament's repeal of the 1678 prohibition on French imports—which repeal alone increased the customs revenue—the Tory Parliament, in June 1685, granted James a very generous duty.

The new 1685 duty substantially raised the imposition on imported colonial tobacco and sugar. The tax on English colonial tobacco rose from 2d to 5d a pound, an increase of 150 percent (the duty on foreign tobacco, for its part, doubled from 6d to 1s). On muscovado sugar the duty rose from just over 1s6d to 3s6d per hundredweight (cwt) (the duty on the foreign product was now 8s per cwt).[8] The new duties retained the partial drawback on reexported tobacco and sugar (reexported tobacco paid duties of only a halfpenny a pound), but the duty increase, on the whole, was quite substantial indeed and predictably, the customs revenue soared. In 1686 London merchants imported and retained within England (without reexportation) 403,911 cwt of muscovado sugar and nearly 15 million pounds of tobacco. The previous rates would have earned duties of just over £30,000 on sugar and £124,000 on tobacco; the new rates, however, earned more than £70,000 for sugar and more than £310,000 for tobacco. (If one also includes the halfpenny duty on the 13,112,200 pounds of reexported tobacco, the total tobacco duties in 1686 amounted to more than £338,000).[9]

The new duties triggered a storm of protest. English merchants feared the tax would discourage consumption in England; colonial planters feared the tax would drive down the farm price of their crops, becoming, effectively, a crushing tax on the staple plantations. The "burden of these heavy Impositions," one planter warned, would soon devastate the "once flourishing English Colonies."[10] In November 1685, the House of Burgesses petitioned the Crown that "the additional duty" was "very ruinous" and would surely "prove destructive to Trade, and too prejudicial to your Majesties Plantations"; "wee cannot support ourselves under the burthen thereof," the burgesses said.[11] The Virginia governor, Lord Howard of Effingham, quickly distanced himself from the petition, apologizing to the Crown for the assembly's "great importunitys"; nevertheless, he informed the Lords of Trade that news of the "late Additional Imposition on Tobacco has soe disturbed the Planters."[12] Sure enough, the farm price of tobacco fell from a penny a pound in 1685 to less than three-quarters of a penny by the end of 1688.[13] Sugar planters, of course, hated the tax as well; on Barbados, the deputy-governor, council, and assembly sent a joint petition to the Crown insisting that the current low price of sugar made them utterly "unable to bear the burden" of the duty.[14] Even the royal governor of Jamaica, Hender Molesworth—friend of the Crown and agent of the Royal African Company—informed William Blathwayt in August 1685 that this "vast discouragement" would surely "ruine all the plantations." "Virginia receives a mortall Stabb, Barbados and the Islands fall into a Hectick fevour, and Jamaica into a Consumption," he wrote; ". . . in 7 yeares the revenue will be much lesse then it was before this additional duty."[15] "They would use us like Sponges, or like Sheep," railed a sugar planter on hearing of the duty; "They think us fit to be squeezed and fleeced."[16]

Sugar fell to its lowest price of the century at the end of 1685. The farm price of muscovado sugar had already fallen from 2–3 pence a pound in the 1660s to just over 1d a pound in the early 1680s. That particular price drop was the result, in part, of expanded production on the French sugar islands, especially Martinique, as well as on the English Leeward Islands and Jamaica. Now, after the effects of the new duty, raw sugar earned less than a penny a pound at farm. According to the Barbadian government, the price tumbled 40 percent from the beginning of 1685 to the end of summer, reducing the island to a "most deplorable Condition."[17] The price drop was obviously the result of James's new tax. "The severity and burthen of the late additional duty," the governor of Barbados reported, has caused much "trouble & apprehension"—"sugar selling very low here."[18] Furthermore, the price of African slave labor had risen more than 10 percent since the early 1680s.[19] RAC agents were now sitting governors on Jamaica and Barbados and doing a better job at curtailing interlopers; meanwhile the largest shareholder of the RAC was none other than James himself. Indeed, only weeks after his coronation, James issued a proclamation declaring his full intent to enforce the RAC monopoly.[20] West Indian debts to the RAC grew more than 40 percent over the decade, totaling £170,000 by the end of the 1680s.[21] Most of the coin that Barbadians had acquired in the early 1680s disappeared in the second half of the decade. Even the island's pro-RAC deputy governor, Edwyn Stede, acknowledged this fact: "Money being soe Scarce here," he wrote in 1687, ". . . that unless the European marketts will afforde a better Price . . . this once flourishing Island will soone Decay." "Wee are in miserable Condition," the deputy governor of Barbados added, "not findeing Money in the Island in any reasonable portion to Supply the Wants of it, nor any meanes to bring Money to us."[22]

Worse, in 1687 the planters learned of a design by James to incorporate a West India Company. The prospective company would monopolize the entire sugar trade, with the king receiving annual dividends as another source of revenue independent of Parliament. If this project of "Indigent and other persons" succeeded, "by them onely are wee to be supplyed with Money and Creditt and all necessaryes," the Barbadian governor protested. "What have we done, or wherein have we offended, that we should be used in this manner?" the island's agent to London, Edward Littleton, asked later in 1689; ". . . These Men seem to be trying Conclusions, whether they can so far provoke us, as to make us desperate. . . . They would make the very Name of *England* hateful to us. They would make our Great and Dear Mother, *England*, to be so cruel and unnatural, as to destroy and devour her own Children."[23]

In Virginia, the king's appetite for independent revenue had prompted not only the hated duty increase but also a separate measure regarding the collection of quitrents. The quitrent was a fee paid directly to the Crown of 1s per annum on every fifty acres of land (the king claimed ultimate ownership of all soil in the colony). Since 1662, quitrents could be settled in either silver coin or tobacco valued at 2d a pound. The market price for tobacco had long fallen far below 2d a pound—sometimes below 1d a pound—yet the Crown continued to collect quitrents at the higher valuation. The infamous Arlington-Culpeper patent in 1673 granted two private proprietors the quitrent for a time, but in 1684 Charles bought back the rights. Then James became king. With no advance warning he decreed that quitrents could henceforth be paid only in *silver money*: no more payment in tobacco, not even at an adjusted rate. The policy change, in many ways, was patently absurd; Virginia was one of the most silver-starved colonies in all of America. It was not even clear whether the measure was the least bit doable, much less prudent. For the next year and a half, the Burgesses and its agents pleaded desperately for a reversal, the inhabitants "not being possible able so to doe, there being noe Specificall monie in this Country." The king's plan, they urged, was "not only ruinous but utterly impossible."[24] Under acute pressure from the burgesses, Governor Effingham (a Roman Catholic and otherwise staunch ally of James) overrode the king's command and temporarily accepted tobacco at 1d a pound pending further negotiations, a compromise that the Crown finally though reluctantly agreed to late in 1686.[25]

Effingham otherwise proved quite the imperious governor in Virginia. In October 1685 he issued a proclamation forbidding all seditious discourse (unwanted criticism of the governor or king); in December he prorogued the House of Burgesses for petitioning the Crown against the new duty. The burgesses met again in October 1686, proclaiming that it was unlawful for the governor to raise taxes without "Our Own Consent." All colonists, they said, have "a Right to and Inheritance in the Lawes of his Majesties Kingdom of England, and the Liberties and Priviledges" thereof.[26] On hearing of these proceedings, King James condemned the burgesses for their "frivolous and unnecessary debates" and ordered Effingham to dissolve the assembly in the king's name—the first time the House of Burgesses had ever been dissolved by royal command.[27]

James II proceeded differently with the more northerly settlements. Most of these were private colonies, whether by charter or proprietorship. Like the Lords of Trade, James deeply distrusted these colonies, preferring instead the Spanish colonial model of large, consolidated viceroyalties, devoid of any representative assemblies. Initially the king acted boldly in this direction: just three months into his reign, he ordered articles of indictment against Rhode Island and Connecticut—the former for violating the Navigation Acts, the latter for not permitting Anglican forms of worship—and a writ was soon out against the Jersey proprietors and Lord Baltimore's proprietorship in Maryland.[28] James's former proprietary colony, New York, became a royal colony immediately upon his accession. Soon afterward, James announced the repeal of the colony's "Charter of Libertyes and Priviledges," a document drafted in October 1683 by the New York legislature—the first assembly to ever meet in the colony—outlining certain political freedoms reserved for the colony, including triennial assemblies, habeas corpus, and consent to all legislation.[29]

Action thereafter, however, was painstakingly slow. James, at first, had wished to combine New York, the Jerseys, and Pennsylvania into a single dominion, governed without a representative assembly.[30] But the plan stalled. Many more pressing issues occupied the king's early administration, namely Monmouth's Rebellion, a failed attempt by Charles's eldest, illegitimate, and Protestant son to overthrow James in the summer of 1685. Consolidating the northern colonies seemed a paltry matter by comparison, and what little attention the king could afford was better spent on the Caribbean or Chesapeake settlements. In the meantime, the people of New England, and Massachusetts especially, anxiously awaited the Crown's next action.

The future of Massachusetts Bay was stuck in an agonizing malaise early in James II's reign. The charter had been legally vacated in October 1684, but the death of Charles in February, and James's many other preoccupations early in his reign, resulted in the colony being left simply as it was. Until May 1686, the General Court—still dominated by the independent faction—continued to sit and to legislate as if nothing had happened, making no official acknowledgment whatsoever of the charter's nullification. The most they could do was to carry on as usual, and to fast and to pray for a miracle.[31]

The Boston mint, like the government, was in a state of limbo. No details at all had been released on whether the Crown planned to resurrect the mint, defunct since June 1682, in altered form. The Lords of Trade took up the question in November 1684—one month after revoking the Massachusetts charter—asking the Commissioners of the Royal Mint in England to report on whether the king shall "continue or set aside the further exercise of such a Mint." Predictably, the mint commissioners advised that the Boston mint either remain closed or have its coins brought to the same standard weight and valuation as the English shilling. The former 1652 stamp corroborated the commissioners' overall suspicion of the mint. "It may also be observed," they noted, "that though they have continued this unwarrantable way of Coyneing of Money ever since the year 1652, yet there is noe alteration of date appears upon their Coynes."[32] A mint under royal direction would not retain the old stamp, but even so, the association between New England sovereignty and coining money persisted, the commissioners argued. The Lords of Trade, uncertain of what to do, delayed their recommendation.

In the meantime, Massachusetts moderates lined up to support the impending royal government. They did so with a disquieting mixture of enthusiasm and anxiousness. One of the leading moderates, Joseph Dudley, urged Randolph in December 1684 that the Crown "betrust the Government wholly to persons among us."[33] But Charles died in February; not until autumn 1685 did James commission a grand council to temporarily preside over the colonies of Massachusetts, New Plymouth, and New Hampshire. The commission for this new interim government did not even arrive in Boston until May 1686, when Randolph returned to Massachusetts with commission in hand (along with writs against the private governments of Rhode Island and Connecticut). The commission named Dudley the council president, with no elected assembly. To Randolph's delight, the Massachusetts General Court adjourned without resistance. Simon Bradstreet, former governor and a moderate, refused his appointment as councillor, citing the lack of any representative assembly; nevertheless, he was the only nominee to do so. All awaited the launch of the announced and more permanent Dominion of New England, which the Crown belatedly decided would be headed by Sir Edmund Andros, the former governor of New York, who had not yet departed London. All other details remained highly tentative.[34]

The Dudley councillors took their oaths of office on May 25, 1686. Four days later, Randolph announced his support for a Boston mint. The about-face was astonishing. Once the mint's foremost enemy, Randolph now insisted that there was an absolutely "necessity" for a Boston coinage, "for since they have Ceased coining, their money is every day shipd off for England. . . . Tis a hard matter to gett £100 in silver." For ten years, Randolph had frantically railed against the mint; now, with his allies in power, a Boston mint under royal direction was not only desirable but indispensable. The Dudley Council agreed, petitioning the king a few days later that "our Trade for want of money is much perplexed and decayed," beseeching "his Majestys Licence, direction and Impress . . . for establishing a Mint in this his Dominion."[35] Randolph's urging aside, in July 1686 the Commissioners of the Royal Mint in London issued a second report on the question, reiterating their opposition and reminding the Lords of Trade that a proposal in 1678 for a Jamaican mint had been "found impracticable." A Boston coinage of any sort was inadvisable, the commissioners insisted; nevertheless, they agreed to contrive "some other Inscriptions more agreeable to the Kings Prerogative to be Stampt upon the Coyne of New England, if a Mint be settled there."[36]

Andros, still in London, weighed in on the matter. He agreed with Randolph and Dudley that New England would benefit greatly from a mint. "Peices of Eight" are of "unequal weight and value," he said in October 1686. Andros even went so far as to defend the founding of the original mint in 1652. This time, however, operations would "be performed by his Majesty's Officers, and the profit that shall arise by the Coinage, applied to his Majesty's use."[37] As governor of New York from 1674 to 1683, Andros was greatly familiar with the pine-tree shilling; it will be remembered, also, that as governor Andros had lobbied (unsuccessfully) for a New York mint. Now, in like manner, Andros believed that a Dominion of New England coinage, besides regularizing the currency, would rapidly enhance the prestige of his new government.

All came to naught. Toward the end of October 1686, the Lords of Trade advised against "Re-establishing a Mint for the Coining of Money in New England." James followed their counsel.[38] In order to fully vanquish any vestiges of an independent Bay colony, any trace of that undoubted symbol of independence, the Boston shilling, must also disappear.

For the short duration of the Dudley government—before Andros arrived in Boston in December 1686—the interim regime commanded only a token of control over New England. The Dudley Council failed to collect any tax revenue, teetering near bankruptcy; the councillors met only sparsely and simply reappointed local officeholders. The lack of any representative assembly had reportedly unsettled several members of the council.[39] Soured, Randolph turned against them. "The independent faction still prevails," he reported a mere three months into the Dudley regime; the council, he claimed, withstood all efforts "to prevent the irregular trade of this place," for "some of the Council are traders." Indeed, one of the first actions of the Dudley Council was to petition the Lords of Trade that New England merchants be exempt from the Navigation Act of 1673. Randolph's seizure that summer of six interloping vessels "inflames the people's malice against me," he reported, and the councillors "openly refused" to assist the prosecution. Some of the councillors "look upon me as the onely enemy of their Country," and "the independent ministers . . . have spoken treasonable words in their pulpits." "The Great favour of liberty of Conscience granted this people may in a short tyme be of ill consequence," he warned; there must be "some limitation to their extravagant use of it."[40]

But the Dudley Council was not entirely disengaged that summer and fall of 1686. On the contrary, the councillors were quite active in promoting an issue of great imperative: at least for their own pocketbooks. Land speculation was foremost on the minds of several of the councillors and, with it, a corresponding proposal for a colonial paper currency. King Philip's War had opened up vast acreage for settlement in central Massachusetts and northeastern Connecticut. Speculators hungrily awaited coming riches. The chief obstacle was confirmation of land title. Massachusetts land titles were notoriously precarious, subject to conflicting political jurisdictions, Indian claims, and competing titles over the same plot of land. The theocratic Puritan government was hardly the proper venue to validate the speculators' claims; prominent ministers like Increase Mather had long roared against land speculation from the pulpit. "Land! Land! hath been the Idol of many in New-England," was Mather's lamentation.[41] Thus royal government, for land speculators, was a promising alternative. From 1676 onward, most speculators aligned themselves closely with Randolph and the moderate faction in Massachusetts politics. Anticipating the inevitability of royal government, a number of land syndicates sprouted up, the most famous of which was the Atherton Company, which hoped to later sell the land at a spectacular profit of £20 sterling per one hundred acres.[42] Beyond the syndicates, individual speculators made enormous purchases, especially in the period after 1683, when the coming dissolution of the charter was imminent. Indeed, the men that Randolph had nominated for the forthcoming Dudley Council, together, laid claim to 397,733 acres, the projected future value of which totaled tens of thousands of pounds sterling.[43]

The king's long delay in establishing a new government over New England surely worried the speculators, but when the king's commission for the Dudley Council arrived in May 1686, the land interest had every reason to be enthusiastic. Nine of the thirteen councillors were members of one or more of the land syndicates, and all but one of the councillors were involved in speculation individually.[44] One councillor, Richard Wharton, was the leading associate of the Atherton Company: he alone laid claim to more than 200,000 acres. Dudley himself claimed nearly 10,000 acres.[45] Furthermore, Randolph bore news that Connecticut and New Hampshire would also be included in the new government, both of which had long been favorite targets for land speculation. Soon after the commission arrived, one group of speculators (including the colony's former agent, William Stoughton) purchased 160,000 acres in Connecticut for the paltry price of £120 sterling.[46] As Randolph became more and more disillusioned with the Dudley Council, he became all the more critical of "the Great Landed men." "In our whole Councill," he said, "not one man but either by private Interest or faction is touch'd." "These will stickle hard," he predicted, "when their titles of Land are questioned."[47]

In September 1686 the Dudley Council endorsed the establishment of a "Bank of Credit," in part to address the land title question.[48] This proposal—from an otherwise languishing council—was daring to say the least. The prospective bank, besides creating an official land registry, would lend paper currency to anybody who mortgaged their land with the bank. Particularly striking was that the bank was the brainchild of a curious newcomer to Boston: Captain John Blackwell.

Captain Blackwell had arrived in Boston only in 1684. An aged merchant, devout Puritan, former treasurer of war under Cromwell, and former member of Parliament under the Commonwealth government, Blackwell had worked the last quarter of a century in Ireland as a financial administrator.[49]

Now in his early sixties, he developed a plan for a Massachusetts land bank. Paper currency was at the heart of Blackwell's scheme. According to his proposal, the initial emission of paper bills would total £10,500, issued in denominations of twenty shillings and upward, with further emissions following. "Bank-bills of Credit will not only answer the Ends of Gold and Silver moneys," he said, "but are Preferrable to both," having greater "ease of Compting and Carriage," as well as "safety in Travelling." Besides, he said, the global supply of silver and gold was simply too "insufficient in this age of the world." Why not back a new paper currency by land?[50]

Blackwell first submitted his application for a bank to the General Court in 1684, a few months after arriving in the colony, just prior to the charter's revocation. Despite support from the upper house of the legislature—consisting mostly of commercial men of the moderate faction—opposition in the independent lower house kept the plan from moving forward.[51] Two years later, however, the assembly had been dissolved, and the way was now clear for legal sanction. In June 1686, just weeks after taking their oaths of office, the Dudley councillors announced the formation of a special committee—headed by Blackwell—to investigate ways in which the council might counter various "obstructions in Trade and Navigation."[52] Randolph blasted the rising influence of this peculiar new figure—"a violent Commonwealth's man," he said of Blackwell, suddenly "consulted with in all public affairs." The councillors were "making all the land in this Government sure to themselves," Randolph warned; ". . . large tracts of Land they have bestowed upon each other."[53]

On September 27, Blackwell and his committee presented to the council their proposal for a "Bank of Credit." The councillors noted that "Persons of approved integrity, prudence and Estates in this Country" supported the project, and after citing the "great decay of trade . . . occasioned by the present Scarcity of Coyne," endorsed the bank as "a publique and usefull invention" and "thinke fitt in his Majesties Name to Declare an Approbation, Allowance and Recommendation thereof."[54] With this pronouncement, Blackwell's loan office became the first government-endorsed financial institution in American history.

Why, exactly, did the Dudley Council approve of the bank? Was it truly out of concern for the "Scarcity of Coyne"? The council claimed that a shortage of money had caused many "obstructions to Manufactures and Comerce in this Countrey." "It is not visible how the same may be remedied," the councillors insisted, "unless some other secure Medium be approved than the Species of Silver, which very injuriously hath been transported into other parts."[55] The Boston mint had vanished, the trade deficit with England was still intolerably high, and country pay alone was clearly out of the question. Blackwell's paper notes seemed the best alternative. Land, indeed, seemed a great way to back a currency; perhaps the council was truly acting in good faith. Randolph had estimated that there were "hundreds of Inhabitants who have above 1000 acres of Land in their possession," and so access to the bank, most likely, would not have been monopolized by an oligarchical few.[56] And yet, of course, with all but one of the councillors actively involved in land speculation, it would be altogether naive to dismiss self-interested motives. The bank would inject much-needed currency into the Dominion, yes, but the councillors (and their friends) would invariably capture a great bulk of that paper money.

The answer on motive may lie in the names of those directly involved in the bank's official organization. Of the twelve available names, all of them, as expected, were highly prominent men. Four of the twelve—Dudley, Stoughton, Wharton, and Wait Winthrop—were also members of the Dudley Council. At least four of the twelve were also members of the Atherton Company: Wharton, Winthrop, Elisha Hutchinson, and John Saffin. And yet four of the twelve had little to no speculative interests at all. At least two of them had previously opposed the moderate faction on the former General Court. Elisha Cooke was also among the bank's organizers. A politician, medical practitioner, and one of the wealthiest men in Boston, Cooke was the most outspoken enthusiast for the old Massachusetts charter, and later, after 1689, played a leading, animated role in opposing royal interference in Massachusetts politics.[57] Clearly, the rationale for supporting the bank varied from man to man. A sincere belief that it would help the larger public likely drove the support of some of the men, especially Cooke and possibly Blackwell. For others, perhaps most, personal profit was simply an added bonus that accompanied the greater public good. And then for others, whom it is impossible to identify with any accuracy, personal profit alone drove their support. For speculators looking to validate their sometimes dubious claims, a successful land bank, with its accompanying land registry, would effectively secure the legality of their titles.

Now that the council had officially endorsed his private banking scheme, Blackwell purchased the printing press, plates, and necessary rolls of paper. He and the council understood that the bills would serve mostly as a subsidiary currency. Notes were no smaller than twenty shillings, the rough equivalent of three full-weight Spanish dollars (themselves inadequate for small change). Only a merchant, landowner, or tradesman of considerable worth would make regular use of notes of such a high denomination.[58] The bank's success or failure hinged entirely upon whether nonsubscribers possessed enough confidence in the notes to give them a regular currency across the whole trading community. With the government's support, it looked like that confidence might just come into being. All that was still needed was Andros's approval.

As Blackwell and the Dudley Council paved the way for New England's first paper currency, Jamaican and Chesapeake planters waged an acutely more familiar battle over the official valuation of Spanish coin. Since 1683 the Jamaican assembly had sought earnestly to raise Spanish dollars from 5s to 6s. Governor Lynch shot down their first attempt; the next governor, Sir Hender Molesworth—agent for the RAC—likewise blocked the measure, and vetoed another bill that would have taxed all coin exported from island.[59] When Molesworth returned to England in 1687, however, his temporary replacement, Christopher Monck, Duke of Albemarle, proved much more sympathetic to the planters' currency demands. That summer Albemarle, first, petitioned the Crown for the "power to Coyne small mony—viz pence, half pence and Farthings of Tynn or Copper," as small change remained scarce on the island.[60] Then, a few months later in March 1688, before the Crown replied, Albemarle signed a bill into law advancing the piece of eight to 6s.[61] The RAC erupted in protest, calling the statute "much detrimentall to trade, especially to such as have debts owing them," reducing the island's collective debt of near £170,000 by 20 percent. Molesworth, now in London, lobbied strongly against the new valuation, calling it an act "against Common Justice" that would cheat "all Creditors," "lessen his Majesties Revenue," and create "uncertainty" in trade.[62] The coming revolution in November 1688 precluded any immediate imperial action on the subject, but finally, in October 1689, the newly crowned William III disallowed the act, returning the piece of eight on Jamaica to 5s—betraying continuity in the midst of revolution.[63]

The battle over the price of a Spanish dollar prevailed also in the Chesapeake. In October 1686 the Maryland assembly again tried to raise the dollar from 4s6d to 6s. The "want of ready money in this province is a very great hindrance," the assemblymen said in their justification. A decade earlier, in 1676, the proprietor had already repealed legislation from 1671 raising the piece of eight to 6s. By the mid-1680s Maryland was the only private colony to still value dollars below 6s and the only colony to still possess the same rate for silver coin as England. The currency bill of 1686 passed through the assembly and received the governor's signature. All for naught: in 1688 the proprietor again repealed the 6s valuation, fearing perhaps that his assent would grant the king all the more reason to seize his proprietorship, already under heavy scrutiny.[64] The piece of eight in Maryland remained stuck at 4s6d. The proprietor did not yet know it, but his heavy-handed, paternalistic style of rule came at a high cost: the allegiance of the Maryland people.

In Virginia, in July 1686 the council petitioned the Crown (again) for a 6s valuation. Just three years earlier, King Charles II had repealed Governor Culpeper's proclamation raising the piece of eight to 6s. In this latest petition, the Virginia council reiterated that a 6s valuation was the best means for "causing considerable quantities of money to be brought in hither by merchants and Traders." Even Governor Effingham gave the petition his blessing.[65] Once the petition reached London, however, the Commissioners of the Customs submitted a formal objection; they called it a "great hindrance and Obstruction to Trade" that will "Conduce only to the advantage of some particular persons." "Noe Rate ought to be sett upon Money other than according to the reall intrinsick Value and Worth," the commissioners argued. James agreed, commanding the governor, "you shall not upon any pretence whatsoever permit any alteration."[66]

The staple plantations were thus the final bastions of the older 5s rate. Though consistent in this regard, the empire's apparent inconsistency in allowing devaluation in other colonies infuriated many of the leading planters in the Chesapeake and Jamaica. The newly royal colony of New York, for example, was allowed to retain its 6s9d rate (adopted in 1684), a valuation 35 percent higher than Virginia or Jamaica. Worse still, in October 1686 the Crown awarded Sir Edmund Andros the freedom to set *any rate at all* on foreign coin in the Dominion of New England—no guidelines or recommendations whatsoever. (The Crown made this decision only a few months before rejecting the Virginia petition to simply raise the dollar from 5s to 6s.) Andros was disappointed with the Crown's decision against a Dominion of New England mint; nevertheless, he accepted with gratitude the power and privilege to freely "regulate the Peices of 8"—something the staple plantations were never remotely afforded.[67]

Sir Edmund Andros arrived in Boston with great ceremony on December 20, 1686. A man of title, military training, and colonial executive experience, the new governor—boasting a lavish coat of scarlet lace—paraded down the streets of Boston with two companies of royal soldiers, in the aristocratic style so befitting the High Stuart age. Accompanying Andros was a commission from the Roman Catholic king of England. Revolting as this was to the independent, Puritan faction in Massachusetts, the moderate, commercial faction was also soon quickly dismayed. To the moderates' shock, the new governor rapidly forsook them. From the beginning, he all but shunned the Dudley Council (now styled the Dominion Council), favoring instead a band of sycophantic New Yorkers who had proven loyal advisers during his seven-year stint as governor of that colony. From December onward, neither Randolph nor the Dominion Council exerted any real political power.[68]

The moderates' lack of influence became most apparent once currency matters arose to the governor's attention. In January 1687, Andros informed the council of a matter of "high Import" that he had not yet revealed to the councillors: his unhindered freedom to raise the value of Spanish coin.[69] Weeks later, on February 23, Richard Wharton—merchant, councillor, and land speculator—read Andros a paper recommending an elaborate plan for devaluation. Wharton, with the support of the other councilors, proposed raising the value of pine-tree shillings by 16 percent, so that six pine-tree shillings (no longer minted, but still in circulation) would now make 7s legal tender. As for Spanish pieces of eight, Wharton recommended raising their value by 12.5 percent, so that a full-weight Spanish dollar would now pass at 6s9d. This was the same rate that dollars passed for in New York and would encourage a temporary stream of incoming Spanish coin to New England. Yet because the advancement of Spanish coin would not be quite as high as the advancement of Boston coin, the old pine-tree shilling would enjoy a comparatively higher value in New England, assuring its continued circulation and encouraging merchants to export Spanish coin instead when shipping money abroad.[70]

After Wharton's currency presentation, the Dominion Council partook in "a long debate about mony." According to the minutes, "Great Complaints were made that unless both the Coyne of New England and pieces of Eight were raised all the money would go out of the Country." "Many of the Councill were very zealous for raiseing the Value of mony," the minutes reported, "saying t'would make mony plenty in the Country and quicken Trade." Some of the councillors, also, were very determined to ensure that "New England money"— that is, pine-tree shillings—remain in the colony, urging that "all possible restriction be made that none may be transported or melted downe upon penalty."[71] Andros, to their shock, utterly disagreed with their prescription for devaluation. "Raiseing mony," he argued, "would help only the Merchants," at the expense of the "Country Inhabitants." The prices for imported goods would rise before the prices for agricultural produce. Thus devaluation would cause a "great Inequality in Trade and Suddainly the Country would be ruined."[72]

After considering the matter for a couple more weeks, Andros rejected Wharton's request for a 6s9d piece of eight. But that was not the worst of it. Andros, instead, raised the piece of eight from 5s10d to 6s—an increase of 3 percent—but without any corresponding increase in the value of the pine-tree shilling.[73] Wharton's plan had called for Boston coin to be overvalued relative to Spanish coin, in order to keep pine-tree shillings inside the colony. Andros's decree *undervalued* Boston coin, with the opposite effect. With the mint long out of operation and the coin now undervalued, the pine-tree shilling would almost surely become extinct within a few years.

The move was a slap in the face of the mercantile interest. Why did Andros take this action? Was it truly out of concern for the "Country Inhabitants"? The day of Wharton's currency presentation, Andros, regarding the pine-tree shilling, "wholy declared against Setting any value upon the New England mony farther than the Intrinsick Value."[74] But why approve raising the value of Spanish money? Why undervalue the pine-tree shilling? Andros likely agreed with the Crown that the continued use of pine-tree shillings undermined the new political order. Andros had wanted a Dominion coinage, not a charter coinage. The old Bay shilling was a hallmark of the deceased charter government. The councillors' attempt to overvalue the coin must have struck Andros as peculiarly suspicious: Why were the councillors so eager to preserve the independent Boston shilling that so proudly championed the year 1652? The councillors' desire to promote and preserve the pine-tree shilling smacked of sedition (at least in Andros's view). But then why did Andros not, at least, raise the value of Spanish money to 6s9d, as requested by Wharton? After all, this was the rating for Spanish coin in New York. But that is where the answer, perhaps, lies. Andros retained deep connections to New York; his closest cadre of advisers all hailed from New York, which was not yet part of the Dominion of New England. If Andros had advanced the coin to 6s9d, Spanish silver would have temporarily drained from New York to Boston. As William Stoughton and other Bostonians later testified, Andros relied primarily on the advice of a few "Strangers to the Countrey . . . persons of known and declared Prejudices against us": "a Crew of abject Persons fetched from New York."[75]

It may seem strange that Wharton and his merchant allies now sided so intently with the pine-tree shilling. After all, they were the faction that had previously urged the General Court to apologize for the mint. But the merchants had always supported a Massachusetts coinage of some sort or another. Unlike the independent faction, the merchants grounded their reasoning solely in economic utility; hence the Dudley Council's petition for a Dominion mint the previous summer. Whether the stamp had a pine tree or the royal arms of England made no difference to them. They simply wanted a uniform currency and therefore wished to see Bay shillings remain the standard money of Massachusetts—not the clipped, disorderly cacophony of foreign coinages. Andros, too, had wanted a mint. For Andros, however, the coin's stamp *absolutely* mattered. He, like Randolph, wanted a Dominion coinage bearing imperial symbols, but also like Randolph, he refused to countenance a politically incendiary coinage. The Crown denied permission for a Dominion mint; Andros, therefore, reconciled himself to a more heterogeneous currency. Any effort to promote the retention and circulation of the old pine-tree shilling was completely out of the question for Andros.

Andros's decision on the valuation of coin represented the opening salvo of the governor's all-out rejection of the goals of the council and merchant interests in Boston. The next battle between him and the council was on the all-important land issue. Andros was well prepared for this contest. He had already begun reviewing the land claims prior to leaving London; he knew well that hundreds of thousands of acres, and many thousands of pounds sterling, depended on his handling of this sensitive topic.

In the month or two preceding Andros's arrival, the colony's great land speculators were already apprehensive about whether the governor would legitimate their claims. For this reason, late in 1686, progress stalled on the setting up of Blackwell's land bank. Not only were the status of the land titles in limbo, but it was still more doubtful whether the Dudley Council had the right to authorize a comprehensive banking scheme. Many of the speculators who backed the plan earlier that summer now hesitated to mortgage their property with the bank—at least not until they might receive some assurance that Andros was on board with the plan. Already by Andros's arrival in December, Blackwell had reduced the number of staff at the bank, hoping it would prove but a temporary measure until confidence returned.[76]

On February 24, 1687, one day after Wharton presented his case for devaluation, Andros presided over a hearing regarding the land claims of the great Atherton Company, of which Wharton was the most interested member. It was hard to imagine Andros not ruling in their favor. To rule against the company would mean alienating some of the most influential men in all of New England. Andros patiently heeded the company's arguments. To the company's shock, however, at the end of the session, he insisted on a second hearing. In May the associates presented their case again. Andros flatly rebuffed all of their land claims. The claims of the other syndicates he rejected as well and then recommended to the Lords of Trade that all absentee land claims be dismissed entirely, de facto, without any further hearings. That summer, Wharton hurried to London to lobby for Andros's removal.[77]

Blackwell tenaciously clung to his bank through the end of 1687, hoping to miraculously persuade Andros to join the scheme. Blackwell even revised the rules of the bank so that goods also, and not just land, would be accepted as security for the bank's paper notes.[78] As late as December 1687, Dudley and Stoughton reaffirmed their support for Blackwell's project; there remained some hope that Wharton's lobbying efforts in London might override Andros's decision regarding the land claims.[79] But the project was doomed in the eyes of many; at best, all confidence had been shattered and would take all but a miracle to restore. The sudden, inglorious crumbling of the bank paralleled the like implosion of the land claims. Outstanding profits had awaited the Massachusetts speculators in the summer of 1686; the bank, they believed, would be the crowning jewel atop the whole ordeal. Andros believed the bank to be little more than a fanciful fraud, propagated by an uppity class of greedy speculators with questionable titles to near-infinite acreage of land. As Thomas Hutchinson, future colonial governor of Massachusetts, wrote much later in his history of the colony, once the land claims collapsed, the "expression in vogue was that 'the calf died in the cow's belly.'"[80]

In this sense, ironically, Andros shared something in common with the likes of Reverend Increase Mather, who also abhorred the land-grabbers and denied the ultimate legality of their claims. Any veneer of similarity ended here, for Andros targeted *all* landowners in New England, including ordinary farmers, vigorously asserting "his Majesties Right to the soile."[81] The governor believed that with the revocation of the charter in 1684, all land in New England had automatically reverted to the Crown. Having swept aside the speculators, Andros, in the spring of 1688, challenged all land titles whatsoever, including indisputable ones issued under the former charter. Every New England landowner, he decreed, must petition for an entirely new land patent, attendant with exorbitant patent fees. Once patented, the landowner must pay, in *silver coin*, an annual quitrent to the Crown of 2s6d per hundred acres. In a society where most middling freeholders owned at least one hundred acres of land, and usually more, the new quitrent would amount to a debilitating drain of at least £1,000 annually from New England (more than three thousand pieces of eight). As one petition read: "All the money in the Countrey wou'd not suffice to patent the Lands."[82]

The new land policy united small and large landowners alike in opposition to Andros, bringing together the disparate factions of independent yeomen and moderate merchant-speculators. The loudest critics of the new requirement for land patents were those of the independent faction, including Mather and Elisha Cooke, who later blasted the effort to turn New Englanders into mere "tennants to the Late King James . . . pretending all to be the Kings." Having "at Vast Charges of their own conquered a Wilderness, and been in possession of their Estates Forty, nay Sixty years," "a parcel of Strangers" was now stripping them of all that "their Fathers before them had laboured for!"[83]

The land issue was the boiling point at which the Dominion lost nearly all support. Many other grievances, of course, made the Dominion extremely unpopular: the loss of representative government and the official establishment of the Church of England in Boston. But some of the leading moderates might have acquiesced—however reluctantly—to the loss of representative government if it meant they still wielded influence as councillors; and religious toleration, for many of them, was perfectly desirable. Rather, the "great matter of Properties and Titles to our Lands" is what finally eviscerated any modicum of support for Andros among the moderate, commercial faction. As one later petition from a group of moderate merchants read, Andros imperiled the "great matter of Properties and Titles to our Lands." "We were every day told, That no Man was owner of a Foot of Land in all the Colony," another public declaration later expressed.[84] The land controversy brought together men so deeply estranged as Wharton and Mather; the former discord between moderates and independents dissipated. In May 1688, Mather joined Wharton in London to lobby for Andros's removal.[85]

Any lingering hope for Blackwell's bank evaporated. On July 5, 1688, Andros received a new commission from the Crown, an implicit endorsement of his land policy. The commission added New York, the Jerseys, Rhode Island, and Connecticut to the Dominion and removed Dudley as the government's deputy and chief judge. Seven days later, Andros prosecuted four leading colonists for not having patented their lands, including one of the bank partners, James Russell. On July 16, four days after the prosecution of Russell and others, Blackwell announced that his bank project had officially ended, the rolling press and reams of paper for the bank's prospective currency now to be sold to the highest bidder.[86]

Andros's aggressive assault on civil liberties stunned the former proud colonists of Massachusetts Bay. Andros prohibited town meetings except for once a year; denied habeas corpus; banned the printing of "unlicensed papers, books or Pamphlets"; and jailed and fined any subject who dared protest the levying of taxes without an elected assembly.[87] The most famous jailing was of Reverend John Wise, whom Andros fined an astounding £50 for saying in a public speech that "taxation without representation is tyranny." (Later, in the early eighteenth century, Wise was the colony's most zealous supporter of paper currency.)[88]

The rapid decay of Boston's money supply highlighted the dire situation. Even Randolph testified to the radical changes in New England fortune. "Money grows very scarce and no trade to bring it in," he wrote in May 1687, adding later, in January 1688, "our money goes all away" with "little or none to supply ordinary occasions."[89] Coming from Randolph, of all people, this was a dreadful assessment indeed. No doubt, a great deal of this exported money took the form of the undervalued pine-tree shilling, though Spanish money also departed the colony. The money shortage caused one councillor to urge Andros "very much to raise the money"—that is, devaluation—but the governor again refused.[90] A few merchants and tradesmen took matters into their own hands and voluntarily agreed to accept clipped dollars at 6s face value, despite the order that money go by weight.[91] The "Country Inhabitants" in particular, said Randolph, have no silver money: "they pay all in oates." Country pay, indeed, was so prolific, reported Randolph, that the Dominion treasury was commonly known as "the Great Grainary."[92]

One of the culprits of this shrinking money supply was the sizable decline in illegal trade. Andros made good on his promise to strictly follow the Crown's instructions to seize all interloping vessels, and then to try them in a juryless admiralty court.[93] Andros also commanded that only five ports in all of New England be allowed to receive incoming vessels and assigned an armed coasting vessel to survey the seaboard.[94] Randolph later recalled that the "Illegal Trade, so Notoriously carried on by the People of New-England, was then stopt," especially the former illegal trade "with the French at Newfoundland"; the end of this commerce, he said, "very much enraged those merchants who traded in great quantityes of brandy and other French goods."[95] Writing from a Boston jail in May 1689, Randolph feared mistreatment from the Massachusetts rebels, who believed him guilty of economic sabotage. "This country is poor," he said in a private letter, "the exact execution of the acts of trade hath much impoverished them." Nor was this a recent realization: in 1687 he wrote Blathwayt that "the Country is very poor and fatally declining. . . . Our shopkeepers break every day. . . . Not twenty Shopps will long be open in Boston."[96] When the rebels overthrew Andros in April 1689, their stated grievances included "the Courses immediately taken to damp and spoyl our Trade." Around the same time in London, Mather likewise noted that "the Country hath mightily declined, and gone to ruin daily, not being now like the place it was Five Years ago."[97]

Smuggling declined across most of English America in the late 1680s. A single month into his reign—April 1685—James directed that the royal navy "seize all forrein shipps or vessells that shall presume to Trade in those plantations contrary to Law." He further commanded all governors to study "the Principall Laws relating to the Plantation Trade," observe strictly all rules regarding bonds and certificates, and maintain detailed lists of all ships arriving to and from each colony.[98] The antismuggling offensive was largely successful. Governor Dongan in New York seized a large number of Dutch ships on the eve of the colony's merger with the Dominion of New England; Lord Effingham in Virginia secured a twelve-gun frigate from England to patrol Chesapeake waters.[99] "The Virginians are very angry that I stay here because I won't lett them cheat the King," wrote the commander of the frigate; "they say I spoile their trade, and the best words I can get from them is old rogue and old dog." A few planters, he said, hired "small vessels to come when I am gone," to ship tobacco "away for Holland"—obviously to earn more money; nevertheless, illicit trade, in the general, significantly diminished.[100]

Piracy was more difficult to stop, but this too abated. In August 1687 James commissioned a vice admiral, Sir Robert Holmes, to lead a "Squadron of Ships" to the Americas to quell the "great numbers of Pirates," something Charles had never seen fit to do. James also instructed governors to retain captured pirates in jail until the Crown appointed a time and place for trial—circumventing autonomous colonial juries—and in January 1688, as part of an antipiracy proclamation, James offered "Full and Ample Pardon" to any who voluntarily turned themselves in.[101] Though results were mixed, and though Holmes could not even begin to adequately cover the whole Atlantic seaboard, these moves still had a noticeable effect and constituted the most action yet the Crown had taken on the subject. Boston, in particular, ceased to be a receptacle for pirates; as of August 1688, Andros had jailed eight suspected buccaneers, some of them having traded with Boston merchants prior to capture.[102] One of the men had brought with him "about nine hundred peeces of eight"; another crew had "great treasure" of "£1000 or £1500 a man," all of whom would have been welcomed there just a few years earlier.[103]

No doubt, colonial economic conditions worsened considerably during the brief reign of King James II. Some colonists attributed the worsened conditions to the new duties on sugar and tobacco, others to the suppression of smuggling and piracy, others to the inability of colonial governments to devalue their currency. When news arrived in America that James had been overthrown, there was no economic basis, at least, for the average colonist to do anything less than to celebrate.

Mercantilism retained its impregnable hold over English economic thought under King James II. Mercantilists were still of one accord with regard to the need for a favorable trade balance; they still viewed an influx of silver and gold—and its subsequent retention within the country—as the most effective means to national glory, prosperity, and strength. Nevertheless, division more than unity characterized the mercantilism of the 1680s. Two distinct brands of mercantilism—monopoly mercantilism and industrial-capital mercantilism—competed for precedence in England in the 1680s. Nicholas Barbon was right when he remarked in 1690 that "there is nothing . . . that men differ more in their sentiments than about the true causes that raise and promote trade."[104] This was no benign disagreement between friendly factions; rather, it manifested in political animus and discord. The two emerging political parties in England, Whig and Tory, identified distinctly with one brand of mercantilism over the other. The Whigs, generally speaking, endorsed industrial-capital mercantilism; the Tories and James II endorsed monopoly mercantilism. Both sides enshrined the balance-of-trade doctrine as the key to power and wealth, but on the means to a more favorable balance of trade, there could not have been starker disagreement. This issue, along with many noneconomic issues, placed the Whigs and Tories at severe if not irreconcilable odds in the late 1680s.

Monopoly mercantilists emphasized the importance of a well-organized trade with the East Indies and Spanish America, believing the reexport sector to be the most profitable branch of overseas commerce. Mercantilists of this type enthusiastically supported state-protected monopolistic ventures, namely the Royal African Company and the East India Company. Overseas trade, monopoly mercantilists insisted, demanded order and regularity; it should not be "subject to such frequent Changes," as characterized more "precarious" and "ungoverned trades."[105] In a highly competitive world order, England could not afford internal competition within the same branch of commerce overseas. As James asserted in April 1685, those who wished to abolish these monopolies favored "private profit before the Publick Good": they sought to organize trade in a "Disorderly manner." The RAC and EIC, he declared, were both "at grèat Charges and Expence in Fortifying and Settling divers Garrisons, Forts and Factories," rendering monopoly all the more necessary (to avoid the free-rider problem).[106] Even the laissez-faire Dutch long ago granted monopoly rights to the Dutch East India Company, after a brief and seemingly failed experiment with free trade. Hence James, in 1687, planned to incorporate a West India Company to monopolize the sugar trade and even flirted with the idea of creating an additional company to monopolize the trade from New England of naval stores and timber.[107]

The emerging Tory party in England was the natural home for monopoly mercantilism. Monopoly mercantilists opposed a "loose, distracted, and disorderly trade," preferring instead the "orderly mannaging of their trade."[108] Tories, in like manner, opposed a loose, disorderly government, preferring instead a tightly organized political and religious regime under the rule of a dynamic and enterprising monarch, financed, in part, by revenue generated from monopoly companies.[109] Monopoly mercantilists viewed the Netherlands as England's foremost economic rival; Dutch merchants, after all, retained their long-standing dominance over the East Indian trade, and they were the RAC's only real competition in the trade of slaves and contraband to Spanish America. James, of course, was director and largest shareholder of the RAC; his chief economic adviser, Sir Josiah Child, was the leading merchant of the East India Company. French trade in the East Indies and Spanish America was negligible at best. Dutch overseas trade appeared to have almost fully recovered from the disastrous 1670s; indeed, the Dutch sent a record number of vessels to the East Indies in the 1680s.[110] A fourth Anglo-Dutch war was certainly not out of the question. "If we should throw off the East-India Trade," Child warned, "the Dutch would soon treble their strength and power in India, and would become sole Masters of all those rich and necessary Commodities of the East; and make the European world pay five times more for them, than now they do, which would so vastly increase their Riches, as to render them irresistible."[111] The argument was certainly compelling; and if monopolies were the best means to combat Dutch trade in the East and in Africa, why not extend the same logic to the colonial trade in sugar, tobacco, naval stores, and timber?

Industrial-capital mercantilists, on the other hand, espoused the necessity of state-protected manufacturing, banking, capital, and labor. Highly critical of East Indian commerce, industrial-capital mercantilists emphasized, not the reexport trade of foreign goods from England, but the export of English-made goods, namely textiles. Domestic manufactures would surely improve the balance of trade, they contended: English-made goods could either be exported abroad or consumed at home, the latter eliminating dependency on imported articles. The importation of calicoes by the East India Company, they argued—paid for with silver and gold—retarded the development of English manufactures. The industrial-capital mercantilist did not oppose corporations per se but only those possessing state-granted monopolies, which Whigs maintained caused an artificial increase in prices that benefited a narrow few at the expense of the greater public. Adding to these grievances, Tories dominated the leadership of most of these monopoly companies, though the great bulk of independent merchants in London were Whigs.[112]

Money, not manufacturing, was the ultimate end goal of industrial-capital mercantilism. In order for gold and silver to increase in England, the industrial-capital mercantilists argued, the kingdom must have a strong manufacturing base, with the aid of protective tariffs (not yet in existence) and outright prohibitions on foreign articles if necessary. Carew Reynell, a proto-Whig in the 1670s, insisted on tripling the tariff on foreign textiles, warning against free trade with the French and East Indies. "Where a Nation Imports by its voluptuousness more than it Exports, it must needs come to ruine; Coin there going out in Specie for the over ballance," he said. "They tempt us with all sort of French Toyes, Indy and Japan trifles, stain'd Callicoes, Silks and such pleasant things, and fetch away our Money and solid wealth. But I say let us make store of all new Manufactures to tempt them with, and not send Money."[113]

Industrial-capital mercantilists found a natural home in the emerging Whig party, whose adherents insisted that France, not Holland, was England's foremost economic (and political) rival. Though France suffered a brief economic slump in the late 1680s—a consequence, in part, of the emigration of Huguenot artisans, capital, and money from France after Louis revoked the Edict of

Nantes—that was no reason to relax any worry.[114] The public revenue in France exceeded that of England by six times, amounting to some £12 million annually.[115] The dogs of war were also rearing their heads. In September 1687, Louis reinstated the former anti-Dutch tariff of 1667, breaking the treaty agreement of 1678; he threatened a military response if the Dutch retaliated with new tariffs of their own.[116] Whigs were naturally sympathetic to the Dutch model of Protestantism fused with civil liberties and merchant-dominated government; nevertheless, they viewed the Netherlands as a power past its prime. France was the genuine threat—a kingdom that had benefited greatly from the economic advice of Jean-Baptiste Colbert, the finance minister and mercantilist mastermind who had instituted a profusion of statutory protection for French manufacturing and industry.[117]

Nearly everything about James's rule horrified the Whigs. The Tory Parliament in 1685 lifted the previous 1678 ban on French imports, resulting in a flood of French goods, including textiles, into England. Between 1686 and 1688, English merchants imported £700,000 worth of French linens, endangering the infant linen industry in England.[118] As Louis amped up aggression toward the Netherlands, the king of England appeared ready to ally with his cousin in a war against the Dutch.[119]

Most critically, however, James alienated moderate Tories. His chilling assault on civil liberties, proud embrace of Roman Catholicism, and overt hostility toward representative government proved too much for many of his initial supporters. Moreover, despite their reservations on Dutch commercial power, a growing number of Tories recognized the hazard in allowing Louis XIV to expand his absolutist empire unchecked. Louis seemed poised to conquer Europe; James, in the meantime, seemed entirely oblivious, if not complacent. In April 1687 James issued the Declaration of Indulgence, unilaterally suspending the requirement that officeholders take Anglican communion, greatly angering many High Anglican Tories. The birth of James Francis Edward Stuart in June 1688 portended a perpetual Catholic monarchy, causing most Protestants in England, regardless of party, to despair.[120] A little more than a quarter-century after the Stuart restoration, England appeared on the precipice of yet another civil war.

By the early months of 1688, a cadre of Whigs and moderate Tories had begun to conspire to either topple James or to compel him militarily to acquiesce to parliamentary demands. Nevertheless, as late as the early summer of 1688, there was little to no sign that a revolution was pending. James remained in a strong position: he commanded a powerful army and navy, with loyalists and sycophants occupying top bureaucratic positions, not to mention his amiable relationship with the French king. Shortly after the birth of James's son in June, the conspirators composed a desperate letter to the Stadtholder of the Dutch Republic, Prince William of Orange, inviting him to invade the British Isles. In exchange they promised that English foreign policy would turn against France. William—a devout Calvinist and arch-enemy of Louis XIV— was a grandson of King Charles I of England, nephew of James II and Charles II, and husband of Mary Stuart, the eldest, Protestant daughter of James. James first learned of the conspiracy in August but astonishingly remained in a state of denial, prepping for battle only belatedly in October after William published a declaration explaining his intent to rescue England from the "Arbitrary and Despotick power" exercised by "Evill Councellours" within James's court.[121]

On November 5, William invaded southwestern England with an army of more than twenty thousand men—mostly Dutchmen, but also some Huguenot, Scotch, and English volunteers—conveyed across the Channel in more than four hundred transport vessels and a fleet of fifty-three warships, with financial backing from Whig merchants and the Dutch government. To James's horror, most of his senior military officers stood down, and within a few weeks James's army had almost completely dissolved. Though James was still in position to negotiate with William, he scurried to France in a panic on December 11, seeking French support as the Dutch prince approached London. But King Louis was not able to immediately counteract the Dutch invasion on James's behalf; weeks before, Louis had crossed the Rhine into Germany with more than seventy thousand troops, initiating what became the Nine Years' War. William arrived in London on December 18 and ordered that all English troops withdraw to more than twenty miles outside of the city. For several months, only Dutch troops—numbering seventeen thousand—were allowed to bear arms in London, placing control of the city firmly within William's command. On February 13, Parliament offered the Crown to William and Mary as joint sovereigns of England, and a new coin bearing their image followed shortly thereafter.[122]

After weeks of unsubstantiated rumors, official word finally reached Boston on April 18 that James had indeed been overthrown. Andros was finished. "The Action was now begun," detailed one first-hand account, "and the Rumour of it running like Lightning through the Town, all sorts of people were presently inspired with the most unanimous Resolution, I believe, that was ever seen. Drums were beaten, and the whole Town was immediately up in Arms."[123] Guided carefully by a coalition of moderate and independent elites in the colony, the rebels—backed by some two thousand militiamen— arrested Andros, Randolph, Dudley, and sundry military and civil officers. Andros, in total humiliation, attempted "an Escape in Womans Apparel, and pass'd two Guards, but was stopped at the third, being discovered by his

Shoes, not having changed them." Soon thousands of men and women, from "all the Country round," streamed into Boston, expressing their "unanimous content" for the peaceful and restorative action. "There was no Bloodshed, nor so much as any Plunder committed," one observer said, ". . . setting aside the intemperate Speeches of some inconsiderate men."[124]

Colonial insurgency thereupon spread southward into New York and Maryland. After Andros's deputy in New York, Francis Nicholson, stalled in proclaiming William and Mary the rightful sovereigns, rebels seized the town fort on May 31 and assumed the reins of government (though Nicholson managed to flee for England). Jacob Leisler—an eccentric German merchant, fervent Calvinist, and captain in the local militia—led the band of New York rebels, consisting primarily of middling and lesser artisans and tradesmen—men who were ordinarily shut out of the political process by the colony's merchant and landowning elite. Weeks later in Maryland, in the month of July, a band of antiproprietor insurgents calling themselves the Protestant Associators deposed the Roman Catholic governor for likewise delaying any proclamation of England's new king and queen.[125] This was the last of the colonial rebellions; colonists now eagerly and anxiously awaited to see how imperial policy would change in the revolution's aftermath.

The Glorious Revolution undoubtedly ranks among the landmark events in English history, politically but also economically. Mercantilism underwent a major transition in England after 1688. The transition neither happened overnight nor was an inevitable consequence of the revolution, but the overthrow of radical Toryism late in 1688 was the decisive turning point. It was still another quarter century before the ultimate triumph of Whiggery was evident; confirmation arrived not until the historic general election in 1715, after which the Tories became a permanent minority in Parliament and a non-factor in executive administration until the year 1760. The industrial-capital brand of mercantilism, not its Tory alternative, guided the English economy through the long eighteenth century.

As colonists soon discovered, mercantilism, more broadly considered, had decidedly *not* been overthrown in 1688. Indeed, mercantilism strengthened after 1688. The underlying doctrines of mercantilism became as good as sacrosanct in the minds of nearly all imperial policymakers far into the eighteenth century. The reasons were many, but the most critical factor in the survival and strengthening of mercantilism in England at the dawn of the new century was the country's desperate need for money in the turbulent 1690s.

CHAPTER 9

Reconstructing a Mercantilist Empire, 1690s

War time calls for more Money than time of Peace.

—Sir Dudley North, *Discourses Upon Trade* (London, 1691)

It is too evident, that Money [in England] is very scarce both in City and Country. . . . The immediate Cause of this Scarcity, is the Exportation of our Money into Forrain Parts. . . . The Plantations therefore are of great weight, to turn the Balance of Trade to our advantage. And therefore we should cherish and encourage the Plantations, and not oppress them as we do.

—Anonymous, *The True Causes of the Present Scarcity of Money* (London, 1690)

On January 22, 1689 the Convention Parliament convened to justify the crowning of William and Mary and to urge the immediate prosecution of war against Louis XIV. The coming Nine Years' War was a war to safeguard the revolution, to secure English commerce overseas—"the very Life-Blood of a Nation," William called it—and to defend the continent of Europe from an "arbitrary and universal monarchy."[1]

It was not yet evident in 1689 how this new political regime would modify either colonial administration or the political economy of empire more generally. At present, rebel provisional governments presided over Massachusetts, New York, and Maryland. Wartime exigencies and communication delays made difficult any rapid transition in colonial governance. What of the empire's move since the 1670s toward tighter economic and political controls? Had these controls also been toppled in 1688? Was the era of coercive consolidation over? For the brief period immediately following the revolution, it indeed seemed plausible that much or all of what had been done since the 1670s would be reversed. And yet, within a short time, it was indisputable that colonial America was as subordinate as ever to English imperial and mercantilist goals. The style and strategy had changed, in enormously consequential ways. But the basic principle of colonial subordination remained. The colonial vision of economic and political equality within the empire subsequently dimmed and in some respects all but vanished. But why?

The principle of colonial subordination survived 1688 because of unstable economic and monetary circumstances in England in the darkest hours of the 1690s. The fiscal demands and realities of war created a desperate situation in England. Starved for revenue, and with the domestic currency falling steadily and frighteningly awry, the English government became more committed than ever to mercantilist principles. This commitment, in turn, reaffirmed the necessity of subordinating the colonial economy to imperial concerns.

To reconstruct a mercantilist empire, however—on lasting, solid ground no less—was no simple task. An all-out return to the more brazen coercion of the 1680s was neither feasible nor expedient after 1688. Neither was the decentralized, autonomous colonial system of the pre-1670s. A new, third way had to be found, one that satisfied the pecuniary aims of the expanding fiscal-military state in England while relaxing colonial jealousies about autocratic government and the loss of political liberties. The program, though imperfectly executed, assured the continuation of England's Atlantic empire, helping to secure the fervent loyalty of England's dependent colonial sphere for more than half a century. After all of the tumult of the previous years, the success of this imperial-colonial program in and after the 1690s was nothing short of astonishing, and it helped to make Britain the most formidable empire of the eighteenth century.

On May 29, 1689, thousands of men and women across Massachusetts Bay converged on Boston to celebrate the crowning of William and Mary. Providence had graciously answered their most desperate and urgent prayers, redeeming New and Old England from subjugation and popery. The declaration of grievances submitted by the Massachusetts rebels explained that Andros had grossly violated their liberties; indeed, Andros's men had "plainly affirmed" that "the People in New-England were all Slaves, and the only difference between them and Slaves is their not being bought and sold." Surely, the colony's former rights and privileges would swiftly be restored, the rebels believed. After all, the people of Massachusetts—the declaration continued—were "true Lovers of their Country," known for their "pure Exercise of the Protestant Religion," and now unequivocally "dutiful and loyal to our King."[2]

Many Bostonians wished to restore the old charter government immediately upon their arrest of Andros in April. Yet other more prominent voices—men of "estates and shipping," according to Randolph, now in prison—insisted on a more prudent course. The city's leadership thus erected a Committee of Safety and then patiently, though anxiously, awaited further orders from London. Eminent men soon filled the interim government, and Simon Bradstreet—the venerable moderate, now ninety years old—returned to the governorship.[3]

They did not know that in London there was already stiff opposition to restoring the old charter. The Lords of Trade—still extant and still dominated by William Blathwayt—urged the drafting of an entirely new Massachusetts charter. Blathwayt was fluent in Dutch and had quickly and skillfully asserted himself as one of King William's most trusted advisers. During the coming war, Blathwayt even accompanied William on his frequent trips to the Low Countries, serving as his acting secretary of state.[4] Blathwayt hoped earnestly that the Crown would retain its tight control over New England; the Dominion, after all, had terminated most of the smuggling and piracy trade and constituted a powerful bulwark against neighboring French Canada. As Reverend Increase Mather himself had recently noted, "He that is Sovereign of New-England, may by means thereof, when he pleaseth, be Emperour of America."[5] Blathwayt and his coterie agreed. Besides, many of the moderate, non-Puritan commercial men in Boston did not wish a return to the old charter; they desired, rather, a broader, more open, cosmopolitan government, one fully incorporated within the greater empire, yet attended by fundamental political liberties, including habeas corpus and representative government.

The vast majority of Bay colonists, nevertheless, desired an unadulterated return to the former charter. Mather represented their interests in London, having already arrived there in May 1688; he was soon joined by Elisha Cooke and Thomas Oakes, sent by the colony as agents to lobby vigorously for a renewal of the old charter and for a prompt resurrection of the Boston mint. "You are to solicite that the liberty of coynage may be allowed us," Governor Bradstreet instructed the agents, together with a "Confirmation of our ancient Charter." King William, in the meantime, recognized the provisional government and ordered the release of Andros, Randolph, and Dudley from jail for immediate transfer to England for questioning.[6]

Mather lobbied Parliament incessantly throughout the summer of 1689 for a full charter renewal, working closely with sympathetic members of Parliament. Later that year, the House of Commons even passed a bill to restore the old charter; however, the bill failed to come to a vote in the House of Lords before William dissolved Parliament in February 1690. This failure doomed Mather's efforts, for the 1689 parliament was predominantly Whiggish, but the mood of the English electorate of late had shifted abruptly toward a more conservative course. The coming general elections awarded the Tories a slight majority in Parliament, and King William, more and more, favored Tory advisors. Indeed, from 1690 through 1693, William's leading minister was none other than Lord Danby, Charles II's chief minister from 1673 to 1679—one of the initial architects of the Lords of Trade and of the imperial-colonial consolidation program more generally. Danby, back then, had been driven by his concern for the government's finances and revenue; the same concerns carried over into the early 1690s.[7]

A relentless assault on the former charter ensued. Opponents charged the previous Massachusetts government with having abused its former "Unlimited Authority," pursuing an "Abominable, Illegal way of Trade." They claimed that the "chief cause of the Revolution" against Andros was to "break all the Laws made for the encouragement and increase of the Navigation."[8] One critic, John Palmer—a former judge and councillor under Andros—argued staunchly against the colonial notion of political equality within the empire. Colonial plantations, he said, were "much differenced from England, and not to have those Privileges and Liberties which England enjoyed"; rather, they are to be "restrained and burthened beyond any in England, as appears by the several Acts made for the increasing of Navigation." They may even be lawfully ruled "without any regard to Magna Charta."[9] Randolph, of course, also chimed in, claiming that the Massachusetts rebels considered themselves the king's "Nominall and not reall Subjects." Already, he said, the Bostonians were conniving to circumvent "the very Laws and Navigation of England, and making themselves as it were Independant to this Crown." Their "cryes of oppression" and "pretensions of grievances" were merely façades: their true intent was to "Restore to themselves a free Trade." "If these People be not prevented of their old way of Trade," Randolph warned, it "must necessarily in a short time destroy the Trade of England."[10]

Renewing the old charter might also result in a full restoration of the Boston mint. According to Randolph, the loss of the mint was one of several reasons for the colony's revolt against Andros. In a new report to parliament, Randolph reminded the body that Boston's assumption of the "Regal Power of Coyning" had been a "weighty consideration" in the Crown's decision to vacate the old charter. One anonymous writer (perhaps Randolph) cited the mint as the *first* piece of evidence that the people of Massachusetts desired full independence. "They Act as a Free and Independent Commonwealth," the author stated; ". . . Now to show the unlimited Authority they pretend to . . . (1) They took upon them to coyn Money in the Name of the Commonwealth as they call it."[11]

Taken aback by the intensity of the opposition, Mather charged Randolph with "Scandalous Libel" and having a long history of "many false Informations and misrepresentations." Mather promised that smuggling would practically disappear upon a return of the old charter: "the whole body of the people," he said, "would rejoyce in the severest Execution of those Acts, and lend their utmost help." As for the mint, there was no treason at all in its initial establishment, for "the mint was set up in 1652, when there was no King in England." Lord Baltimore of Maryland, he recalled, had also coined money during the Interregnum period, and other colonies, besides, exercised monetary autonomy through coin devaluation. "Was not the Value of Coyn altered in Pensilvania?" Mather asked; ". . . Why then should New-England be esteemed more criminal?"[12]

By summer 1690 it was evident that Mather, Cooke, and Oates had lost the debate. Most Englishmen despised James II's domestic policies; his colonial policy, however, was another matter and not entirely objectionable. The extreme fiscal demands of wartime had cast a new light on the prudency of centralization. A few Tories even clamored for a reinstatement of Andros in New England.[13] But this stance was no longer tenable: even most Tories conceded that Mather was generally correct when he said that the Dominion regime violated the "fundamentals of the English Government."[14] Yes, Randolph still noxiously insisted that "force is the Onely Argument to convince & oblige them to a dutyfull & intire Submission."[15] But that was just Randolph being Randolph. To most reasonable observers it was now manifest that a new system must be settled upon: one that credibly safeguarded the mercantilist order, but under a framework more agreeable to basic notions of English political liberty. With this idea in mind, in April 1691, the Lords of Trade, spearheaded by Blathwayt, began drafting a new charter for Massachusetts. Mather, dejected, nonetheless "resolved to get as much Good, and prevent as much Hurt to the Countrey as possible."[16]

The Massachusetts agents were fortunate to win even this concession: Leisler's rebels in New York only wished they had been treated so kindly. Though the New York rebels had eagerly acknowledged William and Mary in summer 1689, the Crown soon declared them traitors for overthrowing the former Dominion regime. The leader of the rebellion, Jacob Leisler—a militia captain who declared himself lieutenant-governor in December 1689—confronted ferocious opposition from New York elites and, unlike his opponents, lacked appropriate contacts in London. Moreover, his behavior was erratic, and his jailing opponents on charges of sedition and treason earned him many enemies. In 1691 the Crown appointed Joseph Dudley, now in New York, chief justice over the court that convicted Leisler and Jacob Milborne (his son-in-law) of treason, hanging them in May. The following year, Colonel Benjamin Fletcher, a Tory, arrived in New York as the royal governor and swiftly allied himself with the anti-Leislerians, setting off a generation-long, factional dispute over the legacy of that rebellion.[17]

The Maryland rebels got off a bit easier, but their example too caused the Massachusetts agents some concern. Shortly after the Maryland revolt in July 1689, King William suspended Lord Baltimore's proprietorship and assumed direct control of the colony, appointing several of the Protestant rebels to the Maryland council. Those appointments caused no unease. But for the colony's lieutenant governor, William appointed none other than Andros's former deputy Francis Nicholson. Nicholson, moreover, had also been appointed lieutenant governor of Virginia. Most shocking of all, in early 1692, William appointed Sir Edmund Andros governor of Virginia, transferring Nicholson full-time to Maryland.[18]

Mindful of these startling developments, Mather maneuvered carefully in his subsequent negotiations with the Crown, hoping and praying for the best in a new charter. Mather knew well that many people in Massachusetts would deeply resent abandoning the old charter; they would certainly never tolerate another Dominion-like regime. Meanwhile, as the Lords of Trade hammered out a new charter, the provisional government at Boston—without seeking any authority from the king—embarked on a radical experiment, not of coinage, but of printing paper money.

Few men in Massachusetts could have possibly foreseen the enormous ramifications of the colony's first emission of paper money in December 1690. The currency emission inaugurated a century-long epoch in American monetary history. Amazingly, the emission began without any knowledge from English officials; indeed, it occurred accidentally, as the product of a failed military expedition.

In autumn 1690, Captain Sir William Phips—a native of Maine, resident of Boston, and renowned adventurer and treasure hunter—assumed command of a naval and land expedition on behalf of the Massachusetts colony against the French at Quebec. Earlier that year, he and seven hundred men compelled the French to surrender Port Royal in Acadia. The new expedition to Quebec included a flotilla of thirty-two ships and more than two thousand men. A successful invasion, he and others believed, would prove the colony's utmost devotion and loyalty to William and Mary, ensuring greater success for the charter negotiations in London. The Quebec expedition was extraordinarily costly, however, and the question of how to finance it loomed. Few merchants in Boston were willing to lend hard money to the Massachusetts treasury, as the future of the interim government was still very much in limbo. Instead, the Massachusetts government took a huge gamble by presuming that the plunder won from victory would adequately finance the mission. Quebec, after all, was only scantily garrisoned.[19]

Phips returned to Boston on November 19, 1690. The mission had utterly failed. News of the intended invasion leaked to the French in time for them to send reinforcements from Montreal, delivering Phips a crushing defeat. The soldiers' wages were not yet paid, nor were the costs of the army and navy's supplies; moreover, an outbreak of smallpox ravaged the camp. Soldiers and officers alike were "upon the point of Mutiny." The humiliating loss cost the colony nearly one thousand lives and swamped the government with "Extreme Debts" amounting close to £100,000, with "not a Penny in the Treasury."[20]

Desperate and all but penniless, the interim Massachusetts government landed on a seemingly benign solution: the government simply *printed* the requisite funds on paper. On December 10, 1690, the provisional government authorized the emission of £7,000 in "bills of credit." The denomination of the bills ranged from 5s to £5 (100s); the bills were printed on paper measuring $4 \times 5\frac{1}{2}$ inches (see figure 11). With these, the treasurer paid the soldiers and settled the colony's debts. A few months later, the government set the ceiling at £40,000 in paper bills, allowed denominations to range from 2s to £10, and made provision for new taxes to draw all the notes back in by 1693.[21]

Many colonists did not yet consider these bills of credit to be *real* money, even though they circulated as a commonly accepted medium of exchange. The colony, in 1690, did not design for the bills to replace coin as money, as indicated by the name *bill of credit*. Each bill, in effect, was a certificate of debt, issued by the government, guaranteeing that the stated amount (2s to £10) was "due from the Massachusetts Colony to the Possessor." The inscription on the bill stated that in "all publick payments," the bill "shall be in value equal to money," meaning that the holder at any time could use the note in lieu of silver money for taxes and fees. The possessor of the bill was the creditor; the government was the debtor. When the treasurer accepted the currency in public payments, he effectively "redeemed" the bill and thus retired that portion of the government's debt.[22]

Not surprisingly, this "New-Coyn'd Money" in Massachusetts was enormously controversial.[23] The "new mint raised here of paper money" (as some merchants called it) won both avid support and fervent opposition.[24] The notes depreciated in value more than 30 percent after leaving the printing press. The notes, for many, were unreliable because the government that issued them was unreliable. It was a provisional government, after all. The Crown, at any moment, might soon repudiate the bills, draw up a new charter invalidating all the laws of the provisional government, and cancel any of the taxes that the government had intended to give backing to the bills. As Reverend Cotton Mather (younger brother to Increase) later recalled, the people were "afraid that the Government would in half a year be so overturned as to convert their Bills of Credit altogether into Wast-paper." "Our Paper money has ruined us," one merchant wrote Francis Nicholson in October 1691—the silver coinage displaced by a currency printed on coarse, flimsy paper.[25] Some colonists considered the bills a "scandal to New-England" and "reproach them as a Grand

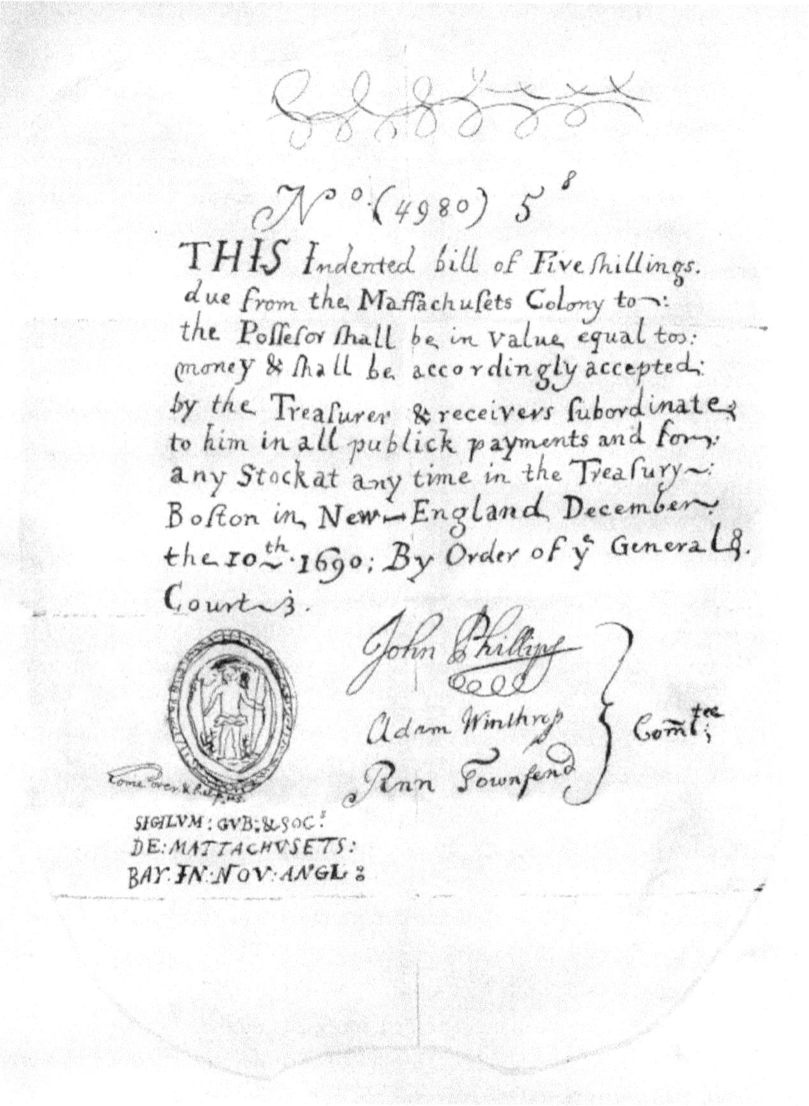
No. (4980) 5s
THIS Indented bill of Five shillings.
due from the Massachusets Colony to:
the Possessor shall be in value equal to:
money & shall be accordingly accepted:
by the Treasurer & receivers subordinate
to him in all publick payments and for:
any Stock at any time in the Treasury:
Boston in New-England December
the 10th. 1690: By Order of ye General
Court.
John Phillips
Adam Winthrop
Penn Townsend
Comtee
SIGILVM: GVB: & SOC:
DE: MATTACHVSETS:
BAY: IN: NOV: ANGL:

Figure 11. Five-shilling bill of credit of the Province of Massachusetts Bay. The original emission was printed, not handwritten; this is a pen-and-ink sketch. Reprinted from *Proceedings of the Massachusetts Historical Society*, 1st ser., vol. 6 (Boston, 1862–1863), p. 428. (Courtesy of the Massachusetts Historical Society.)

Cheat." Others, like Captain John Blackwell, praised the currency as "less Troublesome & Cumbersome than Silver" and "more Portable than Coyn." Cotton Mather agreed, calling the notes "of more Use to the New-Englanders, than if all their Copper Mines had been opened, or the Mountains of Peru had been Removed into these parts." "Why may not Paper-mony be as good as Tobacco-mony, Potato-mony and Sugar-mony?" Blackwell asked, "Yea, do not our Brethren at Connecticut find, Corn-mony will do their business for them?"[26]

However one felt about the bills of credit, the haphazard, tumultuous manner in which they were introduced embodied the wider societal chaos engulfing the Massachusetts colony in 1690–1692. Failed military ventures, uncertainty surrounding the charter, escalating Indian conflicts, high taxes, and £40,000 of a seemingly unstable paper currency sparked a crisis in Massachusetts culture. One minister even called this period "the short *Anarchy* accompanying our late Revolution."[27] Little wonder that 1692 was also the year of the infamous witch trials in Salem. At the height of the frenzy, some colonists, for good luck, carried "witch pieces" in their pockets: silver coins bearing teeth marks and bendings.[28] The abrupt introduction of a strange currency, coupled with war and political instability, rendered people more likely to snap. New England society, like the currency itself, seemed on the verge of completely breaking down. The colony's credit was failing.

The collapse never came. In May 1692 the new charter arrived in Boston, and though the frenzy in Salem still proceeded that summer, the charter's advent signaled a return of at least some semblance of stability to the colony. With the new charter, a popularly elected legislature returned to Massachusetts Bay. Nevertheless, the Crown now possessed the right to veto laws, and the king now appointed the governor and lieutenant governor, both formerly elected by the populace. The Massachusetts council, once popularly elected, was now elected by the General Court, and the governor could veto any of the selections (as happened in 1693 when the assembly elected Elisha Cooke). Accused smugglers could no longer be tried by a jury of their peers, but by juryless vice-admiralty courts administered directly by the Crown. Nevertheless, the General Court still possessed the power of the purse, retaining the ability to withhold a salary from an unfriendly governor. And though the governor could dissolve the assembly at will, the assembly had to convene at least once a year. Moreover, if the Crown failed to repeal a law within three years, the law was permanent unless repealed by the General Court, no matter how offensive to imperial interests. Finally, the new charter extended the franchise to all property-holding men, not simply church members, placing non-Puritan merchants within the electorate for the first time. All things considered, the charter was a reasonably good deal for the colony, now styled the Province of Massachusetts Bay. Though the colony's political privileges were nowhere near their former extent, and still less than private colonies, they were nonetheless greater than a typical royal colony.[29]

There was no mint in the new charter. Mather, with Phips (who ventured to London after his defeat at Quebec to serve as the colony's agent), made a last-minute appeal to the Lords of Trade for the "Liberty of coynage," but to no avail. The two agents, first, appealed to the mint's economic expediency, citing the abundance of clipped Spanish money and dearth of "small mony for Change." But they additionally insisted that the Crown had much to gain politically by reinstating the mint, arguing that such "will tend to convince and satisfie them [the colonists] that they shall be not loosers but gainers by the new Settlement."[30] Mather understood that the new charter would be extremely controversial among the people. A restoration of the pine-tree shilling might have useful psychological benefits, precluding the colonists from thinking that they had surrendered an undue amount of political and economic autonomy. But the Crown disagreed: when the Commissioners of the Royal Mint reported on the question early in 1692, they blasted the idea, and Mather returned to Boston with a mint-less charter.[31]

Neither side was completely pleased with the final text of the charter. Blathwayt and the Lords of Trade regretted some of the more substantial concessions; the Massachusetts agents regretted that the province enjoyed considerably less autonomy than Rhode Island, Connecticut, and other private colonies. Indeed the Crown in 1690 permitted Rhode Island and Connecticut to resume their old governments, with popularly elected governors and no obligation to submit laws to England for approval (something the Crown came to regret later). Not so for Massachusetts. Elisha Cooke and Thomas Oakes, at first, repudiated the new charter, excoriating Mather for compromising unnecessarily on too many critical questions. Mather himself admitted that the new government was "more Monarchical and less Democratical than in former Times." But this was no reason to wholly reject it. "Although there are some things in this New-Charter which are not desirable," he conceded, "yet nothing that is intolerable. Take it with all its Faults, and it is not so bad." The former Dominion of New England had made it impossible to any longer take for granted such liberties as a representative assembly. To reject such a liberal settlement, Mather warned, would usher "fatal Ruine on New-England." Most people in Massachusetts came to agree.[32]

King William permitted Mather to nominate the first royal governor. Mather chose Phips. William Stoughton, the former agent who had challenged Randolph in the late 1670s, became lieutenant governor. Boston merchants dominated the governor's council. Crucially, the new government confirmed the land titles of the great speculators, along with the titles of small landowners. Indeed, when Mather initially described the charter to his compatriots back home, he eagerly announced that "all Mens Properties are Confirmed and Secured."[33] Furthermore, in 1692, the new General Court declared the old pine-tree shillings legal tender.[34]

Most Massachusetts colonists found considerable comfort in the new imperial system. A constitutional, Calvinist monarch now sat on the throne. Colonists perceived a common bond with Parliament over its constitutional resistance to James's arbitrary government; many colonists interpreted the Glorious Revolution as a victory for English political liberties on both sides of the Atlantic. By contrast, leading figures in England viewed the revolution as a localized event, disagreeing that colonists enjoyed the same political liberties as Englishmen residing in England. Nevertheless, many Whigs had great empathy for the colonists' former struggle under Stuart oppression—enough to give the colonial interpretation of the Glorious Revolution some semblance of accuracy, especially given that many of the colonists' most cherished political liberties (like representative government) were in fact restored after 1688.[35] Finally, the advent of a quarter century of global warfare with Roman Catholic, absolutist France introduced a new paradigm into the English world, one in which the Protestant monarch, in league with Parliament, extended protection to colonists in exchange for their allegiance and obedience to the greater aims of empire. Colonists interpreted that protection as including not only military protection from the neighboring French but also the restoration and preservation of basic political liberties. As Mather said, "all English Liberties are restored"—the province "may now expect Protection and Assistance from England."[36]

This new protection-allegiance paradigm was the basis on which colonists tacitly accepted their subordinate place within a Protestant, mercantilist empire. Their general acceptance of this subordinate role was contingent largely upon the preservation of their most fundamental political liberties. To call it contractual would not be accurate—it was more familial, binding, existential, and intimate than the commercial metaphor of contract. The parent-child metaphor was still a more apt description of the relationship. But as the terms of this relationship were never spelled out with any real precision, the particulars remained subject to much contention and bargaining in the decades to follow. In Massachusetts politics, a faction known as the popular party sought continually to neutralize the powers of the royal governor, all the while displaying fervent, sincere, and unremitting loyalty to the British monarch. This generated a great deal of tension between London and Boston in and after the 1690s. Gone, however, was the pre-1688 flirtation in Massachusetts with absolute colonial sovereignty, and gone too was the empire's flirtation with absolute royal command.[37] Back in 1678 the General Court had feared that the closing of their mint would betoken "his majesties signall ouning us."[38] Bay colonists remained markedly jealous of their much-cherished liberty, but after 1688, it was no longer as difficult for them to accept the ultimate sovereignty of Old England over New England matters. As one Bostonian wrote later in the mid-eighteenth century, "Coinage is a Prerogative of the Sovereignty, not of a colony."[39]

The economic rationale for having a mint had not vanished in Massachusetts; people still used irregular Spanish coins in routine transactions. But the supplementary use of paper currency made the need for a mint less urgent. After the new charter arrived, the bills of credit gained slowly but steadily in value; the charter neither repudiated the bills nor prohibited further emissions. Furthermore, in its inaugural session, the reconstituted General Court declared the bills to be legal tender for private debts, not simply for public payments, further boosting the currency's credit. The year 1694 was the final one in which the Massachusetts treasury accepted country pay as legal tender for taxes.[40]

For the next sixty years, paper money became perhaps the most controversial issue in Massachusetts politics. Some Bostonians later cursed the day when the Massachusetts government approved "the first Emission of the fraudulent publick Bills of Credit."[41] Many opponents of the currency reflected nostalgically on the period before its introduction. "As to Silver and Gold we never had much of it in the Country," recalled one writer in 1720, "but we can very well remember, that before we had Paper Money, there was a sufficiency of it Currant in the Country, and as the Bills of Credit came in and multiplied, the Silver ceased and was gone."[42] "Before Paper Money took place in New England, Silver abounded," wrote a prominent (and certainly not unbiased) opponent in 1740; ". . . Silver began to be generally ship'd off as Paper became the Currency."[43]

Silver indeed became less common in Massachusetts Bay after 1690, notwithstanding the hyperbolic quality of some of the above statements. There was reportedly "not one quarter part" of the old pine-tree shillings remaining in circulation by the mid-1690s, though the General Court had declared them legal tender.[44] Merchants exported most of what remained of the old Boston coinage to England and to other colonies; the Carolina legislature in Charlestown, for instance, recognized pine-tree shillings as current money in 1700.[45] By the turn of the century, New England merchants exported to England alone an estimated £18,000 to £30,000 in silver coins every year.[46] Finally, in December 1697—after debating the measure for three years—the General Court prohibited exporting more than £5 of coin at a time from the colony, citing the present "scarcity of money."[47] "Silver in New-England is like the water of a swift Running River," said Cotton Mather in 1691, "always coming, and as fast going away." "If neither Silver can be had, nor Corn brought in without loss both to the Government and People," he said, "what remains but Accounts, Bills, or such like Paper-pay?"[48]

The Crown's refusal to sanction a Boston mint begs the question why the empire, at first, tolerated colonial bills of credit. For one thing, colonial paper financed expeditions against the French. Second, unlike the pine-tree shilling, the new bills of credit acknowledged imperial authority by displaying the royal arms on the lower left-hand corner of the bill. But lastly, imperial officials—at first—viewed bills of credit as something entirely distinct from *money*. Though the paper passed from hand to hand, like all other currency, the bill of credit was technically speaking a promissory note that indebted the colonial government to the noteholder (the creditor). Bills of credit were "in value equal to money"—as the currency read—but money itself remained exclusively silver and gold coin. Not until the 1720s did the Crown pressure colonial governments to curtail their use of paper money. For the time being, men like Captain John Blackwell persuasively dismissed all accusations that paper currency represented a new form of "Treason against the Crown of England."[49]

The pine-tree coinage had finally vanished, at least for now. A couple generations later, the image reappeared. In 1776 the Massachusetts government issued a new coin, a copper coin. On the reverse of the money was the goddess of liberty, seated on a globe. Stamped proudly on the obverse of the coin was a pine tree, which soon also emblazoned the bills of credit used by the colony to fight the War of Independence (figure 12).

The Nine Years' War with France changed England in ways that none could have predicted in 1689. The war's pecuniary demands forever altered English finance and even the character of English government, transforming the latter into what historian John Brewer calls the "fiscal-military state."[50] The transformation, necessitated by war, affirmed anew the wisdom and practicality of mercantilism as the empire's chief economic framework. The matter was extremely urgent. England's military expenditures averaged nearly £5.5 million per annum during the war, comprising almost three-quarters of the government's budget. The surge in government spending forced a doubling of taxes and unprecedented borrowing. The decade before, annual public expenditures averaged under £2 million.[51] The English navy, during the war, swelled from 25 to 234 ships; the army more than doubled in size to help Continental allies battle the army of Louis XIV, more than 250,000 men strong.[52]

FIGURE 12. *Top*, copper pine-tree penny of Massachusetts, 1776. (Courtesy of the Massachusetts Historical Society.) *Bottom*, one shilling bill of credit of Massachusetts, 1779 (ANS 0000.999.29713. Courtesy of American Numismatic Society.)

The growing scarcity of England's money supply compounded the urgency. Between 1688 and 1695, English merchants exported from the country approximately £2,127,000 worth of silver coin and bullion: 1,225,944 ounces of foreign silver coin and 6,754,649 ounces of silver bullion (most of which was melted English coin). Of this total, £698,896 departed England in one year alone, 1694.[53] Output at the Tower Mint was equally appalling. Between 1690 and 1694, mint output averaged only £70,051 per annum (both gold and silver, but mostly gold)—an alarming plunge from the £543,658 average between 1680 and 1688.[54] The impact was devastating. "Money is very scarce both in City and Country," said the author of a 1690 pamphlet entitled *The True Causes of the Pre-*

sent Scarcity of Money; "Want of Money is the common Cry," Sir Dudley North, merchant, wrote in 1691.[55] In 1695 Captain John Blackwell, now living in England, remarked that "the whole Nation is almost destitute of Moneys: Not only for the carrying on the War . . . but for our home Markets." "The Scarcity of Money and the great Complaints of all sorts of Traders for want of Money . . . is a Truth too well known to be denied," another stated in 1694.[56] "Those Streams that brought in our Treasure from Spain and the West-Indies, are evidently diverted into another Channel," wrote a pamphleteer in 1696, ". . . our Coin being very low, and the balance of Trade so much against us."[57] The scarcity was so dreadful that former king James II, in April 1692, penned a declaration to "his Loving Subjects" promising that a Jacobite restoration would "restore Trade . . . bringing back Wealth and Bullion into the Kingdom, which of late has been so much exhausted."[58]

England's overseas trade suffered terribly from the war. "The regular establish'd Methods of Business and Intercourse of the World is broken," observed one Englishman in 1696; the "grievous deadness of Trade," another wrote in 1690, had caused the "Exportation of our Money into Forrain Parts."[59] Merchants withdrew immense sums of capital from overseas commerce; within a couple years, the total tonnage of English shipping had fallen by more than half; woolen exports declined severely; the French navy effectively debarred most English commercial vessels from the Mediterranean, and French privateers captured about four thousand English merchant vessels through the course of the war.[60] The trade deficit with Sweden and the Baltic countries for desperately needed naval stores reached £200,000 per annum, siphoning even more silver from the kingdom.[61]

The Continental side of the war drained England of almost £1 million of silver and gold bullion (but mostly silver), delivered across the Channel to finance the many thousands of troops stationed in Flanders and across northern Europe.[62] England's allies, the Grand Alliance—including the Holy Roman Empire, Spain, the Netherlands, and Austria—were almost wholly dependent on English subsidies and financing. As early as November 1692, King William delivered a speech to Parliament lamenting the "inconvenience of sending out of the kingdom great sums of money" to finance the Continental war.[63] The greater part of these remittances were in bills of exchange, but many of the debts contracted on these bills were later settled in bullion. Indeed, concerns about the draining of specie played a significant role in the Tory ascendancy in 1690–1693, displacing Whigs in Parliament who had proved so hawkish for Continental war in 1689; Tories, by contrast, focused primarily on the naval side of the conflict.[64] "Nothing dreins a Country so much as a Foreign War, where the Troops must be paid abroad," Charles Davenant, a leading Tory, remarked: "it bears off the Species of Mony (the very Life of Trade)," all "sent abroad to pay the Army, which Treasure is partly dispersed about in Germany." Secretary to the Treasury William Lowndes in like manner regretted the "great Expence of our Wealth in Foreign Parts of Europe" and the obligation "to transmit our Moneys into other Countries."[65]

To top it all, the quality of the domestic coinage in England had almost totally deteriorated. Clipping had long plagued the old and still extant hammered silver money, coins that dated back to the early Stuarts and even to the age of Elizabeth. But the problem became extremely severe in the early 1690s, at which point, according to William Lowndes, the silver content in most circulating coins had "Diminished near one Half."[66] The money "loudly cryed for a Reformation"; the "Ruin and Destruction of our Money" by clippers was no longer even remotely endurable.[67] The government delayed recoining the money as long as it could. As one writer later recalled, "it was feared the distraction about the coin would be more fatal than the war with France, and the King of France fully expected the same would bring us into confusion."[68] Nevertheless, by 1695, leading officials concluded that there was no other option but to recoin all of the old hammered silver money, even as the war raged on. In a matter of months, beginning in January 1696, the gargantuan project abruptly ejected from circulation some £4.7 million of silver coins (at face value), paralyzing the economy and costing the government more than £2.3 million in expenses.[69]

All things considered, the Great Recoinage of 1696 worked to the ultimate, long-term benefit of the English economy. The action stabilized confidence in the fundamental soundness and trustworthiness of the pound sterling and, together with the founding of the Bank of England in 1694, prepped the nation for a century of credit expansion and fiscal solidity. In the short term, however, the undertaking proved extraordinarily painful. The government notoriously botched the particulars of the plan's execution, sparking, temporarily, the greatest currency crisis and economic confusion in English history—"a greater Scarcity of Money, and even greater Decay of Trade and Credit than England knew, since they were a trading Nation," said one contemporary.[70] "Extreme Misery" abounded: "there is little Money current," and "necessities for Money are great"; "the people are discontented to the utmost."[71] As diarist John Evelyn wrote in June 1696, "tumults are every day feared, nobody paying or receiving money."[72] Months later, an English minister observed that despite the ongoing war in Europe, "nothing hath more exercis'd the Tongues, and fill'd the Hearts of many this last year, than the difficulties about the Money."[73]

A near-universal war weariness had firmly set in by the mid-1690s. Most Englishmen now tired of the "great difficulty in raising Money for carrying on the War"—that "long and obstinate War in Europe."[74] Even Whigs like John Cary feared that continued warfare "may strain the Nerves and Sinews of our Treasure before it be ended."[75] The currency contraction of the Great Recoinage incapacitated the nation's economy, provoking, among other things, mass bankruptcies and a debilitating run on the infant Bank of England in May 1696. "War annihilates your Money," John Briscoe, merchant and Tory, remarked the same year.[76]

The war for both sides involved "great Expence of Blood and Treasure."[77] France likewise suffered a hemorrhaging of money, coupled with a decay of foreign trade. "Whenever this War ceases," remarked Davenant in 1695, "it will not be for want of mutual Hatred in the opposite Parties, nor for want of Men to fight the Quarrel." Rather, he said, "that side must first give out where Money is first failing." Davenant was correct; the war ended less than two years later for reasons of financial exhaustion. "War is quite changed from what it was in the time of our Forefathers, when, in a hasty Expedition, and a pitch'd Field, the Matter was decided by Courage," he said, "but now the whole Art of War is in a manner reduced to Money."[78] "War is become rather an Expence of Money than Men," another Englishman stated in 1693, "and Success attends those that can most and longest spend Money." "The Wars now adays seem rather to be waged with Gold than with Iron," declared another writer in 1695.[79]

English government was never again the same: the Nine Years' War transformed the state in ways that the mere unseating of James II could never have accomplished on its own. Far from the libertarian revolution that some Whigs anticipated in 1688, the power, role, and scope of the government burgeoned in the aftermath of the revolution. Parliament assumed a much more active role in economic matters in the years and decades after 1688.[80] The state bureaucracy inflated; the number of public employees increased almost fivefold between 1688 and 1714, with some assigned to preexisting departments, and others to entirely new ones.[81] The expenses of war and bureaucratic growth forever altered the state of the nation's finances. Even with the doubling of taxes, government revenue fell significantly short of expenditures (£3.64 million compared to £5.5 million per annum), placing the nation's outstanding debt at £16.7 million by the end of the war.[82] Prior to 1689, government debt rarely exceeded a single year's worth of revenue. The national debt, in turn, sparked a financial revolution, including the formation of elaborate markets in stocks, bonds, and other securities. Most famously, in April 1694, Parliament chartered the Bank of England—the first incorporated bank in English history—in return for a loan to the government of £1.2 million at 8 percent interest, on security of tax revenue marked specifically for this purpose.[83] Public finance had never come easier, but with it arose a new class of "monied Men"—bankers and stockjobbers "enrich'd with the collective Treasure of the Nation," critics warned—and "where the Treasure is, there will be the Power."[84]

All of these changes, whether for good or for ill, bewildered those who lived through the 1690s and the two additional war-filled decades to follow. The war, the bureaucracy, the Bank, the Recoinage, the wartime depredations on commerce: all further validated, it seemed, the mercantilist fixation on money. The "long and expensive War" had demonstrated that government should do everything within its power to increase the sum of gold and silver in England.[85] Gold and silver remained as necessary to empire "as Nerves and Sinews are for the motion of the Natural Body," remarked Sir Josiah Child in 1694. "Ready Money must be had for the Prosecution of the War and bringing down the Power of France," said Dalby Thomas, sugar merchant, in 1695: "if the Foreign Trade were promoted and secured as it might be," he said, "we might easily find Money to carry on a lasting War."[86]

The monetary and fiscal crisis of the 1690s ended a brief flirtation with an antimercantilist impulse that had accompanied the Glorious Revolution. For some years after 1688, a disparate group of economic dissidents in England—including a few radical Whigs, Country politicians, and some pro–East India Company Tories—condemned altogether the balance-of-trade doctrine and the specie objective (the primacy of gold and silver). This group represented, in certain respects, a libertarian alternative to the mercantilist order. Some of the dissidents rejected the mercantilist emphasis on overseas trade, arguing that domestic exchange and the internal market were equally important for the health of the national economy; others repudiated the supposed tension between private and public interest, praising the acquisitive urge as positively good for the economy regardless of its implications for the balance of trade; still others insisted that money was simply one of many different kinds of commodities, "and one sort of Commodity is as good as another."[87] The dissent was short-lived, fading into near-total obscurity by the early eighteenth century. A quarter century of warfare had apparently refuted these ideas. "Some are of opinion that Laws for Regulating of Trade are unnecessary," wrote John Pollexfen, founding member of the Board of Trade, in 1697, but just "as too many Limitations of Trade may be inconvenient, so too much Liberty dangerous."[88]

During and after the 1690s, mercantilism and the balance-of-trade doctrine became even more entrenched as economic orthodoxy. "The necessityes of the Warr have carried away most of the ready money," wrote Davenant, but "if we can protect our Trade to that degree as to be Gainers by the General Ballance, the Expence and Length of the War will not so much affect us." Even Secretary Lowndes—an ardent supporter of devaluation—called the "Ballance of Trade . . . the Original Cause of the Scarcity of Silver in England." England must never suffer "an over-ballancing of Foreign Commodities with our Home Commodities," he urged in 1695, else "our Treasure will be exhausted, which is the Life of Trade and Sinews of War." "Our Coin must decrease," Pollexfen warned in 1699, "unless some alterations be made in the course of trade."[89]

James Whiston, a broker, writer on trade, and publisher of commodity prices, outlined the endgame of mercantilism concisely and frankly. "'Tis high time to awaken all the Vital Powers of State," he urged in 1693; "the Strength or Weakness, Wealth or Poverty of this Kingdom wholly depends upon the Good or Ill Management of Foreign Trade." "Hereby the Nation will be abundantly Enriched," he promised, "and Money being the very Life of War, and Sinews of all Publick Action, we shall be enabled to bring the World into a Dependant Awe, send out our Superfluities at what Profit we please, and also return the richest Commodities of the Remotest Climates at our own Prices: The People will be Contented, and the Exchequer maintained in a Full Spring Tide, ready to encounter all Emergencyes; so that it can't be within the reach of the Worlds United Power to do us prejudice." "A Foreign Trade Managed to the best Advantage," he continued, "will make our Nation so Strong and Rich, that we may Command the Trade of the World, the Riches of it, and consequently the World it self."[90]

Many administrators and mercantilists thus blasted the repeated evasions of imperial trade laws by England's American colonists. Unless the plantations were soon brought into "subjection and dependency upon their Mother-Kingdom," Child warned in 1692, the "Benefit of them would be wholly lost to the Nation." John Cary, a Whig and major tobacco merchant in Bristol, urged that Virginia planters be made to "more absolutely depend on this Kingdom." "All the English Plantations should be bound," insisted Nehemiah Grew, "bound, I mean, to Trade with England alone." "The Breach of the Navigation Act, in our Plantations, will have dangerous Consequences," wrote Davenant, and "if suffer'd we cannot expect to hold 'em long in our Subjection." "These Colonies," he warned, "(if they fall into the Practice of Trading independantly of England) may erect themselves into Independant Commonwealths, or Pyratical Societies, which at last we shall not be able to Master; by which means the Plantations, which now are a main Branch of our Wealth, may become a Strength to be turn'd against us."[91]

The Nine Years' War and English currency crisis highlighted, in an extreme way, the empire's utmost need for colonial economic subordination. And yet the question remained: How were imperial authorities to persuade American colonists, who had so vehemently resisted economic controls in the previous several decades, to submit to and appreciate the realities of empire in a post-1688 world? Four economic issues in particular—each related directly or indirectly to money—vexed imperial authorities in the 1690s: smuggling, piracy, currency devaluation, and colonial manufacturing.

The pecuniary incentive to smuggle was no less in the colonies after 1688 than before. Many foreign traders continued to sell goods at "much lower Rates" and to purchase colonial goods at rates "much higher."[92] When the governor of Jamaica reported of an incoming Dutch vessel in 1690, he added, "the mony of the Dutch ship was the greate Temptation."[93] Dutch manufactured goods, on the whole, remained less expensive than English manufactures; Dutch shipping, moreover, was not as adversely impacted by the war, nor as diverted to wartime uses, allowing the Dutch to freight goods "cheaper than we could do," the merchants in Bristol petitioned in 1696.[94] The Dutch remained particularly active in the English West Indies; the proximity of St. Eustatius, St. Thomas, and Curaçao—"the Dutch our neighbours," said the governor of Jamaica—made it particularly tempting to buy imports "at easy rates."[95]

Trade with the Scots offered up another temptation, especially for middling tobacco planters in Virginia and Maryland. Few English ships visited the Chesapeake during the war because of foreign depredations at sea. The English government responded by instituting a strict convoy system, but one that favored wealthy tobacco planters with personal connections in England, leaving smaller planters with fewer buyers. Scottish interlopers filled the void, feigning English names, forging certificates, or doing business by "some obscure Creek 40 or 50 Miles distant from the [Customs] Collectors Office"; and when delivered to court, the interlopers could count on an acquittal from the colonial jury.[96] A 1695 report from the Commissioners of the Customs estimated that Scotch trade in America diminished the customs by at least £50,000 per annum, warning that "if there were not some Law to prevent the same, the Plantation-Trade would be in Danger to be totally lost."[97] Thus in April 1692 the English government reinstated an exceedingly familiar face: Mr. Edward Randolph. This time, Randolph returned to America as surveyor general of the customs in Virginia, serving there five years. Sir Edmund Andros became governor of Virginia in 1692, a position he retained for six years, while Francis Nicholson—former deputy of the Dominion of New England—became governor of Maryland, disputing with the colonial assembly, council, and courts over "their Darling Illegal Trade," as he called it. The Navigation Acts "are oftener broken than kept," Nicholson claimed.[98]

Illegal trade was especially infectious in private colonies, where partial juries, courts, and government officials persistently hampered regulatory enforcement.

Pennsylvania merchants traded extensively with the Scots off the shore of the Delaware River and continued to send ships of their own to Curaçao, carrying Chesapeake tobacco to the Dutch islanders for European imports, avoiding detection by storing the tobacco in "bread casks covered with flour at each end."[99] In neighboring Jersey (also private) the people were "great favourers of the Scotch Traders"; in Rhode Island and Connecticut, "plain breaches of the Acts of Trade and Navigation" continued unabated.[100] The governor of Rhode Island conceded frankly to the Crown, in 1694, that the Navigation Acts "have been very much violated," yet callously denied that there was anything he could realistically do to stop it.[101] Further south, Carolina retained its reputation as a "center of Illegal Trade," with Charles Town merchants establishing contacts with Dutch merchants on Curaçao, "from whence the Manufacture of Holland is brought."[102] Even in New York, a royal colony, the leading mercantile families—still ethnically and culturally Dutch—imported "great quantitys of European goods" from Holland and Curaçao.[103]

Smuggling persisted also in Massachusetts. The colonial legislature in June 1692 enacted the Naval Office Act, providing for colonial-appointed officers to clear and enter ships in seven different ports in the colony. The act won the support of Governor Sir William Phips, who issued an order declaring that "no further office than the Naval Office established by Act of the Province is necessary for clearing and entering ships," thus bypassing the imperial customs collector, Jahleel Brenton (appointed by the Crown after Randolph's return to England).[104] On one wild occasion in 1693, Phips and a throng of fifty men laid "violent hands" on Brenton for seizing an interloping sloop, reportedly "pushing and dragging him about the wharfe . . . striking him severall blows" with a cane, and with "Barbarous Language threatening to beat him until he broke all his bones." Brenton grudgingly released the confiscated goods and vessel: a sloop appropriately christened the *Good Luck*. (Brenton soon returned to London to lobby for Phips's removal and for the Crown to disallow the Naval Office Act; the Crown disallowed the act in August 1695.)[105]

The swarming of pirates along the North American seaboard presented still another problem for England. The Nine Years' War provoked an explosion in buccaneering in the early to mid-1690s, a period that history remembers as the Golden Age of Piracy. War impelled the commissioning of privateers by the English and French governments, primarily for operations in the Caribbean Sea, but colonial governors too had license again to commission privateers against enemy ships. As encouragement early in the war, King William had issued a "Generall Pardon" to pirates who now offered privateering services "to any of the Governors in his Majestys Plantations in America."[106] William Kidd was the most famous of these wartime privateers. Captain of the *Blessed William*, Kidd had a commission from the governor of Nevis to combat the French on the high seas.[107] As late as 1693, Parliament had passed an act "for the encouragement of privateers," yet it was evident from the beginning that the strategy might back-fire.[108] Privateers rarely stopped with enemy ships; as the Board of Trade regret-ted in 1698, "privateers" had become "a soft name given to Pirates."[109] For the whole of the 1690s, scores of buccaneers, most often with privateering commis-sions (real or counterfeit), scoured the waters east of the Cape of Good Hope, including the east African coast, Red Sea, Arabian Sea, Persian Gulf, and Indian Ocean. The buccaneers plundered Mughal vessels, Muslim pilgrimage vessels, and sometimes—though less commonly—even vessels belonging to the English East India Company. Madagascar was the pirates' primary base of operations; settled since the mid-1680s, Madagascar effectively constituted an independent pirate state.[110]

Pirates and privateers received a warm welcome in most colonial ports, as they had in the early 1680s, all "sharing in the Spoil"—from shopkeepers and shipbuilders, to merchants seeking bargain prices on luxury items, to governors and other officials probing for bribes of silver, gold, and other gifts; indeed, "their sharing in such large summs tempts the people of those parts to goe along with them."[111] Local tradesmen made a habit of selling the buccaneers victuals, repairing and "fitting out the Pirates ships."[112] Restive or disgruntled sailors at port often joined the buccaneers, allured by the prospect of riches and a more democratic experience on the high seas; the pirates' "sharing in such large summs tempts the people of those parts to goe along with them."[113] Many re-spectable colonial merchants helped finance the voyages, motivated "by the great expectations of Riches." In exchange for this capital, the buccaneers agreed to return to the colonial port with the plundered silver, gold, spices, and other booty. To ease the mind of the merchant-investor, the buccaneers sometimes even left behind their "Wives and families as pledges of their returne."[114] Alter-natively, other merchants sent agents directly to Madagascar to sell colonial pro-duce and to purchase "great quantities of East India goods."[115]

The most famous patron of the buccaneers was the governor of New York, Benjamin Fletcher—ironically, a man appointed by the Crown. Colorful, flam-boyant, and eager for the twin prize of popularity and profit, Fletcher, in close alliance with the merchants who dominated his council, turned New York into "a nest of Pirates" and smugglers.[116] When charges were later brought against Fletcher, he justified his actions by recalling that when he first arrived in New York, "the Government was £3000 in debt, no credit left, and the people most unwilling to pay the taxes." Paper currency was not available to Fletcher, but pi-racy was, and with "the Province being then exhausted of men as well as of mony, nothing could be worse than to drive these men [pirates] to other parts."[117]

During Fletcher's governorship (1692–1698), pirates brought into New York an estimated £100,000 of silver and gold per annum.[118] Coin included gold of Turkish, Arabic, and Barbary origin, spent in common street shops, brothels, and alehouses. The city's wealthiest merchants serviced the pirates with clothing, food, "Liquors, Arms and Gunpowder," accepting in return gold, silver, calicoes, spices, and silks.[119] One such pirate vessel, the *Jacob*, had initially been fitted out in Newport, Rhode Island, in December 1690. After a number of successful forays in the Indian Ocean, the *Jacob* arrived at New York in 1693, bearing £800 a man. Fletcher extended the pirates protection in return for "a suitable present of Arabian Gold"—£100 from each crew member—as well as possession of the ship, which the governor then sold for £800 cash.[120] One purported privateer who received a commission from Fletcher—Captain John Hore—announced publicly that he was "bound to the red seas," upon which twenty-two merchants in the city invested in his expedition. Thomas Tew, a buccaneering captain with "considerable spoils of silver and gold," was also "much countenanced" by Fletcher upon his arrival in 1694, "being entertained at dinner with him" and lavishly shown around town in the governor's coach, with "severall presents Interchanged." Tew "publickly declared that he designed for the Red Seas or the Coast of Arabia," pledging to make New York his point of return in exchange for a commission from Fletcher, who readily agreed.[121] All this was "notoriously publick" and "known to most of the City": "openly declared" by Tew in order to recruit additional men for the voyage, allured by the promises of "great riches."[122] All in all, through his whole tenure as governor, Fletcher made an estimated £30,000 for himself, while merchant elites like Frederick Philipse used their gains from investing in piracy to buy massive estates along the Hudson River.[123]

Further pirate sanctuaries included Philadelphia; Carolina; New Jersey; and Newport, Rhode Island. In 1692 the governor at Charles Town sold a privateering commission to a Red Sea pirate for twenty gold guineas (the equivalent of more than one hundred pieces of eight). Just one year before, the *Batchelor's Delight*—a ship of eighty men, possessing £1,100 each—returned from the Indian Ocean to dock at Charles Town.[124] The Rhode Island governor granted privateering commissions with extreme liberality—thirty commissions in the year 1694 alone.[125] Indeed Captain Tew, before heading to New York in 1694, dropped anchor in Newport (his hometown) with "£10,000 in Gold & Silver," by which "the people are Enriched," Randolph reported.[126] Quaker merchants in New Jersey and Philadelphia earnestly supported the privateers. The deputy governor of Pennsylvania, William Markham, confessed to William Penn in 1697 that he accepted "a small present" from men who "went by the name of Privateers"—("they might be Pirats for any thing I know to the contrary")—and that "some of those men at this time have houses of their own & families in this town," one of whom, astoundingly, had married his daughter.[127] Penn understood the temptation: in 1701 he told the Board of Trade that it was hard for colonists to turn pirates away when they "empty their Pockets at our Taverns." "The whole Continent labours under the want of mony to circulate Trade," Penn said; so who could blame them? The New Jersey governor, Jeremiah Basse likewise identified money as the reason for the pirates' popularity: "the generality of our people receivinge no small advantage by the currencie of their monys."[128]

Silver, gold, and luxury goods were a splendid temptation for practically any colonial tradesman. "It is notorious in this Part of the World that Pyrates and Privateers have been very much harboured," wrote an anonymous Virginian in 1701, ". . . those People bringing in great quantities of Money, and other rich Goods."[129] The most spectacular feature of all in this trade was the influx of gold from faraway lands. "Arabian Gold is in great plenty," reported the Earl of Bellomont, successor to Fletcher as New York governor. Arabian gold coins were generally worth twelve to fourteen shillings, the value of two Spanish silver dollars. One English official visiting Pennsylvania for the first time in 1701 remarked, to his shock, that there was "no money to be seen amongst them now but Arabian Gold." "We have a parcell of pirates in these parts," an inhabitant wrote in 1695, "which people call the Red-Sea men, who often get great booty of Arabian Gold."[130]

The idea of a plain American shopkeeper handling Arabian money is striking and curious. What were the thoughts running through his head when he encountered such a piece? At the very least, it reminded him that the world was a huge place—far larger than even the boundaries of the Atlantic Ocean. No doubt he thought the money exotic. And how many opportunities he had to obtain such pieces! In 1692 a crew of one hundred pirates, with £2,000 a man—having captured a treasure-laden Mughal ship—trekked up the American seaboard from Carolina to Rhode Island. Three years later, another vessel from the Red Sea made the same voyage, this time comprising sixty pirates with £1,000–£1,500 a man.[131] One pirate ship reportedly "flushed them at New Yorke with Arabian Gold and East India goods." Another crew of seventy pirates visited Charles Town in 1693 with "a Vast quantity of Gold from the Red Sea." Little wonder that upon their arrival in Charles Town, "they were Entertained & had liberty to stay or goe to any other place."[132]

The testimony of Robert Snead, an English captain commissioned to combat piracy, reveals much about the currency motives of the colonists. In the mid-1690s he had a cordial but frank conversation with William Penn on the matter. Penn confessed that there was indeed "a good understanding between him & the Pyrates," for "the men had been civil to him & they had brought in money which was an advantage to the Countrey."[133] Captain Snead had also witnessed the Pennsylvania governor encourage the entry of pirates: "If people came here and brought mony, he was not obligd to ask them where they came." When Snead arrested a gang of pirates who had brought £1,000 a man to the province, "the Governor was much displeasd att me": evidence, he said, of "how the arrabian gold works with some Consciences."[134]

Pirates received a hostile reception in Jamaica and the Chesapeake, just as they had in the 1680s. Governor Nicholson in Maryland was "a man truly zealous to suppress Pyracy & illegall Trade," reported Randolph, and "very severe" to men suspected of harboring or countenancing pirates.[135] Jamaica's days as a buccaneer's paradise were long gone; instead, the buccaneers "returned with vast Wealth to most of their Majesties Northern Plantations in America," Governor William Beeston wrote in 1693.[136] After Beeston refused a bribe from Red Sea pirates in 1696 (the bribe was supposedly £20,000 in coin, but this must have been an exaggeration), the freebooters ventured northward to the friendlier mainland. The vessel reportedly had £300,000 worth of loot on board.[137] In Jamaica and the Chesapeake, remarked a man from Virginia in 1701, colonists "look upon the Pirates and Privateers to be Robbers and Thieves, but the good People of Pennsylvania esteem them very honest Men for bringing Money into their Countrey, and encouraging their Trade."[138]

Remarkably, as of 1695, the empire still lacked any effective antipiracy law. Piracy was "the pest of all trade," to quote Randolph, especially in the East Indies.[139] Indian and Arab merchants continually petitioned the East India Company regarding attacks on their vessels, and it was generally known in Surat and Bombay that "most of the Pyrates which infest those Seas are fitted out of New York."[140] This fact amounted to the "dishonour of the English name and nation," incurring indignation from the Mughals and others, causing "considerable prejudice to the Company."[141]

Piracy and smuggling worked to the same general advantage for colonies that countenanced the illicit activities. Both increased the overall wealth of a colony: wealth as coin ("abundance of money"), wealth as stuff ("rich East India Bale Goods"), or a combination of the two (additional coin *and* additional goods).[142] As the Board of Trade reported in 1698, piracy and illegal trade "frequently combined into a mutual support of one another."[143] "Some Governours may get more by illegal Trade, pyrats, and privateers, than their Governments are worth," remarked Nicholson the same year.[144]

Other quandaries required urgent attention. What of competitive currency devaluations? A new round of devaluations swept the colonies in the

1690s. These new devaluations coincided (not accidentally) with the decade's unprecedented scramble for pirate money. In December 1691 the Charles Town assembly raised the rating for clipped pieces of eight in Carolina by nearly 11 percent; sure enough, afterward, "great quantityes of light Spanish moneys" poured into Charles Town.[145] New York and Pennsylvania each devalued in 1693, an action coordinated by none other than Benjamin Fletcher, who temporarily served as governor for both colonies while Penn was under investigation in England. With this new devaluation, full-weight pieces received a value of 6s7d in New York and 7s in Pennsylvania. King William had commanded Fletcher a year earlier to "not upon any pretence whatsoever permitt any Alteration to be made in the Value of the currant Coyn"; but Fletcher proceeded with the plan anyway.[146] In 1696 Connecticut became the first New England colony to break the 6s threshold, advancing the full-weight dollar to 6s9d. Soon after, Boston merchants responded by accepting clipped coin by tale instead of by weight, amounting to a de facto devaluation of the currency in Massachusetts. Boston merchants had never before accepted currency by tale, but they felt compelled to this voluntary agreement by the fact that under the new charter government, any bill that passed the Massachusetts assembly (including and especially devaluation) had to be approved by the Crown.[147]

The staple plantations, as before, resented the empire's ostensibly haphazard, discriminatory approach toward devaluation, watching on jealously as surrounding settlements adjusted their rates for coin. Reportedly, Spanish money leaked incessantly across the border between Maryland and Pennsylvania, and Marylanders were right to affix much of the blame on Pennsylvania's higher rating for coin. In 1692, for the third time in its history, the Maryland assembly again passed a statute raising the dollar from 4s6d to 6s, but the law, again, was disallowed in England—this time by the Crown, not the proprietor (who had temporarily lost possession of the colony after the 1689 revolt). The assembly desperately pleaded the colonists' case to the Lords of Trade and even directly entreated the master of the Royal Mint for his support, saying that "the want of Ready money in this Province is detrimentall to their Majesties Interest."[148] Moreover, the Crown had recent reapproved a 6s rating for the dollar in Massachusetts. The appeal did not succeed. Defiant, the assembly then moved to raise the value of a full-weight dollar from 4s6d to 7s4d, far exceeding the 6s rating repealed by the Crown, and even exceeding the rating in Pennsylvania. The governor naturally refused to support the action, calling the assemblymen "ill-bred and ungrateful people," to which the assembly responded by voting "that no more Ports be made until our Act for Advancement of Coins be passed."[149] This effort, too, failed, and the piece of eight remained at 4s6d in Maryland.

The Virginia House of Burgesses embarked on similar efforts, also to no avail. Beginning in 1693 the House of Burgesses passed one bill after another raising the piece of eight from 5s to 6s, only to have them rejected by the Virginia council. When the council finally approved such a bill in 1703, the bill went to England for approval. Out of the forty-two bills sent to England that year from Virginia, the currency bill was the only one rejected.[150] Jamaica and the Leeward Islands encountered similar roadblocks. "Nothing is more obvious than that plenty of money in all countryes is what gives a great encouragement to trade," the assemblymen at Antigua urged the Crown, but to no effect.[151] The entire ordeal of devaluations, across the whole of the empire, was nothing short of a gigantic mess; none could deny that fact, no matter where one stood on the issue.

Of still greater importance to the mercantilist empire was the question of what to do about the ever-looming threat of colonial manufacturing. The Whig party, which regained control of Parliament and William's ministry from 1694 to 1697, championed an industrial future for England. The American colonies were rapidly becoming the most dependable overseas market for English manufactured goods. The colonial population in 1696 totaled some 400,000 persons (including the enslaved and Caribbean populations); more than 90,000 lived in New England, and more than 110,000 in the Chesapeake.[152] By the close of the century, English merchants exported to America more than £500,000 worth of manufactured goods—including English-made and reexported European manufactures—every year.[153]

But what if colonials expanded their own industry? Colonial production of rough textiles, primarily of wool and flax, was gradually on the increase, produced largely during agricultural slack periods. Ever slowly, this production satisfied some of the local demand for clothing. What if northern colonists began exporting rough textiles to the Caribbean? The recent influx of German immigrants to Pennsylvania, for example, threatened to bring linen manufacture to America; residents in Germantown, Pennsylvania, reportedly partook in "weaving Linnin Cloth" from local supplies of flax, and the first colonial paper mill was also founded in Germantown in 1690.[154] "All sorts of very good Paper are made in the German-Town, as also very fine German Linen, such as no Person of Quality need be asham'd to wear," an observer reported in 1698, ". . . besides other Woollen Cloathes, the Manufacture of all which daily improves."[155] Even in the Chesapeake, the low price of tobacco encouraged some planters to "set up several manufactures"—according to a report to Parliament in 1695—producing goods that were "formerly supplied with from England" and "consulting how to set up more."[156] Rudimentary iron manufactures also appeared with some success; Massachusetts colonists alone now produced approximately 1,500 tons of iron per annum.[157] The drive toward import substitution was pecuniary at root, as was England's opposition to the practice. As one Germantown resident wrote in 1700, "We are especially desirous to advance the cultivation of the vine and the weaving of cloth in these parts, in order to keep money in the province."[158]

How to combat these ills—smuggling, piracy, devaluation, and colonial manufacturing—without repeating the mistakes of the last two Stuart kings, was the pressing question of the day. The empire's goal was to make mercantilism work while retaining colonial loyalty to empire. Accomplish this goal, Davenant predicted, and "they will be a lasting Revenue to the King, an inexhaustible Mine of Treasure to England." "Our Interest in America, generally speaking," he said, "may bring an immense profit to this Kingdom if it is well looked after by the Government here."[159] To be "well looked after" meant more than mere councils of trade or greater enforcement of the Navigation Acts. Somehow or other, colonists must be persuaded of the prudence and utility of their dependent station within a powerful, free, Protestant, but mercantilist empire.

Maximum political coercion was extremely tempting given the dire need for colonial reform. The scale of the problem in the 1690s seemed to warrant a similar approach to that taken during the 1670s and 1680s. The Glorious Revolution, after all, had overturned despotism in England, but said nothing about colonial governance (or so went the argument). The revolution most certainly had *not* overturned mercantilism, nor had it overturned the vertical hierarchy of mother country and colony.

And yet in discrediting tyranny at home, 1688 had also discredited, even accidentally, the most abject forms of coercive imperial politics. To be certain, English administrators were still highly averse to colonial political autonomy, and remained so deep into the eighteenth century. But on the whole, the idea of absolutely denying colonial subjects their most cherished and fundamental English liberties—including representative assemblies and habeas corpus—was much less agreeable after 1688 than previously, even in colonies where the Crown still actively intervened in political affairs.

An efficient, though not unduly autocratic, framework of imperial governance was what the empire most needed. As things currently stood, in 1695, imperial administration was thoroughly broken. The Lords of Trade were still extant, and still superintended by William Blathwayt, but the committee had nonetheless fallen into relative obscurity. After 1689 the body met only a couple dozen times a year, at irregular intervals, marred by fluctuating membership and a crippling spirit of indolence, faction, and general ineptitude. The embarrassing failure of the Dominion of New England and other like projects from the 1680s had sapped the life out of the body, now dominated almost exclusively by the single person of Blathwayt.[160]

Pressure mounted for the creation of a more dynamic task force specializing in overseas trade and colonial settlements. French attacks on English commercial shipping had reached catastrophic levels, and England's trade balance with foreign countries reflected this problem. Moreover, "the Plantation-Trade in the State it now is in, is Irregular and Disorderly," a parliamentary committee reported in 1694—a "growing Evil," stated a petition of Bristol and Liverpool merchants in January 1695.[161] In November 1695, in a tract entitled a *Memorial Concerning the Coyn of England*, Davenant entreated that a "Universal Care of Traffick" be quickly established. "Trade is or ought to be an Affair of State," he said; neighboring states had "established Councils of Trade," and England required a new committee to evaluate, "first, how the Balance stands, where we get and where we lose in our Traffick with other Nations."[162]

In January 1696—the same month that the recoinage debacle began—a committee of the House of Commons resolved that a new "council of trade be established, by act of Parliament . . . impowered to consider the Plantation Trade, and all other Trades and Manufactures." According to the resolution, the council would be charged, primarily, with protecting English shipping and "settling the Balance of Trade, for the Benefit of this Kingdom."[163] The motion triggered a great constitutional question. If Parliament established the council of trade, the Crown would lose control of an entire administrative department, and a highly significant one at that: the overseeing of all colonial and overseas commerce. King William, wary of the powers already surrendered by the Crown, acted swiftly. Maneuvering ahead of Parliament, in May 1696 William commissioned a new royal committee called the Lords Commissioners of Trade and Plantations, known popularly as the Board of Trade. Its stated purpose was "for promoting the trade of this our kingdom, and for inspecting and improving our plantations in America."[164]

The Board of Trade consisted of sixteen members, eight of whom were required to attend on a regular basis. The Crown appointed the eight regular attendees, chosen for their expertise in commercial affairs; each of these members received a salary of £1,000 a year (equivalent to 4,444 pieces of eight). Blathwayt was among the original appointees, underlining, again, continuity from the pre-1688 era. John Pollexfen—a prominent merchant, Whig, author on trade, and member of Parliament—was also chosen; so too was John Locke. Sir Isaac Newton later served as an expert adviser, as did Charles Davenant, the preeminent Tory economist. The first president of the Board, the Earl of Bridgewater, was a longtime friend of Edward Randolph, and though Randolph himself was never a member, he maintained a regular correspondence and friendship with leading members of the Board.[165]

The Board of Trade answered to the monarch and possessed no executive power in and of itself; nonetheless, the Board commanded great influence. The Board issued frequent reports and recommendations to the Crown, including recommendations on the appointment of colonial governors and customs collectors. The members diligently compiled mounds of statistics; they administered the establishment of vice-admiralty courts, maintained a regular correspondence with governors and imperial officials, consulted merchant interest groups in London, received agents from the colonies, drafted governors' instructions, and issued annual reports to both chambers of Parliament, attendant with proposals for new legislation. Intent on pursuing their business in a scientific manner, the Board's members spent much of their time consulting experts and economists, interviewing officials, receiving lobbyists, and acquiring commercial data.[166] Decidedly mercantilist in outlook, the Board strenuously investigated ways to improve England's balance of trade, particularly with the Mediterranean and Baltic countries, and most especially with colonial America. The Board was the ultimate consummation of the imperial and mercantilist administrative system as developed since the mid-seventeenth century.

The newly passed Navigation Act of 1696 armed the Board of Trade with the most effective mechanism yet for enforcing trade laws. Weeks prior to William's commissioning the Board, Parliament passed an "act for preventing frauds and regulating abuses in the plantation trade." (Remember that through this entire time in 1696, the coinage of England was abruptly ejected from circulation and chaotically delivered to the mint. It is remarkable that the government got anything else done in those dark months.) The purpose of this final great Navigation Act was to strengthen enforcement of preexisting statutes and to clarify previously ambiguous language. The act established, for the first time, a licensing system, by which all English shipowners involved in colonial trade registered their vessels and testified "that no Foreigner, directly or indirectly, hath any Share, or Part, or Interest therein." Furthermore, under the new Navigation Act, all English or colonial buyers of enumerated goods (for example, tobacco and sugar) had to post bond that they would carry the same to either England or to an English colony, even if they paid the plantation duty; previously, under the Navigation Act of 1673, the shipmaster did not have to post bond if he paid the plantation duty. Finally, and perhaps most important, juryless vice-admiralty courts—already in place in Massachusetts under the new charter—were now to prosecute smugglers in *all* of the colonies, including private ones, thus eliminating the ability of colonial magistrates and juries to nullify the law through questionable acquittals.[167] "The Country Jurys will hardly ever find against them," a frustrated observer reported of colonial smugglers in 1695; Edward Randolph, who helped craft the new act, spoke often of the "generall partiality of Courts and Jurys (byassed by private Interest) in all causes relating to the Crown."[168] But no longer. For these reasons, Thomas Barrow, a twentieth-century economic historian, called the Navigation Act of 1696 "a landmark in the development and execution of English colonial policy." "It presupposed lack of cooperation from the colonists," he wrote, "and elaborated in detail, and at length, a comprehensive program to perfect the machinery of enforcement." "In all its varied aspects the Act of 1696 centered authority on London. Every action was to be checked there, every official concerned with the trade laws appointed or approved there."[169]

Months after the Navigation Act of 1696, the High Court of the Admiralty began setting up the requisite network of courts throughout the colonies, divided into eleven districts. In December 1697, Randolph, as surveyor general, began a general tour of the colonies that lasted through July 1700, working to establish the foundations of a revamped and far more effective colonial customs service. Randolph died in Virginia in April 1703, succeeded as surveyor general by Robert Quary, former admiralty judge of Pennsylvania. The frequency of smuggling gradually declined in the early eighteenth century, even in Boston. By 1710 thirty-four customs districts operated in British America, staffed by forty-two officials.[170]

With the enactment of the new Navigation Act, the imperial state turned its attention more fully to piracy. For years, the East India Company had badgered the Crown about piracy, sounding the alarm that piracy might overturn all EIC business in India. The most flagrant action had come from one Captain Henry Every, whose crew recently captured two vessels in the Red Sea belonging to the Mughal emperor; the two vessels contained Arabian gold and other treasures and jewels, as well as the granddaughter of the Mughal emperor.[171] In August 1696 King William issued a circular letter to colonial governors urging the capture of Every's crew, adding that they might be discovered by "the Greate Quantityes of Gold and Silver of Forreign Coynes they usually have with them."[172] Captain Every himself was never captured, but a few of his comrades were, and their trial in London in November 1696 exposed the many colonial accomplices in Newport, Charles Town, Philadelphia, Boston, and most especially New York.[173] Hence, in April 1697, a group of Indian merchants at Bombay petitioned the EIC that "these Villains [pirates] do relate frequently that they carry their unjust gains to New York . . . spending such Coyn there, in the usuall lavish manner."[174]

The end of the 1690s piracy boom was fast approaching; the execution of Every's men, together with the signing of the Treaty of Ryswick with France in September 1697, signaled the twilight of the era.[175] In April 1698, Richard Coote, Earl of Bellomont, arrived in New York to replace Fletcher as governor. Bellomont immediately published a proclamation against piracy, launched a major investigation into the crimes of the Fletcher administration, and sent Fletcher to London for vigorous questioning. The Crown had also made Bellomont governor of Massachusetts and New Hampshire, as well as captain-general over the militias in Rhode Island, Connecticut, and the Jerseys. In all of these colonies, Bellomont, with the help of allies like Governor Jeremiah Basse of New Jersey, proved marvelously effective at opposing smuggling and piracy, which Bellomont called that "most lycencious Trade with Pyrats, Scotland and Curacao."[176] His actions cost him support from many merchants, especially in New York. "Several Pyrats ships have been hovering about . . . since my arrival here," Bellomont reported, but "on notice of the alteration of the Government returned on board and the ships are gone to some other place."[177] The merchants "say I have ruined the town [New York] by hindering the Privateers (for so they call Pyrats) from bringing in a £100000 since my coming," remarked Bellomont; "this inrages them to the last degree that they have miss'd of all this treasure."[178] The governor targeted illegal trade of all types, seizing unlawful goods directly from warehouses and shops. "The Merchants here [New York] have been so used to unlawful trade," he said, "that they were almost ready to mutiny on some seizures I caused to be made"; "the whole city seem'd to be in an uproar, and lookt on it as a violent seizing of their property. . . . The observance of the laws of trade was so great a Novelty that it gave as great discontent as if it had been an infringement of their charter."[179]

Piracy abated most everywhere in the empire by the turn of the century. With it, colonial attitudes also took a turn. Immense pressure from the Crown and from William Penn (worried over the future of his proprietorship) convinced the Pennsylvania assembly to pass a new act against piracy in May 1699, stipulating that anyone who knowingly entertained, concealed, traded with, or corresponded with pirates, "shall be lyable to be Prosecuted as Accessories." Rhode Island had passed a similar law the previous year.[180] In 1699 the Royal Navy impelled the surrender of most of the 1,500 pirates on Madagascar, on promise of amnesty if they put up no fight. Finally, in March 1700, Parliament passed an "Act for the More Effectual Suppression of Piracy," which authorized juryless vice-admiralty courts to try pirates abroad (at sea or in the colonies) instead of sending them to England for trial—with authorization, moreover, to put convicted pirates (including English subjects) to death. The act also stipulated that if any private colony interfered with the vice-admiralty courts, the colony would immediately have its charter revoked.[181] "We are all quiet, in health, and the country improves, not by piracy or forbidden trade, but honest labour and sobriety," Penn eagerly assured the Board of Trade in 1701.[182]

The famous capture and execution of Captain William Kidd avouched the end of piracy's golden age. Kidd, who had earlier proved an able privateer against the French in the early 1690s, received a commission from the Crown in January 1696 to pursue and assault buccaneers at Madagascar and in the Indian Ocean. During the voyage, however, Kidd turned pirate, his crew seizing a four-hundred-ton merchant ship in the Indian Ocean laden with gold, silver, expensive cloths, silks, and other merchandise. After a brief return to New York (his place of residence), authorities in Massachusetts—at Bellomont's direction—captured Kidd in July 1699. After his transport to England, Kidd was tried and then executed in May 1701.[183]

Smuggling and piracy were the two most immediate colonial economic problems to address, but the potential peril of colonial manufacturing constituted a more enduring, long-term threat. This, too, drew the Board of Trade's attention. The Board's commission in 1696 instructed the members to caution against any colonial activity that "may prove prejudicial to England," especially trades by which colonists might begin "furnishing themselves, or other our colonies, with what hath been usually supplied from England."[184] The mere prospect of a thriving colonial textile and iron manufacturing industry was enough to warrant preventive measures. "This Fear seems very remote," Davenant acknowledged in 1698, but if New Englanders begin to "set up Manufactures, and to cloath as well as feed their Neighbours, their nearness and low Price, would give 'em such Advantages over this Nation, as might prove of pernicious Consequence."[185]

In 1699 the Board of Trade presented a report to the House of Commons arguing that colonial woolens "ought to be prohibited, or discouraged, by the most coercive and proper means." "New-England, and other northern colonies," they said, "have applied themselves too much, besides other things, to the improvement of woollen manufactures amongst themselves."[186] Soon after, Parliament passed the Wool Act of 1699. Under the act, no colonial-made woolens, no matter the form—raw, yarn, or cloth—could be exported from one colony to another. Local exchange of woolens within the colony of production remained legal, but the intercolonial sale of woolens—from Massachusetts to Barbados, for instance—was no longer permissible. The act also applied to Ireland, prohibiting the Irish from exporting woolens to foreign countries, to the colonies, or even to England. Irish woolens had become increasingly popular in the colonies as a cheaper alternative to the English variety;

English clothiers petitioned Parliament in 1698 that Irish woolens sold for at least 20 percent less than English woolens in colonial markets.[187]

Protecting English manufacturing was a major priority of many (though not all) mercantilists in the post-1688 era. In 1701 Parliament prohibited the sale within England (though not the reexportation) of all Chinese and Persian silks and all printed Indian calicoes. Parliament's rationale was that foreign textiles "must inevitably be to the great Detriment of this Kingdom, by exhausting the Treasure thereof, and melting down the Coin, and taking away the Labour of the People."[188] Parliament also overhauled the tariff system: before 1688, a simple 5 percent duty covered most imports and exports—designed mostly for revenue, not protection—but by 1709 the majority of foreign imports paid a rate of 20–25 percent, and with Walpole's customs reform in 1722, industrial protection became a cornerstone of national economic policy.[189] English manufactures were a "means of saving Money to the Nation"—indeed "a great deal of Money," for "we gain Gold and Silver from those Countries" that purchase English manufactures, thus ensuring for "this Kingdom a much greater Fountain of Riches than ever the Gold and Silver Mines of the Indies were."[190] "Money can no way be brought into the Kingdom, but by the Export of our Manufactures," argued William Carter, a clothier, in 1700. "'Tis our Manufactures and Product which furnish this Kingdom with Silver," wrote John Cary in his 1696 *Essay on the Coyn and Credit of England*: "the Vitals of this Kingdom are, our Manufactures, our Fishery, and our Plantations Trade."[191]

The Wool Act of 1699 fit neatly within the industrial-capital mercantilist model. Later, in 1732, Parliament passed the Hat Act, which prohibited the intercolonial sale of American-made hats (every year, English merchants exported tens of thousands of English-made hats to colonists).[192] Regulations like these seemed oppressive to some: Adam Smith later called these exact prohibitions "a manifest violation of the most sacred rights of mankind," all out of a "groundless jealousy of the merchants and manufacturers of the mother country." "The interest of the colonies was sacrificed to the interest of those merchants," alleged Smith.[193]

Nevertheless, most colonists by the turn of the century learned to tolerate such restrictions, which in the grand scheme of things seemed relatively mild. Outside of woolens (and, later, hats), colonists still enjoyed a remarkably free system of intercolonial trade that expanded with each passing decade, bringing considerable wealth to colonial seaports. Colonial labor, besides, was still too expensive for mass manufacturing.

Moreover, some mercantilist programs positively benefited colonial economic interests—for example, Britain's subsidization of colonial naval stores. In the 1690s, England ran a colossal trade deficit with Scandinavia and the

Baltic countries for naval stores. The deficit averaged more than £200,000 per annum, reaching a height of £350,000 in 1699, and over the decade the price of tar had doubled.[194] As Randolph said, this deficit "unavoidably Draines England Yearly of Vast Sumes of ready money"; it was a trade that "carries away such prodigious sums of our best and weightiest money," wrote John Evelyn. "They always drein'd us of Mony," Davenant wrote of these countries, and yet the materials were "so absolutely necessary," Cary noted, "that we must have them, though purchased for Bullion."[195] Worse still, in 1700, war broke out between Sweden and Russia—the Great Northern War, lasting until 1721—causing the price of tar (imported primarily from Sweden) to spike even further.

Colonial naval store production was the logical solution. For several years the Board of Trade received reports of North America's potential for naval store production "sufficient to supply all the navy, which would be a great advantage, and prevent the money from going out of England."[196] Thus, in 1704, Parliament authorized the Bounty Act. The stated purpose of the act was to abate the "great Expence of the Treasure of this Kingdom." The Bounty Act remunerated all colonial producers of tar, pitch, turpentine, rosin, hemp, masts, yards, and bowsprits and added each of these to the enumerated article list under the Navigation Acts (prohibiting their export to foreign countries).[197] King James II and monopoly mercantilists had earlier considered the creation of an exclusive company to monopolize the New England trade in naval stores. But a nonexclusive bounty system was far more amenable to the brand of mercantilism that dominated the British imperial system in the early eighteenth century. Besides, the system would divert colonists from manufacturing. The Bounty Act was not without flaws—hemp and flax, in the aftermath, were still heavily imported from Russia—but in the end, the act proved a success, especially in the Carolinas. Between 1716 and 1726, English merchants imported nearly five times more barrels of pitch and tar from the colonies than from Scandinavia and the Baltics: so much that English merchants even began *reexporting* colonial pitch, tar, and some turpentine to continental Europe.[198] As the Board of Trade reported happily in 1721, "the importation of pitch and tar from the Baltick is greatly decreased, & and much money saved in the balance of our trade."[199]

Another colonial benefit from mercantilism was the boom in colonial shipbuilding. This resulted directly from restrictions built into the Navigation Acts, as colonial ships qualified as legal vessels. In Massachusetts alone, between 1696 and 1713, shipbuilders constructed 1,118 vessels totaling almost seventy thousand tons. Shipbuilding industries of a smaller scale expanded also in New York, Philadelphia, Newport, Charles Town, and even Virginia. Most colonial-built vessels were smaller ships, used for coastal trade, but they alleviated freight costs, and the income earned from the sale of colonial ships to English merchants—which was not uncommon—allowed colonists to buy more imported English goods.[200]

For plantation owners in the Chesapeake and Caribbean, the repeal of the Royal African Company monopoly was among the greatest gains to come from the 1690s. Monopoly mercantilists had dominated the court of King James II, but after 1688, "Egregious Monopolys" like the RAC and EIC faced mounting criticism in England, and the onslaught proved too much for the companies to wholly withstand.[201] In Parliament, Whig and Country politicians blocked any statutory recognition of the two companies, and English courts refused or neglected to prosecute interlopers in the African trade, driving down the price of RAC shares.[202] In 1698 King William granted a charter to the so-called New East India Company, headed by Whigs, to rival the old Tory syndicate (though the two companies merged in 1709). The RAC, for its part, finally secured statutory recognition in 1698, but only on condition that the RAC abandon its monopoly. The law stated that for a period of thirteen years, slave traders outside of the company must pay a 10 percent duty to the RAC to help it maintain garrisons along the African coast. After 1712, the RAC would no longer receive payments from independent slave traders. The act was so effective in opening up the slave trade that by 1701 the RAC's share of England's slave trade from Africa plunged to a mere 8 percent. The RAC was based out of London, but the English outports of Bristol and Liverpool, where many noncompany dealers resided, developed into full-fledged capitals of the international slave trade.[203]

The collapse of the RAC monopoly signaled not a repudiation of mercantilism but a reconstitution of it toward the Whiggish brand. As John Cary predicted in 1695, the "opening [of] the African Trade," by supplying colonial planters "with Negroes on easie Terms," would "render these Plantations more profitable to this Kingdom." Cary called the African trade the "best Traffick the Kingdom hath": it employed many vessels and seamen, provided a market for English manufactures, and provided the labor by which "great Quantities of Sugar, Tobacco, Cotton, Ginger, and Indigo are raised." "This Trade indeed is our Silver Mines," he concluded, "for by the Overplus of Negroes above what will serve our Plantations, we draw great Quantities thereof [silver bullion and coins] from the Spaniard."[204]

As predicted, the volume of slave traffic to the Chesapeake and Caribbean increased dramatically in the early eighteenth century. Between 1698 and 1707, private traders delivered nearly 80,000 slaves to the English Caribbean, whereas the RAC delivered just under 25,000 in the same period. By comparison, between 1680 and 1688, the RAC delivered just over 46,000 slaves; interlopers provided an unknown number, but nowhere near the totals after 1698.[205] The number of transported slaves to mainland North America soared by nearly 300 percent, from 5,500 in the fifteen years before 1698, to 15,000 in the following fifteen.[206] Ironically, the price of slaves rose substantially after 1698; the presence of more English buyers off the West African coast permitted African dealers to fetch a higher price for each slave.[207] Yet Chesapeake and West Indian planters now had a far greater supply of slaves than previously (the former complaint, besides higher prices, was the shortage of slaves), and the bogeyman of monopoly could no longer be blamed for high prices. The repeal of the RAC monopoly thus removed a great grievance in the plantation colonies.

Elite planters in the Chesapeake and Caribbean, in other critical ways, learned the material benefits of empire during and after the 1690s. The Nine Years' War proved terribly disruptive to the plantation trades; French privateers recurrently raided English vessels laden with colonial tobacco and sugar, causing rates for freight and shipping insurance to spike. The English government responded by deploying armed convoys to ensure the safe transport of tobacco and sugar across the militarized Atlantic. The convoy system cost the English government tens of thousands of pounds sterling per annum, all financed directly out of the Royal Exchequer. But wartime resources were highly limited; necessity demanded that the government restrict the convoys to a certain quota of ships. The system favored planter-elites with personal connections in London—chiefly with leading mercantile interest groups in London who lobbied Parliament and executive departments with increasing regularity—binding the planters closer to imperial authority and mollifying their former antagonism to such restrictive measures as the Navigation Acts.[208] The great tobacco and sugar planters became proud subjects of a mercantilist empire.

Finally, the colonial disunity arising from competitive currency devaluations cried out for a definitive resolution. The situation had gotten worse since the mid-1690s. In May 1698, for example, the Pennsylvania assembly shockingly raised the value of a full-weight dollar from 7s to 7s10d. The new rating was 75 percent higher than the rating in Maryland. The Pennsylvania assembly called it "a prudential act to keep money in the province." Two years later, in 1700, the Carolina assembly raised the value of full-weight dollars to 7s6d.[209] Blathwayt, on hearing of this latter rating, blasted devaluation as "a very great grievance . . . it is so ruinous to Trade & contrary to His Majesties pleasure."[210] Several prominent voices now urged that "one certain Standard for all sorts of Coin be setled in all the Plantations on the Continent." Pennsylvania and Carolina, by means of devaluation, "drain all the Money from Virginia and

Maryland"; "the Inconveniences to Virginia, by the drawing away all the Specie, are inexpressible."[211] William Penn, fearing the loss of his proprietorship, recommended to the Crown in 1700 that "it would be convenient that there would be one Standard of coin" for all English America.[212] For a brief period, in 1700, the Board of Trade flirted with the idea of an empire-wide colonial mint, even consulting Locke on the matter, though the Board quickly shelved the idea.[213] "I wish all were at a par," Penn told the Board of Trade in 1703, "that an ounce of silver should be an ounce of silver in all the Dominions." Even the governor of New York, in 1703, came out in favor of a single standard, for "many inconveniences happen for want of such a Regulation." At 6s7d per dollar, New York boasted a relatively high rating, and yet it was still considerably lower than the 7s10d rating in Pennsylvania. "This growing evil requires speedy applycation," the new surveyor general, Robert Quary, wrote the Board of Trade that same year.[214]

On June 18, 1704, Queen Anne issued a proclamation that no colony, anywhere in America, rate full-weight dollars higher than 6s a piece, beginning the following January. Moreover, clipped monies were to be valued by weight, not by tale, with a proportional sum of pence deducted for each missing pennyweight.[215] The proclamation, in theory, should have forced Pennsylvania, Carolina, and New York to lower their rating for coin to 6s, while permitting Maryland, Virginia, Jamaica, and Barbados to raise it beyond 5s to 6s. Nonetheless, the devaluation saga continued; the only provision for enforcement was the queen's mere command, on pain of royal disfavor, with no mechanism in place to punish colonies for disobedience. The proclamation was completely ineffectual, and so finally, in 1708, Parliament passed "An Act for Ascertaining the Rates of Foreign Coins in Her Majesty's Plantations in America." The act stipulated that "if any Person" in the colonies violated the 6s rule after May 1709, they would either "suffer six Months Imprisonment" or pay a fine of £10 sterling money.[216] Even then, several years passed before the colonies complied; nevertheless, the Currency Act of 1708 ultimately succeeded in ridding the colonial world of that particular controversy, just in time for it to be replaced with a similar, yet separate controversy over paper money.

The reconstitution of England's mercantilist empire did not go quite as far as some figures had hoped. Randolph and Blathwayt, in particular, pushed very hard to eliminate private colonies—places "where the governors are not immediately nominated by your Majesty," where smuggling, piracy, and devaluation were rife.[217] This push, together with the desire to administer a more centralized empire during time of war, spawned a two-decade long effort in Whitehall and Westminster to abolish private colonies. Such governments, reported Randolph, "have been long Endeavouring to breake loose & set up for themselves, having no sort of regard to the Acts of Trade."[218] Randolph suggested adding Carolina to Virginia, Connecticut to New York, and Rhode Island to now-royal Massachusetts.[219] Royal colonies "take all possible Care to prevent illegal Trade . . . but it is otherwise in the Charter Governments," wrote an anonymous Virginian in 1701; "Those Governments which are immediately under His Majesty suffer by the other Governments raising and lowering the value of their coins," wrote Governor Nicholson of Maryland in 1699.[220] In 1701, Blathwayt presented a report on behalf of the Board of Trade to the House of Commons, urging the conversion of private colonies into settlements controlled directly by the Crown. The proposal sat in Parliament until 1706 but never won enough support for passage, in part because of the strenuous lobbying of William Penn and a general reluctance in Parliament to violate property rights. The only success from the period was the Crown's purchase of the rights of the proprietors of East and West Jersey in August 1701, combining them into a single royal colony.[221] Over time, South Carolina and North Carolina became royal colonies in 1720 and 1729, respectively, but Pennsylvania and the private New England colonies remained untouched. Perhaps all for the better: an overly aggressive takeover by the Crown would have almost certainly backfired, disrupting the implicit bargain struck in the 1690s of protection in exchange for allegiance. Inadvertently, the failure to convert the remaining private governments to royal colonies in fact strengthened England's hold over the Atlantic colonial system.

In the 1690s and after, empire became an asset in the colonial mind, not a handicap. For most, it meant protection: protection of basic political liberties; protection of relatively free commerce within a circumscribed imperial economic system; and protection from the autocratic, Roman Catholic French. In exchange, colonists for the most part accepted their subordinate place within a free, powerful, Protestant, mercantilist empire. As one English writer, William Burke, later wrote in the mid-eighteenth century, the role of imperial administration was to make America "as useful as possible to the trade of the mother country; to secure its dependence; to provide for the ease, safety, and happiness of the settlers; to protect them from their enemies . . . to preserve them from the tyranny and avarice of their governors." Colonists possessed neither "unbounded liberty," nor did they labor "under a base servitude"; rather, the colonists were dependent "British subjects," attended by a reasonable blend of rights, privileges, duties, and obligations.[222] A general acquiescence to the mercantilist order, and to the principle of colonial economic subordination more broadly, was among the colonists' most essential obligations.

Mercantilist thought carried Britain's economic empire into the beginnings of the long eighteenth century. As late as 1734, the English author of *Money Answers All Things* declared the balance-of-trade doctrine "almost self-evident."[223] It was a "certain Rule in Trade," wrote one Englishman in 1690, "that a Country grows Rich, and gets Money, when it sells more than it buyes. . . . The whole skill of enriching a Country by Trade consists in keeping this Balance right."[224] Of silver and gold, John Cary remarked that "nothing but the Ballance of our Trade brings it in . . . [and] nothing but the Ballance of our Trade with particular places carryes it out." "Whatever we export Yearly, is a certain Wealth to the Kingdom, and is indeed the Foundation of all our Commerce," argued Charles Davenant; "the Wealth of a Country now is the Ballance . . . a Nation which looses in the Generall Ballance had better be without Trade then with it."[225]

By the end of the seventeenth century, the growth of Atlantic commerce and of London as the capital and commercial hub of that empire was nothing less than spectacular. London, the seat of empire, boasted a population of 575,000 in the year 1700 (up from 400,000 in 1650); the second-largest city in England, Norwich, had 30,000 inhabitants (Bristol had 20,000); while Boston, the most populous colonial city, had fewer than 10,000 inhabitants. Eighty percent of all English imports, and 84 percent of England's reexports, went through London, which housed three-quarters of England's entire merchant fleet.[226] In 1660, colonial trade comprised only 4 percent of London's overseas commerce; by 1700, the trade's share had risen to almost 20 percent, and colonial goods accounted for one-third of the value of all goods that London merchants reexported to continental Europe.[227] By 1700, approximately one thousand merchants in London had some sort of trading interest—big or small—in English America, and many of them organized into formal interest groups, meeting regularly in London coffee houses.[228] Tobacco and sugar dominated the English Atlantic trade; by 1700, London merchants reexported more than two-thirds of incoming Chesapeake tobacco to continental Europe (up from one-third a few decades prior), and annual imports of sugar from the West Indies were double what they were in the 1660s.[229] Colonial consumption of English manufactures had also risen substantially and continued to soar through the eighteenth century; by the early 1770s, American colonists purchased more than one-half of all of England's exports of wrought iron, hats, silk, cottons, and linens.[230] As John Briscoe opined in a pamphlet published in London in 1696, England's overseas trade was the "Source and Foundation of all our Wealth, Power and Prosperity." The title of Briscoe's pamphlet was *A Discourse of Money*.[231]

Mercantilist enthusiasm for colonial plantations reached a new apex after 1688. One writer, James Puckle, in 1696, called England's "Fruitful Plantations" as good as "many Mines of Treasure." Charles Davenant, in 1698, praised the colonies as "a Spring of Wealth to this Nation, that they work for us, that their Treasure centers all here, and that the Laws have ty'd them fast enough to us." "Colonies are a Strength to their Mother Kingdom, while they are under good Discipline," he argued, ". . . and while they are kept dependant on it"; "the principal Care will always be, to keep them dependant upon their Mother Countrey, for otherwise they will become more profitable to our Neighbours than to us." John Cary agreed, insisting on the necessity of "better securing our Plantation Trade, so as it may more absolutely depend on this Kingdom." "This was the first Design of settling Plantations abroad," Cary stated in 1695, "that the People of England might better maintain a Commerce and Trade among themselves, the chief Profit whereof was to redound to the Center . . . by which means England would become the Centre of Trade, and standing like the Sun in the midst of its Plantations would not only refresh them, but also draw Profits from them."[232]

Why should colonists embrace such a system? Cary answered: "Standing like the Sun in the midst of its Plantations," England "would not only refresh them, but also draw Profits from them, and indeed it's a matter of exact Justice it should be so, for from hence Fleets of ships and Regiments of Soldiers are frequently sent for their Defence, at the Charge of the Inhabitants of this Kingdom." This system, he said, ensured for the colonists, "the Security of Religion, Liberty, and Property, towards the Charge whereof they contribute little." By no means, then, was the system exploitative. Though necessarily hierarchical—England, after all, was the "Mother Kingdom"—the new imperial system was familial and one of mutuality: an interlocking web and hierarchy of obligations, rights, duties, and benefits. The more obedient the colonists, Cary said, "the more Treasure they bring to the Nation," and the more they enriched England, the more protection they would receive—a grand, near-ingenious system of reciprocity; a transatlantic bulwark of liberty, religion, and property. "These are our Golden Mines," he boasted of America, "and have helpt to support the Ballance of our Trade."[233]

Epilogue
The Grand Settlement

Colonies ought never to forget what they owe to their
mother country, in return for the prosperity and riches
they enjoy. Their gratitude in that respect, and the
duty they owe, indispensably oblige them to be
immediately dependant on their original parent, and
to make their interest subservient thereunto.

—Malachy Postlethwayt, *Britain's Commercial Interest
Explained and Improved* (London, 1757)

We all think ourselves happy under Great-Britain. We
love, esteem and reverence our mother country, and
adore our King. And could the choice of independency
be offered to the colonies, or subjection to Great-
Britain upon any terms above absolute slavery, I am
convinced they would accept the latter.

—James Otis, *The Rights of the British Colonies, Asserted
and Proved* (Boston, 1764)

In July 1671 Edward Montagu, Earl of Sandwich,
and president of the Council for Foreign Plantations, issued miscellaneous
comments and warnings regarding New England and, more particularly, Massachusetts Bay. "They are att present a numberous and thrivinge people," he
reported; in about twenty years, they are likely "to be mighty rich and powerfull," with little mind for "dependance upon old England." If such circumstances were to come about, it would have dire consequences, imperiling the
"vending our owne manufactures," not only to New England, but to the sugar
islands, where plantation owners would grow dependent on New England textiles. "I conceive it impossible," he warned, "to prevent wholly their encrease
and arrivall at this power." Nevertheless, Sandwich continued, great care ought
to be taken "to regulate this people and gett as much hand in theire government as wee can." Such a program "admitts of noe delay . . . for they encrease

fast every yeare both in people, Trade, riches, and multitude of shipps, and will be the apter to disobey."

One might have expected Sandwich to then launch into a screed demanding an end to the Massachusetts charter and the suppression of many of the colonists' most cherished liberties. But Sandwich, instead, urged the use of only "faire meanes to prevent the growing power of the Massachussett Colonye." "I take the way of roughnesse and peremptory orders, with force to backe them, to be utterly unadviseable," he said. "For they are already too strong to be compelled . . . and though I apprehend them yett not at that point to cast us off voluntarily and of choise; yett I beleeve if wee use severity towards them in theire Government civill or religious, that they will (being made desperate) sett up for themselves and reject us."[1]

Sandwich died in May 1672. His more moderate strategy for imperial administration—to secure colonial allegiance by not offending colonists' understandable desire for basic political liberty—had to wait some years longer, about a quarter century, before finally winning favor. The vision of Randolph, in the meantime, won the day. Writing from Boston in June 1676, Randolph urged the newly created Lords of Trade of the absolute necessity of "reducing the Plantation to their due Obedience . . . and force them to an humble & ready Submission."[2]

In following Randolph's more extreme blueprint for imperial rule in America—calling for unconditional and uncompensated obedience—the Stuart empire vastly overreached. Fortunately, for the cause of the early English empire, the stratagem met a quick death, hastened by the Glorious Revolution. The replacement was a view, long standing in England, championing "that unparalell'd Priviledge of Liberty and Property." These words came from a tract authored by William Penn in 1687 entitled *The Excellent Priviledge of Liberty & Property Being the Birth-Right of the Free-born Subjects of England*. The pamphlet included a reprint of Magna Carta—"the Store-house of all our Liberties," Penn called it—so that the reader "may understand what is his Right, and how to preserve it from unjust and unreasonable men." "In France, and other Nations," he wrote, "the meer Will of the Prince is Law." Not so for the English, said Penn, "each man having a fixed Fundamental-Right born with him." This fundamental right, Penn and others believed, extended to colonial Englishmen not living in England.[3]

Charles Davenant of England echoed a similar idea but connected colonial political freedom to imperial economic prosperity. A politically free America would make a more opulent empire. "Without doubt these Colonies will flourish," he predicted in 1698, "if they are intrusted to honest, discreet, and skilful

hands, who will let them perceive they enjoy the Rights and Liberties of English Men, tho' not in England. Industry has its first Foundation in Liberty:
They who either are Slaves, or who believe their Freedom's precarious, can
neither succeed in Trade, nor Meliorate a Country."[4]

In the years after 1688, imperial administrators conceded that colonists possessed a broad but temperate and bounded political liberty. Those in charge
of the empire arrived at this conclusion slowly, often only implicitly, sometimes
reluctantly, and always with certain conditions and limitations that distinguished colonists from Englishmen at home. This political liberty included,
most importantly, a general claim to assembly government, protections from
blatant autocracy, and imperial oversight of a more balanced and constitutional
nature. The 1690s inaugurated "a compromise style of imperial administration in America," writes Richard S. Dunn. Colonists, by and large, welcomed
the change and adjusted their attitudes accordingly. Hence, the immense loyalty that colonists sincerely displayed toward the British king throughout so
much of the eighteenth century—the "cult of benevolent monarchy," Brendan McConville calls it—even as they jealously guarded those same liberties
from royal appointees.[5]

Two critical components of empire survived the Glorious Revolution.
These were distinct but closely related: first, mercantilism; second, colonial
subordination to the political and economic will of the home government in
London. Parliament did not repeal the Navigation Acts, but rather strengthened them; the Board of Trade, far from relaxing imperial intervention, was
just as insistent, and far more effective, in managing and monitoring colonial
behavior than its predecessor. In many ways, the empire's approach toward
colonial America was not that radically different after the 1690s from what it
had been between 1675 and 1688. The tide of centralization was as unrelent-
ing as ever; many of the same men still railed against illegal trade and recalci-
trant assemblies, and the Crown even appointed some of the same officials to
positions of power, including Randolph, Blathwayt, and Andros.

The difference, this time, was in the empire's character. For most colonials,
empire became a lot more tolerable after 1688. Events in the 1690s and early
1700s went a long way toward persuading most colonists that economic subordination to a mercantilist empire was a fairly reasonable price to pay for the
basic protection of their most cherished and fundamental liberties, freedoms
the colonists had learned to appreciate more deeply during the arbitrary and
heavy-handed 1680s. As British historian David Armitage notes, the popular
perception of the British empire by the early eighteenth century was that it
was, above all other empires—past or present—"Protestant, commercial, mar-

itime and free." It became "more intellectually plausible," he tells us, "to argue that liberty and empire might be reconciled."[6]

Colonists, ever gradually, and at different rates and to varying degrees, vowed tacit allegiance to this particular brand of empire—to a free, Protestant, but mercantilist empire—in return for the restoration and future assurance of political and civil liberty, property, and a relatively free system of commerce within imperial boundaries. For these conditions, economic subordination was a sensible exchange. Certainly, this imperial-colonial settlement was haphazard and often ambiguous, subject, thereafter, to much dispute as to its precise terms. Nevertheless, a sea change had unquestionably taken place. Protection from autocratic government—whether from London or from the menacing French—and the corollary assurance of assembly government in the colonies, the rule of law, and a balanced imperial constitution rendered the administration of empire far less repulsive to most colonists than previously. This change ensured a high degree of colonial acquiescence to the mercantilist order.

Adam Smith was mostly though not entirely correct when he wrote in *Wealth of Nations* that "in every thing, except their foreign trade, the liberty of the English colonists to manage their own affairs their own way is complete." Colonial assemblies, he noted, possessed "the sole right of imposing taxes for the support of the colony government," and not even "the most obnoxious colonist, as long as he obeys the law, has anything to fear" from imperial officials. "The government established by the [1688] Revolution" merited immense admiration from colonial Americans, Smith said; it was to the post-1688 government that "all the colonies of America owe the liberty, security, and property which they have ever since enjoyed."[7] Most colonists in prerevolutionary America would not have disagreed.

Writers on both sides of the Atlantic acknowledged and celebrated this protection-allegiance arrangement. As one Englishman, John Mitchell, wrote of the colonies in 1767, "their liberties, safety and security, are a certain pledge for their allegiance and dependence." Mitchell predicted that this "band of union between them and their mother country" would function so long as Britain preserved "the happy constitution they enjoy," for indeed "it is this happy constitution, which the colonies derive from their mother country, that attaches them to her, and makes them willingly and chearfully submit to that auspicious government."[8] James Otis, the later revolutionary in Boston, stated in 1764 that it was "our rights as men and free born British subjects" that made colonists "very happy in comparison with the subjects of any other prince in the world."[9] Decades earlier, in 1701, an anonymous Virginian argued that "the chiefest thing wanting to make the Inhabitants of these Plantations happy, is a good Constitution of Government," which he defined as one allowing colonists to "enjoy their Liberties and Estates, and have Justice equally and impartially administered unto them." The same author clarified that he did not mean "that they should have great Liberties of Trade"; nor did he mean that they should have "any other Liberties or Priviledges that may be thought prejudicial to the King or Kingdom of England." Rather, "a free Constitution of Government," he said, was sufficient to secure colonial allegiance to empire.[10] The product of this arrangement was a mutually beneficial, hierarchical, reciprocal order of duties, obligations, privileges, and liberties.

That being said, the relationship between empire and colony was not contractual in the Lockean or Rousseauian sense. It was a more binding, existential tie—hence the common use in those days of the mother-child metaphor. Persistent abuses of an extraordinary nature could indeed sever that tie. But the nature of the tie was far deeper and more intimate than anything described in modern contract theory. By consequence, the tie was far less capable of being severed. That, of course, did not make the relationship any less tense—as in any familial relationship. There were still immense consequences when either side abused their position or failed to uphold their particular duties and obligations. But only in very rare, extreme hypothetical cases was a complete severing of the tie even a remote possibility from the colonial point of view; it was only ever seriously considered during the turbulent period of the late 1640s and early 1650s, and among a minority of independent leaders in Massachusetts Bay in the 1670s and 1680s. In and after the 1690s, that more radical view had almost completely disappeared. Colonists, by and large, accepted their stationplace within the mercantilist empire.

Doubtless, many colonists were still willing after the 1690s to exploit illicit trade opportunities—that is, if these opportunities promised considerable gain and were reasonably safe from detection. When colonists did so, however, their actions were no longer grounded as frequently in an ideological commitment to some inherent right to free trade. Most colonists now agreed that the many advantages of imperial membership overrode any burden or inconvenience that arose from annoying or unprofitable economic constraints. The Navigation Acts were certainly better than falling prey to France. One could still push back and bend the rules when enforcement was weak or an official appeared especially pliant, as seen with the oft-ignored Molasses Act of 1733. But an open, belligerent, and ideologically rooted defiance of the whole imperial economic order—as seen often in the Restoration period of 1660 to 1688—no longer appealed to most colonists. There were remarkably few colonial complaints about the Navigation Acts in the prerevolutionary eighteenth century.[11]

Working within the mercantilist system, besides, had many material advantages. The armed convoys that protected tobacco and sugar fleets during the Anglo-French Wars taught elite plantation owners in the Chesapeake and Caribbean the immense value of imperial protection. Furthermore, colonial tobacco and sugar possessed a practical monopoly over the consumer market in England, protecting them adequately from foreign competition. English freight rates, and the cost of importing goods from England, fell demonstrably in the eighteenth century. Furthermore, in the eighteenth century, intercolonial commerce continued to flourish, and barring the restriction on colonial woolens and hats, intercolonial exchange was almost completely unhampered and legal. "The most perfect freedom of trade is permitted between the British colonies of America and the West Indies," remarked Smith; ". . . They make a great internal market for produce of one another."[12] A post-1688 boom in colonial shipbuilding resulted, in large measure, from the Navigation Acts; imperial subsidization of colonial naval stores added further to the real benefits of working legally within the mercantilist economy. For the first time, also, colonial interest groups organized and formed an effective lobbying force in London— voicing their opinions, requests, and concerns at Whitehall and Westminster with far more regularity than in the seventeenth century—further integrating the colonies within the imperial system.[13]

For a time, as well, the empire allowed colonial governments to print their own paper money, obviating the need for silver and gold coin in domestic circulation (colonists still needed coin to buy many imported goods). The people of Massachusetts had used paper money for internal exchange since 1690. South Carolina joined Massachusetts in 1703. New York, Connecticut, New Jersey, and New Hampshire issued their first paper money in 1709 and Rhode Island in 1710, all in the name of financing the War of the Spanish Succession, known in America as Queen Anne's War. With paper money, colonial governments exercised far greater influence over the local money supply than they had in the era of competitive currency devaluations. Because the practice effectively serviced the imperial war effort, the Crown, for now, permitted paper money.

Perhaps more than any other people within the empire, English West Indian planters gained most from the empire's new structure. The repeal of the RAC monopoly answered one of their loudest objections from the Restoration, and when the hated 1685 duty on sugar lapsed in June 1693, Parliament elected not to renew it (while renewing the 5d duty on tobacco and even raising it to 6s a pound in 1697). Burgeoning competition from neighboring French sugar islands (France acquired Hispaniola in 1697) bolstered the attractiveness of a closed economic system for English sugar planters; moreover, the imperial government supplied far greater military aid to the islands than to mainland North America. As absentee ownership of the sugar plantations became more and more common, many of the most powerful voices in defense of Caribbean interests resided in London, allowing them ready access to lobby Whitehall and Westminster, wedding the sugar interest ever closer to the imperial center.[14]

For most colonists in the eighteenth century, whether in the Caribbean or on mainland North America, trade was just as profitable through legal channels. As Edmund Burke later said on the floor of the House of Commons in 1774, under any other empire, the Navigation Acts would have lowered the colonists to "a condition of as rigorous servitude as men can be subject to." But "they were indemnified for it by a pecuniary compensation," he said. "Their monopolist happened to be one of the richest men in the world. By his immense capital . . . they were enabled to proceed with their fisheries, their agriculture, their ship-building. . . . This capital was a hot-bed to them. Nothing in the history of mankind is like their progress. . . . America had the compensation of your capital, which made her bear her servitude."[15] For all of his rhetorical flourish, Burke, in essence, was right. If one *had* to trade with a single country in the eighteenth century, Britain was far and away the superior monopolist.

But that was not all. "She had another compensation," Burke continued, "which you are now going to take away from her. She had, except the commercial restraint, every characteristic mark of a free people in all her internal concerns. . . . She was taxed by her own representatives. She chose most of her own magistrates. . . . She had in effect the sole disposal of her own internal government." "This whole state of commercial servitude and civil liberty, taken together," he said, "is certainly not perfect freedom; but comparing it with the ordinary circumstances of human nature, it was a happy and a liberal condition." The colonists, in short, had enjoyed an excellent bargain, rendering it far easier to bear the "principle of commercial monopoly." If Parliament insisted, however, upon "the unlimited and illimitable nature of supreme sovereignty," he warned in 1774, "you will teach them by these means to call that sovereignty itself in question," and "they will cast your sovereignty in your face."[16]

Edmund Burke was not the only one to warn of this risk. In 1720, the two English authors of *Cato's Letters* warned of the same danger, with essentially the same prescription. "There can be but two Ways" to prevent American colonists "from throwing off their Dependence," they said. The first was "to keep it out of their Power"; the second was to keep it "out of their Will." "The first must be by Force"; the second, by prosperity, a reasonable amount of liberty, and gentle persuasion—"using them well" and allowing them even to "get Wealth too," so long as doing so did "not prejudice their Mother-Country." "Force can never be used effectually to answer this End," they said; the answer, rather, lay in a sensible degree of "Liberty and Encouragement" and not "by Power alone." England's colonies were always "intended to increase the Wealth and Power of the native Kingdom, which they will abundantly do, if managed prudently, and put and kept under a proper Regulation . . . returning again to us Silver and Gold." "A few prudent Laws and a little prudent Conduct," they reasoned, "would soon give us far the greatest Share of the Riches of all America."[17]

Long after 1688, the British empire was still a mercantilist empire. Colonists for decades after remained economically subordinate to the empire's pecuniary agenda. Silver and gold were still the primum mobile that moved the spheres; the quest to center money in London still drove imperial action deep into the eighteenth century. The difference now was that most colonists accepted this mercantilist reality as a judicious cost for the many political and economic benefits that accrued to them as subordinate members of that empire. By their actions the colonists conferred on the system legitimacy. They were not reluctant subjects but happy, grateful, and loyal subjects. The empire erred later in presuming this allegiance to be unconditional.

Acknowledgments

Writing a book requires a lot more time and patience than I had ever anticipated. Between the years of researching and writing the initial manuscript, and the subsequent years of seemingly perpetual revisions, I have quite the laundry list of people to acknowledge.

Where else to start but by thanking my wife, Erin? "Her price is far above rubies, the heart of her husband doth safely trust in her." I am eternally grateful for your companionship, mind, beauty, and faithfulness.

Many thanks to Michael McGandy, senior editor at Cornell University Press, for believing in this project and for being so generous and flexible through the process of preparing the book.

Many thanks to Donald Critchlow, my chief mentor and dearest friend at Arizona State University (ASU), for his inestimable guidance and joyful company through the last several years. Many thanks to all of the men and women who support the Political History and Leadership (PHL) program that Don and I administer at Arizona State.

Many thanks to my ASU colleagues in the School of Historical, Philosophical and Religious Studies (SHPRS), for their wonderful advice and friendship since my arrival in 2014. I think in particular of Catherine O'Donnell, Roxane Barwick, Mark Power Smith, Andrew Barnes, Peter de Marneffe, Chris Jones, Adrian Brettle, Calvin Schermerhorn, Victoria Thompson, and Chouki El Hamel. I think also of the current director of the school, Richard Amesbury, as well as past directors Matt Garcia, Matt Delmont, and Tracy Fessenden.

Many thanks to Cynthia Kierner, my former adviser at George Mason University, for her patience, counsel, and guidance as I composed the original manuscript. Thank you for telling me so candidly when my writing or research was shabby. Many thanks to Rosemarie Zagarri, Michael O'Malley, and Christian Koot for their helpful advice and comments on that manuscript. Many thanks also to Larry White for instructing me in monetary theory.

Many thanks to the anonymous readers of the manuscript, for their greatly esteemed suggestions and insight. Many thanks to Clare Jones, acquisitions assistant at Cornell, for helping to get this book into production; to Catherine

Cambron and Mary Ribesky at Westchester Publishing Services for their help with editing; and to Kate Mertes for indexing.

Many thanks to the Institute for Humane Studies, the Institute for Humanities Research, and the Library Company of Philadelphia for their fellowships and grants, which went so far in making this book possible.

Many thanks to the creators and administrators of *Early English Books Online*, *Colonial State Papers*, *Colonial America* (Adam Matthew), *Early American Imprints*, and other digital archives. Many thanks to the archivists and staff at the National Archives at Kew. Many thanks also to the creators of *Zotero*, whose software saved me an incalculable number of hours in organizing the research that went into this book.

Many thanks to my former high school teachers Nancy Kute, Wendy Rorie, and Gary Whetsel, for inspiring me so powerfully many years ago. Many thanks also to Dr. John Orens, instructor at George Mason University, for modeling the most marvelous lectures I have ever witnessed while I was his teaching assistant in his Western Civilization classes at George Mason University. You were truly an extraordinary inspiration for my style in the classroom.

Many thanks to my family—to my father, mother, brother, sister, grandfather, and grandmother—who so tirelessly loved and prayed for me all of these years. Many thanks to Ben Gibbs and Jackson Cooke for introducing me so enthusiastically to topics of currency and banking years ago.

Finally, all thanks to the one and true God Almighty, for so graciously affording me the liberty and luxury to teach and to write history for a living.

Notes

Introduction

1. John Pollexfen, *A Discourse of Trade, Coyn, and Paper Credit* (London, 1697), 2.

2. Alison Games, *The Web of Empire: English Cosmopolitans in an Age of Expansion* (Oxford: Oxford University Press, 2008), 7–10, 47–52; Ralph Davis, *A Commercial Revolution: English Overseas Trade in the Seventeenth and Eighteenth Centuries* (London: Historical Association, 1967), 3–6; Alan G. R. Smith, *The Emergence of a Nation State: The Commonwealth of England, 1529–1660* (Longman: London, 1997), 173–79.

3. Nicholas Mayhew, *Sterling: The Rise and Fall of a Currency* (London: Allen Lane, 1999), 55–58; C. E. Challis, *A New History of the Royal Mint* (Cambridge: Cambridge University Press, 1992), 687–88.

4. James Whiston, *A Discourse of the Decay of Trade* (London, 1693), 2.

5. Nuala Zahedieh, "Overseas Expansion and Trade in the Seventeenth Century," in *The Origins of Empire: British Overseas Enterprise to the Close of the Seventeenth Century*, ed. Nicholas Canny (Oxford: Oxford University Press, 1998), 399.

6. Nuala Zahedieh, *The Capital and the Colonies: London and the Atlantic Economy, 1660–1700* (Cambridge: Cambridge University Press, 2010), 10.

7. Alison Gilbert Olson, *Making the Empire Work: London and American Interest Groups, 1690–1790* (Cambridge, MA: Harvard University Press, 1992), 52.

8. [Slingsby Bethel], *An Account of the French Usurpation upon the Trade of England* (London, 1679), 3.

9. [Joseph Harris], *An Essay upon Money and Coins: Part I, The Theories of Commerce, Money, and Exchanges* (London, 1757), 67; William Wood, *A Survey of Trade*, 2nd ed. (1718; London, 1722), 334; Carew Reynell, *The True English Interest, or an Account of the Chief National Improvements* (London, 1674), 2; Edward Misselden, *Free Trade, or, The Means to Make Trade Flourish* (London, 1622), 28; Thomas Violet, *An Appeal to Caesar: Wherein Gold and Silver is Proved to be the Kings Majesties Royal Commodity* (London, 1660), 1.

10. Baron de Montesquieu, *The Spirit of Laws*, 2 vols. (1748; repr., New York: Colonial Press, 1899), 1:369.

11. Sir Josiah Child, *A Discourse of the Nature, Use and Advantages of Trade* (London, 1694), 18.

12. Whiston, *Discourse of the Decay*, 2.

13. *Defoe's Review, 1704–1714*, ed. John McVeagh and Arthur Wellesley Secord, 9 vols. (London: Pickering & Chatto, 2003–2011), 3:27.

14. Sir Josiah Child, *A New Discourse of Trade* (London, 1693), 93.

15. Whiston, *Discourse of the Decay*, 2.

16. [Josiah Child], *A Treatise Concerning the East-India Trade* (London, 1681), 24–25, 29.

17. Wood, *Survey of Trade*, vi.

18. *An Essay Upon the Government of the English Plantations* (London, 1701), 59.

19. Quotations from Thomas C. Barrow, *Trade and Empire: The British Customs Service in Colonial America, 1660–1775* (Cambridge, MA: Harvard University Press, 1967), 1; Julian Hoppit, *Britain's Political Economies: Parliament and Economic Life, 1660–1800* (Cambridge: Cambridge University Press, 2017), 16. See also L. H. Roper, *Advancing Empire: English Interests and Overseas Expansion, 1613–1688* (New York: Cambridge University Press, 2017), 2–5; David S. Lovejoy, *The Glorious Revolution in America* (New York: Harper & Row, 1972), xiv.

20. John Cary, *An Essay on the State of England, in Relation to its Trade* (London, 1695), 68; John Cary, *An Essay on the Coyn and Credit of England* (Bristol, 1696), 37. For more on Cary's wide influence, see Sophus A. Reinert, *Translating Empire: Emulation and the Origins of Political Economy* (Cambridge, MA: Harvard University Press, 2011).

21. For works that either reject the term *mercantilism* or deny it meaningful coherence, see Steve Pincus, "Rethinking Mercantilism: Political Economy, the British Empire, and the Atlantic World in the Seventeenth and Eighteenth Centuries," *William and Mary Quarterly*, 3rd ser., 69, no. 1 (Jan. 2012): 3–34; Philip J. Stern and Carl Wennerlind, "Introduction," in Stern and Wennerlind, eds., *Mercantilism Reimagined: Political Economy in Early Modern Britain and Its Empire* (Oxford: Oxford University Press, 2014), 3–22; Julian Hoppit, *Britain's Political Economies: Parliament and Economic Life, 1660–1800* (Cambridge: Cambridge University Press, 2017), 6–7, 17, 82–83, 136–37; D. C. Coleman, "Editor's Introduction," in *Revisions in Mercantilism*, ed. Coleman (Suffolk, UK: Methuen & Co., 1969), 1–18.

1. Silver, Mercantilism, and the Impulse for Colonization

1. Andre Gunder Frank, *ReOrient: Global Economy in the Asian Age* (Berkeley: University of California Press, 1998), 150; Charles P. Kindleberger, *A Financial History of Western Europe* (London: George Allen & Unwin, 1984), 23–24.

2. Sevket Pamuk, "The Evolution of Fiscal Institutions in the Ottoman Empire, 1500–1914," in *The Rise of Fiscal States: A Global History, 1500–1914*, ed. Bartolomé Gun-Casalilla and Patrick K. O'Brien (Cambridge University Press, 2012), 304, 307–11; E. L. Jones, *The European Miracle: Environments, Economies, and Geopolitics in the History of Europe and Asia* (Cambridge: Cambridge University Press, 1981), 176–78, 202–4.

3. Charles Tilly, *Coercion, Capital, and European States, AD 990–1992* (Cambridge, MA: Blackwell, 1990), 39–50, 74–89; Charles Tilly, "Reflections on the History of European State-Making," in *The Formation of Nation States in Western Europe*, ed. Charles Tilly (Princeton: Princeton University Press, 1975), 18–21; Lars Magnusson, *The Political Economy of Mercantilism* (London: Routledge, 2015), 55; Jones, *European Miracle*, 102–6, 130–31.

4. Petr Vorel, *From the Silver Czech Tolar to a Worldwide Dollar: The Birth of the Dollar and its Journey of Monetary Circulation in Europe and the World from the 16th to the*

20th Century (New York: Columbia University Press, 2013), 4–5; Kindleberger, *Financial History*, 24.

5. Rory Naismith, "The Social Significance of Monetization in the Early Middle Ages," *Past & Present* 223, no. 1 (May 2014): 4–8; N. J. Mayhew, "Prices in England, 1170–1750," *Past & Present* 219, no. 1 (May 2013): 27–28; Vorel, *Silver Czech Tolar*, 3–7.

6. *The Journal of Christopher Columbus (During his First Voyage)*, ed. Clements R. Markham (London: The Hakluyt Society, 1893), 43, 73, 126; John J. TePaske, *A New World of Gold and Silver*, ed. Kendall W. Brown (Leiden: Brill, 2010), 23–24, 30–31, 69–70.

7. Hernán Cortés, *Letters from Mexico*, trans. and ed. Anthony Pagden (New Haven: Yale Nota Bene, 2001), 100, 266.

8. *Broken Spears: The Aztec Account of the Conquest of Mexico*, ed. Miguel Leon-Portilla (Boston: Beacon Press, 1992), 51.

9. Cortés, *Letters from Mexico*, 92, 171.

10. TePaske, *New World*, 16–7.

11. TePaske, *New World*, 72–73, 84–90, 115, 171, 235; Stanley J. Stein and Barbara H. Stein, *Silver, Trade, and War: Spain and America in the Making of Early Modern Europe* (Baltimore: Johns Hopkins University Press, 2000), 19–31; P. J. Bakewell, *Silver Mining and Society in Colonial Mexico: Zacatecas, 1546–1700* (Cambridge: Cambridge University Press, 1971), 114–80.

12. TePaske, *New World*, 17, 29, 39, 41, 45, 56.

13. TePaske, *New World*, 190.

14. TePaske, *New World*, 113, 145.

15. Frank, *ReOrient*, 144.

16. TePaske, *New World*, 113, 140, 145, 212.

17. Baron de Montesquieu, *The Spirit of Laws*, 2 vols. (1748; repr., New York: Colonial Press, 1899), 1:369.

18. TePaske, *New World*, 112.

19. TePaske, *New World*, 16.

20. John J. McCusker, *Money and Exchange in Europe and America, 1600–1775: A Handbook* (Chapel Hill: University of North Carolina Press, 1978), 7.

21. Alan Knight, *Mexico: The Colonial Era* (Cambridge: Cambridge University Press, 2002), 175; Stein and Stein, *Silver, Trade, and War*, 24.

22. Thomas James Dandelet, *The Renaissance of Empire in Early Modern Europe* (Cambridge: Cambridge University Press, 2014), 112–13, 136–39, 151–56, 161–63, 213–14.

23. Mark G. Hanna, *Pirate Nests and the Rise of the British Empire, 1570–1740* (Chapel Hill: University of North Carolina Press, 2015), 5–7, 46; Janice E. Thomson, *Mercenaries, Pirates, and Sovereigns: State-Building and Extraterritorial Violence in Early Modern Europe* (Princeton: Princeton University Press, 1994), 22–23; Jon Latimer, *Buccaneers of the Caribbean: How Piracy Forged an Empire* (Cambridge, MA: Harvard University Press, 2009), 4–6, 11–23.

24. John Brewer, *The Sinews of Power: War, Money and the English State, 1688–1783* (Cambridge, MA: Harvard University Press, 1988), 10-11.

25. Hanna, *Pirate Nests*, 38–40; Latimer, *Buccaneers of the Caribbean*, 11–23; Wim Klooster, *The Dutch Moment: War, Trade, and Settlement in the Seventeenth-Century Atlantic World* (Ithaca, NY: Cornell University Press, 2016), 11–12, 25–32; Wim Klooster, "Have

You Heard the News about the Silver Fleet?: The Dutch Appetite for Spanish Silver," *Common-Place* 6, no. 3 (Apr. 2006).

26. Hanna, *Pirate Nests*, 43–45; C. G. A. Clay, *Economic Expansion and Social Change: England, 1500–1700*, 2 vols. (Cambridge: Cambridge University Press, 1984), 1:36.

27. Stein and Stein, *Silver, Trade, and War*, 18, 52–54.

28. Quotation in Fernand Braudel, *The Wheels of Commerce: Civilization and Capitalism, 15th–18th Century* (Berkeley: University of California Press, 1992), 171.

29. Stein and Stein, *Silver, Trade, and War*, 3–4, 7, 17–18, 109; J. I. Andres Ucendo and R. Lanza Garcia, "Prices and Real Wages in Seventeenth-Century Madrid," *Economic History Review* 67, no. 3 (2014): 607–26.

30. Nicholas Mayhew, *Sterling: The Rise and Fall of a Currency* (London: Allen Lane, 1999), 39–44; D. C. Coleman, *The Economy of England, 1450–1750* (Oxford: Oxford University Press, 1977), 22–25; Earl J. Hamilton, *American Treasure and the Price Revolution in Spain, 1501–1650*, rev. ed. (Cambridge, MA: Harvard University Press, 1934; New York: Octagon Books, 1970), 186–221.

31. Mayhew, *Sterling*, 39.

32. Thomas Mun, *England's Treasure by Forraigne Trade, Or, The Balance of our Forraign Trade is the Rule of our Treasure* (1628; repr., London, 1664), 34, 61; Rice Vaughn, *A Discourse of Coin and Coinage* (1630; repr., London, 1675), 82; Gerard Malynes, *Consuetudo, vel, Lex Mercatoria: or, the Ancient Law-Merchant*, 3rd ed. (1620; London, 1686), 64.

33. TePaske, *New World*, 20, 29, 49, 56, 67, 113.

34. Kindleberger, *Financial History*, 26.

35. Dennis O. Flynn, "Fiscal Crisis and the Decline of Spain (Castile)," *Journal of Economic History* 42, no. 1 (Mar. 1982): 141; John H. Munro, "The Monetary Origins of the 'Price Revolution': South German Silver Mining, Merchant Banking, and Venetian Commerce, 1470–1540," in *Global Connections and Monetary History, 1470–1800*, ed. Dennis O. Flynn, Arturo Giráldez, and Richard von Glahn (Aldershot, UK: Ashgate Publishing, 2003), 1–27.

36. Craig Muldrew, "'Hard Food for Midas': Cash and its Social Value in Early Modern England," *Past & Present* 170 (Feb. 2001): 109–13.

37. Richard von Glahn, *Fountain of Fortune: Money and Monetary Policy in China, 1000–1700* (Berkeley: University of California Press, 1996), 113–41. For the earlier paper-money period, see pp. 48–72.

38. Von Glahn, *Fountain of Fortune*, 127; William S. Atwell, "International Bullion Flows and the Chinese Economy circa 1530–1650," *Past & Present* 95, no. 1 (May 1982): 82–83.

39. John F. Richards, "Fiscal States in Mughal and British India," in *Rise of Fiscal States*, ed. Yun-Casalilla and O'Brien, 412; Om Prakash, "Precious-Metal Flows into India in the Early Modern Period," in *Global Connections*, ed. Flynn, Giráldez, and Von Glahn, 149–56.

40. [John Locke], *Some Considerations of the Consequences of the Lowering of Interest, and Raising the Value of Money* (London, 1692), 75.

41. Frank, *ReOrient*, 145; Von Glahn, *Fountain of Fortune*, 114.

42. Von Glahn, *Fountain of Fortune*, 115–18; Atwell, "International Bullion Flows," 68–71.

43. Frank, *ReOrient*, 145.

44. Jan de Vries, "Connecting Europe and Asia: A Quantitative Analysis of the Cape-Route Trade, 1497–1795," in *Global Connections*, ed. Flynn, Giraldez, and Von Glahn, 77; Prakash, "Precious-Metal Flows," 149–56; Atwell, "International Bullion Flows," 72–74.

45. De Vries, "Connecting Europe and Asia," 40, 82.

46. Dennis O. Flynn and Arturo Giráldez, "Born with a 'Silver Spoon': The Origin of World Trade in 1571," *Journal of World History* 6, no. 2 (Fall 1995): 203.

47. Frank, *ReOrient*, 143. Andre Gunder Frank mistakenly says that the 42,000 number was America's silver production in the seventeenth century; the number was from 1520, see TePaske, *New World*, 113.

48. Quotation in Von Glahn, *Fountain of Fortune*, 128–29.

49. Edward Misselden, *Free Trade, or, The Means to Make Trade Flourish* (London, 1622), 19–20, 23, 112.

50. Gerrard De Malynes, *A Treatise of the Canker of Englands Common Wealth* (London, 1601), 68–69.

51. TePaske, *New World*, 113; Stein and Stein, *Silver, Trade, and War*, 6, 41–42, 47–54; Knight, *Mexico: Colonial Era*, 175–77.

52. Montesquieu, *Spirit of Laws*, 1:369.

53. Aristotle, *Politics*, trans. Benjamin Jowett (Mineola, NY: Dover Publications, 2000), 43.

54. [John Pollexfen], *A Vindication of Some Assertions Relating to Coin and Trade* (London, 1699), 43.

55. William Wood, *A Survey of Trade*, 2nd ed. (1718; London, 1722), iv–v.

56. Joyce Appleby, *Economic Thought and Ideology in Seventeenth-Century England* (Princeton, NJ: Princeton University Press, 1978), 202–5; E[phraim] Lipson, *The Economic History of England*, 3 vols., 6th ed. (1931; London, A&C Black, 1956), 3:72.

57. *The True Causes of the Present Scarcity of Money* (London, 1690), 6

58. William Petty, *Political Arithmetick* (1676; London, 1690), 18; Pollexfen, *Vindication*, 37.

59. Edward Misselden, *The Circle of Commerce, or, The Balance of Trade* (London, 1623), 116–17; Richard Haines, *The Prevention of Poverty, or, New Proposals Humbly Offered, For Enriching the Nation*, 2nd rev. ed. (1674; London, 1677), 4; Mun, *England's Treasure*, 11.

60. Edward Littleton, *The Groans of the Plantations* (London, 1689), 29; Adam Anderson, *An Historical and Chronological Deduction of the Origin of Commerce*, vol. 1 (London, 1764), x, xxi; Charles Davenant, *An Essay upon Ways and Means of Supplying the War* (London, 1695), 20; Charles Davenant, *A Memorial Concerning the Coyn of England* (1695), in *Two Manuscripts by Charles Davenant* (Baltimore: Johns Hopkins Press, 1942), 12; Jacob Vanderlint, *Money Answers All Things, or, An Essay to Make Money Sufficiently Plentiful Amongst All Ranks of People* (London, 1734), 8.

61. Misselden, *Circle of Commerce*, 142.

62. Henry Robinson, *Certain Proposalls in Order to the Peoples Freedome and Accommodation in Some Particulars* (London, 1652), 18; John Hagthorpe, *Englands-Exchequer, or, A Discourse of the Sea and Navigation* (London, 1625), 7.

63. John Shovlin, "War and Peace: Trade, International Competition, and Political Economy," in *Mercantilism Reimagined: Political Economy in Early Modern Britain and its Empire*, ed. Philip J. Stern and Carl Wennerlind (Oxford: Oxford University Press, 2014), 305–27.

64. Misselden, *Free Trade*, 4; James Whiston, *A Discourse of the Decay of Trade* (London, 1693), 2; Thomas Violet, *An Appeal to Caesar: Wherein Gold and Silver is Proved to be the Kings Majesties Royal Commodity* (London, 1660), 1, 3; [Slingsby Bethel], *The Present Interest of England Stated* (London, 1671), 8.

65. Tilly, *Coercion, Capital, and European States*, 29, 84–9, 99.

66. *Some Observations Upon the Bank of England* (London, 1695), 18; Whiston, *Discourse of the Decay*, 2.

67. Daniel Defoe, *A Plan of the English Commerce* (London, 1728), 52.

68. Davenant, *Memorial Concerning the Coyn*, 6

69. [William Petyt], *Britannia Languens, or, A Discourse of Trade* (London, 1680), 16.

70. Anderson, *Origin of Commerce*, 1:xxi.

71. Whiston, *Discourse of the Decay*, 3; Richard Lawrence, *The Interest of Ireland in Its Trade and Wealth Stated* (Dublin, 1682), 1, 9, both quotations from Lawrence found in David Armitage, *The Ideological Origins of the British Empire* (New York: Cambridge University Press, 2000), 148; Charles Davenant, *An Essay on the East-India Trade* (London, 1696), 7; Davenant, *Memorial Concerning the Coyn*, 49; Mun, *England's Treasure*, 13.

72. Pollexfen, *Vindication*, 37.

73. David Hume, *Of the Balance of Trade*, in Eugene Rotwein, ed., *David Hume: Writings on Economics* (1752; Madison: University of Wisconsin Press, 1955), 75.

74. Samuel Fortrey, *Englands Interest and Improvement* (London, 1663), 3–4.

75. Fortrey, *Englands Interest*, 4.

76. Davenant, *Memorial Concerning the Coyn*, 50.

77. Josiah Child, *A Discourse Concerning Trade, and that in Particular of the East-Indies* (London, 1689), 1; Whiston, *Discourse of the Decay*, 2.

78. Charles Davenant, *An Essay Upon the Probable Methods of Making a People Gainers in the Ballance of Trade* (London, 1699), 11; Petyt, *Britannia Languens*, 7, 11.

79. William Carter, *An Alarum to England: To Prevent its Destruction by the Loss of Trade and Navigation; which at this Day is in Great Danger* (London, 1700), 14.

80. John Blanch, *The Naked Truth, in an Essay upon Trade* (London, 1696), 12.

81. Carew Reynell, *The True English Interest, or an Account of the Chief National Improvements* (London, 1674), 8.

82. Wood, *Survey of Trade*, 332; Arthur Maynwaring, *Remarks Upon the Present Negotiations of Peace* (London, 1711), 26, quotation in Steve Pincus, "Rethinking Mercantilism: Political Economy, the British Empire, and the Atlantic World in the Seventeenth and Eighteenth Centuries," *William and Mary Quarterly*, 3rd ser., 69, no. 1 (Jan. 2012): 27.

83. C. K., *Some Seasonable and Modest Thoughts Partly Occasioned By, and Partly Concerning the Scots East-India Company* (Edinburgh, 1696), 4, quotation in Armitage, *Ideological Origins*, 148.

84. Niccolò Machiavelli, *The Prince* (1513; New York: Dover Publications, 1992), 37; Wood, *Survey of Trade*, v; Whiston, *Discourse of the Decay*, 2; Roger Coke, *A Discourse of Trade* (London, 1670), preface; Misselden, *Free Trade*, dedicatory.

85. [William De Britaine], *The Interest of England in the Present War with Holland* (London, 1672), 1; [Slingsby Bethel], *An Account of the French Usurpation upon the Trade of England* (London, 1679), 4; George Phillips, *The Interest of England in the Preservation of Ireland, Humbly Presented to the Parliament of England* (London, 1689), 16; Lambe, *Seasonable Observations*, 20; Whiston, *Discourse of the Decay*, 3.

86. Thomas Milles, *The Customers Alphabet and Primer* (London, 1608), in *Mercantilist Theory and Practice: The History of British Mercantilism*, ed. Lars Magnusson, 4 vols. (London: Pickering & Chatto, 2008), 1:75; [Robert Kayll], *The Trades Increase* (London, 1615), 39.

87. *The Grand Concernments of England Ensured* (London, 1659), 16–17.

88. Appleby, *Economic Thought*, 114–15; Steve Pincus, "Neither Machiavellian Moment Nor Possessive Individualism: Commercial Society and the Defenders of the English Commonwealth," *American Historical Review* 103, no. 3 (June 1998): 707–8, 712.

89. John Wheeler, *A Treatise on Commerce* (London, 1601), 8.

90. Kayll, *Trades Increase*, 39, 46.

91. *Grand Concernments*, 16; Mun, *England's Treasure*, 10; Mun, *Discourse of Trade*, 1; Bethel, *Present Interest of England*, 3.

92. My treatment of this topic is based largely on the work of Charles Tilly, especially his 1990 book *Coercion, Capital, and European States*, 17–31, 54–70, 90–99.

93. Tilly, "Reflections on the History of European State-Making," 42; Sir William Petty, "Verbum Sapienti" (London, 1664), in *The Economic Writings of Sir William Petty*, ed. Charles Henry Hull, vol. 1 (Cambridge: University Press, 1899): 113.

94. Alan G. R. Smith, *The Emergence of a Nation State: The Commonwealth of England, 1529–1660* (Longman: London, 1997), 10–11, 172–73, 177–78; Clay, *Economic Expansion*, 1:197; Ralph Davis, *A Commercial Revolution: English Overseas Trade in the Seventeenth and Eighteenth Centuries*, 3–5.

95. Robert Gray, *A Good Speed to Virginia* (London, 1609), B2.

96. Robert Thorne, *A Declaration of the Indies and Landes Discovered and Subdued unto the Emperour and the King of Portugale* (London, 1527), in *Divers Voyages Touching the Discoverie of America*, ed. Richard Hakluyt (London, 1582), B4. Also see David Beers Quinn, *England and the Discovery of America, 1481–1620* (New York: Alfred A. Knopf, 1974), 75–81, 93–103, 131–32; Kenneth R. Andrews, *Trade, Plunder and Settlement: Maritime Enterprise and the Genesis of the British Empire, 1480–1630* (Cambridge University Press, 1984), 41–63.

97. "Golden Fleece" quotation used in at least three sources, Blanch, *Naked Truth*, 2; [Thomas Johnson], *A Discourse Consisting of Motives for the Enlargement and Freedome of Trade, Especially that of Cloth, and other Woollen Manufactures* (London, 1645), 3; James Howel, *Londinopolis: An Historicall Discourse of Perlustration of the City of London* (London, 1657), 396.

98. Alison Games, *The Web of Empire: English Cosmopolitans in an Age of Expansion* (Oxford: Oxford University Press, 2008), 47–52; Smith, *Emergence of a Nation State*, 52–53, 173, 178; Davis, *Commercial Revolution*, 3, 6.

99. Games, *Web of Empire*, 7–10, 47–52; Robert Brenner, *Merchants and Revolution: Commercial Change, Political Conflict, and London's Overseas Traders, 1550–1653* (Princeton University Press, 1993), 5, 13, 17–21; Henry S. Turner, "Corporations: Humanism and Elizabethan Political Economy," in *Mercantilism Reimagined*, ed. Stern and Wennerlind, 162–68; Appleby, *Economic Thought*, 3–4, 32; Lipson, *Economic History of England*, 2:315–34.

100. Games, *Web of Empire*, 81–82; Theodore K. Rabb, *Enterprise and Empire: Merchant and Gentry Investment in the Expansion of England, 1575–1630* (Cambridge, MA: Harvard University Press, 1967).

101. *Grand Concernments*, 17; *The Statutes at Large, from Magna Charta* . . . 9 vols. (London, 1763), 2:592–93.

102. C. E. Challis, *A New History of the Royal Mint* (Cambridge: Cambridge University Press, 1992), 687.

103. Challis, *New History*, 731–77.

104. Smith, *Emergence of a Nation State*, 155–58.

105. John C. Appleby, "War, Politics, and Colonization, 1558–1625," in *The Origins of Empire: British Overseas Enterprise to the Close of the Seventeenth Century*, ed. Nicholas Canny (Oxford: Oxford University Press, 1998), 67.

106. Smith, *Emergence of a Nation State*, 210–18, 233; Dandelet, *Renaissance of Empire*, 255–7.

107. Dandelet, *Renaissance of Empire*, 161, 207.

108. Sir George Peckham, *A True Reporte, Of the Late Discoveries, and Possession, taken in the right of the Crowne of Englande, of the New-found Landes* (London, 1583), n.p.

109. Carole Shammas, "English Commercial Development and American Colonization, 1560–1620," in *The Westward Enterprise: English Activities in Ireland, the Atlantic, and America, 1480–1650*, ed. K. R. Andrews, N. P. Canny, and P. E. H. Hair (Detroit: Wayne State University Press, 1979), 153–59.

110. Humphrey Gilbert, *A Discourse of a Discoverie for a New Passage to Cataia* (London, 1576), H1–2; Drake quotation in the introduction to Peckham, *True Reporte*.

111. Letters Patent to Sir Humfrey Gilbert, June 11, 1578, in *The Principal Navigations, Voyages, Traffiques and Discoveries of the English Nation*, ed. Richard Hakluyt, 3 vols. (London, 1600), 3:135–37.

112. [Ralph Lane], *An Account of the Particularities of the Imployments of the Englishmen left in Virginia* (London, 1586), in Hakluyt, *Principal Navigations*, 3:259; Quinn, *England and the Discovery of America*, 282–87; Appleby, "War, Politics, and Colonization," 63–65; Shammas, "English Commercial Development," 157–59.

113. Peckham, *True Reporte*, F2.

114. John Cary, *A Discourse Concerning the East-India Trade* (London, 1699), 2.

115. [Sir Thomas Smith], *A Discourse of the Common Weal of this Realm of England* (1549; New York: MacMillan and Co., 1893), 69.

116. Ralph Davis, *The Rise of the English Shipping Industry in the Seventeenth and Eighteenth Centuries* (London: MacMillan and Co.), 7.

117. Lawrence A. Harper, *The English Navigation Laws: A Seventeenth-Century Experiment in Social Engineering*, repr. ed. (New York: Columbia University Press, 1939; New York: Octagon Books, 1973), 271.

118. Hakluyt to Martine Frobisher, 1576, in *Principal Navigations*, ed. Hakluyt, 3:46; Peckham, *True Reporte*, F2.

119. William Cronon, *Changes in the Land: Indians, Colonists, and the Ecology of New England* (New York: Hill and Wang, 1983), 30, 110.

120. Richard Hakluyt, *A Discourse Concerning Western Planting* (1584; repr., Cambridge Press, 1877), 155, 157; Christopher Carleill, *A Breef and Sommarie Discourse upon the extended Voyage to the hethermoste partes of America* (London, 1583), 5.

121. Kayll, *Trades Increase*, 43. Also see Jonathan Israel, *The Dutch Republic: Its Rise, Greatness, and Fall, 1477–1806* (Oxford: Clarendon Press, 1995), 15–16; Jonathan I. Israel, *Dutch Primacy in World Trade, 1585–1740* (Oxford: Clarendon Press, 1989), 22–24; Lipson, *Economic History of England*, 3:147–53.

122. Kayll, *Trades Increase*, 41. For a similar observation, see Tobias Gentleman, *Englands Way to Win Wealth* (London, 1614), 5.

123. John Smith, *A Description of New England* (London, 1616), 11.

124. James Rosier, *A True Relation of the Most Prosperous Voyage made this Present Yeere 1605* (London, 1605), B1; Edward Haies, *A Report of the Voyage and Successe Thereof, Attempted in the Yeere of our Lord 1583 by Sir Humfrey Gilbert* (London, 1583), in *Principal Navigations*, ed. Hakluyt, 3:153.

125. Kayll, *Trades Increase*, 41, 43. See also Peter E. Pope, *Fish into Wine: The New-foundland Plantation in the Seventeenth Century* (Chapel Hill: University of North Carolina Press, 2004), 13–19.

126. Hakluyt to Marine Frobisher, 1576, in *Principal Navigations*, ed. Hakluyt, 3:46.

127. *The First Voyage Made to the Coasts of America* (1584), in *Principal Navigations*, ed. Hakluyt, 3:248; Lane, *Account of the Particularities*, 259, 265; "Reasons for Raising a Fund for the Support of a Colony at Virginia," n.d., in *The Genesis of the United States: A Narrative of the Movement in England, 1605–1616*, ed. Alexander Brown, 2 vols. (Boston: Houghton, Mifflin and Company, 1890–1891), 1:37.

128. Thomas Hariot, *A Briefe and True Report of the New Found Land of Virginia* (London, 1588), 6.

129. Hariot, *A Briefe and True Report*, 10.

130. Sir Walter Raleigh, *Discoverie of the Large Rich, and Beauutiful Empire of Guiana* (London, 1596), preface.

131. Adam Smith, *An Inquiry into the Nature and Causes of the Wealth of Nations* (1776; New York: Random House, 1937), bk. 4, ch. I, 529.

132. Mayhew, *Sterling*, 57–58; Smith, *Emergence of a Nation State*, 165–67, 233–37; R. B. Outwaite, *Inflation in Tudor and Early Stuart England* (London: Macmillan, 1982), 11–17.

133. Muldrew, "Hard Food for Midas," 95–96; "A Proclamation concerning Coyne, Plate, and Bullion of Gold and Silver," 1600, accessed on *Early English Books Online* (*EEBO*), http://eebo.chadwyck.com.

134. Israel, *Dutch Republic*, 307–19, 328; Israel, *Dutch Primacy*, 17, 22, 43–60, 74.

135. Jan de Vries, *Economy of Europe in an Age of Crisis, 1600–1750* (Cambridge: Cambridge University Press, 1976), 117–18; Israel, *Dutch Republic*, 316; Israel, *Dutch Primacy*, 21.

136. De Vries, *Economy of Europe*, 122.

137. Israel, *Dutch Republic*, 319–21; Israel, *Dutch Primacy*, 67–69, 73, 103; De Vries, "Connecting Europe and Asia," 75.

138. Clay, *Economic Expansion*, 2:130, 164–65; Lipson, *Economic History of England*, 2:269–74, 286–315; Andrews, *Trade, Plunder and Settlement*, 256–79.

139. K. N. Chaudhuri, "Treasure and Trade Balances: The East India Company's Export Trade, 1660–1720," *Economic History Review*, n.s., 21, no. 3 (Dec. 1968): 482–84, 497–98.

140. Sir Josiah Child, *A New Discourse of Trade* (London, 1692), 144.

141. Mayhew, "Prices in England," 26; Mayhew, *Sterling*, 56–57; Nuno Palma, "Reconstruction of Money Supply over the Long Run: The Case of England, 1270–1870," *Economic History Review* 71, no. 2 (May 2018): 376.

142. Smith, *Emergence of a Nation State*, 178, 251–53; Davis, *Commercial Revolution*, 7–9.

143. Virginia Company Patent, April 10, 1606, in *The Federal and State Constitutions* . . . , ed. Francis Newton Thorpe, 7 vols. (Washington, DC: Government Printing Office, 1909), 7:3783–89.

144. George Chapman, et al., *Eastward Hoe* (London, 1605), E1–E2.

145. Sir Walter Cope to the Earl of Salisbury, August 12, 1607, in *Jamestown Narratives: Eyewitness Accounts of the Virginia Colony, the First Decade: 1607–1617*, ed. Edward Wright Haile (Champlain, Virginia: Roundhouse, 1998), 13.

146. William Brewster to the Earl of Salisbury, June 1607, in *Jamestown Narratives*, 127.

147. Michael Drayton, "To the Virginian Voyage," 1606, in *Poems of Michael Drayton*, ed. John Buxton, 2 vols. (Cambridge: Harvard University Press, 1953), 1:123.

148. Richard Hakluyt, *Virginia Richly Valued, By the Description of the Maine Land of Florida, Her Next Neighbour* (London, 1609), A2–3; Robert Johnson, *Nova Britannia: Offering Most Excellent Fruites by Planting in Virginia* (London, 1609), C1.

149. John Bland, *Trade Revived* (London, 1659), 29; Erasmus Philips, *The State of the Nation, in Respect to her Commerce, Debts, and Money* (London, 1725), 5; James Puckle, *England's Path to Wealth and Honour, in a Dialogue Between an English-Man and a Dutch-Man*, 2nd ed. (1696; London, 1700), 3–4.

150. Wood, *Survey of Trade*, 132–33, 135; Charles Davenant, *Discourses on the Publick Revenues, and on the Trade of England*, 2 vols. (London, 1698), 2:239; John Cary, *An Essay on the Coyn and Credit of England* (Bristol, 1696), 37.

151. Mayhew, "Prices in England," 26; Palma, "Reconstruction of Money Supply," 376.

2. The First Decades of English American Settlement, 1607–1639

1. Council of Virginia to the Virginia Company, June 22, 1607, in *The Genesis of the United States: A Series of Historical Manuscripts [GUS]*, ed. Alexander Brown, 2 vols. (Boston: Houghton, Mifflin and Company, 1890–1891), 1:108; Richard L. Morton, *Colonial Virginia*, vol. 1 (Chapel Hill: University of North Carolina Press, 1960), 5–9; Lorri Glover and Daniel Blake Smith, *The Shipwreck That Saved Jamestown: The Sea Venture Castaways and the Fate of America* (New York: Henry Holt and Company, 2008), 34–37.

2. Glover and Smith, *Shipwreck That Saved Jamestown*, 40–46; Morton, *Colonial Virginia*, 12–14.

3. John Smith, *The Generall Historie of Virginia, New-England, and the Summer Isles* (London, 1624), 53.

4. Glover and Smith, *Shipwreck that Saved Jamestown*, 42–47, 179–83; Morton, *Colonial Virginia*, 25–7.

5. "A Breife Declaration of the Plantation of Virginia during the First Twelve Yeares," 1624, in *The National Archives Public Records Office* (Kew, England) [TNA]: CO 1/3, no. 21i, p. 80;

6. Alexander Whitaker, *Good Newes from Virginia* (London, 1613), 38–39.

7. Smith, *Generall Historie*, 148; Sir Francis Bacon, "Of Plantations," in *The Essayes or Counsels, Civill and Morall* (London, 1625), 201–2.

8. [John Smith], *The Proceedings of the English Colonie in Virginia* (Oxford, 1612), 23; Morton, *Colonial Virginia*, 17; Sinclair Snow, "Naval Stores in Colonial Virginia," *The Virginia Magazine of History and Biography [VMHB]* 72, no. 1 (Jan. 1964): 75–80.

9. James I, "A Proclamation against the uttering of light Spanish silver coine," 1613, accessed on *Early English Books Online (EEBO)*, http//eebo.chadwyck.com.

10. John Hagthorpe, *Englands-Exchequer, or, A Discourse of the Sea and Navigation* (London, 1625), 29.

11. Council of Virginia, *A True Declaration of the Estate of the Colonie in Virginia* (London, 1610), 56.

12. Virginia Bernhard, "Bermuda and Virginia in the Seventeenth Century: A Comparative View," *Journal of Social History* 19, no. 1 (Autumn 1985): 57–70; Glover and Smith, *Shipwreck That Saved Jamestown*.

13. Neville Williams, "England's Tobacco Trade in the Reign of Charles I," *VMHB* 65, no. 4 (Oct. 1957): 404–5.

14. *Journals of the House of Burgesses of Virginia [JHB]*, ed. H. R. McIlwaine and John Pendleton Kennedy, 13 vols. (Richmond, 1905–15), 1:17, 57.

15. Russell R. Menard, "The Tobacco Industry in the Chesapeake Colonies, 1617–1730: An Interpretation," *Research in Economic History* 5 (1980): 157.

16. Michael J. Jarvis, *In the Eye of All Trade: Bermuda, Bermudians, and the Maritime Atlantic World, 1680–1783* (Chapel Hill: University of North Carolina Press, 2010), 27–8.

17. *British Royal Proclamations Relating to America, 1603–1783 [BRPA]*, ed. Clarence S. Brigham (Worcester, MA: American Antiquarian Society, 1911), 18.

18. Smith, *Generall Historie*, 157.

19. *The Records of the Virginia Company of London*, ed. Susan Myra Kingsbury, 4 vols. (Washington, DC, 1906–1935), 1:519.

20. *JHB*, 1:8.

21. *JHB*, 1:16.

22. *JHB*, 1:54; Hartwell, Blair and Chilton, *Present State of Virginia*, 66.

23. *The Statutes at Large; Being a Collection of All the Laws of Virginia . . .* , ed. William Waller Hening, 13 vols. (Richmond, Philadelphia, and New York, 1809–1823), 1:216.

24. *The Historye of the Bermudaes or Summer Islands* (n.d.; repr., London, 1882), 295.

25. John Oldmixon, *The British Empire in America*, 2 vols. (London, 1708), 1:203; Henry Hartwell, James Blair and Edward Chilton, *Present State of Virginia, and the College* (1697; repr., London, 1727), 7–8; Petition of New York merchants to Governor Lord Cornbury, June 25, 1705, in *Documents Relative to the Colonial History of the State of New York [DRNY]*, ed. E. B. O'Callaghan and Berthold Fernow, 15 vols. (Albany, 1856–1887), 4:1133.

26. *JHB*, 1:8.

27. Dalby Thomas, *An Historical Account of the Rise and Growth of the West-India Collonies* (London, 1690), 26.

28. Lieutenant Governor Alexander Spotswood to the Board of Trade, December 29, 1713, CO 5/1317, no. 20.

29. Menard, "Tobacco Industry," 157; Russell R. Menard, "A Note on Chesapeake Tobacco Prices, 1618–1660," *VMHB* 84, no. 4 (Oct. 1976): 404–5.

30. *JHB*, 1:53.

31. J. H. Bennett, "The English Caribbees in the Period of the Civil War, 1642–1646," *William and Mary Quarterly*, 3rd ser., 24, no. 3 (July 1967): 360–61, 367–71; *Archives of Maryland: Proceedings and Acts of the General Assembly of Maryland*, ed. William Hand Browne, et al., 72 vols. (Baltimore: Maryland Historical Society, 1883–1972),

1:20; *Acts of Assembly, Passed in the Island of Montserrat, from 1668 to 1740* (London, 1740), 16–18; John J. McCusker, *Money and Exchange in Europe and America, 1600–1775: A Handbook* (Chapel Hill: University of North Carolina Press, 1978), 239.

32. Robert Beverley, *The History and Present State of Virginia* (1705; repr., Chapel Hill: University of North Carolina Press, 1947), 285

33. Governor John Harvey to Secretary Windebank, June 26, 1636, CO 1/9, no. 17, p. 40; Governor Francis Wyatt and the Council of Virginia to the Privy Council, May 17, 1626, CO 1/4, no. 10, p. 22.

34. For more on bills of exchange, see McCusker, *Money and Exchange*, 19–22; Nicholas Mayhew, *Sterling: The Rise and Fall of a Currency* (London: Allen Lane, 1999), 283–84.

35. Hartwell, Blair and Chilton, *Present State of Virginia*, 9.

36. *Statutes of Virginia*, 1:204–5; William Zebina Ripley, *The Financial History of Virginia, 1609–1776* (New York: Columbia College, 1893), 145–46.

37. Smith, *Generall Historie*, 183. Also see *The Historye of the Bermudaes or Summer Islands* (n.d.; repr., London, 1882), 76; Walter Breen, *Walter Breen's Complete Encyclopedia of U.S. and Colonial Coins* (New York: Doubleday, 1988), 9–11.

38. Virginia Company Patent, April 10, 1606, in *The Federal and State Constitutions . . .* , ed. Francis Newton Thorpe, 7 vols. (Washington, D.C.: Government Printing Office, 1909), 7:3786.

39. Governor Harvey to Secretary Windebank, June 26, 1636, CO 1/9, no. 17, p. 40.

40. License to Henry Lord Matravers, 1638, CO 1/9, no. 132, p. 308.

41. *JHB*, 1:57–59, 65.

42. For more on this episode, see Eric P. Newman, "Coinage for Colonial Virginia," *Numismatic Notes and Monographs* 135 (1956).

43. [John Webbe], *A Discourse Concerning Paper Money* (Philadelphia, 1743), 3.

44. Edward Misselden, *Free Trade, or, The Means to Make Trade Flourish* (London, 1622), title page; James I, " A Proclamation for restraint of the exportation, waste, and consumption of Coine and Bullion," 1622, accessed on *EEBO*.

45. Misselden, *Free Trade*, 41. For more on the early 1620s depression, see Carl Wennerlind, *Casualties of Credit: The English Financial Revolution, 1620–1720* (Cambridge, MA: Harvard University Press, 2011), 19–20, 30–33; J.D. Gould, "The Trade Depression of the Early 1620's," *Economic History Review*, n.s., 7, no. 1 (1954): 81–90; J. D. Gould, "The Trade Crisis of the Early 1620's and English Economic Thought," *Journal of Economic History* 15, no. 2 (June 1955): 121–33; B. E. Supple, *Commercial Crisis and Change in England, 1600–1642: A Study in the Instability of a Mercantile Economy* (Cambridge: Cambridge University Press, 1970), 52–72, 184–89; Carlos Eduardo Suprinyak, "Trade, Money, and the Grievances of the Commonwealth: Economic Debates in England During the Commercial Crisis of the Early 1620's," *History of Economic Ideas* 24, no. 1 (2016): 27–55.

46. Thomas Mun, *A Discourse of Trade, from England unto the East-Indies* (London, 1621), 45–47, 50–53; Gerard Malynes, *The Maintenance of Free Trade* (London, 1622), 102.

47. Thomas Mun, *England's Treasure by Forraigne Trade, Or, The Balance of our Forraign Trade is the Rule of our Treasure* (1628; repr., London, 1664), 218–19.

48. Report of the Privy Council, 1626, in *A Select Collection of Scarce and Valuable Tracts on Money*, ed. J. R. McCulloch (London, 1856), 136.

49. Secretary Conway to the Solicitor-General, Apr. 15, 1625, TNA: SP 16/1, f. 81; Charles M. Andrews, *British Committees, Commissions, and Councils of Trade and Plantations, 1622–1675* (Baltimore: Johns Hopkins Press, 1908), 11–12.

50. *BRPA*, 27–30.

51. William Vaughan, *The Golden Fleece*, pt. 3 (London, 1626), 58; Gerard Malynes, *Consuetudo, vel, Lex Mercatoria, or, The Law Merchant*, 3rd ed. (1620; London, 1683), 63.

52. Malynes, *Consuetudo*, 62–63; Malynes, *Maintenance of Free Trade*, 26; Misselden, *Free Trade*, 11–12.

53. *Proceedings and Debates of the British Parliaments Respecting North America* [*PDBP*], ed. Leo Francis Stock, 5 vols. (Washington, DC: Carnegie Institution of Washington, 1924–1941), 1:28, 30, 72.

54. *PDBP*, 1:32–3; Hagthorpe, *Englands-Exchequer*, 19

55. *BRPA*, 35–6, 55–7; Stanley Gray and V. J. Wyckoff, "The International Tobacco Trade in the Seventeenth Century," *Southern Economic Journal* 7, no. 1 (July 1940): 16.

56. *Records of the Virginia Company*, 1:526–8.

57. *Acts of the Privy Council of England, Colonial Series* [*APCC*], ed. W. L. Grant and James Munroe, 6 vols. (Hereford, UK: 1908–12), 1:48–9.

58. Victor Enthoven and Wim Klooster, "The Rise and Fall of the Virginia-Dutch Connection in the Seventeenth Century," in *Early Modern Virginia: Reconsidering the Old Dominion*, ed. Douglas Bradburn and John C. Coombs (Charlottesville: University of Virginia Press, 2011), 93–95; John R. Pagan, "Dutch Maritime and Commercial Activity in Mid-Seventeenth-Century Virginia," *VMHB* 90, no. 4 (Oct. 1982): 485–86; Christian J. Koot, "Anglo-Dutch Trade in the Chesapeake and the British Caribbean, 1621–1733," in *Dutch Atlantic Connects, 1680–1800*, ed. Gert J. Oostindie and Jessica V. Roitman (Leiden: Brill, 2014), 76.

59. Wim Klooster, *The Dutch Moment: War, Trade, and Settlement in the Seventeenth-Century Atlantic World* (Ithaca, NY: Cornell University Press, 2016), 34–38, 146, 150–52, 183–84; Jonathan Israel, *The Dutch Republic: Its Rise, Greatness, and Fall, 1477–1806* (Oxford: Clarendon Press, 1995), 325–27.

60. Violet Barbour, "Dutch and English Merchant Shipping in the Seventeenth Century," *Economic History Review* 2, no. 2 (Jan. 1930), 285; Israel, *Dutch Republic*, 316; Ralph Davis, *The Rise of the English Shipping Industry in the Seventeenth and Eighteenth Centuries* (London: MacMillan & Co., 1962), 44–57, 177.

61. Henry Robinson, *Certain Proposalls in Order to the Peoples Freedome and Accommodation in Some Particulars* (London, 1652), 8.

62. Menard, "Tobacco Industry," 150.

63. *JHB*, 1:49.

64. Governor Harvey to the Lords Commissioners, May 27, 1632, in *VMHB* 8, no. 2 (Oct. 1900): 149–50.

65. *JHB*, 1:58.

66. Gray and Wyckoff, "International Tobacco Trade," 16.

67. David Peterson de Vries, "Voyages from Holland to America, A. D. 1632 to 1644," trans. Henry C. Murphy (New York, 1853), 112–13, 183.

68. Pagan, "Dutch Maritime and Commercial Activity," 486–88; Koot, "Anglo-Dutch Trade," 80–81; Klooster, *Dutch Moment*, 167; Nell Marion Nugent, *Cavaliers and*

Pioneers: Abstracts of Virginia Land Patents and Grants, 1623–1800, vol. 1 (Richmond, VA: Dietz Printing, 1934), 98, 104–5.

69. Klooster, *Dutch Moment*, 164–67; Koot, "Anglo-Dutch Trade," 77–78; Christian J. Koot, *Empire at the Periphery: British Colonists, Anglo-Dutch Trade, and the Development of the British Atlantic* (New York: New York University Press, 2011), 34–38, 54.

70. *APCC*, 1:258.

71. Menard, "Tobacco Industry," 157.

72. Christopher Carleill, *A Breef and Sommarie Discourse upon the Extended Voyage to the Hethermoste Partes of America* (London, 1583), 5.

73. *PDBP*, 1:26; *Records of the Virginia Company*, 3:477.

74. Tobias Gentleman, *Englands Way to Win Wealth, and to Employ Ships and Marriners* (London, 1614), 8; Misselden, *Circle of Commerce*, 140–41.

75. John Smith, *Description of New England* (London, 1616), 1, 21; Smith, *Generall Historie*, 240; John Smith, *New Englands Trials: Declaring the Successe of 80 Ships Employed thither within these Eight Yeares* (London, 1622), E1.

76. Peter E. Pope, *Fish Into Wine: The Newfoundland Plantation in the Seventeenth Century* (Chapel Hill: University of North Carolina Press, 2004), 13–19.

77. Christopher Levett, *A Voyage into New England* (London, 1624), 23–24, 26–27, 29, 31, 36.

78. T. H. Breen and Stephen Foster, "Moving to the New World: The Character of Early Massachusetts Immigration," *William and Mary Quarterly*, 3rd ser., 30, no. 2 (Apr. 1973): 194–200; Susan Hardman Moore, *Pilgrims: New World Settlers and the Call of Home* (New Haven: Yale University Press, 2007), 3, 14, 20–21, 71, 105–6; Virginia DeJohn Anderson, *New England's Generation: The Great Migration and the Formation of Society and Culture in the Seventeenth Century* (Cambridge: Cambridge University Press, 1991), 99, 115.

79. *Records of the Governor and Company of the Massachusetts Bay in New England*, ed. Nathaniel Bradstreet Shurtleff, 5 vols. (Boston, 1853–1854), 1:82. For more on Puritan values in early New England, see Richard L. Bushman, *From Puritan to Yankee: Character and the Social Order in Connecticut, 1690–1765* (Cambridge, MA: Harvard University Press, 1967), 3–25; Jack P. Greene, *Pursuits of Happiness: The Social Development of Early Modern British Colonies and the Formation of American Culture* (Chapel Hill: University of North Carolina Press, 1988), 22–25.

80. Daniel Vickers, "Competency and Competition: Economic Culture in Early America," *William and Mary Quarterly*, 3rd ser., 47, no. 1 (Jan. 1990): 3–29; Richard Lyman Bushman, "Markets and Composite Farms in Early America," *William and Mary Quarterly* 55, no. 3 (July 1998): 351–74; Bushman, *Puritan to Yankee*, 25–28. See also Stephen Innes, *Creating the Commonwealth: The Economic Culture of Puritan New England* (New York: W.W. Norton & Co., 1995), 6–16, 39–63; Carole Shammas, "How Self-Sufficient Was Early America?" *Journal of Interdisciplinary History* 13, no. 2 (Autumn 1982): 247–72; Alan Kulikoff, "The Transition to Capitalism in Rural America," *William and Mary Quarterly* 46, no. 1 (Jan. 1989): 120–44.

81. *Records of Massachusetts*, 1:83, 93, 126.

82. William Bradford, *History of Plymouth Plantation*, repr., *Bradford's History of Plymouth Plantation, 1606–1646*, ed. William T. Davis (New York: Charles Scribner's Sons, 1908), 175.

83. *Records of Massachusetts*, 1:92. Economic historian Richard Lester notes that the ancient Greeks sometimes used corn as a medium of exchange, and, in parts of Norway, residents even deposited corn in banks, see Richard A. Lester, *Monetary Experiments: Early American and Recent Scandinavian* (Princeton: Princeton University Press, 1939; repr. New York: Augustus M. Kelley Publishers, 1970), 12.

84. *Records of Massachusetts*, 1:137, 140.

85. [John Wise], *A Word of Comfort to a Melancholy Country, or the Bank of Credit Erected in the Massachusetts-Bay* (Boston, 1721), 9–10.

86. Winthrop, Jr. to Secretary Lord Arlington, May 7, 1667, CO 1/21, no. 42, p. 78.

87. *Records of New Plymouth*, 10:139.

88. [John Blackwell], *Some Additional Considerations* (1691), in *Colonial Currency Reprints, 1682–1751*, ed. Andrew McFarland Davis, 4 vols. (Boston: Prince Society, 1910–1911), 1:204. For similar remarks from later writers, see [Hugh Vance], *An Inquiry into the Nature and Uses of Money* (Boston, 1740), 22–23; John Law, *Money and Trade Consider'd, with a Proposal for Supplying the Nation with Money* (Edinburgh, 1705), 4.

89. Michael Merrill was one such historian, in a 1977 article entitled "Cash is Good to Eat: Self-Sufficiency and Exchange in the Rural Economy of the United States." Merrill belonged to the Marxist historical school, and in an effort to reject the notion of a market-oriented colonial economy, he sought to prove that the early American settlers engaged in a "non-commodity mode of production." Merrill's evidence: "Where money does not mediate the exchange of products, the social relations among the producers cannot be commodity relations. . . . The absence of any universal equivalent playing its assigned role is *a priori* evidence that we are dealing with a non-commodity mode of production. . . . The inhabitants of rural America, for their part, lived in a non-commodity world. Money did not mediate exchange"; see p. 60. Merrill's error was in assuming that only silver, gold, or paper can be money, dismissing all other media of exchange as mere barter. Conversely, the argument of this chapter is that country pay was indeed money, as much as silver, gold, or paper currencies. Interestingly enough, the very title of Merrill's article echoes our very argument and contradicts his own: "cash is good to eat" implied that country pay was literally cash. See Michael Merrill, "Cash Is Good to Eat: Self-Sufficiency and Exchange in the Rural Economy of the United States," *Radical History Review* 3 (Winter 1977): 42–71.

90. Webbe, *Discourse Concerning Paper Money*, 3. The author went on to instance tobacco in Virginia and Maryland, and rice in South Carolina.

91. *The Public Records of the Colony of Connecticut*, ed. J. Hammond Trumbull and Charles J. Hoadly, 15 vols. (Hartford: Brown & Parsons, 1850–1890), 1:1, 11; *Records of Massachusetts*, 2:86.

92. *Records of Massachusetts*, 1:137, 140; *Records of Connecticut*, 1:13, 18.

93. Quotation in Lester, *Monetary Experiments*, 11.

94. *Records and Files of the Quarterly Courts of Essex County, Massachusetts* [*RFQC*], ed. George Francis Dow, 9 vols. (Salem, MA: Essex Institute, 1911–1975), 8:330. See also 7:384.

95. *RFQC*, 2:186.

96. *Records of the Colony of New Plymouth in New England*, ed. Nathaniel B. Shurtleff and David Pulsifer, 12 vols. (Boston, 1855–61), 12:110.

97. *RFQC*, 7:64; *Records of New Plymouth*, 10:139.

98. For the earliest instance, see *Records of New Plymouth*, 2:82. For later instances in other colonies, especially see the fifth volume of the *Records of Massachusetts*, as well as the third and fourth volumes of the *Records of Connecticut*.

99. *Records of Connecticut*, 3:81.

100. *Records of New Plymouth*, 3:25

101. *Records of New Plymouth*, 4:186.

102. *Records of New Plymouth*, 4:184.

103. Massachusetts General Court to Charles II, October 30, 1684, in *Massachusetts Archives Collection*, vol. 106, p. 336, repr. in Sylvester S. Crosby, *The Early Coins of America, and the Laws Governing their Issue* (Boston, 1875), 76.

104. *Massachusetts Archives*, Pecuniary, vol. 1, cited in Joseph B. Felt, *An Historical Account of Massachusetts Currency* (Boston, 1839), 53.

105. *RFQC*, 4:157.

106. *Records of Massachusetts*, 1:340. Also see *Records of New Plymouth*, 3:25, 4:186.

107. For more on book credit, see Newell, *Dependency to Independence*, 97–101; W. T. Baxter, *The House of Hancock: Business in Boston, 1724–1775* (Cambridge, MA: Harvard University Press, 1945), 18–21; Claire Priest, "Currency Policies and Legal Development in Colonial New England," *Yale Law Journal* 110, no. 8 (June 2001): 1311–12, 1328–30, 1335.

108. Amicus Reipublicae [pseud.], *Trade and Commerce Inculcated* (Boston, 1731), 14; Sarah Kemble Knight, *The Journal of Madam Knight* (1704; Boston: Small, Maynard & Company, 1920), 40–41. For later use of country pay, see W. T. Baxter, *The House of Hancock: Business in Boston, 1724–1775* (Cambridge, MA: Harvard University Press, 1945), 16, 21–25, 32–34.

109. William Cronon, *Changes in the Land: Indians, Colonists, and the Ecology of New England* (New York: Hill and Wang, 1983), 95–103; Daniel K. Richter, *Facing East from Indian Country: A Native History of Early America* (Cambridge, MA: Harvard University Press, 2001), 45–46, 135–37; Nancy Shoemaker, *A Strange Likeness: Becoming Red and White in Eighteenth-Century North America* (Oxford: Oxford University Press, 2004), 43–48, 65–76.

110. Charles Bullock, *Essays on the Monetary History of the United States* (New York: MacMillan Company, 1900), 7; Adriaen van der Donck, *A Description of the New Netherlands* (1653; repr., Syracuse, NY: Syracuse University Press, 1968), 93; Cronon, *Changes in the Land*, 95.

111. Stuyvesant to the WIC Directors, April 21, 1660, in *DRNY*, 14:470; Jaap Jacobs, *New Netherland: A Dutch Colony in Seventeenth-Century America* (Leiden: Brill, 2005), 42, 193–214; Daniel K. Richter, *Trade, Land, Power: The Struggle for Eastern North America* (Philadelphia: University of Pennsylvania Press, 2013), 56–58, 100–101; Susanah Shaw Romney, *New Netherland Connections: Intimate Networks and Atlantic Ties in Seventeenth-Century America* (Chapel Hill: University of North Carolina Press, 2014), 122–37; Mark Peterson, *The City-State of Boston: The Rise and Fall of an Atlantic Power, 1630–1865* (Princeton: Princeton University Press, 2019), 45–46.

112. Simon Middleton, *From Privileges to Rights: Work and Politics in Colonial New York City* (Philadelphia: University of Pennsylvania Press, 2006), 17–18.

113. Patroons of New Netherland to the States General, June 1634, in *DRNY*, 1:87; Answer of the WIC to the Remonstrance from New Netherland, January 31, 1650, in *DRNY*, 1:344.

114. *DRNY*, 1:360.

115. Bradford, *History of Plymouth Plantation*, 234–35; Cronon, *Changes in the Land*, 95–96.

116. Bernard Bailyn, *The New England Merchants in the Seventeenth Century* (Cambridge, MA: Harvard University Press, 1955), 24–25; Alfred A. Cave, *The Pequot War* (Amherst: University of Massachusetts Press, 1996), 54–57.

117. Bradford, *History of Plymouth Plantation*, 235; Bailyn, *New England Merchants*, 26–27; Cave, *Pequot War*, 53, 61; Richter, *Facing East*, 45.

118. Neal Salisbury, *Manitou and Providence: Indians, Europeans, and the Making of New England, 1500–1643* (Oxford University Press, 1982), 147–65; Cave, *Pequot War*, 50; Peterson, *City-State of Boston*, 46–48.

119. Bradford, *History of Plymouth Plantation*, 235–36; Daniel Gookin, *Historical Collections of the Indians of New England . . .* (1674; Towtaid, MA: 1970), 18.

120. Cave, *Pequot War*, 50, 53, 63, 66; Salisbury, *Manitou and Providence*, 148–50, 165, 200–14; Peterson, *City-State of Boston*, 47–48.

121. Richter, *Trade, Land, Power*, 101; Cave, *Pequot War*, 163; Peterson, *City-State of Boston*, 51–52, 69–70.

122. *Records of Massachusetts*, 1:208; *Records of Connecticut*, 1:13.

123. *Records of Massachusetts*, 1:329, 2:42; *RFQC*, 1:119–20, 129, 280.

124. Adrian van der Donck, "Memoir on the Boundaries of New Netherland," Feb. 16, 1652, in *DRNY*, 1:469; Richter, *Trade, Land, Power*, 100–104; Peterson, *City-State of Boston*, 51–53.

125. Petition of New Amsterdam Merchants to the States-General, July 26, 1649, in *DRNY*, 1:269.

126. Peterson, *City-State of Boston*, 38–43; Daniel Vickers, *Farmers and Fishermen: Two Centuries of Work in Essex County, Massachusetts, 1630–1850* (Chapel Hill: University of North Carolina Press, 1994), 91–97; James McWilliams, *Building the Bay Colony: Local Economy and Culture in Early Massachusetts* (Charlottesville: University of Virginia Press, 2007), 37–43.

127. McWilliams, *Building the Bay Colony*, 43–48; Joseph A. Goldenberg, *Shipbuilding in Colonial America* (Charlottesville: University Press of Virginia, 1976), 8–9.

128. For more on the status of merchants in this early period, see Bailyn, *New England Merchants*, 20–23, 32–33, 38–41; McWilliams, *Building the Bay Colony*, 75–86; Innes, *Creating the Commonwealth*, 160–91.

129. Cotton Mather, *The Christian Philosopher: A Collection of the Best Discoveries in Nature, with Religious Improvements* (London, 1721), 120.

130. Mather, *Christian Philosopher*, 121.

131. *Records of Massachusetts*, 1:74, 109–11, 160.

132. For a larger treatment of this subject, see Mark Valeri, *Heavenly Merchandize: How Religion Shaped Commerce in Puritan America* (Princeton: Princeton University Press, 2010).

133. Dudley North, *Discourses Upon Trade* (London, 1691), 16.

134. C. E. Challis, ed., *A New History of the Royal Mint* (Cambridge University Press, 1992), 688–89.

135. Israel, *Dutch Primacy*, 125–36, 149–56, 226; C.G.A. Clay, *Economic Expansion and Social Change: England, 1500–1700*, 2 vols. (Cambridge: Cambridge University Press, 1984), 2:187.

136. Alan G. R. Smith, *The Emergence of a Nation State: The Commonwealth of England, 1529–1660* (Longman: London, 1997), 280.

137. Mayhew, *Sterling*, 72.

138. Ben Coates, *The Impact of the English Civil War on the Economy of London, 1642–50* (Aldershot: Ashgate Publishing, 2004), 9; Smith, *Emergence of a Nation State*, 177.

139. *Historical Statistics of the United States, Colonial Times to 1970*, 2 vols. (Washington, DC: U.S. Bureau of the Census, 1976), 2:1168.

140. *BRPA*, 53. See also J. H. Elliott, *Empires of the Atlantic World: Britain and Spain in America, 1492–1830* (New Haven: Yale University Press, 2006), 117–18.

141. Andrews, *British Committees*, 16.

142. Reprinted in Robert C. Winthrop, ed., *Life and Letters of John Winthrop* (Boston, 1867), 224–27.

143. Smith, *Emergence of a Nation State*, 211, 251–87.

144. Supple, *Commercial Crisis*, 125–28; Mayhew, *Sterling*, 74.

145. Smith, *Emergence of a Nation State*, 287–92, 297–98.

3. Monetary Upheaval, Recovery and the Dutch Infiltration, 1640–1659

1. Ben Coates, *The Impact of the English Civil War on the Economy of London, 1642–50* (Aldershot: Ashgate Publishing, 2004), 79–83; B. E. Supple, *Commercial Crisis and Change in England, 1600–1642: A Study in the Instability of a Mercantile Economy* (Cambridge: Cambridge University Press, 1970), 129–31.

2. Coates, *English Civil War*, 166–69.

3. "Humble Petition of Divers Citizens of London," 1641, in *The English Civil War and Revolution: A Sourcebook*, ed. Keith Lindley (London: Routledge, 1998), 66; second quotation from Coates, *English Civil War*, 20.

4. *A Caution to Keepe Money: Shewing the Miserie of the Want Thereof* (London, 1642), 2; William Lithgow, *The Present Surveigh of London and Englands State* (London, 1643), A3.

5. Alan G. R. Smith, *The Emergence of a Nation State: The Commonwealth of England, 1529–1660* (Longman: London, 1997), 166, 283–84, 291.

6. C. G. A. Clay, *Economic Expansion and Social Change: England, 1500–1700*, 2 vols. (Cambridge: Cambridge University Press, 1984), 1:37; Coates, *English Civil War*, 53–89.

7. Smith, *Emergence of a Nation State*, 307.

8. Nicholas Mayhew, *Sterling: The Rise and Fall of a Currency* (London: Allen Lane, 1999), 74–75; C. E. Challis, "Lord Hastings to the Great Silver Recoinage, 1464–1699," in *A New History of the Royal Mint*, ed. C. E. Challis (Cambridge: Cambridge University Press, 1992), 281–85.

9. Challis, "Lord Hastings," 283; Mayhew, *Sterling*, 76.

10. Charles I, "A Proclamation for making of severall pieces of Forreigne Coyne to be Currant in this Kingdome," March 4, 1644, accessed on *Early English Books Online* (*EEBO*), http://eebo.chadwyck.com.

11. Sir Thomas Roe, Speech in Parliament, 1641, accessed on *EEBO*; Thomas Violet, *A True Discovery to the Commons of England* (London, 1650), 1, 4, 6.

12. Marion H. Gottfried, "The First Depression in Massachusetts," *New England Quarterly* 9, no. 4 (Dec. 1936): 655–56; Bernard Bailyn, *The New England Merchants in the Seventeenth Century* (Cambridge, MA: Harvard University Press, 1955), 45–47; Darrett B. Rutman, *Winthrop's Boston: Portrait of a Puritan Town, 1630–1649* (Chapel Hill:

University of North Carolina Press, 1965), 183–84; Mark Peterson, *The City-State of Boston: The Rise and Fall of an Atlantic Power, 1630–1865* (Princeton, NJ: Princeton University Press, 2019), 42–43.

13. John Winthrop, *The Journal of John Winthrop, 1630–1649*, ed. Richard S. Dunn and Laetitia Yeandle (Cambridge, MA: Belknap Press of Harvard University Press, 1996), 328.

14. *Records of the Governor and Company of the Massachusetts Bay in New England*, ed. Nathaniel Bradstreet Shurtleff, 5 vols. (Boston, 1853–1854), 1:304.

15. Gottfried, "First Depression," 655–56; Bailyn, *New England Merchants*, 47.

16. Winthrop, *Journal*, 342.

17. Winthrop, *Journal*, 353.

18. *Records of Massachusetts*, 1:307.

19. Winthrop, *Journal*, 328, 339.

20. [Patrick Murray], *Thoughts on Money, Circulation, and Paper Currency* (Edinburgh, 1758), 9.

21. *Records of Massachusetts*, 2:20, 29; John J. McCusker, *Money and Exchange in Europe and America, 1600–1775: A Handbook* (Chapel Hill: University of North Carolina Press, 1978), 131.

22. *Records of Massachusetts*, 1:304–7, 329, 340.

23. Gerard Malynes, *The Center of the Circle of Commerce, or, A Refutation of a Treatise, Intituled The Circle of Commerce* (London, 1623), dedicatory; Rice Vaughn, *A Discourse of Coin and Coinage* (1630; repr., London, 1675), 147.

24. [Simon Clement], *A Discourse of the General Notions of Money, Trade, and Exchanges* (London, 1695), 31.

25. Cathy Matson, *Merchants and Empire: Trading in New York* (Baltimore, Johns Hopkins Press, 1998), 71–72, 82–85.

26. Blackwell to William Penn, Jan. 25, 1689, in *The Papers of William Penn*, ed. Marianne S. Wokeck et al., vol. 3 (Philadelphia: University of Pennsylvania Press, 1986), 228–29.

27. Murray, *Thoughts on Money*, 10.

28. Adam Smith, *An Inquiry into the Nature and Causes of the Wealth of Nations* (1776; New York: Random House, 1937), bk. 5, ch. III, p. 883; Gerard Malynes, *The Maintenance of Free Trade* (London, 1622), 13.

29. Vaughn, *Discourse of Coin*, 32–33, 166.

30. *Records of Massachusetts*, 2:29.

31. *Documents Relative to the Colonial History of the State of New York [DRNY]*, ed. E. B. O'Callaghan and Berthold Fernow, 15 vols. (Albany, 1856–1887), 1:203; McCusker, *Money and Exchange*, 156.

32. *The Public Records of the Colony of Connecticut*, ed. J. Hammond Trumbull and Charles J. Hoadly, 15 vols. (Hartford: Brown & Parsons, 1850–1890), 1:86; *The Statutes at Large; Being a Collection of All the Laws of Virginia . . .* , ed. William Waller Hening, 13 vols. (Richmond, Philadelphia, and New York, 1809–1823), 1:308, 397, 410; *Acts, Passed in the Island of Barbados, from 1643 to 1762*, ed. Richard Hall (London, 1764), 450, 463, 468; McCusker, *Money and Exchange*, 156, 205, 239, 276.

33. Quotation from pro-devaluation writer Edward Misselden, *Free Trade, or, The Means to Make Trade Flourish* (London, 1622), 18.

34. [James Hodges], *The Present State of England, As to Coin and Publick Charges* (London, 1697), 85–86.

35. *Records of Massachusetts*, 3:92.

36. *Records of Massachusetts*, 1:294, 303; Nathanael Byfield, *New Englands First Fruits* (London, 1643), 39.

37. Virginia DeJohn Anderson, *New England's Generation: The Great Migration and the Formation of Society and Culture in the Seventeenth Century* (Cambridge: Cambridge University Press, 1991), 134–40; Stephen Innes, *Creating the Commonwealth: The Economic Culture of Puritan New England* (New York: W.W. Norton & Co., 1995), 237–70; James McWilliams, *Building the Bay Colony: Local Economy and Culture in Early Massachusetts* (Charlottesville: University of Virginia Press, 2007), 66–74.

38. Bailyn, *New England Merchants*, 77; Daniel Vickers, *Farmers and Fishermen: Two Centuries of Work in Essex County, Massachusetts, 1630–1850* (Chapel Hill: University of North Carolina Press, 1994), 98–100.

39. Vickers, *Farmers and Fishermen*, 99; Bailyn, *New England Merchants*, 78–79, 82–83.

40. James G. Lydon, "Fish and Flour for Gold: Southern Europe and the Colonial American Balance of Payments," *Business History Review* 39, no. 2 (Summer 1965): 171–75, 182; Peterson, *City-State of Boston*, 55–60, 100.

41. *Some Considerations Upon the Several Sorts of Banks Propos'd as a Medium of Trade* (Boston, 1716), 3; Samuel Danforth, *An Almanac for the Year of Our Lord 1648* (Cambridge, MA, 1648), page for December, cited in Gottfried, "First Depression," 667.

42. Charles F. Carroll, *The Timber Economy of Puritan New England* (Providence, RI: Brown University Press, 1973), 77–79, 87–89; Nuala Zahedieh, *The Capital and the Colonies: London and the Atlantic Economy, 1660–1700* (Cambridge: Cambridge University Press, 2010), 194–95.

43. Winthrop, *Journal*, 353; *Records of Massachusetts*, 1:340.

44. Joseph A. Goldenberg, *Shipbuilding in Colonial America* (Charlottesville: University Press of Virginia, 1976), 11–18; McWilliams, *Building the Bay Colony*, 51–55.

45. Thomas Mun, *England's Treasure by Forraigne Trade, Or, The Balance of our Forraign Trade is the Rule of our Treasure* (1628; repr., London, 1664), 209.

46. Charles Davenant, *An Essay on the East-India Trade* (London, 1696), 155. For more on the importance of invisible earnings, see Curtis Nettels, *The Money Supply of the American Colonies Before 1720* (Madison: University of Wisconsin Press, 1934; repr., Clifton, NJ: Augustus M. Kelley Publishers, 1973), 69–72; Innes, *Creating the Commonwealth*, 274–75; James F. Shepherd and Gary M. Walton, *Shipping, Maritime Trade, and the Economic Development of Colonial North America* (Cambridge: Cambridge University Press, 1972), 116–36.

47. Christian J. Koot, *Empire at the Periphery: British Colonists, Anglo-Dutch Trade, and the Development of the British Atlantic* (New York: New York University Press, 2011), 55; Wim Klooster, *The Dutch Moment: War, Trade, and Settlement in the Seventeenth-Century Atlantic World* (Ithaca, NY: Cornell University Press, 2016), 77–81.

48. John J. McCusker and Russell Menard, *The Economy of British America, 1607–1789* (Chapel Hill: University of North Carolina Press, 1985), 153.

49. Zahedieh, *Capital and the Colonies*, 214.

50. Richard S. Dunn, *Sugar and Slaves: The Rise of the Planter Class in the English West Indies, 1624–1713* (Chapel Hill: University of North Carolina Press, 1972), 84–116.

51. Zahedieh, *Capital and the Colonies*, 259–60.

52. Willoughby to Charles II, September 16, 1667, in *The National Archives Public Records Office* (Kew, England) [TNA]: CO 1/21, no. 108, p. 218; Willoughby to Secretary Henry Bennet, February 18, 1664, CO 1/18, no. 29, p. 63.

53. *Acts and Statutes of the Island of Barbados* (London, 1654), 13–15, 17, 20–26; *Acts of Assembly, passed in the Island of Barbadoes, from 1648, to 1718* (London, 1732), 39–43, 45, 59–51, 61–63, 77–79, 100.

54. *Discourse of the Duties on Merchandize* (London, 1695), 5, cited in Frank Wesley Pitman, *The Development of the British West Indies, 1700–1763* (New Haven, CT: Yale University Press), 140.

55. *Acts and Statutes of Barbados*, 83–84.

56. Governor Christopher Codrington to the Lords of Trade, July 13, 1691, CO 152/38, no. 33.

57. Samuel Davis, "Proposals to the Lords of the Treasury," May 21, 1701, repr. in Sylvester S. Crosby, *The Early Coins of America, and the Laws Governing their Issue* (Boston, 1875), 140.

58. Dalby Thomas, *An Historical Account of the Rise and Growth of the West-India Collonies* (London, 1690), 14; Richard Vines to Winthrop, July 19, 1647, in *Winthrop Papers*, vol. 5 (Boston: Massachusetts Historical Society, 1947), 172.

59. Carroll, *Timber Economy*, 82–84; Dunn, *Sugar and Slaves*, 210; Anderson, *New England's Generation*, 153–54; Nettels, *Money Supply*, 82–84.

60. Bailyn, *New England Merchants*, 84–85; McWilliams, *Building the Bay Colony*, 51–52.

61. *Records and Files of the Quarterly Courts of Essex County, Massachusetts* [RFQC], ed. George Francis Dow, 9 vols. (Salem, MA: Essex Institute, 1911–1975), 1:119–20.

62. Raphael E. Solomon, "Foreign Specie Coins in the American Colonies," in Eric P. Newman and Richard G. Doty, eds., *Studies on Money in Early America* (New York: American Numismatic Society, 1976), 36.

63. *Records of Massachusetts*, 3:92.

64. *Records of Massachusetts*, 2:42, 86, 112, 254, 3:172; *Records of Connecticut*, 1:69, 79, 118.

65. Jacob M. Price, "The Economic Growth of the Chesapeake and the European Market, 1697–1775," *Journal of Economic History* 24 (1964): 496; Russell R. Menard, "The Tobacco Industry in the Chesapeake Colonies, 1617–1730: An Interpretation," *Research in Economic History* 5 (1980): 132–33.

66. Douglas M. Bradburn and John C. Coombs, "Smoke and Mirrors: Reinterpreting the Society and Economy of the Seventeenth-Century Chesapeake," *Atlantic Studies* 3, no. 2 (Oct. 2006): 140–43, 148; April Lee Hatfield, *Atlantic Virginia: Intercolonial Relations in the Seventeenth Century* (Philadelphia: University of Pennsylvania Press, 2004), 52–59.

67. Beauchamp Plantagenet, *A Description of the Province of New Albion* (London, 1648), 5.

68. Jack P. Greene, *Pursuits of Happiness: The Social Development of Early Modern British Colonies and the Formation of American Culture* (Chapel Hill: University of North Carolina Press, 1988), 13–18.

69. *Journals of the House of Burgesses of Virginia* [JHB], eds. H.R. McIlwaine and John Pendleton Kennedy, 13 vols. (Richmond, 1905–1915), 1:100, 107; *A Perfect Description of Virginia: Being, A Full and True Relation of the Present State of the Plantation* (London, 1649), 7.

70. *Statutes of Virginia*, 1:308–9.

71. Little has been written of the prospective Virginia coinage, and most of it is quite old: see Eric P. Newman, "Coinage for Colonial Virginia," *Numismatic Notes and Monographs* 135 (1956); Philip Alexander Bruce, *Economic History of Virginia in the*

Seventeenth Century, 2 vols. (New York: MacMillan Company, 1895; repr., New York: Peter Smith, 1935), 2:502–3, 507–8; William Zebina Ripley, *The Financial History of Virginia, 1609–1776* (New York: Columbia College, 1893), 111–14; Crosby, *Early Coins*, 22.

72. Jonathan Israel, *The Dutch Republic: Its Rise, Greatness, and Fall, 1477–1806* (Oxford: Clarendon Press, 1995), 611–12; Jan de Vries, *Economy of Europe in an Age of Crisis, 1600–1750* (Cambridge University Press, 1976), 101; Jaap Jacobs, *New Netherland: A Dutch Colony in Seventeenth-Century America* (Leiden: Brill, 2005), 228–29, 258.

73. *Records of the Colony of Rhode Island and Providence Plantations, in New England,* ed. John Russell Bartlett, 7 vols. (Providence, 1856–62), 1:126.

74. *Records of Massachusetts*, 2:29; *Records of Connecticut*, 1:86.

75. *Statutes of Virginia*, 1:258.

76. *JHB*, 1:71.

77. Price estimate from Koot, *Empire at the Periphery*, 20. See also pp. 45–46, 74–77; Wim Klooster, "Anglo-Dutch Trade in the Seventeenth Century: An Atlantic Partnership?" in Allan I. Macinnes and Arthur H. Williamson, eds., *Shaping the Stuart World, 1603–1714: The Atlantic Connection* (Leiden: Brill, 2006), 266–74; Violet Barbour, "Dutch and English Merchant Shipping in the Seventeenth Century," *Economic History Review* 2, no. 2 (Jan. 1930): 285.

78. Benjamin Worsley, *The Advocate, Or, A Narrative of the State and Condition of Things Between the English and Dutch Nation, in Relation to Trade* (London, 1651), 5–6.

79. Statistic from Lionel Gatford, *Publick Good without Private Interest, or, A Compendious Remonstrance of the Present Sad State and Condition of the Colonie in Virginea* (London, 1657), 14. See also Israel, *Dutch Republic*, 316; De Vries, *Economy of Europe*, 117–18; John R. Pagan, "Dutch Maritime and Commercial Activity in Mid-Seventeenth-Century Virginia," *Virginia Magazine of History and Biography* 90, no. 4 (Oct. 1982): 487.

80. Henry Robinson, *Certain Proposalls in Order to the Peoples Freedome and Accommodation in Some Particulars* (London, 1652), 8.

81. *Proceedings and Debates of the British Parliaments Respecting North America* [*PDBP*], ed. Leo Francis Stock, 5 vols. (Washington, DC: Carnegie Institution of Washington, 1924–1941), 1:155; *JHB*, 1:74.

82. *Perfect Description*, 4; statistics from Victor Enthoven and Wim Klooster, "The Rise and Fall of the Virginia-Dutch Connection in the Seventeenth Century," in Douglas M. Bradburn and John C. Coombs, eds., *Early Modern Virginia: Reconsidering the Old Dominion* (Charlottesville: University of Virginia Press, 2011), 99. Also see Hatfield, *Atlantic Virginia*, 40–51; Pagan, "Dutch Maritime," 486–93.

83. Coates, *English Civil War*, 174.

84. *Perfect Description*, 15.

85. Koot, *Empire at the Periphery*, 56–57; Klooster, *Dutch Moment*, 167–69.

86. *A Declaration Set Forth by the Lord Lieutenant Generall, the Gentlemen of the Councell & Assembly . . .* (The Hague, 1651), 3; Governor Daniel Searle to the Council of State, October 8, 1652, in CO 1 / 11, cited in Koot, *Empire at the Periphery*, 94.

87. Klooster, *Dutch Moment*, 157.

88. Klooster, *Dutch Moment*, 166–67; Koot, *Empire at the Periphery*, 49–51; Klooster, "Anglo-Dutch Trade," 269–74; Christian J. Koot, "Anglo-Dutch Trade in the Chesapeake and the British Caribbean, 1621–1733," in Gert J. Oostindie and Jessica V. Roitman, eds., *Dutch Atlantic Connects, 1680–1800* (Leiden: Brill, 2014), 82.

89. Koot, "Anglo-Dutch Trade," 82.

90. John Milton, *The Readie and Easie Way to Establish a Free Commonwealth* (London, 1660), 2; John Pollexfen, *A Discourse of Trade, Coyn, and Paper Credit* (London, 1697), 7; Carew Reynell, *A Necessary Companion, or, The English Interest Discovered and Promoted* (London, 1685), preface. See also Israel, *Dutch Republic*, 328–29.

91. Jonathan I. Israel, *Dutch Primacy in World Trade, 1585–1740* (Oxford: Clarendon Press, 1989), 197–98, 224–26; Israel, *Dutch Republic*, 610–11; Coates, *English Civil War*, 189–90, 195–97.

92. Clay, *Economic Expansion*, 2:188.

93. Israel, *Dutch Primacy*, 200–204, 215; Israel, *Dutch Republic*, 713–14.

94. Zahedieh, *Capital and the Colonies*, 35.

95. James Yard to Sir Robert Stone, May 26, 1652, TNA: SP 18/24, pt. 1, f. 33.

96. Jan de Vries, "Connecting Europe and Asia: A Quantitative Analysis of the Cape-Route Trade, 1497–1795," in Dennis O. Flynn, Arturo Giráldez and Richard von Glahn, eds., *Global Connections and Monetary History, 1470–1800* (Aldershot, UK: Ashgate Publishing, 2003), 88; Israel, *Dutch Republic*, 936.

97. Reynell, *Necessary Companion*, 13. Also see De Vries, "Connecting Europe," 75–7; Israel, *Dutch Republic*, 941.

98. Israel, *Dutch Republic*, 938–40.

99. Israel, *Dutch Republic*, 935–36; Klooster, *Dutch Moment*, 146–47, 164–66, 183–84.

100. Robinson, *Certain Proposalls*, 8.

101. Joyce Oldham Appleby, *Economic Thought and Ideology in Seventeenth-Century England* (Princeton: Princeton University Press, 1978), 73–74; Lars Magnusson, *The Political Economy of Mercantilism* (London: Routledge, 2015), 56–58.

102. Worsley, *Advocate*, 1; Mun, *England's Treasure*, 202.

103. Josiah Child, *A New Discourse of Trade* (London, 1692), 92; John Cary, *An Essay on the State of England, in Relation to its Trade* (London, 1695), 123; Francis Brewster, *Essays on Trade and Navigation* (London, 1695), 94; Josiah Child, *Brief Observations Concerning Trade, and Interest of Money* (London, 1688), 3.

104. Quotations in Smith, *Emergence of a Nation State*, 318.

105. Charles M. Andrews, *British Committees, Commissions, and Councils of Trade and Plantations, 1622–1675* (Baltimore: Johns Hopkins Press, 1908), 30–34.

106. Instructions for the Council of Trade, August 1650, in Andrews, *British Committees*, 115–16.

107. Council of State to the Lord General, July 30, 1651, TNA: SP 25/96, f. 317.

108. Smith, *Emergence of a Nation State*, 330; Michael Braddick, *State Formation in Early Modern England, c. 1550–1700* (Cambridge: Cambridge University Press, 2000), 178–80, 215.

109. Braddick, *State Formation*, 219.

110. Henry Robinson, *Briefe Considerations Concerning the Advancement of Trade and Navigation* (London, 1649), preface, 1.

111. Carla Gardina Pestana, *The English Atlantic in an Age of Revolution, 1640–1661* (Cambridge, MA: Harvard University Press, 2004), 99–103; Charles McLean Andrews, *The Colonial Period of American History*, 4 vols. (New Haven, CT: Yale University Press, 1934–8), 4:35–40.

112. *Declaration Set Forth*, 2; *JHB*, 1:75–78.

113. *JHB*, 1:79; *Acts and Statutes of Barbados*, 4.

114. *PDBP*, 1:225; Lawrence A. Harper, *The English Navigation Laws: A Seventeenth-Century Experiment in Social Engineering* (Columbia University Press, 1939; repr., New York: Octagon Books, 1973), 34–41.

115. McCusker and Menard, *Economy of British America*, 40.

116. *The Statutes at Large, from Magna Charta . . .* , 9 vols. (London, 1763), 1:349–51, 2:527.

117. Worsley, *Advocate*, 12; Robinson, *Certain Proposalls*, 10, 18.

118. John Streater, *The Continuation of this Session of Parliament Justified* (London, 1659), 12; S.E., *The Touch-Stone of Mony and Commerce, or, An Expedient for Increase of Trade, Mony, and Shiping in England* (London, 1653), 4.

119. Samuel Lambe, *Seasonable Observations Humbly Offered to His Highness the Lord Protector* (London, 1657), 19; S.E., *Touch-Stone*, 3.

120. Klooster, "Anglo-Dutch Trade," 276; Israel, *Dutch Republic*, 715;

121. Israel, *Dutch Primacy*, 215, 226.

122. Klooster, "Anglo-Dutch Trade," 276.

123. Israel, *Dutch Primacy*, 208–9; Israel, *Dutch Republic*, 715; J. E. Farnell, "The Navigation Act of 1651, the First Dutch War, and the London Merchant Community," *Economic History Review*, n.s., 16, no. 3 (1964): 449–52; Gijs Rommelse, "The Role of Mercantilism in Anglo-Dutch Political Relations, 1650–74," *Economic History Review* 63, no. 3 (Aug. 2010): 597.

124. Rommelse, "Role of Mercantilism," 595–96; Israel, *Dutch Republic*, 714–15.

125. Israel, *Dutch Republic*, 716, 721–22, 727; Israel, *Dutch Primacy*, 209–12; Koot, *Empire at the Periphery*, 47–48.

126. *Statutes of Virginia*, 1:413. Also see *Records of Massachusetts*, 3:354, 4.1:197; *Records of Connecticut*, 1:261; *Records of Rhode Island*, 1:356; Pestana, *English Atlantic*, 174–77.

127. *JHB*, 1:76.

128. Directors of the WIC to Peter Stuyvesant, June 14, 1656, in *DRNY*, 14:350. Also see Enthoven and Klooster, "Virginia-Dutch Connection," 105–7.

129. Koot, *Empire at the Periphery*, 60, 67, 70–72; Klooster, *Dutch Moment*, 168–71; Klooster, "Anglo-Dutch Trade," 276.

130. *Declaration Set Forth*, 3–4.

131. *Records of Massachusetts*, 4.1:229; *Records of Rhode Island*, 1:356, 389.

132. Andrews, *British Committees*, 29–31, 36–37, 48–49; Smith, *Emergence of a Nation State*, 320–31.

133. British Library, Additional Manuscripts., vol. 11411, ff. 11–12, cited in Andrews, *British Committees*, 56–57.

134. British Library, Egerton Manuscripts, vol. 2395, f. 86, cited in Andrews, *British Committees*, 58.

135. *Records of Massachusetts*, 3:261–62, 4.1:84–85.

136. *Records of Massachusetts*, 4.1:104–5. See also Walter Breen, *Walter Breen's Complete Encyclopedia of U.S. and Colonial Coins* (New York: Doubleday, 1988), 12–16; Louis Jordan, *John Hull, the Mint and the Economics of Massachusetts Coinage* (Hanover: Coin Collector's Club, 2002); Crosby, *Early Coins*, 30–76; Mark Peterson, "Big Money Comes to Boston: The Curious History of the Pine Tree Shilling," *Common-Place* 6, no. 3 (Apr. 2006); Peterson, *City-State of Boston*, 104–12; Jonathan Barth, "'A Peculiar

Stampe of Our Owne': The Massachusetts Mint and the Battle over Sovereignty, 1652–1691," *New England Quarterly* 87, no. 3 (Sept. 2014): 490–525.

137. John J. TePaske, *A New World of Gold and Silver*, ed. Kendall W. Brown (Leiden: Brill, 2010), 242; Alan Knight, *Mexico: The Colonial Era* (Cambridge: Cambridge University Press, 2002), 196; Peterson, *City-State of Boston*, 100–103.

138. [John Locke], *Some Considerations of the Consequences of the Lowering of Interest, and Raising the Value of Money* (London, 1692), 150–51; *Diaries of John Hull, Mint-master and Treasurer of the Colony of Massachusetts Bay*, reprinted in *Archaeologia Americana: Transactions and Collections of the American Antiquarian Society*, vol. 3 (Worchester, MA, 1857), 145.

139. Roger Williams, *A Key into the Language of America* [1643], in *Collections of the Massachusetts Historical Society*, vol. 3 (Boston: Munroe & Francis, 1810), 231–32; *Records of Rhode Island*, 1:155. See also Daniel K. Richter, *Facing East from Indian Country: A Native History of Early America* (Cambridge, MA: Harvard University Press, 2001), 100.

140. *Records of Connecticut*, 1:179; *Records of Massachusetts*, 2:261, 4.1:36; *New Haven Town Records*, ed. Franklin Bowditch Dexter, 2 vols. (New Haven, CT: 1917–1919), 1:18, 21–22, 98, 128.

141. *Records of Massachusetts*, 2:279, 3:153, 4.2:4.

142. *Records of Massachusetts*, 3:261–62.

143. *Records of Massachusetts*, 3:353–54; quotation from *Massachusetts Archives Collection*, vol. 100, p. 46.

144. *Acts of Assembly, Passed in the Island of Montserrat, from 1668 to 1740* (London, 1740), 20; Assembly of Nevis, 1672, CO 154/1, p. 4.

145. Peterson, *City-State of Boston*, 68–75, 82–89, 140–45.

146. Edward Randolph to the Earl of Clarendon, June 14, 1682, in *Edward Randolph: Including his Letters and Official Papers from the New England, Middle, and Southern Colonies in America* [*Randolph Letters*], eds. Robert Noxon Toppan and Alfred T. S. Goodrick, 7 vols. (Boston, 1898–1909), 3:159.

147. Rice Vaughn, *A Discourse of Coin and Coinage* (1630; repr., London, 1675), 83.

148. Thomas Bayly, *The Royal Charter Granted Unto Kings by God Himself* (London, 1682), 9, cited in Kevin Sharpe, *Rebranding Rule: The Restoration and Revolution Monarchy, 1660–1714* (New Haven: Yale University Press, 2013), 134.

149. Thomas Hobbes, *Leviathan, or, The Matter, Form, and Power of a Common-Wealth Ecclesiastical and Civil* (London, 1651), 92, 129–30.

150. *Records of Massachusetts*, 4.1:80.

151. Quotation from Marchamont Nedham, *The Case of the Kingdom Stated* (London, 1647), 4. Also see Perry Miller, "Errand into the Wilderness," *William and Mary Quarterly*, 3rd ser., 10, no. 1 (Jan. 1953): 15–18; Smith, *Emergence of a Nation State*, 287–90, 310, 339–42; Pestana, *English Atlantic*, 53–83, 123–48.

152. Sir Richard Saltonstall to John Cotton and John Wilson, 1652, in *The Saltonstall Papers, 1607–1815*, ed. Robert E. Moody, in *Collections of the Massachusetts Historical Society* (Boston, 1972, 1974), 1:1648–49, cited in Pestana, *English Atlantic*, 147. Also see Smith, *Emergence of a Nation State*, 329, 339–45.

153. Increase Mather to Thomas Gouge, 21 Nov. 1683, CO 1/65, no. 73iv, p. 329; [Increase Mather], *New-England Vindicated* (London 1689), 2–3.

154. Peterson, *City-State of Boston*, 92–93, 112–22.

155. *Diaries of John Hull*, 3:186–87.

156. Bailyn, *New England Merchants*, 75, 86, 95–101; Rutman, *Winthrop's Boston*, 181–83, 186–90, 241–42.

157. *Records of Massachusetts*, 4.1:348.

158. *RFQC*, 1:356–57.

159. *Records of Rhode Island*, 1:39.

160. Menard, "Tobacco Industry," 158.

161. Gatford, *Publick Good*, 13–14, 20–21.

162. John Brewer, *The Sinews of Power: War, Money and the English State, 1688–1783* (Cambridge, MA: Harvard University Press, 1988), 11–12, 14–15, 64–65; Braddick, *State Formation*, 219–20.

163. Carla Gardina Pestana, *The English Conquest of Jamaica: Oliver Cromwell's Bid for Empire* (Cambridge, MA: Belknap Press of Harvard University Press, 2017); Pestana, *English Atlantic*, 177–81.

164. Dunn, *Sugar and Slaves*, 35–39; Susan Dwyer Amussen, *Caribbean Exchanges: Slavery and the Transformation of English Society, 1640–1700* (Chapel Hill: University of North Carolina Press, 2007), 35.

165. Dunn, *Sugar and Slaves*, 203.

166. Justin Roberts, "Surrendering Surinam: The Barbadian Diaspora and the Expansion of the English Sugar Frontier, 1650–75," *William and Mary Quarterly* 73, no. 2 (Apr. 2016): 225–36.

167. Zahedieh, *Capital and the Colonies*, 214, 217; Russell R. Menard, "Plantation Empire: How Sugar and Tobacco Planters Built Their Industries and Raised an Empire," *Agricultural History* 81, no. 3 (Summer 2007): 310.

168. John Oldmixon, *The British Empire in America*, 2 vols. (London, 1708), 2:162.

169. Dunn, *Sugar and Slaves*, 237; Zahedieh, *Capital and the* Colonies, 248.

170. John Bland, *Trade Revived* (London, 1659), 10.

4. Mercantilism, Mints, Clipping, Smuggling, and Piracy, 1660–1674

1. Samuel Lambe, *Seasonable Observations Humbly Offered to His Highness the Lord Protector* (London, 1657), 3.

2. Ralph Davis, *The Rise of the English Shipping Industry in the Seventeenth and Eighteenth Centuries* (London: MacMillan and Co., 1962), 18.

3. Charles Davenant, *Discourses on the Publick Revenues, and on the Trade of England*, 2 vols. (London, 1698), 2:204.

4. Sir Francis Brewster, *Essays on Trade and Navigation* (London, 1695), 101.

5. Alison Gilbert Olson, *Making the Empire Work: London and American Interest Groups, 1690–1790* (Cambridge, MA: Harvard University Press, 1992), 2–6, 14–28; Perri Gauci, *The Politics of Trade: The Overseas Merchant in State and Society, 1660–1720* (Oxford: Oxford University Press, 2001).

6. John Streater, *The Continuation of this Session of Parliament Justified* (London, 1659), 11–13.

7. Lambe, *Seasonable Observations*, 2; S.E., *The Touch-Stone of Mony and Commerce, or, An Expedient for Increase of Trade, Mony, and Shiping in England* (London, 1653), 1, 4; John Milton, *The Readie and Easie Way to Establish a Free Commonwealth* (London, 1660), 17.

8. [Slingsby Bethel], *The Present Interest of England Stated* (London, 1671), 2, 8.

9. Lord Clarendon, *The Life of Edward Earl of Clarendon* . . . vol. 2 (1667; repr., Oxford: Clarendon Press, 1827), 231.

10. Charles II, "A Proclamation Against Exportation, and Buying and Selling of Gold and Silver at Higher Rates then in Our Mint," June 10, 1661, accessed on *Early English Books Online*, http//eebo.chadwyck.com.

11. Instructions to the Council of Trade, November 7, 1660, in Charles M. Andrews, *British Committees, Commissions, and Councils of Trade and Plantations, 1622–1675* (Baltimore: Johns Hopkins Press, 1908), 73–74.

12. Instructions for the Council for Forraigne Plantations, December 1, 1660, in *Documents Relative to the Colonial History of the State of New York* [*DRNY*], ed. E. B. O'Callaghan and Berthold Fernow, 15 vols. (Albany, 1856–1887), 3:35.

13. *The Statutes at Large, from Magna Charta* . . . [*SLMC*], 9 vols. (London, 1763), 3:182–85, 267–69; *Proceedings and Debates of the British Parliaments Respecting North America* [*PDBP*], ed. Leo Francis Stock, 5 vols., (Washington, DC: Carnegie Institution of Washington, 1924–1941), 1:278–82, 310–11. Also see Lawrence A. Harper, *The English Navigation Laws: A Seventeenth-Century Experiment in Social Engineering* (New York: Columbia University Press, 1939; repr., New York: Octagon Books, 1973), 53–60, 161–62; Charles McLean Andrews, *The Colonial Period of American History*, 4 vols. (New Haven, CT: Yale University Press, 1934–38), 4:61–91, 108–16.

14. Brewster, *Essays on Trade and Navigation*, 92; Sir Josiah Child, *A New Discourse of Trade* (London, 1692), 91; Edmund Burke, "Speech on American Taxation," April 19, 1774, in *The Works of Edmund Burke*, vol. 1 (Boston, 1839), 455; John Hodges, *How to Revive the Golden Age* (London, 1666); Davenant, *Discourses on the Publick Revenues*, 2:85.

15. Petition of the President, Council and Assembly of Barbados to the Commissioners for Foreign Plantations," May 11, 1661, *The National Archives-Public Records Office* (Kew, England) [TNA]: CO 31/1, p. 46; Petition of the Representatives for Barbados to Charles II, September 5, 1667, CO 1/21, no. 102, p. 207; "Grievances of the Inhabitants of Barbadoes," 1675, CO 1/35, no. 47.

16. Berkeley, "Answer to 'Enquiries to the Governor of Virginia,'" 1671, in *The Statutes at Large; Being a Collection of All the Laws of Virginia* . . . , ed. William Waller Hening, 13 vols. (Richmond, Philadelphia, and New York, 1809–1823), 2:515.

17. William Berkeley, *A Discourse and View of Virginia* (London, 1663), 6.

18. Berkeley, "Answer to Enquiries," in *Statutes of Virginia*, 2:516.

19. John Bland, *The Humble Remonstrance of John Blande of London, Merchant, on the Behalf of the Inhabitants and Planters in Virginia and Mariland* (London, 1661), 1–4.

20. Berkeley, *Discourse and View of Virginia*, 10.

21. Nuala Zahedieh, *The Capital and the Colonies: London and the Atlantic Economy, 1660–1700* (Cambridge: Cambridge University Press, 2010), 208, 225; Russell R. Menard, "The Tobacco Industry in the Chesapeake Colonies, 1617–1730: An Interpretation," *Research in Economic History* 5 (1980): 136.

22. Zahedieh, *Capital and the Colonies*, 199, 216; Menard, "Tobacco Industry," 151; Stanley Gray and V. J. Wyckoff, "The International Tobacco Trade in the Seventeenth Century," *Southern Economic Journal* 7, no. 1 (July 1940): 16.

23. Zahedieh, *Capital and the Colonies*, 214–16.

24. A. P. Thornton, *West-India Policy under the Restoration* (Oxford: Clarendon Press, 1956), 258–59; 108–9; Thomas C. Barrow, *Trade and Empire: The British Customs Service in Colonial America, 1660–1775* (Cambridge, MA: Harvard University Press, 1967), 18–19.

25. *Journals of the House of Burgesses of Virginia* [*JHB*], ed. H. R. McIlwaine and John Pendleton Kennedy, 13 vols. (Richmond, 1905–15), 2:4, 7–8, 14, 19, 42.

26. Heads of the Demise Granted Lord Arlington and Lord Culpeper," February 1672, CO 1/28, no. 20, p. 41.

27. John Oldmixon, *The British Empire in America*, 2 vols. (London, 1708), 2:161; *A Discourse of the Duties on Merchandize* (London, 1695), 5.

28. Petition of Cradock to the King, November 19, 1661, CO 1/15, nos. 88–89, pp. 173–74.

29. Menard, "Tobacco Industry," 132–34, 158–59.

30. Peter D. McClelland, "The Cost to America of British Imperial Policy," *American Economic Review* 59, no. 2 (May 1969): 379.

31. Menard, "Tobacco Industry," 150; Gray and Wyckoff, "International Tobacco Trade," 7–8.

32. Lionel Gatford, *Publick Good without Private Interest, or, A Compendious Remonstrance of the Present Sad State and Condition of the Colonie in Virginea* (London, 1657), 14.

33. Bland, *Humble Remonstrance*, 1.

34. Governor Thomas Lynch to the Lords of Trade and Plantations, August 29, 1682, CO 1/49, no. 35, pp. 134–35; Samuel Hayne, *An Abstract of all the Statutes made concerning Aliens* (London, 1685), 12. Both cited in Christian J. Koot, *Empire at the Periphery: British Colonists, Anglo-Dutch Trade, and the Development of the British Atlantic* (New York: New York University Press, 2011), 121.

35. "Some Observations on the Island of Barbadoes," 1667, CO 1/21, no. 170, p. 332.

36. Richard Ligon, *A True and Exact History of the Island of Barbados* (London, 1657), 40. See also Susan Dwyer Amussen, *Caribbean Exchanges: Slavery and the Transformation of English Society, 1640–1700* (Chapel Hill: University of North Carolina Press, 2007), 16–17, 145–54; Zahedieh, *Capital and the Colonies*, 259–60.

37. S.E., *Toutch-Stone of Mony*, 4. For more on the social significance of silver plate, see Craig Muldrew, "'Hard Food for Midas': Cash and its Social Value in Early Modern England," *Past & Present* 170 (Feb. 2001): 109–13.

38. John J. McCusker and Russell R. Menard, *The Economy of British America, 1607–1789* (Chapel Hill: University of North Carolina Press, 1985), 153.

39. For the early years of the company, see William Pettigrew, *Freedom's Debt: The Royal African Company and the Politics of the Atlantic Slave Trade, 1672–1752* (Chapel Hill: University of North Carolina Press, 2013), 22–26; Zahedieh, *Capital and the Colonies*, 247.

40. Wim Klooster, *The Dutch Moment: War, Trade, and Settlement in the Seventeenth-Century Atlantic World* (Ithaca, NY: Cornell University Press, 2016), 24–25, 81–83, 158–64.

41. *PDBP*, 1:342, 2:34.

42. *SLMC*, 3:268; *PDBP*, 1:310; Bernard Bailyn, *The New England Merchants in the Seventeenth Century* (Cambridge, MA: Harvard University Press, 1955), 127.

43. Report of the Council of Trade to the King, November 1668, in *DRNY*, ed. E. B. O'Callaghan and Berthold Fernow, 15 vols. (Albany, 1856–1887), 3:175. Also see Bailyn, *New England Merchants*, 127, 130, 144, 147.

44. Report of the Council of Foreign Plantations, April 30, 1661, CO 1/15, no. 42, p. 83; Minutes of the Council for Foreign Plantations, December 7, 1663, in *DRNY*, 3:47.

45. Quotation in Thomas C. Barrow, *Trade and Empire: The British Customs Service in Colonial America, 1660–1775* (Cambridge, MA: Harvard University Press, 1967), 9.

46. *SLMC*, 3:381–82; Barrow, *Trade and Empire*, 6–9; Bailyn, *New England Merchants*, 149–53, 182.

47. Minutes of the Council for Foreign Plantations, August 25, 1662, and December 7, 1663, in *DRNY*, 3:44, 47; *Acts of the Privy Council of England, Colonial Series* [*APCC*], ed. W. L. Grant and James Munroe, 6 vols. (Hereford, UK: 1908–1912), 1:366.

48. Victor Enthoven and Wim Klooster, "The Rise and Fall of the Virginia-Dutch Connection in the Seventeenth Century," in *Early Modern Virginia: Reconsidering the Old Dominion*, ed. Douglas M. Bradburn and John C. Coombs (Charlottesville: University of Virginia Press, 2011), 111–12; Koot, *Empire at the Periphery*, 120–24.

49. Joseph Trevers, *An Essay to the Restoring of our Decayed Trade* (London, 1677), 46–47.

50. Nuala Zahedieh, "Defying Mercantilism: Illicit Trade, Trust, and the Jamaican Sephardim, 1660–1730," *Historical Journal* 61, no. 1 (Mar. 2018): 82–84.

51. Minutes of the Council for Foreign Plantations, December 1663, in *DRNY*, 3:47. Also see Klooster, *Dutch Moment*, 167; Simon Middleton, *From Privileges to Rights: Work and Politics in Colonial New York City* (Philadelphia: University of Pennsylvania Press, 2006), 49.

52. George Downing to Lord Clarendon, February 12, 1664, quotation in Koot, *Empire at the Periphery*, 91.

53. Gijs Rommelse, "The Role of Mercantilism in Anglo-Dutch Political Relations, 1650–74," *Economic History Review* 63, no. 3 (Aug. 2010): 602–5; Jonathan Israel, *The Dutch Republic: Its Rise, Greatness, and Fall, 1477–1806* (Oxford: Clarendon Press, 1995), 766–76; Jonathan I. Israel, *Dutch Primacy in World Trade, 1585–1740* (Oxford: Clarendon Press, 1989), 271–79.

54. *PDBP*, 1:325–30.

55. Report of the Council of Trade to Charles II, November 1668, in *DRNY*, 3:175–6; Middleton, *From Privileges to Rights*, 52–58; Koot, *Empire at the Periphery*, 106–7, 153–56; Klooster, *Dutch Moment*, 98–100, 171–72.

56. Justin Roberts, "Surrendering Surinam: The Barbadian Diaspora and the Expansion of the English Sugar Frontier, 1650–75," *William and Mary Quarterly* 73, no. 2 (Apr. 2016): 226–27, 244–45, 255; Israel, *Dutch Republic*, 938.

57. Petition of the President, Council, and Assembly of Barbadoes to the Commissioners for Foreign Plantations, May 11, 1661, CO 31/1, pp. 45–46; Petition of the Representatives of Barbadoes to Charles II, September 5, 1667, CO 1/21, no. 102, p. 207; Petition from the Representatives of Barbados to Charles II, August 3, 1668, CO 1/23, no. 33, p. 68.

58. Nicholas Blake to Charles II, February 28, 1669, CO 1/67, no. 95, p. 326; Symon Lambart, Speaker of the Assembly, to Governor Willoughby, November 17, 1670, CO 31/2, p. 9; Presentments of the Grand Jury in Barbadoes, July 8, 1673, CO 1/30, no. 50, p. 111. Also see Petition of Willoughby to Charles II, November 1668, CO 31/2, p. 30.

59. Modyford to Bennet, May 10, 1664, and February 20, 1665, in CO 1/18, no. 65, p. 137 and CO 1/19, no. 27, p. 40; Report of the Committee of the Privy Council, August 10, 1664, CO 1/18, no. 93, p. 206; Modyford to Arlington, September 20, 1670, CO 1/25, no. 59iii, p. 152.

60. *Archives of Maryland: Proceedings and Acts of the General Assembly of Maryland*, ed. William Hand Browne et al., 72 vols. (Baltimore: Maryland Historical Society, 1883–1972), 3:365, 383–85.

61. *Archives of Maryland*, 1:444.

62. *Archives of Maryland*, 1:414–15.

63. John Ogilby, *America: Being an Accurate Description of the New World* (London, 1670), 188. For more on the Maryland coinage, see Andrews, *Colonial Period*, 2:329–30; Sylvester S. Crosby, *The Early Coins of America, and the Laws Governing their Issue* (Boston, 1875), 123–32; Walter Breen, *Walter Breen's Complete Encyclopedia of U.S. and Colonial Coins* (New York: Doubleday, 1988), 18–20.

64. Talon to Jean-Baptiste Colbert, November 10, 1670, in *DRNY*, 9:70; Colbert to Talon, June 4, 1672, in *DRNY*, 9:89.

65. Samuel Maverick, *A Briefe Discription of New England and the Severall Townes Therein* ([1660]), in *Proceedings of the Massachusetts Historical Society*, 2nd ser., vol. 1 (1884–1885), 241.

66. *Diaries of John Hull, Mint-master and Treasurer of the Colony of Massachusetts Bay*, reprinted in *Archaeologia Americana: Transactions and Collections of the American Antiquarian Society*, vol. 3 (Worchester, MA, 1857), 151–52.

67. Maverick, *Briefe Discription*, 241; John Giffard to Secretary Nicholas, 1661, CO 1/15, no. 45, p. 96.

68. Report of Mason and Godfrey to the King, February 15, 1662, CO 1/16, no.18, p. 37; Stuyvesant to the Directors of the WIC, October 19, 1660, in *DRNY*, 14:484.

69. The following account of this story emerged much later, in a 1768 letter to one Thomas Hollis, but further confirmation of this encounter came from the Massachusetts General Court on October 30, 1684, when they claimed in a letter to London that "in 1662, when our first Agents were in England, some of our Money was showed by Sir Thomas Temple at the Council-Table, and no dislike thereof manifested by any of those right honourable Persons: much less a forbidding of it," *Massachusetts Archives Collection*, vol. 106, no. 336, repr. in Crosby, *Early Coins*, 76. For the 1768 account—from which we have quoted—see *Memoirs of Thomas Hollis, Esq.*, vol. 1 (London, 1780), 397. Also see Mark Peterson, *The City-State of Boston: The Rise and Fall of an Atlantic Power, 1630–1865* (Princeton, NJ: Princeton University Press, 2019), 146–48.

70. George Carr to Arlington, December 14, 1665, CO 1/19, no. 143, pp. 334, 338–41.

71. *Records of the Governor and Company of the Massachusetts Bay in New England*, ed. Nathaniel Bradstreet Shurtleff, 5 vols. (Boston, 1853–1854), 4.2:211; Affidavit of Captain James and Mary Oliver, 1666, in *Massachusetts Archives Collection*, vol. 106, nos., 125, 139.

72. Petition of the Massachusetts General Court to Charles II, August 1, 1665, in *Documents and Records Relating to the Province of New-Hampshire, from the Earliest Period of its Settlement: 1623–1776*, ed. Nathaniel Bouton, 7 vols. (Concord, 1867–1873), 1:295.

73. George Carr to Arlington, December 14, 1665, CO 1/19, no. 143, p. 339.

74. *Records of Massachusetts*, 4.2:317–8; Bailyn, *New England Merchants*, 112–26, 159–60; Peterson, *City-State of Boston*, 149–51; Richard S. Dunn, *Puritans and Yankees: The*

Winthrop Dynasty of New England, 1630–1717 (Princeton, NJ: Princeton University Press, 1962), 151–63, 217–19.

75. Colonel Mathias Nicolls to Arlington, April 9, 1666, CO 1/20, no. 42, p. 82.

76. *Records and Files of the Quarterly Courts of Essex County, Massachusetts* [*RFQC*], ed. George Francis Dow, 9 vols. (Salem, MA: Essex Institute, 1911–75), 2:385; Joseph A. Goldenberg, *Shipbuilding in Colonial America* (Charlottesville: University Press of Virginia, 1976), 18–23; Stephen Innes, *Creating the Commonwealth: The Economic Culture of Puritan New England* (New York: W.W. Norton & Co., 1995), 298–305; James McWilliams, *Building the Bay Colony: Local Economy and Culture in Early Massachusetts* (Charlottesville: University of Virginia Press, 2007), 145–57.

77. *Records of Massachusetts*, 4.1:434, 4.2:88, 421.

78. *Massachusetts Archives Collection*, vol. 100, p. 136, repr. in Crosby, *Early Coins*, 105.

79. *Records of Massachusetts*, 4.2:567–68.

80. [John Woodbridge], *Severals Relating to the Fund* (1682), 1–7. Also see Margaret Ellen Newell, *From Dependency to Independence: Economic Revolution in Colonial New England* (Ithaca: Cornell University Press, 1998), 121–23; Joseph Dorfman, *The Economic Mind in American Civilization*, vol. 1 (New York: Viking Press, 1946; repr., New York: Augustus M. Kelley Publishers, 1966), 93–95; Andrew McFarland Davis, *Currency and Banking in the Province of the Massachusetts-Bay*, 2 vols. (New York: MacMillan Company, 1901), 2:67–69.

81. *Records of Massachusetts*, 4.2:533; *The Colonial Laws of New York, from the Year 1664 to the Revolution*, 5 vols. (Albany, 1894), 1:96–97.

82. *Records of Massachusetts*, 5:351, 373.

83. *SLMC*, 2:552; Roger Coke, *A Treatise Concerning the Regulation of the Coyn of England, and how the East-India Trade may be Preserved and Increased* (London, 1696), 19.

84. *The Acts and Resolves, Public and Private, of the Province of the Massachusetts Bay*, 21 vols. (Boston, 1869–1922), 1:70–71.

85. John Locke, *Further Considerations Concerning Raising the Value of Money* (London, 1695), 13.

86. William Lowndes, *A Report Containing an Essay for the Amendment of the Silver Coins* (London, 1695), 97.

87. Governor Christopher Codrington to the Lords of Trade, July 13, 1691, CO 152/38, no. 33; Minutes of the Council of Barbados, November 26, 1678, CO 31/1, p. 300.

88. *Records of Massachusetts*, 4.2:533.

89. Carla Gardina Pestana, "Early English Jamaica without Pirates," *William and Mary Quarterly*, 3rd ser., 71, no. 3 (July 2014): 339–40, 357; Mark G. Hanna, *Pirate Nests and the Rise of the British Empire, 1570–1740* (Chapel Hill: University of North Carolina Press, 2015), 102–8.

90. Hanna, *Pirate Nests*, 5–7; Janice E. Thomson, *Mercenaries, Pirates, and Sovereigns: State-Building and Extraterritorial Violence in Early Modern Europe* (Princeton, NJ: Princeton University Press, 1994), 22–23.

91. Oldmixon, *British Empire*, 2:161.

92. Lieutenant General D'Oyley to Admiralty Commissioners, June 7, 1659, CO 1/33, no. 56, p. 143; Cornelius Burough to Admiralty Commissioners, April 23, 1659, CO 1/33, no. 55, p. 137. See also Jon Latimer, *Buccaneers of the Caribbean: How*

Piracy Forged an Empire (Cambridge: Harvard University Press, 2009), 120–43; Thornton, *West-India Policy*, 67–76.

93. Hanna, *Pirate Nests*, 112–13.

94. Modyford to Bennet, February 20, 1665, CO 1/19, no. 27, p. 38; Nuala Zahedieh, "Trade, Plunder, and Economic Development in Early English Jamaica, 1655–89," *Economic History Review*, n.s., 39, no. 2 (May 1986): 215–16. See also Latimer, *Buccaneers of the Caribbean*, 144–63; Thornton, *West-India Policy*, 85–123.

95. Minutes of the Council of Jamaica, February 22, 1666, CO 140/1, p. 143.

96. John Style to Secretary Arlington, July 24, 1665, CO 1/19, no. 81, pp. 87–90; *Calendar of State Papers: Colonial Series, America and the West Indies, 1574–1738* [*CSPC*], ed. W. Noel Sainsbury et al., 44 vols. (London, 1860–1969), *1661–8*, no. 1023.

97. [William Burke], *An Account of the European Settlements in America*, 2 vols., 4th rev. ed. (London, 1765), 1:68.

98. Alexander O. Exquemelin, *Bucaniers of America, or, A True Account of the Most Remarkable Assaults Committed of Late Years Upon the Coasts of the West-Indies* (London, 1684), 1:106–7.

99. Nuala Zahedieh, "The Merchants of Port Royal, Jamaica, and the Spanish Contraband Trade, 1655–1692," *William and Mary Quarterly*, 3rd ser., 43, no. 4 (Oct. 1986): 584.

100. "An Account taken from Mr. Harris of New England," April 29, 1675, CO 1/34, no. 66, p. 140.

101. Stanley J. Stein and Barbara H. Stein, *Silver, Trade, and War: Spain and America in the Making of Early Modern Europe* (Baltimore: Johns Hopkins University Press, 2006), 107–8; Klooster, *Dutch Moment*, 174–75, 181–82; Zahedieh, "Defying Mercantilism," 80–82; Zahedieh, *Capital and the Colonies*, 247–48.

102. Zahedieh, *Capital and the Colonies*, 248; Zahedieh, "Merchants of Port Royal," 590.

103. *APCC*, 1:359; Petition of the RAC to the King, 1665, TNA: SP 29/142, f. 1.

104. Klooster, *Dutch Moment*, 13, 175–82; Zahedieh, "Merchants of Port Royal," 571–74.

105. Zahedieh, "Merchants of Port Royal," 592–93.

106. Pestana, "Early English Jamaica," 335–36.

107. Latimer, *Buccaneers of the Caribbean*, 162–81, 202–2; Hanna, *Pirate Nests*, 113–16.

108. Richarde Browne to Secretary Joseph Williamson, August 21, 1671, CO 1/27, no. 24, p. 69.

109. Hanna, *Pirate Nests*, 116.

110. Instructions for Lynch, December 31, 1670, CO 1/25, no. 107, pp. 267–70.

111. Robert Hewytt to Lynch, June 16, 1672, CO 1/29, no. 36i, p. 90. Also see Latimer, *Buccaneers of the Caribbean*, 227–41; Thornton, *West-India Policy*, 214–20.

112. Richard S. Dunn, *Sugar and Slaves: The Rise of the Planter Class in the English West Indies, 1624–1713* (Chapel Hill: University of North Carolina Press, 1972), 157; Hanna, *Pirate Nests*, 123.

113. Zahedieh, "Trade, Plunder, and Economic Development," 207.

114. Dunn, *Sugar and Slaves*, 203.

115. Zahedieh, "Trade, Plunder, and Economic Development," 207.

116. *RFQC*, 5:137, 246.

117. *RFQC*, 4:18.

118. *RFQC*, 6:90–91.

119. *Records of the Colony of New Plymouth in New England*, ed. Nathaniel B. Shurtleff and David Pulsifer, 12 vols. (Boston, 1855–1861), 4:184, 5:137. For other examples of country pay being used in New Plymouth in the 1660s and 1670s, see *Records of New Plymouth*, 4:97, 186, 5:69, 98, 8:121, 140, 11:216.

120. Proclamation of Governor Lord Windsor, October 10, 1662, CO 139/1, pp. 24–25.

121. Willoughby to Arlington, June 27, 1664, CO 1/18, no. 81, p. 174.

122. Hans Sloane, *A Voyage to the Islands Madera, Barbados, Nieves, S. Christophers and Jamaica*, 2 vols. (London, 1707–1725), 1:42. See also Assembly of Montserrat, 1670, in *CSPC, 1669–74*, nos. 372, 374; Assembly of Nevis, 1672, CO 154/1, p. 4.

123. *Acts of Assembly, Passed in the Island of Montserrat, from 1668 to 1740* (London, 1740), 19–20; John J. McCusker, *Money and Exchange in Europe and America, 1600–1775: A Handbook* (Chapel Hill: University of North Carolina Press, 1978), 256–57.

124. *Acts of Assembly, Passed in the Charibbee Leeward Islands, from 1690, to 1730* (London, 1734), 41; Mark Lewis, *Proposals to Increase Trade, and to Advance His Majesties Revenue* (London, 1677), 8.

125. Thomas Ashe, *Carolina, or, A Description of the Present State of that Country* (London, 1698), in *Narratives of Early Carolina, 1650–1708*, ed. Alexander S. Salley, Jr. (New York: Charles Scribner's Sons, 1911), 150. See also Curtis Nettels, *The Money Supply of the American Colonies Before 1720* (Madison: University of Wisconsin Press, 1934; repr., Clifton, NJ: Augustus M. Kelley Publishers, 1973), 113–14; Richard S. Dunn, "The English Sugar Islands and the Founding of South Carolina," *South Carolina Historical Magazine* 72, no. 2 (Apr. 1971): 81–93.

126. Thomas Woodward to John Colleton, June 2, 1665, in *The Colonial Records of North Carolina*, ed. William L. Saunders, 10 vols. (Raleigh, 1886–1890), 1:100.

127. Noeleen McIlvenna, *A Very Mutinous People: The Struggle for North Carolina, 1660–1713* (Chapel Hill: University of North Carolina Press, 2009), 13–45; Jonathan Edward Barth, "'The Sinke of America': Society in the Albemarle Borderlands of North Carolina, 1663–1729," *North Carolina Historical Review* 87, no. 1 (Jan. 2010): 1–12.

128. *Records of North Carolina*, 1:185–87, 219.

129. Menard, "Tobacco Industry," 158–59.

130. Detailed Account of the Public Levy, February 20, 1677, CO 1/39, pp. 101–6.

131. *JHB*, 2:22, 29.

132. *Archives of Maryland*, 2:220.

133. *Archives of Maryland*, 2:286–87.

134. McCusker, *Money and Exchange*, 189.

135. *The Memorial History of the City of New-York, From its First Settlement to the Year 1892*, ed. James Grant Wilson, vol. 4 (New York: New-York History Company, 1893), 298.

136. Cathy Matson, *Merchants and Empire: Trading in New York* (Baltimore: Johns Hopkins Press, 1998), 84–85; Middleton, *From Privileges to Rights*, 75–76; Koot, *Empire at the Periphery*, 167–69.

137. Sir John Werden to Andros, January 28, 1676, in *DRNY*, 3:236. Werden was the duke's secretary; the letter was Werden's reply to Andros's request.

138. York to Andros, April 6, 1675, in *DRNY*, 3:230; Werden to Andros, September 15, 1675, in *DRNY*, 3:234.

139. *Colonial Laws of New York*, 1:96–97.

140. *The Records of New Amsterdam, from 1653 to 1674 Anno Domini*, ed. Berthold Fernow, 7 vols. (New York: Knickerbocker Press, 1897), 6:404, 7:76, 83, 98.

141. [James Hodges], *The Present State of England, As to Coin and Publick Charges* (London, 1697), 85.

142. Minutes of the Council of Jamaica, October 21, 1671, CO 140/1, pp. 248–49; Minutes of the Council of Jamaica, December 21, 1671, CO 140/1, pp. 270–71.

143. Werden to Andros, January 28, 1676, in *DRNY*, 3:236.

5. Empire in Crisis and Flux, 1670–1677

1. Carew Reynell, *The True English Interest, or an Account of the Chief National Improvements* (London, 1674), preface.

2. Sir Joseph Williamson, "Observation on the State of New England," May 1675, *The National Archives-Public Records Office* (Kew, England) [TNA]: CO 324/3, p. 61. Williamson was a member of the Privy Council and the Lords of Trade and Plantations.

3. David Ormrod, *The Rise of Commercial Empires: England and the Netherlands in the Age of Mercantilism, 1650–1770* (Cambridge: Cambridge University Press, 2003), 142; Margaret Priestley, "Anglo-French Trade and the 'Unfavourable Balance' Controversy, 1660–1685," *Economic History Review*, n.s., 4, no. 1 (1951): 44–5.

4. Jan De Vries, *Economy of Europe in an Age of Crisis, 1600–1750* (Cambridge: Cambridge University Press, 1976), 80, 84–85; Joyce Appleby, *Economic Thought and Ideology in Seventeenth-Century England* (Princeton, NJ: Princeton University Press, 1978), 260.

5. Joseph Trevers, *An Essay to the Restoring of our Decayed Trade* (London, 1677), 18, 45; [John Houghton], *England's Great Happiness, or, A Dialogue between Content and Complaint* (London, 1677), 2; Petty, *Political Arithmetick*, preface; Robert Murray, *A Proposal for the Advancement of Trade* (London, 1676), 4. Houghton and Petty did not share these views; they were merely repeating the common opinion of the day.

6. Sir John Craig, *The Mint: A History of the London Mint from A.D. 287 to 1948* (Cambridge: Cambridge University Press, 1953), 155–57; Nicholas Mayhew, *Sterling: The Rise and Fall of a Currency* (London: Allen Lane, 1999), 96.

7. Sir William Petty, *Political Arithmetick* (1676; repr., London, 1690), 110; C. E. Challis, "Lord Hastings to the Great Silver Recoinage, 1464–1699," in *A New History of the Royal Mint*, ed. C. E. Challis (Cambridge: Cambridge University Press, 1992), 382.

8. Nicholas Mayhew estimates that £2.7 million of the £7.5 million in circulation in 1643 had been coined under Elizabeth; see N. J. Mayhew, "Population, Money Supply, and the Velocity of Circulation in England, 1300–1700." *Economic History Review*, n.s., 48, no. 2 (May 1995): 246–47.

9. Sir William Petty, *Quantulumcunque* (1682), in *Select Collection*, 162.

10. Craig Muldrew, "'Hard Food for Midas': Cash and Its Social Value in Early Modern England," *Past & Present* 170, no. 1 (Feb. 2001): 89–90; Appleby, *Economic Thought*, 217–18; Craig, *Mint*, 167.

11. William Lowndes, *A Report Containing an Essay for the Amendment of the Silver Coins* (London, 1695), 99–100.

12. *Diary and Correspondence of John Evelyn*, ed. William Bray, 4 vols. (London, 1857), 1:378; Samuel Fortrey, *Englands Interest and Improvement* (London, 1663), 35.

13. [William Petyt], *Britannia Languens, or, A Discourse of Trade* (London, 1680), 227–28; Dudley North, *Discourses Upon Trade* (London, 1691), 18–19.

14. Mayhew, *Sterling*, 97; Challis, *New History of the Royal Mint*, 699.

15. L.A. Clarkson, *The Pre-Industrial Economy in England, 1500–1750* (London: Batsford, 1971; repr., New York: Schocken Books, 1972), 146.

16. Muldrew, "Hard Food for Midas," 97–104; Christine Desan, *Making Money: Coin, Currency, and the Coming of Capitalism* (Oxford: Oxford University Press, 2014), 257.

17. Muldrew, "Hard Food for Midas," 92–93, 104–5; Richard Grassby, *The Business Community of Seventeenth Century England* (Cambridge: Cambridge University Press, 1995), 246–49.

18. Richard Haines, *The Prevention of Poverty, or, New Proposals Humbly Offered, For Enriching the Nation* (London, 1674), 15–16.

19. Fortrey, *Englands Interest*, 36.

20. John Brewer, *The Sinews of Power: War, Money and the English State, 1688–1783* (Cambridge: Harvard University Press, 1988), 207; J. Keith Horsefield, "The 'Stop of the Exchequer' Revisited," *Economic History Review*, n.s., 35, no. 4 (Nov. 1982): 511–13, 523–25; Mayhew, *Sterling*, 86, 90; R. D. Richards, "The 'Stop of the Exchequer,'" *Economic History: Supplement to the Economic Journal* 2 (1930): 45–62.

21. *Bishop Burnet's History of His Own Time*, vol. 1, ed. Thomas Burnet (1683/1724; repr., London, 1753), 428; J.R., *The Mystery of the New Fashioned Goldsmiths or Bankers* (London, 1676), 6.

22. Horsefield, "Stop of the Exchequer," 514–15.

23. *Diary of John Evelyn*, 2:70–1; Minutes of the Committee of Trade and Plantations, December 23, 1675, CO 391/1, pp. 56–57.

24. Petty, *Political Arithmetick*, preface, 96; Houghton, *England's Great Happiness*, title.

25. Appleby, *Economic Thought*, 25, 261, 264; Steve Pincus, *1688: The First Modern Revolution* (New Haven: Yale University Press, 2009), 50–52, 55–60, 66–67, 83–85, 90; Nuala Zahedieh, *The Capital and the Colonies: London and the Atlantic Economy, 1660–1700* (Cambridge: Cambridge University Press, 2010), 3–4, 20; Ralph Davis, *The Rise of the English Shipping Industry in the Seventeenth and Eighteenth Centuries* (London: Mac-Millan & Co., 1962), 15–21.

26. Petty, *Political Arithmetick*, 87.

27. Richard Haines, *The Prevention of Poverty, or, New Proposals Humbly Offered, For Enriching the Nation*, 2nd rev. ed. (1674; London, 1677), 4; [Slingsby Bethel], *An Account of the French Usurpation upon the Trade of England* (London, 1679), 4; Thomas Violet, *An Appeal to Caesar: Wherein Gold and Silver is Proved to be the Kings Majesties Royal Commodity* (London, 1660), 8, 29.

28. [James Burgh], *Britain's Remembrancer* (1746; 4th ed., London, 1747), 17.

29. Bethel, *French Usurpation*, 6.

30. Bethel, *French Usurpation*; Roger Coke, *A Discourse of Trade* (London, 1670), 38.

31. *The Uses and Abuses of Money, and the Improvements of It* (London, 1671), preface.

32. Fortrey, *Englands Interest*, 22, 28.

33. "An Act . . . for Prohibiting several French Commodities for Prohibiting Several French Commodities" (1678), p. 3, accessed on *Early English Books Online* (*EEBO*), http://eebo.chadwyck.com.

34. K. N. Chaudhuri, "Treasure and Trade Balances: The East India Company's Export Trade, 1660–1720," *Economic History Review*, n.s., 21, no. 3 (Dec. 1968): 497.

35. C. G. A. Clay, *Economic Expansion and Social Change: England, 1500–1700*, 2 vols. (Cambridge: Cambridge University Press, 1984), 2:167. See also Giorgio Riello, *Cotton: The Fabric that made the Modern World* (Cambridge: Cambridge University Press, 2013).

36. Appleby, *Economic Thought*, 166–67; Ralph Davis, *A Commercial Revolution: English Overseas Trade in the Seventeenth and Eighteenth Centuries* (London, Historical Association, 1967), 11–12.

37. John Blanch, *The Naked Truth, in an Essay Upon Trade* (London, 1696), 4–5; [Thomas Johnson], *A Discourse Consisting of Motives for the Enlargement and Freedome of Trade, Especially that of Cloth, and other Woollen Manufactures* (London, 1645), 3.

38. John Bland, *Trade Revived* (London, 1659), 14; William Carter, *A Brief Advertisement to the Merchant and Clothier about the Present State of the Woollen Manufactures of this Nation* (London, 1672), 14.

39. Roger Coke, *England's Improvements* (London, 1675), 57–58; Samuel Lambe, *Seasonable Observations Humbly Offered to His Highness the Lord Protector* (London, 1657), 20; Charles Davenant, *An Essay on the East-India Trade* (London, 1696), 9; Charles Davenant, *Discourses on the Publick Revenues, and on the Trade of England*, 2 vols. (London, 1698), 1:31.

40. Trevers, *Restoring of our Decayed Trade*, 12, 18.

41. Reynell, *True English Interest*, preface.

42. Jonathan I. Israel, *Dutch Primacy in World Trade, 1585–1740* (Oxford: Clarendon Press, 1989), 213–16.

43. Clay, *Economic Expansion*, 2:191; Ormrod, *Commercial Empires*, 277, 284, 309.

44. Wim Klooster, *Illicit Riches: Dutch Trade in the Caribbean, 1648–1795* (Leiden: KITLV Press, 1998), 12, 14.

45. Jan de Vries, "Connecting Europe and Asia: A Quantitative Analysis of the Cape-Route Trade, 1497–1795," in *Global Connections and Monetary History, 1470–1800*, ed. Dennis O. Flynn, Arturo Giráldez, and Richard von Glahn (Aldershot, UK: Ashgate Publishing, 2003), 75–77, 88–90.

46. Thomas James Dandelet, *The Renaissance of Empire in Early Modern Europe* (Cambridge: Cambridge University Press, 2014), 204–29.

47. Jonathan Israel, *The Dutch Republic: Its Rise, Greatness, and Fall, 1477–1806* (Oxford: Clarendon Press, 1995), 739–41, 777–78.

48. Jonathan Israel, *The Dutch Republic: Its Rise, Greatness, and Fall, 1477–1806* (Oxford: Clarendon Press, 1995), 739–41, 777–78; Israel, *Dutch Primacy*, 282–84; Dandelet, *Renaissance of Empire*, 241.

49. Quotation in Peer Vries, *State, Economy and the Great Divergence: Great Britain and China, 1680s–1850s* (London: Bloomsbury Academic, 2015), 325.

50. Israel, *Dutch Republic*, 779–85; Israel, *Dutch Primacy*, 289–92; Dandelet, *Renaissance of Empire*, 235.

51. Geoffrey Holmes, *The Making of a Great Power: Late Stuart and Early Georgian Britain* (London: Longman, 1993), 90, 95.

52. Israel, *Dutch Primacy*, 293–96; Israel, *Dutch Republic*, 796–805; Steven C. A. Pincus, "From Butterboxes to Wooden Shoes: The Shift in English Popular Sentiment

from Anti-Dutch to Anti-French in the 1670s," *Historical Journal* 38, no. 2 (June 1995): 354–56.

53. Algernon Sidney, "Court Maxims," 1666, Warwickshire SRO, 152, quotation in Pincus, *1688*, 313; Andrew Marvell, *An Account of the Growth of Popery and Arbitrary Government in England* (Amsterdam, 1677), 16, quotation in Pincus, *1688*, 314.

54. Algernon Sidney, "Court Maxims," Warwick County Record Office, p. 177, quotation in Pincus, "Butterboxes," 341.

55. Examination of Thomas Joyce by Henry Coventry, December 26, 1672, Longleat House, Coventry MSS XI, fo. 51, quotation in Pincus, "Butterboxes," 343.

56. Sir Thomas Clarges, January 12, 1674, in Anchitell Grey, *Debates of the House of Commons from the Year 1667 to the Year 1694* (London, 1763), 1:232, quotation in Pincus, "Butterboxes," 344; Hentry Ball to Sir Joseph Williamson, September 19, 1673, in *Letters Addressed from London to Sir Joseph Williamson*, ed. W. D. Christie (London, 1874), 2:20, quotation in Pincus, "Butterboxes," 344. For more on English opposition to the Third Anglo-Dutch War, see Pincus, "Butterboxes," 341–61; Holmes, *Making of a Great Power*, 100–101, 112–16.

57. Israel, *Dutch Primacy*, 295–301; Israel, *Dutch Republic*, 812–13; Pincus, "Butterboxes," 360–61.

58. Israel, *Dutch Primacy*, 313–19; Klooster, *Illicit Riches*, 12–14.

59. Dandelet, *Renaissance of Empire*, 232; Richard Bonney, "The Rise of the Fiscal State in France, 1500–1914," in *The Rise of Fiscal States: A Global History, 1500–1914*, ed. Bartolomé Yun-Casalilla and Patrick K. O'Brien (Cambridge University Press, 2012), 93.

60. Zahedieh, *Capital and the Colonies*, 225.

61. Dandelet, *Renaissance of Empire*, 240–41; Wim Klooster, *The Dutch Moment: War, Trade, and Settlement in the Seventeenth-Century Atlantic World* (Ithaca, NY: Cornell University Press, 2016), 172–74; Philip P. Boucher, *France and the American Tropics to 1700: Tropics of Discontent?* (Baltimore: Johns Hopkins University Press, 2008), 168–228.

62. Pincus, "Butterboxes," 358–59; Holmes, *Making of a Great Power*, 90–101.

63. Petty, *Political Arithmetick*, preface.

64. Brewer, *Sinews of Power*, 12.

65. Klooster, *Dutch Moment*, 157–48, 175–82; Israel, *Dutch Republic*, 766–67, 934–41; Pincus, "Butterboxes," 336–38.

66. [William De Britaine], *The Interest of England in the Present War with Holland* (London, 1672), 2–3.

67. Pincus, "Butterboxes," 338–41, 355–58; Pincus, *1688*, 309–15.

68. Bethel, *French Usurpation*, 1–3, 6–7.

69. Pincus, *1688*, 315–16.

70. *The Statutes at Large, from Magna Charta . . .* [SLMC], 9 vols. (London, 1763), 3:391.

71. Holmes, *Making of a Great Power*, 115–16, 134; J. R. Jones, *Country and Court: England, 1658–1714* (Cambridge, MA: Harvard University Press, 1978), 180–96.

72. Brewer, *Sinews of Power*, 14–15, 20, 38, 89.

73. Bethel, *French Usurpation*, 7.

74. Zahedieh, *Capital and the Colonies*, 44.

75. Bethel, *French Usurpation*, 23–24.

76. [Slingsby Bethel], *The Present Interest of England Stated* (London, 1671), 9–10.

77. For more on this conflict of visions, see Craig Yirush, *Settlers, Liberty, and Empire: The Roots of Early American Political Theory, 1675–1775* (Cambridge: Cambridge University Press, 2011), 8–11, 16–19, 41–42, 49, 75–76; Jack P. Greene, *Negotiated Authorities: Essays in Colonial Political and Constitutional History* (Charlottesville: University Press of Virginia, 1994); Jack P. Greene, *Peripheries and Center: Constitutional Development in the Extended Polities of the British Empire and the United States, 1607–1788* (Athens: University of Georgia Press, 1986).

78. Thomas Hobbes, *Leviathan, or, The Matter, Form, and Power of a Common-Wealth Ecclesiastical and Civil* (London, 1651), 131; Instructions for the Council for Foreign Plantations, July 30, 1670, in Charles M. Andrews, *British Committees, Commissions, and Councils of Trade and Plantations, 1622–1675* (Baltimore: Johns Hopkins Press, 1908), 117.

79. John Hull to William Stoughton and Peter Bulkeley, December 22, 1677, *John Hull Letter Book, 1670–1685* (Worcester, MA: American Antiquarian Society), sec. 15, cited in John J. McCusker, "British Mercantilist Policies and the American Colonies," in *The Cambridge Economic History of the United States*, ed. Stanley L. Engerman and Robert E. Gallman, vol. 1 (Cambridge: Cambridge University Press, 1996), 355.

80. For more on this alternative colonial account of rights and law within the empire, see Yirush, *Settlers, Liberty, and Empire*, 8–9, 16–19, 49, 75–76.

81. For more on the colonial and merchant interests in London during this period, see Alison Gilbert Olson, *Making the Empire Work: London and American Interest Groups, 1690–1790* (Cambridge, MA: Harvard University Press, 1992), 27–29, 36–49.

82. Quotation in Thomas C. Barrow, *Trade and Empire: The British Customs Service in Colonial America, 1660–1775* (Cambridge, MA: Harvard University Press, 1967), 9.

83. Andrews, *British Committees*, 67–68, 75–80, 84–86.

84. Instructions for the Council for Foreign Plantations, July 30, 1670, in Andrews, *British Committees*, 117, 121–22, 126. See also Andrews, *British Committees*, 96–104; I. K. Steele, *Politics of Colonial Policy: The Board of Trade in Colonial Administration, 1696–1720* (Oxford: Clarendon Press, 1968), 5.

85. Instructions for the Council of Trade and Foreign Plantations, September 27, 1672, in Andrews, *British Committees*, 128–31. Also see Andrews, *British Committees*, 106–11; Steele, *Politics of Colonial Policy*, 6–7.

86. *SLMC*, 3:381–82.

87. Holmes, *Making of a Great Power*, 115–16, 134; Jones, *Country and Court*, 49, 180–96.

88. *Acts of the Privy Council of England, Colonial Series*, ed. W. L. Grant and James Munroe, 6 vols. (Hereford, UK: 1908–1912), 1:620.

89. Steele, *Politics of Colonial Policy*, 8–9; Greene, *Peripheries and Center*, 13–15; Greene, *Negotiated Authorities*, 47–48; Winfred T. Root, "The Lords of Trade and Plantations, 1675–1696," *American Historical Review* 23, no. 1 (Oct. 1917): 23–24, 31.

90. Barbara C. Murison, "Blathwayt, William (bap. 1650, d. 1717)," accessed on *Oxford Dictionary of National Biography* (Oxford University Press, 2004), http://www.oxforddnb.com.ezproxy1.lib.asu.edu/view/article/2626.

91. Stephen Saunders Webb, *The Governors-General: The English Army and the Definition of the Empire, 1569–1681* (Chapel Hill: University of North Carolina Press, 1979).

92. Greene, *Peripheries and Center*, 14–15; Greene, *Negotiated Authorities*, 48; Philip S. Haffenden, "The Crown and the Colonial Charters, 1675–1688: Part I," *William and Mary Quarterly*, 3rd ser., 15, no. 3 (July 1958): 308–9.

93. See for example, Stephen Saunders Webb, *1676: The End of American Independence* (New York: Alfred A. Knopf, 1984); Yirush, *Settlers, Liberty, and Empire*, 57.

94. Jill Lepore, *The Name of War: King Philip's War and the Origins of American Identity* (New York: Knopf, 1998); James David Drake, *King Philip's War: Civil War in New England, 1675–1676* (Amherst: University of Massachusetts Press, 1999); Mark Peterson, *The City-State of Boston: The Rise and Fall of an Atlantic Power, 1630–1865* (Princeton: Princeton University Press, 2019), 122–26; Webb, *1676*, 221–44.

95. Richard S. Dunn, "Imperial Pressures on Massachusetts and Jamaica, 1675–1700," in *Anglo-American Political Relations, 1675–1775*, ed. Alison Gilbert Olson and Richard Maxwell Brown (New Brunswick, NJ: Rutgers University Press, 1970), 57.

96. Peterson, *City-State of Boston*, 126–29; Curtis Nettels, *The Money Supply of the American Colonies Before 1720*, repr. ed. (Madison: University of Wisconsin Press, 1934; Clifton, NJ: Augustus M. Kelley Publishers, 1973), 251.

97. *Records of the Governor and Company of the Massachusetts Bay in New England*, ed. Nathaniel Bradstreet Shurtleff, 5 vols. (Boston, 1853–1854), 5:120–21.

98. William Douglass, *A Summary, Historical and Political, of the First Planting, Progressive Improvements, and Present State of the British Settlements in North-America*, 2 vols. (Boston, 1749–1751), 1:525.

99. [John Wise], *A Word of Comfort to a Melancholy Country* (Boston, 1721), 8.

100. Russell R. Menard, "The Tobacco Industry in the Chesapeake Colonies, 1617–1730: An Interpretation," *Research in Economic History* 5 (1980): 152, 159; Zahedieh, *Capital and the Colonies*, 199, 208–9.

101. Sir John Knight to Shaftesbury, October 29, 1673, in *Documents Relative to the Colonial History of the State of New York*, ed. E. B. O'Callaghan and Berthold Fernow, 15 vols. (Albany, 1856–1887), 3:209–10.

102. Menard, "Tobacco Industry," 159; Charles Wetherell, "'Boom and Bust' in the Colonial Chesapeake Economy," *Journal of Interdisciplinary History* 15, no. 2 (Autumn 1984): 189.

103. Richard L. Morton, *Colonial Virginia*, vol. 1 (Chapel Hill: University of North Carolina Press, 1960), 193, 215–16; Wilcomb E. Washburn, *The Governor and the Rebel: A History of Bacon's Rebellion in Virginia* (Chapel Hill: University of North Carolina Press, 1957), 31; Thomas J. Wertenbaker, *Virginia Under the Stuarts, 1607–1688* (Princeton: Princeton University Press, 1914), 127–33.

104. Warren M. Billings, "The Causes of Bacon's Rebellion: Some Suggestions," *Virginia Magazine of History and Biography* 78, no. 4 (Oct. 1970); 424–27; Morton, *Colonial Virginia*, 216–24.

105. Webb, *1676*, 18–9; Billings, "Causes of Bacon's Rebellion," 418–19; Morton, *Colonial Virginia*, 220–23.

106. *The Statutes at Large; Being a Collection of All the Laws of Virginia, from the First Session of the Legislature in the Year 1619*, ed. William Waller Hening, 13 vols. (Richmond, Philadelphia, and New York, 1809–1823), 2:23, 106.

107. *The Statutes at Large . . . of Virginia*, 2:282.

108. Morton, *Colonial Virginia*, 230–39; Billings, "Causes of Bacon's Rebellion," 424; Washburn, *Governor and the Rebel*, 19–32, 40; James D. Rice, "Bacon's Rebellion in Indian Country," *Journal of American History* 101, no. 3 (Dec. 2014): 726–50.

109. Morton, *Colonial Virginia*, 238–46; Washburn, *Governor and the Rebel*, 17–19.

110. Morton, *Colonial Virginia*, 247–61.

111. Declaration of Nathaniel Bacon in the Name of the People of Virginia, July 30, 1676, in *Massachusetts Historical Society Collections*, 4th ser. vol. 9 (1871), 184–87.

112. Morton, *Colonial Virginia*, 265–77.

113. *Journals of the House of Burgesses of Virginia* [*JHB*], ed. H. R. McIlwaine and John Pendleton Kennedy, 13 vols. (Richmond, 1905–15), 2:101–3, 107–9.

114. Beverley, *History and Present State of Virginia*, 74–75, 78.

115. Affidavit of Timothy Biggs, August 15, 1679, in *The Colonial Records of North Carolina*, ed. William L. Saunders, 10 vols. (Raleigh, 1886–1890), 1:291–93; Robert Holden to the Commissioners of the Customs, June 10, 1679, CO 1/43, no. 71, pp. 124–26; Barrow, *Trade and Empire*, 24–27; Bailyn, *New England Merchants*, 151; Noeleen McIlvenna, *A Very Mutinous People: The Struggle for North Carolina, 1660–1713* (Chapel Hill: University of North Carolina Press, 2009), 46–70; Jonathan Edward Barth, "'The Sinke of America': Society in the Albemarle Borderlands of North Carolina, 1663–1729," *North Carolina Historical Review* 87, no. 1 (Jan. 2010): 13–15.

116. A. P. Thornton, *West-India Policy under the Restoration* (Oxford: Clarendon Press, 1956), 39–46, 51–56, 60–62, 167–68; Agnes M. Whitson, *The Constitutional Development of Jamaica, 1660–1729* (Manchester: Manchester University Press, 1929), 20–35, 154–56.

117. Minutes of the Council of Jamaica, in *Calendar of State Papers: Colonial Series, America and the West Indies, 1574–1738* [*CSPC*], ed. W. Noel Sainsbury et al., 44 vols. (London, 1860–1969), *1669–74*, nos. 642, 705.

118. Lynch to Worsley, July 8, 1673, CO 1/30, no. 49, p. 109.

119. Instructions for Lynch, December 31, 1670, CO 1/25, no. 107, p. 265.

120. *CSPC, 1669–74*, nos. 1206, 1232, 1241.

121. Journals of the Lords of Trade and Plantations, July 1676, CO 1/37, no. 31, p. 108. Also see Whitson, *Constitutional Development*, 73–74; Richard S. Dunn, *Sugar and Slaves: The Rise of the Planter Class in the English West Indies, 1624–1713* (Chapel Hill: University of North Carolina Press, 1972), 158; William Pettigrew, *Freedom's Debt: The Royal African Company and the Politics of the Atlantic Slave Trade, 1672–1752* (Chapel Hill: University of North Carolina Press, 2013), 26.

122. Coke, *Discourse of Trade*, 5, 13–14; Reynell, *True English Interest*, 7–8. For more on demographic concerns in the 1670s, see Paul Slack, "William Petty, the Multiplication of Mankind, and Demographic Discourse in Seventeenth-Century England," *Historical Journal* 61, no. 2 (June 2018): 301–25.

123. John Cary, *An Essay on the State of England, in Relation to its Trade* (Bristol, 1695), 65.

124. Cary, *Essay on the State of England*, 68; Petty, *Political Arithmetick*, 96, 99; William Penn, *Some Account of the Province of Pennsilvania* (London, 1681), 1–2.

125. Petty, *Political Arithmetick*, 88, 95.

126. Greene, *Peripheries and Center*, 15; David S. Lovejoy, *The Glorious Revolution in America* (New York: Harper & Row, 1972), 178–79.

6. Showdown in English America, 1675–1684

1. *Calendar of State Papers: Colonial Series, America and the West Indies, 1574–1738* [*CSPC*], ed. W. Noel Sainsbury, et al., 44 vols. (London, 1860–1969), *1675–76*, no. 403; Robert Southwell to the Duke of Ormond, November 13, 1677, Hist. MSS Commis-

sion, *Ormond*, new ser., vol. V, p. 386, cited in John C. Rainbolt, "A New Look at Stuart 'Tyranny': The Crown's Attack on the Virginia Assembly, 1676–1689," *Virginia Magazine of History and Biography* 75, no. 4 (Oct. 1967): 392.

2. Report of the Council of Foreign Plantations, April 30, 1661, CO 1/15, no. 42, p. 83; Sir William Petty, *Political Arithmetick* (1676; repr., London, 1690), 88.

3. *Diary and Correspondence of John Evelyn*, ed. William Bray, 4 vols. (London, 1857), 2:59–61.

4. Richard L. Bushman, *From Puritan to Yankee: Character and the Social Order in Connecticut, 1690–1765* (Cambridge, MA: Harvard University Press, 1967), 18–21.

5. Minutes of the Lords of Trade and Plantations [LTP], December 1, 1675, *The National Archives-Public Records Office* (Kew, England) [TNA]: CO 1/35, no. 50, p. 269.

6. Tim Harris, *Politics Under the Later Stuarts: Party Conflict in a Divided Society, 1660–1715* (London: Longman, 1993), 52–109; W. A. Speck, *Reluctant Revolutionaries: Englishmen and the Revolution of 1688* (Oxford University Press, 1988), 31–38; J. R. Jones, *Country and Court: England, 1658–1714* (Cambridge, MA: Harvard University Press, 1978), 197–216; Geoffrey Holmes, *The Making of a Great Power: Late Stuart and Early Georgian Britain* (London: Longman, 1993), 120–31.

7. York to Andros, January 28, 1676, in *Documents Relative to the Colonial History of the State of New York* [DRNY], ed. E. B. O'Callaghan and Berthold Fernow, 15 vols. (Albany, 1856–1887), 3:235.

8. Michael Garibaldi Hall, *Edward Randolph and the American Colonies, 1676–1703* (Chapel Hill: University of North Carolina Press, 1960), 1, 20; Thomas C. Barrow, *Trade and Empire: The British Customs Service in Colonial America, 1660–1775* (Cambridge, MA: Harvard University Press, 1967), 16–17, 30–34; Mark Peterson, *The City-State of Boston: The Rise and Fall of an Atlantic Power, 1630–1865* (Princeton: Princeton University Press, 2019), 153–55.

9. Hall, *Randolph*, 21–24, 30–31; Richard S. Dunn, *Puritans and Yankees: The Winthrop Dynasty of New England, 1630–1717* (Princeton: Princeton University Press, 1962), 214–16.

10. Bernard Bailyn, *The New England Merchants in the Seventeenth Century* (Cambridge, MA: Harvard University Press, 1955), 112–14, 143, 159–60, 168–69; Dunn, *Puritans and Yankees*, 217–19.

11. Randolph to Secretary Henry Coventry, June 17, 1676, in *Edward Randolph: Including his Letters and Official Papers . . . [Randolph Letters]*, ed. Robert Noxon Toppan and Alfred T. S. Goodrick, 7 vols. (Boston, 1898–1909), 2:205.

12. Randolph, "An answer to severall heads of enquiry . . . ," October 12, 1676, in *Randolph Letters*, 2:225. See also Hall, *Randolph*, 26–30; David S. Lovejoy, *The Glorious Revolution in America* (New York: Harper & Row, 1972), 139–40.

13. *Randolph Letters*, 2:229.

14. Minutes of the Council for Foreign Plantations, 21 June 1671, CO 1/26, no. 78, p. 200.

15. Increase Mather, *An Earnest Exhortation to the Inhabitants of New-England* (Boston, 1676), 1, 22. The classic work on this subject is Perry Miller, "Errand into the Wilderness," *William and Mary Quarterly*, 3rd ser., 10, no. 1 (Jan. 1953): 3–32.

16. *Records of the Governor and Company of the Massachusetts Bay in New England*, ed. Nathaniel Bradstreet Shurtleff, 5 vols. (Boston, 1853–1854), 4.2:211.

17. Petition of Mason to Charles II, July 1676, in *Documents and Records Relating to the Province of New-Hampshire, from the Earliest Period of its Settlement: 1623–1776*, ed.

Nathaniel Bouton, 7 vols. (Concord, 1867–1873), 1:325; Sir Joseph Williamson, "Observation on the State of New England," May 1675, CO 324/3, p. 60; Minutes of the LTP, December 1, 1675, CO 1/35, no. 50, p. 269.

18. *Randolph Letters*, 2:231–2, 249.

19. *Randolph Letters*, 2:235–6, 249–50, 253–54, 258.

20. *Randolph Letters*, 2:266.

21. Objections against the Massachusetts Charter, July 20, 1677, CO 1/41, no. 35, p. 85.

22. Memoranda concerning New England, July 20, 1677, CO 1/41, no. 32, p. 75.

23. Journals of the LTP, July 19, 1677, *Randolph Letters*, 2:276–7; Answer of the Agents of the Massachusetts, July 20, 1677, CO 1/41, no. 31, pp. 72–73.

24. Journals of the LTP, July 27 and August 2, 1677, *Randolph Letters*, 2:277–79, 283.

25. Answer of the Agents of the Massachusetts, July 20, 1677, CO 1/41, no. 31, p. 72.

26. Sylvester S. Crosby, *The Early Coins of America, and the Laws Governing their Issue* (Boston, 1875), 133–34.

27. *Records of Massachusetts*, 5:203.

28. *Records of Massachusetts*, 5:163.

29. *Records of Massachusetts*, 5:155.

30. Hall, *Randolph*, 39–41.

31. Journals of the LTP, March 25, 1678, *Randolph Letters*, 2:285–87.

32. Randolph to the LTP, n.d. [March or April 1678], *Randolph Letters*, 6:72–75.

33. Stoughton and Bulkeley to the LTP, June 28 and July 2, 1678, *Randolph Letters*, 2:269, 3:7–8, 14–16.

34. Stoughton and Bulkeley to the LTP, n.d., *Randolph Letters*, 6:75–77; *Acts of the Privy Council of England, Colonial Series [APCC]*, ed. W. L. Grant and James Munroe, 6 vols. (Hereford, UK: 1908–1912), 1:843; Hall, *Randolph*, 42–46.

35. "Randolph's Welcome Back Againe," January 1680, *Randolph Letters*, 3:61–64; Randolph to Governor Josiah Winslow, January 29, 1680, in *Randolph Letters*, 3:65.

36. Randolph to Sir Edmund Andros, January 3, 4, and 7, 1680, CO 1/44, no. 31, pp. 75–76.

37. *APCC*, 2:22–23; Hall, *Randolph*, 55–58; Bailyn, *New England Merchants*, 166–67.

38. Henry Ashurst, Elisha Cooke, Increase Mather, and Thomas Oakes, "An Answer to Mr. Randolph's Account Touching Irregular Trade Since the Late Revolution," 1689, in *The Andros Tracts: Being a Collection of Pamphlets and Official Papers . . .* , ed. William H. Whitmore, 3 vols. (Boston: Prince Society, 1868–1874), 2:128.

39. Hall, *Randolph*, 58–60.

40. *Records of Massachusetts*, 5:192–93, 200.

41. George Carr to Secretary Lord Arlington, December 14, 1665, CO 1/19, no. 143, p. 338; second quotation in Lovejoy, *Glorious Revolution*, 125.

42. Randolph to Andros, January 4 and 28, 1680, CO 1/44, no. 31, pp. 75–77; LTP to Charles II, September 15, 1680, CO 5/904, pp. 87–88.

43. Petition of Randolph to Charles II, April 6, 1681, *Randolph Letters*, 3:90; Randolph to Sir Leoline Jenkins, April 20, 1681, *Randolph Letters*, 6:90–94.

44. Culpeper to the LTP, August 9, 1681, CO 1/47, no. 44, p. 93.

45. Report of the LTP, October 1681, CO 1/47, no. 79, pp. 188–90.

46. Dunn, *Puritans and Yankees*, 217–19; Hall, *Edmund Randolph*, 59–60; Lovejoy, *Glorious Revolution*, 146–50.

47. Letter from Randolph, December 21, 1681, CO 1/48, no. 112, p. 348.

48. Instructions to Joseph Dudley and John Richards, February 15, 1682, CO 1/48, no. 32, p. 147.

49. Randolph to the Earl of Clarendon, June 14, 1682, *Randolph Letters*, 3:159; Dudley Council, June 2, 1686, *Proceedings of the Massachusetts Historical Society*, 2nd ser., vol. 13 (Boston, 1899–1900), 244.

50. *Randolph Letters*, 3:229–34; Mather to Thomas Gouge, November 21, 1683, CO 1/65, no. 73iv, p. 329. See also Hall, *Edmund Randolph*, 61–83; Philip S. Haffenden, "The Crown and the Colonial Charters, 1675–1688: Part I," *William and Mary Quarterly*, 3rd ser., 15, no. 3 (July 1958): 300–307.

51. Hall, *Randolph*, 79–83; Haffenden, "Colonial Charters, Part I," 307; Lovejoy, *Glorious Revolution*, 156–57.

52. Sir John Knight to the Earl of Shaftesbury, October 29, 1673, in *DRNY*, 3:209–10.

53. Richard L. Morton, *Colonial Virginia*, vol. 1 (Chapel Hill: University of North Carolina Press, 1960), 207–11; Lovejoy, *Glorious Revolution*, 36–42; Thomas J. Wertenbaker, *Virginia Under the Stuarts, 1607–1688* (Princeton: Princeton University Press, 1914), 123–26.

54. Petition of Virginia agents, November 1675, in John Burk, *The History of Virginia, from its First Settlement to the Present Day*, vol. 2 (Petersburg, 1805), xlv-liii.

55. Petition of Virginia Agents, 1676, in Burk, *History of Virginia*.

56. Draft of the Virginia Charter, March 3, 1676, in *Virginia Magazine of History and Biography* [*VMHB*] 56, no. 3 (July 1948): 264–65; Report of the Privy Council, November 19, 1675, in *The Statutes at Large; Being a Collection of All the Laws of Virginia, from the First Session of the Legislature in the Year 1619*, ed. William Waller Hening, 13 vols. (Richmond, Philadelphia, and New York, 1809–1823), 2:528–32.

57. Petition of Virginia Agents, 1676, in Burk, *History of Virginia*, lx; "Remonstrances against the stoppage of the charter," 1676, in *Statutes of Virginia*, 2:539.

58. Petition of Sarah Bland to Charles II, April 22, 1676, in *VMHB* 20, no. 4 (Oct. 1912): 850–52.

59. "Draft of the Virginia Charter," 265.

60. "Remonstrances against the stoppage," 2:534–36; Order of the King in Council, May 31, 1676, in *CSPC, 1675–76*, no. 935.

61. Proposals of Thomas Ludwell and Robert Smith, 1676, in *VMHB* 1, no. 4 (Apr. 1894): 433–35; "Remonstrances against the stoppage," 2:541.

62. Bland to Sir Joseph Williamson, April 28, 1676, in *VMHB* 20, no. 4 (Oct. 1912): 352–55; Bland to Thomas Povy, July 8, 1676, CO 1/37, no. 81.

63. Blathwayt to the Earl of Carlisle, May 31, 1679, cited in Lovejoy, *Glorious Revolution*, 50; Berkeley to Secretary Coventry, June 3, 1676, Coventry MS, LXXVII, p. 103, cited in John C. Rainbolt, "A New Look at Stuart 'Tyranny': The Crown's Attack on the Virginia Assembly, 1676–1689," *VMHB* 75, no. 4 (Oct. 1967): 391.

64. Virginia Charter, October 10, 1676, in *Statutes of Virginia*, 2:532–33.

65. Proclamation of Charles II, October 10, 1676, in *Statutes of Virginia*, 2:423–24; Instructions to Berkeley, November 13, 1676, in *Statutes of Virginia*, 2:424–26.

66. Rainbolt, "New Look at Stuart 'Tyranny,'" 389; Lovejoy, *Glorious Revolution*, 51.

67. William Harbord to the Earl of Essex, December 17, 1676, in *Selections from the Correspondence of Arthur Capel, Earl of Essex, 1675–77*, ed. Clement Edwards Pike (London, 1913), p. 87, cited in Rainbolt, "New Look at Stuart 'Tyranny,'" 389.

68. Commissioners for Virginia to Thomas Watkins, March 27, 1677, CO 1/39, no. 52; Commissioners for Virginia to Secretary Coventry, April 5, 1677, CO 5/1371, pp. 182–87.

69. *CSPC, 1675–76*, no. 599; *CSPC, 1677–80*, no. 360; Morton, *Colonial Virginia*, 291–96; Lovejoy, *Glorious Revolution*, 53–55; Rainbolt, "New Look at Stuart 'Tyranny,'" 393–97.

70. Francis Moryson to Blathwayt, October 25, 1678, in *VMHB* 24, no. 1 (Jan. 1916): 78; Order of the Privy Council, October 30, 1678, CO 1/42, no. 356.

71. Instructions to Culpeper, December 5, 1679, in *VMHB* 14, no. 4 (Apr. 1907): 361; Lovejoy, *Glorious Revolution*, 55–57; Rainbolt, "New Look at Stuart 'Tyranny,'" 398–400. For the original treatment on the institutionalization of "garrison government" in this period, see Stephen Saunders Webb, *The Governors-General: The English Army and the Definition of the Empire, 1569–1681* (Chapel Hill: University of North Carolina Press, 1979).

72. *Statutes of Virginia*, 2:466–69; Morton, *Colonial Virginia*, 298–99; Lovejoy, *Glorious Revolution*, 78–79; Rainbolt, "New Look at Stuart 'Tyranny,'" 398–400.

73. *Journals of the House of Burgesses of Virginia* [*JHB*], ed. H. R. McIlwaine and John Pendleton Kennedy, 13 vols. (Richmond, 1905–1915), 2:141, 146.

74. Culpeper to the LTP, December 12, 1681, CO 1/47, no. 105, p. 262; Journal of the LTP, December 20, 1681, and January 21, 1682, CO 391/3, pp. 328–29, 340; Instructions to Culpeper, January 27, 1682, CO 5/1356, p. 58.

75. Culpeper to the LTP, October 25, 1681, CO 1/47, no. 80, p. 193.

76. Russell R. Menard, "The Tobacco Industry in the Chesapeake Colonies, 1617–1730: An Interpretation," *Research in Economic History* 5 (1980): 159.

77. *JHB*, 2:145.

78. Lovejoy, *Glorious Revolution*, 58–59; Morton, 304–5; Nicholas Spencer to Secretary Leoline Jenkins, May 3, 1682, and Sir Henry Chichley to Jenkins, May 1682, in *VMHB* 28, no. 2 (Apr. 1920): 120.

79. *Executive Journals of the Council of Colonial Virginia* [*EJCV*], ed. H. R. McIlwaine and Wilmer L. Hall, 5 vols. (Richmond, 1925–1945), 1:35–36, 44–45.

80. Journal of the LTP, September 27, 1683, CO 391/4, p. 200.

81. *Statutes of Virginia*, 2:521–22. In 1681 Arlington had disposed of his share entirely to Culpeper.

82. Morton, *Colonial Virginia*, 310–13, 316; Wertenbaker, *Virginia Under the Stuarts*, 240; Lovejoy, *Glorious Revolution*, 60–63.

83. *CSPC, 1681–5*, nos. 1273, 1342–43; Morton, *Colonial Virginia*, 317, 330–31.

84. *LJCV*, 1:66.

85. *JHB*, 2:228–29, 243, 249; Lovejoy, *Glorious Revolution*, 67.

86. Menard, "Tobacco Industry," 138, 150.

87. Culpeper to the LTP, December 12, 1681, CO 1/47, no. 105, pp. 260–61.

88. Journal of the LTP, April 14, 1679, in CO 391/2, p. 326; Instructions to Culpeper, January 27, 1682, CO 5/1356, p. 39.

89. *EJCV*, 1:46.

90. *Statutes of Virginia*, 3:23–24; Rainbolt, "New Look at Stuart 'Tyranny,'" 403–4.

91. Richard S. Dunn, *Sugar and Slaves: The Rise of the Planter Class in the English West Indies, 1624–1713* (Chapel Hill: University of North Carolina Press, 1972), 203.

92. Mark G. Hanna, *Pirate Nests and the Rise of the British Empire, 1570–1740* (Chapel Hill: University of North Carolina Press, 2015), 134.

93. Nuala Zahedieh, *The Capital and the Colonies: London and the Atlantic Economy, 1660–1700* (Cambridge: Cambridge University Press, 2010), 233.

94. C. E. Challis, *A New History of the Royal Mint* (Cambridge: Cambridge University Press, 1992), 689–90.

95. F. Hanson, *The Laws of Jamaica* (London, 1683), preface.

96. William Pettigrew, *Freedom's Debt: The Royal African Company and the Politics of the Atlantic Slave Trade, 1672–1752* (Chapel Hill: University of North Carolina Press, 2013), 22–25, 30.

97. Zahedieh, *Capital and the Colonies*, 248; Nuala Zahedieh, "The Merchants of Port Royal, Jamaica, and the Spanish Contraband Trade, 1655–1692," *William and Mary Quarterly*, 3rd ser., 43, no. 4 (Oct. 1986): 590.

98. *APCC*, 2:35.

99. Curtis Nettels, *The Money Supply of the American Colonies Before 1720*, repr. ed. (Madison: University of Wisconsin Press, 1934; Clifton, NJ: Augustus M. Kelley Publishers, 1973), 18–20; Zahedieh, "Merchants of Port Royal," 589.

100. Dunn, *Sugar and Slaves*, 234; William A. Pettigrew, "Free to Enslave: Politics and the Escalation of Britain's Transatlantic Slave Trade, 1688–1714," *William and Mary Quarterly*, 3rd ser., 64, no. 1 (Jan. 2007): 25.

101. Justin Roberts, "Surrendering Surinam: The Barbadian Diaspora and the Expansion of the English Sugar Frontier, 1650–75," *William and Mary Quarterly* 73, no. 2 (Apr. 2016): 251; Hanna, *Pirate Nests*, 132.

102. Zahedieh, *Capital and the Colonies*, 117–18; Pettigrew, *Freedom's Debt*, 26, 218.

103. Hanna, *Pirate Nests*, 185.

104. *CSPC, 1669–74*, nos. 1206, 1232, 1241.

105. Journals of the LTP, July 1676, in CO 1/37, no. 31, p. 108. For another case, see *CSPC, 1675–6*, nos. 987–89. Also see Hanna, *Pirate Nests*, 129–30.

106. *CSPC, 1675–6*, nos. 471, 536–38; *CSPC, 1677–80*, nos. 39, 172, 174, 208, 270, 313, 368, 375, 398, 402; A. P. Thornton, *West-India Policy under the Restoration* (Oxford: Clarendon Press, 1956), 167–72; Agnes M. Whitson, *The Constitutional Development of Jamaica, 1660–1729* (Manchester: Manchester University Press, 1929), 27–28, 48, 56–72.

107. *CSPC, 1677–80*, nos. 412, 457, 465, 480, 641; Thornton, *West-India Policy*, 169–75; Whitson, *Constitutional Development*, 78–84; Lovejoy, *Glorious Revolution*, 22–23; Craig Yirush, *Settlers, Liberty, and Empire: The Roots of Early American Political Theory, 1675–1775* (Cambridge: Cambridge University Press, 2011), 57–58.

108. Journals of the LTP, July 1676, in CO 1/37, no. 31, p. 108.

109. Memorial of Carlisle to the LTP, 10 Nov. 1677, CO 1/41, no. 102, p. 248; Order of the King in Council, November 16, 1677, CO 1/42, no. 118, p. 312.

110. Carlisle to Secretary Coventry, August 14, 1678, in CO 138/3, p. 246.

111. *CSPC, 1677–80*, nos. 779, 786, 794, 807, 815–16; Whitson, *Constitutional Development*, 84–8; Thornton, *West-India Policy*, 176–77.

112. Carlisle to Coventry, September 10, 1678, CO 138/3, p. 250; Carlisle to Williamson, October 24, 1678, CO 1/42, no. 137.

113. Carlisle to the LTP, November 15, 1678, CO 1/42, no. 145.

114. Carlisle to Coventry, October 24, 1678, CO 138/3, pp. 277–84; Carlisle to Williamson, October 24, 1678, CO 1/42, no. 137.

115. LTP to Charles II, May 28, 1679, CO 138/3, p. 293; LTP to Carlisle, May 31, 1679, CO 138/3, p. 313.

116. Order of the King in Council, November 16, 1677, CO 1/42, no. 118, p. 312; Journal of the LTP, December 6, 1678, CO 391/2, pp. 270–71.

117. Henry Slingesby to the LTP, February 7, 1679, CO 1/43, no. 15, p. 24.

118. Journal of the LTP, February 21, 1679, CO 1/43, no. 20, pp. 31–32; LOT to Carlisle, 22 February 22 1679, CO 138/3, p. 262.

119. Carlisle to the LTP, June 20, 1679, CO 1/43, no. 76, p. 136.

120. LOT to Carlisle, February 22, 1679, CO 138/3, p. 262.

121. John J. McCusker, *Money and Exchange in Europe and America, 1600–1775: A Handbook* (Chapel Hill: University of North Carolina Press, 1978), 105, 157, 168, 189, 239–40, 246, 256, 276.

122. Carlisle to the LTP, June 20, 1679, CO 1/43, no. 76, p. 136.

123. Carlisle to the LTP, September 15, 1679, CO 1/43, no. 118, p. 209.

124. Lynch to the LTP, December 18, 1679, CO 1/43, no. 172, p. 326; *CSPC, 1677–80*, nos. 1559–61, 1566, 1571–72; Whitson, *Constitutional Development*, 98–110; Thornton, *West-India Policy*, 195–202.

125. Speech of Lynch to the Assembly, October 19, 1683, CO 1/53, no. 13, p. 63; *CSPC, 1681–5*, nos. 174, 227, 262, 668, 699, 711, 714, 743, 745, 948, 963, 966, 1236–37, 1275, 1311; Thornton, *West-India Policy*, 202–3, 208–10; Whitson, *Constitutional Development*, 116–27; Hanna, *Pirate Nests*, 141.

126. Haffenden, "Colonial Charters, Part I," 307.

127. Blathwayt to Effingham, December 9, 1684, quotation in Lovejoy, *Glorious Revolution*, 172–73.

7. Economic Rebellion, Competition, and Growth in English America, 1680–1685

1. Carlisle to Secretary Coventry, January 26, 1679, *The National Archives-Public Records Office* (Kew, England): CO 138/3, p. 287.

2. Mark G. Hanna, *Pirate Nests and the Rise of the British Empire, 1570–1740* (Chapel Hill: University of North Carolina Press, 2015), 141; Jon Latimer, *Buccaneers of the Caribbean: How Piracy Forged an Empire* (Cambridge: Harvard University Press, 2009), 260–61; Cyril Hamshere, *The British in the Caribbean* (Cambridge: Harvard University Press, 1972), 88–91.

3. Report of the Privy Council, January 27, 1681, CO 1/46, no. 89, p. 177.

4. Latimer, *Buccaneers of the Caribbean*, 223–41.

5. Vaughan to the LTP, April 4, 1676, CO 1/36, no. 40, p. 71; Hanna, *Pirate Nests*, 131.

6. Memorial of the Comte de Bergeyck, Spanish Envoy, April 10, 1677, CO 1/40, no. 57, p. 86; Petition of Dom Andreas de Camargo and John de Molina, September 16, 1676, CO 324/2, p. 101.

7. Secretary Henry Coventry to Vaughan, June 8, 1676, quotation in Richard S. Dunn, "Imperial Pressures on Massachusetts and Jamaica, 1675–1700," in *Anglo-American Political Relations, 1675–1775*, ed. Alison Gilbert Olson and Richard Maxwell

Brown (New Brunswick, NJ: Rutgers University Press, 1970), 60; Thomas Lynch, "Reflections on the State of Jamaica," June 20, 1677, CO 1/40, no. 111, p. 245.

8. Jamaica Council to the LTP, May 20, 1680, CO 1/44, no. 62, p. 414.

9. Alan Knight, *Mexico: The Colonial Era* (Cambridge: Cambridge University Press, 2002), 133, 177.

10. Lynch to the Lord President of the Council, June 20, 1684, CO 1/54, no. 132, p. 362.

11. Hanna, *Pirate Nests*, 132–35, 142.

12. Morgan to the LTP, July 14, 1681, CO 1/47, no. 29; Jamaica Council to the LTP, May 20, 1680, CO 1/44, no. 62, p. 414.

13. *Acts of Assembly, Passed in the Island of Jamaica, from the Year 1681 to the Year 1769*, 2 vols. (Kingston, 1787), 1:6–7.

14. Lynch to William Blathwayt, February 22, 1683, CO 1/51, no. 43, p. 102; Lynch to Secretary Sir Leoline Jenkins, July 26, 1683, CO 1/52, no. 35, pp. 66–69.

15. Deposition of Simon Calderon, 1682, CO 1/49, no. 139; translation from original Spanish in *Calendar of State Papers: Colonial Series, America and the West Indies, 1574–1738 [CSPC]*, ed. W. Noel Sainsbury et al., 44 vols. (London, 1860–1969), *1681–5*, no. 872. See also Hanna, *Pirate Nests*, 149.

16. Latimer, *Buccaneers of the Caribbean*, 244–62; Hamshere, *British in the Caribbean*, 88–91.

17. Governor Richard Coney to the Earl of Nottingham, October 21, 1684, CO 1/55, no. 53, p. 231; Carlisle to the LTP, November 23, 1679, CO 1/43, no. 157, p. 277.

18. Examination of Richard Arnold, August 4, 1686, CO 1/60, no. 20i, pp. 34–37; Robert C. Ritchie, *Captain Kidd and the War against the Pirates* (Cambridge, MA: Harvard University Press, 1986), 19, 25, 80–83; Latimer, *Buccaneers of the Caribbean*, 245–62; Hamshere, *British in the Caribbean*, 88–91.

19. Lynch to the LTP, February 28, 1684, CO 1/54, no. 41, p. 97.

20. Hanna, *Pirate Nests*, 13–16, 167; Ritchie, *Captain Kidd*, 19; Curtis Nettels, *The Money Supply of the American Colonies Before 1720*, repr. ed. (Madison: University of Wisconsin Press, 1934; Clifton, NJ: Augustus M. Kelley Publishers, 1973), 88–89.

21. Dyre to Secretary Jenkins, September 12, 1684, CO 1/55, no. 36, p. 98.

22. Letter from Cranfield, October 7, 1683, CO 5/904, p. 195; Relation of T. Thacker, Deputy-Collector, August 16, 1684, CO 1/55, no. 36ii, p. 102. For more on the sheltering of pirates in Rhode Island, see Hanna, *Pirate Nests*, 154–56.

23. Dyre to Secretary Jenkins, September 12, 1684, CO 1/55, no. 36, p. 98.

24. Nettels, *Money Supply*, 87n; Hanna, *Pirate Nests*, 136.

25. Cranfield to the LTP, August 25, 1684, CO 1/55, no. 25, p. 67.

26. *Edward Randolph: Including his Letters and Official Papers . . . [Randolph Letters]*, ed. Robert Noxon Toppan and Alfred T. S. Goodrick, 7 vols. (Boston, 1898–1909), 4:117, 279–80, 5:13.

27. *Some Considerations Upon the Several Sorts of Banks Propos'd as a Medium of Trade* (Boston, 1716), 3; John Colman, *The Distressed State of the Town of Boston Once More Considered* (Boston, 1720), 9.

28. Kevin P. McDonald, *Pirates, Merchants, Settlers, and Slaves: Colonial America and the Indo-Atlantic World* (Oakland: University of California Press, 2015), 45; Hanna, *Pirate Nests*, 150–54; Proprietors to Governor Joseph Moreton, February 1686, CO

5/288, pp. 75–76; Proprietors to Colleton, March 3 and October 17, 1687, CO 5/288, pp. 103–5, 124.

29. *An Essay on Currency* (August 1732; repr., Charlestown, 1734), 6.

30. Nicholas Spencer to Secretary Jenkins, July 16, 1683, CO 1/52, no. 29, p. 54.

31. *Acts of the Privy Council of England, Colonial Series [APCC]*, ed. W. L. Grant and James Munroe, 6 vols. (Hereford, UK: 1908–1912), 2:62.

32. Janice Thomson, *Mercenaries, Pirates, and Sovereigns: State-Building and Extraterritorial Violence in Early Modern Europe* (Princeton, NJ: Princeton University Press, 1994), 50; Hanna, *Pirate Nests*, 145–46, 178–79.

33. James II to William Penn, October 13, 1687, in *Pennsylvania Archives, First Series*, ed. Samuel Hazard, 12 vols. (Philadelphia, 1852–1856), 1:97; James II to Governor Thomas Dongan, October 13, 1687, in *Documents Relative to the Colonial History of the State of New York [DRNY]*, ed. E. B. O'Callaghan and Berthold Fernow, 15 vols. (Albany, 1856–1887), 3:490.

34. John J. McCusker, *Money and Exchange in Europe and America, 1600–1775: A Handbook* (Chapel Hill: University of North Carolina Press, 1978), 105, 157, 168, 189, 239–40, 246, 256, 276.

35. *The Public Records of the Colony of Connecticut*, ed. J. Hammond Trumbull and Charles J. Hoadly, 15 vols. (Hartford: Brown & Parsons, 1850–1890), 3:119; *Documents and Records Relating to the Province of New-Hampshire, from the Earliest Period of its Settlement: 1623–1776*, ed. Nathaniel Bouton, 7 vols. (Concord, 1867–1873), 1:480; *The Statutes at Large of South Carolina*, ed. Thomas Cooper and David James McCord, 10 vols. (Columbia, 1836–1841), 2:v; *The Statutes at Large of Pennsylvania, from 1682 to 1801*, ed. James T. Mitchell, Henry Flanders, Jonathan Willis Martin, Hampton L. Carson, and Gail McKnight Beckman, 17 vols. (Harrisburg and New York, 1896–1976), 1:152–3; McCusker, *Money and Exchange*, 175, 215.

36. James II to Dongan, May 29, 1686, in *DRNY*, 3:375; McCusker, *Money and Exchange*, 168.

37. *Statutes of Pennsylvania*, 1:152–3; *Minutes of the Provincial Council of Pennsylvania*, 16 vols. (Philadelphia and Harrisburg, 1851–1853), 1:72; Minutes of the Barbados Council, November 26, 1678, CO 31/1, pp. 299–300; *Records of the Governor and Company of the Massachusetts Bay in New England*, ed. Nathaniel Bradstreet Shurtleff, 5 vols. (Boston, 1853–1854), 4.2:533, 5:351, 373; McCusker, *Money and Exchange*, 175, 239–40.

38. Captain Thomas Wenham to the Board of Trade, November 2, 1704, in *DRNY*, 4:1119; second quotation from Thomas Lord Culpeper in 1676, cited in William Zebina Ripley, *The Financial History of Virginia, 1609–1776* (New York: Columbia College, 1893), 124.

39. Governor John Blackwell to Penn, January 25, 1689, in *The Papers of William Penn*, ed. Marianne S. Wokeck et al., vol. 3 (Philadelphia: University of Pennsylvania Press, 1986): 229–30.

40. Petition of New York merchants to Governor Lord Cornbury, June 25, 1705, in *DRNY*, 4:1133.

41. *The Grants, Concessions, and Original Constitutions of the Province of New Jersey [GCOC]*, ed. Aaron Leaming and Jacob Spicer (Philadelphia, n.d.), 285–86.

42. Governor Lord Cornbury to the Board of Trade, February 19, 1705, in *DRNY*, 4:1131.

43. *A Letter Humbly Offer'd to the Consideration of all Gentlemen, Yeomen, Citizens, Freeholders* (London, 1696), 19; Captain Thomas Wenham to the Board of Trade, November 2, 1704, in *DRNY*, 4:1119.

44. John Locke, *Further Considerations Concerning Raising the Value of Money* (London, 1695), 14; [John Locke], *Some Considerations of the Consequences of the Lowering of Interest, and Raising the Value of Money* (London, 1692), 144–45.

45. Petition of RAC, October 23, 1683, CO 1/53, no. 19, pp. 78–80.

46. Lynch to the Jamaica Assembly, September 21, 1683, CO 1/52, no. 100, pp. 247–48; Richard S. Dunn, *Sugar and Slaves: The Rise of the Planter Class in the English West Indies, 1624–1713* (Chapel Hill: University of North Carolina Press, 1972), 160.

47. Petition of RAC, October 23, 1683, CO 1/53, no. 19, pp. 78–80.

48. Lynch to the Jamaica Assembly, September 21, 1683, CO 1/52, no. 100, p. 248.

49. Petition of the RAC, January 12, 1683, CO 1/51, no. 6; Answer of Jamaicans, January 28, 1683, CO 1/51, no. 20.

50. Petition of Nathaniel Weare and others to the LTP, July 11, 1684, CO 1/55, no. 6i, p. 13; Cranfield to the LTP, October 16, 1684, CO 1/55, no. 50.

51. LTP to James II, April 8, 1685, in *Documents of New-Hampshire*, 1:570; LTP to Cranfield, April 29, 1685, in *Documents of New-Hampshire*, 1:572.

52. Commissioners of Customs to the LTP, September 27, 1684, in CO 1/55, no. 44, p. 166.

53. Rice Vaughn, *A Discourse of Coin and Coinage* (1630; repr., London, 1675), 164–65; Commissioners of the Mint to the Lords of the Treasury, September 27, 1684, CO 1/55, no. 45, pp. 168–69.

54. *Records and Files of the Quarterly Courts of Essex County, Massachusetts* [*RFQC*], ed. George Francis Dow, 9 vols. (Salem, MA: Essex Institute, 1911–1975), 3:456. For gold possession, see pp. 3:359–60, 372, 415–16, 8:349–50.

55. *RFQC*, 6:169, 8:9, 445.

56. *RFQC*, 6:197, 8:204.

57. *RFQC*, 7:64.

58. Nettels, *Money Supply*, 204.

59. *RFQC*, 5:204.

60. *Records of Connecticut*, 3:297.

61. *Records of Connecticut*, 3:119; *Documents of New-Hampshire*, 1:480–1.

62. *Records of the Colony of New Plymouth in New England*, ed. Nathaniel B. Shurtleff and David Pulsifer, 12 vols. (Boston, 1855–1861), 8:304, 11:223. For more, see pp. 5:168, 6:173, 197–99, 8:300–303, 310, 11:247.

63. *RFQC*, 7:255.

64. *RFQC*, 7:340.

65. *RFQC*, 7:384.

66. *RFQC*, 6:219–20.

67. *RFQC*, 6:420–21.

68. *Records of Massachusetts*, 5:269.

69. *Records of New Plymouth*, 6:54, 90, 11:247.

70. *Records of the Colony of Rhode Island and Providence Plantations, in New England*, ed. John Russell Bartlett, 7 vols. (Providence, 1856–1862), 3:236.

71. Louis Jordan, *John Hull, the Mint and the Economics of Massachusetts Coinage* (Hanover, NH: The Colonial Coin Collectors Club, 2002), 102–17; Mark Peterson, *The City-State of Boston: The Rise and Fall of an Atlantic Power, 1630–1865* (Princeton: Princeton University Press, 2019), 92, 110–11.

72. Peterson, *City-State of Boston*, 111–12.

73. Letter of Thomas Newe, 1682, *Narratives of Early Carolina, 1650–1708*, ed. Alexander S. Salley, Jr. (New York: Charles Scribner's Sons, 1911), 187.

74. *Executive Journals of the Council of Colonial Virginia*, ed. H. R. McIlwaine and Wilmer L. Hall, 5 vols. (Richmond, 1925–1945), 1:45.

75. John C. Coombs, "The Phases of Conversion: A New Chronology for the Rise of Slavery in Early Virginia," *William and Mary Quarterly*, 3rd ser., 68, no. 3 (July 2011): 336, 343, 358; Douglas Bradburn and John C. Coombs, "Smoke and Mirrors: Reinterpreting the Society and Economy of the Seventeenth-Century Chesapeake," *Atlantic Studies* 3, no. 2 (Oct. 2006): 139–43; April Lee Hatfield, *Atlantic Virginia: Intercolonial Relations in the Seventeenth Century* (Philadelphia: University of Pennsylvania Press, 2004), 52–54.

76. Coombs, "Phases of Conversion," 343, 359–60; Bradburn and Coombs, "Smoke and Mirrors," 142, 151.

77. John J. McCusker and Russell R. Menard, *The Economy of British America, 1607–1789* (Chapel Hill: University of North Carolina Press, 1985), 134–36.

78. Dutton to the LTP, November 16, 1682, CO 1/49, no. 104, p. 136; Dutton to the LTP, March 24, 1685, CO 1/57, no. 70, p. 175.

79. Minutes of the Barbados Council, November 26, 1678, CO 31/1, p. 300.

80. *RFQC*, 5:339.

81. Nuala Zahedieh, *The Capital and the Colonies: London and the Atlantic Economy, 1660–1700* (Cambridge: Cambridge University Press, 2010), 259–60; Dunn, *Sugar and Slaves*, 85.

82. Dunn, *Sugar and Slaves*, 87; McCusker and Menard, *Economy of British America*, 153.

83. Hans Sloane, *A Voyage to the Islands Madera, Barbados, Nieves, S. Christophers and Jamaica*, 2 vols. (London, 1707–1725), 1:42; Council Minutes, Montserrat, March 14, 1669, CO 155/2, p. 542; Governor Christopher Codrington to the LOT, July 13, 1691, CO 152/38, no. 33. Also see Dunn, *Sugar and Slaves*, 131, 137.

84. Lynch to the LTP, August 29, 1682, CO 1/49, no. 35, p. 131; Lynch to the Jamaica Assembly, September 21, 1683, CO 1/52, no. 100, p. 247.

85. F. Hanson, *The Laws of Jamaica* (London, 1683), preface.

86. Cathy Matson, *Merchants and Empire: Trading in New York* (Baltimore: Johns Hopkins Press, 1998), 74, 90–93, 111–12, 116; Christian J. Koot, *Empire at the Periphery: British Colonists, Anglo-Dutch Trade, and the Development of the British Atlantic, 1621–1713* (New York: New York University Press, 2011), 154, 205–8.

87. Matson, *Merchants and Empire*, 60–63, 90; James G. Lydon, "Fish and Flour for Gold: Southern Europe and the Colonial American Balance of Payments," *Business History Review* 39, no. 2 (Summer 1965): 177.

88. Wim Klooster, *The Dutch Moment: War, Trade, and Settlement in the Seventeenth-Century Atlantic World* (Ithaca, NY: Cornell University Press, 2016), 109, 133, 170–72, 180–83; Wim Klooster, *Illicit Riches: Dutch Trade in the Caribbean, 1648–1795* (Leiden: KITLV Press, 1998), 41–71.

89. Sloane, *Voyage to the Islands*, 1:xix, lvi; Koot, *Empire at the Periphery*, 205.

90. Nettels, *Money Supply*, 86–87.

91. Nettels, *Money Supply*, 107, 110; Matson, *Merchants and Empire*, 73; Joseph A. Goldenberg, *Shipbuilding in Colonial America* (Charlottesville: University Press of Virginia, 1976), 26–27; Simon Middleton, *From Privileges to Rights: Work and Politics in Colonial New York City* (Philadelphia: University of Pennsylvania Press, 2006), 7–8, 76–77, 103.

92. Sir John Werden to Dongan, August 27, 1684, in *DRNY*, 3:350; Dongan to Werden, February 18, 1685, in *DRNY*, 3:356.

93. Daniel Denton, *A Brief Description of New-York: Formerly Called New-Netherlands* (London, 1670), 15–17.

94. US Bureau of the Census, *Historical Statistics of the United States, Colonial Times to 1970*, vol. 2 (Washington, DC, 1975), 1168.

95. James T. Lemon, *The Best Poor Man's Country: A Geographical Study of Early Southeastern Pennsylvania* (Baltimore: Johns Hopkins Press, 1972), 3–5, 12–25, 42.

96. Francis Daniel Pastorius to the German Company, November 1684, in *Narratives of Early Pennsylvania, West New Jersey and Delaware, 1630–1707* [*NEP*], ed. Albert Cook Myers (New York: Barnes & Noble, Inc., 1912), 376.

97. *Statutes of Pennsylvania*, 1:152, 163.

98. Francis Daniel Pastorius, *Positive Information from America, Concerning the Country of Pennsylvania* (Philadelphia, 1684), in *NEP*, 397.

99. William Penn, *A Further Account of the Province of Pennsylvania* (London, 1685), 17.

100. Lemon, *Best Poor Man's Country*, 27–29; Lydon, "Fish and Flour," 177.

101. Thomas Budd, *Good Order Established in Pennsilvania & New-Jersey in America* (London, 1685), 16–17.

102. Gabriel Thomas, *An Historical and Geographical Account of the Province and Country of Pensilvania* (London, 1698), 9.

103. McCusker and Menard, *Economy of British America*, 309–10, 325, 329; Matson, *Merchants and Empire*, 248–49.

104. Denton, *Brief Description*, 17.

105. Budd, *Good Order*, 17.

106. Zahedieh, *Capital and the Colonies*, 58, 257, 263–64.

107. *The Present State of the Colony of West-Jersey* (1681), in *NEP*, 191; Zahedieh, *Capital and the Colonies*, 260–61; Lemon, *Best Poor Man's Country*, 30.

108. Denton, *Brief Description*, 18.

109. Zahedieh, *Capital and the Colonies*, 58, 263.

110. Not all historians agree with the argument that smuggling declined; English scholars tend to emphasize the persistence of smuggling in the colonies late into the seventeenth century. Nevertheless, many colonial American historians now seem to believe that smuggling substantially declined in the 1670s and into the early 1680s. Three of the more prominent include Nuala Zahedieh (excepting the contraband trade out of Jamaica), John J. McCusker, and Russell R. Menard; see Zahedieh, *Capital and the Colonies*, 6–7, 40–41; McCusker and Menard, *Economy of British America*, 77; John J. McCusker, "British Mercantilist Policies and the American Colonies," in *The Cambridge Economic History of the United States*, ed. Stanley L. Engerman and Robert E.

Gallman, vol. 1 (Cambridge: Cambridge University Press, 1996), 353–57. More recently, Christian Koot, in his study of English-Dutch interaction in the seventeenth century Caribbean, challenges this view; see Koot, *Empire at the Periphery*, 120; Christian J. Koot, "Anglo-Dutch Trade in the Chesapeake and the British Caribbean, 1621–1733," in *Dutch Atlantic Connects, 1680–1800*, ed. Gert J. Oostindie and Jessica V. Roitman (Leiden: Brill, 2014), 87–92.

111. McCusker and Menard, *Economy of British America*, 104, 136, 154.

112. Russell R. Menard, "Plantation Empire: How Sugar and Tobacco Planters Built Their Industries and Raised an Empire," *Agricultural History* 81, no. 3 (Summer 2007): 320; Zahedieh, *Capital and the Colonies*, 201.

113. Zahedieh, *Capital and the Colonies*, 173–83.

114. Cosmopolite [Joseph Cawthorne], *A Plan to Reconcile Great Britain and Her Colonies, and Preserve the Dependency of America* (London, 1774), 29–30. See also Nettels, *Money Supply*, 63.

115. Randolph to Parliament, 1689, in *Randolph Letters*, 5:11–2.

116. Minutes of the LTP, December 1, 1675, CO 1/35, no. 50, p. 269.

117. Memorial of the Commissioners of Customs, December 11, 1683, CO: 389/8, pp. 287–88.

118. James II to Governor Thomas Dongan, June 20, 1686, in *DRNY*, 3:385; *APCC*, 2:81.

119. Josiah Child, *A New Discourse of Trade* (London, 1693), preface; John Palmer, *An Impartial Account of the State of New England, or, The Late Government There, Vindicated* (London, 1690), 40.

120. Lynch to the LTP, August 29, 1682, CO 1/49, no. 35, pp. 134–35.

121. Matson, *Merchants and Empire*, 83–85.

122. Dyre to the Commissioners of the Customs, June 30, 1685, CO 1/57, no. 169, p. 417; *Archives of Maryland: Proceedings and Acts of the General Assembly of Maryland*, ed. William Hand Browne et al., 72 vols. (Baltimore: Maryland Historical Society, 1883–1972), 5:428–29.

123. LTP to Andros, January 12, 1687, in *Randolph Letters*, 4:145–47; Koot, *Empire at the Periphery*, 208.

124. Nathaniel Bacon Sr. to Blathwayt, August 26, 1682, quotation in David S. Lovejoy, *The Glorious Revolution in America* (New York: Harper & Row, 1972), 61.

125. Robert C. Nash, "The English and Scottish Tobacco Trades in the Seventeenth and Eighteenth Centuries: Legal and Illegal Trade," *Economic History Review*, n.s., 35, no. 3 (Aug. 1982): 363–64.

126. Randolph to the Commissioners of Customs, December 7, 1695, CO 324/5, p. 353; Victor Enthoven and Wim Klooster, "The Rise and Fall of the Virginia-Dutch Connection in the Seventeenth Century," in *Early Modern Virginia: Reconsidering the Old Dominion*, ed. Douglas M. Bradburn and John C. Coombs (Charlottesville: University of Virginia Press, 2011), 111–12.

127. George Muschamp to the Lords Proprietors, April 11, 1687, CO 1/62, no. 19, p. 93.

128. Memorandum of Commissioners of Customs, March 30, 1685, CO 1/57, no. 75, p. 188; Petition of Sir Richard Dutton to the King, September 7, 1681, CO 1/47, no. 27, p. 59; Koot, *Empire at the Periphery*, 120–24; Koot, "Anglo-Dutch Trade," 88; Susan Dwyer Amussen *Caribbean Exchanges: Slavery and the Transformation of English Society, 1640–1700* (Chapel Hill: University of North Carolina Press, 2007), 104.

129. Report of Captain St. Lowe, May 1687, CO 1/62, no. 62, pp. 224–25.

130. Zahedieh, *Capital and the Colonies*, 117–18, 216; David W. Galenson, "The Atlantic Slave Trade and the Barbados Market, 1673–1723," *Journal of Economic History* 42, no. 3 (Sept. 1982): 504.

131. Petition of the Royal African Company, September 9, 1680, in *APCC*, 2:8; Dunn, *Sugar and Slaves*, 232–33.

132. William Pettigrew, *Freedom's Debt: The Royal African Company and the Politics of the Atlantic Slave Trade, 1672–1752* (Chapel Hill: University of North Carolina Press, 2013), 26.

133. Letter to the RAC from factors on Barbados, May 30, 1681, CO 1/47, no. 96, p. 231.

134. Dunn, *Sugar and Slaves*, 235–37.

135. Koot, "Anglo-Dutch Trade," 87–90.

136. Ralph Davis, *A Commercial Revolution: English Overseas Trade in the Seventeenth and Eighteenth Centuries* (London: Historical Association, 1967), 4, 9–14; Ralph Davis, "English Foreign Trade, 1660–1700," *Economic History Review*, n.s., 7, no. 2 (1954): 158–59; Perry Gauci, *Emporium of the World: The Merchants of London, 1660–1800* (London: Hambledon Continuum, 2007), 18–27.

137. C. G. A. Clay, *Economic Expansion and Social Change: England, 1500–1700*, 2 vols (Cambridge: Cambridge University Press, 1984), 2:167; Davis, *Commercial Revolution*, 12.

138. Marchamont Nedham, *The Case of the Kingdom Stated* (London, 1647), 10; [William Petyt], *Britannia Languens, or, A Discourse of Trade* (London, 1680), 225.

139. C. E. Challis, *A New History of the Royal Mint* (Cambridge: Cambridge University Press, 1992), 689–90.

140. Zahedieh, *Capital and the Colonies*, 126.

141. Report of Stoughton and Bulkeley to the LTP, July 1678, in *Randolph Letters*, 2:269.

142. Ralph Davis, *The Rise of the English Shipping Industry in the Seventeenth and Eighteenth Centuries* (London: MacMillan & Co., 1962), 17–18; Zahedieh, *Capital and the Colonies*, 137–39.

143. McCusker and Menard, *Economy of British America*, 40.

144. Zahedieh, *Capital and the Colonies*, 267–75; Margaret Ellen Newell, *From Dependency to Independence: Economic Revolution in Colonial New England* (Ithaca: Cornell University Press, 1998), 94–96.

145. Dalby Thomas, *An Historical Account of the Rice and Growth of the West-India Collonies* (London, 1690), 28.

146. *The True Causes of the Present Scarcity of Money* (London, 1690), 7.

147. Nuala Zahedieh, "Overseas Expansion and Trade in the Seventeenth Century," in *The Origins of Empire: British Overseas Enterprise to the Close of the Seventeenth Century*, ed. Nicholas Canny (Oxford: Oxford University Press, 1998), 410.

148. Zahedieh, "Overseas Expansion," 404, 410; Amussen, *Caribbean Exchanges*, 40–14.

149. Zahedieh, *Capital and the Colonies*, 58, 189, 214.

150. Dunn, *Sugar and Slaves*, 85, 203.

151. Zahedieh, "Overseas Expansion," 411.

152. Thomas, *West-India Collonies*, 9, 21–23.

153. Pettigrew, *Freedom's Debt*, 30.

154. Zahedieh, *Capital and the Colonies*, 249; Pettigrew, *Freedom's Debt*, 30.

155. Zahedieh, *Capital and the Colonies*, 248; Nuala Zahedieh, "The Merchants of Port Royal, Jamaica, and the Spanish Contraband Trade, 1655–1692," *William and Mary Quarterly*, 3rd ser., 43, no. 4 (Oct. 1986): 590.

156. Zahedieh, *Capital and the Colonies*, 231.

157. Thomas, *West-India Collonies*, 9.

158. Reynell, *True English Interest*, 88–89.

159. Zahedieh, "Overseas Expansion," 410.

160. Russell R. Menard, "The Tobacco Industry in the Chesapeake Colonies, 1617–1730: An Interpretation," *Research in Economic History* 5 (1980): 159.

161. Menard, "The Tobacco Industry," 152.

162. Thomas, *West-India Collonies*, 27.

163. Zahedieh, *Capital and the Colonies*, 199.

164. *Journals of the House of Burgesses of Virginia*, ed. H. R. McIlwaine and John Pendleton Kennedy, 13 vols. (Richmond, 1905–1915), 2:228.

165. John Cary, *An Essay on the State of England, in Relation to its Trade* (Bristol, 1695), 69–70; John Pollexfen, *A Discourse of Trade of Trade, Coyn, and Paper Credit* (London, 1697), 91; Child, *New Discourse*, 204–6.

166. Jacob M. Price, "Colonial Trade and British Economic Development, 1660–1775," *Lex et Scientia: The International Journal of Law and Science* 14 (1978): 111–12; Goldenberg, *Shipbuilding in Colonial America*, 33, 99–106.

167. Child, *New Discourse*, 207; Reynell, *True English Interest*, 91.

168. Zahedieh, *Capital and the Colonies*, 264; Zahedieh, "Overseas Expansion," 415.

169. Edward Littleton, *The Groans of the Plantations* (London, 1689), 24.

170. Zahedieh, *Capital and the Colonies*, 263–64.

171. Carew Reynell, *The True English Interest, or an Account of the Chief National Improvements* (London, 1674), preface.

172. Petyt, *Britannia Languens*, 27, 150.

173. Littleton, *Groans of the Plantations*, 23, 30.

8. Revolutions of 1685–1689

1. C. E. Challis, *A New History of the Royal Mint* (Cambridge: Cambridge University Press, 1992), 690.

2. Steve Pincus, *1688: The First Modern Revolution* (New Haven: Yale University Press, 2009), 92, 96, 99–101, 104; David S. Lovejoy, *The Glorious Revolution in America* (New York: Harper & Row, 1972), 106, 160–67, 173, 236–37.

3. J. R. Jones, *The Revolution of 1688 in England* (New York: W.W. Norton, 1972), 55–56; J. R. Jones, *Country and Court: England, 1658–1714* (Cambridge, MA: Harvard University Press, 1978), 11; J. R. Western, *Monarchy and Revolution: The English State in the 1680s* (Totowa, NJ: Rowman and Littlefield, 1972), 83–85; W. A. Speck, *Reluctant Revolutionaries: Englishmen and the Revolution of 1688* (Oxford University Press, 1988), 31–32.

4. Pincus, *1688*, 121–25, 132, 316–23; Jones, *Revolution*, 11–13, 57, 129.

5. Tim Harris, *Politics Under the Later Stuarts: Party Conflict in the Divided Society, 1660–1715* (London: Longman, 1993), 119–24; Pincus, *1688*, 99–102; Jones, *Revolution*, 58–60; Speck, *Reluctant Revolutionaries*, 41–47; Tim Harris, *Revolution: The Great Crisis of the British Monarchy, 1685–1720* (London: Allen Lane, 2006), 46–61.

6. Pincus, *1688*, 144; Speck, *Reluctant Revolutionaries*, 55; Harris, *Revolution*, 187–91.

7. Pincus, *1688*, 125–26, 132–34, 145–46, 158–62, 178; Speck, *Reluctant Revolutionaries*, 56, 62–63, 171; Harris, *Politics Under the Later Stuarts*, 12, 117, 124; Harris, *Revolution*, 191–99, 229–36; Jones, *Revolution*, 21–23, 31–34, 62–67; Holmes, *Making of a Great Power*, 168–71, 181–85.

8. *The Statutes at Large, from Magna Charta . . .* 9 vols. (London, 1763), 3:405–8.

9. Nuala Zahedieh, *The Capital and the Colonies: London and the Atlantic Economy, 1660–1700* (Cambridge: Cambridge University Press, 2010), 189, 199.

10. Edward Littleton, *The Groans of the Plantations* (London, 1689), 1, 12.

11. *Legislative Journals of the Council of Colonial Virginia [LJCV]*, ed. H. R. McIlwaine, 3 vols. (Richmond, 1918–1919), 1:72–73.

12. Effingham to the Earl of Sunderland, November 13, 1685, in *The National Archives-Public Records Office* (Kew, England): CO 5/1357, p. 76; Effingham to Blathwayt, November 14, 1685, CO 5/1357, p. 80.

13. Russell R. Menard, "The Tobacco Industry in the Chesapeake Colonies, 1617–1730: An Interpretation," *Research in Economic History* 5 (1980): 138–39, 159.

14. Deputy-Governor, Council, and Assembly of Barbados to the LTP, September 14, 1685, CO 1/58, no. 56, p. 153.

15. Molesworth to Blathwayt, August 29, 1685, CO 1/58, no. 44, pp. 102–3.

16. Quotation in K. G. Davies, "The Revolutions in America," in *The Revolutions of 1688*, ed. Robert Beddard (Oxford: Clarendon Press, 1991), 249.

17. Deputy-Governor, Council, and Assembly of Barbados to the LTP, September 14, 1685, CO 1/58, no. 56, p. 153; Richard S. Dunn, *Sugar and Slaves: The Rise of the Planter Class in the English West Indies, 1624–1713* (Chapel Hill: University of North Carolina Press, 1972), 196, 205; Zahedieh, *Capital and the Colonies*, 214, 217.

18. Deputy-Governor Edwyn Stede to the LTP, September 21, 1685, CO 1/58, no. 59.

19. David Eltis, Frank D. Lewis, and David Richardson, "Slave Prices, the African Slave Trade, and Productivity in the Caribbean, 1674–1807," *Economic History Review*, n.s., 58, no. 4 (Nov. 2005): 679.

20. Proclamation of James II, April 1, 1685, in *British Royal Proclamations Relating to America, 1603–1783 [BRPA]*, ed. Clarence S. Brigham (Worcester, MA: American Antiquarian Society, 1911), 137–38; William A. Pettigrew, "Free to Enslave: Politics and the Escalation of Britain's Transatlantic Slave Trade, 1688–1714," *William and Mary Quarterly*, 3rd ser., 64, no. 1 (Jan. 2007): 11; Dunn, *Sugar and Slaves*, 160.

21. Joseph E. Inikori, *Africans and the Industrial Revolution in England: A Study in International Trade and Economic Development* (Cambridge: Cambridge University Press, 2002), 326.

22. Deputy-Governor Edwyn Stede to the LTP, September 19 and October 19, 1687, CO 1/63, nos. 38, 45, pp. 211, 220.

23. Stede to the LTP, October 19, 1687, CO 1/63, no. 45, p. 211. Littleton, *Groans of the Plantations*, 12, 18. Also see Richard S. Dunn, "The Glorious Revolution and America," in *The Origins of Empire: British Overseas Enterprise to the Close of the Seventeenth Century*, ed. Nicholas Canny (Oxford University Press, 1998), 453; Zahedieh, *Capital and the Colonies*, 41, 50.

24. *Journals of the House of Burgesses of Virginia [JHB]*, ed. H. R. McIlwaine and John Pendleton Kennedy, 13 vols. (Richmond, 1905–1915), 2:267.

25. *LJCV*, 1:75; *JHB*, 2:273.

26. *LJCV*, 1:117; Richard L. Morton, *Colonial Virginia*, vol. 1 (Chapel Hill: University of North Carolina Press, 1960), 316–24.

27. James to Effingham, August 1, 1686, in *The Statutes at Large; Being a Collection of All the Laws of Virginia, from the First Session of the Legislature in the Year 1619*, ed. William Waller Hening, 13 vols. (Richmond, Philadelphia, and New York, 1809–1823), 3:40–41.

28. Philip S. Haffenden, "The Crown and the Colonial Charters, 1675–1688: Part II," *The William and Mary Quarterly*, 3rd ser., 15, no. 4 (Oct. 1958): 452–56; Jack P. Greene, *Negotiated Authorities: Essays in Colonial Political and Constitutional History* (Charlottesville: University Press of Virginia, 1994), 48; Lovejoy, *Glorious Revolution*, 69, 97.

29. David S. Lovejoy, "Equality and Empire: The New York Charter of Libertyes, 1683," *William and Mary Quarterly* 21, no. 4 (Oct. 1964): 504–15; Craig Yirush, *Settlers, Liberty, and Empire: The Roots of Early American Political Theory, 1675–1775* (Cambridge University Press, 2011), 62–63.

30. Haffenden, "Colonial Charters, Part II," 461.

31. Michael Garibaldi Hall, *Edward Randolph and the American Colonies, 1676–1703* (Chapel Hill: University of North Carolina Press, 1960), 97–99; Lovejoy, *Glorious Revolution*, 155–57.

32. Blathwayt to Henry Guy, November 22, 1684, CO 5/904, p. 218; Commissioners of the Mint to the Lords of the Treasury, January 15, 1685, CO 1/60, no. 88iii, pp. 262–63.

33. Dudley to Randolph, December 1, 1684, in *Edward Randolph: Including his Letters and Official Papers . . . [Randolph Letters]*, ed. Robert Noxon Toppan and Alfred T. S. Goodrick, 7 vols. (Boston, 1898–1909), 3:336.

34. Lovejoy, *Glorious Revolution*, 159, 169–70; Hall, *Randolph*, 90–99.

35. Randolph to Blathwayt, May 29, 1686, in *Randolph Letters*, 6:172; Dudley Council, June 2, 1686, in *Proceedings of the Massachusetts Historical Society [PMHS]*, 2nd ser., vol. 13 (Boston, 1899–1900), 244.

36. Commissioners of the Mint to the Lord Treasurer, July 15, 1686, CO 1/60, no. 88ii, p. 260.

37. [Andros], "Reasons for a Mint in New-England," October 13, 1686, CO 1/60, no. 88v, p. 266.

38. Journals of the LTP, October 23, 1686, CO 391/6, p. 23; LTP to James II, October 13, 1686, CO 5/904, p. 325; Order of the King in Council, October 27, 1686, CO 1/60, no. 88, p. 256.

39. Hall, *Randolph*, 104–7; Richard S. Dunn, *Puritans and Yankees: The Winthrop Dynasty of New England, 1630–1717* (Princeton, NJ: Princeton University Press, 1962), 231–33.

40. Randolph to the Lord Treasurer, August 23, 1686, and Randolph to the LTP, August 23, 1686, in *Randolph Letters*, 4:113, 116–17.

41. [Mather], *An Earnest Exhortation to the Inhabitants of New-England* (Boston, 1676), 9; Theodore B. Lewis, "Land Speculation and the Dudley Council of 1686," *William and Mary Quarterly*, 3rd ser., 31, no. 2 (Apr. 1974): 256–57, 261; J. M. Sosin, *English America and the Revolution of 1688: Royal Administration and the Structure of Provincial Government* (Lincoln: University of Nebraska Press, 1982), 65.

42. Lewis, "Land Speculation," 258, 266.

43. Lewis, "Land Speculation," 261, 270.

44. Lewis, "Land Speculation," 260, 264–66, 269–71; Sosin, *English America*, 60, 65.

45. Lewis, "Land Speculation," 265, 271.

46. Lewis, "Land Speculation," 264, 270.

47. Randolph to Blathwayt, March 14 and 31, 1687, in *Randolph Letters*, 6:215, 218.

48. Dudley Council, September 27, 1686, in *PMHS*, 13:20, 272.

49. G. E. Aylmer, "Blackwell, John (1624–1701)," *Oxford Dictionary of National Biography* (Oxford University Press, 2004), accessed on http://www.oxforddnb.com/view/article/37197.

50. [John Blackwell], *A Discourse in Explanation of the Bank of Credit* (Boston, 1687), in *Colonial Currency Reprints, 1682–1751* [*CCR*], ed. Andrew McFarland Davis, 4 vols. (Boston, 1910), 1:122–26, 135–40; [John Blackwell], *A Model for Erecting a Bank of Credit: With a Discourse in Explanation Thereof* (London, 1688), 22. This latter pamphlet was a London reprint (with only slight modifications) of a lost edition printed in Boston in 1684. For secondary literature on Blackwell's banking scheme, see Dror Goldberg, "Why Was America's First Bank Aborted?" *Journal of Economic History* 71, no. 1 (Mar. 2011): 211–22; J. Keith Horsefield, "The Origins of Blackwell's Model of a Bank," *William and Mary Quarterly* 23, no. 1 (Jan. 1966): 121–35; Katie A. Moore, "The Blood That Nourishes the Body Politic: The Origins of Paper Money in Early America," *Early American Studies: An Interdisciplinary Journal* 17, no. 1 (Winter 2019): 15–23; Bernard Bailyn, *The New England Merchants in the Seventeenth Century* (Cambridge, MA: Harvard University Press, 1955), 184–87; Margaret Ellen Newell, *From Dependency to Independence: Economic Revolution in Colonial New England* (Ithaca, NY: Cornell University Press, 1998), 120–26; Joseph Dorfman, *The Economic Mind in American Civilization*, 2 vols. (New York: Viking Press, 1946; repr., New York: Augustus M. Kelley Publishers, 1966), 1:96–102.

51. Theodore Thayer, "The Land-Bank System in the American Colonies," *Journal of Economic History* 13, no. 2 (Spring 1953): 147.

52. Dudley Council, June 2, 1686, in *PMHS*, 13:248–49.

53. Randolph to the Lord Treasurer, August 23, 1686, and Randolph to the LTP, August 23, 1686, in *Randolph Letters*, 4:113, 116–17.

54. Dudley Council, September 27, 1686, in *PMHS*, 13:272.

55. Dudley Council, September 27, 1686, in *PMHS*.

56. Randolph to Blathwayt, March 31, 1687, in *Randolph Letters*, 6:218.

57. *Massachusetts Archives Collection*, vol. 127, p. 66; Davis, *CCR*, 1:148; Newell, *Dependency to Independence*, 123–24.

58. Blackwell, *Discourse in Explanation*, 126.

59. Molesworth to the Earl of Sunderland, April 28, 1686, CO 1/59, no. 63, p. 230; Minutes of the Jamaica Council, July 1, 1686, CO 140/4, pp. 117–23.

60. Memorandum of the LTP, June 3, 1687, CO 1/62, no. 68, p. 250; Memorandum of Albemarle, 1 July 1687, CO 1/62, no. 82, p. 281.

61. Minutes of the Jamaica Council, March 29–31, 1688, CO 140/4, pp. 216–18.

62. Memorandum of the RAC, July 19, 1688, CO 1/65, no. 26, p. 50; Molesworth, "Reasons against the bill,'" March 9, 1688, CO 1/64, no. 32, p. 142.

63. *Acts of the Privy Council of England, Colonial Series*, ed. W. L. Grant and James Munroe, 6 vols. (Hereford, UK: 1908–1912), 2:834.

64. *Archives of Maryland: Proceedings and Acts of the General Assembly of Maryland*, ed. William Hand Browne, et al., 72 vols. (Baltimore: Maryland Historical Society, 1883–1972), 13:142–44.

65. *Executive Journals of the Council of Colonial Virginia [EJCV]*, ed. H. R. McIlwaine and Wilmer L. Hall, 5 vols. (Richmond, 1925–1945), 1:79; Address of the Virginia Council to James II, July 2, 1686, CO 1/59, no. 113, p. 356; Memorandum of Effingham, April 3, 1687, CO 1/62, no. 18, p. 83.

66. Commissioners of the Customs to the Lords of the Treasury, April 30, 1687, CO 1/62, no. 31, p. 127; *EJCV*, 1:518.

67. Order of the King in Council, October 27, 1686, CO 1/60, no. 88, p. 256; LTP to James II, October 13, 1686, CO 5/904, p. 325; Journals of the LTP, October 23, 1686, CO 391/6, p. 23.

68. Richard S. Dunn, "Imperial Pressures on Massachusetts and Jamaica, 1675–1700," in *Anglo-American Political Relations, 1675–1775*, ed. Alison Gilbert Olson and Richard Maxwell Brown (New Brunswick, NJ: Rutgers University Press, 1970), 65; Bailyn, *New England Merchants*, 175–76; Hall, *Randolph*, 107–10; Lovejoy, *Glorious Revolution*, 183, 214.

69. Minutes of the Dominion Council, January 22, 1687, in *Proceedings of the American Antiquarian Society [PAAS]*, vol. 13 (Worcester, MA, 1899–1900), 247–49.

70. "Mr. Wharton's paper about raising of money," February 23, 1687, in *Massachusetts Archives Collection*, vol. 100, no. 162, repr. in Sylvester S. Crosby, *The Early Coins of America, and the Laws Governing their Issue* (Boston, 1875), 106–7.

71. Minutes of the Dominion Council, in *PAAS*, 13:252, 262–63.

72. Minutes of the Dominion Council, in *PAAS*, 13:252–54.

73. Minutes of the Dominion Council, in *PAAS*, 13:263.

74. Minutes of the Dominion Council, in *PAAS*, 13:252.

75. William Stoughton, et al., *A Narrative of the Proceedings of Sir Edmond Androsse and his Complices* (London, 1691), 4; "The Declaration of the Gentlemen, Merchants, and Inhabitants of Boston," April 18, 1689, in *The Andros Tracts: Being a Collection of Pamphlets and Official Papers . . .* , ed. William H. Whitmore, 3 vols. (Boston: Prince Society, 1868–1874), 1:13.

76. Blackwell, *Discourse in Explanation*, 1:143; Bailyn, *New England Merchants*, 185–87.

77. Lewis, "Land Speculation," 258, 266–69; Dunn, *Puritans and Yankees*, 245–46; Sosin, *English America*, 72; Lovejoy, *Glorious Revolution*, 215.

78. *Massachusetts Archives Collection*, vol. 127, pp. 66–69; *Massachusetts Archives Collection*, vol. 129, pp. 55–62; Goldberg, "America's First Bank," 217.

79. Andrew McFarland Davis, *Currency and Banking in the Province of the Massachusetts-Bay*, vol. 2 (New York: MacMillan Company, 1901), 79.

80. Thomas Hutchinson, *The History of Massachusetts, from the First Settlement thereof in 1628, until the Year 1750*, 2 vols., 3rd ed. (Boston, 1764/7; Salem, MA, 1795), 2:231.

81. Randolph to Blathwayt, May 21, 1687, in *Randolph Letters*, 6:221.

82. Stoughton, et al., *Narrative of the Proceedings*, 9; Dunn, *Puritans and Yankees*, 248; Lewis, "Land Speculation," 267–68; Lovejoy, *Glorious Revolution*, 186–87; T. H. Breen, *The Character of the Good Ruler: A Study of Puritan Political Ideas in New England, 1630–1730* (New Haven, CT: Yale University Press, 1970), 138, 146–47.

83. Henry Ashurst, et al., "An Answer to Mr. Randolph's Account Touching Irregular Trade Since the Late Revolution," 1689, in *Andros Tracts*, 2:129; *The Revolution in New-England Justified, and the People There Vindicated* (Boston, 1691), 12.

84. Stoughton, et al., *Narrative of the Proceedings*, 8; "Declaration of the Gentlemen," 1:16.

85. Dunn, *Puritans and Yankees*, 245–50; Sosin, *English America*, 75–78; Lovejoy, *Glorious Revolution*, 220–26.

86. Letter from Captain John Blackwell, July 16, 1688, in *Andros Tracts*, 3:84–86; Goldberg, "America's First Bank," 217–18.

87. Minutes of the Dominion Council, January 28, 1687, in *PAAS*, 13:249.

88. Breen, *Character of the Good Ruler*, 144–45; Yirush, *Settlers, Liberty, and Empire*, 65–66.

89. Randolph to John Povey, May 21, 1687 and January 24, 1688, in *Randolph Letters*, 4:163, 199.

90. Randolph to Blathwayt, November 23, 1687, in *Randolph Letters*, 6:235–36.

91. Randolph to Povey, January 24, 1688, in *Randolph Letters*, 4:199.

92. Randolph to Blathwayt, November 23, 1687, in *Randolph Letters*, 6:235.

93. LTP to Andros, January 12, 1687, in *Randolph Letters*, 4:145–47; Minutes of the Dominion Council, August 24, 1687, in *PAAS*, 13:475; Order of Andros to Randolph, June 24, 1687, in *Randolph Letters*, 4:164–65. For more on the decline of smuggling under the Dominion, see Lovejoy, *Glorious Revolution*, 190–91; Viola Florence Barnes, *The Dominion of New England: A Study in British Colonial Policy* (New Haven, CT: Yale University Press, 1923; repr., New York: Frederick Ungar Publishing Co., 1960), 169–71; Hall, *Randolph*, 111; Dunn, *Puritans and Yankees*, 239.

94. Minutes of the Dominion Council, March 8, May 25, and August 24, 1687, in *PAAS*, 13:261–62, 467.

95. Randolph to Parliament, 1689, in *Randolph Letters*, 5:14; Randolph to the LTP, May 29, 1689, in *Randolph Letters*, 4:279.

96. Randolph to Governor Edwyn Stede, May 16, 1689, in *Randolph Letters*, 4:266; Randolph to Blathwayt, March 31, 1687, in *Randolph Letters*, 6:219.

97. "Declaration of the Gentlemen," 1:13; [Increase Mather], *A Brief Relation of the State of New England, From the Beginning of that Plantation to this Present Year, 1689* (London, 1689), 6.

98. Order of the King in Council, April 1, 1685, CO 1/57, no. 83, p. 208; Commissioners of Customs to the Governors of the Plantations, August 10, 1685, CO 324/4, pp. 151–67.

99. Christian J. Koot, *Empire at the Periphery: British Colonists, Anglo-Dutch Trade, and the Development of the British Atlantic, 1621–1713* (New York: New York University Press, 2011), 171–72.

100. Report of Thomas Allen, CO 1/63, pp. 278–81, quotation in Victor Enthoven and Wim Klooster, "The Rise and Fall of the Virginia-Dutch Connection in the Seventeenth Century," in *Early Modern Virginia: Reconsidering the Old Dominion*, ed. Douglas M. Bradburn and John C. Coombs (Charlottesville: University of Virginia Press, 2011), 114.

101. Proclamation of James II, January 20, 1688, in *BRPA*, 140–41; James to Penn, October 13, 1687, in *Pennsylvania Archives, First Series*, ed. Samuel Hazard, 12 vols. (Philadelphia, 1852–56), 1:97; James to Dongan, October 13, 1687, in *Documents Relative to the Colonial History of the State of New York* [*DRNY*], ed. E. B. O'Callaghan and Berthold Fernow, 15 vols. (Albany, 1856–1887), 3:490–91. See also Mark G. Hanna, *Pirate Nests and the Rise of the British Empire, 1570–1740* (Chapel Hill: University of North Carolina Press, 2015), 179–81.

102. Francis Nicholson to Thomas Povey, August 31, 1688, in *DRNY*, 3:552. Also see Barnes, *Dominion of New England*, 166–68; Lovejoy, *Glorious Revolution*, 190.

103. Minutes of the Dominion Council, August 10 and 24, 1687, in *PAAS*, 13:475; Randolph to Blathwayt, October 19, 1688, in *Randolph Letters*, 6:275–76.

104. Nicholas Barbon, *A Discourse of Trade* (London, 1690), A3.

105. Charles Davenant, *Discourses on the Publick Revenues, and on the Trade of England*, 2 vols. (London, 1698), 2:421, 423; Edward Misselden, *Free Trade, or, The Means to Make Trade Flourish* (London, 1622), 54.

106. Proclamation of James II, April 1, 1685, in *BRPA*, 137–38.

107. Zahedieh, *Capital and the Colonies*, 41, 50; Dunn, "Imperial Pressures," 61. For more on the arguments in favor of monopolies, see Tim Keirn, "Monopoly, Economic Thought, and the Royal African Company," in *Early Modern Conceptions of Property*, ed. John Brewer and Susan Staves (London: Routledge, 1995), 439–44; Philip J. Stern, "Companies: Monopoly, Sovereignty, and the East Indies," in Philip J. Stern and Carl Wennerlind, *Mercantilism Reimagined: Political Economy in Early Modern Britain and its Empire* (Oxford: Oxford University Press, 2014), 181–84.

108. Misselden, *Free Trade*, 75–76.

109. Harris, *Politics under the Later Stuarts*, 94–102; Geoffrey Holmes, *British Politics in the Age of Anne* (London: Macmillan, 1967), 58–59.

110. Jonathan I. Israel, *Dutch Primacy in World Trade, 1585–1740* (Oxford: Clarendon Press, 1989), 103, 313–24, 329–39; Jonathan Israel, *The Dutch Republic: Its Rise, Greatness, and Fall, 1477–1806* (Oxford: Clarendon Press, 1995), 843, 939; Pincus, *1688*, 326, 372–75, 380–81.

111. Sir Josiah Child, *A Discourse Concerning Trade, and that in Particular of the East-Indies* (London, 1689), 3, 6.

112. Nuala Zahedieh found that of the twenty big merchants in London trading with the colonies, fifteen were Whigs and only five were Tories; moreover, all five of these Tory merchants were involved in the core management of monopoly companies, namely the RAC; see *Capital and the Colonies*, 114–16.

113. Carew Reynell, *The True English Interest, or an Account of the Chief National Improvements* (London, 1674), 8, 10.

114. Israel, *Dutch Republic*, 844.

115. Charles Davenant, *An Essay upon Ways and Means of Supplying the War* (London, 1695), 22.

116. Israel, *Dutch Republic*, 844–49.

117. Pincus, *1688*, 86–87, 311–12, 372–75.

118. Jacob M. Price, "Colonial Trade and British Economic Development, 1660–1775," *Lex et Scientia: The International Journal of Law and Science* 17 (1978): 117.

119. Pincus, *1688*, 323–27; Jones, *Revolution*, 177–87.

120. Jones, *Revolution*, 34–35, 51–52, 61–67, 129; Pincus, *1688*, 180, 199–201, 208–11, 316–26; Speck, *Reluctant Revolutionaries*, 48–51, 56–69; Harris, *Politics Under the Later Stuarts*, 123–32; Holmes, *Making of a Great Power*, 172–74, 181–85.

121. "The Declaration of His Highnes William Henry, Prince of Orange," October 10, 1688 [original date, September 30], accessed on *Early English Books Online* (*EEBO*), http//eebo.chadwyck.com. See also Jones, *Revolution*, 176–77, 188–90, 209–49, 262–66; Pincus, *1688*, 180–82, 224–26; Holmes, *Making of a Great Power*, 185–86.

122. Speck, *Reluctant Revolutionaries*, 71–91; Jones, *Revolution*, 5–6, 280–310; Harris, *Revolution*, 3–6, 269–307; Holmes, *Making of a Great Power*, 176–79, 187–90; Israel, *Dutch Republic*, 849–53.

123. A.B., *An Account of the Late Revolutions in New-England* (London, 1689), 4.

124. Nathanael Byfield, *An Account of the Late Revolution in New-England* (Boston, 1689), in *Andros Tracts*, 1:8; A.B., *Late Revolutions*, 5. See also Lovejoy, *Glorious Revolution*, 238–45; Davies, "Revolutions in America," 246–49, 259–60; Owen Stanwood, *The Empire Reformed: English America in the Age of the Glorious Revolution* (Philadelphia: University of Pennsylvania Press, 2011), 97–103.

125. Lovejoy, *Glorious Revolution*, 251–68, 281–85; Davies, "Revolutions in America," 261–64; Dunn, "Glorious Revolution," 455–59; Stanwood, *Empire Reformed*, 103–12, 129–35.

9. Reconstructing a Mercantilist Empire, 1690s

1. *The Speech of the Prince of Orange, to some Principle Gentlemen of Somersetshire and Dorsetshire* (Exeter, 1688); *Proceedings and Debates of the British Parliaments Respecting North America [PDBP]*, ed. Leo Francis Stock, 5 vols. (Washington, DC: Carnegie Institution of Washington, 1924–1941), 2:4.

2. "The Declaration of the Gentlemen, Merchants, and Inhabitants of Boston," April 18, 1689, in *The Andros Tracts: Being a Collection of Pamphlets and Official Papers . . .*, ed. William H. Whitmore, 3 vols. (Boston: Prince Society, 1868–1874), 1:12–17; Richard L. Bushman, *King and People in Provincial Massachusetts* (Chapel Hill: University of North Carolina Press, 1985), 16.

3. Randolph to the Governor of Barbados, May 16, 1689, in *Edward Randolph: Including his Letters and Official Papers . . . [Randolph Letters]*, ed. Robert Noxon Toppan and Alfred T. S. Goodrick, 7 vols. (Boston, 1898–1909), 4:265–66; David S. Lovejoy, *The Glorious Revolution in America* (New York: Harper & Row, 1972), 244–45, 277–78; Michael Garibaldi Hall, *Edward Randolph and the American Colonies, 1676–1703* (Chapel Hill: University of North Carolina Press, 1960), 123.

4. Barbara C. Murison, "Blathwayt, William (bap. 1650, d. 1717)," accessed on *Oxford Dictionary of National Biography* (Oxford University Press, 2004), http://www.oxforddnb.com/view/article/2626.

5. [Increase Mather], *A Narrative of the Miseries of New-England* (London, 1688), 1.

6. Bradstreet to Massachusetts Agents, January 24, 1690, in *Andros Tracts*, 3:59–60; Order of William III, July 30, 1689, in *Randolph Letters*, 4:290–91; Lovejoy, *Glorious Revolution*, 227–34, 279–80, 340; J. M. Sosin, *English America and the Revolution of 1688: Royal Administration and the Structure of Provincial Government* (Lincoln: University of Nebraska Press, 1982), 75–78, 83–84.

7. *PDBP*, 2:1–2, 8–9; Lovejoy, *Glorious Revolution*, 231–33, 341; Hall, *Randolph*, 124–32, 155–56; Steve Pincus, *1688: The First Modern Revolution* (New Haven: Yale University Press, 2009), 357; Julian Hoppit, *A Land of Liberty? England, 1689–1727* (Oxford: Clarendon Press, 2000), 144–49.

8. *A Short Discourse Shewing the Great Inconveniences of Joyning the Plantation Charters with those of England in the General Act of Restoration* (London, 1689), 1–2; C. D., *New England's Faction Discovered . . .* (London, 1690), 3.

9. John Palmer, *An Impartial Account of the State of New-England, the Late Government There, Vindicated* (London, 1690), 25, 40.

10. *Randolph Letters*, 4:278, 285, 5:10, 15, 37.

11. Randolph to Parliament, 1689, in *Randolph Letters*, 5:12; Randolph to the LTP, May 29, 1689, in *Randolph Letters*, 4:280; *Short Discourse*, 2.

12. [Increase Mather], *New-England Vindicated* (London, 1689), 1–3; Ashurst, Cooke, Mather, and Oakes, "An Answer to Mr. Randolph's Account . . . ," 1689, in *Andros Tracts*, 2:129; [Increase Mather], *A Vindication of New-England, from the Vile Aspersions Cast upon that Country* (Boston, 1690), 16–17.

13. Owen Stanwood, *The Empire Reformed: English America in the Age of the Glorious Revolution* (Philadelphia: University of Pennsylvania Press, 2011), 135, 146; Lovejoy, *Glorious Revolution*, 231–33, 341–42; Craig Yirush, *Settlers, Liberty, and Empire: The Roots of Early American Political Theory, 1675–1775* (Cambridge University Press, 2011), 69–73.

14. [Increase Mather], *A Brief Relation of the State of New England* (London, 1689), 7.

15. Randolph to the Bishop of London, October 25, 1689, in *Randolph Letters*, 4:307.

16. [Increase Mather], *A Brief Account Concerning Several of the Agents of New-England* (London, 1691), in *Andros Tracts*, 2:279–83.

17. Lovejoy, *Glorious Revolution*, 255–57, 274–77, 295–302, 312–40, 354–63; Richard S. Dunn, "The Glorious Revolution and America," in *The Origins of Empire: British Overseas Enterprise to the Close of the Seventeenth Century*, ed. Nicholas Canny (Oxford University Press, 1998), 458–63; Patricia U. Bonomi, *A Factious People: Politics and Society in Colonial New York* (New York: Columbia University Press, 1971), 76–77.

18. Lovejoy, *Glorious Revolution*, 272–74, 302–10, 364–70; Dunn, "Glorious Revolution," 459; Richard L. Morton, *Colonial Virginia*, vol. 1 (Chapel Hill: University of North Carolina Press, 1960), 334–44.

19. Address of New England merchants to William III, October 1690, in *The National Archives-Public Records Office* (Kew, England): CO 5/855, no. 122; Dunn, "Glorious Revolution," 460; Mark Peterson, *The City-State of Boston: The Rise and Fall of an Atlantic Power, 1630–1865* (Princeton, NJ: Princeton University Press, 2019), 181–83.

20. [Cotton Mather], *Pietas in Patriam: The Life of His Excellency Sir William Phips* (London, 1697), 43–44.

21. Andrew McFarland Davis, *Currency and Banking in the Province of the Massachusetts-Bay*, 2 vols. (New York: MacMillan Company, 1901), 1:267–70. See also Dror Goldberg, "The Massachusetts Paper Money of 1690," *The Journal of Economic History* 69, no. 4 (Dec. 2009): 1092–1106; Katie A. Moore, "The Blood That Nourishes the Body Politic: The Origins of Paper Money in Early America," *Early American Studies: An Interdisciplinary Journal* 17, no. 1 (Winter 2019): 3–4, 24–27.

22. For more on the functioning of colonial bills of credit, see E. James Ferguson, "Currency Finance: An Interpretation of Colonial Monetary Practices," *William and Mary Quarterly*, 3rd ser., 10, no. 2 (Apr. 1953): 173–74; Curtis Nettels, *The Money Supply of the American Colonies Before 1720*, repr. ed. (Madison: University of Wisconsin Press, 1934; Clifton, NJ: Augustus M. Kelley Publishers, 1973), 257–65.

23. Quotation is from a later recollection of this incident: *The Second Part of the South-Sea Stock, Being an Inquiry into the Original of Province Bills or Bills of Credit* (Boston, 1721), 6.

24. Letter from Boston merchants, February 2, 1691, CO 5/856, no. 138.

25. Mather, *Pietas in Patriam*, 44; Francis Foxcroft to Nicholson, October 26, 1691, CO 5/1037, no. 64.

26. [John Blackwell], *Some Additional Considerations* (Boston, 1691), 12, 18–20; Cotton Mather, *Some Considerations on the Bills of Credit now passing in New-England* (Boston, 1691), 8; Mather, *Pietas in Patriam*, 44.

27. Rev. Samuel Willard, *Character of a Good Ruler* (Boston, 1694), 3, quotation in T. H. Breen, *Puritans and Adventurers: Change and Persistence in Early America* (New York: Oxford University Press, 1980), 105.

28. Walter Breen, *Walter Breen's Complete Encyclopedia of U.S. and Colonial Coins* (New York: Doubleday, 1988), 12.

29. *The Acts and Resolves, Public and Private, of the Province of the Massachusetts Bay*, 21 vols. (Boston, 1869–1922), 1:1–20.

30. Memorial of Phips and Mather, November 9, 1691, CO 5/856, no. 202.

31. Commissioners of the Mint to the Lords Commissioners of the Treasury, January 19, 1692, repr. in Sylvester S. Crosby, *The Early Coins of America, and the Laws Governing their Issue* (Boston, 1875), 96–97.

32. Mather, *Brief Account*, 2:285, 289–90; Lovejoy, *Glorious Revolution*, 340–48, 370–72; Bushman, *King and People*, 104–6.

33. Mather, *Brief Account*, 2:296; Goldberg, "Massachusetts Paper Money," 1096; Richard S. Dunn, *Puritans and Yankees: The Winthrop Dynasty of New England, 1630–1717* (Princeton, NJ: Princeton University Press, 1962), 262–64.

34. *Acts and Resolves of Massachusetts*, 1:70.

35. Yirush, *Settlers, Liberty, and Empire*, 76–79; Stanwood, *Empire Reformed*, 1–4.

36. Mather, *Brief Account*, 2:288–89.

37. For more on these themes, see Bushman, *King and People*, 13–24, 88–111; Yirush, *Settlers, Liberty, and Empire*, 76–79; Stanwood, *Empire Reformed*, 4, 20; Brendan McConville, *The King's Three Faces: The Rise and Fall of Royal America, 1688–1776* (Chapel Hill: University of North Carolina Press, 2006), 40–41.

38. *Records of the Governor and Company of the Massachusetts Bay in New England*, ed. Nathaniel Bradstreet Shurtleff, 5 vols. (Boston, 1853–4), 5:202–3.

39. William Douglass, *A Summary, Historical and Political, of the First Planting, Progressive Improvements, and Present State of the British Settlements in North-America*, 2 vols. (Boston, 1749–51), 1:434.

40. *Acts and Resolves of Massachusetts*, 1:35–36; Davis, *Currency and Banking*, 1:267–70; Nettels, *Money Supply*, 209.

41. Douglass, *Summary, Historical and Political*, 1:525n.

42. *Boston News-Letter*, April 18, 1720.

43. [William Douglass], *A Discourse Concerning the Currencies of the British Plantations in America, Especially with Regard to their Paper Money* (Boston, 1740), 34.

44. Petition of Sir Mathew Dudley, January 1694, CO 5/858, p. 64.

45. *The Statutes at Large of South Carolina*, ed. Thomas Cooper and David James McCord, 10 vols. (Columbia, 1836–1841), 2:163.

46. Nettels, *Money Supply*, 91.

47. *Acts and Resolves of Massachusetts*, 1:306.

48. Mather, *Some Considerations*, 6.

49. Blackwell, *Additional Considerations*, 13.

50. John Brewer, *The Sinews of Power: War, Money and the English State, 1688–1783* (Cambridge, MA: Harvard University Press, 1988).

51. Brewer, *Sinews of Power*, 30, 38, 40, 89, 137; Pincus, *1688*, 351; P. G. M. Dickson, *The Financial Revolution in England: A Study in the Development of Public Credit, 1688–1756* (Macmillan and Company, 1967; repr., Aldershot, UK: Gregg Revivals, 1993), 46.

52. Jon Latimer, *Buccaneers of the Caribbean: How Piracy Forged an Empire* (Cambridge, MA: Harvard University Press, 2009), 280–81; Brewer, *Sinews of Power*, 11–12, 27, 31.

53. D. W. Jones, *War and Economy in the Age of William III and Marlborough* (Oxford: Basil Blackwell, 1988).

54. C. E. Challis, *A New History of the Royal Mint* (Cambridge: Cambridge University Press, 1992), 690.

55. *True Causes of the Present Scarcity*, 3; North, *Discourses Upon Trade*, 11.

56. John Blackwell, *An Essay towards Carrying on the Present War against France* (London, 1695), 2; John Briscoe, *A Discourse on the Late Funds of the Million-Act, Lottery-Act, and Bank of England* (London, 1694), 22.

57. John Blanch, *The Naked Truth, in an Essay Upon Trade* (London, 1696), 6–7.

58. James II, "His Majesties Most Gratious Declaration to all his Loving Subjects, Commanding their Assistance against the Prince of Orange, and his Adherents" (Saint-Germain-en-Laye: 1692).

59. John Briscoe, *A Discourse of Money* (London, 1696), 112; *True Causes of the Present Scarcity*, 3.

60. Joyce Appleby, *Economic Thought and Ideology in Seventeenth-Century England* (Princeton: Princeton University Press, 1978), 248–49, 261; Brodie Waddell, "The Politics of Economic Distress in the Aftermath of the Glorious Revolution, 1689–1702," *English Historical Review* 130, no. 543 (Apr. 2015): 322–23; Jones, *War and Economy*, 17–18, 130–31, 145–61; Joseph A. Goldenberg, *Shipbuilding in Colonial America* (Charlottesville: University Press of Virginia, 1976), 31–33.

61. Justin Williams, "English Mercantilism and Carolina Naval Stores, 1705–1776," *Journal of Southern History* 1, no. 2 (May 1935): 172.

62. Hoppit, *Land of Liberty*, 128; Jones, *War and Economy*, 18, 37–40, 77–94.

63. Quotation in Henry Horwitz, *Parliament, Policy and Politics in the Reign of William III* (Newark: University of Delaware Press, 1977), 104.

64. Pincus, *1688*, 307–8, 350–58; Geoffrey Holmes, *The Making of a Great Power: Late Stuart and Early Georgian Britain* (London: Longman, 1993), 236–37.

65. Charles Davenant, *Discourses on the Publick Revenues, and on the Trade of England*, 2 vols. (London, 1698), 2:10, 101; [William Lowndes], *A Further Essay for the Amendment of the Gold and Silver Coins* (London, 1695), 3–4.

66. William Lowndes, *A Report Containing an Essay for the Amendment of the Silver Coins* (London, 1695), 107.

67. *A Letter Humbly Offer'd to the Consideration of all Gentlemen, Yeomen, Citizens, Freeholders* (London, 1696), 19; William Hodges, *The Groans of the Poor, the Misery of Traders, and the Calamity of the Publick* (London, 1696), 3.

68. *The Autobiography of William Stout of Lancaster, 1665–1752*, ed. J. D. Marshall (Cambridge: Chadwyk-Healey, 1978), 109.

69. John Craig, *The Mint: A History of the London Mint from A.D. 287 to 1948* (Cambridge: Cambridge University Press, 1953), 187–94; C. E. Challis, "Lord Hastings to the

Great Silver Recoinage, 1464–1699," in Challis, *New History of the Royal Mint*, 383–91; Nicholas Mayhew, *Sterling: The Rise and Fall of a Currency* (London: Allen Lane, 1999), 95–101; Appleby, *Economic Thought*, 217–39.

70. [James Hodges], *The Present State of England, as to Coin and Publick Charges* (London, 1697), 20.

71. Hugh Chamberlen, *A Collection of Some Papers Writ Upon Several Occasions, Concerning Clipt and Counterfeit Money, and Trade* (London, 1696), 17; [Hugh Chamberlen], *Positions Supported by their Reasons, Explaining the Office of Land-Credit* (London, 1696), 5; Edmund Bohun to John Cary, July 31, 1696, British Library, MS 5540, fo. 64r, cited in Challis, "Lord Hastings," 388.

72. *Diary and Correspondence of John Evelyn*, ed. William Bray, 4 vols. (London, 1857), 2:343.

73. *A Sermon on the Restoring of the Coyn* (London, 1697), 17, cited in Mark G. Hanna, *Pirate Nests and the Rise of the British Empire, 1570–1740* (Chapel Hill: University of North Carolina Press, 2015), 227.

74. [Dalby Thomas], *Some Thoughts concerning the Better Security of our Trade and Navigation, and Carrying on the War Against France more Effectually* (London, 1695), 3; Briscoe, *Discourse of Money*, 112.

75. John Cary, *An Essay on the State of England, in Relation to its Trade* (London, 1695), preface.

76. Briscoe, *Discourse of Money*, 115.

77. Charles Davenant, *An Essay upon Ways and Means of Supplying the War* (London, 1695), 26.

78. Davenant, *Ways and Means*, 26–27.

79. James Whiston, *A Discourse of the Decay of Trade* (London, 1693), 2; *Some Observations upon the Bank of England* (London, 1695), 18.

80. Julian Hoppit, *Britain's Political Economies: Parliament and Economic Life, 1660–1800* (Cambridge: Cambridge University Press, 2017).

81. J. H. Plumb, *The Growth of Political Stability in England, 1675–1725* (1967; repr., London: Macmillan Press, 1979), 99–100, 112–13; Brewer, *Sinews of Power*, 65–67, 137–38, 142–43; Holmes, *Making of a Great Power*, 257–65.

82. Brewer, *Sinews of Power*, 30, 89.

83. Dickson, *Financial Revolution*, 46–50, 343–49; Sir John Clapham, *The Bank of England: A History*, 2 vols. (Cambridge: Cambridge University Press, 1966), 1:15–24.

84. Briscoe, *Discourse on the Late Funds*, 19; Briscoe, *Discourse of Money*, 137–39.

85. Davenant, *Discourses on the Publick Revenues*, 2:163–64.

86. Sir Josiah Child, *A Discourse of the Nature, Use and Advantages of Trade* (London, 1694), 18; Thomas, *Some Thoughts*, 2–3.

87. Nicolas Barbon, *A Discourse Concerning Coining the New Money Lighter* (London, 1696), 40. For more on this subject, see Appleby, *Economic Thought*, 242–48, 262–63; Joyce Appleby, "Ideology and Theory: The Tension between Political and Economic Liberalism in Seventeenth-Century England," *American Historical Review* 81, no. 3 (June 1976): 499–511.

88. John Pollexfen, *A Discourse of Trade, Coyn, and Paper Credit* (London, 1697), 147–50.

89. Charles Davenant, *A Memorial Concerning the Coyn of England* (1695), in *Two Manuscripts by Charles Davenant* (Baltimore: Johns Hopkins Press, 1942), 42; Davenant, *Ways*

and Means, 29; Lowndes, *Report Containing an Essay*, 90; Lowndes, *Further Essay*, 2–3; [John Pollexfen], *A Vindication of Some Assertions Relating to Coin and Trade* (London, 1699), 78.

90. Whiston, *Decay of Trade*, 1–3.

91. Sir Josiah Child, *A New Discourse of Trade* (London, 1692), 94–95; Cary, *Essay on the State of England*, preface, 38; Nehemiah Grew, *The Meanes of a Most Ample Encrease of the Wealth and Strength of England in a Few Years*, repr., *Nehemiah Grew and England's Economic Development* , ed. Julian Hoppit (Oxford University Press, 2012), 70; Davenant, *Discourses on the Publick Revenues*, 2:84–86, 205.

92. George French, *The History of Col. Park's Administration whilst he was Captain-General and Chief Governor of the Leeward Islands* (London, 1717), 198, cited in Christian J. Koot, *Empire at the Periphery: British Colonists, Anglo-Dutch Trade, and the Development of the British Atlantic, 1621–1713* (New York: New York University Press, 2011), 188.

93. Earl of Inchiquin to the LTP, July 6, 1690, CO 137/2, no. 72.

94. *PDBP*, 2:152; Koot, *Empire at the Periphery*, 188; Nuala Zahedieh, *The Capital and the Colonies: London and the Atlantic Economy, 1660–1700* (Cambridge: Cambridge University Press, 2010), 37, 41.

95. Extract from a letter of Sir William Beeston to Blathwayt, March 18, 1697, in *Calendar of State Papers: Colonial Series, America and the West Indies, 1574–1738 [CSPC]*, ed. W. Noel Sainsbury et al., 44 vols. (London, 1860–1969), *1696–7*, no. 824; Christian J. Koot, "Anglo-Dutch Trade in the Chesapeake and the British Caribbean, 1621–1733," in *Dutch Atlantic Connects, 1680–1800*, ed. Gert J. Oostindie and Jessica V. Roitman (Leiden: Brill, 2014), 92–93.

96. Randolph to the Commissioners of Customs, October 16, 1695, in *Randolph Letters*, 5:118. Also see *PDBP*, 2:204; Robert C. Nash, "The English and Scottish Tobacco Trades in the Seventeenth and Eighteenth Centuries: Legal and Illegal Trade," *Economic History Review*, n.s., 35, no. 3 (Aug. 1982): 357, 364, 371.

97. *Journals of the House of Commons [JHC]*, vol. 11 (London, 1803), 252.

98. Nicholson to Board of Trade [BOT], July 13, 1697, CO 5/725, p. 122; Nicholson to BOT, March 27, 1697, CO 5/714, no. 16.

99. Memorial of Sir Thomas Laurence, June 25, 1695, CO 5/713, no. 115. See also *Acts of the Privy Council of England, Colonial Series [APCC]*, ed. W. L. Grant and James Munroe, 6 vols. (Hereford, UK: 1908–1912), 2:272; *CSPC, 1693–6*, nos. 289ii, 1139i, 2303; *CSPC, 1696–7*, nos. 149, 862, 1338; *CSPC, 1697–8*, no. 796; *CSPC, 1699*, no. 694.

100. Memorial of Randolph to the Commissioners of Customs, November 10, 1696, in *Randolph Letters*, 5:157; Report of the Earl of Bellomont, November 27, 1699, in *Records of the Colony of Rhode Island and Providence Plantations, in New England*, ed. John Russell Bartlett, 7 vols. (Providence, 1856–1862), 3:387.

101. Governor John Easton to the LTP, September 6, 1694, CO 5/858, no. 39.

102. Memorial of Sir Thomas Laurence, June 25, 1695, CO 5/713, no. 115; Report of Randolph, November 10, 1696, in *Randolph Letters*, 5:155–56.

103. T. Weaver to the BOT, January 9, 1698, in *Documents Relative to the Colonial History of the State of New York [DRNY]*, ed. E. B. O'Callaghan and Berthold Fernow, 15 vols. (Albany, 1856–1887), 4:462. See also Bonomi, *Factious People*, 60–68; Cathy Matson, *Merchants and Empire: Trading in New York* (Baltimore: Johns Hopkins University Press), 86–87.

104. *Acts and Resolves of Massachusetts*, 1:34–35; *CSPC, 1689–92*, no. 2561.

105. Petition of Jahleel Brenton to the Lords of the Treasury, 1693, CO 5/857, no. 87i. See also *APCC*, 2:237, 285; *CSPC, 1689–92*, no. 2031; *CSPC, 1693–6*, nos. 1507, 2202, 2342.

106. *APCC*, 2:153.

107. Robert C. Ritchie, *Captain Kidd and the War Against the Pirates* (Cambridge, MA: Harvard University Press, 1986), 26, 30, 151–52.

108. *PDBP*, 2:76.

109. BOT to the Lords Justices of England, October 19, 1698, in *DRNY*, 4:385.

110. Hanna, *Pirate Nests*, 185–89, 201–11; Ritchie, *Captain Kidd*, 19, 25, 80–83; Janice E. Thomson, *Mercenaries, Pirates, and Sovereigns: State-Building and Extraterritorial Violence in Early Modern Europe* (Princeton: Princeton University Press, 1994), 47–48.

111. Davenant, *Discourses on the Publick Revenues*, 2:88.

112. Bellomont to the BOT, August 31, 1697, in *DRNY*, 4:306.

113. Memorial of Sir Thomas Laurence, June 25, 1695, CO 5/713, no. 115.

114. Jeremiah Basse to Secretary William Popple, July 15, 1697, in *Documents Relating to the Colonial History of the State of New Jersey [DRNJ]*, ed. William A. Whitehead, Frederick W. Ricord, William Nelson, and A. Van Doren Honeyman, 33 vols. (Newark, 1880–1928), 2:151.

115. Bellomont to the BOT, August 31, 1697, in *DRNY*, 4:304.

116. Bellomont to the BOT, May 18, 1698, in *DRNY*, 4:304. For more on Fletcher and piracy, see Thomas J. Archdeacon, *New York City, 1664–1710: Conquest and Change* (Ithaca: Cornell University Press, 1976), 68–69, 123–25; Hanna, *Pirate Nests*, 217–19; Ritchie, *Captain Kidd*, 33–39.

117. Fletcher to the BOT, December 24, 1698, in *DRNY*, 4:443–44.

118. Matson, *Merchants and Empire*, 82.

119. Bellomont to the BOT, June 22, 1698, in *DRNY*, 4:323.

120. Peter De La Noy to the LTP, June 13, 1695, in *DRNY*, 4:223; Report of the BOT, 28 Nov. 1698, in *DRNY*, 4:433; Ritchie, *Captain Kidd*, 37–38; Hanna, *Pirate Nests*, 215.

121. Attorney-General of New York to Bellomont, May 4, 1698, CO 5/1041, no. 4iii. Also see Hanna, *Pirate Nests*, 192–93, 218.

122. Bellomont to the BOT, May 18, 1698, in *DRNY*, 4:307.

123. Hanna, *Pirate Nests*, 188, 219; Jacob Judd, "Frederick Philipse and the Madagascar Trade," *New-York Historical Society Quarterly* 55, no. 4 (Oct. 1971): 354–74.

124. Instructions from the Lords Proprietors, November 8, 1691, in *The Colonial Records of North Carolina*, ed. William L. Saunders, 10 vols. (Raleigh, 1886–1890), 1:383; Hanna, *Pirate Nests*, 188–89.

125. Hanna, *Pirate Nests*, 215–16.

126. Randolph to the Commissioners of Customs, November 10, 1696, in *Randolph Letters*, 5:158–59.

127. Markham to Penn, April 24, 1697, CO 5/1257, no. 6xiv.

128. Penn to the BOT, March 6, 1701, CO 5/1260, no. 99; Basse to Secretary Popple, July 15, 1697, in *DRNJ*, 2:152.

129. *An Essay Upon the Government of the English Plantations* (London, 1701), 24.

130. Bellomont to the BOT, July 22, 1699, in *DRNY*, 4:532; George Larkin to the BOT, December 5, 1701, in *CSPC, 1701*, no. 1054, cited in Hanna, *Pirate Nests*, 193; Peter De La Noy to the LTP, June 13, 1695, in *DRNY*, 4:223.

131. Nicholson to the LTP, July 16, 1692, *CSPC, 1689–92*, no. 2344; Memorial of Sir Thomas Laurence, June 25, 1695, CO 5/713, no. 115; Hanna, *Pirate Nests*, 190.

132. Bellomont to the BOT, August 24, 1699, in *DRNY*, 4:551; Randolph to the Commissioners of Customs, November 10, 1696, in *Randolph Letters*, 5:155.

133. Narrative of Captain Robert Snead, April 1697, CO 323/2, no. 114i.

134. Snead to Sir John Houblon, September 20, 1697, CO 5/1233, no. 31.

135. Randolph to Secretary Popple, May 12, 1698, CO 323/2, no. 114; Morton, *Colonial Virginia*, 373–74; Hanna, *Pirate Nests*, 216–17.

136. Beeston to the LTP, June 10, 1693, CO 137/3, no. 17.

137. Beeston to the BOT, June 15, 1696, CO 137/4, no. 6.

138. *Essay Upon the Government*, 24.

139. Randolph to the Commissioners of Customs, October 16, 1695, in *Randolph Letters*, 5:124.

140. Letters to the EIC, October 15, 1696, and January 15, 1697, CO 323/2, no. 80i.

141. BOT to Fletcher, February 1, 1697, in *DRNY*, 4:255; Letter to the East India Company, October 15, 1696, CO 323/2, no. 80i.

142. Colonel Robert Quarry to the BOT, June 1, 1699, in CO 5/1258, no. 30.

143. BOT to the Lords Justices of England, October 19, 1698, in *DRNY*, 4:385.

144. Nicholson to the BOT, August 20, 1698, CO 5/714, no. 52, pp. 9–10.

145. Carolina effected this devaluation a bit subtly by switching the valuation of coins from weight to tale. Since 1683, full-weight dollars in Carolina passed for 6s, and clipped dollars for less, via a sliding scale based on pennyweights. With this new legislation, however, the Carolina assembly declared that all Spanish dollars weighing 13 dwt or more pass at 5s a piece. Full-weight coin (17.5 dwt) decreased in value by this new legislation, but clipped coin rose in value by approximately 10 percent. Previously, coins of 13 dwt (one-quarter clipped) passed for 4s6d: now, the same coin passed for 5s. Thus, after this act, virtually no full-weight money made way to Charles Town. See *Statutes of South Carolina*, 2:72–73, 94–95.

146. Before March 1693, the rating in New York was 6s (the former Dominion of New England rating). The new law, besides raising full-weight coin from 6s to 6s7d, established that 4.5d be deducted for each missing pennyweight from clipped money. Three months later, Fletcher's lieutenant governor in Pennsylvania, William Markham—another patron of pirates—declared that full-weight dollars pass in Pennsylvania at 7s, but with only 2d deducted for each missing pennyweight (thus keeping Philadelphia a center for light money despite having abolished pure currency by tale). Formerly, in Pennsylvania, Spanish dollars passed at 6s regardless of weight. See *DRNY*, 4:1134; *Statutes of Pennsylvania*, 1:205–6.

147. *The Public Records of the Colony of Connecticut*, ed. J. Hammond Trumbull and Charles J. Hoadly, 15 vols. (Hartford: Brown & Parsons, 1850–90), 4:166, 176–7; *DRNY*, 4:1134; *CSPC, 1702–3*, no. 590.

148. *Archives of Maryland: Proceedings and Acts of the General Assembly of Maryland*, ed. William Hand Browne, Clayton Colman Hall, and Bernard Christian Steiner, 72 vols. (Baltimore: Maryland Historical Society, 1883–1972), 8:357, 13:493–95, 38:5, 19:47, 252, 360, 23:62, 351.

149. *Archives of Maryland*, 19:48, 302.

150. *Journals of the House of Burgesses of Virginia*, ed. H. R. McIlwaine and John Pendleton Kennedy, 13 vols. (Richmond, 1905–1915), 2:436, 444, 476, 3:67, 147–48, 151–52.

151. Act of the Antigua Assembly, March 26, 1699, repr. in Robert Chalmers, *A History of Currency in the British Colonies* (London, 1893), 66; APCC, 2:128, 834; John J. McCusker, *Money and Exchange in Europe and America, 1600–1775: A Handbook* (Chapel Hill: University of North Carolina Press, 1978), 246, 257.

152. Zahedieh, *Capital and the Colonies*, 238–39, 257, 279; John J. McCusker and Russell R. Menard, *The Economy of British America, 1607–1789* (Chapel Hill: University of North Carolina Press, 1985), 104, 136.

153. Zahedieh, *Capital and the Colonies*, 240, 257–58.

154. Richard Frame, *A Short Description of Pennsilvania* (Philadelphia, 1692), in *Narratives of Early Pennsylvania, West New Jersey and Delaware, 1630–1707*, ed. Albert Cook Myers (New York: Barnes & Noble, Inc., 1912), 304–5.

155. Gabriel Thomas, *An Historical and Geographical Account of the Province and Country of Pensilvania, and of West-New-Jersey in America* (London, 1698), in *Narratives of Early Pennsylvania*, 42.

156. *PDBP*, 2:111.

157. Edwin Perkins, *Economy of Colonial America*, 2nd. ed. (New York: Columbia University Press, 1980; New York: Columbia University Press, 1988), 25; Zahedieh, *Capital and the Colonies*, 260–62; McCusker and Menard, *Economy of British America*, 325, 329; Margaret Ellen Newell, *From Dependency to Independence: Economic Revolution in Colonial New England* (Ithaca, NY: Cornell University Press, 1998), 68.

158. Francis Daniel Pastorius, *Circumstantial Geographical Description of Pennsylvania* (1700), in *Narratives of Early Pennsylvania*, 383.

159. Davenant, *Discourses on the Publick Revenues*, 2:238–40.

160. I. K. Steele, *Politics of Colonial Policy: The Board of Trade in Colonial Administration, 1696–1720* (Oxford: Clarendon Press, 1968), 9; Winfred T. Root, "The Lords of Trade and Plantations, 1675–1696," *American Historical Review* 23, no. 1 (Oct. 1917): 35–39; Charles McLean Andrews, *The Colonial Period of American History*, 4 vols. (New Haven, CT: Yale University Press, 1934–8), 4:274–75, 284–85, 374.

161. Parliamentary Committee, "The Irregular and Disorderly State of the Plantation-Trade," 1694, in *Annual Report of the American Historical Association for the Year 1892* (Washington, 1893), 40; second quotation in *JHC*, 195.

162. Davenant, *Memorial Concerning the Coyn*, 51–53.

163. *JHC*, 11:423–24.

164. *PDBP*, 2:213; Root, "Lords of Trade," 39–41; Andrews, *Colonial Period*, 4:285–90.

165. Andrews, *Colonial Period*, 4:292; Peter Laslett, "John Locke, the Great Recoinage, and the Origins of the Board of Trade: 1695–1698," *William and Mary Quarterly*, 3rd ser., 14, no. 3 (July 1957): 372–73, 378, 402.

166. *PDBP*, 2:216; Andrews, *Colonial Period*, 4:290–94, 305; Yirush, *Settlers, Liberty, and Empire*, 88–89.

167. *The Statutes at Large, from Magna Charta . . . [SLMC]*, 9 vols. (London, 1763), 3:609–13, 720. Also see Andrews, *Colonial Period*, 4:159–74; Thomas C. Barrow, *Trade and Empire: The British Customs Service in Colonial America, 1660–1775* (Cambridge, MA: Harvard University Press, 1967), 53–59.

168. Memorial of Sir Thomas Laurence, June 25, 1695, CO 5/713, no. 115; Randolph to the Commissioners of Customs, August 17, 1696, CO 323/2, no. 6.

169. Barrow, *Trade and Empire*, 53, 59.

170. Barrow, *Trade and Empire*, 59–73.

171. *APCC*, 2:299–300; Hanna, *Pirate Nests*, 189, 238.

172. *APCC*, 2:301.

173. Hanna, *Pirate Nests*, 238–42.

174. Letter to the EIC, April 28, 1697, CO 323/2, no. 94.

175. Hanna, *Pirate Nests*, 249–50; Latimer, *Buccaneers of the Caribbean*, 278–81.

176. Bellomont to the BOT, May 25, 1698, in *DRNY*, 4:317. Also see Hanna, *Pirate Nests*, 256–68; Ritchie, *Captain Kidd*, 51–55, 169–82; Matson, *Merchants and Empire*, 63, 86; Archdeacon, *New York City*, 129–30.

177. Bellomont to the Lords of the Admiralty, May 18, 1698, in *DRNY*, 4:313.

178. Bellomont to Secretary Popple, July 7, 1698, CO 5/1040, no. 84; Bellomont to the Lords of the Treasury, November 14, 1698, in *DRNY*, 4:538.

179. Bellomont to the BOT, May 18 and 25, 1698, in *DRNY*, 4:303–6, 318–19.

180. *The Statutes at Large of Pennsylvania, from 1682 to 1801*, ed. James T. Mitchell, Henry Flanders, Jonathan Willis Martin, Hampton L. Carson, and Gail McKnight Beckman, 17 vols. (Harrisburg and New York, 1896–1976), 1:238; *Records of Rhode Island*, 3:335–38.

181. Hanna, *Pirate Nests*, 289–90; Ritchie, *Captain Kidd*, 153; Thomson, *Mercenaries, Pirates, and Sovereigns*, 49–50; Latimer, *Buccaneers of the Caribbean*, 280.

182. Penn to the BOT, July 2, 1701, CO 5/1261, no. 8a, cited in Hanna, *Pirate Nests*, 291.

183. *DRNY*, 4:532, 551, 583; Ritchie, *Captain Kidd*, 56–79, 89–126; Hanna, *Pirate Nests*, 230–31; Latimer, *Bucceaneers of the Caribbean*, 281.

184. *PDBP*, 2:214.

185. Davenant, *Discourses on the Publick Revenues*, 2:227.

186. *PDBP*, 2:265.

187. *SLMC*, 4:9–12; Francis G. James, "Irish Colonial Trade in the Eighteenth Century," *William and Mary Quarterly*, 3rd ser., 20, no. 4 (Oct. 1963): 577–78.

188. *SLMC*, 4:47–9.

189. Ralph Davis, "The Rise of Protection in England, 1689–1786," *Economic History Review*, 2nd ser., 19, no. 2 (Aug. 1966): 306–17; Holmes, *Making of a Great Power*, 301–2; Appleby, *Economic Thought*, 249.

190. [Theodore Janssen], "General Maxims in Trade," 1713, in *The British Merchant; or, Commerce Preserv'd*, ed. Charles King, 3 vols. (London, 1721), 1:5, 21; Petition of British Manufacturers, 1737, repr. in *Memoirs of Wool, Woolen Manufacture, and Trade*, ed. John Smith, vol. 2 (London, 1756), 65–66.

191. William Carter, *An Alarum to England, to Prevent its Destruction by the Loss of Trade and Navigation* (London, 1700), 27; John Cary, *An Essay on the Coyn and Credit of England* (Bristol, 1696), 21, 34.

192. *PDBP*, 4:132–33, 145–47; Zahedieh, *Capital and the Colonies*, 270.

193. Adam Smith, *An Inquiry into the Nature and Causes of the Wealth of Nations* (1776; repr., New York: Random House, 1937), bk. IV, ch. VII, pp. 549–50.

194. Williams, "English Mercantilism," 171–73, 177.

195. Randolph to the BOT, July 24, 1696, CO 323/2, no. 4; Evelyn to Lord Godolphin, June 16, 1696, in *Diary of John Evelyn*, 3:356; Davenant, *Discourses on the Publick Revenues*, 2:86; John Cary, *A Discourse Concerning the East-India Trade* (London, 1699), 2.

196. Robert Quary to the BOT, June 16, 1703, in *DRNY*, 4:1059.

197. *SLMC*, 4:181–83.

198. Williams, "English Mercantilism," 175–79; Sinclair Snow, "Naval Stores in Colonial Virginia," *Virginia Magazine of History and Biography* 72, no. 1 (Jan. 1964): 82–87, 91–93.

199. *DRNY*, 5:628.

200. Nettels, *Money Supply*, 69–70; Goldenberg, *Shipbuilding in Colonial America*, 31–36, 45–53, 99.

201. Quotation from Grew, *Meanes of a Most Ample Encrease*, 91.

202. Tim Keirn, "Monopoly, Economic Thought, and the Royal African Company" in *Early Modern Conceptions of Property*, ed. John Brewer and Susan Staves (London: Routledge, 1995), 433–35; William A. Pettigrew, *Freedom's Debt: The Royal African Company and the Politics of the Atlantic Slave Trade, 1672–1752* (Chapel Hill: University of North Carolina Press, 2013), 27–42; William A. Pettigrew, "Free to Enslave: Politics and the Escalation of Britain's Transatlantic Slave Trade, 1688–1714," *William and Mary Quarterly*, 3rd ser., 64, no. 1 (Jan. 2007): 11–16.

203. *SLMC*, 3:710–11; Pettigrew, *Freedom's Debt*, 37–39, 219; Pettigrew, "Free to Enslave," 5, 33; Keirn, "Monopoly," 435–37.

204. Cary, *Essay on the State of England*, 71, 74–76.

205. Richard S. Dunn, *Sugar and Slaves: The Rise of the Planter Class in the English West Indies, 1624–1713* (Chapel Hill: University of North Carolina Press, 1972), 234; Pettigrew, *Freedom's Debt*, 14.

206. Pettigrew, "Free to Enslave," 33.

207. Pettigrew, *Freedom's Debt*, 38; David Eltis, Frank D. Lewis, and David Richardson, "Slave Prices, the African Slave Trade, and Productivity in the Caribbean, 1674–1807," *Economic History Review*, n.s., 58, no. 4 (Nov. 2005): 679.

208. Douglas Bradburn, "The Visible Fist: The Chesapeake Tobacco Trade in War and the Purpose of Empire, 1690–1715," *William and Mary Quarterly*, 3rd ser., 68, no. 3 (July 2011): 362–67, 372, 377–78, 385; Koot, *Empire at the Periphery*, 188; Dunn, *Sugar and Slaves*, 211–12.

209. *Statutes of Pennsylvania*, 1:232; *Minutes of the Provincial Council of Pennsylvania*, 16 vols. (Philadelphia and Harrisburg, 1851–1853), 1:558; *Statutes of South Carolina*, 2:163.

210. Blathwayt to Secretary William Popple, August 22, 1701, CO 5/1046, no. 34.

211. *Essay Upon the Government*, 56; Henry Hartwell, James Blair, and Edward Chilton, *Present State of Virginia, and the College* (1697; repr., London, 1727), 14; Robert Beverley, *The History and Present State of Virginia* (1705; repr., Chapel Hill: University of North Carolina Press, 1947), 285.

212. Report of Penn, December 9, 1700, in *DRNY*, 4:757.

213. *CSPC, 1700*, nos. 607, 614, 616.

214. Penn to the BOT, April 21, 1703, in *CSPC, 1702–3*, no. 604; Cornbury to the BOT, 30 June 1703, in *DRNY*, 4:1059; Robert Quary to the BOT, June 16, 1703, in *DRNY*, 4:1047–49.

215. *British Royal Proclamations Relating to America, 1603–1783*, ed. Clarence S. Brigham (Worcester, MA: American Antiquarian Society, 1911), 161–62.

216. *SLMC*, 4:324–25; *PDBP*, 3:188, 197.

217. *PDBP*, 2:205.

218. Randolph to the Commissioners of Customs, August 17, 1696, CO 323/2, no. 6i.

219. *Randolph Letters*, 7:474–77.

220. *Essay Upon the Government*, 22; Nicholson to the BOT, July 1, 1699, CO 5/1310, no. 2.

221. *PDBP*, 2:382–89, 386, 392–401; Yirush, *Settlers, Liberty, and Empire*, 89–95; I. K. Steele, "The Board of Trade: The Quakers, and Resumption of Colonial Charters, 1699–1702," *William and Mary Quarterly*, 3rd ser., 23, no. 4 (Oct. 1966): 596–619.

222. [William Burke], *An Account of the European Settlements in America*, 2 vols. (London, 1757), 2:293–94.

223. Jacob Vanderlint, *Money Answers All Things, or, An Essay to Make Money Sufficiently Plentiful Amongst All Ranks of People* (London, 1734), 8.

224. *True Causes of the Present Scarcity*, 5.

225. Cary, *Essay on the Coyn*, 19; Davenant, *Discourses on the Publick Revenues*, 2:3; Davenant, *Ways and Means*, 20; Davenant, *Memorial Concerning the Coyn*, 12.

226. Zahedieh, *Capital and the Colonies*, 20–21; Clay, *Economic Expansion*, 2:182.

227. Zahedieh, *Capital and the Colonies*, 31, 284.

228. Alison Gilbert Olson, *Making the Empire Work: London and American Interest Groups, 1690–1790* (Cambridge, MA: Harvard University Press, 1992), 27–28, 52–55.

229. Zahedieh, *Capital and the Colonies*, 208, 214.

230. Jacob M. Price, "What Did Merchants Do? Reflections on British Overseas Trade, 1660–1790," *Journal of Economic History* 49, no. 2 (June 1989): 276.

231. Briscoe, *Discourse of Money*, 23.

232. James Puckle, *England's Path to Wealth and Honour, in a Dialogue Between an English-Man and a Dutch-Man* (1696; rev. ed., London, 1700), 3; Davenant, *Discourses on the Publick Revenues*, 2:204, 207, 231; Cary, *Essay on the State of England*, preface, 68, 70.

233. Cary, *Essay on the State of England*, 70–73; Cary, *Essay on the Coyn*, 37.

Epilogue: The Grand Settlement

1. Earl of Sandwich, "Comments Upon New England," July 2, 1671, repr. in F. R. Harris, *The Life of Edward Mountagu, K.G. First Earl of Sandwich (1625–1672)*, 2 vols. (London, 1912), 2:337–41.

2. Randolph to Secretary Coventry, June 17, 1676, in *Randolph Letters*, 2:207–8. *Edward Randolph: Including his Letters and Official Papers . . .* [*Randolph Letters*], ed. Robert Noxon Toppan and Alfred T. S. Goodrick, 7 vols. (Boston, 1898–1909), 2:207–8.

3. [William Penn], *The Excellent Privilege of Liberty & Property Being the Birth-Right of the Free-born Subjects of England* (Philadelphia, 1687), preface, introduction, 23.

4. Charles Davenant, *Discourses on the Publick Revenues, and on the Trade of England*, 2 vols. (London, 1698), 2:252.

5. Richard S. Dunn, "The Glorious Revolution and America," in *The Origins of Empire: British Overseas Enterprise to the Close of the Seventeenth Century*, ed. Nicholas

Canny (Oxford: Oxford University Press, 1998): 447; Brendan McConville, *The King's Three Faces: The Rise and Fall of Royal America, 1688–1776* (Chapel Hill: University of North Carolina Press, 2006), 8. See also Richard L. Bushman, *King and People in Provincial Massachusetts* (Chapel Hill: University of North Carolina Press, 1985).

6. David Armitage, *The Ideological Origins of the British Empire* (Cambridge University Press, 2000), 7, 146–47. See also Bernard Bailyn, *The Origins of American Politics* (New York: Alfred A. Knopf, 1968), 16–23.

7. Adam Smith, *An Inquiry into the Nature and Causes of the Wealth of Nations* (1776; New York: Random House, 1937), bk. 4, ch. I, p. 551, and bk. 5, ch. III, pp. 896–97.

8. [John Mitchell], *The Present State of Great Britain and North America* (London, 1767), 307n, 362–63.

9. Otis, *Rights of the British Colonies*, 34.

10. [An American], *An Essay Upon the Government of the English Plantations on the Continent of America* (London, 1701), 2–4, 13.

11. Oliver M. Dickerson, *The Navigation Acts and the American Revolution* (Philadelphia: University of Pennsylvania Press, 1951); John J. McCusker, "British Mercantilist Policies and the American Colonies," in *The Cambridge Economic History of the United States*, ed. Stanley L. Engerman and Robert E. Gallman, vol. 1 (Cambridge: Cambridge University Press, 1996), 352–57.

12. Smith, *Wealth of Nations*, bk. 4, ch. I, p. 547.

13. Alison Gilbert Olson, *Making the Empire Work: London and American Interest Groups, 1690–1790* (Cambridge, MA: Harvard University Press, 1992).

14. Dunn, "Glorious Revolution," 460–65; Andrew J. O'Shaughnessy, "The Formation of a Commercial Lobby: The West Indian Interest, British Colonial Policy and the American Revolution," *Historical Journal* 40, no. 1 (1997): 71–95.

15. Edmund Burke, "Speech on American Taxation," April 19, 1774, in *The Works of Edmund Burke*, vol. 1 (Boston, 1839), 457–58.

16. Burke, "Speech on American Taxation," 456–58, 490.

17. [Thomas Gordon and John Trenchard], *Cato's Letters*, 4 vols. (London, 1720), 3:284–87.

INDEX

Page numbers in *italics* refer to figures.

Africa: gold from, 13, 14, 140; piracy in, 196–97, 270; slave trade in, 103, 112, 128, 145, 187, 285

agricultural money. *See* country pay

American Indians. *See* Native Americans

Anderson, Adam, 24, 25

Andros, Edmund: arrest of, 247–48, 250, 251; calls for reinstatement of, 253; on currency devaluation, 134, 135; in Dominion of New England, 230–31, 236–42; mint requests from, 134, 210; in New York, 133–35, 166, 176, 210; revolt against, 242, 252; in Virginia, 254, 268

Anglo-Dutch wars. *See specific wars*

Anglo-Spanish War (1585–1604), 18, 35

Anne (queen of England), 286

Aristotle, 22

Armitage, David, 292–93

Asia: Dutch East India Company in, 148; overland trade routes to, 13; pieces of eight utilized in, 16; silver shipments from Europe to, 20–21. *See also* East Indies; *specific countries*

asiento, 128–29, 135

Atherton Company, 232, 234, 239

Backwell, Edward, 141

Bacon, Francis, 43

Bacon, Nathaniel, 159–60

Bacon's Rebellion (1676), 158–60, 163, 170, 181–82

balance of power, 15, 67

balance of trade: colonization and, 32, 34, 39, 41; currency devaluation and, 77, 78; in economic recovery, 75, 79–81; as government priority, 104, 107–8, 135; mercantilist views of, 3–5, 13, 22–26, 142, 243–45, 288; money supply impacted by,

3–4, 33, 43, 79, 267; state intervention in, 25–26. *See also* trade deficits; trade surpluses

Bank of Credit, 232–34

Bank of England, 264, 265

Barbados: clipped money in, 126, 208; in colonial trade, 82–83, 86, 93, 219; currency by tale method in, 200–201, 208; currency devaluation in, 78, 190, 199; on free trade, 90, 93, 109; mint requests from, 82, 117; money supply in, 207–8; population of, 70, 103; as royal colony, 110; slave trade in, 81–83, 103, 112, 208; sugar production, 81–82, 90, 103, 131, 227; tobacco production, 46; wealth accumulation in, 112

Barbon, Nicholas, 243

Barrow, Thomas, 279

bartering, 59–61, 64, 82–83, 101, 218

Basse, Jeremiah, 272, 280

Bay shillings: circulation of, 97–98, 101; denominations of, 95; design of, 95–96, *96*, 120–21, *121*, 168–69; motivations for production, 96–97; output records for, 206; as political symbol, 98–100, 117, 123; silver content of, 97, 124, 170; undervaluing of, 237–38, 241

Beeston, William, 195, 273

Bennet, Henry, earl of Arlington, 179–80

Berkeley, William, 86, 90, 93, 109–10, 114, 159–60, 182–83

Bermuda coinage, 48, *48*, 99

Bethel, Slingsby, 28, 106–7, 142–43, 149–51

Beverley, Robert, Jr., 160, 183

bills of credit, 255–57, *256*, 260–62, *262*

bills of exchange: characteristics of, 47; in colonial trade, 83, 123, 194, 207, 209; during economic crises, 75; in reexport trade, 103; as wartime finance, 263

Lightning Source UK Ltd.
Milton Keynes UK
UKHW010740270122
397802UK00003B/154